ook may be kept three weeks. It is to be
d on / before the last date stamped below.
f 20 will be charged for e   week
ve   book is overdue.

D1357273

COUNTER-TERRORIST LAW AND EMERGENCY POWERS
IN THE UNITED KINGDOM
1922–2000

Counter-terrorist Law and Emergency Powers in the United Kingdom
1922–2000

LAURA K. DONOHUE

Harvard University

IRISH ACADEMIC PRESS
DUBLIN • PORTLAND, OR

First published in 2001 by
IRISH ACADEMIC PRESS
44, Northumberland Road, Dublin 4, Ireland

and in the United States of America by
IRISH ACADEMIC PRESS
c/o ISBS, 5804 NE Hassalo Street,
Portland, OR 97213 3644

Website: www.iap.ie

© Laura K. Donohue 2001

British Library Cataloguing in Publication Data
Donohue, Laura K.
    Counter-terrorist law and emergency powers in the United Kingdom 1922–2000.
    – (New directions in Irish history)
    1. Terrorism – Law and legislation – Great Britain   2. Terrorism – Great Britain
    – Prevention – History – 20th century   3. Executive power – Great Britain –
    History – 20th century.
    I. Title
    345.4'1'0231

    ISBN 0–7165–2687–5

Library of Congress Cataloging-in-Publication Data
Donohue, Laura K., 1969–
    Counter-terrorist law and emergency powers in the United Kingdom, 1922–
2000/Laura K. Donohue.
        p. cm. — (New directions in Irish history)
    Includes bibliographical references and index.
    ISBN 0–7165–2687–5 (hb)
    1. War and emergency powers—Great Britain—History. 2. Terrorism—Great
Britain—History. I. Title. II. Series.
    KD6004.D66 2000
    342.41'0412—dc21   00–035043

Typeset in 10.5 pt on 13 pt Sabon
by Carrigboy Typesetting Services, County Cork
Printed by Creative Print and Design (Wales), Ebbw Vale

Dedicated to
Susan L. Donohue

and in memory of
Allen C. Donohue

Contents

List of Acts

Acknowledgements

IN THE COURSE of this research a number of individuals generously provided assistance. Matthew Kramer's invaluable insight and critical analysis, particularly on issues of jurisprudence and political thought, substantially influenced the manuscript. Keith Jeffery and Paul Arthur meticulously read the text and lent input on the historical and political context into which the Northern Ireland and British governments introduced emergency measures. Brice Dickson contributed feedback throughout the research as well as in the final editing stages. Conor Gearty also reviewed the manuscript and offered his valuable perspective on the development of emergency law in Westminster. James Loughlin and Richard Holm commented on the historical context, and Colm Campbell directed me to important source material. Melissa Lane also provided advice during the research and writing stages. Mark Goldie has been unfailing in his support. I am obliged to him and to Quentin Skinner, who provided tremendous insight and guidance.

Josie Templeton and Sheenagh Johnston at the Public Record Office Northern Ireland assisted in obtaining papers relating to the Northern Ireland Office of Home Affairs. Paul Seaward from the House of Commons helped to locate parliamentary papers and arranged for my attendance at annual debates on emergency legislation. Bill Noblett and the staff in Government Publications at the University Library, University of Cambridge aided in procuring a number of vital documents.

It was while I was at Stanford University as a Visiting Scholar that I was able to complete the research for this book. I am grateful to the Center for International Security and Cooperation and the Gould Center for Conflict Resolution. In particular, I would like to thank Scott Sagan, Lynn Eden, Steve Stedman, Dean Wilkening, and Byron Bland. During the editing stages of the book Susan Wright helped greatly. I am obliged to her and to Linda Longmore at the Irish Academic Press for helping to finalise the manuscript.

Numerous individuals and organisations contributed to the costs of writing this book. In particular, I am most grateful to Nancy Roberts Bowen for her generosity in funding much of the research. P.E.O.

International and the United Kingdom's Overseas Research Students' Award Scheme also helped to cover the institutional costs. The Managers of the Prince Consort and Thirlwall Fund, the Trustees of the Sutasoma Trust, the General Board of the Faculties at the University of Cambridge, the Managers of the Smuts Memorial Fund, Churchill College and the Frederic William Maitland Memorial Fund at the University of Cambridge funded further field research.

In addition to the above individuals and institutions, I would like to thank the communities in Northern Ireland who have welcomed me and taught me much about the conflict. I have learned a tremendous amount from Vera Curran, Daniel Curran, Martin Whyte, Michael Campbell, Bridie Campbell, Michael Brady, Eileen Brady, Nolene Magee, Michael Magee and others. Although it is not possible to name each person, their kindness is much appreciated. Sally Visick, Keith Jeffery, and numerous individuals also opened their homes to me during my research. To them I am most grateful. With Richard Clutterbuck I developed a more informed view of many of the issues addressed in this book; his camaraderie is deeply missed. Jack Shepherd and Kathleen Shepherd have both professionally and personally encouraged me to pursue many of the enquiries that come to fruition in this book. Jack's help and guidance over the past decade deeply influenced the course of my research. I also extend my appreciation to Susan Donohue, Juliette Donohue, Stephen Donohue and Shannon Donohue for their steadfast support. It is to Susan Donohue and Allen Donohue that I dedicate this work. Finally, with deep gratitude I thank Tansel Özyar, who has not only offered comments on the material enclosed, but who has been a constant source of strength and encouragement.

LAURA K. DONOHUE
Cambridge
May 2000

Introduction

T HE STORY OF Irish history is a tale punctuated by the assumption
and exercise of extraordinary State power. From the 1351 Treason
Act and the Coercion Acts of the nineteenth century, through the 1998
Northern Ireland (Emergency Provisions) Act, political forces repeatedly
turn to the codification of emergency powers as a means to secure the
State, North or South. Powers of detention and internment, special courts,
extensive powers of entry, search and seizure, the waiving of the right to
silence, and the imposition of limits on freedom of movement have
marked – and continue to characterise – emergency law *vis-à-vis* Ireland.

These powers both limit and perpetuate violence. In the short term,
they provide for extensive intelligence gathering and they remove from
society individuals who may well be involved in the planning and
execution of violence. They also convey a collective moral aversion
towards the use of violence for political ends. In the long term, however,
such statutes do substantial damage to political and social dynamics.
Indeed, the Unionist government's exercise of the 1922–43 Civil
Authorities (Special Powers) Acts (SPAs), introduced into a time of great
violence, ultimately served to divide the province further. Between 1920
and 1922 political violence claimed 428 lives in Northern Ireland and
accounted for over 1,766 injuries. This represented a staggering increase
in the number of deaths in the nineteenth century. Between 1813 and
1907, sixty-eight deaths in total resulted from political violence, and of
these, half were in 1886.[1] However, the extreme powers introduced to
quell this violence immediately following partition were levied well
beyond the initial incidents of violence. The 1922 Special Powers Act
empowered the Civil Authority to impose curfew, close premises, roads
and transportation routes, detain and intern, proscribe organisations,
engage in censorship, ban meetings, processions and gatherings, alter the
court system, ban uniforms, weapons and the use of cars. Amongst other
provisions, it granted extensive powers of entry, search and seizure, and, in
a Draconian catch-all phrase, empowered the Civil Authority 'to take all
such steps and issue all such orders as may be necessary for preserving
the peace and maintaining order'. Almost exclusively levied against the

minority population from 1922 to 1972, the 1922–43 SPAs became one of the central grievances leading to the Civil Rights movement of the late 1960s and the civil unrest that, ultimately, led to the suspension of the Northern Parliament.

In spite of the pivotal role played by this legislation, virtually no secondary research exists on the specific regulations introduced under its auspices and the manner in which the unionist regime used these powers throughout the tenure of Stormont. In 1936 the National Council for Civil Liberties conducted a review of the regulations in place at the time. More recently Colm Campbell has examined the formation of the legislation and its operation from 1918 to 1925.[2] Aside from these works, there are virtually no other analyses that treat the legislation in any significant detail. Further, these sources only examine the statute up to 1936 and 1925, respectively. Most accounts of twentieth century Northern Irish history either pay scant attention to the 1922–43 SPAs or mention the occasional event in which the government exercised some of its powers under the 1922 SPA.[3] One historian has gone so far as to assert that, 'It would . . . be unjust to lay too much emphasis upon the special powers that the Northern Ireland government has from time to time made use of'.[4] Yet, this same author recognises the deep grievance bred by the SPA: '[the house searches conducted in July 1970] further worsened the relations of the troops with the civilian population and especially the Catholics, by whom the new measure came to be regarded as almost as objectionable as the Special Powers Act itself'.[5] So, if the Northern Ireland government only occasionally made use of the SPAs, how did they come to be seen as so objectionable? The answer is that the government actually made extensive use of emergency powers throughout the fifty years of Stormont; yet the dearth of research on the statute itself has led to either the omission or misinterpretation of the manner in which the Unionist government maintained control of Northern Ireland from 1922 to 1972.

This book attempts to fill the lacunae in our understanding of Northern Irish history since 1922. Chapter one explores the circumstances surrounding the inception of Northern Ireland and discusses the web of emergency measures instituted to secure the constitutional position of the North. The 1920 Government of Ireland Act established what matters fell within the auspices of the new parliament. Enabled by this statute to make laws to preserve the 'peace, order and good government' of Northern Ireland, the new Executive immediately introduced the 1921 Local Government (Emergency Powers) Act (Northern Ireland), which provided the Ministry of Home Affairs with extensive powers regarding the composition of local councils and town commissions. The 1922 Criminal Procedure Act (Northern Ireland) created special courts for the trying of offences linked to political violence. Although the Northern government never invoked this statute, together with the formation of the local security forces, the Royal Ulster Constabulary and the Ulster Special Constabulary, the primacy of issues of law and order can be seen. By far the most significant measure introduced at this time, however, was the 1922 Civil Authorities (Special Powers) Act. The chapter focuses on the introduction of this statute, its annual renewal and the 1928 five year extension. In 1933 the Northern government made the statute indefinite, with further amendments introduced in 1943.

The second chapter details the more than 100 regulations introduced under the 1922–43 Special Powers Acts. Contrary to what has been asserted elsewhere, this legislation became part of the fabric of daily control to address the republican, nationalist and even communist threats perceived by the Northern government. The chapter focuses on the evolution of these measures: the government initially used the statute to establish order in the North. As violence declined, the Northern Executive began to use the regulations to prevent the expression of republican and nationalist ideals. A change in justification for the emergency powers coincided with this shift. From being required to establish law and order, unionists soon hailed them as necessary to maintain peace. In this context the government determined unacceptable any public support for ideals undermining the State's authority; this included both nationalist and republican aspirations.

While the 1922–43 Special Powers Acts might be viewed by some to be an instrument of the past, a detailed examination of the regulations introduced from 1922 to 1972 reveals that many of the same measures that alienated the minority community in Northern Ireland continue in existence today. In 1972 Britain prorogued Stormont and introduced direct rule. Although the government immediately announced its intent to repeal the 1922–43 Civil Authorities (Special Powers) Acts and Regulations and to replace them with new emergency legislation, the resultant 1973 Northern Ireland (Emergency Provisions) Act (EPA) did not so much revoke the previous statutes as simply rename and expand them. The vast majority of powers included in the 1973 EPA echoed regulations introduced under the 1922–43 SPAs, the 1920 Restoration of Order in Ireland Act, and the 1914–15 Defence of the Realm Acts. Their direct inclusion into the 1973 EPA was overshadowed by the prominence of the Diplock Report, the attention elicited by changes in trial by jury and the continued use of internment. Chapter three also highlights events leading up to the suspension of the Northern Parliament and Britain's subsequent adoption of the 1973 EPA. It examines the recommendations of the Diplock Commission and the extent to which Britain incorporated these recommendations into the 1973 EPA. The chapter then demonstrates that the British government transferred a significant number of prior emergency measures, such as detention, internment, the closing of licensed premises, the blocking up of roads, the prohibition of vehicle usage, powers of entry, search and seizure, possession of property and land, compensation, the prohibition of meetings, assemblies and processions, proscription and the collection of information on security forces, from the 1922–43 SPAs. In many cases, these measures in fact bear much longer histories, reaching back to the 1920 Restoration of Order in Ireland Act, the 1914–15 Defence of the Realm Acts and previously.

In spite of claims that the legislation would be temporary in nature, following the introduction of the 1973 EPA, Britain maintained and expanded emergency powers in Northern Ireland. Chapter four follows the evolution of special powers and their gradual inclusion into ordinary criminal law. It discusses the statute's amendment in 1975, its replacement in 1978, and further Northern Ireland (Emergency Provisions) Acts in 1987, 1991 and 1996. These measures can only be understood in the political context within which they operated: civil disorder in the early 1970s and attempts at an early political settlement met with minimal success. Following the government's implementation of Ulsterisation and criminalisation, the H-Block campaign ignited public opinion, spurring the introduction of additional security measures. The so-called 'supergrass' system and the advent of Anglo-Irish relations can be seen as a complement to counter-terrorist statutes. Supplementary provisions such as the 1988 broadcast ban, the formal recognition of MI5's role in the North, and the 1988 Criminal Evidence (Northern Ireland) Order, which restricted an individual's right to silence, both reflected and strengthened the government's use of extraordinary powers. The chapter concludes with an examination of the 1991 and 1996 EPAs against the backdrop of the Brooke-Mayhew talks and the beginning of the peace process.

Not only did extraordinary powers operate in Northern Ireland, but gradually emergency measures seeped their way into Great Britain. Throughout the twentieth century Westminster expanded regular criminal statutes and enacted special counter-terrorist law aimed at preventing Northern Irish political violence on the mainland. The powers included in these statutes reflected those introduced in Northern Ireland under the 1922–43 Special Powers Acts. In 1939 the British government responded to the Irish Republican Army mainland bombing campaign with the introduction of the 1939 Prevention of Violence (Temporary Provisions) Act. This statute introduced powers of expulsion, prohibition, arrest and detention. Like Stormont's initial intentions with regard to the 1922 SPA and Westminster's later introduction of the 1973 EPA, the government intended the 1939 PVA to act as an interim statute. Although the IRA's mainland bombing campaign ceased within a year of the statute's introduction, it was not until 1953 that the 1939 Act was allowed to expire and it was not repealed until 1973. Largely in response to the Birmingham bombings, in 1974 Westminster reintroduced powers contained in the 1939 Act, with the addition of proscription, a provision employed under the 1922–43 SPAs and the 1973 EPA. Again, Westminster intended for this legislation to be in place for a limited period. Chapter five examines the 1939 PVA and 1973 PTA and looks at the evolution of the later statute: its successive renewal, its replacement in 1976, 1984, and 1989, and additional powers granted under the PTA in 1996.

From its initial application to Northern Irish violence, by 1996 some 50 per cent of the cases prosecuted under the PTA related to international terrorism. Having been faced for years with Northern Irish political violence, the British government adapted its powers under the PTA to apply to violence instigated by non-domestic terrorist organisations. From 1996 to 2000 Parliament's acceptance of extraordinary powers accelerated to the point where Westminster began considering the permanent codification of counter-terrorist law. Cease-fires in Northern Ireland and the progression of the negotiations suggested that the 'emergency' situation to which the government appealed to justify its measures, was changing. New statutes, such as the 1996 Northern Ireland (Entry to Negotiations) Act, 1997 Northern Ireland Arms Decommissioning Act and 1998 Public Processions (Northern Ireland) Act, Police (Northern Ireland) Act, Northern Ireland Act and Human Rights Acts sought to address the political issues in Northern Ireland. The British government complemented these 'political' alterations with the continued application of counter-terrorist measures. As the Labour party swept to victory in the general election, the new government dropped powers of internment and exclusion. Together with the revival of Lord Lloyd's review, it appeared as though the government might relinquish some of its extraordinary powers. The sudden introduction of the 1998 Criminal Justice (Terrorism and Conspiracy) Act in the wake of the Omagh bombing, however, crushed such hopes. This statute created more stringent forfeiture provisions, made incursions into a suspect's right to silence, and allowed the testimony of a police officer to serve as evidence of membership in a specified organisation. Perhaps the most surprising of the powers assumed at this time were those related to the conspiracy to engage in terrorist activity overseas. Chapter six concludes with discussion of Labour's December 1998 White Paper and subsequent discussions in Parliament on the formal adoption of counter-terrorist legislation.

At a time when the Western World appears increasingly concerned with the dissemination of liberal, democratic thought, Britain, one of the countries leading the establishment of liberal norms, repeatedly derogates from the standards it sets while it takes steps to institute the permanent suspension of various civil liberties. What has brought the United Kingdom to the point where it would contemplate codifying the permanent sus-pension of these liberties? In one sense, these moves simply acknowledge the status quo. Although repeatedly claimed to be temporary in nature, there is very little new – and there is nothing temporary – about emergency law in the United Kingdom. As chapters one through six demonstrate, emergency powers have a long, protracted history in Northern Ireland and Great Britain. Chapter seven explores the reasons for this. It suggests that the answer lies in a confluence of factors. The first section examines the nature of emergency legislation, suggesting that its formal structure, duplication of existing criminal offences, symbolic importance and perceived effectiveness contributed to the retention of the Special Powers. The second section highlights historical considerations: the persistence of the Northern Ireland conflict, as reinforced by deep divisions in the province and the sporadic resurgence of paramilitary activity, Britain's previous use of emergency law in Ireland and the continued perception in Westminster of Northern Ireland as somehow different from Great Britain. The final section suggests that the justification offered by the Northern Ireland government for the use of emergency measures differed from that invoked by Westminster. The Unionist government appealed to reason of state to entrench emergency law. In contrast, Britain appealed to a Lockean concept of the right of the people to life and property and the duty of the government to act to protect this right. These justifications created room within which emergency measures could be exercised. In Northern Ireland, owing to the type of justification being invoked, the government constructed a wider interpretation of what was acceptable than that claimed by Westminster. The context within which the British State operated, while it mitigated the more extreme aspects of emergency law, nevertheless supported the establishment and operation of emergency measures. The Northern Ireland Parliament and Westminster also dealt differently with what might otherwise be seen as a clash of rights inherent in the operation of emergency law. From 1922 to 1972 the

Northern government largely regarded the Special Powers as only infringing on the rights of one portion of the population. Those subject to its provisions had chosen to forego such rights through the adoption of violent means. In contrast, Westminster largely recognised that emergency law infringed the rights of all citizens within the State. However, Parliament justified this incursion by appeal to what might be termed a 'hierarchy of rights'. The right to life and property provided a trump card over 'lesser rights', such as the right to silence, the right to free speech and the right to a jury trial. The international arena, for its part, served to validate and verify the borders set by, particularly, the British government, in its appeal to *salus populi suprema lex*. While the European Court of Human Rights did adjudicate on the more extreme aspects of emergency law, such as the use of the five torture techniques employed in the early 1970s and extended detention, it nevertheless recognised the right of the State to defend itself. So while some attention was paid to the domestic development of counter-terrorist measures, minimal concrete requirements or limitations were presented. Simultaneously, the right of the State to defend itself and a general condemnation of terrorism as a means to a political ends supported Britain's use of some sort of emergency law. These elements contributed to the retention and extension of counter-terrorist measures well beyond their intended life.

It is possible that in the 21st century the use of terrorism for political recognition will grow as international boundaries solidify, weapons, technology and communication systems become increasingly sophisticated, and the contradiction in the international arena between self-determination and State sovereignty remains unresolved. It remains less than clear, though, how States can and should respond to challenges to their political legitimacy. The exact type and nature of such challenges vary widely. Even in the Northern Ireland context the type of threat faced by the Northern government differed radically from that confronting Westminster. At the inception of Northern Ireland, unionists viewed the State as a bulwark against Roman Catholicism. The State had to be maintained to protect the unionist, largely Protestant, community from the dangers of 'Rome rule'. Unionists perceived any attempt on the part of nationalists or republicans to gain power as an attack on the constitutional structure of the State. The defence of this structure entailed both a political and a religious or sectarian orientation, in terms of the types of policies adopted and the manner in which they were implemented from 1922 to 1972. The Special Powers became levied almost exclusively on the Catholic population, becoming inextricably linked to the political issues in the North. Westminster, in turn, viewed the challenge as an attack on the life and property of citizens within the State. In order for the government to fulfill its duties and to maintain its political legitimacy, it had to institute measures to mitigate the more extreme effects of political intransigence. In both circumstances counter-terrorist legislation gave birth to new offences, extensive powers and new procedures, all of which impinged on the civil liberties of the population. The measures themselves became part of the political equation, and rather than being separable from the political process, they became fundamentally entrenched in the dynamics of Northern Ireland.

CHAPTER ONE

Emergency Powers and the Inception of the Northern State

The Government has definitely recognised that there are two distinct elements among the population – Those that are loyal to the British Crown and Empire, and those who are not. The Government is asking the help of all loyalists in Ulster, and proposes to arm with Firearms all those called on for duty, to confer certain privileges, to recognise them, and to indemnify them for injuries incurred by the performance of their duties.

Lt.-Col. William Spender[1]

BURGEONING UNIONIST and republican militance throughout the late nineteenth and early twentieth century brought the issue of Irish independence to a head.[2] From the signing in 1912 of Carson's Solemn League and Covenant and the creation of the Ulster Volunteer Force (UVF), through the 1916 Easter Rising and subsequent emergence of the Irish Republican Army (IRA), the British government found itself embroiled in an increasingly unpopular Anglo-Irish war. Sinn Féin swept the 1918 General Election in Ireland. Candidates refused to take their seats in Westminster and instead formed Dáil Éireann in Dublin. In January 1919 the Dáil pledged itself to the Irish Republic and elected Eamonn de Valera, the most senior officer in the aftermath of the Easter Rising, as president of the new republic. Arthur Griffith, who founded Sinn Féin in 1905, served as first deputy, and Michael Collins, who orchestrated intelligence operations in Dublin, took control of the military. In the North Edward Carson a barrister and an administrator in the Conservative government and James Craig, from 1906 MP for East Down, emerged as central figures in the movement to maintain ties to the British government. From 1927 Viscount Craigavon, Craig was to serve as the first Prime Minister of Northern Ireland 1921–40. In anticipation of

1

events that were to lead to the partition of Ireland, peaceful but massive demonstrations gave way to threats of armed resistance in both the North and the South.

Responding to these developments in Ireland, the British Prime Minister, David Lloyd George, strongly encouraged the northern unionists to find accommodation with the southern nationalists. In the end, his Liberal and Conservative coalition served to secure Ulster's separate position within the United Kingdom. The British Cabinet's Irish sub-committee recognised the strong resistance in the upper northeast of Ireland to the creation of an all-Ireland parliament. It also determined that the exclusion of the North from the South, with direct rule from Westminster, would be unacceptable. This would enable 'opponents of Great Britain . . . to say either that Great Britain is ruling nationalist majorities against their will, or that it is giving its active support to Ulster in its refusal to unite with the rest of Ireland'.[3] The sub-committee instead recommended the establishment of a regional parliament in the North subservient to Westminster. Although unionists had not sought a home parliament, they accepted regional administration as security against control administered from Dublin. Recognising that minimal sympathy existed for them across the Irish Sea, and fully aware of Lloyd George's nationalist leanings, they feared that Westminster might try to force Irish unity. A parliament of their own meant safety, 'for we believe that once a parliament is set up and working well . . . we should fear no one, and we feel that we would then be in a position of absolute security . . . and therefore I say that we prefer to have a parliament, although we do not want one of our own'.[4]

In an effort to alleviate the drain on British resources and to go some way towards meeting the conflicting demands in Ireland – while protecting what it saw as British interests – the Lloyd George administration in 1920 secured the passage of the Government of Ireland Act.[5] The statute created two Irish parliaments. The six northeastern counties, incorporating a majority unionist population, were to be governed from Belfast and the remaining twenty-six counties, predominantly nationalist and republican, were to be administered from Dublin. The Act provided for limited powers to be transferred to the two bodies, with Westminster retaining financial control. It required that both parts of Ireland send representatives to Westminster and it allowed for the Crown to appoint members of the regional parliaments. In addition, the legislation provided for a Council of Ireland to address common affairs in the North and in the South, with the possibility of eventually expanding its jurisdiction to govern the entire island.

Although the North formed a parliament in accordance with the 1920 Act, Dáil Éireann in the South rejected it and refused to recognise the subsequent elections. Violence increased and Sinn Féin and the IRA continued to press for a united Ireland. In response Lloyd George invited northern and southern leaders to meet in London to renegotiate the Government of Ireland Act. Discussion eventually resulted in the 1921 'Articles of Agreement for a Treaty between the Irish Free State and Britain'. This document granted the island dominion status, required Members of Parliament to take an oath of allegiance to Britain, and allowed Ireland to conduct domestic and international affairs with a high degree of independence. The North had the right to opt out of the new State within a year, and, if it chose to do so, a border commission would verify the new boundary. Collins and Griffith, negotiating on behalf of the Provisional government, understood the underlying agreement to be that either the boundary revision would result in reducing the size of Northern Ireland to an untenable entity, thus forcing eventual Irish unification, or that up to one third of the northern province would be forfeit.[6] They conveyed this intention to border nationalists, who felt let down by a Treaty that formally acknowledged partition. The isolated nationalist minority in north-east Ulster – particularly Joseph Devlin's supporters in West Belfast – also viewed an all-Ireland Parliament as preferable to a boundary commission that would be unlikely to relinquish those areas in which they lived.[7] In the South the Dáil narrowly passed the Treaty, and a violent civil war ensued between those willing to accept the twenty-six county unit with ties to Britain and those who wanted to press for full Irish independence. The IRA, with some 100,000 members, split sharply as to whether the Treaty should be accepted or whether the fight for a thirty-two county republic should continue. Pro-Treaty factions became absorbed into the Provisional military forces, and the newly established Southern government took clear steps to subdue those opposing the agreement. By the end of the Civil War in the South, 24 May 1923, more than 12,000 IRA members had been imprisoned and seventy-seven sentenced to death.[8] Although militarily and politically defeated, the IRA continued over the next fifty years to claim to be the only legitimate government in Ireland, rejecting the treaty and the border established by partition. Other historians provide excellent accounts of the evolution of political affairs north and south at this time.[9] For our purposes it is worth noting the atmosphere in the North at the time of partition and the legislative framework within which the Northern State operated.

Within five months of signing the Treaty, the North exercised its right to secede. The Civil War in the South demonstrated the strength of anti-partition sentiment just over the border, and the presence of a sizable minority within Northern Ireland who claimed allegiance to the South intensified unionist fear that the North would be drawn into a united Ireland. The Northern Ireland Ministry of Home Affairs saw the IRA as, 'carrying on a systematic and persistent attempt to render the government of Northern Ireland impossible'.[10] Internal documents cited the murder of police constables and government officials, ambushes of the police, the destruction of bridges and property, arson, the laying of ground mines, larcenies of materials, raids on post offices, the cutting of telegraph wires, sniping across the border and kidnapping as evidence of these activities.[11] Confrontation at a street level within the North further emphasised internal rejection of partition. At no time was this more apparent than during the marching season. For example, on 9 July 1921, in the midst of preparations for the 12th of July, an IRA attack on three Royal Irish Constables in the Falls Road area of Belfast spurred a five hour street battle in which fourteen individuals lost their lives and a further eighty-six suffered injury.[12] Further rioting occurred in August and September. Various attempts by southern nationalists to raise the issue of border revision in London served to emphasise further the precarious nature of the new State. Liberal leaders, sympathetic to Irish unity, continued to bring pressure on northern leaders to concede to an all-Ireland constitutional structure.

Not only did the North feel under attack physically and diplomatically, but economically the province continued to spiral downward. Unemployment had grown steadily in the northern shipbuilding and textile industries, leaving large numbers of soldiers returning from World War I out of work. Allegations that Catholics had 'peacefully penetrated' industry while Protestants had been away at war ignited further sectarian action. In 1921 attacks began on Catholics in the northern engineering and some parts of the linen industries, and within a week over 8,000 expulsions had occurred.[13] The 'pogrom' continued until July 1922, in the course of which 267 Catholics and 185 Protestants died.[14] Republicans in the South responded to the eviction of Catholic workers by introducing an economic embargo on goods being shipped from Northern Ireland, thus exacerbating economic tension. Under the guidance of W.T. Cosgrave, the Dáil Minister for Local Government, the General Council of County Councils organised a boycott of Belfast goods. The blacklist initially included banks and insurance companies whose headquarters were located in Belfast. A Craig-Collins Pact of 21 January 1922 did little to stem the tide of violence and the expulsion of Catholic workers. The second clause of the agreement declared that Collins would endeavour to

end the Belfast Boycott in turn for Craig trying to get Catholics returned
to the shipyards. No changes immediately ensued, however, and northern
nationalists suspected that Collins had simply been outmanoeuvred by
not demanding any concrete guarantees from Craig.[15] Sinn Féin subsequently extended the boycott to include all goods manufactured and/or
distributed from Belfast, Newtownards, Lisburn, Banbridge and Dromore,
and Collins authorised the formation of a specially paid IRA unit, the
seventy member 'Belfast City Guard' to protect Catholics from sectarian
attack.[16] While the boycott officially lasted until 1922, unofficially it
extended far beyond that.[17] More important that the direct economic
consequences of the boycott on the North was the considerable
psychological impact it bore. Not only did it serve to solidify the division
between the Catholic/Nationalist and Protestant/Unionist identities, but
it also gave a concrete form to 'Protestant fears of discrimination – or
worse – at the hands of a Nationalist government'. As Townshend
concludes, 'It can only have cemented opposition to republicanism and
fostered a determination to use any means to preserve the reality of
Ulster separation'.[18]

In concert with the boycott, Collins' government engaged in a policy
of non-recognition of the northern government. From the end of January
1922, the provincial government paid the salaries of teachers at Catholic
schools in Northern Ireland. Those teachers who refused to recognise the
authorities in the North could count on support from the Southern
government. As discrepancies over Craig and Collins' interpretation of
the Boundary Commission became more apparent, the political situation
in the North degenerated into what Churchill referred to as a 'return to
that hideous bog of reprisals'.[19] Viewing the previous British response to
violence in Ireland as inadequate, unionists insisted at the creation of the
new parliament that the new State implement more severe measures.

The 1920 Government of Ireland Act, which continued to govern the
North's relationship with Britain, empowered the Northern Ireland
Parliament to make laws to preserve the 'peace, order and good
government' of Northern Ireland.[20] The legislation delineated a number
of broad restrictions: Britain withheld the authority to wage war, conduct
foreign relations, enter into international treaties, maintain armed forces,
create currency, grant titles of honour, govern communication networks,
or legislate for issues of treason, treason felony or immigration.[21] In
addition to these excepted matters, the British Parliament also retained
authority over Northern Ireland for legislation applying to the United
Kingdom. The Northern Ireland government could neither repeal nor
alter any provision of the 1920 Act, nor any other act passed by

Westminster. Further, it declared void any statute passed by the Northern Ireland Parliament that contradicted any act of Westminster, or orders, rules or regulations made under such an act.[22] Additional matters reserved for British jurisdiction under the 1920 Act included the postal service, particular savings banks, the issuance of stamps, an all-Ireland Public Record office, land purchase and railway charges. Although withheld from the Northern Parliament, these powers had the potential to be granted to an all-Ireland assembly in the event of agreement between the Northern and Southern parliaments. The all-Ireland assembly never materialised. As a result, Westminster retained these areas. The 1920 Act also transferred some administrative and legislative affairs to the North. Among the most significant of these powers were those relating to electoral arrangements and responsibility for internal law and order. These areas fell under the jurisdiction of the Prime Minister and the Ministry of Home Affairs, two of the six ministries created to administer transferred or devolved matters. The other ministries included Agriculture, Commerce, Education, Finance and Labour.

The 1920 Government of Ireland Act went some way towards offering protection for the minority community: legislation passed by the government could neither directly nor indirectly discriminate based on religious beliefs:

> In the exercise of [its] power to make laws under this Act the Parliament of Northern Ireland shall [not] make a law so as either directly or indirectly to establish or endow any religion, or prohibit or restrict the free exercise thereof, or give a preference, privilege, or advantage, or impose any disability or disadvantage, on account of religious belief or religious or ecclesiastical status . . . or take any property without compensation. Any law made in contravention of the restrictions imposed by this subsection shall, so far as it contravenes those restrictions, be void.[23]

The statute required that the Supreme Court of Judicature of Northern Ireland and in the final instance the House of Lords determine the validity of Acts passed by the Northern Ireland Parliament.[24] In practice, the Northern Parliament refrained from legislating in areas reserved for Westminster. Correspondingly, the British Parliament refrained from commenting on issues that fell within the domain of the Northern Ireland government. In 1939 the British Secretary of Home Affairs emphasised this point in Westminster: 'May I remind you, Mr Deputy Speaker, that Mr Speaker has more than once ruled that the maintenance of law and order in Northern Ireland is the responsibility of the Government of Northern Ireland and not of this House?'[25] Sir Dennis

Herbert assured Sir Samuel Hoare that, 'The Ruling of Mr Speaker was that matters which were entirely for the Northern Ireland Parliament could not be criticised in this House'.[26] The British government also refrained from encouraging judicial scrutiny of the constitutional relationship.[27] The entrenchment of proportional representation for the election of members to the Northern Ireland House of Commons provided some further protection of the minority community.[28] However, the statute gave the Northern Ireland Parliament the power to alter, after three years, 'the qualification and registration of the electors, the law relating to elections and the questioning of elections, the constituencies, and the distribution of the members among the constituencies'.[29]

Although Westminster maintained ultimate jurisdiction over the North, short of abolition, Britain held no recourse to effective parliamentary or executive scrutiny of provincial affairs. Westminster failed to create either a Secretary of State for Northern Ireland or a Northern Ireland Committee, answerable to the British Parliament. Thus, within the broad limits highlighted above, the British government provided the Northern Ireland government a high degree of autonomy to develop its own social, political and economic institutions:

> All existing laws, institutions, and authorities in [Northern Ireland], whether judicial, administrative, or ministerial, and all existing taxes in [Northern] Ireland, shall, except as otherwise provided by this Act, continue as if this Act had not passed, but with the modifications necessary for adapting them to this act and subject to repeal, abolition, alteration, and adaptation in the manner and to the extent authorised by this Act . . . [The Crown] may place under the control of the Government of . . . Northern Ireland, for the purposes of that Government, . . . such of the lands, buildings, and property in . . . Northern Ireland . . . vested in or held in trust for His Majesty, and subject to such conditions or restrictions (if any) as may seem expedient.[30]

At an informal level, Westminster only applied statutes to the North with the prior agreement of unionist politicians.[31] The virtual absence of Nationalist MPs ensured that the minority community obtained minimal say in such matters. Assurances that Britain would 'reinforce Ulster as much as she wanted',[32] placed the provincial Parliament, also predominantly unionist, in the forefront of policy decisions. Much of this support derived from the conservative camp in Britain. Following the 1921 Treaty tension quickly arose between the Treasury, run by the liberal Lloyd George camp, and the Colonial Office, headed by Winston Churchill, with regard to Northern Ireland. The Treasury resented the profligacy of unionists with regard to public funds, as well as the establishment of a Joint Exchequer

Board to arbitrate disputes between Belfast and the Treasury, thus diminishing strict Treasury accountability. As Churchill became an implacable supporter of Ulster Unionism, the Treasury contingent viewed him as undermining the Free Staters. Following Michael Collins' death, the Churchill camp ultimately prevailed. Not only could the British government relinquish its role in bolstering Collins' credibility, but the eruption of the Civil War in the South went some way towards justifying a stronger Northern government.[33]

Although tension existed between the Northern Government and the British Treasury, unionists clearly called the shots in the North. For instance, in response to questions in the imperial Parliament, the British Home Secretary replied: '[Regulation 22 of the Special Powers Act] is made under an Act of the Parliament of Northern Ireland, and is not a responsibility of my Rt. Hon. Friend'. When pressed further on the subject Lloyd rejoined: 'The Rt. Hon. Baronet is no doubt aware that the legislature of Northern Ireland have power to make laws for the peace, order and good government of Northern Ireland'.[34] Unionists in the North shared this view of the relative autonomy of the province. Both the government and those entrusted with security in the region viewed themselves as bearing the ultimate responsibility for the North. As the Belfast Royal Irish Constabulary division commissioner circulated to the district inspectors: 'While the defence of Ulster from hostile invasion may ultimately be the inalienable duty of the British government, the maintenance of law and order and the protection of life and property in the cities, in the interior and on the border must primarily rest in the hands of the RUC and Special Constabulary'.[35] This *de facto* isolation from Westminster left the unionists in Northern Ireland in virtually complete control of regional affairs. Accordingly, the new government, headed by James Craig, swiftly enacted a number of emergency statutes to consolidate control of the new State.

EMERGENCY MEASURES

The 1920 local elections in the northern Six Counties resulted in nationalist control of twenty-five local councils. By the time of partition, many of these had already indicated their allegiance to Dáil Éireann. As the question of a Boundary Commission arose in London, the Northern government became alarmed that local government support would prove a strong argument for the transfer of a number of border areas to the South. The new Northern Ireland Minister of Home Affairs and Unionist

MP for East Belfast and Victoria, Sir Richard Dawson Bates, distributed a circular to the local authorities, requesting that they cooperate with the Northern government. In response, the Tyrone County Council refused to recognise the Northern Parliament and reaffirmed its commitment to Dáil Éireann. The Royal Irish Constabulary subsequently confiscated the local records and documents, and the government swept the 1921 Local Government (Emergency Powers) Act (Northern Ireland) through Parliament.[36] This statute provided the Ministry of Home Affairs for Northern Ireland with extensive powers regarding the composition of local councils and town commissions. The 1921 Local Government Act enabled the government to replace any recalcitrant local authority with a paid official administrator, until the reconstitution of the local body could be arranged. On the day that the Ministry of Home affairs transferred Tyrone's local government power to Belfast, the Fermanagh County Council passed a resolution pledging allegiance to Dáil Éireann. The Ministry of Home Affairs seized council offices, expelled council officials and dissolved the council. Armagh, Keady and Newry Urban Councils, Downpatrick Town Commissioners, Cookstown, Downpatrick, Kilkeel, Lisnaskea, Strabane, Magherafelt, and Newry No. 1 and No. 2 Rural Councils suffered the same fate. By April 1922 a number of Boards of Poor Law Guardians had all been dissolved and commissioners appointed to conduct their affairs. Derry Corporation remained the only nationalist controlled local council whose powers were not transferred to a commissioner appointed by the Unionist government.[37]

Intended as a temporary measure, the Northern Parliament annually renewed the 1921 Local Government Act through the Expiring Laws Continuance Acts. In order to provide for more permanent unionist control of the political system, the following year the government passed the Local Government Act (Northern Ireland).[38] In addition to addressing the annual election and retirement of members and controlling applications to the county borough of Belfast, Belfast City and District water commissioners, this Act provided for the method of voting and electoral divisions. The statute eliminated proportional representation in local elections and, to ensure the loyalty of all members of the political system, required that a declaration of allegiance be made within one month of appointment. The oath read: 'I . . . hereby declare that I will render true and faithful allegiance and service to His Majesty King George the Fifth, His heirs and successors according to law and to His Government of Northern Ireland'.[39] Most significantly, it empowered the Ministry to establish orders for constituting electoral divisions:

The Ministry may from time to time make orders:
(a) dividing a borough, urban district or town into wards and fixing the boundaries of such wards, altering the number and boundaries of the wards, or altering the boundaries of the wards without altering their number, and apportioning the borough councillors and aldermen, urban district councillors or town commissioners among the wards;
(b) dividing a county into county electoral divisions, altering the boundary of a county electoral division, or the number of county councillors and county electoral divisions for a county, and, in case of an urban district forming one county electoral division, assigning more than one county councillor to that division.[40]

With such wide-sweeping powers allocated to the Executive, this Act effectively established a basis for gerrymandering that maintained predominantly unionist councils in areas where significant Catholic communities resided. In 1920 nationalists controlled twenty-five out of eighty councils; by 1926 they controlled only two of the eighty. Even accounting for a nationalist boycott in many areas to protest the new boundaries and oath of allegiance, subsequent elections demonstrated the effectiveness of the gerrymandered constituencies. In the Omagh Rural Council area, where Catholics held a sixty-one and a half per cent Catholic majority, nationalists won twenty-six seats in 1920 to thirteen held by unionists. After the Northern government redrew the electoral boundaries, unionists held the council twenty-one seats to eighteen.[41] In Tyrone the government provided 70,595 Catholic voters with nine seats and 57,000 unionists with eighteen seats.[42] In March 1934 the Ministry of Home Affairs dissolved the Armagh Urban Council on grounds of corruption. However, the suspension of powers lasted twelve years, at the conclusion of which it encompassed new wards and a unionist majority. In 1936 the Northern government again redrew the local election boundaries for Derry and for the Omagh Urban Council. As late as 1967, in the Londonderry County Borough, where Catholics represented 62 per cent of the total voting population, the government allowed Catholic areas to elect only eight out of twenty councillors on the corporation.[43] Throughout the tenure of the Unionist government, the nationalist community failed to reclaim a single local council that had become unionist as a result of gerrymandering, and as time progressed, the majority of local seats were left uncontested.[44] Between 1923 and 1955 the average number of uncontested seats was around 96 per cent for rural councils, 94 per cent for county councils and 60 per cent for urban and borough councils.[45] The government accompanied the suspension of local councils and subsequent gerrymandering with a restricted franchise in which only ratepayers and their spouses could vote. The government also granted limited companies up to six votes according to their rateable valuation, the exercise of which was undertaken by the company directors. This structure worked to the advantage of the more economically sound Protestant community, removing direct access to the political system from a significant portion of the Catholic population. The 1921 Act also became the cornerstone for subsequent discrimination in housing, employment and social services. As the Cameron Commission later reported:

> In certain areas . . . the arrangement of ward boundaries for local government purposes has produced in the local authority a permanent unionist majority which bears little or no resemblance to the relative numerical strength of unionists and non-unionists in the area . . . we have good reason to believe the allegation that these arrangements were deliberately made and maintained with the consequence that the unionists used and have continued to use the electoral majority thus created to favour Protestant or unionist supporters in making public appointments – particularly those of senior officials – and in manipulating housing allocations for political and sectarian ends.[46]

Unhappy with the elimination of proportional representation, for a number of months the British government withheld royal assent from the 1922 Act. British civil servants viewed this legislation as *ultra vires* the Northern Ireland government, 'an abrogation of the rights of the minority . . . and . . . a fatal obstacle to conciliatory efforts'.[47] Nevertheless, the Crown eventually granted royal assent, with the incident being the first and last time that Britain interfered in the passage of an act of the Northern Parliament.

More than two decades later the Labour government in Westminster introduced universal suffrage in Great Britain, which abolished the restricted franchise for local government. Unionist politicians made sure that Northern Ireland was not included in the Act and introduced the 1946 Representation of the People Bill, which not only ensured a restricted franchise, but tightened it further by removing votes from non-ratepaying lodgers. The Unionist government retained company votes and extended their use to elections to the Northern Ireland Parliament. The Northern Ireland government Chief Whip, Major L.E. Curran, stated that the objective of the Bill was to prevent nationalists from gaining control of the border counties and of Derry City. He added: 'The best way to prevent the overthrow of the government by people who had no stake in the country and had not the welfare of the people of Ulster at heart was to disenfranchise them'.[48] Although *Hansard* was edited to leave this statement out, the official records retained reference to the Opposition's outrage.[49]

In response to rising violence associated with republican demands for Home Rule, immediately prior to partition Loyalists in the North reformed the Ulster Volunteer Force. As in 1912, an élite group that maintained a close relationship with the police and army led the 1920 UVF. A decentralised and localised force, Loyalists formed the body with the tacit approval of the British government. Britain later called upon the 1920 UVF to assist the regular Crown forces. Relations between the Crown forces and members of the UVF were uneasy. The British Commander-in Chief reported to his superiors that employing the local militia amounted to 'the arming of Orange bigots'. Concern at the military's perspective of the UVF, and resentment expressed within the UVF at the dangerous night-time duties imposed on the loyalist volunteers, led to unionist leaders' insistence that the force be put on an official footing. The threat of anarchy, should matters be taken into the hands of the loyalist rank and file, motivated the British government to agree to the incorporation of the UVF into the newly formed police and military institutions. The regular police force, the Royal Ulster Constabulary (RUC), drew from the Royal Irish Constabulary and the UVF. The Northern government initially sought a police force with proportional Catholic and Protestant representation. Violence in the North, the Civil War in the South, pressure within the nationalist and republican communities, and the increasing sectarian nature of government in the North quickly undermined this goal. While the RUC in 1923 reached some 21.1 per cent Catholic members, the percentage subsequently dropped to 10 per cent or less.

In addition to a strong police force, unionist leadership also viewed the creation of a military force with sole responsibility to the Northern government as an indispensable objective of the new State. Although the 1920 Act prohibited the North from raising its own armed force, the 1882 Special Constables Act enabled the government to establish the Special Constabulary.[50] The Northern Executive swiftly supplemented the RUC with the Ulster Special Constabulary (USC), consisting of three 'classes' of members: class 'A' for officers engaged in full-time duty and willing to be posted anywhere in Northern Ireland; class 'B' for part-time officers operating in their own locality, and class 'C' for individuals reserved for emergency duty. By August 1922 the security forces included 1,200 full-time RUC members, 7,000 'A' specials, 20,000 'B' specials and 17,000 'C' specials.[51] After the boundary question dropped by the wayside at the end of 1925, the Unionist government stood down the A and C Specials. The government retained the B Specials, however, whose average membership was between 11,000 and 12,000. Almost exclusively Protestant and largely drawn from the ranks of the UVF, the B Specials served as an unofficial army of the unionist regime. It was only much later, in the wake of Terence O'Neill's reforms, that the government reduced their number to 8,500 and in 1970 the government disbanded the B Specials.[52]

At the time of partition the Unionist government insisted on the formation and retention of these security forces. Collins vehemently objected to the Colonial Secretary about the use of the Ulster Special Constabulary but his objections fell on deaf ears.[53] Civil war had erupted in the South, and the British government wanted to avoid direct confrontation over the development of a paramilitary force that seemingly violated the 1920 Act. Republicans in the North sought to overturn the Constitution of the new State. The distance between the Northern Parliament and Westminster can clearly be seen in Britain's refusal to interfere with even the operation of the Special Constabulary. Major-General Solly-Flood, appointed in 1922 as Military Adviser to Northern Ireland, submitted evidence in the same year, criticising the RUC and B Specials, to a secret inquiry conducted by Barrington Ward, KC, appointed to investigate the June 1922 murder of three Catholics in Cushendall.[54] Solly-Flood's final report strongly criticised the security forces, but instead of addressing the concerns the British Cabinet took steps to suppress the report. Following Solly-Flood's subsequent resignation, later attempts by the War Office to install a new Military Advisor in the North met with strong resistance from the unionist establishment. One of the unionist leadership's objectives at that time was to retain a military force with sole responsibility to the Northern government. The Executive sought to institutionalise this force permanently, thus underscoring the refusal of the North to be coerced into a united Ireland. As such, Orangemen bore the duty to consider serving on the force:

> The more Orangemen we have in [the Ulster Special Constabulary] the better it will be for the Protestant interests and the success of the Orange body itself. This seems perfectly patent. We must remember the old adage 'He who is not with me is against me'. Orangemen must come out now or be very sorry later that they have been neutrals, when they see nationalists filling the ranks of an armed force where they might have been.[55]

The creation of the USC both reflected and accelerated the relative autonomy of the Northern Parliament over issues of law and order.

In concert with the above measures, in 1922 the Northern Parliament passed the Criminal Procedure Act (Northern Ireland).[56] Drawn from clause four of the Craig-Collins pact, this Act allowed for the removal of juries and the creation of special courts for trials involving serious crime. The Act defined 'serious crime' as, 'any offence punishable with death, penal servitude, or imprisonment for a term exceeding six months'.[57] This was not the first time that non-jury trial had been initiated in Ireland. The 1881 Protection of Person and Property Act[58] created 'Special Resident Magistrates' to address trial without juries. One resident magistrate defended the statute's powers and his role in their use: 'to send persons for trial before a jury was but to advertise the weakness of the law; and as my object was to assert its strength, I avoided this course during my magisterial administration'.[59] In 1882 Britain also instituted the Prevention of Crime (Ireland) Act.[60] In the wake of the Phoenix Park murders, this legislation suspended the right to trial by jury in acts of treason, murder and assaults on dwelling houses. If the Lord-Lieutenant believed that an impartial trial could not be obtained under regular law, he had the power to assign cases to a three-judge tribunal. Britain incorporated similar provisions into the discarded Criminal Justice Administration (Ireland) Bill of 1920.[61] The measure proposed a special commission court constituted by a President and two additional members, all appointed by the Lord-Lieutenant. Under the Bill the Lord Lieutenant had the power to refer cases to the court for charges relating to treason, murder and explosives. The special court had the option of inflicting the death penalty. In order to convict, the bench had to be unanimous.[62] In response to the widespread intimidation of juries in evidence at the time, the legislation established a special commission composed of three judges of the High Court in Ireland. The statute allowed appeal to the Court of Criminal Appeal, with five other judges of the High Court present. The Act, however, never operated, and its institution spurred the resignation of one of the leading justices of the time.

The 1922 Criminal Procedure Act specified that special courts be comprised of the Lord Chief Justice of Northern Ireland and one of the two judges of the Court of Appeal of Northern Ireland. The statute required that these two judges hear cases either at the request of the accused or by designation of the Northern Ireland Attorney General, with no appeal from the court possible. The schedule to the Act applied serious crimes to treason or treason felony, murder or manslaughter, assault either causing bodily harm or conducted with the intent to cause grievous bodily harm, arson, any crime or offence involving (a) the breaking into, firing at or otherwise attacking or injuring a dwelling house (b) larceny or robbery with threats or violence (c) malicious injury, damage, or destruction of property (including any crime or offence under the 1861 Malicious Damage Act, any crime or offence against the 1883 Explosive Substances Act or the 1920 Firearms Act), and any involvement with the commission of such crimes.

During the introduction of the Bill, the main argument made against the adoption of this legislation in the House of Commons centred on the concern that with two judges, it was unlikely that mitigating circumstances would be taken into account. Members of the Northern Ireland Parliament viewed the elimination of the jury as akin to the removal of human sympathy.[63] Owing to doubts expressed in the North as to the powers of the Northern Parliament to legislate on matters affecting the judiciary, unionists arranged for concurrent legislation to be introduced into Westminster. They hoped in this way to validate the Criminal Procedure Act. Winston Churchill directed at the time, however, that the Bill drafted to confirm the Criminal Procedure Act not be introduced into the imperial Parliament and that the Northern government refrain from instituting any proceedings under the Act.

Although the Northern Executive refrained from invoking this statute, its content indicates the approach of the Northern government towards violence linked with the political structure of the North. Significantly, during the introduction of the 1922 Act, Richard Best, the Northern Ireland Attorney General, failed to give any examples where a jurist had actually been intimidated, or a jury had returned an unfair verdict. When the British government previously introduced similar measures in Ireland, a comparable lack of evidence marked their introduction. Even at the height of the Ribbon crisis in 1871, the Viceroy of Ireland, Earl Spencer, suggested that 'proof cannot be given to the idea . . . that Ireland is not fit for juries'. Under the 1881 Protection of Person and Property Act the government created special resident magistrates to oversee jury-less courts. The government followed this statute with the 1882 Prevention of Crime (Ireland) Act, which empowered the Lord-Lieutenant to assign cases to a three-judge tribunal, in the event that the Lord-Lieutenant believed an impartial trial to be impossible. In each instance, however, minimal information was provided as to the number of and extent to which cases of intimidation had arisen.[64] Members of Parliament later voiced concern in 1973 at the same lack of hard data to back up the government's plea for the suspension of jury trial. Chapter three looks at this in greater detail and explores the introduction of the Diplock courts. Essentially, immediately following partition, the 1921 Local Government (Emergency Powers) Act, the 1922 Local Government Act and the formation of the RUC and Special Constabulary worked together to consolidate unionist control of the province. The 1922 Criminal Procedure Act further indicates the length to which the Unionist government would go to secure the State. By far the most pervasive and extensive powers employed at this time, however, were contained in an entirely different piece of legislation. The 1922 Civil Authorities (Special Powers) Act (SPA) enabled the Unionist government to establish order and to consolidate its hold on the North.[65]

1922–33 SPECIAL POWER ACTS

Between 6 December 1921 and 31 May 1922, 236 people died and a further 346 sustained injuries in Northern Ireland as a result of political violence. Those who died numbered sixteen members of the Crown forces, 147 Catholics and seventy-three Protestants. Of those injured, thirty-seven served in the Crown forces, 166 were Catholic and 143 were Protestant.[66] Responding directly to this violence, in 1922 the Northern Ireland government enacted the Civil Authorities (Special Powers) Act (Northern Ireland), also known as the Special Powers Act (SPA).[67] This legislation, drawn from statutes previously employed by the British government, quickly became the cornerstone of Unionist security policy. The Unionist government renewed the 1922 SPA annually from 1923 through 1927[68] and extended it in 1928 through the Civil Authorities (Special Powers) Act (Northern Ireland).[69] In 1933 the government noted the efficacy of the legislation and made it permanent through the 1933 Civil Authorities (Special Powers) Act (Northern Ireland).[70] On one further occasion, in 1943, the Executive further amended the SPA.[71]

Throughout the tenure of the Stormont regime the 1922–43 Special Powers Acts were recognised as being inequitably applied to the two communities in Northern Ireland. Following the 1935 riots in the North the Council for Civil Liberties issued a report which stated: 'The Northern Government has used Special Powers towards securing the domination of one particular political faction and, at the same time, towards curtailing the lawful activities of its opponents . . . the Government's policy is thus driving its opponents into the way of extremists'.[72] The British-appointed Cameron Commission later underscored these claims. This body concluded that the presence and disparate application of the Special Powers Acts had generated widespread resentment among the Catholic population. Indeed, this statute constituted one of the central grievances highlighted by the Civil Rights campaign of the late 1960s and featured prominently in demands made by organisations such as the Northern Ireland Civil Rights Association and the People's Democracy.

Initial claims regarding the Bill's non-partisan character soon gave way to recognition of how the Unionist government applied the legislation.[73] The 1922 SPA evolved out of the 1920 Restoration of Order in Ireland Act (ROIA),[74] which, in turn, drew itself from the 1914–15 Defence of the Realm Acts (DORA).[75] The first Defence of the Realm Act granted power to 'His Majesty in Council' to issue regulations, 'for securing the public safety and the defence of the realm'.[76] Regulations introduced under the Act focused on preventing communication with the enemy and ensuring the safety of all railways, docks, harbours and communication networks. Regulations under DORA granted the competent military authority numerous emergency powers, such as occupation of land and buildings, the confiscation of property, control of petrol, control of lands, control of movements of the civil population, the power to make by-laws, powers of search, interrogation and arrest. They also provided for the trial of offences via courts-martial or a court of summary jurisdiction. The United Kingdom government introduced the ROIA to retain provisions of the DORA in relation to Ireland, while repealing the rest of the statute for Great Britain.[77] The 1920 ROIA stated: 'Where it appears to His Majesty in Council that, owing to the existence of a state of disorder in Ireland, the ordinary law is inadequate for the prevention and punishment of crime or the maintenance of order, His Majesty in Council may issue regulations under the Defence of the Realm consolidation Act, 1914, for securing the restoration and maintenance of order in Ireland'.[78] The ROIA assumed every DORA Regulation in force at the time of its enactment. In addition, whereas the DORA had only dealt with offences against the Act, Westminster constructed the 1920 ROIA to apply to criminal charges as well. Any criminal case referred to the Attorney General could be investigated and punished under the ROIA and its Regulations.

In November 1921 the new Northern Ireland Ministry of Home Affairs proposed that the government introduce a bill to transfer the powers held by the military authority under the Restoration of Order in Ireland Regulations (ROIR) to the Civil Authority. The Ministry also requested that in lieu of courts martial, special courts be created to impose the penalties detailed by the new legislation. Outside courts martial, no precedent existed which would allow an authority lower than a County Court to impose flogging or the death penalty. The government viewed the special court as useful in cases where the courts anticipated that juries would act in a manner partial to offenders belonging to their own party. In the Northern Parliament and in personal correspondence the Ministry of Home Affairs highlighted the aim of the government in removing the powers from the military and transferring them to the Civil Authority. For instance, in a written response by the Minister of Home Affairs to the Lord Mayor of Belfast, who had contacted the Ministry with the concern that the new legislation would undermine his authority, Dawson Bates, wrote:

> [The Special Powers Act] in no way interferes with the prerogative vested in you as Lord Mayor of Belfast. It proposes to confer certain additional powers with the object of increasing the penalty for certain offences, and increasing the power of certain courts to inflict sentences; shortly, it proposes to transfer to the Civil Authorities (that is the Government of the day) the various powers which were vested, and still are vested, in the Military Authorities under the Restoration of Order in Ireland Act.[79]

The Unionist government later claimed that the effect of the SPA was, 'to give the Minister of Home Affairs, designated the Civil Authority, power to make Regulations corresponding to the Restoration of Order in Ireland Regulations, and to make orders under such of those Regulations as were of an enabling character'.[80] The Special Powers Act so effectively transferred powers from the ROIR, that by 1926 the Ministry of Home Affairs determined that the revocation of the 1920 Act would not involve, 'the abrogation of any important or essential powers' which the government either didn't hold or couldn't obtain under the SPA.[81] Westminster did not, however, repeal the 1920 Act at this time. The two main reasons for retaining the legislation related to measures providing for courts martial for charges levied on the security forces and limiting the movement of arms into and out of Northern Ireland. Under the 1920 Government of Ireland Act, Britain reserved for the imperial government all matters relating to import and export. Unionist Members of Parliament cited additional concerns that it might be difficult to get similar legislation passed through Parliament in the future, should an administration less 'sympathetic' come to power.[82] The Home Office agreed to retain the ROIR but encouraged the Northern government to arrange for the Civil Authority to begin acting on the powers granted to the Military Authority in the ROIR and duplicated in the 1920 Firearms Act. Westminster finally repealed the ROIA and ROIR through the 1953 Statute Law Revision Act.[83]

The urgency evinced by violence in the province can be seen clearly in the vigour with which the Unionist government introduced the 1922 SPA. Hugh Smith Morrison, MP for Queen's University, exclaimed: 'I say, we cannot help ourselves. We are up against a wall, and we must make a fight for our lives'.[84] Repeatedly, Unionist Members of the Northern Ireland Parliament highlighted the need to regain control of the province. Robert Megaw, Unionist MP for Co. Antrim and Parliamentary Secretary in the Ministry of Home Affairs 1921–5, announced: 'All that we have got to do is to restore the supremacy of law and order within our area'.[85] Dehra Chichester, Unionist MP for Londonderry County and Derry City 1921–9, similarly asserted: 'We feel that the strongest measures are absolutely needed now, and that in the present state of the country, it is only the very strongest measures which can strike the necessary fear into the hearts of the criminals'.[86] The incidence of rising violence immediately preceding the introduction of the Special Powers Act prompted this concern. For example, an internal report in November 1921 stated:

> While a number of individual outrages have recently taken place, an organised outbreak by gunmen appears to have been designed to synchronise with the taking over of the administration of Law and Justice by the Northern Government. On Saturday and Sunday, 20th and 21st November a good deal of sniping took place . . . On the evening of the 21st, the disturbances assumed more threatening proportions. The trouble started in the early morning with an attack by snipers on shipyard workers proceeding to work at Newtownards Road. Military and police were hurried to the scene and checked the firing. Sniping, however, continued and several persons were hit . . . In the after-noon the trouble spread to the York Street area, where a number of casualties occurred . . . there were in all three persons killed, and nine wounded. On [22 November] the disturbances assumed a most serious character. In the Newtownards Road district a fierce outbreak of shooting took place on passers-by . . . No less than three bomb outrages were perpetrated . . . No less than 10 persons were killed, and over 50 wounded on this date . . . The disturbances were again renewed on the 23rd November . . . There were . . . three killed and 15 wounded. On the 24th instant, a further dreadful bomb outrage took place . . . There were four men killed and 10 wounded on 24th November.[87]

The government also sought to create a strong administration and consistent policy in contrast to the vacillation and conciliation seen by unionists as characterising previous British governments in Ireland. Members of the Northern Ireland Parliament asserted: 'Vacillation and ineptitude almost beyond belief have characterised some of the past governments of our country,'[88] and, 'We have a heritage given us by the

British Government, a state of things rendered unbearable because of the misgovernment under which we have lived and laboured for the last 15 years in Ireland'.[89] The Northern Ireland government's fundamental aim was to avoid being terrorised or driven into a united Ireland. The subsequent Bill incorporated a number of the regulations employed under the 1920 Act and created a special tribunal for courts martial. It also substituted the Civil Authority for the competent Military or Naval Authority as the authority to direct charges and prosecutions for both offences and crimes, defining the Civil Authority as, in relation to offences, the Minister of Home Affairs (or some person authorised by him in that capacity), and with regard to crimes, the Northern Ireland Attorney General.

The government justified the legislation when it was first introduced into the Northern Ireland House of Commons by appealing to the exceptional nature of the violence and the development of the social and political situation in Northern Ireland. Unionist ministers asserted: 'This is an exceptional time and requires exceptional measures. We may require stronger measures still'.[90] Robert Lynn added: 'We are living not in normal, but in very abnormal times . . . Is civilisation going to be allowed to exist, or is there going to be anarchy?'[91] This appeal to extraordinary circumstances met the tests laid out in both the 1914 Defence of the Realm Act and the 1920 Restoration of Order in Ireland Act, which dictated under what conditions emergency regulations could be issued. The new parliament also looked to the past for justification of measures introduced, with reference not merely to the content of previous emergency statutes, but to the manner in which such legislation would be executed. 'The measure places no hardship whatever on men who are lawfully disposed. Some of us . . . remember the introduction of the Crimes and Coercion Acts in the early seventies and eighties, and no one, at least in the Northern Area, ever thought for one moment that their rights were in any way challenged.'[92] The idea that the Act only applied to individuals who broke the law carried through public and parliamentary discussion of the emergency measures. The *Belfast Newsletter* and the *Northern Whig* carried similar statements. Such sentiments continued to be voiced throughout the fifty years that the 1922 Special Powers Act operated. During the Senate debates on the 1943 Special Powers Act Members of the Northern Ireland Parliament asserted: 'No innocent man need be afraid of the law in Northern Ireland; it is only the criminal who need be afraid of it'.[93] Unionists in the North further sought to legitimise the far-reaching powers through appeal to the international arena. Robert Lynn asserted: 'The demand that the Government is making of this House is not an extreme one at all, because I think there is scarcely a regulation or clause in this Bill, or a regulation that will be made under it, that every civilised Government does not hold at the present time'.[94] In 1922 the Civil Authoritie's Bill received widespread support in the Northern Parliament, with members proposing even greater powers during the second reading. Of the entire House, only one member opposed the Bill, and this opposition was voiced with an eye towards increasing military measures instead. It should be remembered that at this time the nationalist boycott meant that the House was almost wholly comprised of the unionist community.

In accordance with the charter granted the Northern Parliament under the 1920 Government of Ireland Act, the Special Powers Act set out to empower the government to take steps, 'for preserving the peace and maintaining order in Northern Ireland'. Colonel Meyler, Robert Megaw and Samuel Watt, the Permanent Secretary in the Ministry of Home Affairs, drafted the measure. Through this legislation Northern MPs surrendered a great deal of the parliamentary authority allocated by the 1920 Act and transferred it to the Northern Ireland Executive. The first section of the SPA allowed the Civil Authority, '. . . to take all such steps and issue all such orders as may be necessary for preserving the peace and maintaining order'.[95] The framers added a slight caveat providing that the ordinary course of law and the enjoyment of property bear minimal disturbance according to the exigencies of the situation in question. This clause was drawn from the Restoration of Order in Ireland Regulations which read:

> The ordinary avocations of life and the enjoyment of property will be interfered with as little as may be permitted by the exigencies of the measures required to be taken for securing the restoration or maintenance of order in Ireland, and ordinary civil offences will, except so far as measures to the contrary are taken under these regulations, be dealt with by the civic tribunals in the ordinary course of law.[96]

The government included this section in the 1922 Special Powers Act with the understanding that although the elimination of disorder was their first priority, the Civil Authority would attempt to avoid interfering with 'law abiding' people.[97] In accordance with these concerns, the 1922 Special Powers Act provided for the right to compensation from the Civil Authority for property damages incurred in the course of the exercise of powers embedded in the Act. Section 11 became governed by rules issued 7 December 1922 by Denis Stanislaus Henry, the first Lord Chief Justice of Northern Ireland, who was distinguished also for being a Catholic unionist.[98] The rules, drafted by John C. Davison, Law Adviser to the Ministry of Home Affairs, used the Workmen's Compensation Rules of 1917 as a precedent. James Cooper, a solicitor in Fermanagh, prompted the creation of these rules. Cooper sent a missive to the Secretary of the Ministry of Home Affairs that referred to a claim against the government that a local firm planned to file. During a search on the 30 May 1922 the security forces had damaged the Coulter Brothers' premises and confiscated their motor car. The Restoration of Order Act dictated that certain rules be made by the Lord Chief Justice of Northern Ireland concerning the procedure to be adopted in making claims against the government of Northern Ireland. In his letter Cooper requested that the Ministry of Home Affairs supply a copy of the current rules governing compensation. In the absence of such a document, the Ministry drafted and issued a set of rules under section 11 of the Special Powers Act.[99] The decision for settlement rested with a County Court or an arbitrator to be appointed by that Court. As discussed in chapter three, similar provisions for compensation were later incorporated into section 25 of the 1973 Emergency Provisions Act.

The first section of the 1922 SPA effectively extended to the Executive the authority that had been vested in the Northern Parliament to make laws. The statute empowered the Civil Authority not just with the general power to take action and to make, vary or revoke regulations, but with specific powers reflected in the regulations themselves. As with the 1920 Restoration of Order in Ireland Act, all regulations made under the legislation had to be laid before both Houses of Parliament 'as soon as may be' after their creation, at which time each House had fourteen days to dispute the regulation.[100] The legislature, however, had no right to disallow any of the Minister's regulations. The statute merely provided that the Northern Ireland Parliament had the option of petitioning for the revocation of any regulation. The authority to annul measures rested in the hands of the Lord-Lieutenant, whom the Executive advised on whether to accept or decline the petition. Although the constitutional structure incorporated direct scrutiny from Britain, in practice the Lord-Lieutenant exercised almost no influence over provincial affairs. The 1921 Local Government (Emergency Provisions) Act, discussed earlier, is the only instance in which Britain exercised any censorship of Northern Irish legislation. Even then, the Act was merely delayed for two months and no amendments or alterations were made to the resulting statute. Westminster never invoked the power of annulment with relation to the 1922–43 SPAs, in the course of which unionists introduced or amended more than 100 regulations. The ease with which such regulations were passed is illustrated in the complaints in the Northern Ireland Parliament as to their absence even from the table.[101] Members of the Northern Parliament did not even need to read the measures. The Executive simply issued regulations, and at the expiry of the two week period, copies of the new measures were circulated to the RUC and Special Constabulary.

The 1922 Act made it an offence not only to act against a regulation created in pursuance of the legislation, but to incite or endeavour to persuade another person to commit an offence, or to harbour any person in the knowledge, or reasonable grounds for supposition, of having acted in contravention to the regulations.[102] Any individual with the knowledge or reasonable belief that another individual was acting, had acted, or was about to act in such a manner, would be found guilty of an offence upon failing to inform the civil authorities of the fact.[103] The government extracted the wording of the revocations of Regulations directly from Regulation 66 of the Restoration of Order in Ireland Act. In a vague, catch-all phrase, the 1922 legislation further stated: 'If any person does any act of such a nature as to be calculated to be prejudicial to the preservation of the peace or maintenance of order in Northern Ireland and not specifically provided for in the regulations, he shall be deemed to be guilty of an offence against the regulations'.[104] This clause allowed virtually any action to be prosecuted if determined by the unionist establishment to threaten the peace of the State. Thus, not only did the legislation fail to require the consent of the legislature for the enactment of specific regulations, but the Ministry of Home Affairs could declare any action unlawful even without introducing a new regulation. Beyond granting these powers to the Executive, the Act provided for them to be delegated further by the Civil Authority.

Delegations under the 1922–33 SPAs

According to section 1(2), the powers granted to the Minister of Home Affairs for Northern Ireland could be delegated to any police officer, either unconditionally or subject to conditions the Minister deemed necessary. The government exercised these powers with caution during the operation of the SPAs. In general, the Minister of Home Affairs only granted the RUC Inspector General and Deputy Inspector General powers under Regulations 23 and 4.[105] After 1933 the Ministry delegated to the Parliamentary Secretary the overall power to act as the Civil Authority. One reason for the conservative use of section 1(2) was the ambiguity concerning who exactly could be counted as a 'chief officer of police'. In the absence of a definition in the 1922 SPA, the Chief Crown Solicitor interpreted this as similar to the definition put forth in the 1920 Firearms Act: that of County Inspector and above, and in Belfast the officer discharging the duty of the City Commissioner. Arthur Black, the Northern Ireland Attorney General 1939–41, finally resolved the debate by drafting a new statutory instrument to reflect Ewing Gilfillan's requirements.[106] This instrument amended Regulation 23(B) to read, 'Inspector General' or 'Deputy Inspector General'.[107] Early in the operation of the SPA, a second reason for reluctance to delegate power under the Act seems to have centred on whether such delegation would impair the power of the Minister himself. To keep the powers of the Minister of Home Affairs intact, subsequent orders specifically stated that the delegation of such powers in no way diminished the existing powers of the Civil Authority or others acting on behalf of the Civil Authority. In each case the Minister of Home Affairs granted authorisation by issuing an order with the names of the individuals to whom he extended his power.

In 1922 Dawson Bates authorised Charles George Wickham, RUC Inspector General 1922–45, and John Fizugh Gelston, Commissioner of Police for Belfast and later RUC Deputy Inspector-General, to exercise the powers of arrest, detention and internment under Regulation 23. Later in the year Bates extended the same power to Gelston in his new position as RUC Deputy Inspector General. Although in 1925 the Minister issued an order granting Wickham the authority to prohibit meetings, assemblies and processions under Regulation 4, Dawson Bates sent with it strict instructions that this authority should only be exercised having first consulted with the Ministry of Home Affairs. Dawson Bates allowed the delegation in this particular case to enable Wickham to prohibit a meeting of the Unemployed Workers in Belfast scheduled for 6 October 1922. The warrant authorising Wickham to prohibit such meetings accompanied a draft order for the Inspector General to sign prohibiting the march. Although delegation generally under the SPA could be made to any chief officer of police (section 1(2), the power of prohibiting meetings could be delegated to 'any magistrate or chief officer of police'.[108] The Ministry of Home Affairs delegated further powers under Regulation 4 to subsequent RUC Inspector Generals, but the policy of informing the Ministry before the issuance of orders continued in practice throughout the operation of the SPAs. As H.C. Montgomery, Secretary to the Ministry of Home Affairs, wrote in 1945 to Captain Richard Pike Pim, the second RUC Inspector General, 'I am . . . to state that while the authority conferred on you to prohibit meetings or processions under Regulation 4 is of a general nature the Minister desires that this power shall not be exercised without previous reference to the Ministry'.[109] This policy, in a sense, however, was meaningless, as nearly all of the information on the basis of which the Ministry of Home Affairs prohibited meetings, assemblies and processions under Regulation 4 was based on reports supplied by the RUC. Between 1922 and 1972 the RUC issued only a few orders banning meetings, and these were enacted only in prior consultation with Home Affairs. In 1926 Dawson Bates extended powers under Regulation 23 to Frederick Ambrose Britten, RUC Deputy Inspector General, in 1935 to Ewing Gilfillan, RUC County Inspector, and in 1942 to Joseph Roger Moore, RUC County Inspector. In 1945 the Minister of Home Affairs further delegated powers under Regulations 23 and 4 to Richard Pike Pim, the newly-appointed RUC Inspector General. Although at the time the Ministry had orders in place with regard to the Inspector General and County Inspector, the Minister of Home Affairs deemed delegation to a third member of the RUC necessary. Moore's recent appointment as head of the Crime Special Branch made him responsible for matters arising out of the Special Powers Acts. In any event, the impetus for extending powers to the RUC came from the RUC itself.[110] As in the early 1920s, all detention orders under Regulation 23 had to be sent through the Home Affairs office before signature by the RUC.[111]

Section 3(2) of the 1922 SPA empowered the Attorney General to delegate the authority to prosecute for offences against the SPA and its Regulations. In the first year of the operation of the SPA, Best liberally applied this section by extending such authorisation to all officers and members of the Constabulary Forces.[112] Best directed at the time that, in line with the procedures followed for other offences, cases of a more serious character be submitted for special directions.[113] He sent a second circular to the RUC with guidelines for prosecutions. For firearms cases, every case had to be submitted for the specific directions of the Attorney General.[114] Although some question soon arose as to whether the general authorisation dated 28 April 1922 would suffice in later years, the Ministry of Home Affairs indicated that the RUC should wait until a challenge to the power arose in court, at which time a special order would be issued to protect the prosecuting police officer. 'The Minister [of Home Affairs] is advised that the general authority dated 28 April 1922 is still valid and effective. As, however, it may be difficult to prove this authority if the question is seriously challenged in court, a special authority will be issued in important or special cases where a vigorous defence is anticipated. In minor cases the general authority may be acted upon and if seriously challenged the court may be asked to adjourn the case in order that proof of the authority may be produced.'[115] In part because of this concern and partially as a result of the diminishing number of prosecutions under the Special Powers Acts, the practice gradually evolved that the RUC submit all cases under the 1922–43 SPAs or the Regulations to the Attorney General for specific authorisation. With the advent of the Second World War, however, and the tremendous increase in case load due to the introduction of identity cards under the Special Powers Act, Wickham requested that John Clarke MacDermott, Northern Ireland Attorney General and former Unionist MP for Queen's University, issue an order authorising District Inspectors to prosecute in cases arising under Regulation 1A.[116] The original papers delegating authority had been lost.[117] MacDermott responded to Wickham's request by asserting that section 3(2) had been designed to protect individuals from the broad powers encapsulated in the Act. Although he disagreed with the wide interpretation of the section, he extended the power to Deputy Inspectors to prosecute for offences against Regulation 1 or 1A because of the heavy case load and various delays caused by the issuance of identity cards:

> I think there can be little doubt that the primary intention of Section 3(2) of the Civil Authorities (Special Powers) Act (Northern Ireland) 1922 was to provide a safeguard for the individual in respect of the very drastic powers vested in the executive by that statute. I would be slow therefore to delegate authority as widely as was apparently done in 1922. But while a consideration of individual cases by the Attorney General should, I feel, be regarded as the normal course in complying with Section 3(2) I am satisfied that the terms of this subsection are sufficiently broad to allow of a more general authorisation and that an authorisation of this nature may properly and as a matter of practical sense be given in respect of cases under Regulation 1A.

In order to expedite the processing of cases related to offences under Regulation 1A, he was prepared to derogate his powers of prosecution:

> At present these cases are very numerous and there is inevitable delay as the file has to go from district to county to HQ to me and then back. All cases do not get back and this delay is especially unfortunate in custody cases, particularly as the sum of cases to date shows that they are usually simple breaches of Regulation 1A without any very complicated or serious element . . . In order therefore to facilitate and expedite dealing with offences under Regulation 1A I am prepared under Section 3(2) to authorise each DI to prosecute these offences in

his district save in such cases as I direct generally or specifically to be brought to me in the first instance . . . My general direction is that any cases under Regulation 1A which are unusually serious in their nature or implications or in which the person to be charged is a national of an allied power should be brought to my notice before proceedings are started; and further, that I should be acquainted with the facts of any case in which the defendant appeals.[118]

On assumption of office, all District Inspectors automatically received the authority from 1942–46 to prosecute these offences in their districts, save any cases viewed as unusually serious in their nature or implications, or in which the person to be charged was a national of an allied power.[119] The courts upheld this decision. The King's Bench Division of the High Court ruled on the 15 July 1942 in *Sweny* v. *Carroll* that the Attorney General could grant a general authorisation to the police to prosecute cases under Regulation 1A. In *Sweny* v. *Carroll* District Inspector N.H. Sweny alleged that Michael Carroll, the defendant, arrived in Northern Ireland from Éire in April 1942. Charging him with failing to produce an identity document, Sweny directed a prosecution by virtue of a general authorisation granted to him by MacDermott in March 1942. Two resident magistrates, W.F. McCoy and J.H. Campbell, had dismissed the charge against Carroll, holding that the facts relating to each alleged offence had to have been considered by the Attorney General before authority could be delegated and a prosecution brought. MacDermott suggested that a general order was sufficient to support a prosecution and that section 3(2) did not require specific directions. The Lord Chief Justice ruled that the wording of the section was consistent with the general consent given by the Attorney General.[120]

In 1957 Richard Pim once again sought permission for District Inspectors to prosecute cases under the Special Powers Acts, this time for curfew. Brian Maginess, Northern Ireland Attorney General (1956–64), accordingly issued an order authorising such officers to prosecute under Regulation 19. This practice continued until 1971. On the 16 April 1971 the Northern government announced the recommendations issued by a working party on public prosecutions, which had been set up under the chairmanship of Lord McDermott, Lord Chief Justice of Northern Ireland. The committee proposed the establishment of a system of public prosecutors, in place of the practice whereby the RUC acted as prosecutors in summary proceedings. The police continued to prosecute only for minor offences normally handled within four hours after arrest.

Mode of Trial and Penalties

As previously mentioned, in the absence of courts martial, the 1922 Act provided for the creation of special courts. The Act required that all trials conducted under its auspices be tried summarily by a court of two or more magistrates, with preliminary proceedings conducted by a single resident magistrate. As with the 1920 Restoration of Order in Ireland Act, appeal against convictions lay with a Court of Quarter Sessions, with the appellate tribunal consisting of a recorder or County Court judge sitting alone. In response to concerns that the first hearing of a case should be sufficiently strong in order that the accused be assured that the courts adjudicated fairly and legally, the government responded that it was more economical to employ only one individual for preliminary hearings. As Mr Coote stated in the House:

> I think that all the Attorney General asks for is that powers which are vested in two resident magistrates may be vested in one. I think that is a very simple request. It is a very economic request. If you will insist on having two resident magistrates going over the country for all these preliminary hearings it will mean a great deal of work and a great deal of expense . . . we are not here with any interest other than that of peace. We are here in order to afford such an instrument as will protect the law-abiding and the well-disposed people in our area.[121]

The statute specified that offences against the Act be considered in addition to offences determined under existing statutes. Thus, the maximum sentence of two years imprisonment, with or without hard labour, and a fine of £100 was additional to penalties already imposed for the transgression in question. 'The Regulations do not supersede the ordinary law. A man who throws a bomb is liable to penal servitude for life, and the possession of the bomb itself renders him liable to penal servitude for fourteen years. The two years' term does not apply to a bomb at all.'[122] The statute also amended ordinary law with regard to punishment, powers of arrest, the reading of depositions and the prohibition of inquests. Section five of the 1922 Special Powers Act centred on whipping, as defined by Section 37 of the 1916 Larceny Act. Flogging in this section related to any crime cited under the 1883 Explosive Substances Act, any offence regarding firearms under the 1920 Firearms Act, any offence against the Larceny Act relating to menacing demands with intent to steal, and any act of arson or any offence punishable on indictment under the 1861 Malicious Damage Act.[123] The Unionist government employed flogging as a punishment in numerous cases, both immediately following partition and during the IRA's 1938 campaign.[124] The government levied the vast majority of such sentences only on the Catholic population.[125] Immediately following the enactment of the 1922 SPA, between 26 April and 17 July, twenty-one prisoners received sentences of both extended imprisonment and lashes of either the cat or the birch. Of the twenty-one, only three were Protestants (all Presbyterian), and the rest Catholics. By July four of the floggings had been conducted and appeals for clemency in the other cases had been denied. Although both Britain and the Irish Free State later placed considerable pressure on the North to remit the outstanding sentences on nationalists, and in spite of the fact that Craig claimed that he was inclined to be lenient, Dawson Bates insisted that the law should take its course. These sentences provoked severe criticism from Britain and the Irish Free State.[126]

Responding to increased incidents of bombing, section 6 of the 1922 SPA introduced the death penalty for violations against section 2 and 3 of the 1883 Explosive Substances Act. Section 2 of this previous act provided that 'any person who unlawfully and maliciously causes by any explosive substance an explosion of a nature likely to endanger life or to cause serious injury to property shall, whether any injury to person or property has been actually caused or not, be guilty of felony, and on conviction shall be liable to penal servitude for life, or for any less term (not less than the minimum term allowed by law) or to imprisonment with or without hard labour for a term not exceeding two years'. Thus, even if no damage had occurred the death penalty could be applied. Section 3 of the 1922 Act read:

> Any person who within or (being a subject of Her Majesty) without Her Majesty's dominions unlawfully and maliciously – (a) does any act with intent to cause by an explosive substance, or conspires to cause by an explosive substance, an explosion in the United Kingdom of a nature likely to endanger life or to cause serious injury to property; or (b) makes or has in his possession or under his control any explosive substance with intent by means thereof to endanger life, or cause serious injury to property in the United Kingdom, or to enable any other person by means thereof to endanger life or cause injury to property in the United Kingdom, shall, whether any explosion does or does not take place, and whether any injury to person or property has been actually caused or not, be guilty of felony, and on conviction shall be liable to penal servitude for a term not exceeding twenty years, or to imprisonment with or without hard labour for a term not exceeding two years, and the explosive substances shall be forfeited.

Similar to section 4 of the 1883 Explosive Substances Act, the 1922 Act placed the onus of proof on individuals to demonstrate the lawfulness of the possession. Offences against section 3 of the 1883 Explosive Substances Act were formerly punishable by penal servitude not exceeding twenty years, or imprisonment with or without hard labour for a period not exceeding two years. The SPA provided that these offences could be punishable by death, but it did not bring such offences, which were considered felonies, within the jurisdiction of the summary courts; therefore, they still had to be tried by a judge and jury. The government introduced this last alteration not in the original Bill itself but in a later amendment reflecting concerns voiced by members of the House during the second reading of the Bill. Although eleven executions occurred in Northern Ireland from 1922 to 1972, none of these was conducted under the auspices of the 1922–43 SPAs.[127] Section 7 of the 1922 Act extended powers of arrest, and section 9 allowed for the reading of depositions where the attendance of witnesses could not be procured.

Control of Inquests

Section 10 of the 1922 SPA made further provision for the Minister of Home Affairs to control and prohibit the holding of inquests by coroners. Craig ensured that this section's clauses be included in the statute to protect the security forces from prosecution while they exercised powers under the Act. As Samuel Watt wrote to Richard Best during the drafting of the legislation:

> The Prime Minister is particularly anxious to secure that any member of the police or military forces, who, in what he bona-fide believes to be the execution of his duty, either wounds or kills an individual, should be indemnified so as to render him immune from any form of legal action. I do not know whether it would be possible to go farther in this direction than is provided by Clause 6(b) and (c) of the new Bill. No doubt, it will be permissible under that clause to arrange that the officer holding an inquest should be the superior officer of the force in which the man whose acts are called in question may be serving.[128]

Clauses 10(a), (b) and (c) of the final Act addressed coroners' inquests. In order to avoid controversial findings the government retained the power to appoint its own coroner and coroner's jury, prevent particular inquests and prohibit inquests in any area of Northern Ireland. During the committee stage of the Bill, Members of the Northern Ireland Parliament raised concerns about the extension of this power. Morrison noted: 'If these inquests are prohibited it raises a suspicion that will enable the enemy to blacken us further as far as that may be possible'.[129] He added: 'the holding of inquests is a very necessary thing under ordinary and other circumstances that may arise. They satisfy public opinion'.[130] The government countered these tentative points of opposition with the observation that not all coroners in the province shared the political inclination of the majority in the Northern Ireland Parliament. Richard Best stated: 'We cannot shut our eyes to the fact that there are some areas where the coroners are not in sympathy with us – where they are absolutely hostile to us, and the Minister of Home Affairs wishes, under these circumstances, to be able to prohibit inquests from being held in these particular areas'.[131] Once again the government appealed to the Restoration of Order in Ireland Act, and in particular to Regulation 81, which specified that the Lord-Lieutenant, for purpose of securing order, could prohibit the holding of inquests either by geographic area or by particular case. Best, stated bluntly: 'If you do not grant us this power under the Bill, we still have got it under the Restoration of Order in Ireland Regulations'.[132] Within weeks of the passage of this measure the Royal Irish Constabulary submitted a detailed report to the Ministry of Home Affairs, indicating which coroners were, 'not likely to be impartial where party feeling would be concerned'. The police listed one coroner from Co. Armagh and one from Co. Fermanagh. The RIC provided two more names for Co. Tyrone with a brief discussion of their political affiliations.[133] In the event that individual police officers did not feel that a coroner's inquest was expedient, Dawson Bates requested that they submit an application containing, 'sufficient information to show the necessity for the Special Inquest', to the RUC Divisional Commissioner, who would then forward the document to the Ministry of Home Affairs for consideration.[134]

1933–43 SPECIAL POWERS ACTS

The Northern Parliament renewed the 1922 SPA annually from 1923 through 1927 and in 1928 extended it for a five year period. In 1933 the government made the statute indefinite, with later amendments introduced in 1943. As early as 1927 the Northern Executive considered making the powers permanent. The question arose at Cabinet meetings on 30 July and 30 September in connection with the Expiring Laws Continuance Bill, which had already been introduced into the Northern Ireland House of Commons. The Cabinet deferred the question until the following year, by which time a report could be solicited from Anthony Brutus Babington, the Northern Ireland Attorney General. With his subsequent approval, in April 1928 the Cabinet decided to introduce a special bill to make the 1922 Act permanent. In the intervening period the 1922 Act had been amended in two ways: (a) the government shortened the period within which an address could be presented by either House of the Northern Ireland Parliament to the governor to ten days,[135] and (b) the Executive repealed sub-section 7 of section 2 of the Act (applying particular British enactments enabling accused persons to be competent witnesses for the defence) and re-enacted its effect in general terms by the 1923 Criminal Evidence Act (Northern Ireland).[136]

In 1927, when the issue of making the statute permanent came up for discussion, the Executive recognised that a state of relative peacefulness existed in Northern Ireland. The powers conferred by the Act and its Regulations had been used with increasing infrequency. That year the government brought only one prosecution under the Act, and that related to an offence (breach of an order under Regulation 23A) committed in 1926.[137] According to the RUC the chief value of the Act during this period centred on the power it gave to prohibit 'anything which may result in a breach of the peace, such as Republican and Communist meetings'.[138] Nevertheless, the government pointed to the expanding power of Fianna Fáil, the recent southern IRA campaign, the continued presence of a disaffected 'undercurrent', and the possible difficulty that might arise in trying to introduce similar measures to a future parliament less favourably disposed to special powers, as making it imperative that the Special Powers Act be extended once and for all. Internal memos voiced resentment at Britain's previous vacillation in security policy, claiming that such actions had played a central role in the Troubles of the early 1920s: 'In the old days the Imperial Parliament acted in the most inconsistent manner in connection with repressive legislation and this was, undoubtedly, one of the reasons why the Country was so unsettled. My feeling is, accordingly, that it would be desirable to place the Act permanently on the Statute Book, utilising it only if necessary'.[139] Ministers further appealed to the fact that the government passed the Defence of the Realm Acts and Regulations not at a time of disorder, but during the war as a way to be able to deal promptly with any emergency situations which might arise.[140] Although the government initially proposed that the Special Powers Act be made permanent, the Bill, as passed, continued the statute for five years only.[141]

Following the enactment of the 1922 SPA, the border defining Northern and Southern Ireland, intended as a temporary measure, became a permanent division. The Civil War in the South and opposition from the Northern Ireland government delayed the Boundary Commission from reporting. It did not begin work until 1924. Although its members reached internal agreement on border changes by 1925, the government suppressed the final report. The Commission advised the transfer of 183,000 acres and 31,000 people from Northern Ireland to the Irish Free State and the exchange of 50,000 acres and 7,500 people from the South to the North. Before the Commission could publish its recommendations, however, information was leaked to the *Morning Post*, and the Irish government's representative, Eoin MacNeill, resigned. The border remained as it had been drawn in 1921.

The elimination of the Border Commission failed to dissipate tension in the North. In the South republicans formed a distinct and increasingly Irish, Catholic State. In the 1932 Free State General Election, Eamonn deValera and Fianna Fáil gained control of the Southern Parliament. DeValera had vigorously opposed the 1921 Treaty and was determined to move the Free State towards independence from Britain and unity with the North. On his first day in office he lifted the ban on the IRA, announced the release of all IRA prisoners, and sent two of his ministers to Arbor Hill prison to meet the IRA as they exited. He demanded that Britain return some £30 million that had been paid in Land Annuities.[142] DeValera abolished the oath of allegiance from the Dáil and dropped the Union Jack as the Irish flag. Under his influence, northern nationalists boycotted the Northern Parliament at Stormont. Although some returned in 1933, sporadic participation marked the next decade, during which the southern regime continuously raised the issue of partition with the British government. In 1937 deValera instituted a new Constitution, renaming the Free State Éire and claiming jurisdiction over all of Ireland. In concert with these moves in the South, the formation of the Anti-Partition League in the North marshalled the energies of a full-time secretary, branches and regular meetings, to unite 'all those opposed to partition into a solid block'.[143] Britain, in turn, occasionally applied pressure to the Northern government to reconsider partition. In July 1945 Britain returned to power a Labour government led by Clement Attlee. With an overall majority, the Labour Party consistently criticised the evolution of affairs with regard to Northern Ireland. In 1945 some thirty Labour MPs formed an organisation called 'Friends of Ireland,' committed to unifying Ireland and remedying the grievances of northern Catholics.

Not only did developments in the Irish Free State/Éire and in Britain emphasise the lack of acceptance of the Treaty and, with it, the border, but various moves in the South further accentuated the Irish and Catholic nature of the State. In 1933 the Fianna Fáil government abolished the right of appeal from Irish courts to a judicial committee of the Privy Council in London. Seen as a minority guarantee, this move particularly alarmed both northern and southern Protestants.[144] The Irish Nationality and Citizenship Act of 1935 cancelled British citizenship for Irish citizens. The 1923 Censorship of Films Act, the 1929 Censorship of Publications Act, compulsory Irish lessons in all schools, the banning of education on contraception and, until the 1937 Constitution, the erection of obstacles to divorce, defined the Free State as a distinctively Catholic entity. Throughout this period the number of Protestants in the South dropped sharply: from 314,000 Protestants in 1911, only about 148,900 were resident by 1946.[145]

In the midst of these developments, on 25 January 1933 the Northern Ireland Minister of Home Affairs submitted two bills to the Cabinet; the first provided for the indefinite extension of the SPA while the second limited it to an additional five years. During a Cabinet meeting held on 31 January, however, the Executive opted for the first Bill. Although members of the Senate proposed during the committee stage to limit the duration of the 1922 SPA to three years, enabling the government to draft alternate legislation to be incorporated into ordinary law, the Committee defeated the amendment two to fourteen.[146] The rationale for securing the Act both in 1928 and in 1933 was antithetical to the reasons for which the government had first introduced it. While the Northern Executive claimed that 1922 Act focused on a return to civil order in the province, in 1933 the government argued that it was precisely because the North was tranquil that the legislation should be entrenched: 'The Government are not yet satisfied that those malcontents in our community have yet learned the lesson that Ulster will not stand for further outbreaks or disorders . . . Although peace prevails throughout the Province and law and order have rapidly improved in recent years, it is desirable to avoid as far as possible the yearly debates which have taken place on this particular measure during recent years'.[147] The extension of the Act became permanent in all but the wording of the statute. Craig decided in 1933 that the legislation should be secured, but he still objected to the word 'permanent' in the legislation itself. As a result, the statute reads: 'unless Parliament otherwise determines'. From 1933, Stormont made the 1922 SPA indefinite, effectively transforming the legislation from a temporary emergency measure into a constant feature of Northern Irish legislation.

Section 1(2) of the 1933 Civil Authorities (Special Powers) Act amended the 1922 statute to enable the Minister of Home Affairs to delegate all powers of the Civil Authority under the Special Powers Act to the Parliamentary Secretary of the Ministry of Home Affairs. Craig initially intended for the Minister of Home Affairs, as the Civil Authority, to be able to delegate his powers to 'any Minister'. However, when this proposal was circulated, other members of the Executive felt that it would be derogatory for one minister to receive delegation at the hands of another. As a result, Babington inserted a clause into the Bill empowering the Minister to delegate his powers to a 'Parliamentary Secretary'.[148] The Ministry of Home Affairs cautiously extended these powers to subsequent parliamentary secretaries, who only rarely acted in place of the Minister as the Civil Authority under the Special Powers Acts. The first delegation took place in 1935, when Dawson Bates granted all authority to George Boyle Hanna. The Minister of Home Affairs revoked this order on 6 August 1937. On 13 September 1937, as a result of the Minister's plans to go on a three week leave from the 15 of the month, the Minister of Home Affairs delegated all of his authority under the Special Powers Acts to John Clarke Davison, the Parliamentary Secretary. When it was suggested upon the Minister's return that this power be revoked, the Ministry decided not to, as 'We may find it useful to have Mr Davison available in the Minister's absence from Belfast at any time'.[149] On the 26 August 1938 the Minister of Home Affairs extended the power of the authority to Edmond J. Warnock, Davison's successor as Parliamentary Secretary. The Ministry of Home Affairs revoked these powers on 10 June 1940 and extended them to the new Parliamentary Secretary, William Lowry. On 13 May 1943 William Lowry, who himself became Minister of Home Affairs, issued an order empowering his replacement, Sir Wilson Hungerford, to act as the Civil Authority.

Five years after the government made the 1933 Act permanent, the IRA launched a number of attacks in Northern Ireland, and in September 1939 it initiated a bombing campaign in Great Britain. Explosions began with bombs in London, Birmingham and Manchester in January 1939. More bombing incidents followed on the 4, 5 and 6 of February and became more numerous throughout the year. By July, 127 explosions had occurred. On the 24 July Westminster introduced the Prevention of Violence Bill, which allowed the government to require all Irish people living in Britain to register and empowered the government to deport Irish citizens. A bomb two days later at King's Cross killed one man and injured fifteen others. It took only five days for Westminster to pass the Bill, and seven days for it to become law, forty-eight people had been expelled and five prohibited from entering Britain. The bombings continued into August and September, but Britain's entry into the war on 3 September 1939 effectively ended the campaign. The IRA lacked a sympathetic community from which to operate and, in light of the severe measures imposed by the British government their activities dwindled down.[150]

In Northern Ireland, as in 1922, the number of individuals apprehended by the northern security forces immediately increased. However, the government perceived the measures available for securing the conviction of republican leaders who did not have firearms or explosives in their possession at the time of arrest, as inadequate. Only two possible routes of prosecution existed. Members of the IRA could be charged with a violation of the 1922 SPA under Regulation 24A, which specified that 'any person who becomes or remains a member of an unlawful association or who does any act with a view to promoting or calculated to promote the objects of an unlawful association or seditious conspiracy' be found guilty of an offence against the regulations. Unlawful organisations listed in Regulation 24A included the Irish Republican Brotherhood, Irish Republican Army, Irish Volunteers, Cumann na mBan, Fianna na hÉireann, Saor Éire and the National Guard.[151] Second, the individual could be charged with treason felony under the 1848 Treason Felony Act. If charged under the former, the trial had to be before a court of summary jurisdiction composed of two or more resident magistrates, with a maximum punishment of two years' hard labour and a fine not exceeding £100. MacDermott saw such sentences as inappropriate for leaders of the republican movement, particularly during World War II, when the Law Department sought to secure 'exemplary' sentences. The alternative to Regulation 24A was to proceed on indictment on a charge of treason felony. Although it was not as technical an offence to prove as high treason, the charge was nevertheless complicated and difficult. In each case both the nature of the IRA as a paramilitary organisation and treasonable conspiracy had to be proved. It involved the production of numerous witnesses, as well as a tremendous amount of time to prepare and to present the case. The Deputy Inspector charged with combatting the activities of the IRA had to give evidence in each trial. To protect his time and ensure his safety, as the number of prosecutions increased it became inadvisable to focus attention on his position. No doubt existed that treason felony could be applied to terrorist crime: several trials for treason felony occurred in Northern Ireland between 1922 and 1942. Although the Attorney General suggested that treason felony remained 'the most apt charge' on which to arraign an important member of the IRA – who was found without arms or explosive substances in his possession – he also conceded that it was cumbersome and impractical. As a result, the government often prosecuted cases under the weaker auspices of Regulation 24A, attempting to demonstrate membership of an unlawful organisation. MacDermott wrote to Dawson Bates: 'The difficulties of proving an offence under the Treason Felony Act have from time to time resulted in the case being sent for trial before the Magistrates on a charge under the Regulations with the consequence that the punishment awarded does not meet the gravity of the crime'.[152]

The Northern Ireland Ministry of Home Affairs had no power to streamline the process under the 1848 Act. According to section 4(1) (6) of the 1920 Government of Ireland Act, the Northern parliament's legislative jurisdiction did not extend to either treason or treason felony. The Ministry of Home Affairs, acting in concert with the Prime Minister and the Attorney General, concluded that the simplest way to proceed would be to amend the 1922 Special Powers Act by increasing penalties for offences against the regulations. The Northern Ireland Parliament amended the SPA by means of the 1943 Civil Authorities (Special Powers) Act (Northern Ireland).[153] In consultation with Wickham and MacDermott, the Ministry of Home Affairs decided to make any offence under the Act or the regulations triable either summarily or on indictment. Amendments to sections 3 and 4 provided that a person convicted on indictment should be liable to: a) penal servitude for not less than three years or more than fourteen years, b) imprisonment for not more than two years with or without hard labour, c) a fine not exceeding £500, or d) either penal servitude or such imprisonment and such fine.[154] The Ministry also instituted changes in the makeup of the summary courts: for minor offences, such as curfew or documents of identity, the new statute provided for the court to be composed of one resident magistrate and not two as previously specified. This proposal had first been made in 1941 by the RUC when it claimed that requiring two resident magistrates for prosecutions under Regulation 1A was 'unwieldy and expensive'.[155] The Ministry denied the request at the time on the basis that it failed to provide sufficient reason to draft an entirely new amendment to the legislation. The amending statute provided the opportunity to insert appropriate measures into the 1943 Act.

The government instituted the adjustment to the courts immediately following the enactment of the 1943 SPA.[156] This regulation set a maximum sentence of six months or a fine not exceeding fifty pounds for offences arising under regulations addressing curfew, documents of identity, closing of licensed premises and possession of petrol, placing prosecution of such offences within the jurisdiction of a single magistrate sitting alone.[157] Dawson Bates summarised the overall changes of the 1943 Act, stating that they would, 'enable cases of a more serious nature to be dealt with expeditiously without having recourse to the somewhat cumbersome and impracticable procedure which would be necessary if such cases were brought under the Treason Felony Act of 1848, while . . . cases which may be regarded as minor offences against the Regulations [could] be disposed of with less expense and inconvenience and will make for expedition generally'.[158] Specific reference to the IRA in this memorandum suggests that the government specifically targeted the IRA with these amendments. The government gave the same reasons during the second reading in the Northern Ireland House of Commons, 9 March 1943 and in the Senate, 23 March 1943.[159]

The Northern Cabinet initially proposed that the 1943 Amending Bill include a provision giving police and prison officers the same powers with regard to the escape or attempted escape of internees from custody as the police had at Common Law in the case of escape or attempted escape of felons. However, the Attorney General's office recommended instead that the matter be dealt with by simply making an amendment to Regulation 23. The final paragraph of this regulation made it an offence for any person to assist the escape of a person in custody under the regulation. Section 7 of the 1922 statute empowered any person authorised by the Civil Authority, or any police constable – where necessary for the purpose of effecting an arrest in respect of an offence against the regulations – to exercise the like powers as for Common law. The Ministry of Home Affairs inserted an additional paragraph at the end of Regulation 23 to the effect that if any person in custody under the regulations escaped or attempted to escape, he would be guilty of an offence against the regulations. This enabled section 7 to be brought into operation.[160] From 1943 until 1972 the government refrained from instituting any further amendments to or replacements of the 1922–43 Special Powers Acts.

CONCLUSION

Sectarian violence and instability surrounding the creation of the Northern State lent urgency to Craig's regime. The 1921 Local Government (Emergency Powers) Act, 1922 Local Government Act and 1922 Criminal Procedure Act went some way towards meeting the challenge posed by the disorder. Complemented by the formation of the Royal Ulster Constabulary and Ulster Special Constabulary, the 1922 Special Powers Act was by far the most extreme measure implemented at the inception of the Northern government. At the time of its enactment, unionists justified the SPA by appealing to necessity: republican elements in the midst of the province, aided by sympathetic anti-Treatyists in the South, sought to overturn the constitutional structure of the State. Within months of the statute's introduction, violence plummetted. Rather than repeal the legislation, though, the perceived effectiveness quickly became part of the defence for its continued use:

> The Civil Authorities (Special Powers) Act was passed by the Parliament of Northern Ireland in April 1922 and within six months republican activity had been almost wholly suppressed as is indicated by the fact that the weekly number of murders due to political crime fell to zero, and of woundings to less than one. Since then, although there have been sporadic outbursts which the Civil Authority by the use of the powers which the Act confers, has been able to suppress with all speed, there has been nothing approaching the return of the appalling conditions which prevailed in the first half of 1922 . . . The interference with the ordinary principles of law which is caused by the Act and the regulations made under it by which these results have been achieved . . . is in practice comparatively trifling.[161]

A later report stated:

> The reason[s] for the continuance of the Civil Authorities Act . . . [are] first, . . . the existence of the Statute has undoubtedly proved that the powers under it which are reposed in the Authorities, act as a valuable deterrent on those who would otherwise be prepared to resort to any measures of violence to subvert the Constitution . . . second . . . the Authorities are only too well aware that the various disloyal and illegal organisations which were responsible for such a holocaust of murder and outrage still exist.[162]

Thus, while the statutes effectively addressed the violence in the province, the threat to the Constitution remained. In fact, as it soon emerged, the central use of the 1922–43 SPAs lay not in the main provisions of the statute, but in the statutory rules and orders introduced under the legislation. This legislation became a blunt weapon, exercised on behalf of and by one community in the North, and levied almost exclusively against the Catholic population. Chapter two focuses on the breadth and exercise of the powers so obtained by the Northern government.

CHAPTER TWO

Regulating Northern Ireland
1922–1972

I N THE EARLY 1920s the Unionist government drew on regulations under the 1922–43 Civil Authorities (Special Powers) Acts (SPAs) that focused on averting the immediate violence and civil unrest in Northern Ireland.[1] The Minister of Home Affairs, entrusted under the 1920 Government of Ireland Act with issues of law and order, extensively employed orders for detention, internment and restriction, curfew, restrictions on licensed premises, the sale and transfer of explosives, the blocking up of roads and powers of entry, search and seizure. These measures seemed to accomplish their goal. Within five months of the passage of the Special Powers Act the number of murders had plummeted from a high of eighty to one and the number of attempted murders from fifty-eight to eleven. The totals continued to decline for the balance of 1922 and well into 1923. Appendix A details the monthly murders and attempted murders in Northern Ireland from November 1921 to May 1923. As the Northern Ireland Imperial Secretary wrote to the Home Office in June 1923, 'These figures demonstrate in a convenient form the return of Northern Ireland during the last year to a peaceful internal condition. In comment upon that table I may add that all the four murders shown as committed since October 1922 were all definitely non-political'.[2]

Although it is difficult to judge the extent to which each regulation played a role in decreasing levels of violence, collectively they had a significant impact. In pleading for the permanent entrenchment of the 1922 SPA, Dawson Bates stated: 'If it had not been for the existence of the Civil Authorities Act on the Statute Book, and the powers which are utilised under it, there would have been no constitutional Government left in Ulster to-day'.[3] The government, however, gradually shifted its emphasis from broad measures designed to return civil order to the North to more preventative regulations aimed at suppressing the threat posed by nationalist and republican aspirations. The late 1920s to the mid 1950s witnessed an increase in the use of regulations prohibiting meetings, assemblies and processions, the flying of the Tricolour, the wearing of the

Easter Lily the singing of nationalist and republican songs, the circulation of newspapers, the printing of nationalist or republican documents and the operation of republican organisations. By the early 1950s the republican threat appeared to be largely contained. Together with the normalisation of some of the emergency powers into other statutes, such as the 1951 Public Order Act and the 1951 Criminal Procedure Act (Northern Ireland), the 1954 Flags and Emblems (Display) Act (Northern Ireland), and in conjunction with the revocation of the Offences Against the State Act in the South, between 1949 and 1951 the Unionist government repealed the vast majority of regulations under the SPA.[4]

Various elements contributed to the repeal of regulations at this time. World War II certainly had a direct impact: having demonstrated loyalty in contrast to the South's neutrality, northern unionists could look upon their continued links to Britain with increased confidence. With Winston Churchill, a devout Orange supporter, in power their position was even more secure. Moreover, the 1949 Ireland Act, enacted to respond to the 1948 declaration of the Irish Republic, reaffirmed that Northern Ireland would remain part of the United Kingdom until a majority in the Northern Parliament decreed otherwise. Unionists had established such a clear hold on the political machinery that the possibility of losing a majority in the Northern Ireland Parliament looked further off than ever. The newly found confidence gained under these circumstances, together with the relative calm in the North and the lack of immediate threat from the IRA, contributed to the repeal of emergency provisions. Thus, although divisions were still present in the province, the degree of security felt by the unionists, in juxtaposition to the constitutional threat wielded by nationalism and republicanism, had grown. An IRA bombing campaign from 1956 to 1962, however, while unsuccessful in its execution, spurred Stormont to reintroduce a number of the regulations. Thus, by the outbreak of the civil rights movement in the mid to late 1960s, many of the measures were back in place. As civil unrest increased, the government reverted to regulations aimed at obtaining civil order, and it is this legacy that the British government inherited with the proroguement of Stormont in 1972. Westminster's subsequent implementation of the 1973 Northern Ireland (Emergency Provisions) Act specifically incorporated regulations designed to obtain civil order, retaining only a few measures aimed at denying legitimacy to the nationalist or republican ideology.[5] Chapter three examines the measures incorporated into the 1973 legislation in more detail.

The shift to provisions designed to counter the constitutional challenge posed by republicanism accompanied a transformation in the justification for the Act. While the rationale for enacting the legislation in 1922 was based on a need to establish law and order in the province, in 1933 the government argued that it was precisely because the North was tranquil that the legislation should be made permanent:

> The Government are not yet satisfied that those malcontents in our community have yet learned the lesson that Ulster will not stand for further outbreaks or disorders . . . although peace prevails throughout the Province and law and order have rapidly improved in recent years, it is desirable to avoid as far as possible the yearly debates which have taken place on this particular measure during recent years.[6]

A later report stated:

> The reasons[s] for the continuance of the Civil Authorities Act . . . [are] first, . . . the existence of the Statute has undoubtedly proven that the powers under it which are reposed in the Authorities, act as a valuable deterrent on those who would otherwise be prepared to resort to any measure of violence to subvert the Constitution . . . second . . . the Authorities are only too well aware that the various disloyal and illegal organisations which were responsible for such a holocaust of murder and outrage still exist.[7]

The republican threat remained. Thus, although the 1922–43 SPAs had been effective in returning the province to a state of order, they became viewed as indispensable for maintaining peace. As an internal memo of the Northern Executive stated:

> The Civil Authorities (Special Powers) Act was passed by the Parliament of Northern Ireland in April 1922 and within six months republican activity had been almost wholly suppressed as is indicated by the fact that the weekly number of murders due to political crime fell to zero, and of woundings to less than one. Since then, although there have been sporadic outbursts which the Civil Authority by the use of the powers which the Act confers, has been able to suppress with all speed, there has been nothing approaching the return of the appalling conditions which prevailed in the first half of 1922.[8]

The efficacy of the measures led to the entrenchment of emergency legislation. Chapter seven examines factors which influenced this move towards permanency; for now, let us turn to a more detailed consideration of the regulations introduced by the Northern Ireland government from 1922 to 1972.

ADDRESSING CIVIL DISORDER: REGULATIONS IMMEDIATELY
FOLLOWING PARTITION

The majority of prosecutions in Northern Ireland that arose from the violence that immediately followed partition did not fall under the 1922 Special Powers Act. From July 1922 to December 1924, only eighteen cases were brought under the 1922 SPA, compared to 345 under the 1920 Firearms Act. Of seventy-two people brought to trial for charges under the SPA, only thirty-seven were convicted, as opposed to 397 and 296 under the Firearms Act.[9] The dismissal rate for cases under the Special Powers Act during this time was 47 per cent – nearly twice the 25 per cent rate under the Firearms Act. Instead of prosecuting offences against the statute, the government initially made the most use of regulations authorising the Ministry to exercise extended powers.[10] The thirty-five original regulations empowered the Civil Authority to impose curfew, to close licensed premises, to prohibit public meetings and processions, to ban military drilling, military uniforms and uniforms indicating membership of proscribed organisations, and to establish stringent requirements for the possession of firearms, explosives or petrol. In consultation with the Royal Irish Constabulary, the government drew these regulations directly from the 1920 Restoration of Order in Ireland Act (ROIA).[11] The Minister for Home Affairs, and members of the police force acting at his discretion, possessed virtually unlimited power to search for and to seize contraband and to detain those suspected of subversive activity. Interference with the railways, telephones, or telegraphs was banned as was the spreading of false statements or reports, statements, 'intended or likely to cause disaffection to His Majesty'.[12]

Members of the Northern Ireland Parliament expressed concern during the House debates that this clause would suppress criticism of the government altogether. Assuring the objector that it would be pursued only with regard to deliberately false statements relating to the government, the Northern Ireland Attorney General once again appealed to precedent. Best stated: 'This is nothing new; we are simply taking an existing regulation, one that is in full force and effect in the [Restoration of Order in Ireland Act]. We wish to put it in operation ourselves without having to invoke the aid of the military who have other and more necessary work to do'.[13] The Civil Authority was granted the ability to prohibit the circulation of any newspaper as deemed necessary. As mentioned in chapter one, the 1922 SPA further empowered the Civil Authority 'to take all such steps and issue all such orders as may be necessary for preserving the peace and maintaining order'.[14] In accordance with this section, the government quickly replaced or amended many of the initial regulations, particularly those governing powers of detention and curfew, and introduced a number of new regulations authorising additional powers, such as internment, restriction and exclusion orders. In 1922 alone the Northern Executive introduced fourteen amendments and additions to the regulations. Appendix C details the additional regulations introduced as statutory rules and orders under the 1922–43 Civil Authorities (Special Powers) Acts (Northern Ireland). By 1972 the Northern government had issued over 100 statutory rules and orders. These were shielded from effective parliamentary scrutiny because MPs could only petition the Lord-Lieutenant to consider their revocation.

Detention, restriction and internment

From 1922 to 1949, Regulations 23, 23A, 23B, 23C and 23D of the 1922–43 SPAs governed powers of detention, restriction and internment. Of these, only a few paragraphs of Regulation 23 had been included as part of the original schedule to the Act. The government amended this regulation within six weeks of the statute's enactment to allow for the detention of individuals wherever specified by the civil authorities and under whatever conditions the Civil Authority deemed appropriate.[15] The five regulations operated together during the first few years of the Northern government, at which time they were used to quell civil disorder.

Regulation 23, as amended in the first year of the operation of the SPA, allowed for the arrest without warrant of any individual suspected of acting, having acted, or being about to act in a manner prejudicial to the preservation of the peace or maintenance of order,[16] or upon whom any items were found which could be interpreted as prejudicial to the preservation of peace. In the latter case, the Civil Authority had the power to dispose of any items thus declared. The National Council for Civil Liberties later challenged the constitutionality of this clause, but no cases were brought before the courts.[17] An individual arrested under Regulation 23 could be detained either in the prisons or wherever was specified in the order, under whatever conditions the Civil Authority directed, until either discharged under the direction of the Attorney General or brought before a court of summary jurisdiction.[18] In each case in which the police determined that an individual should be detained, an application had to be made through the Inspector General and submitted to the Ministry of Home Affairs in order to secure a detention order.[19] The regulation specified that at the end of the period of detention, if the individual was not to be allowed to leave custody, twenty-four hours' notice in writing be given the detainee regarding the nature of the charge before he or she could be brought to court.[20]

Gradually the provisions governing detention became more extreme. Within a month of the enactment of the original regulation, the Civil Authority obtained the power to appoint the place of trial for detainees. An additional order dropped the demand of 'reasonable grounds' for detention. The text of Regulation 23, 'whom he suspects of acting or of having acted or of being', was replaced by the words, 'whose behaviour is of such a nature as to give reasonable grounds for suspecting that he has acted or is acting'.[21] Provisions for taking photographs and finger-prints of detainees were also made.[22] Any person found helping to plan another's escape or harbouring the individual during his or her escape would be found guilty of an offence against the regulations.

Regulation 23A gave the Civil Authority the power to prohibit individuals from residing in or entering certain areas, or to prevent individuals from leaving regions in which they resided. An order made under this regulation could also impose any number of conditions about reporting to the police, residence, movement, and the like.[23] In practice, the Minister of Home Affairs tended to issue restriction orders under Regulation 23A independent of internment or detention. The government continued to use restriction orders until the late 1940s. Restriction of movement served as a precursor to powers of exclusion, introduced to counter republican violence in Britain by the 1939 Prevention of Violence Act. Chapter five discusses this statute in more detail.

From 1922 to 1972 in Northern Ireland, during general elections the Ministry instructed the RUC to enforce all orders already served under Regulation 23A, but to refrain from serving any new orders until after the election. No republican demonstrations or processions were to be allowed during the 1933 General Election. In 1938 the same policy held, although Wickham instructed the force to allow considerable latitude to the speakers of all parties at election meetings in expressing their opinions in support of candidates. 'Election meetings should not as a rule be interfered with, except a speaker uses language directly inciting his hearers to the commission of outrage'.[24] The Ministry also issued restriction and exclusion orders under Regulation 23B as conditions for the release of internees. Until March 1923, the Ministry rarely used this aspect of Regulation 23B. However, in that month Charles Wickham issued a letter to the City Commissioners in Belfast and Derry and all County Inspectors, encouraging them to make use of restriction orders under Regulation 23B, particularly in cases relating to released internees.[25] More broadly, this regulation empowered the Minister of

Home Affairs, on the recommendation of a chief officer of police, a police officer of higher rank, or an advisory committee, to intern any individual *suspected of acting, having acted or being about to act* in a manner prejudicial to the peace and maintenance of order.[26] The government modeled this regulation on Regulation 14B of the 1920 Restoration of Order in Ireland Regulations.

In the exercise of the regulation, the RUC, with the advice of the Special Constabulary, took on the primary role. Although the Ministry retained the final say on all matters, it adopted virtually all of the RUC's recommendations. Conferences at the Ministry of Home Affairs governing the exercise of internment powers from 1922 to 1924 involved the Inspector General, the Deputy Inspector General, the District Inspector, the County Inspectors for Antrim, Armagh, Down, Fermanagh, Londonderry and Tyrone, and the County Commandants for Armagh, Down and Tyrone, as well as a number of officers of the Special Constabulary. The only government representatives present at these meetings were the Minister of Home Affairs, the Parliamentary Secretary and the Secretary of the Ministry of Home Affairs. Most of the Ministry's responsibilities seem to have been passed to the Parliamentary Secretary, removing the Minister of Home Affairs from having any impact on the process other than signing the final documents. The Advisory Committee played almost no role at all. The Ministry extended the power to suggest individuals for internment to the Advisory Committee in December 1923, after which point the body only recommended three persons for confinement.[27] It was appointed by the Minister of Home Affairs and presided over by an individual who had held a high judicial office, been a recorder, County Court judge, or a practicing barrister for at least ten years. Although a person in respect of whom an internment order had been made could make representation to the committee protesting the order, the representation rarely, if ever, changed the circumstance of the internee. As of January 1923 out of 542 internees, only 147 had appeared before the Advisory Committee.[28] When approaching the committee the internee was not allowed legal representation.

The Ministry obtained complete authority over the movement of internees through additional regulations that allowed the Civil Authority to remove any individual interned to wherever his or her presence was required for the purpose of entering into a recognisance, or in the interests of justice, or for the purpose of public inquiry.[29] The government extended these powers from a previous measure, Regulation 23D, which allowed for any person undergoing a sentence of imprisonment in Northern Ireland to be removed to any place where his presence was required.[30]

The Executive did not limit the place of internment to prisons.[31] The government implemented these changes to the regulation within a month of the 1922 Act, as the number of internees proved too large for the initial internment facilities.

Regulation 23C governed visits to and communication with both detainees and internees:

1. A person detained or interned under the regulations shall not, except with the sanction of the civil authority, be permitted to be visited by any person other than an officer of the place of detention or internment . . .
2. (a) Except with the consent of the civil authority no communication may be sent by a person detained under these regulations whilst so detained. All communications from or to such person shall be examined by the said officer in charge or by another officer appointed by him for the purpose . . .
   (b) No communications may be sent or received by a person interned under the regulations except such as have been examined and passed by the said officer in charge or by another officer appointed by him for the purpose.[32]

The government extended further restrictions in a subsequent regulation requiring that all communications from prisoners be written on prison-issued post cards and limiting visits as deemed appropriate by the Civil Authority.[33] The Ministry of Home Affairs further expanded these rules to address issues of neatness and cleanliness and to give prison officers the ability to grant and withhold books, papers, documents or other articles in the prisoner's possession at the time of his arrest.[34] On the same day that Dawson Bates issued these restrictions, he issued a regulation allowing prisoners to send letters regarding urgent business or family issues if approved by the prison officer. As with the earlier order, it required that the prison officer examine any post cards, letters or parcels either sent or received by the prisoner. The Ministry issued numerous other provisions at this time (for example, that prisoners cut their hair in accordance with orders issued by the medical officer, that prisoners maintain the facilities in a neat and orderly manner, that the prison guards restrict smoking to specific places and hours, that books and newspapers not found objectionable to the prison officer be supplied by the prisoner at his or her own expense, and that prisoners be kept to a particular diet, adapted for punishment reasons).

The government employed powers of detention throughout unionist control of the North.[35] However, the Ministry of Home Affairs only combined internment and restriction orders once – from May 1922 to December 1924. Unionists introduced internment three additional times during the operation of the Northern government – from December 1938 to December 1946, from December 1956 to December 1961, and from August 1971 to December 1975. Although Britain repealed the 1922–43 Special Powers Acts in 1973, Westminster retained powers of internment in the 1973 EPA. Chapter three examines more in detail Britain's use of this measure.

In 1922 the police arrested individuals for internment prior to the creation of the regulation empowering the Civil Authority to intern. On 22 May the Royal Ulster Constabulary arrested and detained two hundred men throughout Northern Ireland. It was not until the 1 June, however, that the Ministry of Home Affairs issued Regulation 23B, authorising internment. On the 28 June the Minister distributed orders interning 278 people.[36] Precipitating subsequent internment and exclusion orders, the RUC issued a circular detailing internment procedures. This document instructed the police to place arrested individuals into one of two categories. Category one consisted of dangerous organisers of crime, men suspected of having committed murder, arson, or attacks on Crown forces or railways, and actual or potential criminals possessing expert knowledge. The second category included individuals of minor importance from a military or police point of view who, 'whilst being potential criminals, differ in no material particulars from the general rebel population'.[37] Those individuals listed as class II were to be asked three questions: 'Are you a member of the IRA?', 'Are you a loyal subject of HM King George V?', and 'Do you acknowledge the authority of the Government of Northern Ireland?' If the prisoner answered in the affirmative to question one, or in the negative to questions two or three, he was required to sign a paper stating that he would leave Northern Ireland. After thumb prints and photos were taken, the RUC formally released and deported the prisoner. The government constructed a court to carry out the procedure outlined with regard to those classified under Class II, in order to screen for deportation.

By the end of June 1922, police had remanded 282 men into custody. In the following two months the RUC effected approximately 150 more orders. Thereafter the numbers dropped to between twenty and thirty a month, until May 1923, by which time some 575 individuals were interned.[38] Over half of those interned came from Belfast and Co. Tyrone.[39] From this peak the total number steadily declined, until the last internees were released in December 1924. Although violence had spread throughout both communities in Northern Ireland, internment was almost exclusively levied against republicans. From 1922 to 1924 between ten and twenty loyalists were interned, as opposed to more than 700 on the republican side.[40] In order to house the large number of internees, in June 1922 the government bought the S.S. *Argenta* and converted it to an internment facility. Between April and October 1922 the number of individuals in northern jails nearly doubled from 470 to 870. The total number of internees eventually exceeded 500.[41] The conditions on the internment ship were dismal.[42] It was moored in Belfast Lough but later moved to Larne harbour. As the numbers steadily rose, by August 1922 it became clear that a second facility would be required. The RUC accordingly took over the workhouse at Larne and adapted it for use as an internment camp. In addition to the placement of some of the internees in Londonderry Prison and Belfast Prison, from 1922 to 1924 the RUC interned seven women in Armagh Female Prison. The government later also used the Malone Reformatory for the housing of internees.

The internment process required that the RUC submit a short report to the Ministry, detailing the name and address of individuals recommended for internment, their rank (if any) in the IRA, and additional information as to the individuals' associates, activities and political views. For instance, one such record indicated that the individual recommended for internment, '[h]as always kept the company of prominent Sinn Féiners. Is a prominent member of the Gaelic League and a great enthusiast of Gaelic Games. Has frequently expressed his views in favour of the Sinn Féin party and most likely is a member of the IRA but because of the position he occupies did not openly drill or march with them'.[43] Another report stated: 'Prominent organiser of Sinn Féin and a member of the Sinn Féin Executive. Has been active in the movement since the beginning. Was known to march and drill with the Irish Volunteers. Very unfriendly disposed towards the police. There can be little doubt but he is a member of the IRA possessed of extreme views'.[44] The RUC Inspector General then submitted a certificate to the Ministry, in which he declared that the named person was suspected of being about to act in a manner prejudicial to the preservation of the peace.[45] After this the Minister of Home Affairs issued an order directing that the individual be confined. For a variety of reasons the role of the Advisory Committee during the first round of internment was minimal. The first members of the Advisory Committee were John Leach, KC as Chair, and Lieutenant-Colonel Ford Hutchinson, D.S.O., as a member. A.P. Henry, B.L. was added after the third sitting of the committee. The RUC served all internees, on arrival at their place of internment, with a copy of the order instructing their detention, in which they were told of their right to make representations for the consideration of the committee. The first sittings were held on the S.S. *Argenta* on 1 and 2 August 1922. Of the forty-one internees who applied to come before the committee, only twenty-one actually appeared. Some internees were afraid that recognition of the Advisory Committee might prejudice the prospect of an 'acquittal' in later IRA courts martial. Others believed that the committee used these inquiries to incriminate other persons, and so a widespread campaign discouraged individuals from attending. In response to the intimidation, no further sittings of the committee were held on the S.S. *Argenta*: 'It appeared very doubtful whether any internees would appear under the conditions then existing'.[46] When Larne Workhouse was opened, individuals requesting to appear before the board were transferred there and subsequently met with the Advisory Committee. In total, forty-five sittings were held, with some 488 of the 732 persons interned in total appearing before the committee.[47] After it was decided to offer conditions to the internees, the appearances decreased, until the last sitting was held on the 1 May 1924.

Unionists used internment not just to eliminate the threat posed by potential troublemakers, but as an opportunity to gain insight into the workings of the republican movement and to prevent information from being passed to and between internees. The Ministry of Home Affairs retained the authority to grant or withhold all visits. The Ministry then referred all applications for visits to the police for a report regarding the desirability or otherwise of granting them. After February 1924, though, visits by immediate relatives were generally authorised by the Ministry without previously consulting the police. In November 1924 when a number of internees received nominations as candidates for the parliamentary election, the Ministry authorised visits from their election agents. With regard to correspondence, the prison directors forwarded all letters or parcels received by prisoners to Larne Workhouse to be censored. An official appointed by the CID resided there permanently. An experienced warder assisted the censor, with the manual labour done by two internees. From January 1923 until December 1924 excerpts from the letters appeared in weekly reports which were submitted to the Ministry of Home Affairs and forwarded to the RUC. The Ministry eventually expanded the distribution of the weekly, secret report to the Governor, Deputy Governor, and various intelligence officers and occasionally the Ministry forwarded sections of the letters to the Prime Minister as well. Unionists used these reports to put together a picture of general discussion related to the release of the internees, the friends, family and acquaintances of the prisoners, patterns of emigration and connections in Scotland and England. In a few cases the government used the system to uncover plans to raise legal charges against the government or the police, and steps were taken to ensure that the case would fall through.

Overall, the information obtained through censorship was seen by the prison officials, the RUC and the Ministry of Home Affairs as proof of the efficacy of internment:

> Systematic censoring is proving (were proof needed) that a very large percentage of the men interned are in the right place, this is shown by the fact that they receive letters from men who were known rebels (many now in the Free State Army) and the string of names often mentioned only goes to show that the internee and correspondent were closely associated previously along with others of like tendency.[48]

Major E.W. Shewell became intimately involved in the procedure. As controversy grew regarding whether prisoners would accept the condition of bail for release, the Ministry of Home Affairs instructed the RUC: 'Will you please direct the censor office at Larne that, when letters are received for internees the object of which is to deter them from going before the Advisory Committee, he should hold them up and not allow them to be delivered to the addresses unless he had some special reason for doing so, such as a desire to encourage the correspondence'.[49] The censor forwarded some of the letters subsequently intercepted to the Advisory Committee and others to the Ministry of Home Affairs. The authorities disposed of at least sixty-four letters by simply placing them in the internees' files.[50] Censorship began in January 1923 with 947 letters and 349 parcels examined during the last week of the month by officials in Larne. This number remained steady throughout the next six months, and from June through July 1923, a weekly average of 1020 letters and 376 parcels belonging to the internees was censored by the government.[51] This number decreased towards the end of 1923 and into 1924 as the number of prisoners declined.

During the first round of internment prisoners initiated a few attempts to organise hunger strikes. With one exception these lasted but a short time and received little support, being based on individual grievances. On 25 October 1923, however, 131 men on the S.S. *Argenta* instigated a hunger strike based on the assertion that the strike would continue until the government unconditionally released the men. The next day prison authorities transferred the hunger strikers to Belfast Prison. On the 29 October a second and third hunger strike began in Larne Workhouse internment camp and in Londonderry Prison. The numbers on strike increased steadily until 31 October, at which time there were 229 hunger strikers: 133 in Belfast Prison, sixty-nine in Larne Workhouse and twenty-seven in Londonderry Prison. On 2 November the government removed twenty-five strikers from Larne Workhouse to Belfast Prison, and, the following day, forty from Larne Workhouse to Londonderry Prison. The numbers gradually decreased until the strike ended in mid-November. In all, 269 individuals went on the strike during which no deaths and no releases ensued.

At the peak of internment in May 1923, Dawson Bates deemed the security situation in Northern Ireland sufficiently improved to suggest to Wickham that the cases of those interned more than six months be considered to determine which internees could be released.[52] The RUC suggested that the release of the internees would remove the principal grounds for propaganda against the Northern government. It would further serve to indicate that the country was returning to normal.[53] In November and December 1923 each county conducted a review in which the local County Inspector, the County Commandant, an officer from Inspector General's office and the Parliamentary Secretary examined the internees' cases. Those whose discharge was agreed were offered release, subject to entering into a personal bail of £10 to keep the peace for six months. In each case either a member of the Advisory Committee or the prison governors made the offer to the internee. By January 1924 the number of individuals interned had decreased, the S.S. *Argenta* had closed, and all remaining internees had transferred to Larne Workhouse.

Although some of the internees in Larne Workhouse agreed to the terms, a number refused and held out for unconditional release. By the 5 May 1924, 249 internees were still imprisoned, seventy-five of whom Wickham had recommended for unconditional release and had refused the conditions being offered. Concern grew within the Ministry of Home Affairs over the legality of retaining individuals whose release had been formally recommended by the Inspector General. As a result the Ministry of Home Affairs decided to offer unconditional release to the internees, with restriction orders subsequently issued under Regulation 23A. Major Shewell, in a Minute of 2 May 1924, raised doubts as to whether the government could legally retain the men after their unconditional release had been advised by the police, if the recommendation by a chief officer of police was necessary *before* an internment order could be made. J.W. E.Poynting responded that while it might not hold as a point of law, 'it may be doubted whether the continued internment of these 75 men is in accordance with the intention of Regulation 23B'.[54] In concurrence with Poynting and Shewell, the Parliamentary Secretary agreed to release the men unconditionally and raised the matter at the next general conference on internment at the Ministry of Home Affairs. The RUC, USC and a few Home Affairs officials attended this meeting. At the gathering Wickham agreed that those who had refused the earlier conditions be released as soon as possible, as they, 'had been kept in internment some months longer than they otherwise would have been'. It was felt that although the internees represented minimal threat, they would take steps to deliberately violate any subsequent restriction orders placed on them. Therefore, the conference attendees decided not to impose any conditions upon their discharge.

The use of restriction orders for released internees had been agreed in January 1923 at a meeting attended by representatives of the Ministry of Home Affairs, the RUC and the Special Constabulary. Restrictions subsequently set under Regulation 23B directing the release of the internee set limits on the geographic area in which the ex-internee could reside or enter, established bail, detailed requirements for reporting place of residence and regularly registering at specific times and dates at the nearest RUC station, required the ex-internee to carry an identity card and demanded that the ex-prisoner report any intention to stay out between 11.00 p.m. and 5.00 a.m. The exact nature of the conditions, which were set by the RUC and sent to the Ministry of Home Affairs for approval, varied with each case. At the meeting in January 1923 it was agreed that in the event that the internee refused release on the conditions set, he or she would be let out unconditionally and subsequently issued with restriction orders detailing the same provisions under Regulation 23A. In accordance with this policy, in response to the prisoners refusing bail in May 1924, the Ministry decided to release all seventy-five over a period of three weeks. Influencing the timing and conditions set on each internee was the political tenor of the region to which the internee was being returned. The RUC suggested that although Co. Down and Co. Armagh seemed to be peaceful, reprisals from loyalists could be expected on internees returned to Co. Tyrone. The head of the RUC repeatedly voiced and supported this view. For example: 'The County Inspector, Tyrone has gone carefully into the question of unconditional release and is of opinion that some safeguard is necessary owing to local feeling generally'.[55] It was agreed that men from the Cookstown area would remain interned and that those outside of the area would be issued further restrictions upon their discharge.[56] As the RUC expected that those from Co. Tyrone would not agree to the conditions, the Inspector made arrangements to serve them detailed restriction orders under Regulation 23A.[57] (As with internment orders, restriction orders had to be preceded by a formal recommendation from the RUC Inspector General and the relevant County Inspector.)[58]

Throughout the balance of 1924 the government released groups of between three and twelve internees daily, with the last group discharged on 23 December 1924. The Ministry of Home Affairs issued the majority of restriction orders under Regulation 23B, as part of the internees' conditions for release. Remnants of these orders remained in place until 30 April 1926, at which time the government revoked the final seventeen. Shewell brought the issue of the remaining restriction orders to the attention of Dawson Bates, who subsequently sent the list of individuals subject to restriction to Wickham to see if there was any reason why they should not be withdrawn. With their agreement, Shewell arranged for the lifting of the orders. The police then informed the individuals concerned of the revocation. On average the Ministry issued restriction orders under this regulation for a minimum of three months and a maximum of three years. By 12 January 1924, the Ministry had revoked ninety-six orders of restrictions under Regulation 23B, of three months standing or over, out of 134 total (both over and under three months). Internees subject to restriction orders came from across the North: 12 from Belfast, 17 from Antrim, 19 from Armagh, 6 from Down, 1 from Fermanagh, 10 from Londonderry, and 31 from Tyrone. The Ministry arranged for cases less than three months to be taken up at the next review.[59]

Aside from being directed against internees refusing release with conditions, unionists mainly used restriction orders under Regulation 23A to issue exclusion orders against individuals coming to the North. Owing to the departure of nearly all the persons against whom exclusion orders had been made, as of January 1924 only six cases under Regulation 23A still had to be addressed.[60] The RUC used restriction orders not just to pacify public opinion following the release of internees and to prevent individuals from operating in certain areas or in Northern Ireland as a whole, but also to test individuals' loyalties towards the new Northern Ireland State, to prevent republicans from meeting and to demonstrate the power of the Northern Ireland government.

In December 1922 a number of men returned to Antrim after six months in the Free State Army. Suspicious that they were being planted in the North, the RUC enacted restrictions on each individual and demanded that they provide information on the state of affairs in the South. At the suggestion of the County Inspector, the police required a number of individuals to sign an oath of allegiance to the North and to declare their loyalties. The County Inspector for Antrim first suggested this measure in a letter to Charles Wickham on 8 December 1922.[61] Similar cases in County Armagh had been dealt with by restricting individuals' movements within the county. When the inspector proposed that the men from Antrim be restricted to a radius area within four, five or six miles of either their home or the nearest police station, Poynting had some misgivings, as he wanted to deal with each case under the same general principles.[62] The County Inspector protested that it would be useless to restrict individuals to an entire county, as the returning soldiers could simply join up with groups in the area to commit outrages. 'The object which I have in view when making these recommendations is to prevent suspects from one district from getting into close touch with others in another and also to impress upon them the fact that they are not being let off and may yet be punished for past outrages.'[63] In accordance with the County Inspector's recommendation, Wickham wrote to Dawson Bates, recommending restrictions. Immediately following this event the Ministry distributed a circular to the RUC to encourage the use of such restriction orders in similar cases. In total, of the 726 persons interned from 1922 to 1924, the police released 284 on bail. The RUC directed that seventy report to the police, ninety-eight leave Northern Ireland, twenty submit to other conditions and 254 be released unconditionally.[64]

In response to rising tension surrounding the Boundary Commission Report, in November 1925 the Northern government interned a number of individuals. Within 2 months, though, they were released. Between this event and the second time the Unionist government introduced internment on a large scale basis, December 1938, the Executive only directed two additional internments. (Although Farrell claimed that the Northern government used internment during a royal visit in 1950, the absence of any regulation at the time governing its introduction suggests that the Ministry detained, not interned the republicans.[65] Boyle, Hadden and Hillyard also cite the internment of leading republican politicians during a royal visit to Northern Ireland in 1951.)[66]

From 1938 to 1946 the Ministry of Home Affairs introduced internment on a widespread basis for the second time. An IRA campaign, which began with the bombing of a number of customs posts on 28 and 29 November, prompted this move. From two explosions or attempted explosions in 1935, one in 1936 and eight in 1937, as a result of the campaign the number jumped to twenty-two in 1938.[67] In response the RUC increased their level of activity: the B Specials began patrolling and on the 22 December Dawson Bates reintroduced internment with the arrest of thirty-four men. When Britain entered the Second World War in September 1939, the Northern government interned another forty-five republicans. Soon afterwards Craigavon announced that the internees would be incarcerated until the end of the war. In order to house them the government purchased an old merchant ship, the S.S. *Al Rawdah* and by August 1940 held 214 suspected republicans on board.[68] Conditions on the vessel were so deplorable and gave rise to such controversy that by November 1940 the government was forced to abandon it and the internees were transferred to Belfast and Londonderry Prisons. Although internment both north and south of the border had a significant impact on the IRA campaign, the IRA's northern command in March 1942 further resolved to sabotage war industries and British military objectives.[69] Following a number of incidents in September, the RUC picked up over 120 men in Belfast and subsequently interned ninety of them. Outside the city the government arrested nearly 200 more individuals, tripling the number of internees overnight. By mid-October, the Executive held more than 400 men and a few women with no formal charges laid against them.[70] Although the IRA campaign was almost completely exhausted by this time, the government did not authorise the release of internees until the end of the war.

The Ministry of Home Affairs revoked regulations 23, 23A, 23B and 23C in 1949.[71] Within a few years, however, the government reinstated the power to arrest individuals without warrant as Regulation 10. This 1955 statutory instrument included the added proviso that a person could not be detained more than twenty-four hours for the purpose of interrogation.[72] In 1957 the government extended detention without warrant to forty-eight hours.[73] Immediately prior to this, with the advent of a new IRA campaign, the Ministry reintroduced word for word the previous Regulation 23 as Regulation 11, the former Regulation 23B as Regulation 12 and the prior Regulation 23C as Regulation 13.[74] This statutory instrument also reintroduced a measure stating that the powers conferred by the regulations be treated in addition to and not in derogation of any powers exercisable by the Civil Authority (as Regulation 14), requirements that an individual acting under the regulations provide a permit or proof of permission (as Regulation 15), powers to exclude the public from court proceedings (as Regulation 16) and provisions for a court of summary jurisdiction (as Regulation 17).

Unionists introduced internment for the third time under Regulation 12. This time the period of internment lasted from 1956 to 1962. Once again, republican agitation prompted the introduction of the measure. In early December 1956 the IRA established four 'flying columns' of twenty-five men each along the border in the Republic of Ireland with the plan of linking up with IRA units in Northern Ireland. The IRA engineered 'Operation Harvest' to attack the security forces and to sabotage communications, public buildings and property. The aim was to create 'liberated' zones along the border. The campaign began with a single incident on 11 December, followed by 341 incidents in 1957. Ten days after the first attack the RUC arrested and detained numerous republicans, both IRA members and supporters of Saor Uladh. The

South followed suit in July 1957. Eventually the Northern government interned 256 men and one woman.[75] As part of its effort to counter the IRA campaign, the Minister of Home Affairs introduced Regulation 37 to require that no one disembark a ship moored in Northern Ireland.[76] Internal quarrelling, lack of military equipment and economic viability, poor organisation and a high arrest rate all played a part in bringing the campaign to a spluttering end. There were twenty-seven incidents in 1959 and twenty-six in 1960; by its conclusion in 1962 the campaign had dwindled to isolated sniping incidents.

In 1938 and again in 1956 the government employed internment to thwart republican campaigns aimed at obtaining a united Ireland. The threat posed to the government in each instance arose from concerted IRA plans to overthrow the State. Basil Brooke's (from 1952 Viscount Brookeborough's) premiership of Northern Ireland from 1943 to 1963 thus served to maintain the status quo. With Terence O'Neill's election in 1963, however, the government began to make overtures to improve relations with the Republic of Ireland and to address the economic and political concerns of the Catholic population. For the most part, however, the basis of the reform programme consisted of structural changes to existing agencies and not the creation of legally enforceable rights. Nevertheless, when unionists again introduced internment in 1971, what faced the government was a very different situation. O'Neill's limited reforms in the 1960s created expectations for further reforms within the broader Catholic community that remained unmet. The resulting civil rights movement tapped into latent frustration in the province and quickly became much larger than either the IRA or, as William Craig suggested, the Communist Party, had planned. The civil rights movement certainly drew on republican roots. The Northern Ireland Civil Rights Association originated from an August 1966 conference of the Wolfe Tone Society – a group that had been established in 1964 from the committee organised for the 1963 commemorations. In 1966 the republican movement sought to take advantage of the opportunities afforded by the civil rights movement, though, and not necessarily to be the sole instigator and organiser of the civil rights campaign. Opportunism is not the same as organising a movement. In an interview with the *Belfast Telegraph* in February 1969, Cathal Goulding asserted that while republicans were not the sole organisers, and had not 'infiltrated' the movement, they did encourage members to become involved. This reflected the tendency within republican circles at that time to view political activity as a necessary precursor to eventual military action. Thus, while the republican movement supported social and economic issue agitation, 'nowhere do they contain blueprints that correspond with the objectives, structure or activities of NICRA'.[77] Various individuals who have conducted extensive studies of IRA activity support this view: 'It seemed for a moment that in one year the civil rights' movement had done more to end injustice than fifty years of anti-partition policies had begun to do. Where was the IRA during all this? Apparently not there at all as an organised body'.[78] And 'Throughout the life of the civil rights movement unionist politicians claimed that it was a front for the resurgence of the IRA. Many still believe that. Despite the involvement of many IRA members and Republicans . . . the charge is untrue'.[79] The Scarman Tribunal also supported this finding, as it determined that neither a concerted plot to overthrow Stormont, nor any evidence of an armed insurrection existed at the time.[80] With the IRA's 1956–62 campaign barely past, however, unionists immediately viewed the action as an instance of republicanism. The fact that unionists controlled the State augmented this interpretation. Any resistance to the government was viewed as an attack on the majority community. Since republicans had historically constituted the enemy of the government, unionists assumed that the republicans were orchestrating the civil unrest in order to undermine the Northern government. Nevertheless, in the late 1960s and early 1970s, the IRA did not constitute a serious paramilitary force. In actuality the government faced not just republicans, but also a number of unarmed citizens who believed in civil rights. The massive RUC response and the government's extensive use of special powers were more than inappropriate. It was precisely such actions that had motivated the civil rights marchers in the first place.[81] The Unionist government's partisan response to the civil rights' campaign, and most particularly its use of internment and the treatment of detainees, caused events in the province to spiral out of control, rallying support behind the IRA and playing a key role in the proroguement of Stormont. The tension surrounding the civil rights marches and the outbreak of the current round of Troubles is well documented elsewhere.[82]

In response to rising violence, in 1970 Stormont began openly discussing the reintroduction of internment. William Craig suggested that it be reinstated along with a rearming of the police.[83] James Chichester-Clark, the Northern Ireland Prime Minister, stated that internment without trial would not be employed unless the Security Committee advised it. If so advised, the government would not stand in the way of its introduction. John Taylor, Minister of Home Affairs, added that internment would be used only as a last resort, if and when the government felt it was necessary.[84] The British Home Secretary, Reginald Maudling, urged that internment only be introduced if a 'strong and convincing argument' existed. On 31 March 1971 he said: 'Internment is a very ugly thing, but political murder is even uglier'.[85] In response to accusations levied by unionist politicians, he later denied that he was blocking the introduction of internment, protesting that he was prepared for it to be adopted in the event that Westminster, Stormont and the security forces agreed.[86] He added that the IRA and British Army were in a state of war.

On 28 June 1971 Brian Faulkner, the Northern Irish Prime Minister, H. Kirk, the Minister of Finance, Roy Bradford, the Minister of Development, Harry West, the Minister of Agriculture, and Nat Minford and John D. Taylor, Minister of Home Affairs and Parliamentary Secretary, went to Brownlow House, Lurgan, the headquarters of the Royal Black Institution, for talks with leaders of the Orange, Black and Apprentice Boys Orders about forthcoming parades. The following day, the government announced that an additional 900 soldiers would be sent to Northern Ireland within the next two weeks to support the security forces over the 'Twelfth' parades. This brought the total number of troops in Northern Ireland to 11,800.[87] The British government announced the arrival of another 1,000 troops on 5 August 1971, immediately prior to the introduction of internment.

'Operation Demetrius' commenced on 9 August 1971 at 4.00 a.m. with the arrest of 342 Catholic men. By November the RUC had arrested an additional 648 individuals.[88] The quality of information supplied by the RUC Special Branch for the initial sweep, however, left much to be desired. Among those picked up during the operation were elderly, long-retired republicans, young revolutionaries, trade unionists, middle-class civil rights activists, a drunk picked up at a bus stop and numerous people held on mistaken identity. In addition, several people listed were dead.[89] Of those initially arrested, the security forces released 116 within forty-eight hours.[90] These releases did little to appease the growing anger of the minority population and rioting erupted throughout the province. By the end of the first day of internment, more than 100 homes had been set on fire, a number of Protestant and Catholic families had been forced to leave their dwellings and ten people had been killed. Bus services were suspended in Belfast as crowds set up barricades of burning vehicles and attacked troops in Andersontown and Ballymurphy. The violence quickly spread to Newry, Strabane and Derry with further attacks and numerous shops and factories burned. Requests made to the army for protection of both Protestant and Catholic areas were denied as the rioting strained security forces to their limits. On the following day, violence continued in Belfast and Derry. Thirteen more people died in widespread shooting and an additional 240 houses in Ardoyne burned to the ground following reports of intimidation. By the end of the second day of internment the death toll had risen to twenty-three. The Community Relations Commission estimated that by 24 September about 2,000 families had left their homes because of violence or intimidation, with more than 10,000 people forced to move.[91] The operation of the measure was clearly partisan. Not only were the vast majority of those interned Catholic, but a statement issued by the amalgamated committee of the Orange, Black and Apprentice Boys Orders, called on members to give their active support to the security forces in defending the constitution and supporting the use of internment.

Unlike the introductions of internment in 1938 and 1956, which were paralleled by similar measures in the South, in 1971 the Irish Prime Minister, Jack Lynch, made a public statement calling on the British government to replace the Stormont administration by an impartial alternative assembly or commission. The next day Brian Faulkner responded to Lynch by asserting that the Republic had no role to play in a political settlement in Northern Ireland. The British Prime Minister, Edward Heath, echoed these sentiments within a week in a telegram to Lynch, stating that the Republic's attempt to interfere in the affairs of the UK were unjustified, unacceptable and in no way contributing towards peace in the region. John Taylor, Minister of Home Affairs in Northern Ireland, further urged that the Republic immediately introduce internment as it had during both World War II and the 1956 IRA campaign, as the IRA continued to use the South as a base for raids on the North. The South had indicated to the Northern government in 1970 that they would be in a position to introduce internment without trial, if it was found necessary to deal with the large-scale bank robberies and threats to kidnap diplomatic officials in the Republic.[92] In the meantime over 7,000 northern Catholics moved to southern army camps that had been established along the border.

Organised and clear opposition to internment existed within Northern Ireland. Following a meeting on the 14th of August in Belfast attended by nine opposition MPs, Gerry Fitt announced that a non-violent campaign of civil disobedience would begin as a protest against internment. The purpose would be, 'to demonstrate that a large section of the community had withdrawn its consent from the system of government'.[93] Again, although not organised by the republican movement, the civil disobedience campaign went some ways towards meeting the republican agenda. On 25 October 1971 at the Sinn Féin Ard-Fheis in Dublin, Ruairí Ó Brádaigh, president of Provisional Sinn Féin, said that the most desirable prelude to a 32 county republic would be to make the North ungovernable and to bring down Stormont. The Chief of Staff of the Provisional IRA, Seán Mac Stiofáin, called for a further extension of the civil disobedience campaign to include non-payment of motor tax, hire purchase payment and mortgages. A series of one-day shutdown strikes began in various towns throughout the province. On 26 August business in Newry, Derry and Strabane came to a standstill, and in Armagh the postal services ran up to three hours late. In Fermanagh many people stayed away from work and in some places factories closed completely. The rent and rates strike conducted under the auspices of the campaign soon forced the Northern Ireland government to pass emergency legislation under the Payment for Debt (Emergency Provisions) Act.[94] As from 21 October 1971 amounts due to have been paid for rent and rates began to be deducted either directly from wages of employed people or recovered from State payments.

Widespread civil protest accompanied the rent and rates campaign. On 19 August 1971 thirty prominent Catholics in Derry announced that they would withdraw immediately from public office in protest against internment. Two days later Basil Glass, chairman of the Alliance Party, sent a telegram to the British Prime Minister, urging that interment be repealed and that criminal charges be brought against internees where prima-facie evidence of their crimes existed. By 11 September the Community Relations Commission issued a statement in which it called for the replacement of internment by the normal process of law as soon as possible in order to pave the way for Catholic participation in political talks. On 22 September Harold Wilson announced in Westminster that the decision to introduce internment and the way it had been carried out had created a new and grave situation in Northern Ireland.[95] On 19 October five Northern Irish Members of Parliament began a forty-eight hour hunger strike outside No. 10 Downing Street in protest against internment and the treatment of internees. Five days later eight Catholic priests refused to pay fines for failing to fill in census forms. In a statement issued after the court proceedings the priests said that they wished to identify with innocent people who had suffered imprisonment without trial. The unrest extended to the internment camps as well. A 26 October riot at Long Kesh internment camp took two hours before it could be brought under control by troop reinforcements. Internees set fire to one of the huts and held four warders as hostages. CS gas was used to restore orders. Two days later internees at Long Kesh Camp ended a forty-eight hour hunger strike in protest against bad food and living conditions. The strike involved men in a different compound to that in which the riot had recently occurred.

In the exercise of Regulations 11 and 12, in 1971 the Ministry of Home Affairs issued 260 detention orders in August, seventy-two in September and 101 in October. Of those so detained the Ministry released eighteen in August, seventy-two in September and seven in October. As from 31 October, the government had 281 people interned and ninety-six individuals detained, bringing to 377 the number of individuals being held without trial.[96]

Initially the government held internees in Crumlin Road Jail and the H.M.S. *Maidstone*, a depot ship moored in Belfast harbour. Because of overcrowding, however, on 6 January 1972 the prison system opened a second internment camp at Magilligan, Co. Londonderry. Within ten days the Northern Ireland government transferred men from H.M.S. *Maidstone* to Magilligan.

During this time the violence not only continued but increased. In July 1971 seventy-eight explosions using 830 lbs of gelignite occurred. In August 131 explosions, using 1,465 lbs of gelignite, and in September 196 explosions employing 1,898 lbs detonated. October witnessed 117 explosions, caused by 1,574 lbs of gelignite.[97] Protests against internment continued into 1972 up to the proroguement of Stormont. On the 2nd of January 1972, in contravention of the Northern government's ban on meetings, assemblies and parades that had been introduced simultaneously with internment, about 5,000 people attended an anti-internment rally in Falls Park, Belfast. On 22 January additional rallies were held in Armagh and at Magilligan. On 29 January the RUC imprisoned James Daly, a Lecturer in Scholastic Philosophy at Queen's University, for refusing to fill in the census form as a protest against internment. On the 12th of February a deputation from the Alliance Party met Edward Heath and Harold Wilson in London to urge the government to desist from internment if a new political initiative could be found. The following day about 7,000 Northern Resistance Movement supporters held an anti-internment march at Enniskillen. On 5 March the RUC prevented an anti-internment march, attended by 400–500 demonstrators, from proceeding along the main road from Pomeroy to Carrickmore, and on 11 March an anti-internment march at Magilligan was disrupted by the RUC, who allowed only a few demonstrators to pass their checkpoint every seven minutes. The 19th of March witnessed about 20,000 people attend an anti-internment rally in Casement Park.

By the time Britain dissolved the Northern Parliament, unionists had interned some 940 persons in Northern Ireland.[98] Once again, the government inequitably applied the measures to the two communities. Even after the prorogation of Stormont, republicans constituted the vast majority of internees. At the height of the Ulster Worker's Council strike there were only seventy loyalist detainees. Otherwise, the number resided around fifty. In contrast, the number of republicans detained reached almost 640 in December 1973 and stayed above 550 until Rees' phased releases began in July 1974.[99] Spjut suggests that one of the reasons for this imbalance was that there existed little political pressure on the Secretary of State for Northern Ireland to detain loyalists. Further, 'HM Government explained to the Human Rights Commission and Court that one of its reasons for restricting the scale of loyalist detention was its fear of further violent reaction by loyalist terrorists'.[100] Britain slightly altered provisions governing detention and internment throught the 1972 Detention of Terrorists Order.[101] Westminster later incorporated these measures into the 1973 Northern Ireland (Emergency Provisions) Act (EPA). Internment remained on the statute books through 1996.[102]

Curfew

The very first regulation of the 1922–43 SPAs empowered the Ministry of Home Affairs to impose curfew. The Unionist government issued the majority of curfew orders within the first three years of partition. Part of the original schedule to the 1922 Special Powers Act, Regulation 1 derived from Regulation 13 of the ROIR, which provided the competent military authority the power to require inhabitants to remain indoors. Within twenty days of the enactment of Regulation 1 Dawson Bates added the qualification: 'A person shall be deemed to be or to remain out between such hours if he is found between such hours elsewhere than at his usual place of abode'.[103] The government provided permits for those requiring to be out during these hours, such as doctors, nurses, veterinary surgeons and church ministers. In 1949 unionists revoked Regulation 1, but within a few years it was reintroduced as Regulation 19 in order to address disorder arising from the IRA's 1956 campaign.[104] Although the final decision to make curfew orders rested with the Minister of Home Affairs, the Parliamentary Secretary, the Secretary, the RUC Inspector General, the RUC Deputy Inspector General and the RUC District Inspector attended meetings to determine the extent and duration of curfew orders. Under powers transferred by the Attorney General under section 3(2) of the 1922–43 SPAs, the police carried out almost all of the prosecutions of alleged violations of this measure.

As was previously mentioned, the Unionist government issued most of the curfew orders under the regulations immediately following partition. Between 27 April 1922 and 10 December 1924 the Ministry issued some seventeen such orders. The government applied the vast bulk of these to

Belfast, with only six addressed to areas outside the city or to Northern Ireland as a whole. (See Table 2a.) During the Belfast riots in the 1930s, the government once again imposed curfew – once in 1932 and twice in 1935. Unionists only issued curfew orders in a few other instances – once in 1942 and twice in 1957. Although the government declared a Lower Falls curfew in 1970, courts later determined its enforcement by the British military unconstitutional.

Closing of Licensed Premises

Similar to the authorisation of curfew, the new Northern government drew the measure governing the closing of licensed premises directly from the ROIR and included it in the original schedule to the 1922 SPA. The government only used Regulation 2 in a few instances in the early years of the Northern government and then suspended it until disorder once again erupted in the late 1960s. At the time of its adoption, the RUC, the Prime Minister and the Ministry of Home Affairs regarded this regulation as one of the most effectual remedies to violence.[105] The British government had used the corresponding Regulation 10 of the ROIR extensively, and the new government expected such closures to serve as an intermediary step after curfew in returning order to the North. As with curfew, Regulation 2 aimed to avert civil disorder and not, necessarily, to thwart any concerted republican threat. As a result, this provision lay dormant after 1924 until it was finally revoked in 1949.[106] The authority to close licensed premises did not return to the books until it was reintroduced in 1969 as Regulation 39.[107] On the day of its reintroduction the Ministry of Home Affairs issued an order closing all licensed premises in Belfast over the weekend. The Minister issued similar orders within two weeks and again in January 1970. During June, July and August 1970, the government required that all licensed premises in Belfast close after 8.00 p.m. indefinitely, and then after 8.00 p.m. each Friday and Saturday night. The government lifted these bans, however, for the 12 July loyalist marches. In only one instance did closure orders affect licensed premises outside of Belfast, and that was in accordance with an order issued on 7 August 1970, requiring that all such premises in Derry close on the 12 August. The Ministry lifted the final order requiring Belfast licensed premises to close after 8.00 p.m. on the weekends on 27 August 1970. Britain later incorporated Regulation 9 into schedule 3(5) of the 1973 EPA.

Table 2a: Curfew Orders Issued in Northern Ireland 1922–1972
under Regulation 1 (1922–1949) and Regulation 19 (1956–1972)
of the Civil Authorities (Special Powers) Acts

ORDER DATE	SPECIFIED LOCATION	TIMES	COMMENTS
27.4.22	Belfast	11.00 pm–6.00 am	
13.5.22	Areas of Belfast	9.00 pm–7.00 am	
17.5.22	Areas of Belfast	9.00 pm–7.00 am	
25.5.22	Rest of Northern Ireland	11.00 pm–5.00 am	
31.5.22	Co. and City of Belfast	11.00 pm–5.00 am	
8.6.22	[Pubs in Belfast] Belfast	[10.00 am–9.30 pm] 11.00 pm–6.00 am	Cancels 13.5.22 and 15.5.22
20.7.22	Areas of Belfast	9.30 pm–6.00 am	
24.7.22	Areas of Belfast	11.00 pm–6.00 am	Cancels 20.7.22, applies 8.6.22 to areas specified in 20.7.22
23.9.22	Belfast	11.30 pm–6.00 am	Changes 8.6.22 curfew hours but not pub times
21.10.22	Bangor, areas outside Belfast	11.30 pm–5.00 am	
3.1.23	Belfast	11.30 pm–5.00 am	Cancels 23.9.22, varies 8.6.22
6.4.23	Belfast and rest of Northern Ireland	12.00 am–5.00 am	Cancels 25.5.22, 31.10.22, 3.1.23, varies 8.6.22
25.6.23	[Pubs in Belfast]	[lifts 10.00 am– 9.30 pm]	Cancels pub portion of 8.6.22
20.12.23	Northern Ireland	2.00 am–5.00 am	Only for 25, 26, 27.12.23 and 1.1.24; otherwise 6.4.23 order in force: 12.00 am–5.00 am 28, 29, 30.12.23, 1.1.24
22.5.24	Derry	11.00 pm–5.00 am	6.4.23 remains in force for rest of Northern Ireland
13.6.24	Northern Ireland	12.00 am–5.00 am	Lifts 22.5.24; applies 6.4.23 throughout Northern Ireland
18.12.24	Northern Ireland	Temporarily lifted	Lifts curfew 24.12.24– 3.1.25, returns to 12.00am– 5.00 am as from midnight, 3.1.25
30.12.24	Northern Ireland	Lifted	Lifts curfew in province, revokes 6.4.23 and 18.12.24
11.10.32	Belfast	11.00 pm–5.00 am	
18.10.32	Belfast	Lifted	Revokes 11.10.32
10.5.35	Areas of Belfast	10.00 pm–5.00 am	
14.5.35	Areas of Belfast	Lifted	Revoked 10.5.35
13.7.35	Belfast	10.00 pm–6.00 am	
9.10.42	Nationalist areas of Belfast	8.30 pm–6.00 am	Issued by William Lowry, PS
16.8.35	Belfast	Lifted	Revokes 13.7.35
12.8.57	Newry, areas of Armagh and Co. Down	11.00 pm–5.30 am	
9.9.57	Newry, areas of Armagh and Co. Down	Lifted	Revokes 12.8.57

Sale and Transfer of Explosives

Regulation 3 of the original schedule to the 1922 SPA made provision for the Civil Authority to issue orders prohibiting or restricting, 'the carrying, having or keeping of firearms, military arms, ammunition or explosive substances', in any area in Northern Ireland. The government created this provision to address the disorder surrounding the drawing of the border. Because the 1920 Government of Ireland Act restricted Northern Irish legislation to issues within the provincial domain, the Northern government could only apply Regulation 3 on a limited basis. Instead, the unionist regime continued to rely on Regulation 31 of the Restoration of Order in Ireland Act to prohibit the import or export of explosives from Great Britain to Northern Ireland, or vice versa, without a permit from the competent military authority. Orders issued in 1916 and 1917 under Regulation 30 of the Defence of the Realm Regulations required additional permits for the manufacture, sale, purchase, transfer, or disposal of firearms, ammunition and explosive substances within Northern Ireland. These orders also required individuals dealing in arms or explosives to keep a detailed register of people to whom such items were transferred. General Maxwell issued the first order on 28 September 1916, with B. Mahon promulgating the second on 31 March 1917. Continued in operation by the Restoration of Order in Ireland Regulations, these measures complemented Regulation 3 of the 1922 SPA.

By 1926, the only regulations made under the ROIR that continued to be effective in Northern Ireland included: Regulations 21 and 21A, dealing with the importing, keeping or carrying of carrier pigeons, Regulation 22, dealing with wireless telegraphy, Regulation 19A, dealing with the safe custody of documents, Regulation 24A, dealing with sending letters in invisible ink, Regulation 29B, giving power to establish special military areas, Regulation 30, giving power to make orders to control the manu-facture, sale, purchase, transfer or disposal of firearms, ammunition and explosive substances, Regulation 31, regarding a permit for the removal of firearms and ammunition from Great Britain to Northern Ireland and vice versa, Regulation 42, dealing with the causing or inciting to mutiny amongst HM Forces, and Regulation 58D relating to, the right of a serving soldier to be tried for an indictable offence by court martial. The govern-ment only brought a few charges under these regulations in the years immediately following partition, as the courts dealt with the vast majority of firearms and ammunition cases with under the 1920 Firearms Act.[108] By the early 1930s Regulation 3 of the 1922–43 SPAs and Regulations 30 and 31 of the 1920 ROIA had fallen from use altogether.

In 1933 the police attempted to bring an explosives case under Regulations 30 and 31 of the Restoration of Order in Ireland Act. As the prosecution was being prepared, the police discovered a number of loopholes: in order to bring charges the original order would have to be produced and the police would have to prove that the order was still in force. Although the latter could be accomplished by producing the statutory instrument[109] and the Table of Chronological Statutes, the original orders, which had not been published in the *Dublin Gazette*, had been lost. Next, it would have to be shown that an officer of the Royal Ulster Constabulary was an officer of the Royal Irish Constabulary. Although subsection 4, section 1 of the 1922 Constabulary Act (Northern Ireland) would be sufficient for these purposes, the subsequent question of whether an order of the competent military authority, dated 26 September 1916, constituted a provision of law would arise. Consequently, Wickham recommended that either the military authorities issue a new order under ROIR or the civil authorities issue a new regulation under the 1922–33 SPAs in order to address the receipt and control of explosives. The utility of the ROIR orders at the time pertained to explosives, as the 1920 Firearms Act granted the authorities ample powers to control arms and ammunition. Although the only cases being pursued related to individuals who had obtained explosives for poaching and similar acts, the Ministry of Home Affairs determined that, in order to avert the possibility of gelignites being used for public attacks, the regulation of explosives should be more carefully carried out. Dawson Bates decided to bring into force a new regulation under the 1922–33 SPAs in order to grant the civil authorities the same power which the naval or military authorities held under Regulation 30. Regulation 3A prohibited the manufacture, sale, purchase, transfer or disposal of any explosive substance within Northern Ireland unless certain conditions, such as the possession of permits and keeping of registers, were met.[110]

The Unionist government further expanded Regulations 3 and 3A in the late 1930s in response to the republican bombing campaign. From 1920 to 1922 the IRA had used 'paxo', the name given by the IRA to a combination of potassium chlorate and paraffin wax, as an explosive. Following thirteen explosions, two attempted bombings and two accidental explosions in Belfast between November 1937 and November 1938, Britain's Inspector of Explosives, H.E. Watts, discovered in 1939 that several large batches of potassium chlorate had been purchased from Great Britain by firms in both Éire and Northern Ireland. Watts immediately informed Wickham, who pushed for the introduction of a regulation under the 1922–33 SPAs to limit access to this material in

Northern Ireland. However, the Ministry of Home Affairs did not support the introduction of this regulation. As E.W. Scales wrote in 1939, 'Although the Inspector General seems very keen on having these regulations made I am personally very doubtful if any good purpose will be served. I had an opportunity of discussing the matter with Captain Fawcett, His Majesty's Inspector of Explosives, during his recent visit, and his view is that the regulations are unlikely to achieve their object'.[111] Nevertheless, the Ministry issued Regulation 3B, which limited the possession and sale of potassium chlorate and aluminum powder.[112] Once again, although the government could not limit the export and import of these substances to and from Northern Ireland, it could legislate on their use within the province itself. The Northern government introduced additional restrictions on explosives in 1939.[113] This later regulation required wholesalers to register the amount and description of all substances received.

Blocking Up of Roads

In an effort to prevent attacks from IRA columns based in the South, the northern security forces, with the verbal assent of the Minister of Home Affairs, destroyed roads along the border two months before the passage of the 1922 SPA. As from 1 May 1922, no roads had been blocked in Belfast, Co. Antrim, Co. Armagh or Co. Down. The security forces had closed twenty-five roads in Co. Fermanagh, thirteen roads and bridges in Co. Londonderry and fifteen roads in Co. Tyrone.[114] The Ministry issued Regulation 7A, based on Regulation 5 of the ROIR and issued in May 1922, in order to legalise these actions *ex post facto* and to authorise the military and police to obstruct roads and passageways in the future.[115] On the same day that the government created first Regulation 7A, the Ministry issued Regulation 18A, which made it an offence for one's premises to be used for the discharge of firearms.[116] This measure provided the basis for the first case to be brought under the Special Powers Act on 4 June 1922.

The government accompanied amendments to Regulation 7A a few weeks later with the introduction of Regulations 22A, 23A and 23B. The statute implied that roads could be blocked only as a matter of police or military necessity to prevent attack. The police already held this power at common law, but it was not sufficient for a permanent stopping up of roads. The police also raised at this time the issue of whether they were either empowered or required to install lights on the roads that had been so closed. The amending regulation declared that it was not necessary for the security forces to illuminate the area, but that they must contact the Ministry of Home Affairs as soon as the barrier had been constructed. Under pressure from the RUC, the Minister within three weeks extended the length of time for blockage of public ways from specified to indefinite periods.[117] Similar to internment, the government designed these measures to meet a specific situation that had already occurred. The unionist regime used these powers extensively during the Civil War in the South and the initial period of instability in the North. As the urgency of both situations dissipated, the measures became increasingly less critical until the government finally revoked them in 1949. In 1955 the government reinstated the measures as Regulation 9, and on the assumption of Direct Rule Britain incorporated them into part II, section 17 of the 1973 EPA.[118] An order issued by the Ministry of Home Affairs in March 1972 further empowered the police to prohibit the use, waiting, or leaving unattended of vehicles within any area or road declared a 'designated zone'.[119]

Powers of Entry, Search and Seizure

Perhaps the most widely used powers granted to the Civil Authority and the security forces under the 1922–43 SPAs were those relating to entry, search and seizure of property. Most of the regulations sought to thwart the republican campaign initiated immediately following the introduction of the border. Although the Unionist government routinely employed these powers throughout the fifty years of the Northern government, no complete available records detail the extent to which the government exercised the relevant provisions. Regulation 18 in the original schedule to the 1922 SPA authorised the Civil Authority, or any member of the security forces on duty, to enter any house, building, land, vehicle, vessel, aircraft or other premises at any time of day or night if reason existed to suspect that these places were being, had been, or were about to be constructed, used or kept for any purpose prejudicial to the preservation of the peace or at which place an offence against the regulations was being or had been committed. The person entering the area had the power to search and to inspect any part of the properties and to seize anything found therein if there were reasonable grounds for suspecting that the seized item was being used or intended to be used in contravention of the regulations. The measure granted the Civil Authority the power to order that anything seized either be destroyed or otherwise discarded.

The Ministry of Home Affairs expanded Regulation 18 soon after the enactment of the SPA to include provision for entering and searching premises employed for instigating violence.[120] This measure, Regulation

18A, required each individual owning, frequenting or occupying such premises to demonstrate ignorance of the use to which the premises were being put, in order to avoid being found guilty of an offence under the regulations. It also provided for the Civil Authority to close the premises altogether.

In 1922 the government added a further provision: Regulation 18B required the registration of all occupants renting rooms in lodgings.[121] The book had to be produced to the security forces on demand, with details each lodger's name, address and occupation inscribed. Drawn from the ROIR, this measure further empowered the Civil Authority to enter, if need be by force, any such building at any time of day or night and to interrogate any person found therein. The Northern government rarely, if ever, used this power.

The final expansion of this set of regulations occurred in 1923 when the Executive extended powers of search and seizure to private financial records. Regulation 18C provided the Civil Authority with the power to demand bank documents and seize funds held in any account.[122] On 26 May a local police force sent a plea for such extended powers to the District Inspector of the RIC in Newry:

> Can authority be obtained please! for local police officers to ascertain, by inspection of all cheques, or other forms of exchange, from what sources large sums are lodged to the credit of persons in comparatively poor circumstances. I have reason to believe that sums of money amounting to thousands of pounds sterling have been lodged within a month to the credit of a man known to be intimately connected with Sinn Féin and IRA activities in this district. Access to bank books would be necessary in this case. Due care will be taken to ensure that the matter is treated as confidential and that only a commissioned officer of the police is allowed access to the books and documents in suspect cases.[123]

As the powers were not available at the time, the District Inspector forwarded the request to the Minister of Home Affairs, who, in turn, directed it to Richard Best. Finding no provision in the Special Powers Act that would adequately cover the case, the Ministry of Home Affairs took steps to enact Regulation 18C. Although this power was used from time to time, the government levied it most heavily from 1923–24.[124]

Other provisions in the original schedule granted wide powers of search and seizure. Regulation 19 allowed the Civil Authority, or any superior officer of police, to authorise a police constable to attend any meeting or assembly in the event that an offence against the regulations was expected to occur. Regulation 21 granted any police officer or constable the power to stop any vehicle travelling along any public road and, in the event of reasonable suspicion, to search and seize the vehicle or anything found therein which was presumed to be against the regulations or maintenance of peace in Northern Ireland. According to the Ministry of Home Affairs, the government extensively used the power to stop and search vehicles. However, because the police already had such wide powers under the Motor Vehicles Acts, it was hard to say whether the stoppage of any individual vehicle was actually carried out under the provisions of the Acts rather than by the Regulation.[125]

Through Regulation 8, the SPA empowered the Civil Authority to take possession of any land and to construct any building or road on it as may be deemed necessary. It also empowered the Civil Authority to take possession of any buildings or other property, including gas, electricity and water works, and any sources of water supply. The police, acting in this capacity, could destroy any building or structure, take possession of any arms, ammunition, explosive substances, equipment or stores and do any other act involving interference with private property. Should a person sell or remove such items after being informed of the Civil Authority's intention to remove them, he or she would be found guilty of an offence. Based on Regulation 2 of the ROIR, the constabulary employed this measure most frequently immediately following partition.

Although the Executive revoked all of these regulations in 1949, in 1954 the Unionist government reintroduced a number of them.[126] The new Regulation 4 re-enacted almost word for word Regulation 18, governing the entry and search of premises and the seizure of any items found therein. The new Regulation 5 duplicated Regulation 21, empowering the security forces to stop and search vehicles and to seize any articles located there. In both cases the new statutory rules and orders dropped the requirement of reasonable suspicion and replaced it with just suspicion. The Ministry of Home affairs later incorporated this alteration into section 17 of 1973 EPA.[127] The new Regulation 6 combined some of the earlier regulations, empowering any police officer or constable to stop and search a person and to seize any firearms, ammunition, or explosive substances thus found. In addition, the new Regulation 36 authorised the Civil Authority to order anything seized by virtue of the regulations to be disposed of in such a manner as it may think fit. As was previously stated, while these measures were used throughout the tenure of the Northern government, they were particularly designed to be employed during times of disorder. Numerous complaints arose, particularly during the civil unrest in the late 1960s and early 1970s, that the security forces unfairly levied the powers of search against the Catholic population. As late as April 1971 Gerry Fitt, leader of the nationalist Social Democratic and Labour Party, met with Richard Shaples, British Minister of State in the Home Office, to warn him that 'serious consequences' could ensue if the searches in the sealed-off Catholic areas in West Belfast continued exclusively in non-unionist areas. In May 1971 residents held a series of meetings in New Lodge Road, Britton's Parade and Whiterock Road to protest at the soldiers' actions in Catholic areas.

Addressing Republicanism

The powers discussed thus far illustrate the type of measures employed by the Unionist government immediately following partition. As the province reached a level of stability, the government turned its focus from establishing order to eliminating the threat posed by republicanism. Invoking reason of state in defence of the powers exercised, the Ministry introduced and used a number of regulations under the 1922–43 SPAs to protect the constitutional structure of Northern Ireland. This included banning republican meetings, assemblies and processions, imposing censorship of printed matter, films and gramophone records, prohibiting the erection of republican monuments, eliminating the flying of the Tricolour and renderings of 'A Soldier's Song', and proscribing republican organisations. An alteration in rationale for maintaining the Act accompanied this shift – the justification for the introduction of the 1922 SPA revolved around establishing law and order. By 1933 the government argued that because the North was stable, such legislation should be retained. Unionists perceived the 1922 SPA as indispensable for maintaining peace. This section evaluates the government's attempt to stem the threat posed by republicanism through the introduction and use of Special Powers Regulations.

Prohibition of Meetings, Assemblies and Processions

Between 1922 and 1950, the Northern Ireland Ministry of Home Affairs banned more than ninety meetings, assemblies and processions. As recognised by the Ministry of Home Affairs itself, the powers assumed by the Ministry under Regulation 4 of the 1922 SPA did not differ considerably from those held under common law. Under the latter, an assembly of three or more persons who had intentions to carry out any common purpose, lawful or unlawful, in such a manner as to endanger the public peace – or to give 'firm and courageous persons' in the neighbourhood of such assembly reasonable grounds to apprehend a breach of the peace in consequence of it – constituted an 'unlawful assembly'.[128] (See Table 2b) Nevertheless, the government made extensive use of Regulation 4. The Ministry regularly promulgated orders issued under this section through the *Belfast Gazette* and the four Belfast newspapers: the *Irish News, Northern Whig, Belfast Telegraph* and *Belfast Newsletter*. Depending on the jurisdiction affected by the order in question, the government also used other county-wide and local papers, such as the *Londonderry Standard*, the *Londonderry Sentinel* and the *Derry Journal*.[129]

In 1933 the government extended Regulation 4, one of the most frequently used regulations, to include the ability to prohibit the establishment of camps.[130] In July 1931 and 1932 the McKelvey Club near Carnlough ran an IRA camp. The security forces terminated it the second year when members of the group were spotted drilling in the nearby hills. The police sentenced the leader of the club to a month's imprisonment for illegal drilling as specified by Regulation 5 of the 1922–33 SPA. In 1933 Wickham received information that the annual training would be conducted again in early July. However, the government did not base its subsequent decision to ban the club from camping near Carnlough on the substance of the exercises; rather, the concern was that it might agitate the local civilian defence league: 'As a result of what took place last year, if this camp is established it is likely that it may be fired into by certain Protestant elements in the neighbourhood – members of the local branch of the Protestant Defence League, which has been established there. I am of the opinion, therefore, that steps should be taken to prevent this club assembling at this place'.[131] Rather than preventing the League from engaging in violent behaviour, the RUC and Ministry of Home Affairs preferred to prohibit the meeting. Wickham consulted Babington, then Northern Ireland Attorney General, to enquire whether the group could be banned from setting up a camp in the area under the existing Regulation 4. Although he believed it was possible, Babington recommended that a new regulation under the Special Powers Acts be written which would more clearly cover the Carnlough case. The government introduced the amended regulation on 30 June and prepared a draft order to prohibit the meeting at Carnlough. However, on 8 July the RUC discovered that the meeting was not going to be held and as a result the government did not issue the specific order. Nevertheless, Regulation 4, as amended, remained in place.

The Ministry of Home Affairs revoked Regulation 4 in 1951, at which time the 1951 Public Order Act became the primary vehicle for banning

*Table 2b: Meetings, Assemblies and Processions Prohibited in
Northern Ireland 1922–1950 under Regulation 4 of the
Civil Authorities (Special Powers) Acts*

DATE OF ORDER	DATE OF PLANNED EVENT	GROUP ORGANISING AND REASON FOR MEETING/PROCESSION	PLACE CITED IN PROHIBITING ORDER
16.6.22	17.6.22	Republican meetings	w/in 3 mi. radius of Belleek, Co. Fermanagh
3.10.25	6.10.25	Unemployed Workers in Belfast	procession to parliament buildings
3.4.26	4.4.26	Easter Commemoration	at/near Milltown Cemetery in Belfast
21.7.26	25.7.26	Sports Meeting	Tattymacall, Lisbellow, Co. Fermanagh
13.4.27	17.4.27	Easter Commemoration	at/near Milltown Cemetery in Belfast
14.4.27	17.4.27	Easter Commemoration	at/near Brandywell Cemetery in Derry
29.3.28	8.4.28	Easter Commemoration	at/near Milltown Cemetery in Belfast
3.4.28	8.4.28	Easter Commemoration	at/near Brandywell Cemetery in Derry
18.6.28	24.6.28	Meetings at McArt's Fort	w/in 4 mi. radius of McArt's Fort, Cavehill
20.3.29	31.3.29	Easter Commemoration	at/near Milltown Cemetery or elsewhere in Belfast
20.3.29	31.3.29	Easter Commemoration	at/near Brandywell Cemetery or elsewhere in Derry to process to/from
20.3.29	31.3.29	Easter Commemoration	at/near Milltown Cemetery or elsewhere in Belfast with idea of proceeding to/from Milltown
26.3.29	31.3.29	Easter Commemoration	at/near St Patrick's Cemetery or elsewhere in City of Armagh for purpose of organising/holding procession to/from St Patrick's
30.3.29	31.3.29	Easter Commemoration	St Mary's Old Chapel Cemetery/elsewhere in the town of Newry for procession to/from cemetery
11.4.30	20.4.30	Easter Commemoration	at/near Brandywell Cemetery or elsewhere in City of Derry
11.4.30	20.4.30	Easter Commemoration	at/near Milltown Cemetery or City of Belfast
15.4.30	20.4.30	Easter Commemoration	at/near St Patrick's Cemetery or elsewhere in City of Armagh
16.4.30	20.4.30	Easter Commemoration	Carickmore
16.4.30	20.4.30	Easter Commemoration	Donaghmore
16.4.30	20.4.30	Easter Commemoration	Dungannon
6.6.30	29.6.30	Meetings at McArt's Fort	w/in 4 mi. radius of McArt's Fort, Cavehill
19.6.30	22.6.30	Meetings at McArt's Fort	w/in 4 mi. radius of McArt's Fort, Cavehill
1.4.31	5.4.31	Easter Commemoration	Newry
1.4.31	5.4.31	Easter Commemoration	Dungannon
1.4.31	5.4.31	Easter Commemoration	Carickmore
1.4.31	5.4.31	Easter Commemoration	Donaghmore
1.4.31	5.4.31	Easter Commemoration	City of Derry
1.4.31	5.4.31	Easter Commemoration	at/near Milltown Cemetery or elsewhere in Belfast
18.6.31	21.6.31	Meetings at McArt's Fort	w/in 4 mi. radius of McArt's Fort, Cavehill
23.3.32	27.3.32	Easter Commemoration	Hannahstown, Co. Antrim
23.3.32	27.3.32	Easter Commemoration	Carrikmore or near/in Coalisland
23.3.32	27.3.32	Easter Commemoration	at/near Brandywell Cemetery in City of Derry

→

DATE OF ORDER	DATE OF PLANNED EVENT	GROUP ORGANISING AND REASON FOR MEETING/PROCESSION	PLACE CITED IN PROHIBITING ORDER
23.3.32	27.3.32	Easter Commemoration	at/near Milltown Cemetery or elsewhere in City of Belfast
23.3.32	27.3.32	Easter Commemoration	to/from Old Chapel Graveyard, Newry
9.6.32	Indefinite	Protest against imprisonment of Thornbury and Connolly	Northern Ireland
10.10.32	11.10.32	Union Workhouse Procession	to/from Union Workhouse, Belfast
13.1.33	14.1.33	Derry Unemployed Procession	City of Derry
14.1.33	15.1.33	Derry Unemployed Procession	City of Belfast
14.1.33	15.1.33	Derry Unemployed Procession	Abbey Yard or elsewhere in Newry
13.4.33	16.4.33	Easter Meeting	Milltown Cemetery, Belfast
13.4.33	16.4.33	Easter Meeting	St Patrick's Cemetery, Armagh
13.4.33	16.4.33	Easter Meeting	St Columbs' RC Church, Derry
13.4.33	16.4.33	Easter Meeting	Old Chapel Graveyard, Newry
23.7.33	24.3.33	Ulster Democratic League	at/near Library Street or elsewhere in Belfast
4.10.33	8.10.33	Irish Unemployed Workers' Movement	City of Belfast
10.10.33	10–15.10.33	Irish Unemployed Workers' Movement	City of Belfast
8.10.33	14.10.33	Irish Unemployed Workers' Movement	City of Belfast
9.10.33	11.10.33	Irish Unemployed Workers' Movement	City of Belfast
28.3.34	1.4.34	Easter Commemoration	to/from Milltown Cemetery or elsewhere in Belfast
28.3.34	1.4.34	Easter Commemoration	to/from City Cemetery or elsewhere in City of Derry
28.3.34	1.4.34	Easter Commemoration	to/from Old Chapel Graveyard or elsewhere in Newry
9.10.34	11.10.34	Irish Unemployed Workers' Movement	City of Belfast
9.1.35	11.1.35	Ceilidh for release of republican prisoners	Co. Armagh and Co. Down
27.2.35	1.3.35	Ceilidh for released republican prisoners, under name of Plunkett's GFC, Armagh	Any part of Co. of Armagh and Down and urban district of Dungannon
17.4.35	21.4.35	Easter Commemoration	City of Belfast
17.4.35	21.4.35	Easter Week Commemorations	Newry
17.4.35	21.4.35	Easter Commemoration	City of Derry
18.6.35	18.6.35	All parades	City of Belfast (revoked 26.6.35)
30.3.36	31.3.36	Films planned to be shown in Kilrea, Co. Londonderry	Kilrea, Co. Londonderry
7.4.36	24–31.4.36	Easter Commemoration	Northern Ireland
22.3.37	24–31.3.37	Easter Commemoration	Northern Ireland
11.4.38	13–20.4.38	Easter Commemoration	Northern Ireland
17.11.38	19.11.38 20.11.38 21.11.38	Anti-partition meeting	Within 15 mile radius of Newtownbutler, Co. Fermanagh

→

Date of Order	Date of Planned Event	Group organising and reason for meeting/procession	Place cited in Prohibiting Order
24.11.38 27.11.38 28.11.38	26.11.38	Anti-partition meeting	Within 15 mile radius of Newtownbutler, Co. Fermanagh
2.12.38 4.12.38	3.12.38	Anti-partition meeting	Within 15 mile radius of Newtownbutler, Co. Fermanagh (4.12.38) or within 12 mile radius of Dungannon, Co. Tyrone (3.12.38 and 4.12.38)
4.12.38	17.12.38	Larne GAA Junior Championship	
8.12.38	10.12.38 11.12.38	Anti-partition and counter loyalist meeting (GAA match in Pomeroy also banned)	Within 5 mile radius of Claudy, Co. Londonderry
8.12.38	10.12.38 11.12.38	Anti-partition meeting	Within 12 mile radius of Dungannon, Co. Tyrone
8.12.38	11.12.38	Anti-partition meeting	Within 5 mile radius of Newtownbutler, Co. Fermanagh
3.3.39	5.3.39	Anti-partition meeting	City of Derry
4.4.39	10.4.39	Anti-partition meeting	City of Derry or any portion of Co. Londonderry west of the River Foyle
	5.3.39		City of Derry
14.3.39	17.3.39	Anti-partition meeting held by Northern Council of Unity	Within radius of 10 miles of Carnlough, Co. Antrim
3.4.39	5–12.4.39	Easter Commemoration	Northern Ireland
1940	1940	All processions banned under Ministries Act (NI) 1940, except for funerals	
10.2.40	11.2.40	Protest against execution of Barnes and Richards at Birmingham 7.2.40	Northern Ireland
18.2.40	18.2.40	Protest against execution of Barnes and Richards at Birmingham 7.2.40	City of Belfast
19.3.40	20–27.3.40	Easter Commemoration	Northern Ireland
13.6.40	16.6.40	Silverwood Pine Band	Lurgan Urban District
7.4.41	9–16.4.41	Easter Commemoration	Northern Ireland
24.3.42	1–8.4.42	Easter Commemoration	Northern Ireland
9.4.43	21–28.4.43	Easter Commemoration	Northern Ireland
24.3.44	6–12.4.44	Easter Commemoration	Northern Ireland
19.3.45	29.3.45– 4.4.45	Easter Commemoration	Northern Ireland
8.4.46	18–23.4.46	Easter Commemoration	Northern Ireland
14.3.47	3–8.4.47	Easter Commemoration	Northern Ireland
7.3.48	17.3.48	AOH St Patrick's Day anti-partition meeting	City of Derry
9.9.48	11.9.48 13.9.48 19.9.48	1798 rebellion celebrations	City of Belfast
7.3.49	17.3.49	St Patrick's Day gathering	City of Derry
11.4.49	17.4.49 18.4.49	Easter Commemoration	Northern Ireland
15.3.50	17.3.50	AOH St Patrick's Day meeting	Within 3 mile radius of Moneymore, Co. Londonderry

marches and processions.[132] The government introduced similar powers, however, in 1970. Regulation 40 empowered the Civil Authority to prohibit the holding of processions or meetings where there appeared reason to comprehend that such gatherings would give rise to public disorder or cause undue demands to be made upon the police or military forces.[133] The measure retained the same definition of 'public procession' and 'public meeting' as cited in the 1951 Public Order Act. The government also introduced other, related powers under the 1922–43 SPAs. In 1966 the Ministry created Regulation 38, empowering any member of the RUC not below the rank of head constable to prevent any assembly of three or more persons if it was suspected that such a gathering would give rise to a breach of the peace or serious disorder.[134] The government extended this measure in 1969 with Regulation 38A, which allowed the Civil Authority to restrict the use of premises or any class of premises for the purpose of any entertainment, exhibition, performance, amusement, game or sport to which members of the public were admitted.[135]

The vast majority of prohibited events under the 1922–43 SPAs were republican in nature and perceived by the Unionist government as a direct attack on the Northern Irish State. Although the government targeted the regulation to prevent events that would, 'give rise to grave disorder and conduce to a breach of the peace', it repeatedly used the measure to prohibit gatherings not because of any immediate threat they posed peace in the province, but because of their ideological, anti-constitutional basis and their tendency to 'promote disaffection'. In no instance did the government directly prohibit a loyalist gathering under Regulation 4 of the SPA. The government swiftly scotched any suggestion that loyalist marches should be banned. For instance, in 1948 Eddie McAteer raised question in the Northern Ireland House of Commons about a loyalist demonstration scheduled to be held in an overwhelmingly nationalist area. The Minister of Home Affairs answered his inquiry thus: 'I am aware of the meeting referred to, but there is no reason why it should not be held'.[136] In the event that the government inadvertently banned a loyalist meeting in an attempt to avoid counter-demonstrations, not only did the government fail to prosecute a number of loyalists who defied the ban, but the Minister of Home Affairs prepared an extensive public apology to be issued in the Northern Ireland House of Commons:

> I made an order in general terms prohibiting all processions in the City of Belfast, other than the one for which I have prescribed an area. At that time I had no knowledge that any other processions had been arranged in any other parts of the City by any person or by any

organisation. In fact, as I subsequently learned, on the Thursday, to be exact, that the Cumberland Orange Lodge had long previously arranged to hold their Annual Church Service on that afternoon at St Donard's Church, Bloomfield. Though I had no such intention this procession was caught by the Order . . . It is perfectly clear that the Order was violated by those persons who marched to St Donard's Church, and I had to consider whether the participants, who numbered perhaps a couple of hundred should be prosecuted. I came to the conclusion that they should not . . . I am, in fact, more to blame for this difficulty than any one else. My order was badly drafted and . . . I feel a very considerable sense of personal responsibility for this situation. If I had suspected that any other procession had been arranged the Order would have taken a very different form and I must express to the House and to the public my regrets.[137]

Events that did come under official censorship included 1916 Easter Uprising commemorations, 1798 Rebellion remembrances, St Patrick's Day celebrations, Gaelic sports events, anti-partition meetings, ceilidhs for released republicans, protests over issues related to republican prisoners, Ancient Order of Hibernians' functions and unemployed workers' gatherings. In commemorating the 1932 Belfast riots the Unemployed Workers in Belfast, the Derry Unemployed Workers and the Irish Unemployed Workers' Movement invited southern Irish citizens to participate as speakers and attendees. Seen as an attempt by socialist republicans to infiltrate the North and to subvert the authority of the Northern government, the Ministry banned these meetings.[138] Orders banning meetings decreased neither with falling levels of violence in the province, nor with the establishment of the Northern State – between 1922 and 1928 only eight orders were issued under Regulation 4. From 1929 to 1936, however, some forty-seven orders were made. Although the Minister of Home Affairs issued virtually all of the orders under Regulation 4, from 2 October 1925 Dawson Bates authorised Wickham to issue orders under the regulation. Wickham exercised this power the day after he received it to ban a demonstration of unemployed workers in Belfast scheduled for the 6 of that month. However, the RUC rarely exercised this power thereafter. One of the central reasons for the general increase in the use of Regulation 4 was the advent of prohibitions on Easter Week commemorations.

From 1926 until 1949 the prohibitions on Easter celebrations steadily expanded from a ban on a single meeting in Belfast on Easter Sunday, to the prohibition of any commemorative meeting in Northern Ireland for the whole of Easter Week. Republican remarks made during graveside orations on Easter Sunday 1925 spurred the enactment of these orders. At Wickham's prompting, in 1926 the government prohibited any similar commemoration on Easter Sunday at or near Milltown Cemetery in Belfast. Shewell and Wickham played a central role in accomplishing the Easter Week bans. Although the RUC tended to issue a written report of planned events prior to the government enacting an order under Regulation 4, the police did not strictly follow this procedure: 'The Inspector General reports by telephone that Easter Day demonstrations have been announced at Dungannon, Carickmore and Donaghmore at the Roman Catholic Graveyards and recommends their prohibition. The order doing this as regards all these places is attached'.[139] The following year the government extended the ban to a graveside ceremony planned at the Brandywell in Derry. Annually re-enacted, the Ministry applied the order by 1929 to any ceremonies or processions relating to the two cemeteries in the cities of Belfast and Derry, to St Patrick's Cemetery in the city of Armagh, or to St Mary's Old Chapel Cemetery in the town of Newry. By 1930 the government banned all meetings and processions on Easter Sunday in the cities of Derry, Belfast and Armagh, as well as Carickmore, Donaghmore, Dungannon and Newry. In 1932 the Ministry added Hannahstown, Co. Antrim to the list of proscribed sites for Easter commemorations and in 1936 the government extended the ban to all of Northern Ireland for the entire Easter week. The Ministry renewed this ban annually through 1949. Impetus for the renewal of these orders stemmed not just from the original republican object of the 1925 meeting, but from changes in the South, which continued to cause fear among northern unionists.[140]

As with the St Patrick's Day marches, the Ministry did not release the orders until just before Easter week. The government's own stated aim in doing this was to cause the maximum possible disruption and to make it difficult for alternative plans to be made. As the Ministry of Home Affairs made clear: 'Ordinarily publication of [orders] is withheld until the last minute in order to giver the IRA, etc. the minimum space of time in which to adapt'.[141] The Ministry of Home Affairs directed the RUC not only to prohibit any meetings from taking place, but to remove republican flags and notices or posters of the planned events. The police frequently removed posters even when meetings were not banned, if the object of the proposed meeting was nationalist in character.[142] Until 1949 Regulation 16 of the 1922–43 SPAs empowered the police to prosecute individuals found putting up posters in connection with Easter Commemorations and to prevent the public sale or wearing of Easter Lilies. Republicans sold lilies, a symbol of both the Easter Uprising and the republican flag, over the holiday to raise money for the movement.

The Ministry of Home Affairs instructed the police to prohibit the public sale of lilies and, in many instances, the wearing or distribution of these items.[143] The government did try to take this a step further but in 1928 was forced to abandon a draft order banning the use of the lilies as a symbol of republicanism or of a proscribed organisation. The Minister of Home Affairs concluded that it was impossible to define the emblem that the government aimed to prohibit. In addition, the Ministry suggested that the issuance of the order might actually weaken the government's hand in banning the emblem, as it prohibited the wearing of lilies on only one day, 8 April 1928, whereas by section 2(4) of the 1922 Act such attire was an offence at any time. Instead of issuing the order, Shewell instructed the police to advise the organisers of nationalist or republican demonstrations *in advance* that any similar emblem would be prejudicial to the preservation of the peace. The security forces would then have the complete authority not only to insist on its removal, but to prosecute anyone wearing, selling or distributing a lily.[144] As well as these powers, the Ministry instructed the police to report back with a complete account of nationalist activities over the Easter period. Reports were to include the number and location of any wreaths laid on republican plots, the location and participants in graveside prayer services, the number of individuals wearing Easter Lilies, the activities of suspected IRA members, the names and addresses of individuals involved in proceedings and an account of any flags or posters removed.[145]

The RUC initially enforced the orders by locking the gates to the graveyards and only allowing family members to enter to place flowers on family graves. As the ban became more widespread, the police prevented any public Easter meetings or orations from taking place. Although sporadic attempts to defy both the Easter week bans and other orders issued under Regulation 4 occurred,[146] for the most part republicans cancelled events subject to orders under Regulation 4.[147] The Unionist government exercised this measure in a sectarian manner. It went out of its way to ensure that the Easter bans prevented republican gatherings, while loyalist meetings could be executed as planned. For example, over Easter Week 1949, William Brian Maginess, Minister of Home Affairs from 1949 to 1953, decided to ban meetings on Sunday, 17 April and Monday, 18 April. He decided not to include Saturday, 16 April in the ban, as a number of Orange Lodges from No. 9 district had planned a march for Saturday, 16 April and no republican plans were made for the day. Pim informed the Ministry that the following two days were largely republican in character. On Sunday Clann na Poblachta planned to celebrate the coming into force of the Republic of Ireland Bill, the IRA organised a wreath laying ceremony at Milltown Cemetery, a commemoration demonstration was to be held in Armagh, the Newry Anti-Partition League planned a procession to St Mary's Cemetery, a ceilidh was planned in Newry's Town Hall, and plans had been made to lay wreaths at the City Cemetery in Derry on the graves of deceased republicans. On the following day, the Apprentice Boys were planning demonstrations in Belfast, Antrim, Armagh and Down, anti-partition demonstrations were scheduled in Armagh, Down and Londonderry, a Gaelic Athletic Association football match was to take place in Armagh, and the Ancient Order of Hibernians planned a trip to the South. For these two days the government issued orders banning all meetings and processions. On Easter Tuesday Junior Orange demonstrations were planned in Antrim, but the government refrained from issuing any orders prohibiting meetings on this day.[148]

In the implementation of Regulation 4, the government received strong support from the unionist population and most particularly from the Orange Lodges. Not only did Orangemen and loyalist institutions send letters prior to planned events, urging the Minister of Home Affairs to take steps to prohibit nationalist and republican gatherings; in addition, Orange Lodges frequently passed resolutions after the fact, demonstrating approval of government action. They forwarded these motions to the Ministry. For instance, on the 7 March 1948 Edmond Warnock, the Northern Ireland Minister of Home Affairs from 1944 to 1949, banned an anti-partition demonstration planned for St Patrick's Day. Following the ban, the Minister of Home Affairs received a letter from the Falls Road Methodist Church Defenders, L.O.L. No. 1433, thanking him for imposing the ban: 'We feel that if more of our leaders were as faithful and fearless in their duties, Ulster would truly be great'. A letter of appreciation sent by the Coleraine Drumming Club on the 26 March 1948 stated: 'Long may you occupy the position to keep those Popish rebels in check. No Surrender. God Save the King'. A slew of similar letters was sent to the Ministry from around the province: the Apprentice Boys of Derry Club, the Middle Liberties Unionist Association, the Cromac Unionist Association, the Glenavy Branch Unionist Association, the No Surrender Club of the Apprentice Boys of Derry, the Duncairn Women's Unionist Association, the Bloomfield and Pottinger Unionist Association, the Ulster Unionist Labour Association, the Ulster Association of Loyal Workers, Dee Street Unionist Branch, St Jude's Polling Station, the East Belfast Unionist Association, the National Union of Protestants, the Working Committee of the Derry Unionist Association, Lord Arthur Hill Memorial L.O.L. No. 144, Brown's Dental Depot, the Working

Committee of the South Derry Unionist Association and various individuals forwarded similar expressions of support.[149] Many constituents wrote threatening letters. For instance, from Cookstown, the Moneymore District L.O.L., No. 10, wrote to Maginess, 'Tentative arrangements are being made by the loyalists to decorate the Village with Union Jacks and Bunting from end to end, and woe betide anyone who tries to pull down the decorations . . . Tentative arrangements are being made by the loyalists to hold a monster Drumming match at the same time as the proposed Demonstration'.[150]

Loyalist support for the banning of nationalist or republican meetings partly stemmed from the perception that anti-partition sentiments represented a direct attack on Northern Ireland. Their opposition to such sentiments can clearly be seen in the strategy of counter-demonstration adopted in late 1938. On 3 November the Ancient Order of Hibernians (AOH) decided to hold an anti-partition meeting in Newtownbutler on 20 of November the AOH arranged for a number of MPs and TDs to address the demonstration. On 13 November local Orangemen announced a counter-demonstration for the same day, stating their intent to bus in supporters from Armagh, Tyrone and Fermanagh to attend the demonstration. In response on 17 November the government issued an order banning all meetings on the 19, 20 and 21 of that month. Attempts to hold the meeting the following weekend were met by the announcement of a second counter-demonstration and a subsequent ban. This pattern continued for the next two weekends, prompting claims by the Ancient Order of Hibernians AOH that loyalists were attempting to stifle anti-partition speech.[151] This was not far off the truth. In order to give loyalists an opportunity to meet and to prove whether they had serious intentions of holding a meeting on a Sunday, the AOH offered to suspend the meeting planned for 11 December. The loyalists responded that if no anti-partition meeting took place, then there would be no need for a counter-demonstration. As the pattern continued the AOH decided to wait until after 6 January 1939 to hold a rally. In the event the government banned the next meeting, arranged for Derry on 5 March 1939, and the anti-partitionists met in Donegal instead.

Although Pim and Maginess wanted the November anti-partition meeting banned at the outset, Craigavon's initial impulse was to allow the meetings to be held as an outlet for anti-partition sentiment.[152] In response to the announced counter-demonstration, however, the government shifted its position to a more conservative stance. Thereafter, the government made a policy decision to ban anti-partition meetings on the strength of their political import alone. At no time did the government consider allowing the anti-partition meetings and banning the counter-demonstrations as being temporally subsequent to the announcement of the meetings. At a meeting on 1 December 1938 at which Wickham, Dawson Bates and E.S. Murphy, the Northern Ireland Attorney General, were present, it was discussed whether a general order could be issued banning all anti-partition meetings. They decided instead to deal with each case individually: 'The Inspector General has been instructed to report immediately when any other meetings of this kind are proposed to be held so that orders may be issued prohibiting them'.[153] This decision clearly did not include any consideration of either the circumstances or location of the proposed meeting, or the likelihood of its leading to a breach of the peace, or whether a counter-demonstration had been declared for the same time at a nearby location. Within a few months Dawson Bates banned a St Patrick's Day anti-partition gathering, in spite of there being no announced counter-demonstration.[154]

Unionists perceived anti-partition views as a threat to the peace and stability of the North. Any concerted questioning of the current constitutional position of the North was not to be condoned either by the loyalist population in general or by key members of the Unionist government. Immediately following the November 1938 incident Dawson Bates, stated: 'I found [the banning of the anti-partition meetings] necessary in the interests of law and order and in order to ensure that we loyalists in Ulster may be allowed to live in peace'. He added: 'When one finds an increase in the number of crimes committed by people whose motives are to break up our Constitution, is it reasonable for one moment to suggest that we should sit down and do nothing? During the present year, no less than 35 outrages have been committed for the purpose of intimidating the loyalists and government of Northern Ireland'.[155] The prohibition of meetings on the basis of them being republican extended to other events. The Ministry of Home Affairs issued instructions in 1933 to the RUC to prohibit all Easter meetings, even if they were not specifically banned by the order. In a confidential memo of 12 April 1933, Warnock raised his concerns at this manner of operation:

> The orders relate to known meetings at specified places. The minister however wants an instruction to be issued to police to the effect that if any similar meetings are unexpectedly held elsewhere, they are to be stopped, under the general powers of police. As far as I can see, the police in order to stop meetings must be able to show that a breach of the peace is likely, and as some meetings might very possibly be mere hole and corner affairs – perhaps on private grounds – it might not

always be possible to disperse them on the breach of peace principal. I don't want the police to take some drastic actions which might turn out to be illegal.[156]

In January 1935 the government banned a reception and ceilidh that had been organised to celebrate the release of republican prisoners. The objection in this instance was, 'the object for which the dance has been advertised to be held'.[157] Similarly, with regard to a banned meeting of the Irish Unemployed Workers' Movement in October 1934, the report from Wickham advocating its prohibition noted that the demonstration was likely to be supported by the Republican Congress Party, the Communist Party, the Irish Labour Defence League and similar organisations, and, as a result, '[h]aving regard to the object for which the procession is being arranged, I recommend that it be prohibited'.[158] The Ministry subsequently issued the order on the basis of principle alone, and not because it was a particularly emotive, or even important event. 'I have spoken to Mr Gilfillan about the proposed order. He seems to anticipate that the demonstration this year will be of little importance, and . . . is still rather doubtful that it should be prohibited.'[159] The objection to republicanism, *per se*, underlay the government's decision to ban a number of the proposed meetings, assemblies and processions. When asked in Parliament on 8 July 1948 whether the 12 July parades would proceed, the Minister of Home Affairs responded: 'Since I am assured that none of the processionists will be carrying a Republican flag, I see no risk to public order by the usual 12th of July demonstrations'. The onus clearly lay on the republican elements to avoid confrontation with the Unionist State.

Not only did the government prohibit numerous republican meetings, but the RUC also submitted detailed reports to the Ministry of Home Affairs on various nationalist meetings that had not been banned. These documents included copies of speeches made, proceedings, votes taken, influential leaders and other similar information. The RUC reported on the movement of nationalist Members of Parliament and trailed individuals outspoken in their criticism of the Unionist government. For instance, a 1928 report sent by Wickham to the Secretary, Ministry of Home Affairs, read:

> I beg to report that information had been received that the nationalist Members of Parliament for Northern Ireland intend to hold a meeting at Belfast early in March, for the purpose of forming a new branch of the Nationalist Party, under the leadership of Mr J. Devlin, MP. Apparently the object of the proposed meeting is to consolidate and strengthen the ranks of the Nationalist Party.[160]

Similar reports were sent to the Ministry reporting nationalist meetings held on 3 October 1922, 29 October 1922, 9 April 1924, 20 August 1924, 6 and 11 January 1926, and 7, 9 and 10 March 1926.

Not only did the RUC send updates to the Ministry regarding the movement of nationalist MPs, but the police also monitored and reported on nationalists' private correspondence: 'Within the past week Mr Joseph Devlin MP wrote to a prominent nationalist in Enniskillen, asking him to convene a meeting of Nationalists to call on Messers Healy and McHugh to resign their seats unless they took their place in the northern parliament'.[161] Similarly, details of the content of a letter from President Cosgrave in the Republic to Joseph Devlin, Nationalist MP at Westminster from 1902 to 1922 and from 1929 to 1934 and Northern Ireland MP for West Belfast from 1921 to 1929, were reported by Sergeant Patrick Kelly in Armagh to Wickham and forwarded to the Ministry. The RUC also sent records to the Ministry of Home Affairs regarding various comments made by both MPs and city councillors indicating republican or communist sympathies. In the file of William McMullan, MP the RUC wrote: 'With regard to the Boundary question, no Boundary existed as far as he was concerned'. A different file cited Samuel Kyle, MP, as appealing to all workers to join the Workers' Union with the possibility of one day being able to storm the citadel of political power in Northern Ireland, scale the ramparts, and find themselves seated in the places of power in the Northern Parliament. Further reports quoted the city councillor, later Labour MP for the Belfast Dock constituency, Harry Midgley as saying: 'The workers of Ireland will settle it when they learn that they are at present being used as tools for a few of the Imperialist and Capitalist classes,' and again, 'Some consolation was to be found in the fact that Imperialism, like its foster parent Capitalism, was tottering to its doom'.[162] This close collusion between the security forces and the dominant political party raises serious questions as to the role of the police in relation to the Unionist government. It also neatly illustrates the degree to which the unionist regime perceived the aims of republicanism – the realisation of a nationalist ideal – as a threat to the State.

A multitude of letters from loyalist associations to the government claimed the 'right' to be free from being confronted with either the rhetoric or the symbols of Irish republicanism. For example, a letter dated 8 March 1948 stated: 'We are extremely proud to know that we have such a loyal advocate of our liberties that no encroachment can come without being noticed'.[163] Another one referred to '[t]he Popish trial of strength as between the forces of Roman tyranny and Protestant freedom'.[164] In disapproving of republican gatherings, the Orange Lodges voiced particular concern with regard to the flying of the Tricolour. Letters stated: 'We demand that necessary steps and precautions should be taken to make sure that the Republican Tricolour is not carried or displayed. We are of opinion that the display of this flag in the heart of our country would be an insult to our loyal people and the sign of a threat to attack our northern government'.[165] Private letters tended to be more emotive in their rejection of both the flag and republicanism in general. For instance: 'I am proud to see that you . . . have got the guts to defy those who would desecrate the walls of the maiden city by their filthy flags and their disloyal music'.[166] In juxtaposition to loyalist claims to the right not to be offended, nationalists, republicans and nationalist politicians raised the issue of the right to free speech and free assembly. However, in response to a question asked in the Northern Ireland House of Commons, as to whether the Minister could, 'give a guarantee that the liberty of the citizen and the right of free speech and assembly will not be interfered with through the enforcement of the Civil Authorities (Special Powers) Act', the Minister of Home Affairs responded that these rights did not apply to political ideas whose aim was to undermine the State: 'If the Hon. Member in his reference to the liberty of the citizen and the right of free speech and assembly, means to imply liberty to take part in activities calculated to subvert the Constitution or to provoke breaches of the peace and the right to make speeches in furtherance of such unlawful objects, the answer . . . is most emphatically in the negative'.[167]

Although withdrawn as part of the general revocations in 1951, the government incorporated Regulation 4 into ordinary law through the Public Order Act, which controlled the holding of processions.[168] The legislation empowered the Minister and police to regulate and prohibit all meetings and processions and any other 'provocative conduct'. It required forty-eight hours' written notice of the intended time and route to be submitted to the constabulary station nearest to the proposed place where the procession was to commence. If any officer or head constable of the RUC maintained reasonable grounds for suspecting that the procession would lead to a breach of the peace or serious public disorder, he could impose whatever conditions were viewed as necessary to preserve public order. The statute further empowered the Minister of Home Affairs to ban all processions either in a particular location or of a certain class, for up to three months. The statute banned any threatening, abusive or insulting words or behaviour, and prohibited anyone from allowing such conduct on lands or premises within his or her care, leading to public disorder or a likely breach of peace. The Unionist government further amended and strengthened the 1951 Public Order Act by the 1970 Public Order (Amendment) Act (Northern Ireland), which established minimum sentences for breaches of the legislation.[169] Under this statute, from July 1970 the government placed a ban on all processions in Northern Ireland. This order expired at midnight, 31 January 1971. In April of that year the Northern Ireland Security Committee announced that only parades specifically sanctioned by the security forces would be allowed to take place over the Easter period. Two marches, one republican and one loyalist, which had been arranged to take place in the traditional Loup area near Moneymore, Co. Londonderry, fell under the ban. On the introduction of internment in August the Minister of Home Affairs issued a further six month ban on all parades in Northern Ireland, and on 18 January 1972 Brian Faulkner announced the extension of the order for another year, including the traditional summer parades. Within a few days the Grand Orange Lodge of Ireland had declared that, 'in the absence of such convincing reason and clear demonstration of its effectiveness the Government could hardly expect our people to observe [the ban on marches and parades]'.[170]

Censorship

Similar to the provisions prohibiting meetings and assemblies, the unionist regime increasingly used measures governing the censorship of printed matter after violence had declined in the North. In addition, as with Regulation 4, orders issued under Regulation 26 and later Regulation 8, focused almost exclusively on expressions of republican ideals. Regulation 26 of the 1922 SPA empowered the Civil Authority to prohibit the circulation of any newspaper for any length of time. The government expanded this measure in 1943 to prohibit the publication, as well as circulation, of any newspaper, periodical, book, circular or other printed matter.[171] Although the Ministry revoked this regulation in 1949,[172] within five years it reintroduced the provision as Regulation 8.[173] In 1971 the Ministry amended the regulation to make it unlawful for any person to print, publish, circulate, distribute, sell, offer or expose for sale, or have in possession for purposes of publication, circulation, distribution or sale, any document advocating: (a) an alteration to the constitution or laws of Northern Ireland by some unlawful means, (b) the raising or maintaining of a military force, (c) the obstruction or interference with the administration of justice or the enforcement of the law, or (d) support for any organisation which participates in any of the above.[174] Further, any individual whom the security forces reasonably believed to have such a document in his or her possession would be found guilty of an offence against the regulation if he or she failed to turn the document over to the security forces on demand. The measure explicitly exempted government ministers, the Northern Parliament, and the court system from any infraction of the regulation. No longer was the Civil Authority required to issue orders banning specific publications; the last such order expired on 31 December 1971.

Until this time, the Northern government issued approximately fifty-two orders under these regulations, banning over 140 publications. (See Table 2c) The vast majority of banned materials expressed republican views. Those publications prohibited by the Unionist government that did not explicitly adopt this perspective were largely socialist or communist in character. For instance, banned newspapers such as *Workers' Life* and *The Irish World and American Industrial Laborer* had strong socialist leanings as well as republican undertones, while the Communist Party issued *The Red Hand* and the *Irish Workers Weekly*. The Ministry's main contention in prohibiting the publication or circulation of these periodicals was that they contained statements, 'intended or likely to cause disaffection'.

The government banned the first publication, under Regulation 26, *Éire, The Irish Nation*, in March 1924 after levels of violence in the province had dropped. It followed with a second order in December of the same year by the banning of *Poblachta na hÉireann* and *Sinn Féin*. As with most of the orders so issued, the directive limited the period of prohibition to one year. The Northern government renewed a number of bans, however, on an annual basis. From 1926 to 1945 the Ministry annually issued orders banning *An Phoblacht*; from 1927 to 1945 *Irish Freedom – Saoirse na hÉireann*, and from 1930 to 1945 *The Irish World and American Industrial Laborer*. For the most part, the government retained bans on publications only as long as they remained in print. Thus, the Executive prohibited *Fianna* from 1926 to 1927 and then again from 1934 to 1945, *Workers' Life* from 1927 to 1930, *The Nation* from 1930 to 1932, and *Republican Congress* from 1934 to 1945. The ban placed in June 1940 on the *Derry Journal*, the main local newspaper in Derry, provided the exception to this rule. Due to widespread protest, the Ministry lifted the ban after only a fortnight. From 1932 the Ministry began coordinating the date of expiry of orders under Regulation 26 in order to provide for annual extensions of the bans through issuing a single order, with between three and eleven publications banned in annual orders issued from 1931 to 1945. Without going into too much detail on each publication and the bans placed on them, the prohibition of *An Siol*, or *The Seed* (1936–45) offers some insight into the rationale and process behind the Northern government's decisions.

Table 2c: Printed Matter Prohibited in Northern Ireland 1922–1972
under Regulation 26 (1922–1949) and Regulation 8 (1954–1972)
of the Civil Authorities (Special Powers) Acts

DATE OF ORDER	DURATION OF PROHIBITION	MATERIAL BANNED
19.3.24	19.3.24–18.3.25	*Éire, the Irish Nation*
12.12.24	12.12.24–11.12.25	*Poblachta na hÉireann*
30.12.24	1.1.25–31.1.25	*Sinn Féin*
7.1.26	11.1.26–31.12.26	*An Phoblacht, The Republic,* or *The Loyalist*
15.7.26	16.7.26–15.7.27	*Fianna – the Official Organ of Fianna na hÉireann*
3.12.26	1.1.27–31.12.1927	*An Phoblacht, The Republic,* or *The Loyalist*
14.2.27	15.2.27–14.2.28	*Irish Freedom – Saoirse na hÉireann*
1.3.27	1.3.27–29.2.28	*Workers' Life*
1.2.28	15.2.28–14.2.29	*Irish Freedom – Saoirse na hÉireann*
10.12.28	1.1.29–31.12.29	*An Phoblacht, The Republic,* or *The Loyalist*
17.1.29	1.2.29–31.1.30	*The Irish World and American Industrial Liberator*
9.2.29	15.2.29–14.2.30	*Irish Freedom – Saoirse na hÉireann*
19.2.29	1.3.29–28.2.30	*Workers' Life*
31.12.29	1.1.30–31.12.30	*An Phoblacht, The Republic,* or *The Loyalist*
13.1.30	1.2.30–31.1.31	*The Irish World and American Industrial Liberator*
27.1.30	15.2.30–14.2.31	*Irish Freedom – Saoirse na hÉireann*
3.3.30	9.3.30–8.3.31	*The Nation*
6.12.30	1.1.31–31.12.31	*An Phoblacht, The Republic,* or *The Loyalist*
7.1.31	1.2.31–31.1.32	*The Irish World and American Industrial Liberator*
16.1.31	15.2.31–14.2.32	*Irish Freedom – Saoirse na hÉireann*
4.3.31	9.3.31–8.3.32	*The Nation*
23.12.31	1.1.32–31.12.32	*An Phoblacht, The Republic, The Loyalist* or *The Republican Press; The Irish World and American Industrial Laborer;* and *Irish Freedom* or *Saoirse na hÉireann*
6.12.32	1.1.33–31.12.33	*An Phoblacht, The Republic, The Loyalist* or *The Republican Press; The Irish World and American Industrial Laborer;* and *Irish Freedom* or *Saoirse na hÉireann*
15.3.34	9.3.34–31.12.34	*Fianna*
22.5.24	23.5.34–31.12.34	*Republican Congress*
5.12.34	1.1.35–31.12.35	*An Phoblacht, The Republic, The Loyalist* or *The Republican Press; The Irish World and American Industrial Laborer; Irish Freedom* or *Saoirse na hÉireann; Fianna;* and *the Republican Congress*
5.12.35	1.1.36–31.12.36	*An Phoblacht, The Republic, The Loyalist* or *The Republican Press; The Irish World and American Industrial Laborer; Irish Freedom* or *Saoirse na hÉireann; Fianna;* and *the Republican Congress*
4.2.36	4.2.36–31.12.36	*An Siol* or *The Seed*
15.12.36	1.1.37–31.12.37	*An Phoblacht, The Republic, The Loyalist* or *The Republican Press; The Irish World and American Industrial Laborer; Irish Freedom* or *Saoirse na hÉireann; Fianna;* the *Republican Congress;* and *An Siol* or *The Seed*
12.10.37	12.10.37–31.12.37	*Wolfe Tone Weekly*

Date of Order	Duration of Prohibition	Material Banned
29.12.37	1.1.38–31.12.38	*An Phoblacht, The Republic, The Loyalist* or *The Republican Press; The Irish World and American Industrial Laborer; Irish Freedom* or *Saoirse na hÉireann; Fianna;* the *Republican Congress; An Siol* or *The Seed;* and *Wolfe Tone Weekly*
16.12.38	1.1.39–31.12.39	*An Phoblacht, The Republic, The Loyalist* or *The Republican Press; The Irish World and American Industrial Laborer; Irish Freedom* or *Saoirse na hÉireann; Fianna;* the *Republican Congress; An Siol* or *The Seed;* and *Wolfe Tone Weekly*
27.3.39	27.3.39–31.12.39	*Irish Freedom*
6.5.39	6.6.39–31.12.39	*The Sentry*
18.12.39	1.1.40–31.12.40	*An Phoblacht, The Republic, The Loyalist* or *The Republican Press; Irish World and American Industrial Laborer; Fianna; The Republican Congress, An Siol* or *The Seed; Irish Freedom* or *Saoirse na hÉireann; Wolfe Tone Weekly;* and *The Sentry*
5.4.40	5.4.40–31.12.40	*The Irish Workers' Weekly*
1.6.40	3.6.40–31.12.40	*The Derry Journal*
14.10.40	14.10.40–31.12.40	*Red Hand*
20.11.40	20.11.40–31.12.40	*The Critic*
21.12.40	1.1.41–31.12.41	*An Phoblacht, The Republic, The Loyalist* or *The Republican Press; Irish World and American Industrial Laborer; Fianna; Republican Congress, An Siol* or *The Seed; Irish Freedom* or *Saoirse na hÉireann; Wolfe Tone Weekly; The Sentry; Irish Workers' Weekly; Red Hand;* and *The Critic*
18.12.41	1.1.42–31.12.42	*An Phoblacht, The Republic, The Loyalist* or *The Republican Press; Irish World and American Industrial Laborer; Fianna; Republican Congress, An Siol* or *The Seed; Irish Freedom* or *Saoirse na hÉireann; Wolfe Tone Weekly; The Sentry; Irish Workers' Weekly; Red Hand;* and *The Critic*
18.12.42	1.1.43–31.12.43	*An Phoblacht, The Republic, The Loyalist* or *The Republican Press; Irish World and American Industrial Laborer; Fianna; Republican Congress, An Siol* or *The Seed; Irish Freedom* or *Saoirse na hÉireann; Wolfe Tone Weekly; The Sentry; Irish Workers' Weekly; Red Hand;* and *The Critic*
18.12.43	1.1.44–31.12.44	*An Phoblacht, The Republic, The Loyalist* or *The Republican Press; Irish World and American Industrial Laborer; Fianna; Republican Congress, An Siol* or *The Seed; Irish Freedom* or *Saoirse na hÉireann; Wolfe Tone Weekly; The Sentry; Irish Workers' Weekly; Red Hand;* and *The Critic*
7.1.44	7.1.44–31.12.44	*Orange Terror* (book – still Regulation 26)
14.12.44	1.1.45–31.12.45	*An Phoblacht, The Republic, The Loyalist* or *The Republican Press; Irish World and American Industrial Laborer; Fianna; Republican Congress, An Siol* or *The Seed; Irish Freedom* or *Saoirse na hÉireann; Wolfe Tone Weekly; The Sentry; Irish Workers' Weekly; Red Hand;* and *The Critic*
29.12.55	1.1.56–31.12.56	*The United Irishmen; Resurgent Ulster;* and *Gair Uladh*
25.4.56	25.4.56–31.12.56	*The Writings of Philip Clarke* (the Omagh prisoner)
28.12.56	1.1.56–31.12.59	*The United Irishmen; Resurgent Ulster; Gair Uladh;* and The Writings of Philip Clarke (the Omagh prisoner)
23.9.57	24.9.57–31.12.59	*The Irish Republican Bulletin*
15.12.59	1.1.60–31.12.62	*The United Irishmen; Resurgent Ulster; Gair Uladh; Glor Uladh;* and the printed matter entitled *The Irish Republican Bulletin*
30.9.65	30.9.65–31.12.68	*The United Irishmen*
23.12.68	1.1.39–31.12.71	*The United Irishmen*

Source: *Belfast Gazette,* 1922–1972

The Republican Publicity Bureau in Belfast issued *An Siol: the Voice of the Resurgent North* on a fortnightly basis. The paper included Gaelic Athletic Association scores, republican poetry, quotations, recent government raids or actions, calls to arms to fight the English and the IRA's position on social issues. Wickham recommended the prohibition of the paper due to its content, the political views and activities of those responsible for issuing it and the steady improvement in its printing and circulation. The editor, Charles Leddy, had admitted to Irish Free State officials that he was a Brigade Officer in the IRA. Sentenced to two years imprisonment by an Irish Free State military tribunal, he had been released on the 23 December 1935. While serving his sentence he had been put forward during the general election as the republican candidate for West Belfast. Following the issuance of an order prohibiting the circulation of *An Siol*, the Lord Chief Justices of Northern Ireland, William Moore (in 1936) and James Andrews (in 1937), signed warrants authorising the detention of all copies of *An Siol, The Seed*, or any other manifestation of this publication.

Until 1943 prohibited materials fell under the definition of newspaper as constituted by the regulation. The security forces did not always wait for an order to be issued before seizing printed materials. For instance, in 1924 the police removed posters announcing a nationalist meeting at which Eamonn de Valera would be in attendance. They also took down numerous other posters announcing nationalist meetings – even when the government had not issued orders banning the gatherings. In 1933 the police confiscated the *Dungannon Observer* for printing an 'in memoriam' to the 1916 rebels.[175] However, in 1943 the periodical, *Ulster Protestant*, fell less clearly within the definition. Although MacDermott, the Northern Ireland Attorney General, asserted that he was prepared to meet such a challenge, he suggested that other cases might arise in the future where challenges could not be successfully met.[176] Accordingly, the Ministry of Home Affairs amended Regulation 26 to include books as well as periodicals.[177] Under the expanded regulation the Ministry immediately took steps to ban *Orange Terror*, an anti-unionist supplement published by the Catholic religious journal, *Capuchin Annual*.

As with many of the other measures, the government revoked Regulation 26 in 1949.[178] Five years later the Minister of Home Affairs directed that two newspapers, *The United Irishman* and *Resurgent Ulster*, be banned. In the absence of any measure specifically authorising such prohibition, the Ministry issued Regulation 8, which essentially reintroduced Regulation 26.[179] Lest there be any doubt that the regulation was specifically drafted to allow the banning of the two publications, the draft of the regulation and the draft orders banning the publications were circulated together. Under Regulation 8 the Ministry extended the period for which materials could be banned from annual renewal, as under Regulation 26, to periods of up to three years. On 1 February 1971 Chichester-Clark, Prime Minister, announced that the newspaper, *The United Irishman*, which had been banned from 1955 to 1971, was no longer considered subversive and that proceedings would not be taken against those who sold it. This did not indicate a change in government policy, however, as he simultaneously announced that the law would be strengthened to enable police to take action against any newspaper publishing 'subversive or seditious' material.[180]

While Regulation 26 under the 1922–43 SPAs governed the banning of printed materials, Regulation 26A, issued in 1930, empowered the Civil Authority to prohibit films and gramophone records.[181] This measure departed from what would have been an offence under Regulations 8 and 26 banning printed material. Under Regulation 26A mere possession of the prohibited matter constituted an offence:

> in the case of newspapers it was not desirable to make mere possession an offence, since individuals may be sent a single copy of a newspaper without any intention on their part of possessing or circulating it, but it is obvious that nobody becomes possessed of a cinematograph film or gramophone record unless by his own deliberate intention and with a previous knowledge of the subject.[182]

The powers of search and seizure included in Regulation 26A duplicated those of Regulation 3(4)(a) regarding firearms or explosive substances kept or suspected to be kept in contravention of an order under that regulation.

Unlike the other regulations, that were directed towards either civil disorder or nationalist and republican activity, the primary purpose of Regulation 26 was to stop the communist threat:

> I must say that this Regulation has been rendered necessary by the fact that the extreme communist element throughout the world is endeavouring to use both the cinematograph film and the gramophone record for purposes of propaganda to further their doctrines. Many of those films and gramophone records, which are believed to be circulated by Russian Soviet Agents, are subversive not only of established law and order, but also of religion and morality and calculated to be far more dangerous than any firearm or explosive substance.[183]

Members of Parliament echoed this fear that communism would attack religion and morality. George Hanna announced: 'It is the intention of the government to prevent the introduction into this country of any films or gramophone records that would be subversive of law and order or that would interfere with religion or morality'.[184] Unionist newspapers recognised this purpose: 'The regulation is designed to cope with the menace of secret Soviet propaganda in Northern Ireland. The communists of Moscow have for some time past been concentrating on efforts to secure a dominant position in the British Labour movement . . . it is to combat [the] attempts upon the part of the Soviet to spread its doctrines in Northern Ireland that the order has been issued'.[185] The main actors driving the enactment of this regulation appear to have been the great triumvirate of security policy in the North – Shewell, Hanna and Wickham. They cited films and records that the imperial authority had already ordered to be detained if found in the course of their importation to Great Britain.

Films banned by the Home Office prior to Regulation 26A included: *Storm Over Gothland, The Mother, Sacco & Vanzetti, The End of Holy Petersburg, Ten Days that Shook the World, Black Sunday, Strike, In the Land of Lenin, Armoured Cruiser Potemkin, The Road to Damascus, The Fall of the Poison, The Great Romanoff Dynasty, The Great Road, The Ship of Death, Shanghai Documents,* and *The Descendant of Genghis Khan/Storm over Asia.*[186] Warrants issued by the Secretary of State in Britain, however, were created by virtue of a common law power forming part of the inherent prerogative of the Crown. It was unclear whether they could be applied to Northern Ireland.

With the additional concern raised by the formation in 1929 of the Belfast Workers' Film Guild, the RUC and the Ministry of Home Affairs decided to adopt similar powers for the North. The 1920 Government of Ireland Act prohibited the Northern Parliament from legislating on import and export issues. As a result, Regulation 26A addressed the actual presence of such films and records within the province itself. In the month after it was published the Ministry of Home Affairs directed the police not to seize any films or records except in pursuance of an order made under the regulation. 'In the event of any film or record which may be prejudicial to the preservation of the peace or maintenance of order, coming under the notice of the police, an immediate report giving an outline of the subject should be furnished to this Ministry, together with your recommendation as to whether an Order of prohibition should be made or not.'[187] Whilst the RUC Inspector General instructed the police to report any information received regarding films or records 'of a seditious description' which had been, or were about to be, imported into Northern Ireland, he recommended to the Ministry of Home Affairs that the films already banned by the British government not be banned under Regulation 26A.

Although the Unionist government directed the regulation at preventing communist propaganda, the only film banned under its auspices
was republican in character. On 24 November 1936 William Grant, a
Unionist MP, introduced a discussion into the Northern Ireland Parliament
concerning whether the Ministry was going to allow *Ourselves Alone*, a
fictitious story about Sinn Féin, made by a British film company and
previously released in Britain, to be shown at the Hippodrome. The next
evening, the Minister of Home Affairs, the Parliamentary Secretary, the
Inspector General of the RUC and the Belfast City Commissioner
attended a private viewing of the movie. On the following day, the
Belfast Corporation Police Committee also saw it and determined that
there was no reason to interfere with its release in the province. In
response to a telephone call from the RUC Inspector General to the
Minister of Home Affairs, however, on 27 November 1936 the
government issued an order prohibiting the film, sending it to the four
main Belfast papers.[188]

Erection of Monuments

As with a number of regulations introduced under the 1922–43 Special
Powers Acts, the government sought to prohibit the erection of monuments in order to eliminate visible representations of republican ideals.
In 1931 an association called the East Tyrone Republican Association
collected subscriptions in the United States for the construction of a
monument in Carrickmore, County Tyrone to commemorate former IRA
activists. The RUC Inspector General submitted a report to the Ministry
of Home Affairs on the 18 of July, outlining the work that had been
completed on the monument and suggesting that it would serve as a
rallying place for 'the disloyal element in the whole county' on republican
holidays. Concern that it would thus tempt 'loyal elements' in the
neighbourhood to demolish it, he recommended that the monument be
destroyed. In response on the 25 of July the Minister of Home Affairs
created Regulation 8A, which provided for the Civil Authority to make
orders prohibiting the erection of any monuments or memorials deemed
sympathetic to the aims of a proscribed organisation. Within two days
the Ministry issued an order directing that the Carrickmore monument
be destroyed.[189] This was the first of only two orders ever issued under
this regulation, before its revocation in 1951.

The second occasion occurred in 1938. Reacting to a decision to allow
the construction of a British Legion War Memorial at Trevor Hill, Newry,
the Northern Old IRA proposed the erection of an IRA memorial at Hyde

Park. The application stated that the intent of the memorial was, '[f]or the purpose of honouring the memory of all who fell in the struggle for Irish Independence and of Irish patriots generally throughout the ages'. An inscription on the Celtic cross was to read in Gaelic: 'To the Memory of Irish Patriots of All Time'. Next to it would be inscribed a verse from a Protestant scholar, Dr John Kells Ingram, translated by the Protestant president, Dr Douglas Hyde. A majority on the Newry Council agreed to the construction, subject to the same terms and conditions as they had applied to the British Legion's proposed memorial. However, in response to a letter sent from the Newry Unionist Association outlining their objections and suggesting that the Newry Urban District Council be dissolved and a Commissioner appointed to take charge of town affairs,[190] the Minister of Home Affairs issued an order on 24 October 1938 banning the erection of the republican monument.

Flying of the Tricolour and Rendering of 'A Soldier's Song'

In reaction to a multitude of letters from Orange Lodges and other unionist constituents decrying the presence of the Irish flag in Northern Ireland, the Unionist government in 1933 issued a regulation specifically prohibiting the Tricolour from being displayed:

> Any person who has in his possession, or displays, or causes to be displayed, or assists in displaying or in causing to be displayed in any public place . . . any emblem, flag or other symbol consisting of three vertical or horizontal stripes coloured respectively green, white and yellow purporting to be an emblem, flag or symbol representing the Irish Republican Army . . . an Irish Republic . . . or . . . any . . . unlawful association shall be guilty of an offence.[191]

With the police thus authorised to remove the flag even where a breach of the peace was not likely to occur, it was clear that it was the political symbolism of the flag to which the Unionist government objected. Soon after the regulation was issued the Ministry of Home Affairs sent a circular to the RUC Inspector General indicating that the *only* time the flag should *not* be removed was when it was specifically being displayed as a flag of the Irish Free State. At the direction of the Minister of Home Affairs, the aim of the police in carrying out Regulation 24C was to be first towards getting the parties responsible to take down the flag and second towards initiating prosecutions under the regulation.

> When the flag is not displayed genuinely as the flag of the Irish Free State the action of the Police should be directed in the first instance

towards having it removed by those responsible for it, and failing this, towards instituting a prosecution, rather than towards removing it themselves. It is undesirable that the police should be drawn into situations involving climbing or cutting down poles or trees for the purpose of removing flags, or proceeding in strong parties to remove flags in places where no question of a breach of the peace arises.[192]

The Ministry replaced this circular by a directive of 2 March 1948, which differed only from the earlier directions in its substitution of 'Éire' for 'Irish Free State'.[193] Although the RUC often removed the Tricolour after these directions had been issued, there were some circumstances when the RUC did not proceed with a prosecution. The security forces expressed concern as to whether the courts would find that any offence had occurred when there was no possibility of a breach of the peace. In one such situation, the RUC recommended that the function at which the Tricolour was displayed simply be banned the following year to prevent the flying of the flag.[194]

According to the 1920 Government of Ireland Act, the Northern Ireland Parliament could not legislate in general terms on matters of foreign policy; this prevented the government from banning the Irish flag outright. An exchange in the Northern Ireland House of Commons indicates the prevailing attitude at the time: when the issue of whether the Irish Free State flag had been outlawed was raised, George Boyle Hanna, the Northern Ireland Minister of Home Affairs from 1953 to 1956, replied that although the Northern Ireland Parliament had not passed a law making it illegal to display the South's flag in Northern Ireland, 'it is an offence under the Civil Authorities Regulations to display emblems, flags, etc., purporting to represent the Irish Republican Army'. When pursued over the recent arrest of three young men for flying the flag at a football match, a Unionist MP responded in place of the Minister that it was a 'rebel flag'. The Nationalist MP, Mr Stewart, waiving the emblem responded, 'This is the flag of the Irish Free State', to which the Speaker derisively inserted: 'The Hon. Member must not make a speech, but he is entitled to bring any handkerchief he pleases into the House'.[195] The Minister of Home Affairs issued a second directive to the RUC in February 1934 indicating that the police should also remove the Tricolour when deliberately flown as an emblem of the Republic at election meetings.[196] Decisions to ban parades and marches took into consideration whether the republican flag would be flown. In referring to one of the bannings of a St Patrick's Day parade, Edmond Warnock stated at Stormont: 'So long as this government lasts and so long as I am

Minister of Home Affairs, I shall not permit the Republican flag to be carried through Derry City . . . No Surrender'.[197]

In spite of these measures, letters continued to arrive at the Ministry of Home Affairs complaining about being forced to bear witness to the Irish flag in the North. The number of missives skyrocketed particularly after the declaration of the Irish Republic and the passage of the 1949 Government of Ireland Act, which precipitated a slightly more lenient attitude from the Unionist government towards the flying of the Tricolour. A litany of organisations forwarded letters to the Ministry protesting this shift: the Fermanagh and Tyrone Unionist Association, Dungannon Volunteer L.O.L., No. 178, Dungannon Total Abstinence L.O.L., No. 1229, County Tyrone Grand Orange Lodge, National Union of Protestants, Braid District L.O.L., No. 18, Newtownbreda and Purdysburn branch of the Mid-Down Unionist Association, Moybrone Orange Lodge, No. 501, Eniskillen District L.O.L., No. 5 and the Amalgamated Committee for South Down Apprentice Boys of Derry.

Not only did they object to the shift in government policy, but an avalanche of resolutions passed against the flying of the Tricolour in *any circumstance* were subsequently forwarded to the Ministry of Home Affairs. Such resolutions were passed by the Grand Orange Lodge of Ireland, Associated Clubs of Apprentice Boys, Cookstown District L.O.L., West Down Unionist Association, City of Londonderry and Foyle Unionist Association, General Committee of the Apprentice Boys of Derry, Tempo Unionist Association, Fermanagh Unionist Association, County of Londonderry Grand Orange Lodge, No Surrender Branch Club of the Apprentice Boys of Derry, Ulster Orange and Protestant Committee, Mid-Down Unionist Association, Lecale District Royal Black Chapter No. 2, Mourne Unionist Association, Strabane District L.O.L. and County Tyrone Grand Orange Lodge.

These letters often included thinly veiled threats which declared that, unless legislation was passed banning the flying of the Irish flag altogether, the 'loyal people' would take the law into their own hands. For instance, from the Unionist Party headquarters in Enniskillen read: 'The loyalist population are not prepared indefinitely to stand aside and see Police abused and the authority of the Northern Government treated with contempt'.[198] The City of Londonderry and Foyle Unionist Association wrote: 'We solemnly warn the Government that if there is a continuance of [flying the Tricolour in a manner that provokes Loyalists] . . . it will be impossible to guarantee that restraint will be maintained'.[199]

Responses sent from the Ministry of Home Affairs were frequently addressed 'Dear Brother' and signed 'Fraternally yours', and without exception indicated agreement with the general sentiments of the letters. They also explained the 'difficult' position in which the Ministry found itself: 'You will appreciate that the official recognition of the Irish Republic under the Imperial Act passed this year does alter the situation',[200] and:

> The Government is most anxious . . . that the peace of the City should be maintained at all costs, but you will appreciate that a complication arises from the fact that the Irish Republic is now officially recognised by the Government of the UK, of which Northern Ireland forms a part. This recognition covers Northern Ireland and therefore there is difficulty in prohibiting the flying of this flag any more than the flag of any other foreign country.[201]

Northern newspapers frequently covered instances in which the Tricolour had been flown.[202] Correspondence congratulating the government for occasions on which security forces prevented the Tricolour from being flown was amplified with assertions that, so long as the Unionist government had the support of the 'loyal people' of the North, the government would 'maintain for our own and succeeding generations the privileges and the liberties which have been purchased for us by our forefathers at so great a price'.[203]

Partly as a result of the tremendous support demonstrated by the unionist population, the aim of Regulation 24C of the 1922–43 Special Powers Acts became incorporated into non-emergency legislation. In 1954 the Northern government passed the Flags and Emblems (Display) Act (Northern Ireland).[204] In 1975 the Standing Advisory Commission for Human Rights recommended repeal of this legislation. The commission argued that the law should concentrate on whether any particular conduct was likely to lead to a breach of the peace. Since any flag, including the Union Jack, might generate a breakdown in law and order, the distinction should ride on the actions of individuals and not on the character of the flag itself. In addition, it proffered the argument that Northern Irish legislation should be brought into line with the rest of the United Kingdom.[205] This statute forbade any interference with the flying of the Union Jack, while allowing the police to forbid any flags or emblems likely to lead to a breach of the peace.

Directions issued to the RUC and circulated by the Inspector General in 1954 indicated: 'In no circumstances should the Police direct or advise that the Union Jack should not be flown or displayed on premises'. Contrarily:

> [i]f, in the opinion of the Police, the display of the Tricolour is likely to lead to a breach of the peace it shall be the duty of the Police to warn

the person responsible and ask him to remove it forthwith. If this is not done the Police should remove it and should institute proceedings against the person responsible for any offences against the Flags and Emblems (Display) Act (Northern Ireland), 1954 and the Public Order Act (Northern Ireland), 1951.[206]

Not only did the flag evoke strong emotions among the population, but renderings of the anthem of the Irish Free State, 'A Soldier's Song', gained increased notoriety amongst loyalists from the 1930s through the 1950s. As with the display of flags, the Ministry of Home Affairs received a spate of letters requesting that the song be banned. In response, the Ministry issued a second election circular on 8 November 1935, suggesting that 'A Soldier's Song' not be allowed at any election meetings. The RUC Inspector General protested at this directive, claiming that under the current regulations the song could be stopped only if it would lead to a breach of the peace. Nevertheless, in parts of the North, which were primarily nationalist or republican in orientation, the singing of the anthem was not likely to spark opposition and, if a constable intervened, he or she could be taken to criminal or civil court.[207] This led the government to draft a new regulation on 29 November 1935, banning any rendering of 'A Soldier's Song'. Although it was originally proposed that the new regulation allow the prohibition of any song, empowering the Ministry then to issue an order specific to 'A Soldier's Song', the Ministry decided that this would give nationalists and republicans grounds to request the banning of various loyalist songs:

> I think . . . on the whole it is better to make a definite Regulation prohibiting 'The Soldier's Song' only. If you produced a Regulation in general terms the other side would immediately press for having orders made prohibiting 'Dolly's Brae,' etc., and although they will probably do the same in regard to this Regulation, the point is not quite so obvious as if we did the thing in the form originally intended.[208]

The first regulation made it an offence to reproduce any song, 'in such a manner as is likely to cause a breach of the peace or to give offence to any of His Majesty's subjects'. The second and final version made it an offence to render either vocally or instrumentally the 'Soldier's Song' in a manner likely to cause a breach of the peace or to give offence to any of HM's liege subjects.[209] Although the government held this regulation in preparedness, it did not issue the regulation in 1935. However, in response to increased calls for a ban during the next general election, the government resurrected the measure in 1938. Captain Perceval Maxwell, of the East Down Unionist Association sent a letter to Dawson Bates on

6 November 1938, protesting that 'A Soldier's Song' had been sung at the end of a recent meeting in Downpatrick. The meeting, sponsored by the Northern Council of Unity, had lasted just over an hour and involved some 1,200 people. The RUC Inspector General once again protested the implementation of this regulation:

> The police already have ample powers to deal with any conduct liable to lead to a breach of the peace and the proposed Regulation would place them in no stronger position. It would create a new offence and in practice would be almost impossible to enforce. It would tend towards encouraging the use of the Song simply for the purpose of defying the police and would lead to complaints from the Protestant side that the Regulation was not being enforced when to do so would only aggravate what probably was already a difficult situation . . . On the whole I would strongly oppose the proposed Regulation as being unlikely to effect the purpose for which it is intended but rather to encourage the use of the Song and the production of disorders which otherwise would not occur. Its greatest danger is that it will lessen the respect for the police as they will not be able properly to enforce it which will lead to organised defiance on every possible occasion.[210]

Although the police enforced an informal ban on the song during the 1938 General Election,[211] and prosecuted numerous individuals for rendering the music 'in a manner likely to lead to a breach of the peace',[212] the regulation specifically banning 'A Soldier's Song' was never enacted. Other regulations prepared by the government also went unused. For instance, on 16 May 1924 the government prepared Regulation 8A, which authorised the billeting of the police and Special Constabulary during emergencies. Although the Ministry never enacted the measure, it kept the regulation in readiness for use when expedient. As was previously noted, the government also prepared a regulation banning the Easter Lily. However, the Ministry later discarded the regulation on the grounds that (a) it would be too difficult to describe the Easter Lily accurately, and (b) the 1922–43 SPAs already covered breaches of the peace arising from the wearing of the symbol.

Proscription

Prior to the creation of Northern Ireland, the British government deemed a number of republican organisations in Ireland unlawful. In 1918 the imperial government proclaimed the Sinn Féin Organisation, Sinn Féin Clubs, the Irish Volunteers, Cumann na mBan and the Gaelic League to be dangerous.[213] The following year Britain prohibited the same organisations. These bans were never formally revoked. The new Northern government adopted Regulation 14 of the ROIR, by virtue of which these associations were banned, as Regulation 24 of the original schedule to the 1922 SPA.[214] This measure made it an offence for any person to act with a view towards promoting the objects of an unlawful association, or to have in one's possession any document relating or purporting to relate to the affairs of such an organisation. The regulation placed the burden of proof on the defendant, on whose premise or person documents relating to the illegal group were found, to demonstrate his or her absence of association with the proscribed entity. Similarly, the owners or occupants of any premises involved in crimes committed under the Special Powers Acts also became subject to penalties provided for by the legislation.[215] The government expanded this measure within weeks of its introduction through Regulation 24A, which made it an offence to become or remain a member of an unlawful association or to act so as to promote either the objects of an unlawful association or of a 'seditious conspiracy'.[216] It also maintained the shift in burden of proof, making possession of documents relating to the organisation sufficient proof of membership. The government made periodic additions to the list of proscribed groups. In 1933 the Ministry extended this measure with the introduction of Regulation 24B, making it an offence to declare membership of an unlawful association while in a court of law, or, when brought up on such charges, to refuse to recognise the court.[217] As with many other regulations, the government revoked proscription in 1949 and withdrew Regulation 24B two years later.[218] Regulation 24A, however, remained on the statute book through the prorogation of Stormont in 1972. On the suspension of the Northern Parliament Britain incorporated proscription into the 1973 EPA. During the reign of the Northern government, in addition to being published in the *Belfast Gazette*, orders announcing the banning of the organisations were sent to the *Belfast Evening Telegraph*, the *Belfast Newsletter*, the *Northern Whig* and the *Irish News*.

Immediately following the passage of the 1922 SPA, Solly-Flood recommended on 13 May that the Irish Republican Brotherhood, Irish Republican Army, Cumann na mBan, Fianna na hÉireann, Sinn Féin Organisations and Sinn Féin Clubs be banned. It was suggested within the Ministry of Home Affairs that the Northern government could proceed in a similar manner to the imperial government, by proclamation under an 1887 Act, in order to ban these associations. The advantage so gained would be to identify the imperial government with the suppression of the groups. However, a number of individuals in the

Ministry of Home Affairs were afraid of causing 'trouble' with the imperial government. As a result, the Minister of Home Affairs decided to issue an order under Regulation 24A of the 1922 SPA.[219] The subsequent list, derived from Solly-Flood's recommendations and included the Irish Republican Brotherhood, the Irish Republican Army, the Irish Volunteers, Cumann na mBan and Fianna na hÉireann.[220]

On 7 May 1936 officers of Cumann na mBan and Clann na nGaedheal, an American organisation, met in Barry's Hotel, Dublin to form a new political party, Cumann Poblachta na hÉireann. Their manifesto read: 'The true road of national endeavour is to repudiate British rule and domination and to supplant British institutions by the free democratic institutions of the sovereign people'. Its constitution stated that the Irish people bore a right to be a free and separate people, denied any right to Britain to partition the island, and claimed allegiance to the 1916 Irish Republic. The organisation vowed 'to fight resolutely any effort to drag the people into England's imperial wars'. The issue of *An Phoblacht* which contained the Constitution and manifesto was intercepted in Strabane and forwarded to the Ministry of Home Affairs by the postmaster surveyor. The Ministry then sent the copy to the RUC, who prepared a report based on the newspaper article, and submitted it back to the Ministry with the recommendation that the organisation be banned. Within a month the Ministry added Cumann Poblachta na hÉireann to the list of proscribed organisations.[221]

During the 1930s the Northern government banned Saor Éire, a left-wing republican group formed in Dublin in 1931, and the National Guard, a fascist organisation that grew from the Blueshirts.[222] Although the National Guard was formed in accordance with the Blueshirts, among its aims was the attainment of a united Ireland. Throughout the tenure of the Northern government, the Ministry banned considerably less organisations than the number declared illegal in the South. For example, as of 21 October 1931, the Irish Free State had prohibited Saor Éire, the IRA/Oglaigh na hÉireann, Cumann na mBan, Friends of Soviet Russia, the Irish Labour Defence League, the Workers' Defence Corps, the Women Prisoners' Defence League, the Workers' Revolutionary Party (Ireland), the Irish Tribute League, the Irish Working Farmers' Committee and the Workers' Research Bureau.[223] In the North the Ministry issued an order banning Saor Uladh in 1955, following it in 1956 with one banning Sinn Féin and Fianna Uladh.[224] These organisations were nationalist or republican in their orientation, claiming a united Ireland as their ultimate goal.

As the Unionist government instituted limited reforms in the 1960s, an immediate response from loyalist forces ensued. A few weeks after the fifty year commemoration of the Easter Uprising, a paramilitary group calling itself the Ulster Volunteer Force mounted a petrol bomb attack against a Catholic-owned pub on the Shankill Road. Although unsuccessful in the attack, the UVF issued a statement immediately afterwards: 'From this day on we declare war on the IRA and its splinter groups. Known IRA men will be executed mercilessly and without hesitation'.[225] The UVF became the first and only loyalist organisation to be banned by the Northern government.[226] In his address to the Northern Ireland House of Commons announcing the banning of the UVF, O'Neill stated: 'Let no one imagine there is any connection whatever between the [1920 UVF and the present UVF]; between men who were ready to die for their country on the fields of France, and a sordid conspiracy of criminals prepared to take up arms against unprotected fellow citizens. No, this organisation now takes its proper place alongside the IRA in the schedule of illegal bodies'.[227]

The following year, in response to increased civil rights agitation within republican circles, the Ministry of Home Affairs banned Republican Clubs.[228] All the same, no serious attempt was made to enforce the order. Only one case was brought against an individual before the ban was lifted in March 1973. In March 1968 the police charged Mr McEldowney with being a member of the Slaughtneil Republican Club. Local magistrates dismissed the charge on the grounds that the club in question was not a threat to the peace and order in Northern Ireland within the terms of the regulation.[229] The Northern Ireland Court of Appeal reversed the magistrates' decision, claiming that the Minister of Home Affairs bore the sole responsibility for which organisations should be proscribed. Lord Chief Justice MacDermott, former Attorney General and Lord Chief Justice of Northern Ireland from 1951 to 1971, dissented from the decision, claiming that the regulation was too vague to relate to the specifications laid out in the 1922 Special Powers Act. In April 1969 the case reached the House of Lords, where the second appeal was dismissed by a majority of three to two. The majority held that in the absence of proof of bad faith on the part of the Minister of Home Affairs, it was up to him to determine which organisations were subversive. The minority held that since the first court had cleared the club in question of seditious pursuits, the argument that all Republican Clubs had unlawful aims was destroyed. Moreover, the description of Republican Clubs as named in the order was too broad to comfortably fall within the gamut of the 1922 SPA. The majority opinion held and the order prohibiting Republican Clubs stood. By the time Britain assumed direct rule, the Unionist government had banned eleven organisations, nine of which were distinctly republican in character.

ADDITIONAL POWERS EXERCISED UNDER THE 1922–43 SPAs

Refusal to Recognise the Court

The Unionist government employed numerous other measures to counter the republican challenge. The Ministry directed some of the provisions not towards general disorder, nor towards republicanism *per se*, but towards situations that arose within the context of republicanism's challenge to the State. For instance, at the prompting of Babington, the Northern Ireland Attorney General, the Ministry of Home Affairs in January 1933 issued Regulation 24B, which made it an offence to refuse to recognise a court during proceedings related to the 1922 SPA.[230] Babington subsequently sent a circular to the RUC Inspector General with directions for the cases arising in relation to the offence. The memo directed that the prosecuting officer, a District Inspector, request that an offending person be remanded on the first charge, and not on a breach of Regulation 24B. The Inspector was then to consult with Babington as to how the charges should be pursued: 'When a defendant commits a breach of [Regulation 24B] in open Court, the District Inspector prosecuting should ask to have such person remanded on the first charge, so as to enable the directions of the Attorney General to be obtained as to a breach of this Regulation'.[231]

Three years later Babington modified his instructions, directing that in the event of a defendant's refusal to recognise the court, the District Inspector should take a detailed note, to be able to prove it on a future occasion:

> In dealing with the charge then before the court, no reference should be made to this further breach of the Regulations, but the matter should be reported at once for the directions of the Attorney General. If convicted on the original charge, the defendant after he has served his sentence can be brought up again on the fresh charge and dealt with accordingly. When this is done the attention of the court should be drawn to the seriousness of the charge and an exemplary sentence applied for.[232]

The RUC issued further instructions the following year, stating: 'When prisoners refuse to recognise the court, the police should ask the Court to impose a rule of bail. This rule will apply whether a conviction has been obtained in cases before the court or not'.[233] The Inspector General omitted this paragraph in the following year's circular. Following the 1943 Special Powers Act amendments, the Inspector indicated that offences against Regulation 24B should be taken into account in determining whether to proceed by summary trial or on indictment for violations of Regulation 24A. 'Where a person is known to be a member of the IRA, and is likely to refuse to recognise the court, the police, in seeking direction as to a prosecution under Regulation 24A of the Civil Authorities (Special Powers) Act, may take such circumstances into consideration as being relevant to their recommendation as to the mode of trial, i.e., summary or on indictment.'[234]

Powers of Questioning

Security forces used the general powers of questioning obtained via the Special Powers Acts throughout unionist control of Northern Ireland. In 1933 the Ministry added new provisions that aimed at imprisoning republicans. Regulation 22 in the original schedule to the Act provided for the Civil Authority to require by order any person to furnish whatever information may be specified. The measure allowed for the person to attend at such time and such place as specified in the order to furnish the information. Failure to do so would be considered an offence against the regulations. The government effectively amended this regulation within a month to extend similar powers to the security forces. Regulation 22A required that an individual stopped by the security forces answer any question put to him or her to the best of his or her ability and knowledge.[235] It reproduced clause 1, Regulation 53 of the Defence of the Realm Act, which had been revoked on 25 November 1919 and had not been reintroduced into the ROIR. The main impetus for introducing the measure came from Richard Best.[236] Wickham specified that police officers were not to use these powers until every effort had been made to get the person to disclose information voluntarily. The RUC Inspector General believed that such compulsory questioning would not stand up in a court of law, and therefore it should be used only as a last resort:

> The police are not to make a practice of questioning persons as to their loyalty. These instructions are not, however, to be taken as to depriving the police of the powers conferred on them by Regulation 22A of putting reasonable questions, that is questions requiring reasonable information regarding the movements etc. of third parties or of the person questioned. The police should not, however, use the compulsory powers conferred by this Regulation in questioning a person as to his own movements until they had given him every opportunity of voluntarily disclosing them. The answers to questions put under these compulsory powers would not be admissible in evidence on any criminal charge, excepting [sic] one under this Regulation for failure to answer.[237]

The government further expanded this regulation in 1933 by extending powers of examination to resident magistrates.[238] In 1924 the committee appointed to review the provisions of the 1920 Restoration of Order in Ireland Act had highlighted the absence of this power. In its report the committee indicated:

> There is . . . no power of obtaining compulsorily information from persons who have knowledge of the commission or intended commission of crimes until criminal proceedings have been actually commenced. We suggest for consideration whether there should not be some power to compel them to state to the magistrate what they know; such statements being not evidence against any person of the facts stated but simply information bearing upon the question whether a prosecution should be instituted.[239]

Where the police suspected that an offence had been, was being, or was about to be committed, a constable without a warrant could bring before a resident magistrate any person from whom there was reason to believe information could be obtained. The magistrate could then examine the individual under oath, take a deposition concerning the offence and bind the individual by recognisance to appear and give evidence at the next petty sessions (or when called upon, within three months). Offences for which the individual could be questioned included any felonies or mis-demeanors and also any offences against the 1922–33 SPAs or against the regulations. Most critically, a *'person examined under this Regulation shall not be excused from answering any question on the ground that the answer thereto may criminate or tend to criminate himself'*.[240] Any statement made, except in cases pursued by indictment or any other criminal proceedings for perjury, was admissible in later proceedings against the individual. Regulation 22B barred the magistrate conducting the examination from taking part in the later hearing if pursued by summary conviction, and from taking depositions against the individual for proceedings by indictment.

The regulation removed any legal representation from the individual being so questioned: 'No person other than the Magistrate, or such official person as the Magistrate shall direct, shall be present as such Inquiry'.[241] In the event that an individual refused to answer a question, refused to recognise the court or acknowledged membership of an unlawful organisation, the magistrate certified the evidence which was then used in further prosecutions under the regulations.

The government introduced this power for a specific purpose and made use of it immediately after its enactment. In October 1933 security forces arrested and detained forty to fifty suspected republicans. Michael Farrell claims that in the absence of violence at the time, the government was reluctant to intern the individuals so arrested. He considers the subsequent issuance of Regulation 22B as designed particularly for this situation.[242] A report to the Home Office in 1939 states that the power was inserted into the regulations, 'to meet a special and isolated case', and was rarely used thereafter. This seems to support Farrell's claim that the regulation was created for use in a specific instance.[243] After the arrest and detention of the republicans the Ministry issued Regulation 22B. The resident magistrate subsequently examined the men and when they refused to answer questions put to them by the magistrate, the courts convicted them of an offence against the regulations.[244]

Identity Documents

The Unionist government first required identity documents in 1940 as part of their wartime security measures.[245] The decision to introduce identity cards was taken at a Cabinet meeting on 15 June 1940. The aim of the measure was to ensure that the police could ascertain on demand particulars as to the name and permanent address of any individual in Northern Ireland.[246] Although Regulation 1A represented the first such measure to be passed under the 1922–33 SPAs, similar provisions had been made prior to the 1922 Anglo-Irish Treaty, and again in 1923 as part of Regulation 23B. With regard to the first instance, on 29 September 1921 the government drafted an order to issue identity certificates in the event of talks breaking down and martial law being declared in Southern Ireland. Under ROIR Rule 35, no individual over the age of sixteen would be allowed to embark or disembark in Ireland without a permit issued by the General Officer Commanding in Ireland. The order required that all males aged from sixteen to sixty years carry identification documents issued by the military authority. Without these papers and permission to travel, they would be prohibited from proceeding more than ten miles from their residences or travelling at speeds exceeding four mph. Once the Treaty was signed and partition implemented in the North, however, the Northern government discarded these plans.[247]

Regulation 1A, drafted as a result of the Cabinet meeting in June 1940, required every individual over the age of fourteen to carry some form of identification and to produce it to the police on demand. Various documents could serve as identification: an ID card issued pursuant to the provisions of the 1939 National Registration Act, a valid passport, a travel permit card or an identity document issued by a constable of the

RUC in charge of a station.[248] Further orders approved British seamen's identity cards[249] and certificates issued to members of HM Forces temporarily released from service.[250] The Northern government complemented these measures by regulations restricting movement into Northern Ireland. Three days after the Minister issued the first order prescribing approved documents of identity, the government introduced Regulation 1A(2), which required visitors to Northern Ireland to satisfy the police that their presence in Northern Ireland was *essential* for legitimate business of importance to the national interests of the UK.[251] The government never printed this measure. The Ministry revoked it within a week through Regulation 1B, which required that any individual entering Northern Ireland satisfy the police that his presence was not for any purpose detrimental to the preservation of peace and the maintenance of order in Northern Ireland.[252]

Although identity cards quickly became part of the wartime effort, by 1945 it had become clear that Éire presented minimal immediate threat. That year, the RUC granted concessions for people passing through Northern Ireland from the South, stipulating that, as long as they did not leave the trains, they would not be required to carry documents. In May 1946 the RUC Inspector General requested that the Ministry of Home Affairs revoke Regulation 1A.[253] From a security perspective the checking of passengers on public transportation had proven a drain on resources which had yielded minimal results. The RUC claimed that the revocation of the measure would reduce police work along the border and eliminate the inconvenience to cross-border traffic. His sentiments were shared by the Registrar General and the Board of Trade for Northern Ireland who met with the Ministry of Home Affairs in August 1946 to seek an end to the measures. Although the regulations fell under the Special Powers Acts and not under General Defence, identity documents had been absorbed into the wartime administration, especially with regard to national registration, food rationing clothes rationing and residence permits. Provisions of the Defence Regulations reciprocated the overlap between the Special Powers Act and wartime measures. For example, S.R.O. 1774/1941 referred specifically to the power to detain individuals from Éire. Thus, attempts to lift the regulation initially met with resistance from the National Registration Office, the Ministry of Food and other bodies dependent on the cards for administrative matters. Nevertheless, the Northern government rescinded Regulation 1A in August 1946 and did not reintroduce such powers again during the Unionist government of Northern Ireland.[254]

Military Drilling and Use of Military Uniforms

Regulation 5 of the original schedule to the 1922 Special Powers Act provided for the Civil Authority to declare in force in any area a prohibition on military drilling for any person other than a member of the police force. The Unionist government drew this measure from Regulation 9E of the ROIR, which had acted in concert with regular statute law. The 1819 Unlawful Drilling Act prohibited all drilling unless the Lord-Lieutenant or two Justices of the Peace granted authority. A penalty of up to seven years penal servitude could be inflicted for such an offence. Under Section 16 of the 1920 Firearms Act, the power of granting such authority became vested solely in the Minister of Home Affairs. The only object in making such a regulation under the SPA was to enable an offence of this sort to be dealt with as an offence against the regulations by two resident magistrates.

The Executive supplemented the regulation in 1931 with the Military Exercise and Drill (Northern Ireland) Order, which allowed for the RUC Inspector General to issue permits allowing military exercises to be conducted by non-police force members.[255] The following month the police issued an order allowing specific organisations to drill. The order cited the Boy Scouts (Baden Powell), Church Lads' Brigade, Boys' Brigade, Girl Guides, Catholic Boy Scouts (St Vincent de Paul), Catholic Girl Scouts (St Vincent de Paul), Sea Cadets, and recognised branches of the British Legion on Armistice Day. On 28 June 1943 the RUC added the National Fire Service and members of civil defence organisations to the list of bodies allowed to drill. None of the organisations was allowed the use of firearms.

Also in the original schedule, Regulation 3 empowered the Civil Authority to make orders prohibiting or restricting in any area the wearing of uniforms or badges of a naval, military or police character, or uniforms indicating membership of any body as specified in the order. Within a month of the enactment of the statute the Ministry issued Regulation 10A, which further outlawed the unauthorised wearing or possession of any 'official' uniforms supplied by the security forces.[256] It also made it an offence for an individual to represent himself falsely as a person entitled to wear such a uniform.

This measure reproduced, word for word, Regulation 41 of the Restoration of Order in Ireland Act. Unlike most of the other regulations, created by the Ministry of Home Affairs in consultation with the RUC or by the Attorney General in order to expedite prosecutions under the Act, the decision to issue Regulation 10A was the result of an agreement reached between Dawson Bates and Solly-Flood. Section 68 of the 1939 Civil Defence Act later incorporated this measure into ordinary law. Regulations 3 and 10A were repealed in 1949. On 13 February 1971 the Northern Ireland Prime Minister signed two new orders banning the wearing of military style uniforms indicating membership of the IRA or other 'subversive organisations' and making it obligatory for any person to inform the authorities if he or she had knowledge of death or injuries known to be caused by gunshot, explosive devices or other offensive weapons. The RUC arrested three men soon thereafter for wearing military style uniforms and carrying hurling sticks at a funeral in Belfast. A march protesting the arrests and the issuance of the order was held on 21 February 1971, when six women in combat jackets and black berets marched through Belfast. A second protest on 26 February resulted in the arrest of about thirty men and women.

Miscellaneous Provisions

The Unionist government adopted various additional powers under the 1922–43 SPAs. For instance, Regulation 10 of the original act made it an offence to collect information on members of HM Forces or Constabulary. Although the Ministry repealed this measure in 1951,[257] it reintroduced the provision five years later in response to the IRA's 1956–62 campaign.

In 1957 the Ministry issued Regulation 37, empowering the Minister to prevent individuals who were entering Northern Irish ports from coming ashore. In January the cargo ship, *City of Waterford*, arrived into Belfast harbour. Acting on rumours that arms and ammunition were concealed on board, Walter William Buchanan Topping, Unionist MP for Larne and Minister of Home Affairs from 1956 to 1959, issued a regulation empowering the Civil Authority to prevent individuals entering Northern Ireland from ships moored offshore. The same day he issued an order under Regulation 37 prohibiting all but two crew members to step onshore. In its search of the vessel, the government found only the declared shipment of fruit, flax and beer that had been brought from Rotterdam. After two days in port, the ship left on 31 January to return to its home port of Dublin. Regulation 37 remained on the books.[258]

Also in 1957 the government extended various powers enshrined in the 1922–43 SPAs' regulations to the armed forces. The court system later found this extension of powers of search to be unconstitutional, as it violated stipulations laid out in the 1920 Government of Ireland Act. On 23 February 1972 appeals lodged by five people, two of whom, John Hume and Ivan Cooper, were MPs, were successful in the High court, in

Belfast. Their convictions under the Special Powers Act for remaining in an assembly after it had been ordered to disperse were quashed by the judgment of Robert Lowrey, Justice O'Donnell and Justice Gibson, which determined that the limitations stipulated by the 1920 Government of Ireland Act did not permit the government of Northern Ireland to order the armed forces of the Crown to take action. The regulation passed by the Northern Ireland government under the Special Powers Act in 1957 empowering them to do so therefore contravened the 1920 Act. As a result of the High Court decision, the British government immediately introduced a bill at Westminster to legalise all action hitherto taken by the British Army in Northern Ireland. The Home Secretary, Mr Maudling, emphasising the need for speedy legislation, said that the Act would declare that 'the law as far as the armed forces are concerned is and always has been what it was hitherto been believed to be'. The 1972 Northern Ireland Bill passed both Houses of Parliament and received royal assent within hours of the Belfast High court ruling.[259]

Immediately following partition the Northern government carried over to the 1922–43 SPAs the powers that had operated under the ROIR. After the first few years of the Northern government, the government refrained from invoking many of these measures. I have already discussed a number of these, for instance, the closing of licensed premises, taken from Regulation 10 of the ROIR and included under the SPA as Regulation 2 and later Regulation 39, was not used after June 1923 until 1969. Similarly, Regulations 5, 6, 7 and 7A dealing with illegal drilling and the right of access to land or buildings and the closing of roads were not extensively used after 1922. Regulation 8 of the 1922 SPA, which governed the commandeering of buildings and land for police purposes, was based on Regulation 2 of the ROIR. Although it was employed in the early days of the Northern government, it quickly fell into disuse.

There are numerous additional provisions, however that I have not yet addressed, which also fall into this category: Regulation 3 of the original schedule to the 1922 SPA was drawn from Regulations 9A and 9AA of the ROIR. It governed meetings, assemblies, processions and possession of badges or uniforms. Owing in large part to the incorporation of similar powers in other regulations, this provision went unused after the first year of the Northern government. Regulation 9 of the 1922 SPA, addressing the use and possession of motor spirit, was taken directly from Regulation 15A of the ROIR. The government never made use of this measure. Regulation 11 covered any attempt to tamper with telegraphic or telephonic messages or to engage in illegal signalling or the transmission of wireless messages. The Ministry lifted it from Regulations 20 and 22 of the

ROIR, and following partition rarely exercised these powers. Regulation 12, dealing with the use of cipher or code messages, duplicated Regulation 22A of the ROIR. The unionist regime did not use this measure after 1922. Regulation 13, prohibiting any attempt to damage the railways, reintroduced Regulation 22 of the ROIR. Although the Northern government never enacted this provision, the British government later resurrected it under the 1973 EPA. Such cases as arose in conjunction with the railways during unionist control of Northern Ireland were dealt with under other statutes. Likewise, the government did not make use of Regulation 13A, dealing with the deliberate inaction of individuals charged with providing electricity, gas or water, after the establishment of Northern Ireland.

The government also made minimal use of other regulations after the initial violence of 1922. The Ministry took Regulation 14 of the 1922 SPA from Regulation 29 of the ROIR. This measure empowered the Civil Authority to prohibit individuals from approaching defence works within a specified distance. Regulation 15, making it illegal to discharge firearms or otherwise endanger the safety of any police officer, drew from Regulation 32 of the ROIR. Regulation 16, prohibiting any act intended or likely to cause mutiny, sedition or disaffection among the security forces or civilian population, duplicated Regulation 42 of the ROIR. Regulation 17 combined Regulations 43 and 43A of the ROIR, making it an offence to obstruct the security forces in the exercise of their duties. None of these four measures – Regulations 14, 15, 16, and 17 – was used after 1922. Similarly, no prosecutions were held under Regulation 25, drawn from Regulation 27 of the ROIR, which dealt with the printing of false reports and statements. No action was taken under Regulation 27, either, which was drawn from Regulation 27A of the ROIR. This measure prohibited the publication of confidential information with regard to the Northern government.

Regulation 18A of the original schedule to the SPA granted the Civil Authority the power to deal with the alteration of buildings. Although the security forces found this measure to be useful to counter shiping incidents in the early days of the Northern government, the regulation soon fell into disuse. The government never made direct use of Regulation 20, which empowered a justice of the peace to order premises to be closed. The government also refrained from acting specifically on Regulation 22, which required persons to submit such information as may be required by order. And finally, the Northern government never exercised Regulation 32, which allowed for proceedings to be held in camera. The absence of use of these powers can be seen more as a consequence of the other, extensive powers that were exercised by the Northern government, rather than as a sense of leniency or admission that special powers were not necessary. The powers in the regulations overlapped considerably with each other; indeed, the RUC continually reminded the Ministry of Home Affairs of the need to ensure that actions taken would be found by the courts to be constitutional. The government was very careful to ensure that the actions of the Ministry and of the security forces would be found compatible with the law. This led to the withholding of a few regulations and the strengthening and extension of numerous others.

CONCLUSION

The Unionist government used the 1922–43 SPAs and their regulations to quell what were perceived as republican – and in some cases communist – threats to the Northern government. The government supplemented these measures with changes to ordinary legislation, particularly in the mid to late 1960s, at the outbreak of the civil rights movement. The 1969 Firearms Act (Northern Ireland),[260] as amended by the 1971 Firearms (Amendment) Act (Northern Ireland),[261] prohibited the possession of guns or ammunition in suspicious circumstances and transferred the burden of proof to the accused to demonstrate that weapons thus found were to be used for a lawful purpose. The 1969 Protection of the Person and Property Act (Northern Ireland)[262] and 1970 Explosives Act (Northern Ireland)[263] banned, *inter alia*, the construction, possession or use of Molotov cocktails, again transferring the burden of proof to the accused. The 1970 Criminal Justice (Temporary Provisions) Act (Northern Ireland),[264] eventually repealed by the 1973 EPA, established minimum penalties for more serious terrorist offences and for certain types of non-violent civil disobedience, such as sit-ins. This measure was mainly levied against Sinn Féin and members of the Catholic Campaign for Social Justice. The 1970 Prevention of Incitement to Hatred Act (Northern Ireland)[265] created new offences of incitement to hatred and circulation of certain false statements, false reports and imposition of penalties. The government only brought one prosecution, however, under the 1970 Act.

During the tenure of the Northern government occasional voices raised opposition to the 1922–43 SPAs and its powers. The *Irish Times, Irish News*, and various nationalist and republican papers routinely criticised the use of these measures. For instance, following the five year extension of the SPA in 1928, on 16 May the *Irish News/Belfast Morning News* headline read, '1,250,000 Slaves'.[266] In addition, various associations made periodic attempts to encourage the government to relinquish its powers. In

1933 the Belfast Trades and Labour Council and the National Union of Vehicle Builders wrote to the Ministry of Home Affairs, lodging their protest against the SPA. The government received similar letters in 1934 from the Labour Party Northern Ireland, in 1935 from the National Union of Railwaymen and in 1936 from the Irish Trade Union Congress. A campaign launched by the West Belfast Labour Party in June 1936 failed to garner any significant support. An RUC report detailing the proceedings of the first meeting stated: 'Judging from the attendance . . . the police are of opinion, that it will be very difficult for the Communist Party, or any other organisation, to arouse enthusiasm among members of the working class, in respect of a campaign of propaganda or agitation against the Special Powers Act'.[267]

By far the most trenchant criticism of the SPA arose in 1936, when the National Council for Civil Liberties (NCCL) issued a report stating that although there might have been an emergency situation justifying the initial introduction of the 1922 SPA, the conditions had long since ceased to exist. In this light, the emergency measures still in use by the government lacked justification. The Unionist government, anticipating the negative publicity that would be sparked off by the *ad-hoc*, self-appointed inquiry conducted from London, closely monitored all visits to Northern Ireland by members of the NCCL.[268] Prior to the publication of the report of the inquiry, the editor of the *Northern Whig* contacted the Prime Minister on 20 May 1936 to obtain an article detailing the government's position which could be printed jointly with a summary of the NCCL report. The subsequent government statement became the main unionist response to the inquiry. However, as it was written before the Cabinet had actually read the NCCL report, it failed to answer in any coherent or effective manner the specific charges laid by the NCCL.

Not surprisingly, the Ancient Order of Hibernians and Northern Ireland Labour Party passed resolutions congratulating the NCCL.[269] Public discussion in Britain of the Special Powers Acts suddenly appeared and summaries of the NCCL report appeared in publications as far away as the Australian *Sydney Morning Herald* and the South African *Star*.[270] The widespread public response to the NCCL report only served to entrench unionist defence of the 1922–33 SPAs further. The Prime Minister of Northern Ireland, James Craigavon, announced that as long as he was in office the 1922–43 SPAs would remain. He also stated that he would make the statute the central issue at the next general election. The Grand Orange Lodge of Ireland, the Omagh Royal Black Chapter, the Imperial Grand Black Chapter at Lurgan and various other orange associations shared the government's condemnation of the NCCL report.

Craig attended the Grand Orange Lodge meeting at which the organisation passed a resolution denouncing the report. He summed up his response in his speech at the luncheon following the meeting, where he proclaimed that the Northern government 'would always be ready to see that nothing under heaven would interfere with their rights and privileges as members of the British Empire'.[271] The government maintained a relatively straightforward position: the legislation had to be retained in order to keep subversives in check. Apart from this general principle, the government launched a campaign of character defamation against members of the inquiry and maintained that the report was a lie.[272] The government claimed that 'all law-abiding citizens in Northern Ireland enjoy the same liberties as other members of the British Empire'.[273] They were aided in their stance by the relative autonomy of the province from Britain. Even as the NCCL sent a delegation of MPs to Stanley Baldwin, British Prime Minister, to discuss Northern Irish affairs, the *Belfast Newsletter* observed: 'The probability is that Mr Baldwin will remind the deputation that the responsibility for maintaining law and order in Northern Ireland rests entirely with the Ulster government'.[274]

Throughout unionist control of the North the government appealed to reason of state to justify its use of emergency powers. Intended to obtain order in the North, vindication for the continued use of the 1922 SPA soon shifted to its use in maintaining peace. In conjunction with this transfer came a change in the type of regulation employed by the government. From measures aimed at returning civil order, the government increasingly turned to regulations designed to prohibit the expression of republican ideals. While these actions took place in the context of a military response to the republican threat, they were further supported by the claim of the majority population to the 'right' not to be confronted with the manifestation of republican ideals. By denying a voice to the republican aim of a united Ireland, however, and not only to violence as a means of obtaining that goal, the government failed to distinguish between republicanism and nationalism. As a result, the manner in which the regulations were applied denied legitimacy to the political aspirations of a broad portion of the minority community and not just the republican element in Northern Ireland.

Periodic attempts were made after the NCCL report to protest against the 1922–43 SPAs. For example, on 27 November 1938 some 1,500 people attended a meeting in Peel Street, Belfast, protesting at the continued operation of the SPA. The police – rather accurately – perceived the meeting as composed entirely of republican sympathisers. After flying the Tricolour and singing a 'Soldier's Song', those attending the meeting were dispersed by a baton charge.[275] However, it was not until the outbreak of the civil rights marches in the late 1960s that a more visible effort was made. On 1 September 1970 Gerry Fitt, leader of the SDLP, met with John Taylor, Minister of Home Affairs, to discuss RUC and Army abuses in the exercise of the 1922–43 SPAs.[276] On 18 April 1971 Republican Clubs called for the boycott of census forms as an act of disobedience against repressive legislation – particularly the SPA and Public Order Act. On 25 April republicans in the New Lodge Road area of Belfast made a bonfire of 200 census forms and announced that a further 1,000 would be publicly burned at a mass rally to be held later, and on the following day a group of over forty priests launched a protest about the operation of the law in Northern Ireland. A group of Catholic teachers joined the clergy in refusing to fill out the forms. The 1922–43 statute played a key role in these activities: 'The notorious Special Powers Act, with which we have lived since 1922 . . . has been responsible for the alienation and polarisation of the communities . . . and has brought untold trouble'.[277] Not only did these measures induce a backlash against the statute itself, but it engendered an erosion of the perceived legitimacy of the judicial system as well. On 27 April 1971 Fitt met with the Lord Chancellor, Lord Hailsham, to bring to his notice the discontent building up in Northern Ireland over the operation of the judicial system. On 5 May members of the Opposition at Stormont tabled a motion of censure against the Attorney General, Basil Kelly, and called on the Governor to remove (previously Minister of Home Affairs and now Judge) Topping from his position as Recorder of Belfast. In June 1971 an eight person committee, consisting of members of the Bar Council and the Incorporated Law Society of Northern Ireland, was established to ascertain whether cause for concern existed over the administration of law in Northern Ireland. While the 1922–43 SPAs constituted one portion of the issues thus examined, they significantly contributed to the increasing crisis of legitimacy embedded in the Northern Ireland legal system.

Calls for the revocation of the SPAs formed part of the Northern Ireland Civil Rights Association's platform, and in 1969 the Hunt Committee recommended the repeal of these measures. The lack of judicial scrutiny, the centralisation of State power, and the way in which these measures had been used had served to create a pervasive grievance among the minority population. As violence in the province escalated, Britain reclaimed government of the region. Far from repealing the offensive measures, however, Britain retained many of the regulations. The following chapter details Westminster's subsequent use of and alterations to emergency powers in Northern Ireland.

CHAPTER THREE

Special Powers Re-Named:
Direct Rule and the Transfer of Emergency Powers 1972–1973

D URING THE LATE 1960s civil unrest steadily increased in Northern Ireland.[1] In 1969 Britain deployed troops in the North to buy time for a reform of the local security force. The Hunt Committee Report, published two months later, recommended that the RUC be disarmed and relieved of its paramilitary duties, that a police authority be created to which the RUC would be accountable, and that the RUC complaints procedure be revised.[2] These changes sought to eliminate the para-military nature of the police force, to separate the RUC from its close identification with the Unionist government, and to establish legal restraints on police operations. Hunt also recommended that the 1922–43 Special Powers Acts be repealed in order to bring northern legislation into line with the rest of the United Kingdom and that a Director of Public Prosecutions be created to relieve the police of their role in prosecuting offences. In addition, the report advocated the disbandment of the Ulster Special Constabulary and the formation in its place of a locally recruited, part-time defence force answerable to the British Army. The 1969 Ulster Defence Regiment Act subsequently created the Ulster Defence Regiment (UDR), and on 1 April 1970 Britain instituted this regiment as a section of the British Army.[3]

The newly-created Joint Security Committee oversaw the movement of British troops into the province and the institution of the reforms advocated by the Hunt Committee. Westminster designed this body to guarantee that the British government could force through the Hunt Committee's recommendations even if they were rejected by the Northern Ireland Parliament. The committee consisted of the Northern Ireland Prime Minister and various senior colleagues, a number of British civil servants based in the province, the GOC of the British Army and the RUC Chief Constable. While Westminster, through the committee, began to have a more active role in security matters, legislative affairs largely remained the responsibility of the Northern government. The social and economic reforms instituted by Stormont, however, were clearly a case of 'too little too late', and adjustments to security measures, such as the 1969 Firearms Act and Protection of the Person and Property Act, the 1970 Public Order Act, Explosives Act and Prevention of Incitement to Hatred Act proved insufficient deterrents to the rising civil disorder.[4] Most significantly the nature of violence in the province gradually shifted. The IRA reorganised and communal rioting gave way to paramilitary engagement with the security forces. This republican revival prompted the entombment of institutional reform in favour of more aggressive action against the IRA.

Brian Faulkner, the Northern Ireland Prime Minister and Minister of Home Affairs, strove to keep Britain from being drawn further into Northern Irish affairs. Westminster accordingly granted him a wide reign, resulting on 9 August 1971 with the introduction of internment. The decision to introduce it into the region required the consent of the British government: '[a] decision for internment is a decision taken by the Northern Ireland government after consultation with the government of the UK'.[5] However, the primary responsibility for the collection of information rested with the RUC Special Branch.[6] Immediately following 'Operation Demetrius', violence in the province escalated. From thirty-seven explosions in April 1971, forty-seven in May, fifty in June and seventy-eight in July, in August the number soared to 131, followed by 196 in September and 117 in October. In order to combat the rising violence, in November the government rearmed the RUC, but by the end of the year the number of deaths had tripled from thirty pre-internment to 174.[7] As was discussed in the previous chapter, much of the violence stemmed from the minority community's revulsion at the manner in which internment was carried out. Diplock later commented that, 'the scale of the operation led to the arrest and detention of a number of persons against whom suspicion was founded on inadequate information'.[8] The British government, however, was still reluctant to assume direct rule of the province.[9] The treatment of detainees began to attract widespread attention and pressure steadily increased on Britain to re-evaluate whether the provincial government or Westminster should take the lead in security matters.

Prior to the introduction of internment in 1971, no more than occasional allegations of ill-treatment had been lodged against members of the RUC. Once internment began, however, a flood of complaints against the behaviour of security forces ensued.[10] For example, on 17 August 1971 the Civil Rights Association and the Association for Legal

Justice held a joint press conference in Belfast, alleging the ill-treatment of detainees by the security forces, including making them run barefoot over barbed wire and broken glass. Kevin Boyle announced that a member of Amnesty International was in Belfast and would look into the allegations and would consider making a full inquiry. Later in the month Gerry Fitt met in New York with the Secretary General of the United Nations to discuss the ill-treatment of detainees by troops in Northern Ireland. On 27 August Amnesty International announced that the observer, Dr Zbynek Zeman, had spent two days in Belfast investigating the conditions of detainees with special regard to their legal rights. At that time 239 internees were being held in Belfast.[11] On 1 November 1971, 387 priests signed a statement alleging the commission of brutality and torture against men arrested under the Special Powers Act. Copies of the statement were sent to all Westminster MPs, General Tuzo, Jack Lynch, Graham Shillington, the Secretary-General of the UN and the International Red Cross. On 9 November Amnesty International called for an independent international commission of inquiry into, 'serious and apparently substantiated allegations of ill-treatment of internees,' in Northern Ireland, and later in the month the Republic of Ireland announced that it would be placing allegations of brutality by troops in Ulster before the European Court of Human Rights.

Widespread condemnation of the techniques being employed to extract information from Northern Irish prisoners spurred the British government to commission an inquiry. Conducted by Sir Edmund Compton, Edgar Fay and Dr Ronald Gibson, the commission determined in its report of 3 November 1971 that while physical ill-treatment of detainees had occurred, the interrogation procedures did not constitute brutality:

> Where we have concluded that physical ill-treatment took place, we are not making a finding of brutality on the part of those who handle these complainants. We consider that brutality is an inhuman or savage form of cruelty, and that cruelty implies a disposition to inflict suffering, coupled with indifference to, or pleasure in, the victim's pain.[12]

This subtle distinction between brutality and cruelty failed to gain universal acceptance.[13] For instance, in its report of 13 March 1972 Amnesty International claimed that the ill-treatment amounted to brutality and therefore violated clauses of the Declaration of Human Rights and the European Convention for the Protection of Human Rights and Fundamental Freedoms relating to 'torture or inhuman or degrading treatment'. The techniques being used to interrogate suspects

– wall-standing, hooding, noise, a bread and water diet and deprivation of sleep – had been developed post World War II as part of British counter-insurgency operations in Palestine, Malaya, Kenya, Cyprus, the British Cameroons, Brunei, British Guiana, Aden, Borneo/Malaysia and the Persian Gulf.[14] The aim of using these techniques was to create a strict and hostile atmosphere in which the prisoner, completely isolated, would be afraid of what would happen next. In April 1971 officers and staff from the English Intelligence Centre held a seminar on these procedures in Northern Ireland to teach the RUC how to use them. It was claimed at the time that many of the techniques served dual purposes. For example, wall-standing minimised the risk of violence against the guards or other detainees when the subjects were outside the rooms. Hooding prevented detainees from identifying or being identified by each other and constant noise prevented the detainee from hearing or being overheard by others. Furthermore, bread and water formed part of the 'atmosphere of discipline'. As Lord Gardiner pointed out in his minority report, the teaching was done orally, with no written directive, order, syllabus or training manual to support it.[15]

The inquiry examined eleven out of twelve cases of individuals who had been subject to 'interrogation in depth' using these measures in the two days following the August 1971 introduction of internment. A second report issued by Edmund Compton on 14 November considered the interrogation of one of two men similarly questioned between 11 and 18 October 1971. Both documents revealed that the five techniques had been used to excess. In some instances individuals had been at the wall for total periods of up to forty-three and a half hours and for continuous periods of up to sixteen hours.

Bitter criticism greeted the Compton Report, particularly with regard to the thin distinction drawn between 'ill-treatment' and brutality. In response on 16 November 1971 Britain commissioned a second inquiry to examine whether the procedures being employed in Northern Ireland to interrogate detainees warranted change. The committee reported in March 1972 with divided findings: the Chairman, Lord Parker of Waddington and John Boyd-Carpenter submitted the majority report, and Lord Gardiner the minority one.[16] Both the majority and minority reports found that the five techniques had been used excessively by the security forces in Northern Ireland. They surmised that one of the reasons for this was the absence of any rules indicating the degree to which the techniques could be employed. They also observed that, while a UK Minister had never banned the use of the techniques, neither had anyone officially authorised them. The authority cited for the Army's method of questioning was the *Joint Directive on Military Interrogation in Internal Security Operations Overseas*, promulgated first on 17 February 1965 and amended on 10 February 1967. This directive, however, did not apply to the civilian security forces. Lord Gardiner further suggested that the Prison Rules and Directions made by the Minister for Home Affairs did not extend the ordinary police powers of interrogation to the counter-insurgency techniques. The majority report recommended introducing safeguards on the extent to which the techniques could be applied, such as requiring the presence of a senior RUC officer, the use of highly skilled interrogators, the use of the procedures only in special circumstances, the presence of a psychiatric doctor at interrogation centres and the creation of a complaints board. Lord Gardiner, in contrast, found the procedures to be illegal and immoral and not to be continued under any circumstances. Westminster accepted the findings of the minority report and announced in March 1972 that the five techniques would be abandoned.[17]

Allegations of mistreatment continued through the balance of the 1970s. In 1976 The European Commission on Human Rights later determined that the five techniques employed in 1971 constituted torture and that other treatment used by the police was inhuman and degrading.[18] The following year Britain informed the Court that it would in no instance invoke the five techniques as an aid to interrogation again.[19] As late as June 1978 the subject was still being raised in the Commons – largely as a result of the Amnesty International report issued alleging the continued ill-treatment of detainees.[20] In spite of international attention drawn to the issue, however, there was a sharp drop in the prominence of the subject following the Gardiner Report.

Not only did the increase in violence, the shift in the nature of the disorder and the attention drawn towards the methods of interrogation bring the issue of security accountability to the forefront, but on 30 January 1972 thirteen deaths resulting from 'Bloody Sunday' highlighted the importance of more direct control from Westminster over the situation in the North. In the course of a civil rights demonstration members of the Parachute Regiment shot a number of, what were claimed to be, unarmed civilians. As the relationship between the unionist and nationalist communities further deteriorated, on 23 February the courts determined in *Regina (Hume and Others)* v. *Londonderry Justices*[21] that the basis for army operations in Northern Ireland, S.R.O. 71/1957, 16.4.57 of the 1922–43 Special Powers Acts, violated section 4(1) of the 1920 Government of Ireland Act. The case before the court related to an incident earlier in the year, at which time five people had been convicted under the 1922–43 SPAs for remaining in an assembly after it had been ordered to disperse. Robert Lowrey, Justice O'Donnell and Justice Gibson upheld their appeal determining that the 1920 Act did not permit the Northern Ireland government to order the armed forces of the Crown to take action. According to their interpretation, Section 4(1) was limited to security forces covered by transferred matters. With the statutory rule in contravention of the 1920 Act, the army could only exercise those powers it held under common law: the duty of the citizen to aid the civil authorities in suppressing disorder. While Westminster's assumption had been that under the terms of the 1922–43 SPAs the army was acting in support of the civil power, the Army's role, which involved searches, arrests, enforcement of curfew and the stopping of vehicles, had become far more involved than this. As a result of the High Court decision, the British government immediately introduced a Bill into Westminster to legalise all action taken by the British Army in Northern Ireland.[22] The Home Secretary, Mr Maudling, emphasised the need for speedy legislation and stated that the Act would declare that, '[t]he law as far as the armed forces are concerned is and always has been what it was hitherto been believed to be'. The Northern Ireland Bill was passed by both Houses and received Royal Assent within hours of the Belfast High Court ruling. Not only did the 1972 Northern Ireland Act establish a legal framework for the use of the army, but it retrospectively legalised all security force actions since the army was first deployed in 1969.[23]

As a result of the growing concern over the manner in which security affairs were being conducted in the province, on 22 March the British Prime Minister, Edward Heath, proposed to Faulkner that complete security control be transferred to Westminster. Faulkner resigned the following day in protest, at which time the British government introduced direct rule.[24] Britain officially prorogued Stormont from 30 March 1972 by virtue of section 1(3) of the Northern Ireland (Temporary Provisions) Act 1972, which empowered Her Majesty by order in council to make laws in place of the Northern Ireland Parliament.[25] The newly-appointed Secretary of State for Northern Ireland assumed direct responsibility for social and economic planning, constitutional matters and the administration of law and order in the North. William Whitelaw, the first to hold this position, immediately undertook to review all 900 internment cases and to examine the operation of the 1922–43 SPAs. Although the drawbacks to internment were apparent, a renewed IRA campaign in July 1972 and an increase in violence in the province made the British government reluctant to discard it. In an effort to develop a more long-term strategy, however, Westminster appointed the Diplock

Commission to find an alternative means than internment to 'bring to book' individuals involved in terrorist activities. The government's review of the SPAs, together with the final report of the Diplock Commission, formed the basis of emergency legislation introduced by Westminster to address violence in Northern Ireland.

THE DIPLOCK COMMISSION

The Diplock Commission marked the beginning of the replacement of executive detention with prosecution through the court system in an attempt to eliminate the difference between political violence and 'ordinary' crime.[26] It also marked a shift in the prosecution of terrorist cases. From focusing on a trial as the ultimate objective of arrest, the purpose of the inquiry and subsequent alterations in the judicial procedure was to convict individuals so arrested.[27] The inquiry examined trial by jury, arrest procedure, requirements for bail, onus of proof with regard to possession of firearms and explosives, the admissibility of confessions and written statements and the issue of young offenders in Northern Ireland. While the final report advocated changes in a number of these areas, the Commission determined that the principal reason for employing detention rather than engaging in a trial revolved around the intimidation of witnesses. The tragic shooting of Mr. Agnew, a bus driver in East Belfast shot the day before he was due to testify in a terrorist case, highlighted this concern.[28] In order to overcome this issue, the Commission advocated changes in the trial process itself. It operated under the premise that judicial proceedings for terrorist cases meet the minimum standards safeguarded by Article 6 of the European Convention for the Protection of Human Rights and Fundamental Freedoms.[29] This Article required that individuals charged with a criminal offence be entitled to 'a fair and public hearing within a reasonable time by an independent and impartial tribunal established by law'. In addition to the presumption of innocence, the Article detailed a number of minimum rights: that the individual charged be (a) promptly informed of charges to be brought against her or him, (b) given adequate time and facilities to prepare a defence, (c) granted access to legal assistance, (d) allowed to examine witnesses or have witnesses examined against her or him, and (e) provided with an interpreter. Although Article 15 of the Convention allowed for some relaxation of these rights 'in time of war or other public emergency threatening the life of the nation . . . to the extent strictly required by the exigencies of the situation', and in spite of the

Diplock Commission's view that such a situation existed in Northern Ireland, the Commission considered it preferable not to allow criminal trials to fall below the minimum standards as set out in Article 6. In cases, therefore, where the State could not ensure the safety of the witnesses involved, and where public safety required the confinement of the suspected terrorist, internment, on a limited basis, would have to continue:

> We are . . . driven inescapably to the conclusion that until the current terrorism by the extremist organisations of both factions in Northern Ireland can be eradicated, there will continue to be some dangerous terrorists against whom it will not be possible to obtain convictions by any form of criminal trial which we regard as appropriate to a court of law . . . so long as these remain at liberty to operate in Northern Ireland, it will not be possible to find witnesses prepared to testify against them in the criminal courts . . . The only hope of restoring the efficiency of criminal courts of law in Northern Ireland to deal with terrorist crimes is by using an extra-judicial process to deprive [terrorists] of their ability to operate in Northern Ireland . . . the only way of doing this is to put them in detention by an executive act and to keep them confined, until they can be released without danger to the public safety and to the administration of criminal justice.[30]

For such situations the Commission recommended the retention of safeguards laid out in the 1972 Detention of Terrorists (Northern Ireland) Order.[31]

Although some cases would still have to be dealt with through extra judicial processes, the Diplock Commission sought to adjust existing criminal procedures in a manner consistent with Article 6 of the European Convention, thus allowing for the transfer of more cases from detention to the criminal system. In order to accomplish this, the inquiry re-examined the mode of trial and concluded that in light of the possible intimidation of jurors and the bias of jurors deriving from communal loyalties, trial by judge alone for scheduled offences should take the place of jury trial for the duration of the emergency. Although not specifically stated by Diplock, this measure reflected statutes previously employed by both Stormont and the British government in Ireland. Unlike the 1922 Criminal Procedure Act or the 1922–43 SPA, however, the Commission rejected the use of two or more judges in a juryless trial, citing lack of qualified individuals and appropriate resources to enable the judiciary to handle the case load effectively. Under Diplock the jurisdiction of the single judge sitting alone was to extend both to lesser and to scheduled offences.

The Diplock Commission recommended extending powers of arrest to the military, granting soldiers a period of up to four hours to arrest an individual without warrant in order to establish the identity of the individual so detained. The inquiry also advocated that restrictions be set on the granting of bail for persons charged with scheduled offences. Determining the onus of proof for possession and the rules of admissibility of confessions to be two further stumbling blocks to securing the conviction of individuals charged with terrorist offences, the Commission suggested that where it could be demonstrated that firearms, explosives or incendiary devices were found on premises occupied by an individual, the burden of proof lay on the defendant to demonstrate either that his or her use of such an item was for a lawful purpose, or that he or she was ignorant of its existence. While the first instance was already accounted for by the 1969 Firearms Act (Northern Ireland) and 1970 Explosives Act (Northern Ireland), the security forces operating under those Acts had had to prove knowledge of the existence of such weapons in order to demonstrate possession.[32] The proposed changes left untouched the common law defence of acting under duress.

The Diplock Commission recommended further changes with regard to inculpatory admission as administered under the Judges' Rules in Northern Ireland. The Judges' Rules classified as involuntary any admission made in the course of a situation constructed to induce confessions, and thus forbade the use of the admission in a court of law.[33] Although specifically rejecting the interrogation techniques cited in both the 1971 Compton Report and the 1972 Parker Report, the Diplock Commission highlighted the effectiveness of interrogation in obtaining confessions and recommended that the technical rules governing the admissibility of confessions be suspended with regard to scheduled offences for the duration of the Northern Irish emergency. The inquiry suggested that a provision be inserted into the rules allowing for such statements unless they were obtained through torture or inhuman or degrading treatment, thus shifting the burden of proof from the prosecution to the defence. Common law required that the prosecution demonstrate that any confession which it wished to use as evidence was given voluntarily.[34] This language drew on Article 3 of the European Convention which was used as a gauge of the appropriateness of the British response to Northern Ireland. 'Any inculpatory admission made by the accused may be given in evidence unless it is proved on a balance of probabilities that it was obtained by subjecting the accused to torture or to inhuman or degrading treatment.'[35] The Commission also recommended that signed, written statements be allowed in cases where the witness was dead, outside the province or missing.

With regard to persons aged from fourteen to sixteen and found guilty of terrorist offences, Diplock advocated the swift establishment of a secure young offenders' centre. Although provisions had been made in the 1968 Children and Young Persons Act (Northern Ireland) for constructing additional institutions for young individuals, no such edifices had been constructed.[36] Determining that neither the training centres nor prison would be appropriate for such cases, the Commission suggested that the process of building a remand home be accelerated and that the restriction set on the judiciary, limiting the imposition of detention for young people to cases involving offences accompanied by fourteen or more years' sentence for an adult, be withdrawn for the duration of the emergency.

For the relatively severe changes that the Diplock Commission recommended, a surprisingly scarce amount of information was obtained. Only three written documents were submitted in the seven weeks during which the Commission sat. Most of the evidence was heard orally and almost exclusively in London. Only two trips were made to Northern Ireland – both by Lord Diplock himself. While there, the chairman only met with those directly involved in the administration of justice and with members of the civil and armed security forces. Virtually all of those giving evidence were members of the Protestant community. Not only did this mean that no attempt was made to legitimise the Diplock Commission in the eyes of the minority community, but it also meant that there were practically no opportunities for the commission to discuss the possible impact of the changes in policy on the Catholics in Northern Ireland. In reflection of the limited information gathered by the inquiry, and in spite of allegations about the potential intimidation of jurors, no evidence regarding actual cases of intimidation was produced. It was not until the end of the second reading of the 1973 Emergency Provisions Bill that the government provided any examples of intimidation of jurors, and these were on an *ad hoc*, unsystematised basis. The Attorney General, Peter Rawlinson, claimed at the time that thirty cases of witness intimidation had occurred over the past year and suggested that the climate of fear played a large part in the role played by jurors in the judicial proceedings.[37] Prior to this, on 16 November 1972 a question had been put in the House of Commons requesting that the Secretary of State for Northern Ireland,

> [S]eek to ascertain in how many of the cases of those persons in Northern Ireland awaiting trial following committal proceedings the delay is due to the difficulty of persuading witnesses to come forward, intimidation of witnesses or fear that a wrongful verdict will be

brought in by the jury because of actual or feared threats of intimidation of the jury.

The Attorney General replied: 'I am not aware of any case in which delay in bringing a person to trial following committal proceedings is due to any of the factors to which the Hon. Member refers'.[38] The intimidation of judges and magistrates, however, was well documented as a number of individuals had lost their lives through terrorist attacks.[39] On 16 September 1974 the killing of Judge Conaghan further underscored the danger of the judiciary in dealing with terrorist cases.[40] Nevertheless, in response to opposition demands for evidence the Attorney General conceded that at the time the 1973 EPA was being discussed, 'the evidence might not have been sufficient to justify the step proposed but stated that he must have regard to "what might happen in the future"'.[41] Pressed further, Whitelaw would only go so far as to say that 'some of the verdicts given have been rather hard to understand'.[42] Diplock's claim to perverse acquittals was attacked from both sides of the sectarian divide. Bernadette Devlin stated in the House of Commons:

> We have not heard from the government, and certainly not from Lord Diplock, one concrete point of evidence to show that it is necessary for this step to be taken. We have heard of packed juries. But where is the statistical evidence? How many packed juries have there been? What is the percentage of juries that have been packed one way or the other? If there have been perverse judgments, convictions, or acquittals, what is the percentage?[43]

Loyalist politicians likewise attacked the elimination of juries on the basis of alleged intimidation and perverse acquittals.[44] Although some studies later lent support to the perverse acquittals thesis,[45] no evidence was provided at the time. In addition, even if that had been the case, it did not automatically follow that the suspension of jury trial was the most appropriate solution.[46]

THE 1973 NORTHERN IRELAND (EMERGENCY PROVISIONS) ACT

The House of Commons published the results of the Diplock inquiry on 20 December 1972, at which time the government moved to incorporate the vast majority of the recommendations into new counter-terrorist legislation. A White Paper on Northern Ireland heralded the government's decision to incorporate the Diplock Commission's recommendations into an emergency statute. Issued after the commission had reported and before the debate in Parliament regarding the emergency legislation, paragraphs 9, 19 and 60 indicated that the government would introduce many of the Diplock provisions as well as other powers viewed as necessary to contain the situation in Northern Ireland. Whitelaw assured the House that the passage of the proposed measures would result in the repeal of the 1922–43 SPAs and that, given the exceptional nature of the measures incorporated in the legislation, the 1973 statute would be subject to annual renewal. Neither of these points provided sufficient safeguards, as the legislation incorporated a great deal of the powers enshrined in the regulations issued under the 1922–43 SPAs. Put simply, this made their repeal irrelevant. Furthermore, the annual renewal was subject either to support or opposition, barring the possibility of introducing further amendments. Because there had been minimal focus on the actual tenets of the 1922–43 from SPAs 1922 to 1972, most of the discussion surrounding the 1973 EPA revolved around Lord Diplock's recommendations. Nevertheless, there was a general sense within the nationalist community that the previous emergency measures were simply replaced with the new ones:

> The existence of the [1922–43 SPAs] was a big factor in the commencement of the civil rights movement in 1968. One of the demands then made was for the abolition of the Special Powers Act. It had been a running sore in Northern Ireland since the day it went on the Statute book in 1922. The Special Powers Act was taken off the statute book in 1972 by the Conservative Government and replaced by the Northern Ireland (Emergency Provisions) Act.[47]

The previous measures were not so much replaced, however, as re-enacted under a different name and augmented by changes recommended by Diplock, particularly with regard to the judicial process. Although Labour accepted in principle the need for emergency measures and the simultaneous relaxation of common law practices aimed at protecting individuals accused of crime, they preferred a more diluted statute than that presented by the Conservative government.[48] In the event, Labour followed a strategy of abstention during the initial consideration of the measures.

Part I of the 1973 Northern Ireland (Emergency Provisions) Act consolidated the Diplock Commission's recommendations with regard to the administration of justice.[49] The departures from the Diplock Commission's recommendations related to the offences listed in schedule 4 to the Act, which incorporated fewer offences than those advocated by Lord Diplock. The schedule also allowed for the Attorney General to issue a certificate to remove particular cases from being treated as scheduled offences. The trial of scheduled offences on indictment was changed to consist of a judge sitting alone, without a jury, with existing rights of appeal unaffected.[50] While in committee Members of Parliament changed the Bill in a vote of thirteen to eleven to include three judges instead of a single judge for scheduled offences. Committee members argued that a three-judge tribunal would inspire greater confidence in the judiciary, reduce the risk of judicial error and lower the risk to the lives of those adjudicating the cases.[51] The inclusion of the clause stipulating three judges struck a compromise between the abolition of the jury and the substitution of one judge in its place. This decision was later reversed during the report stage in the House of Commons by a vote of eighty-six to fifty-four.[52] Members also introduced a clause limiting trial without jury to cases referred by a judge, who had determined that a fair trial in the particular case was unlikely. However, it was defeated by seventy-six votes to ninety-three.[53] Attempts to limit the number of peremptory challenges in order to avoid stacked juries was also defeated.[54] Restrictions on the granting of bail were set. Only a judge of the High Court was allowed to grant bail on cases involving scheduled offences. The legislation required the judge to be satisfied that the applicant would comply with whatever conditions were set, would not interfere with any witness and would not commit any offence while on bail.[55] For the more serious cases, in order to receive bail the defendant would have to demonstrate further either that he or she had been remanded in custody for a fixed period without being tried or committed for trial or that to refuse bail would cause exceptional hardship. The statute required all trials of scheduled offences to be conducted in Belfast and allowed for the Lord Chief Justice of Northern Ireland to employ county court judges to try scheduled offences. Although the Diplock Commission did not recommend these last changes, the government claimed them as necessary for enhanced security and minimal delays.[56]

The 1973 EPA incorporated the Diplock Commission's recommendations regarding the admissibility of statements as evidence, both from witnesses and inculpatory admissions on the part of the defendant.[57] From 30 March 1972 to 13 April 1973, the statements of twenty-one accused had been held inadmissible on the grounds that they had not been made freely and voluntarily.[58] The onus of proof lay on the accused to demonstrate whether torture, inhuman or degrading treatment had been used in order to extract the confession.[59] The statute also shifted the onus of proof in relation to possession of proscribed materials:[60]

> Where a person is charged with possessing a proscribed article . . . and
> it is proved that at the time of the alleged offence – (a) he and that
> article were both present in any premises; or (b) the article was in
> premises of which he was the occupier or which he habitually used . .
> . the court may accept the fact proved as sufficient evidence of his
> possessing that article at that time unless it is further proved that he
> did not at that time know of its presence in the premises in question,
> or if he did know, that he had no control over it.

Proscribed articles included those listed under the 1883 Explosive
Substances Act, the 1969 Firearms Act (Northern Ireland), and the 1969
Protection of the Person and Property Act (Northern Ireland).[61]

The final section of Part I dealt with the treatment of young offenders.
Section 8 extended the ability of the court to give a fixed custodial
sentence to individuals aged from fourteen to sixteen years found guilty
of scheduled offences, normally punishable by five years' imprisonment
or more. In keeping with the intent of the Diplock Commission, the
Secretary of State announced the construction of a new institution, part
training school and part remand home, for young offenders.[62] The
government also transferred from the courts to the Ministry the
responsibility for allocating offenders to training schools.[63]

SPECIAL POWERS RE-ENACTED

The balance of the 1973 EPA drew from regulations introduced under
the 1922–43 Special Powers Acts. In part owing to the lack of secondary
research on the earlier legislation, however, and in part related to the
prominence and almost wholesale inclusion of the Diplock Commission's
recommendations into subsequent emergency law, analyses of the 1973
EPA have tended to focus only on the impact of the Diplock Report on
the subsequent measures. Yet, the British government directly incorporated
measures from the 1922–43 SPAs relating to detention, internment, the
closing of licensed premises, the blocking up of roads, the prohibition of
vehicle usage, powers of entry, search and seizure, possession of property
and land, compensation, the prohibition of meetings, assemblies and
processions, proscription and the collection of information on security
forces. The 1973 EPA also maintained, with some alterations, provisions
relating to the delegation of powers in the prosecution of offences and
the introduction of additional statutory instruments to supplement the
existing regulations. Not only is much of the substance and language of
these provisions drawn directly from regulations introduced under the

1922–43 Special Powers Acts, but these powers reflect those initially included in the 1920 Restoration of Order in Ireland Act and the 1914–15 Defence of the Realm Acts. There is very little new about emergency legislation in the United Kingdom enacted with regard to Irish – or Northern Irish – political violence. The balance of this chapter focuses on the incorporation of previous emergency powers into the 1973 EPA.

Detention and Internment

Echoing regulations instituted under the 1922–43 Special Powers Acts, the 1973 EPA granted extensive powers of arrest, detention and internment. As will be recalled from the previous chapter, Regulation 23 from the original schedule to the 1922 SPA obtained these powers for the Civil Authority. These regulations allowed for the arrest without warrant of any individual suspected of acting, having acted, or being about to act in a manner prejudicial to the preservation of peace or maintenance of order. Under the 1914–15 Defence of the Realm Acts and 1920 Restoration of Order in Ireland Act, similar powers had previously been granted the military authority in Ireland. Within weeks of the introduction of the 1922 Special Powers Act, the Northern government supplemented it with further powers of internment through Regulation 23B, which detailed conditions for the release of detainees.[64] The Northern Ireland Ministry of Home Affairs revoked these regulations in 1949, but in 1956 reintroduced them almost word for word as Regulations 11 and 12.[65] Regulation 11(1) conferred powers of arrest where an individual was 'acting or about to act in a manner prejudicial to the preservation of peace or maintenance of order'. Under this regulation no limit to the length of detention existed. The object of such an arrest was to determine if the individual would be suitable for detention under Regulation 11(2): internment. Regulation 12 empowered the Civil Authority to restrict the movement of individuals to within a defined radius and to make provision for the removal and internment of persons in Northern Ireland. Following the reintroduction of these provisions, in 1957 Topping, as Minister of Home Affairs, replaced Regulation 10 of the principal regulations with a new Regulation 10, providing that, 'Any officer of the Royal Ulster Constabulary, for the preservation of the peace and maintenance of order, may authorise the arrest without warrant and detention for a period of not more than 48 hours of any person for the purpose of interrogation'.[66] The Ministry did not design this power towards engineering a prosecution in the courts. It required neither reasonable suspicion nor appearance before a competent judicial authority. Instead the northern Executive intended the measure as a means to facilitate intelligence gathering.[67] The wide powers of arrest granted under the 1973 EPA and later the 1974 PTA swiftly became subject to accusations that they were being levied in a similar manner.[68]

Following the proroguement of Stormont, on 1 November 1972 the British Secretary of State issued an order under the Northern Ireland (Temporary Provisions) Act 1972 that made changes to the existing 1922–43 Special Powers Acts' regulations regarding detention and internment.[69] The Detention of Terrorists (Northern Ireland) Order 1972 replaced Regulations 11 and 12.[70] This instrument sought to distinguish between internment and detention, where the former was 'imprisonment at the arbitrary diktat of the Executive Government' and the latter the deprivation of liberty resulting from an extra-judicial process.[71] The acceptance of this distinction as being significant was far from widespread. The Detention of Terrorists Order (DTO) imposed a quasi-judicial format on the former internment structure. It limited the initial period for which an individual could be detained and inserted a review commission to determine whether the detention order should stand. The DTO also provided for the creation of an appeal body. The ultimate authority for each safeguard, though, still remained with the Secretary of State, who, in the place of the Minister of Home Affairs, continued to control powers of detention and internment. Lord Gardiner viewed this order as 'an immense improvement on the existing situation, from the point of view of human rights'.[72] Considering the limited changes that were made at the time, this view goes some way towards explaining the later recommendations of the Gardiner Report.

The statutory instrument worked in the following manner: the Detention of Terrorists Order allowed for the Secretary of State to issue an interim custody order, which allowed an individual to be detained up to twenty-eight days from the date of the order. At the end of that period, either the individual was to be released or the Chief Constable would refer the case to a commissioner appointed by the Secretary of State. The first three commissioners appointed by William Whitelaw included Judge James Leonard, an English Circuit Judge, Sir Ian Lewis, a judge from Nigeria, and Sheriff John A. Dick, a former public law lecturer in Edinburgh. Although the length of time an individual could be held pending actual appearance before a commissioner was not specified, the schedule to the DTO provided that the accused be informed of the nature of charges to be brought against them no less than three days before the hearing. (Under Regulation 11 of the 1922–43 SPAs, a minimum of only twenty-four hours notice in writing had been required.) Departing somewhat from Regulations 10 and 11 of the 1922–43 SPAs, Part III, section 13 (2) of the schedule to the 1972 Detention of Terrorists Order allowed for the internee to be represented by a counsel or solicitor. However, it was almost immediately followed by a clause empowering the commissioner to remove the solicitor and/or detainee from the proceedings:

> Where in relation to any part of the proceedings, it appears to the commissioner that it would be contrary to the interests of public security or might endanger the safety of any person for that part of the proceedings to take place in the presence of the respondent, the respondent and his representatives shall be excluded accordingly.[73]

The DTO required that the commissioner hear evidence to determine whether the interim custody order should be sustained. This hearing substantially departed from the ordinary judicial process – the session was to be held in private, with normal rules of evidence waived. On the basis of both public and private information – unavailable to either the detained individual or his or her solicitor – the commissioner could issue an indefinite detention order. 'What this necessarily means is that the Commissioners must rely upon reports and information received from sources the identity of which cannot be disclosed to the accused or his lawyers or, indeed to the Commissioners themselves.'[74] An automatic right of appeal allowed the detainee twenty-one days to indicate in writing the grounds of appeal and any new evidence which had come to light to a three person tribunal, the members of which were also appointed by the Secretary of State. Sir Gordon Wilmer, a former British Justice of Appeal, chaired the first Detention Appeal Tribunal.[75]

The government announced the creation of the Detention of Terrorists Order on the 1 November and enacted it as of the 7 November 1972. Nevertheless, it was not until the 11 December, the day before it was due to expire, that Whitelaw introduced the DTO into the House of Commons for consideration. By that time the detention commissioners had already completed some 125 cases.[76] At the time of the commission's appointment 284 men were being held in Northern Ireland under the Special Powers Act, including 167 internees and 117 detainees.[77] A number of MPs expressed concern at both the nature of powers enshrined in the provision – that such far-reaching measures should be introduced through Order in Council rather than by statute – as well as the lack of time afforded for debate of the regulation. (Although the obligation under the affirmative order procedure specified one and a half hours, the Secretary of State extended the discussion to a three hour time-frame. Concern, however, was still expressed at the inadequacy of three hours for consideration of the issues involved.)[78] Nevertheless, the House passed the measure 179 votes to 32.[79] The introduction of the DTO did not directly affect the Diplock Commission, which sidestepped the issue of internment by focusing on procedures for bringing suspected terrorists to trial, the manner in which trial was conducted and the composition of the court itself. On the issue of detention, as was previously mentioned, Lord Diplock recommended that the 1972 order be retained.

This pattern – the swift introduction of measures with far-reaching implications – marked Westminster's handling not just of the DTO, but of subsequent emergency measures. As with later powers, such provisions passed at a time of haste became standard references, unexceptional pieces of legislation, that Parliament simply continued. In this instance, the Conservative government included the 1972 Detention of Terrorists Order into the new statute *in toto*, adding one additional 'safeguard': mandatory review of all detention cases by a commissioner after the first year of detention and then at intervals of six months thereafter. The government incorporated the DTO into sections 10 and 11 of the 1973 EPA, authorising the police to arrest without warrant any individual suspected of terrorism or any offence under the Act.[80] The clause employed by the 1973 EPA for the type of individual subject to arrest differed from that used in the regulations under the 1922–43 SPAs. The later statute substituted 'any individual suspected of terrorism' for any individual suspected of acting, having acted, or being about to act, 'in a manner prejudicial to the preservation of the peace or maintenance of order'.

Like Regulation 23 and later Regulation 11 of the 1922–43 SPAs, section 11 of the 1973 Act aimed at facilitating detention without trial: 'The aim was explicitly not bringing a suspect before the court; section 11(3) EPA made it clear that the requirement to bring an arrested individual before the court as soon as practicable did not apply'.[81] This intent echoed that of Regulation 10 of the 1922–43 SPAs. Part II, section 12 of the 1973 EPA further incorporated the Diplock Commission's recommendation that the army be granted powers of arrest without warrant for up to four hours.[82] Although Diplock recommended that four hour detention by the military be allowed only to establish a suspect's identity, the government did not include this limitation in the Act. The rationale behind its omission lay in the circumstances under which a soldier might make an arrest. Under sniper fire or a hail of stones within a no-go area, it would be difficult to state precisely the grounds of arrest and which regulations under which he or she was acting. At the time Westminster enacted the EPA, under the 1967 Criminal Law (Northern Ireland) Act,[83] soldiers, like civilians, had the power to arrest without warrant persons 'reasonably' suspected of committing an offence punishable by five or more years in prison.[84] In spite of this power, however, Westminster voted to authorise military personnel to detain individuals for up to four hours. Table 3a highlights the powers of detention and internment contained in the 1922 SPA, 1922–43 SPAs and the 1973 EPA.

Unionists in Westminster recognised the inclusion of the 1972 Detention of Terrorists Order into the 1973 EPA as essentially continuing the previous Northern Ireland government's policy: '[The 1972 DTO] vindicates the controversial policy of the late Stormont Administration – a policy with which Her Majesty's Government were never able to find fault and which they are now essentially continuing'.[85] Although the new legislation was intended to replace internment altogether, the net result was the introduction of measures running in parallel with the system of internment. Thus, while the government aimed to keep the erosion of the judicial system separate from the regular operation of the courts, the impact of the overall removal of safeguards for innocent people was to discredit further the operation of legislation in Northern Ireland.[86]

Closing of Licensed Premises

As was previously mentioned, not only did powers incorporated into the 1973 Emergency Provisions Act echo regulations and powers employed during the reign of Stormont, but many of the measures harkened back to even earlier emergency legislation. Regulation 10 of the 1920 Restoration of Order in Ireland Act empowered the Civil Authority to close licensed premises to maintain civil order. The Northern Ireland government reintroduced this provision as Regulation 2 of the 1922 SPA: 'The civil authority may by order . . . require all or any licensed premises within any area specified in the order to be closed, either altogether, or subject to such exceptions as to hours and purposes, and to compliance with such directions, as may be specified in the order'. As was mentioned in the previous chapter, the Northern government revoked this measure in 1949, only to reintroduce it in 1969 as Regulation 39. Following the assumption of direct rule, the British government incorporated similar provisions into the 1973 EPA. Schedule 3(5) of the 1973 EPA empowered the Secretary of State to close licensed premises and clubs

Table 3a: Detention and Internment under the 1922–43 Special Powers Acts and the 1973 Northern Ireland (Emergency Provisions) Act

1922 CIVIL AUTHORITIES (SPECIAL POWERS) ACTS (NORTHERN IRELAND)	1922–43 CIVIL AUTHORITIES (SPECIAL POWERS) ACTS (NORTHERN IRELAND)	1973 NORTHERN IRELAND (EMERGENCY PROVISIONS) ACT
Regulations 23 and 23B; revoked 1949; reintroduced 1956 as Regulations 11 and 12 Any person authorised for the purpose by the Civil Authority, or any police constable, or member of any of His Majesty's Forces on duty . . . may arrest without warrant any person whom he suspects of acting or of having acted or of being about to act in a manner prejudicial to the preservation of the peace or maintenance of order, or upon whom may be found any article, book, letter, or other document, the possession of which gives ground for such a suspicion, or who is suspected of having committed an offence against these regulations or of being in possession of any article or document which is being used or intended to be used for any purpose or in any way prejudicial to the preservation of the peace or maintenance of order. **SRO 34/1922, 20.5.1922, B.G. 26.5.1922** Any person so arrested may, on the order of the Civil Authority be detained either in any of His Majesty's Prisons or elsewhere, as may be specified in the order, upon such conditions as the Civil Authority may direct, until he has been discharged by direction of the Attorney-General or is brought before a court of Summary	**1972 Detention of Terrorists (Northern Ireland) Order** 4. (1) Where it appears to the Secretary of State that a person is suspected of having been concerned in the commission or attempted commission of any act of terrorism or in the direction, organisation or training of persons for the purpose of terrorism the Secretary of State may make an order . . . for the temporary detention of that person . . . (3) A person shall not be detained under an interim custody order for a period of more than twenty-eight days from the date of the order unless his case is referred by the Chief Constable to a commissioner for determination 5. (1) Where the case of a person detained under an interim custody order is referred to a commissioner, the commissioner shall enquire into that case for the purpose of deciding whether or not he is satisfied that (a) the respondent has been concerned in the commission or attempted commission of any act of terrorism or the direction, organisation or training of persons for the purpose of terrorism; and (b) his detention is necessary for the protection of the public.	**Schedule 1 (11–13) and sections 10–12** 11. (1) Where it appears to the Secretary of State that a person is suspected of having been concerned in the commission or attempted commission of any act of terrorism or in the direction, organisation or training of persons for the purpose of terrorism, the Secretary of State may make an interim custody order for the temporary detention of that person . . . (3) A person shall not be detained under an interim custody order for a period of more than twenty-eight days from the date of the order unless his case is referred by the Chief Constable to a commissioner for determination . . . 12. Where the case of a person detained under an interim custody order is referred to a commissioner, the commissioner shall enquire into that case for the purpose of deciding whether or not he is satisfied that (a) the respondent has been concerned in the commission or attempted commission of any act of terrorism or the direction, organisation or training of persons for the purpose of terrorism; and (b) his detention is necessary for the protection of the public. 13. Not less than seven days before the hearing of a case for determination under paragraph 12 above, the

→

Jurisdiction. Any person to be brought before a Court under this regulation shall receive at least twenty-four hours' notice in writing of the nature of the charge preferred against him.

S.R.O. 39/1922, 23.6.1922

Any person so arrested shall, if so ordered by the Civil Authority, or by a chief officer of police, or by a police officer of higher rank, be photographed and finger-print impressions of the fingers and thumbs of both his hands taken, and if such person refuses to allow his photograph or such impressions to be taken or obstructs the taking thereof he shall be guilty of an offence against these regulations.

S.R.O. 36/1922, 1.6.1922

When it appears to the Minister of Home Affairs for Northern Ireland . . . that for securing the preservation of peace and maintenance of order in Northern Ireland it is expedient that a person who is suspected of acting or having acted or being about to act in a manner prejudicial to the preservation of the peace and the maintenance of order in Northern Ireland . . . the Minister . . . may by order require that person forthwith, or from time to time, either to remain in, or to proceed to and reside in, such place as may be specified in the order . . . Any person interned under this regulation may, without prejudice to any other powers of removal, be removed on the order of the Civil Authority to any place where his presence is required . . . and may be detained in such place for such time as his presence is so required there, and whilst being so removed or detained he shall be deemed to be interned.

respondent shall be served with a statement in writing as to the nature of the terrorist activities which are to be the subject of the inquiry.

Main text, sections 10 and 11

10. (1) Any constable may arrest without warrant any person whom he suspects of being a terrorist . . . (3) A person arrested under this section shall not be detained in right of the arrest for more than seventy-two hours after his arrest . . .

(4) Where a person is arrested under this section, an officer of the Royal Ulster Constabulary not below the rank of chief inspector may order him to be photographed and to have his finger prints and palm prints taken by a constable, and a constable may use such reasonable force as may be necessary for that purpose.

11. (1) Any constable may arrest without warrant any person whom he suspects of committing, having committed, or being about to commit a scheduled offence or an offence under this Act which is not a scheduled offence.

12 (1) A member of Her Majesty's Forces on duty may arrest without warrant, and detain for not more than four hours, a person whom he suspects of committing, having committed or being about to commit any offence.

licensed under the 1971 Licensing Act (Northern Ireland) or the 1967 Registration of Clubs Act (Northern Ireland).[87] The government viewed these provisions as critical in establishing civil order. Although the wording of the various regulations under Stormont and in the post 73 period varied slightly, they invoked similar powers for the Civil Authority and, after 1973, for the Secretary of State for Northern Ireland. (See Table 3b.)

Blocking up of Roads and Use of Vehicles

Section 17(3) of the 1973 EPA empowered members of HM Forces on duty, any constable, or any person specifically authorised by or on behalf of the Secretary of State to close highways. This provision, traditionally reserved for periods of extreme civil unrest, received virtually no comment in the parliamentary debates on the enactment of the EPA. Rather focused the discussion clearly on the judicial alterations proposed by the Diplock Commission. As highlighted in chapter two, the power to block up roads drew from Regulation 5 of the 1920 ROIR, later Regulation 7A of the 1922–43 SPAs,[88] and from 1955 Regulation 9(1) of the 1922–43 SPAs.[89] (See Table 3c) In a departure from the 1922–43 Special Powers Acts, schedule 3(3) of the 1973 EPA included provisions for the Secretary of State, or any officer of the RUC not below the rank of assistant chief constable, to interfere with railway traffic. The government inserted this provision to increase the security force's ability to search for arms being transported into the North from across the border. Reflecting the changing times, the 1973 EPA dropped the additional language relating to the security forces' ability to block any public road, lane, passage, pathway or ferry, to cut trenches or to demolish or render impassable any bridge.[90] The Northern government had lifted these clauses from the 1920 ROIA and the 1914–15 DORAs, which reflected wartime conditions. Similar to provisions under the 1922–43 Special Powers Acts, the 'new' legislation also forbade any interference in the Civil Authority's attempts to block up roadways or waterways. Section 17(4) of the 1973 EPA, which prohibited any person from interfering with the powers or exercise of the powers under the section, echoed Regulation 17 of the 1922 SPA and, more specifically, from 1955 Regulation 9(3) of the 1922–43 SPAs.[91]

Not only were the roads subject to special clauses under the 1973 EPA, but schedule 3(2) of the statute empowered the Secretary of State to make orders prohibiting, restricting or regulating the use of vehicles in any specified area. Once again, the wording used for this regulation duplicated almost word for word Regulation 33 of the 1922–43 SPAs.[92] Where

Table 3b: Closing of Licensed Premises under the 1922–43 Special Powers Acts and the 1973 Northern Ireland (Emergency Provisions) Act

1922 CIVIL AUTHORITIES (SPECIAL POWERS) ACT (NORTHERN IRELAND)	1922–43 CIVIL AUTHORITIES (SPECIAL POWERS) ACTS (NORTHERN IRELAND)	1973 NORTHERN IRELAND (EMERGENCY PROVISIONS) ACT
Regulation 2 [Revoked by S.R.O. 147/ 1949, 20.8.49] The Civil Authority may by order: (1) Require all or any licensed premises within any area specified in the order to be closed, either altogether, or subject to such exceptions as to hours and purposes, and to compliance with such directions, as may be specified in the order; (2) Make such provisions as he thinks necessary for the prevention of the practice of treating in any licensed premises within any area specified in the order. Any order of the Civil Authority under this regulation may be made to apply either generally or as respects all or any members of the police or other forces mentioned in the order, and may require copies of the order to be exhibited in a prominent place in any licensed premises affected thereby. If any person contravenes or fails to comply with any of the provisions of an order made under this regulation or any conditions or res trictions imposed thereby, he shall be guilty of an offence against these regulations, and the Civil Authority may cause such steps to be taken as may be necessary to enforce compliance with the order. In this regulation the expression 'licensed premises' includes any premises or place where the sale of intoxicating liquor is carried on under a licence.	**Regulation 39, S.R.O. 281/1969, 16.10.69** (1) The Civil Authority may by order fix the closing hour of premises licensed under the provisions of the Licensing Acts (Northern Ireland) and of premises registered under the provisions of the Registration of Clubs Act (Northern Ireland) 1967. (2) If any person contravenes or fails to comply with any of the provisions of an order made under this regulation he shall on summary conviction be liable to imprisonment for a term not exceeding three months or to a fine not exceeding twenty-five pounds or to both such imprisonment and fine.	**Schedule 3, Regulation 5** 5. The Secretary of State may by order require that premises licensed under the Licensing Act (Northern Ireland) 1971, premises registered under the Registration of Clubs Act (Northern Ireland) 1967 or any place of entertainment or public resort shall be closed and remain closed, either for an indefinite period or for a period, or until an event, specified in the order or shall be closed at a particular time either on all days or on any day so specified.

Regulation 33 stated: 'The Civil Authority may order, prohibit, restrict or regulate in any areas the use of vehicles or any class of vehicles on highways or the use of vehicles of specified roads or classes of roads, either generally or in such circumstances as may be specified', the 1973 EPA simply substituted: 'The Secretary of State' for 'The Civil Authority'. (See Table 3c.)

Table 3c: Blocking up of Roads, Interference with the Blocking Up of Roads, and Use of Vehicles under the 1922–43 Special Powers Acts and the 1973 Northern Ireland (Emergency Provisions) Act

1922 CIVIL AUTHORITIES (SPECIAL POWERS) ACT (NORTHERN IRELAND)	1922–43 CIVIL AUTHORITIES (SPECIAL POWERS) ACTS (NORTHERN IRELAND)	1973 NORTHERN IRELAND (EMERGENCY PROVISIONS) ACT
Blocking up of Roads **Regulation 7A [S.R.O. 32/ 1922, 18.5.22] [Revoked by S.R.O. 147/1949, 20.8.49]** 7A. Any military or police officer in any case where he considers it necessary to do so for the purpose of preventing an armed attack on His Majesty's Forces or on a police force or on the civilian population, and in any other case where he considers it necessary so to do, having regard to the military or police necessities of the situation, may close, stop or otherwise render impassable any road, lane, passage, pathway or ferry, or may cut trenches in such road, lane, passage or pathway, or may demolish or otherwise render impassable any bridge without publishing or giving any notice thereof or setting up any warning lights, but any military or police officer taking such action as aforesaid shall immediately give notice thereof to the Civil Authority.	**Regulation 9(1) [S.R.O. 176/1955, 30.11.55]** 9(1). It shall be lawful for the Civil Authority, if he considers it necessary so to do for the preservation of the peace and maintenance of order, to authorise: (a) the total or partial stopping up or diversion of any road by means of barricades or road blocks, or in such other manner as may be considered necessary for that purpose. (b) the prohibition, restriction, or regulation of the use of vehicles of any description on any road either generally or in such circumstances, and subject to such conditions.	**Part II, section 17(3)** 17(3). Any member of Her Majesty's Forces on duty, any constable or any person specifically authorised to do so by or on behalf of the Secretary of State may, so far as he considers it immediately necessary for the preservation of the peace or the maintenance of order, wholly or partly close a highway or divert or otherwise interfere with a highway or the use of a highway, or prohibit or restrict the exercise of any rights of way or the use of any waterway.
Interference with the Blocking Up of Roads **Regulation 17** 17. . . . If any person obstructs, impedes, or otherwise interferes with	**Regulation 9(3)** 9(3) If any person without lawful authority, damages or interferes with any barricade or road block or	**Part II, section 17(4)** 17(4) Any person who, without lawful authority or reasonable excuse (the proof of which lies on him), inter-

———→

any member of any police or other authorised force in the execution of his duties, he shall be guilty of an offence against these regulations.	other obstruction, erected placed or set up on or near any road, by or on behalf of the Civil Authority, or defaces or otherwise tampers with any notice or sign so erected placed or set up, he shall be guilty of an offence against these regulations.	feres with works executed, or any apparatus, equipment or any other thing used, in or in connection with the exercise of powers conferred by this section shall be liable on summary conviction to imprisonment for a term not exceeding six months or to a fine not exceeding £400, or both.
Use of Vehicles **Regulation 21** [Revoked by S.R.O. 147/ 1949, 20.8.49] 21. Any police officer or constable may stop any vehicle travelling along any public road, and, if he has reason to suspect that any vehicle upon any public road is being used for any purpose or in any way prejudicial to the preservation of the peace or maintenance of order, or otherwise unlawfully, may search and seize the vehicle and seize anything found therein which he has reason to suspect is being used or intended to be used for any such purpose as aforesaid.	**Regulation 33** [S.R.O. 3/1957, 11.1.57] 33. The Civil Authority may by order prohibit, restrict or regulate in any area the use of vehicles or any class of vehicles on highways or the use by vehicles of specified roads or classes of roads, either generally or in such circumstances as may be specified.	**Schedule 3(2)** 2. The Secretary of State may by order prohibit, restrict or regulate in any area the use of vehicles or any class of vehicles on highways or the use by vehicles or any class of vehicles of roads or classes of roads specified in the order, either generally or in such circumstances as may be so specified.

Powers of Entry, Search and Seizure

The Conservative government inserted wide powers of entry, search and seizure into the 1973 Northern Ireland (Emergency Provisions) Act, in order to effect arrest,[93] search for arms and explosives,[94] and to search for people unlawfully detained.[95] Although most of these were exercisable only under suspicion, some were operable in its absence: any search of premises other than dwelling-homes for munitions and explosives,[96] any public search of vehicles and persons for the presence of munitions and explosives,[97] and any search of premises for individuals kidnapped and in life-threatening danger.[98] Extremely similar in substance, these provisions departed in one way from Regulations 3, 21 and 22 of the 1922 SPA and from 1954 Regulations 4, 5, 6 and 7 of the 1922–43 SPAs, which required suspicion in each of these cases. The measures instituted by the British government actually went further, then, than prior emergency law in Northern Ireland.

The British government drew section 17 of the 1973 EPA almost entirely from the 1922–43 SPAs. Section 17(1) duplicated powers of entry as specified by Regulation 18 of the 1922 SPA. The latter statute empowered the Civil Authority, or any person duly authorised by the Civil Authority, to enter any premises that were being used to disturb the peace. The 1973 EPA in more concise form replicated these powers for any constable or any member of Her Majesty's Forces on duty. Section 18(1), (2) and (4) also picked up on powers listed in Regulation 18 of the 1922 SPA and, from 1954, Regulation 4 of the 1922–43 SPAs.[99] (See Table 3d.) This gave any member of HM Forces on duty the power to enter and search any premises, if need be by force, if considered necessary for the maintenance of order.

Possession of Property and Land

Beyond entering properties and searching for material suspected to be used in the commission of terrorist acts, section 17(2) of the 1973 EPA granted members of HM Forces, the constabulary, or individuals acting on behalf of the Secretary of State the authority to take possession of any land or property. The statute empowered the security forces to take steps to place structures in a state of defence, to detain or to destroy such property, or to interfere with private rights in cases of operational necessity. Regulation 2 of the ROIA had provided similar powers to the military authority and Regulation 8 of the 1922 SPA had transferred these powers to the Civil Authority. Although the Northern Ireland Ministry of Home Affairs revoked this measure in 1949, it reinstated it in modified form in 1957 as Regulation 34A. The progression of this regulation can clearly be seen from its enactment in 1922 to its inclusion in the 1973 EPA. (See Table 3e.)

Compensation

Compensation regarding the possession of property and land and other infringements of private property rights in execution of the legislation, cited under section 25 of the 1973 EPA, duplicated almost word for word section 11 of the 1922 SPA.[100] The former statute read: 'Where, under the powers conferred by this Act or the regulations, any lands, buildings, goods, chattels or other property are taken, occupied or destroyed, or any other act is done involving interference with private rights of property, compensation shall, subject to the provisions of this section, be payable by the civil authority'. The 1973 EPA stated: 'Where

Table 3d: Powers of Entry, Search, and Seizure under the 1922–43 Special Powers Acts and the 1973 Northern Ireland (Emergency Provisions) Act

1922 Civil Authorities (Special Powers) Act (Northern Ireland)	1922–43 Civil Authorities (Special Powers) Acts (Northern Ireland)	1973 Northern Ireland (Emergency Provisions) Act
Regulation 18 [Revoked by S.R.O. 147/1949, 20.8.49] 18. The Civil Authority, or any person duly authorised by him, or any police constable, or any member of any of His Majesty's Forces on duty, may, if he has reason to suspect that any house, building, land, vehicle, vessel, aircraft, or other premises or any things therein are being or have been, or are about to be, constructed, used or kept for any purpose or in any way prejudicial to the preservation of the peace or maintenance of order, or that a crime or an offence against these regulations is being or has been committed thereon or therein, enter, if need be by force, the house, building, land, vehicle, vessel, aircraft, or premises at any time of the day or night, and examine, search and inspect the same or any part thereof, and may seize anything found therein or any such vehicle or vessel which he has reason to suspect is being used or intended to be used for any such purpose as aforesaid, or is being kept or used in contravention of these regulations, and the civil authority may order anything so seized to be destroyed or otherwise disposed of.	Regulation 4 [S.R.O. 90/1954, 16.6.54] 4. Any police officer or constable [or member of any of Her Majesty's Forces on duty inserted by S.R.O. 71/1957, 16.4.57] may, if he suspects that any house, building, land vehicle, vessel, aircraft, or other premises or anything therein are being or have been or are about to be constructed, used or kept for any purpose or in any way prejudicial to the preservation of the peace or maintenance of order, or that a crime or offence against these regulations is being or has been committed thereon or therein, enter, if need be by force, the house, building, land, vehicle, vessel, aircraft or premises at any time of the day or night and examine, search and inspect the same or any part thereof and may seize anything found thereon or therein or any such vehicle, vessel or aircraft which he suspects is being used or intended to be used for any such purpose as aforesaid or is being kept or used in contravention of these regulations.	Part II, sections 17 and 18 17. (1) Any member of Her Majesty's Forces on duty or any constable may enter any premises or other place – (a) if he considers it necessary to do so in the course of operations for the preservation of the peace or the maintenance of order; or (b) if authorised to do so by or on behalf of the Secretary of State. 18. (1) Any power conferred by this Part of this Act – (a) to enter any premises or other place includes power to enter any vessel, aircraft or vehicle; (b) to search any premises or other place includes power to stop and search any vehicle or vessel or any aircraft which is not airborne and search any container; and in this Part of this Act references to any premises or place shall be construed accordingly and references to a dwelling-house shall include references to a vessel or vehicle which is habitually stationary and used as a dwelling. (2) Any power so conferred to enter any place, vessel, aircraft or vehicle shall be exercisable, if need be, by force. (3) Any power conferred by virtue of this section to search a vehicle or vessel shall, in the case of a vehicle or vessel which cannot be conveniently or thoroughly searched at the place where it is, include power to take it or cause it to be taken to any place for the purpose of carrying out the search. (4) Any power conferred by virtue of this section to search any vessel, aircraft, vehicle or container includes power to examine it.

Table 3e: Possession of Property and Land under the 1922–43
Special Powers Acts and the 1973 Northern Ireland
(Emergency Provisions) Act

1922 CIVIL AUTHORITIES (SPECIAL POWERS) ACT (NORTHERN IRELAND)	1922–43 CIVIL AUTHORITIES (SPECIAL POWERS) ACTS (NORTHERN IRELAND)	1973 NORTHERN IRELAND (EMERGENCY PROVISIONS) ACT
Regulation 8 [Revoked by S.R.O. 147/1949, 20.8.49] 8. It shall be lawful for the Civil Authority and any person duly authorised by him, where for the purposes of this Act it is necessary so to do: (a) To take possession of any land and to construct works, including roads, thereon, and to remove any trees, hedges and fences therefrom; (b) To take possession of any buildings or other property, including works for the supply of gas, electricity or water, and any sources of water supply; (c) To take such steps as may be necessary for placing any buildings or structures in a state of defence; (d) To cause any buildings or structures to be destroyed, or any property to be moved from one place to another, or to be destroyed; (e) To take possession of any arms, ammunition, explosive substances, equipment, or stores intended or liable to be used for purposes prejudicial to the preservation of the peace or the maintenance of order; to take possession of any horses, vehicles or mechanically propelled vehicles, or other means of transport, or require them to be placed at the disposal of any Government Department or person specified by the Civil Authority in that behalf, either absolutely or by the way of hire, and either for immediate or future use. (f) To do any other act involving interference with private rights of property which is necessary for the purposes of this Act.	**Regulation 34A** **[S.R.O. 3/1957, 11.1.57]** 34A. It shall be lawful for the Civil Authority and any person duly authorised by him: (a) to take possession of any land and to construct works, including roads, thereon, and to remove any trees, hedges, and fences therefrom; (b) to take possession of any buildings or other property; (c) to take such steps as may be necessary for placing any buildings or structures in a state of defence; (d) to cause any buildings or structures to be destroyed or any property to be moved from one place to another, or to be destroyed; (e) to do any other act involving interference with private rights of property.	**Part II, section 17(2)** 17. (2) Any member of Her Majesty's Forces on duty, any constable or any person specifically authorised to do so by or on behalf of the Secretary of State may, if authorised to do so by or on behalf of the Secretary of State: (a) take possession of any land or other property; (b) take steps to place buildings or other structures in a state of defence; (c) detain any property or cause it to be destroyed or moved; (d) do any other act interfering with any public right or with any private rights of property, including carrying out any works on any land of which possession has been taken under this subsection.

under this Act any real or personal property is taken, occupied, destroyed or damaged, or any other act is done interfering with private rights of property, compensation shall, subject to the provisions of this section, be payable by the Ministry'. Any questions regarding the compensation to be granted was to be referred to a county court or to an independent arbitrator so designated by the court. Under both statutes, the proceedings were to be conducted according to rules issued by the Lord Chief Justice of Northern Ireland. Any individual, however, who had been found guilty of an offence under the 1973 EPA, immediately waived any rights to compensation under the Act. These provisions reflected almost exactly those in place under the 1922 SPA. Table 3f highlights the similarities with regard to compensation.

Prohibition of Meetings, Assemblies and Processions

As will be recalled from chapter two, prior to direct rule the Stormont government normalised special powers relating to the formal prohibition of meetings, assemblies and processions in the 1951 Public Order Act. Section 21 of the 1973 EPA further enabled security force members to disperse any additional assembly deemed to be a threat to the peace. Section 21 empowered commissioned officers of HM Forces, or any officer of the RUC at the rank of chief inspector or above, to disperse assemblies of three or more persons when of the opinion that such gatherings may lead to a breach of the peace. This section resurrected powers enshrined in Regulation 4 of the 1922 SPA. Section 22 of the 1973 EPA increased the maximum penalty for riotous and disorderly behaviour. Previously governed by section 9(1) of the Criminal Justice (Miscellaneous Provisions) Act this section extended from six months to eighteen months imprisonment where the breach of the peace was likely to be occasioned in a public place.[101]

In addition to meetings and assemblies, schedule 3(4) further allowed any officer of the RUC of the rank of chief inspector and above to interfere with funeral proceedings. In the heightened political tension in Northern Ireland, funerals were becoming political incendiaries. In the event that it appeared to an officer that a funeral may occasion a breach of the peace or serious public disorder, or cause undue demands to be made on Her Majesty's Forces or the police, Schedule 3, section 4 empowered the officer to impose whatever conditions as appeared to him to be necessary for preserving public order, including prescribing the route to be taken, prohibiting the funeral from entering any place specified in the directions, and requiring persons taking part in the funeral to travel in vehicles. These provisions echoed regulations of the 1922–43 Special Powers Acts relating to meetings, assemblies and public processions. (See Table 3g.)

*Table 3f: Rules for Compensation under the 1922–43
Special Powers Actsand the 1973 Northern Ireland
(Emergency Provisions) Act*

1922 Civil Authorities (Special Powers) Act (Northern Ireland)	1922–43 Civil Authorities (Special Powers) Acts (Northern Ireland)	1973 Northern Ireland (Emergency Provisions) Act
Section 11 11.(1) Where, under the powers conferred by this Act or the regulations, any lands, buildings, goods, chattels or other property are taken, occupied or destroyed, or any other act is done involving interference with private rights of property, compensation shall, subject to the provisions of this section, be payable by the Civil Authority out of moneys provided by Parliament. (2) If any question arises as to such compensation, such question, if not settled by agreement, shall be referred for settlement to the county court or an arbitrator to be appointed by that court, and all questions in dispute shall be settled in accordance with such procedure as may be prescribed by rules made by the Lord Chief Justice of Northern Ireland after consultation with the Civil Authority. (3) Nothing in this section shall be construed as giving to any person, where an offence against the regulations has been committed, any right to compensation in respect of lands, buildings, goods, chattels or other property taken, occupied or destroyed in connection with such offence.	**Section 11** [As in column one; this section was not altered 1922–72]	**Part IV, section 25** 25.(1) Where under this Act any real or personal property is taken, occupied, destroyed or damaged, or any other act is done interfering with private rights of property, compensation shall, subject to the provisions of this section, be payable by the Ministry. (2) Any question as to compensation under this section shall, in default of agreement, be referred for determination to the county court or an arbitrator to be appointed by that court, and the procedure for determining any question so referred shall be that prescribed by rules made by the Lord Chief Justice of Northern Ireland after consultation with the Ministry. (3) Nothing in this section shall be construed as giving to any person by whom an offence has been committed any right to compensation in respect of property taken, occupied, destroyed or damaged or in respect of any other act done in connection with the offence.

Table 3g: Prohibition of Meetings, Assemblies, and Processions under the 1922–43 Special Powers Acts and the 1973 Northern Ireland (Emergency Provisions) Act

1922 CIVIL AUTHORITIES (SPECIAL POWERS) ACT (NORTHERN IRELAND)	1922–43 CIVIL AUTHORITIES (SPECIAL POWERS) ACTS (NORTHERN IRELAND)	1973 NORTHERN IRELAND (EMERGENCY PROVISIONS) ACT
Regulation 4 Where there appears to be reason to apprehend that the assembly of any persons for the purpose of the holding of any meeting will give rise to grave disorder, and will thereby cause undue demands to be made upon the police forces, or that the holding of any procession will conduce to a breach of the peace or will promote disaffection, it shall be lawful for the Civil Authority, or for any magistrate or chief officer of police who is duly authorised for the purpose by the Civil Authority, or for two or more of such persons so authorised, to make an order prohibiting the holding of the meeting or procession, and if a meeting or procession is held or attempted to be held in contravention of any such prohibition, it shall be lawful to take such steps as may be necessary to disperse the meeting or procession or prevent the holding thereof; and every person taking part in any such prohibited meeting or procession shall be guilty of an offence against these regulations.	**S.R.O. 80/1933, 7.6.1933, BG 7.7.1993** Where there appears to be reason to apprehend that the assembly of any persons . . . will give rise to grave disorder or conduce to a breach of the peace or promote disaffection and thereby cause undue demands to be made upon the police force, it shall be lawful for the Civil Authority . . . to make an order prohibiting the holding of such assembly, meeting or procession, and if an assembly, meeting, or procession is held or attempted to be held in contravention of such prohibition it shall be lawful to take such steps as may be necessary to disperse the assembly, meeting, or procession or prevent the holding thereof, and every person taking part in any such prohibited assembly, meeting, or procession shall be guilty of an offence against these regulations.	**Section 21** 21.(1) Where any commissioned officer of Her Majesty's Forces or any officer of the Royal Ulster Constabulary not below the rank of chief inspector is of opinion that any assembly of three or more persons may lead to a breach of the peace or public disorder or may make undue demands on the police or Her Majesty's Forces he, or any member of those forces on duty or any constable may order the persons constituting the assembly to disperse forthwith. (2) Where an order is given under this section with respect to an assembly, any person who thereafter joins or remains in the assembly or otherwise fails to comply with the order shall be liable on summary conviction to imprisonment for a term not exceeding six months or to a fine not exceeding 400, or both.

Proscription

In 1973 the British government resurrected the powers of proscription enshrined in Regulation 24A of the 1922–43 SPAs as Part III, section 19 of the 1973 EPA.[102] As was discussed in the previous chapter, the Northern Ireland Ministry of Home Affairs introduced Regulation 24A immediately after the passage of the 1922 SPA. This measure reflected powers already found in Regulation 24. As was observed in chapter two, the new Northern government drew Regulation 24 directly from the 1920 Restoration of Order in Ireland Act and the 1914–15 Defence of the Realm Acts. Although the Northern Ireland Minister of Home Affairs withdrew Regulation 24 in 1949,[103] Regulation 24A, by virtue of which the Unionist government issued all orders banning organisations, remained on the books until the creation of the 1973 EPA. The main difference between Regulation 24A and Part III, section 19 of the 1973 EPA was that the previous measure focused only on actual membership of associations as well as the presence of documents indicating membership, whereas the 1973 EPA extended the measure to address fundraising for proscribed organisations. Annex 733 to the 1973 statute also made it an offence for any person to solicit membership for an unlawful association.

These last two additions signified a change in approach between that taken by the Unionist government in Northern Ireland and that pursued by Britain subsequent to direct rule. The unionist regime sought to deflect republicanism's challenge to the State by not allowing the expression of republican ideals. Britain, in contrast, sought to separate the paramilitary element from the communities in which they had previously found support. By also making fundraising and recruiting an offence, Westminster essentially sought to cut off the support system for the paramilitary organisations. This change in attitude is also reflected in the pure prospectivity of the EPA. Whereas Regulation 24A of the 1922–43 SPAs made it an offence to become or remain a member of an unlawful group, the 1973 EPA specified that the individual had to have taken part in the activities of the organisation after the statute had been brought into force in order to be found guilty of an offence under section 19. The new regulation avoided the retroactive punishment previously incorporated in the 1922–43 SPAs. (See Table 3h.) On 28 February 1972 a motion, signed by about fifty Conservative MPs, had been tabled at Westminster urging the British government to make the IRA an illegal organisation. The 1973 EPA accomplished this. Schedule 2 provided a list of the organisations proscribed, all but one of which were republican in orientation: Sinn Féin, the IRA, Cumann na mBan, Fianna na hÉireann, Saor Éire and the Ulster Volunteer Force (UVF). The Labour government's decision not to ban the UDA did come under fire in the House of Commons.[104] Before the enactment of the 1973 statute, William Whitelaw issued a regulation under the 1922–43 SPAs removing republican clubs from the list of unlawful associations.[105] The British government decided not to ban the Irish Republican Brotherhood, Irish Volunteers, National Guard, Cumann Poblachta na hÉireann, Saor Uladh and Fianna Uladh, previously prohibited under the 1922–43 SPAs.

Table 3h: Proscription under the 1922–43 Special Powers Acts and the 1973 Northern Ireland (Emergency Provisions) Act

1922 CIVIL AUTHORITIES (SPECIAL POWERS) ACT (NORTHERN IRELAND)	1922–43 CIVIL AUTHORITIES (SPECIAL POWERS) ACTS (NORTHERN IRELAND)	1973 NORTHERN IRELAND (EMERGENCY PROVISIONS) ACT
Regulation 24 [Revoked by S.R.O. 147/1949, 20.8.49] 24(1) Any person who does any act with a view to promoting or calculated to promote the objects of an unlawful association within the meaning of section 7 of the Criminal Law and Procedure (Ireland) Act, 1887, shall be guilty of an offence against these regulations. (2) If any person, without lawful authority or excuse, has in his possession any document relating or purporting to relate to the affairs of any such association, or emanating or purporting to emanate from an officer of any such association, or addressed to the person as an officer or member of any such association, that person shall be guilty of an offence against these regulations unless he proves that he did not know or had no reason to suspect that the document was of any such character as aforesaid or that he is not an officer or member of the association. Where a person is charged with having in his possession any such document and the document was found on premises in his occupation, or under his control, or in which he has resided, the document shall be presumed to have been in his possession unless the contrary is proved.	**Regulation 24A** [S.R.O. 35/1922, 22.5.22] 24A. Any person who becomes or remains a member of an unlawful association or who does any act with a view to promoting or calculated to promote the objects of an unlawful association or seditious conspiracy shall be guilty of an offence against these regulations. If any person without lawful authority or excuse has in his possession any document relating to or purporting to relate to the affairs of any such association or emanating or purporting to emanate from an officer of any such association or addressed to the person as an officer or member of any such association or indicating that he is an officer or member of any such association that person shall be guilty of an offence against these regulations unless he proves that he did not know or had no reason to suspect that the document was of any such character as aforesaid or that he is not an officer or member of the association. Where a person is charged with having in his possession any such document, and the document was found on premises in his occupation, or under his control, or in which he is found or has resided, the document shall be presumed to have been in his possession unless the contrary is proved. The following organisations shall for the purposes of this Regulation be deemed to be unlawful associations . . .	**Part III, section 19** 19.(1) Subject to subsection (7) below, any person who: (a) belongs or professes to belong to a proscribed organisation; or (b) solicits or invites financial or other support for a proscribed organisation, or knowingly makes or receives any contribution in money or otherwise to the resources of a proscribed organisation, [(c) solicits or invites any person to become a member of a proscribed organisation or to carry out on behalf of a proscribed organisation orders or directions given, or requests made, by a member of that organisation, added by Annex 733. 1973, Pt. II, pp. 1588/1589] shall be liable on summary conviction to imprisonment for a term not exceeding six months or to a fine not exceeding £400, or both, and on conviction on indictment to imprisonment for a term not exceeding five years or to a fine, or both. (2) The court by or before whom a person is convicted of an offence under this section may order the forfeiture of any money or other property which at the time of the offence he had in his possession or under his control for the use or benefit of the proscribed organisation. (3) The organisations specified in schedule 2 to this Act are proscribed organisations for the purposes of this section; and any organisation which passes under a name mentioned in that schedule shall be treated as proscribed, whatever relationship (if any) it has to any ⟶

		other organisation of the same name. (4) The Secretary of State may by order add to schedule 2 to this Act any organisation that appears to him to be concerned in terrorism or in promoting or encouraging it. (5) The Secretary of State may also by order remove an organisation from schedule 2 to this Act. (6) The possession by a person of a document addressed to him as a member of a proscribed organisation, or relating or purporting to relate to the affairs of a proscribed organisation, or emanating or purporting to emanate from a proscribed organisation or officer of a proscribed organisation, shall be evidence of that person belonging to the organisation at the time when he had the document in his possession.

Section 23A of the 1973 EPA also made it an offence for a person to dress or behave in public, 'in such a way as to arouse reasonable apprehension that he is a member of a proscribed organisation'. These particular stipulations exceeded what might have been successfully prosecuted under the 1936 Public Order Act, which also prohibited the wearing of political uniforms. The 1936 Public Order Act, as amended by the 1963 Public Order Act, banned the wearing of political uniforms in public and prohibited participation in any organisation created with the aim of taking over police or military functions.[106] The statutes made illegal the promotion of political ends through the display of physical force and authorised the police to regulate public procession routes when reasonable ground existed for expectation of serious disorder. The city of London was not subject to this particular provision as the 1839 Metropolitan Police Act already provided such powers to the police.[107] The police also bore a common-law right to attend public meetings conducted on private premises, if they were under reasonable suspicion that their presence was necessary to prevent an incitement to violence.[108] The Public Order Acts also prohibited the possession of offensive weapons and displaying provocative behaviour in public places. Although introduced during a time of fascist disorder in Great Britain, most active fascists in Britain, including Sir Oswald Moseley, were interned under regulations issued in accordance with the 1939 Emergency Powers (Defence) Act.[109] The British Attorney General rarely authorised prosecutions under the Public Order Acts. In 1974, however, prior to the enactment of the Prevention of Terrorism Act, the Attorney General did authorise prosecutions related to Northern Irish political violence under the 1936 and 1963 Public Order Acts. A London magistrate fined twelve members of Provisional Sinn Féin £50 each for wearing black berets at a meeting in Hyde Park at Speakers' Corner.[110] As will be recalled from chapter two, the 1936 Public Order Act drew its provisions from Regulation 3 of the 1922 SPA, which covered the wearing of uniforms and the carrying of weapons. The government viewed these as indicating paramilitary membership. The emergency powers introduced on a temporary basis had become subsumed into more permanent legislation. The 1973 EPA resurrected similar powers for counter-terrorist law.

Collection of Information on the Security Forces

Section 20 of the 1973 EPA made it an offence to collect, record, publish, communicate or attempt to elicit information on HM Forces or constabulary which was of a nature so as to be useful to terrorists. This section duplicated almost precisely the wording of Regulation 10 of the 1922 SPA, repealed in 1951 and re-enacted as Regulation 22 of the 1922–43 SPAs.[111] (See Table 3i.) The main difference between the two provisions lay in the 1973 EPA's use of the word 'terrorist' in place of the Unionist government's reference to individuals 'hostile or opposed to the preservation of the peace or maintenance of order'. 'Terrorist' was defined under the 1973 EPA as, 'a person who is or has been concerned in the commission or attempted commission of any act of terrorism or in directing, organising or training persons for the purpose of terrorism'; with 'terrorism' understood as 'the use of violence for political ends [including] any use of violence for the purpose of putting the public or any section of the public in fear'.[112] The wording of this clause drew from the 1972 Detention of Terrorists (Northern Ireland) Order, introduced under the 1922–43 Special Powers Acts.

Prosecution of Offences

Section 3(2) of the 1922 Special Powers Act allowed the Northern Ireland Attorney General to delegate all powers of prosecution. As was noted in chapter one, the Northern government used this instrument to

Table 3i: Collection of Information on the Security Forces
under the 1922–43 Special Powers Acts and the 1973
Northern Ireland (Emergency Provisions) Act

1922 CIVIL AUTHORITIES (SPECIAL POWERS) ACT (NORTHERN IRELAND)	1922–43 CIVIL AUTHORITIES (SPECIAL POWERS) ACTS (NORTHERN IRELAND)	1973 NORTHERN IRELAND (EMERGENCY PROVISIONS) ACT
Regulation 10 [Revoked by S.R.O. 187/1951, 12.10.51] 10. No person shall, without lawful authority, collect, record, publish or communicate, or attempt to elicit, any information with respect to the movement, numbers, description, condition, or disposition of any police force, or with respect to the plans or conduct, or supposed plans or conduct, of any operations by any such force, or any information of such a nature as is calculated to be or might be directly or indirectly useful to persons hostile or opposed to the preservation of the peace or maintenance of order, and if any person contravenes the provisions of this regulation, or without lawful authority or excuse has in his possession any document containing any such information as aforesaid, he shall be guilty of an offence against these regulations.	**Regulation 22** [S.R.O. 199/1956, 21.12.56] 22. No person shall, without lawful authority, collect, record, publish or communicate, or attempt to elicit, any information with respect to the movement, numbers, description, condition, or disposition of any police force, or with respect to the plans or conduct, or supposed plans or conduct, of any operations by any such force, or any information of such a nature as is calculated to be or might be directly or indirectly useful to persons hostile or opposed to the preservation of the peace or maintenance of order, and if any person contravenes the provisions of this regulation, or without lawful authority or excuse has in his possession any document containing any such information as aforesaid, he shall be guilty of an offence against these regulations.	**Section 20** 20. No person shall, without lawful authority or reasonable excuse (the proof of which lies on him), collect, record, publish, communicate or attempt to elicit, any information with respect to the police or Her Majesty's Forces which is of such a nature as it likely to be useful to terrorists, or have in his possession any record of or document containing any such information.

various degrees during its tenure. For the most part, the police were delegated powers to prosecute cases brought under the 1922–43 SPAs. During the passage of the 1972 Northern Ireland (Temporary Provisions) Act, Britain's Attorney General announced the creation of the Prosecution of Offences (Northern Ireland) Order 1972.[113] In accordance with recommendations of the Hunt Committee Report, this instrument established an office and department for a Director of Public Prosecutions in Northern Ireland. The MacDermott Report on public prosecutions had recommended a similar move.[114] The 1972 Order allowed for greater resources to handle the prosecution of offences in Northern Ireland, separating the police from their previous role and enabling them to focus on 'ordinary' policing duties – including, but not limited to, the exercise of special powers. By establishing an external body with the power to prosecute offences under the 1922–43 SPAs, the government at one level sought to legitimise the actual powers being employed: the Director of Public Prosecutions (DPP) constituted a seemingly 'objective' office. Its very creation and its ability to prosecute cases under the 1922–43 SPAs assumed the normalisation and continuation of emergency law. It also removed the focus from government action, establishing a median body between the police and Parliament that bore the responsibility for the fair application of legislation. It was not the subject of the law itself that was under scrutiny, but the manner in which it was applied. The DPP would have the ability, seemingly, to rise above the sectarian charges levied against the Northern Ireland police and to focus on the fair and equitable prosecution of cases under current legislation. The police then would be charged solely with the exercise of emergency powers in order to combat violence. The creation of the DPP allowed the British government to sidestep many of the charges levied against the exercise of emergency powers by the police in Northern Ireland. This paved the way for the retention of many of the measures introduced by the Stormont government. The 1973 EPA maintained the changes instituted by the 1972 Order. Part IV, section 26(1) of the 1973 Act placed the Director of Public Prosecutions in the role formerly occupied by the Northern Ireland Attorney General, with institution of prosecutions only allowed by, or with the express consent of, the Director of Public Prosecutions for Northern Ireland.

PROVISION FOR THE DISCRETIONARY INTRODUCTION OF FURTHER MEASURES

In a catch-all phrase reminiscent of section 1 of the 1922 SPA, which empowered the Minister of Home Affairs 'to make regulations for making further provision for the preservation of the peace and maintenance of order', section 24 of the 1973 EPA stated: 'The Secretary of State may by regulations make provision additional to the foregoing provisions of this Act for promoting the preservation of the peace and the maintenance of order'. Owing to its wide provisions, in parliamentary debates this clause earned the title, 'Henry VIII subsection'. In response to critics Labour moved that the affirmative resolution procedure to which any orders enacted by the Minister were subject made the situation considerably different than that at work during the reign of Henry VIII. Section 24 broadly transferred to the Secretary of State for Northern Ireland the powers borne previously by the Minister of Home Affairs. Unlike the mechanism employed in the 1922–43 SPAs, however, all orders and regulations made under the 1973 EPA had to be approved by both Houses of Parliament within forty days of their enactment.[115] As with so many of the other emergency powers retained by the British government, the power to introduce virtually any new measure deemed necessary stemmed from the 1920 Restoration of Order in Ireland Act and the 1914–15 Defence of the Realm Acts. Thus, not only did Westminster adopt the less encompassing, more specific regulations, but likewise, the most wide-sweeping measures were carried forward into the new regime.

CONCLUSION

The 1973 EPA preserved, in some form, provisions from the 1922–43 Special Powers Acts relating to detention, internment, the closing of licensed premises, the blocking up of roads, the prohibition of vehicle usage, powers of entry, search and seizure, possession of property and land, compensation, the prohibition of meetings, assemblies and processions, proscription and the collection of information on security forces. It also maintained provisions relating to the delegation of powers and the introduction of additional measures.[116] It differed slightly in its delegation of the powers so conferred and by its insertion of the affirmative resolution procedure for regulations introduced by the Secretary of State.

Powers from the 1922–43 SPAs not included in the new statute included curfew, military drilling and the use of military uniforms, the sale and transfer of explosives, control of the parking of cars, capital punishment and identity documents. Other statutes already covered the first three of these. The fourth, omitted for reasons which were less than clear, was soon resurrected through the Northern Ireland (Emergency Provisions) Regulations 1975,[117] and the latter two would be widely debated by Parliament throughout the coming years.[118] In the interim, capital punishment was addressed in Part 1, section 1 of the 1973 EPA, which reversed section 6 of the 1922 SPA and removed the death penalty from the scope of the new legislation. The clause was inserted into the Bill during the committee stage.[119] From 1922 to 1972 there had been eleven executions in Northern Ireland, only two of which had occurred after 1944 (the last one having taken place in 1961.) None of these had been conducted under the 1922–43 Special Powers Acts.[120] The debate on whether to withdraw the death penalty followed the Secretary of State's 1973 decision to reprieve Albert Brown, a Protestant member of the UDA who had been found guilty of murdering an RUC member, from facing execution. During the Emergency Provisions Act debates a similar case was pending for William Gerard Holden, a Northern Irish Catholic awaiting execution for the murder of a soldier in 1972. Pressure had been steadily increasing on Whitelaw to issue a second reprieval. In the politically charged atmosphere, it was widely acknowledged that an execution would only spark off an even more violent situation. Not only was it impractical to enforce the sentence, but the May 1973 discussion closely followed an 11 April refusal by the House to consider legislation to reintroduce capital punishment in Great Britain. Given that the death penalty had recently been eliminated from Great Britain, the removal of the death penalty from the statute was seen as necessary in order to bring Northern Irish legislation into line with the rest of the UK. The clause banning capital punishment was passed during committee stage 253 to 294.[121] After its inclusion in the 1973 EPA, Part I, section 1 was exempted from requirements regarding the annual review of the emergency statute.

Significantly, many of the provisions from the 1922–43 SPAs that limited the expression of republican ideals also were absent from the 1973 EPA. The British government dropped measures related to the censorship of printed matter, films and gramophone records, the erection of monuments and the flying of the Tricolor. The clear shift away from executive detention and towards a reconsideration of the judicial process in order to bring offenders to book accelerated in the following years. This related to the changing nature of violence in the North – from civil unrest to paramilitary activity – and, correspondingly, to the fall in violence during this time. From a high of 467 deaths in 1972, the numbers dropped to 250 in 1973 and to 216 in 1974.[122] As the Labour government returned to power, the new Secretary of State, Merlyn Rees, emphasised the use of criminal justice procedures and the role of the local security forces in order to fight terrorism. This policy of 'criminialisation' and 'Ulsterisation' influenced the development of emergency legislation and accelerated the movement away from detention and towards the use of the judicial process to bring terrorist offenders 'to book'.[123] The next chapter examines the evolution of the Northern Ireland (Emergency Provisions) Act as influenced by government inquiries, reviews, parliamentary debates, and public pressure from 1973 to 1996.

CHAPTER FOUR

The Northern Ireland
(Emergency Provisions) Act Evolves:
Counter-terrorist legislation in Northern Ireland 1973–1996

IN DECEMBER 1973 the British and Irish governments, the Ulster Unionist Party, the Social Democratic and Labour Party and the Alliance Party held talks at the Sunningdale Civil Service College. Participants agreed to establish an Executive for Northern Ireland, an all-Ireland Council to address affairs affecting both parts of the island, and a Joint Law Commission to address legal treatment of terrorists apprehended North and South. In addition the Republic of Ireland conceded the establishment of a southern police authority to work with the security forces in Northern Ireland. The British government agreed to end detention at the earliest opportunity. Intended to establish an 'Irish dimension' to the Northern Irish conflict, and to create a new political framework to replace Stormont, the political power-sharing experiment soon collapsed. Loyalists opposed to the Sunningdale exercise – Harry West, Ian Paisley and William Craig – were not invited to the talks. Together with Glenn Barr, a founding member of the revived UVF, they formed the Ulster Worker's Council (UWC) to lead a loyalist strike. In May 1974 the UWC brought the province to a standstill. By cutting power supplies and drawing on intimidatory tactics carried out by loyalist paramilitaries, the UWC halted all industrial activity, and within two weeks unionist members were forced to resign from the power-sharing Executive, thus rendering it ineffective. The only element of the Sunningdale Agreement ever implemented both north and south of the border was the Joint Law Commission's report. Their input led to reciprocal legislation, permitting a person accused of a terrorist offence to be brought to trial on whichever side of the border they were arrested.

Immediately prior to the collapse of Sunningdale, Merlyn Rees, Secretary of State for Northern Ireland, announced that a committee would be established to examine the operation of the 1973 EPA. Expressing concern that the Diplock Commission had been too narrow in focusing on how to increase the number of convictions of suspected terrorists, Rees cited the need to consider emergency legislation within the wider framework of civil liberties and human rights.[1] New legislation would be introduced in accordance with the Gardiner Committee's findings. The British government set as Lord Gardiner's frame of reference, 'to consider what provisions and powers, consistent to the maximum extent practicable in the circumstances with the preservation of civil liberties and human rights, are required to deal with terrorism and subversion in Northern Ireland, including provisions for the administration of justice, and to examine the working of the Northern Ireland (Emergency Provisions) Act 1973; and to make recommendations'.[2] In the interim Rees requested a six month renewal of the 1973 EPA, as opposed to the twelve months required by the initial Act. The Gardiner Committee had not yet reported as of December 1974, however, and so the government requested another extension of six months. Although a bill based on Gardiner's report to amend the 1973 EPA finally received its first reading in the House of Commons at the end of June 1975, the 1973 statute had to be formally extended for an additional six months. This was done through the Northern Ireland (Various Emergency Provisions) (Continuance) Order 1975. During its first reading of the order the government noted that the nature of violence in Northern Ireland had changed since the commencement of the January 1975 cease-fire. Although there were some incidents of violence, such as the killing of a policeman in Derry during the second weekend in May, for the most part the Provisional IRA maintained a steady cease-fire during the first six months of 1975. The government came under considerable fire in the House of Commons during the first reading of the 1975 Continuance Order, as members of the House suspected that the Ministry had cut a deal with the paramilitaries to reduce security force activities in return for a lull in violence. Séamus Twomey, leader of the Belfast Provisional IRA, Dáithí Ó Conaill, a leading strategist of the republican movement and Ruairí Ó Brádaigh, President of Provisional Sinn Féin from 1970 to 1983, also claimed that the IRA was engaged in ongoing negotiations with the British Government.[3] Printed sources, such as *The Times* and the *Guardian*, made repeated reference to a 'truce' between the IRA and the British Government.[4]

During this time, although terrorist incidents had fallen steadily, inter-factional violence, particularly in Belfast and Derry, had increased significantly. This was largely seen as a response to the lull in the immediate campaign and the emergence of rivalries within and between the paramilitary movements. These incidents evolved into a full-scale feud between the Official and Provisional IRA, and the Ulster Defence Association and Ulster Volunteer Force, resulting in 157 sectarian or inter-factional murders by November 1975. The number of kneecappings in the first ten months of 1975 also reached a high of 168, compared with 127 for the whole of 1974, and seventy-four for 1973.[5] The British government established incident centres to increase communication with the Provisional IRA during the cease-fire. As attacks on the security forces diminished, the Secretary of State refrained from signing any new interim custody orders. The government claimed that the incident centre network acted to inform the authorities who was responsible for various violent acts during the cease-fire.[6] The RUC announced during this time the creation of a special centralised CID unit, to be known as the A Squad. This group was to be a mobile, co-ordinated detective squad able to respond in support of the local police to address situations throughout the province. The 1975 Continuance Order dealt not just with the 1973 EPA but with the Northern Ireland (Young Persons) Act 1974, which had been introduced in August 1974 to enable the authorities to imprison young people who had escaped from remand homes.[7] It provided for the Secretary of State to issue a directive that a young person charged with a scheduled offence be held in custody in prison rather than in a remand home. Between August 1974 and June 1975, the government issued fifteen such directions.[8] From July 1974 the House of Commons held their debates on the renewal of the 1973 Northern Ireland (Emergency Provisions) Act concurrently with consideration of the extension of the 1974 Northern Ireland (Young Persons) Act.

REITERATING DIPLOCK

In January 1975 Merlyn Rees presented the Gardiner Committee Report to Parliament.[9] The government did not provide Members with the opportunity to debate the report as its own; rather the discussion took place in the context of the amending legislation to the 1973 Act. As has been mentioned, the inquiry's aim was to evaluate what powers were needed to deal with terrorism and subversion, while preserving, to the maximum extent practicable, civil liberties and human rights.[10] The report stated from the outset that some of those giving evidence had argued that the powers enshrined by the 1973 EPA constituted a basic violation of human rights and therefore should be abolished immediately.[11] However, it continued:

We are unable to accept this argument. While the liberty of the subject is a human right to be preserved under all possible conditions, it is not, and cannot be, an absolute right because one man may use his liberty to take away the liberty of another and must be restrained from doing so. Where freedoms conflict, the state has a duty to protect those in need of protection.[12]

Like the Diplock Commission, the Gardiner Committee cited the 1950 European Convention for the Protection of Human Rights and Fundamental Freedoms with regard to the general right to liberty and security of person and noted that it was offset by the negation of the right 'to engage in any activity or perform any act aimed at the destruction of the rights and freedoms set forth'.[13] Although the Gardiner Committee also cited the right of derogation under Article 15 with regard to obligations under Article 5 in times of war or public emergency, it did not view the 1973 EPA as a derogation from these commitments. The committee stated that the suspension of normal legal safeguards for the liberty of individuals was sometimes necessary to counter greater evils, but it emphasised that both the scope and duration of such provisions had to be limited. The report recognised the past ill-treatment of prisoners, as described in the Compton Report and Parker Committee Report, and observed that although the practices had ceased, the resentment caused was 'intense, widespread and persistent'.[14] The report also asserted that any solution to the Troubles would have to be political in nature and would need to address issues of social justice. Along these lines the committee recommended the immediate implementation of the Van Straubenzee Report, *Discrimination in the Prime Sector of Employment*, further improvements in housing, the adoption of a new approach to community relations and consideration of the enactment of a bill of rights.

In the twelve months following the enactment of the 1973 EPA, the government had banned the Official and Provisional IRA, Official and Provisional Sinn Féin, Cumann na mBan, Fianna na hÉireann, the Ulster Freedom Fighters (UFF) and the Red Hand Commandos (RHC). The government proscribed both the UFF and RHC on 12 November 1973. In May 1974 the Labour government deproscribed Official and Provisional Sinn Féin and the UVF.[15] Labour claimed at the time that there were signs that many of the members wanted to return to political activity. The decision to lift the ban imposed on the organisations sought to encourage this. The UVF formed a political arm, and the resultant Volunteer Political Party entered the October General Election. With the escalation of sectarian violence, though, it became increasingly clear that the UVF was still engaged in violence. Incidents such as the Miami Show Band murders and the indiscriminate killings of Catholics on 2 October 1975 pushed the government to re-enact the order banning the UVF. The Northern Ireland (Emergency Provisions) Act 1973 (Amendment) Order 1975 was confirmed by the affirmative resolution of both Houses on 4 November 1975.[16]

Just as the Labour government appealed to the Commons to proscribe the IRA in Britain under the 1974 PTA, considering its prohibition in the Republic and in Northern Ireland, the Gardiner Committee cited the continued proscription of the IRA in Britain and the Republic as justification for retaining the policy of proscription. This was to become a convenient excuse in the years to come; although Britain claimed that the Republic had no business involving itself in the affairs of Northern Ireland, the British government repeatedly cited the law in the Republic as justification for increasingly severe emergency powers introduced in both Northern Ireland and Great Britain.

The Gardiner Committee noted the uneven application of proscription in Northern Ireland with regard to republican and loyalist associations. Although the report stopped short of alleging sectarian application of section 19, it suggested that the government retain the provision and take steps to make further use of its powers. The Standing Advisory Commission on Human Rights echoed these sentiments and noted the disparate treatment of terrorist organisations. SACHR wrote: 'we recommend that all organisations engaged in terrorist activities should be placed on a similar footing'.[17] Britain had formed the Standing Advisory Commission on Human Rights under section 20 of the 1973 Northern Ireland Constitution Act. The body issued its first report on 26 September 1975, covering the period from 1 December 1973 through to 30 June 1975. SACHR aimed: (a) to identify fields in which discrimination either existed or was alleged to exist and to determine the degree of actual discrimination, (b) to examine social, economic, religious and political circumstances surrounding discrimination, and (c) to inform the public of the dangers inherent in discrimination. Acting in an advisory role, the Commission's first report focused on the 1970 Prevention of Incitement to Hatred Act, 1954 Flags and Emblems (Display) Act (Northern Ireland), and the 1973 and 1975 Emergency Provision Acts.[18] Similar to SACHR, a number of Members of Parliament also expressed dissatisfaction with regard to the inequitable application of proscription.[19]

The Gardiner Committee found as an incidental effect of proscription that, in connection with the 1968 Criminal Injuries to Persons (Compensation) Act (Northern Ireland) and the 1971 Criminal Injuries to Property (Compensation) Act (Northern Ireland), proscription under section 19 of the 1973 EPA provided a basis on which the Chief Constable could certify that an 'unlawful organisation' had been responsible for an act, thus considerably simplifying the claims procedure.[20] About twenty-eight prosecutions had been conducted under section 19 of the 1973 EPA, which governed proscription. Of these, twenty-two had been successful. The government followed the Gardiner Committee's recommendation to the extent that it retained the powers of proscription in section 19 of the 1973 Act. The Northern Ireland (Emergency Provisions) (Amendment) Act 1975, however, stopped short of adding any new names to the list.[21]

Responding to widespread public discussion regarding the reintroduction of the death penalty for terrorist offences, the Gardiner Committee upheld the abolition of capital punishment, citing the inflammatory reaction that such a penalty would engender. The inquiry also supported the status quo with regard to the Diplock courts. Although the committee suggested that, in principle, trial by jury presented the best form of adjudication, it considered it untenable in the Northern Irish environment. However, similar to Diplock, Gardiner failed to cite a single instance of intimidation of jurors or perverse acquittals. In the evidence presented to the Gardiner Committee, though, details were provided of 482 instances between 1 January 1972 and 31 August 1974 in which witnesses were either too afraid to make a statement or, after giving one, refused to give evidence in court.[22] Likewise the Committee assumed that jurors would be vulnerable to intimidation and recommended the continued use of a single judge and no jury. From the evidence heard, Gardiner concluded that the administration of justice had not suffered as a result of the elimination of juries. In accordance with his recommendations, the government retained the use of the Diplock courts for scheduled offences. The Gardiner Committee also upheld changes regarding the onus of proof that had been introduced by the 1973 Emergency Provisions Act. It found nothing unusual in the measures that echoed similar shifts of the burden of proof in at least twenty-nine other UK acts and four Northern Ireland statutes. For example, section 4 of the 1883 Explosive Substances Act made it an offence for a person to have explosives in her or his possession. The burden of proof lay on the accused to demonstrate that it was intended for lawful ends.[23]

STRIKING NEW GROUND

The Gardiner Committee departed from the existing statutes in a few minor areas. Concerning changes in the admissibility of evidence introduced under section 5 of the 1973 EPA, the Gardiner Committee noted that outside the Northern Ireland context unsworn statements would be inadmissible as hearsay. The committee objected to the inability of the accused to challenge the verity of such statements through cross-examination. On the 7 August 1973 the Director of Public Prosecutions had issued a direction to the Chief Constable demanding that statements made under section 5 not be tendered in any court without his authority. In the time that had elapsed since the introduction of the EPA, the police had not made use of section 5. Gardiner recommended that the provision be eliminated. Clause 1 of the 1975 EPA brought the law on the admission of written statements into line with the law in Great Britain. Clause 7 repealed section 5 of the 1973 Act, which had allowed written statements to be admitted as evidence in trials for scheduled offences where the witness was unable or unfit to attend the trial or could not be found. The Gardiner Committee also advocated the insertion of a sub-section to make explicit the discretion of the judges presiding over trials for scheduled offences to exclude or disregard a statement if, in the view of the court, the interests of justice so required. Although the subsequent 1975 EPA did not adopt this recommendation, it did make section 6 inapplicable to summary trials for less serious offences.

The Gardiner Committee demonstrated concern at the length of time elapsing between remand and trial.[24] This was to become a preoccupation of official reviews of the emergency legislation. Following the introduction of the EPA, the average length of time had increased from twenty-five weeks in October 1973 to 35.5. weeks in September 1974 for those in custody and to 39.1 weeks for those on bail.[25] These numbers reflected the immense strain that had been imposed on the legal system in Northern Ireland as a result of the use of emergency legislation. Clause three of the amending act subsequently enabled scheduled and non-scheduled offences to be tried together where such offences were closely related. Clause four broadened the number of judges empowered to grant bail to an individual charged with a scheduled offence and freed persons being tried summarily for such offences from any restrictions on the grant of bail. The government also streamlined the process of application for legal aid through clause 5, in order to make it simpler for an accused to receive such help.

Among the new measures considered necessary for the government to include in emergency legislation, the Gardiner Committee recommended a change in the right to silence. For scheduled offences, preliminary inquiry proceedings only commenced at the request of the prosecution and acquiescence of the defence.[26] However, with regard to terrorist offences, it was often the case that the accused refused to recognise the court. The law was unclear as to whether silence indicated assent or dissent, and so the Gardiner Committee recommended that the statute be changed to indicate that silence implied acceptance. Clause 2 of the 1975 EPA went further than Gardiner's recommendation, waiving the accused's right to have a preliminary investigation altogether. It vested in the court the decision to have either a preliminary investigation involving witnesses or a preliminary inquiry based on written depositions at the initial hearing of a scheduled offence. By transferring the decision to the court, which could take into account any representations made by the accused or his or her representative, the interpretation of silence could be bypassed. As with the Diplock Committee, the underlying aim was to secure more convictions. This emphasis on gaining convictions threatened the perception of justice in the exercise of the law.

The Gardiner Committee noted a discrepancy in the case of prisoners, namely, that in the case where two prisoners – one convicted of a scheduled offence and the other a detainee – escaped from the Maze, the convicted prisoner would be entitled to a trial by jury, whereas the detainee would not. The offence of escaping under the 1953 Prison Act (Northern Ireland) was not listed in the schedule to the 1973 EPA, but the offence of escaping from prison while under detention was triable by a judge sitting without a jury, because of its inclusion in paragraph 38 of schedule 1 to the 1973 EPA.[27] The Gardiner Committee recommended that the inconsistency be removed by inserting in the list of scheduled offences the offence of escape and related offences such as assisting escapes and rescuing persons under sections 25 to 33 of the 1953 Act, when the prisoner involved had been convicted of, or charged with a scheduled offence.

Citing difficulties in proving criminal conspiracy for those responsible for orchestrating terrorism, the Gardiner Committee proposed the creation of the new offence of being 'concerned in the commission or attempted commission of any act of terrorism or in directing, organising, training or recruiting persons for the purpose of terrorism', punishable by imprisonment not to exceed fifteen years.[28] Section 19 of the 1973 EPA had made membership in a proscribed organisation an offence, avoiding some problems of proving conspiracy, but the maximum penalty was set at five years' imprisonment. The Gardiner Committee viewed the penalty as inadequate for individuals placed high in the leadership of paramilitary organisations. Labour rejected the Committee's recommendation that a general offence of terrorism should be created. Rees stated: 'If a person commits an act of violence we consider that the proper course of action is to bring that person to trial for his crime and not to convict him under some "catch-all" provision such as an offence of terrorism'.[29] However, it did regard Gardiner as having uncovered two deficiencies in the law with regard to bringing to justice persons recruiting others to be part of a proscribed organisation and individuals engaged in weapons training. Accordingly, section 12 of the amending act added to the list of scheduled offences, 'solicit[ing] or invit[ing] any person to become a member of a proscribed organisation, to carry out on behalf of a proscribed organisation orders or directions given, or requests made, by a member of that organisation'. In addition section 15 made it an offence punishable by five years' imprisonment to train others or to receive training in the use of firearms or explosives, unless the accused could demonstrate that the training was for some lawful purpose.

On the subject of detention, Gardiner acknowledged that it was an executive and not a judicial process. He suggested that it could be justified only 'in times of the gravest emergency, for the purpose of the greater protection of the public'. He added:

> Detention involves a decision by Government to deprive individuals of their liberty without trial and without the normal safeguards which the law provides for the protection of the accused. It is an executive and not a judicial process. It is not known to the common law, and is only justified in a democratic society in times of the gravest emergency, for the purpose of the greater protection of the public. *The continuation of such a system in Northern Ireland for a period of more than three years raises serious questions.*[30]

In the sixteen months since the British government had implemented the 1973 EPA, the government had released 473 detainees. During the same period, 484 new interim custody orders had been made. This brought the total number of individuals in detention at the time of the report to 540.[31] The hearing of the detention cases took place in front of one of approximately twenty commissioners, varying in qualities, experience and aptitudes. (Commissioners were required to have had experience as a judge, barrister, advocate or solicitor in the UK for at least ten years. Their professions ranged from sheriffs and circuit judges, to part-time recorders, and all were operating outside their normal jurisdictions in Great Britain.) All hearings took place in the Maze with decisions taken independently from the Executive. Commissioners held the hearings, which had become adversarial in form, in private. The sessions lasted between one and four days. While the Crown paid for counsel on both sides, the counsel for the Crown were invariably members of the English

Bar and the counsel for the respondents members of the Northern Ireland Bar. The government believed that this procedure reduced the risk to the Northern Ireland members. As the overall hearing could not be held in the absence of the respondent, the refusal of republicans to attend the hearings prevented the commissioners from disposing of any significant number of republican cases.

Evidence for the Crown derived almost exclusively from the testimony of members of the Army and the RUC Special Branch. The convention had become for advice to be given from behind screens, sometimes with voice scramblers. The respondent's counsel could not cross-examine in great detail any evidence that was given, which was mainly hearsay. Much of it depended on information gained from paid informers who received sums of money and favours from the security forces. The informers themselves, however, did not attend the hearings. In order to examine the pedigree of hearsay, the respondent and lawyers would be excluded from the room and evidence given in camera. Thus, although the respondent could be cross-examined, the accuser could not be. At the close of the restricted session, the commissioners informed both the respondent and his or her lawyers of the nature of the evidence given in camera and the reasons for excluding them from the proceedings. In the event that a detention order was served the respondent could appeal to a tribunal. Initially commissioners were not allowed to sit as members of a tribunal, which had the result that the tribunal was unfamiliar with the procedure followed and the tenure of the commissioners' hearings. If the appeal was unsuccessful, the individual could be released either by the Secretary of State or by a commissioner, when the case was referred for review. This combination of executive and quasi-judicial action created an ambiguity around final responsibility for the incarceration and release of detainees. The review process depended on information regarding the nature and general level of terrorist activity in the detainee's home community, but it was provided with minimal information about the individual in question, who had been incarcerated in the Maze in a large compound for numerous months. The result of this policy was twofold. First, the government held detainees in part on the basis of events beyond their control – their geographic location. Second, because the majority of detainees had been lifted from Catholic areas, detention had the effect of alienating the minority population even further.

Gardiner justified the use of detention in terms of the extraordinary circumstances existing in Northern Ireland. Furthermore, he noted that the Heath government's previous attempt to release detainees when direct rule had been introduced in March 1972 had failed to placate hardliners. The programme of releases aimed at restoring a sense of 'goodwill' had resulted in 562 releases in four months and few new detention orders. Far from abating, violence reached new heights during this time, with nearly 6,000 shooting incidents, 192 deaths caused by over 500 explosions and a particularly devastating campaign waged on 'Bloody Friday', 21 July 1972. In a single day seven soldiers and nine civilians were killed and more than 100 civilians injured in the bombing campaign levied by PIRA in Belfast. Thus, although the Gardiner Committee suggested that detention could not serve as a long-term policy, it viewed detention as an effective short-term method of containing violence.

The Gardiner Committee's focus on the possible statistical increase in violence in the event of an end to detention ignored the more devastating result of the detention system. Delays of up to six months in having cases reviewed, the admission of hearsay evidence, the inability of either the respondent or counsel to cross-examine witnesses, the lowered standard of proof, the executive/quasi-judicial manner of release and perceptions of detention as a political bargaining tool all placed the system in disrepute. In addition, the alienation of individuals interned under the system guaranteed that those held in prisons became increasingly sympathetic to anti-government paramilitary activity. The conditions in which the government held special category prisoners significantly alienated portions of the minority community. Further, not only was the system itself in disrepute, but, if indeed, as the government claimed, those in detention had committed violent acts in Northern Ireland, the suggestion that their release would be part of a political bargain meant that such individuals would escape the punishment given their counterparts who had been found guilty in a regular court. This tainted both the quasi-judicial process and the normal rule of law. The detention system also introduced an atmosphere of secrecy and distrust, with information gained from paid informers serving as 'evidence'. Employed during the 1922–72 period by the Unionist government and almost exclusively levied against the Catholic population, the operation of detention measures clearly brought the law into contempt. Members of Parliament highlighted the miserable failure of detention during discussions in the House of Commons. Even loyalists in Northern Ireland were appalled at the manner in which Britain conducted detention. The Revd Ian Paisley commented: 'the commissioners' hearings have become an absolute farce. It must be emphasised that there must be a respect for the law. If the judicial process is seen to have become the farce it now is, there can be no respect for the judicial system.'[32]

Gardiner proposed a number of changes with regard to the detention procedure to amend the more egregious areas of detention until such a time as the extraordinary power could be relinquished. To counter delays, Gardiner recommended that the law be changed with regard to the length of time before which respondents had to be brought before a commissioner. Under the 1973 EPA the Secretary of State had twenty-eight days to refer the case; this did not mean that the detainee would necessarily be brought before a commissioner in that time. The Gardiner Committee advocated a limit of seven days (from the date of the initial order) for written notice to be served upon a detainee, stating the nature of the terrorist activities being alleged against him. Within twenty-one days a Detention Advisory Board would have to submit a written report to the Secretary of State, after which the Secretary of State would have seven days to decide whether to make a confirmed custody order or to direct the detainee's release. Any non-compliance with these time limits would entitle the detainee to automatic release. In order to address the variance between commissioners in terms of quality and consistency of approach, the Committee recommended that the ultimate responsibility for detention should be that of the Secretary of State. It suggested that a seven member detention advisory board, uniformly drawn from the judiciary in England, Scotland and Wales, investigate the cases of individuals proposed for detention. Their inquiries were to be conducted in private, with witnesses questioned individually and without legal representation. The Committee suggested that the detainee should be given the right to make written representations to the Secretary of State, who then had the option to refer the case to the board for advice. The detainee would be given the right to appear before the board.

In contrast to the haphazard release of detainees, the Gardiner Committee advocated an ordered release policy, with a release advisory committee established to advise the Secretary of State. Gardiner asserted:

> Wherever possible detainees should not be returned to home circumstances in which they are likely to be intimidated or persuaded back into paramilitary activity by neighbourhood or home contacts . . . The Committee would have power to advise the Secretary of State to impose conditions on release, such as a requirement to move to a fresh area, with the sanction that the breaking of conditions might result in re-detention.[33]

The suggestion to remove an individual completely from his or her home community is alarming, particularly in the light of the failure of the government even to gain a conviction in a court of law. Gardiner openly acknowledged the falsity of detention as a judicial process: 'less regard should be paid to the past (*which is a matter of allegation, since [the detainee] has not been convicted in a court of law*) than to the probability of a stable and peaceful future'.[34] And yet, on the basis of allegation, the detainee could be completely separated from his or her community from that point onwards. With regard to the stigma attached to detention, it would be difficult to ensure the safety of detainees outside their home neighbourhood. Kevin McNamara, chair of the Labour Party's Northern Ireland Committee, supported this point in the House of Commons, stating: 'Once a detainee is released from detention he is a marked man. No matter how innocent he may have been, there is always the suspicion that he was involved on the side of either Republican or Protestant extremism. His life is in danger after he has been released'.[35] Further, the suggestion that an individual could be severed from his or her home ties suggests a completely uninformed perspective on Northern Irish culture. The history of Northern Ireland is one built on deep familial and community ties, and to suggest that such ties could be pre-emptorially severed by a quasi-judicial process imposed by England – and that such a move might in some way lessen paramilitary activity – reveals a deep ignorance of the society. The Gardiner Committee also suggested that even wider powers be granted to the detention board, as, 'The very success of the Committee will depend upon its ability to operate without a legal strait-jacket'.[36] Yet it is just such a 'straight jacket' that is required for the law to be held in any regard; discarding legality was akin to surrendering any legitimacy that might otherwise be maintained.

Labour partially incorporated Gardiner's suggestions into clause 9 of the 1975 EPA, which repealed schedule 1 of the principal Act and provided new detention arrangements. The new Act abolished commissioners and appeal hearings and established a new advisory procedure. The government sought to address the steady erosion of confidence in the quasi-judicial procedure and to eliminate delays. By eliminating the commissioners, no façade of 'quasi-legality' would be attempted. As Gerry Fitt, the Nationalist MP from Northern Ireland, commented: 'The commissioners gave the procedure a veneer of respectability, but it brought the whole judicial process into disrepute. There was no legal justification for it'.[37] Under the changes introduced by Labour, unless a detention case was referred to an advisor within fourteen days of the initial order, the order would cease to have effect. The new statute required an advisor to consider the case and to submit a report to the Secretary of State indicating whether the detention of the person was necessary for the protection of the public. On receipt of the report, the Secretary of State was only required to take it into consideration before making his decision. The changes fell short of Gardiner's recommendation that a detention advisory board should be created, consisting of seven members of the judiciary, three of whom would be assigned to each case. Viewing this demand on resources as impractical, the government amended the 1973 EPA to require a single advisor holding, or having held judicial office in the UK, or a barrister, advocate or solicitor of not less than ten years' standing. The government also rejected calls for a pre-release detention centre, claiming that the nature of detention required that the detainees not be informed of release beforehand. Merlyn Rees, Secretary of State for Northern Ireland, argued: 'It is not easy to meet the committee's proposal that a form of special assistance should be provided for the detainees on the lines of a family fund. This would mean, in effect, a scheme financed out of public funds which excluded other members of the community who have suffered from the effects of violence'.[38] The government also inserted an overall limit of seven weeks from the initial date of the interim custody order.[39] If a formal detention order had not been issued by this time, the individual had to be released. The responsibility for instigating a review of the detainee's case was transferred to the detainee, who had to request a twelve month review or additional reviews at periods of six months thereafter.[40]

The Gardiner Committee recommended that the government create a new offence with regard to disguise. It cited the 1974 Prevention of Terrorism (Temporary Provisions) Act as creating a precedent for disguises worn by members of proscribed associations, and suggested that a scheduled offence be created for donning any disguise, whether or not it be connected with a paramilitary organisation.[41] Labour adopted this recommendation under section 16 of the 1975 amending act, which made it an offence to adopt any disguise. 'Any person who in a public or open place or in the vicinity of a dwelling house . . . wears any form of disguise shall be liable on summary conviction to imprisonment for a term not exceeding six months or to a fine not exceeding £400 or both, provided always that it shall be a defence that there was just cause or reasonable excuse for such behaviour'.[42] While condemning the 'spurious glamour' granted terrorist organisations by the media, the Gardiner Committee stated: 'There can be no question of introducing censorship in a free society in time of peace'. However, the committee added: 'This does not mean that nothing can be done', and recommended that it be made a summary offence for newspaper editors, printers or publishers to publish anything purporting to be an advertisement for or on behalf of an illegal organisation.[43] The government followed this recommendation in section 12 of the amending act to the extent that it prohibited any advertisements soliciting or inviting readers to join proscribed organisations. The Gardiner Committee also recommend that the governors of the BBC and the Independent Broadcasting Authority re-examine their policies on contact with terrorist organisations and reporting of views and activities. There is substantial evidence that, under pressure from the government, this did occur.

With regard to powers of arrest both by police and military, Gardiner reported: 'Witnesses who appeared before us left us in no doubt that sections of the minority community, and some parts of the majority community, consider that the use made by the army of these powers is excessive and constitutes a real and continuing source of grievance and friction'.[44] The Committee alleged that powers were being used to harass certain individuals and groups, with the army operating primarily in the minority community. Boyle, Hadden and Hillyard suggest that the army's and police's use of emergency powers differed in their intentions and in the use made of the powers. Whereas the police conducted searches with an eye towards prosecution, the army's aim was to gather intelligence. This would explain, in part, the minority community's claims that the army was using its powers under the 1973 EPA for harassment.[45]

Although the Gardiner Report clearly stated that the powers of the security forces should be curtailed, the recommendations it made actually expanded the powers of the police and military. The Gardiner Committee viewed it as 'impracticable' to require that reasons for arrest actually be given at the time of arrest, or that reasonable suspicion should serve as a prerequisite of arrest. It advised expanding powers of search and seizure to include communications equipment and clarifying the ability of security forces to stop an individual solely to establish identity. Labour substantially followed these recommendations in sections 10 and 11 of the 1975 EPA.

Gardiner highlighted various studies underway to examine ways to deal with the creation and transport of incendiary and proxy bombs and urged that utmost attention be given to these additional reports. Although the Gardiner Committee stopped short of advocating the immediate introduction of identity cards, it suggested that the issue remain open for future consideration. Noting the widespread belief that complaints against members of the security force were not taken seriously, the Gardiner Committee asserted that they viewed complaints as fully investigated when made in the 'proper quarter'. The Committee suggested that the lack of public confidence in the police force derived not from any procedural problems, but to a system in which the police were responsible for investigating complaints against themselves. As a result, the Committee suggested the introduction of an independent means of investigating complaints against the RUC and consideration of new measures to handle complaints against the army. The Standing Advisory Commission for Human Rights (SACHR) echoed this advice, urging the creation of an independent means for investigating complaints against the police and army. In its first report SACHR wrote: 'It is essential not only that justice is done but that it is seen to be done'.[46] Simultaneously, in order to combat effectively the continued challenge posed to the security forces, the Gardiner Committee supported the expansion of the RUC Reserve and a strengthening of the Criminal Investigation Department of the RUC. Far from limiting the security forces, these measures enhanced their role in the province. This contradicted the Committee's stated recommendation that additional limits be placed on the forces themselves.

Following seventeen attacks on members of the Northern Irish judiciary, the British government took the opportunity provided by the introduction of amending legislation to try to protect those involved in the administration of justice. Section 20 of the 1973 EPA, itself based on Regulation 10 of the 1922 SPA, had made it an offence to collect information about the armed forces or police. Clause 13 of the 1975 EPA extended this provision to information about persons holding judicial office, court officers and prison officers. By the time the Baker Committee reported in 1984 (see subsequent text), every member of the judiciary had at one time or another been threatened by paramilitaries. In 1972 William Staunton RM was killed, and in 1974 Judge Conaghan and Martin McBirney RM were shot dead at their homes. The same year Judge McGrath was seriously injured in a shooting incident. Five years later Lord McDermott was injured in a bomb explosion, and in 1982 Lord Lowry, the Lord Chief Justice, was targeted in an attack. Also in 1982 Judge Watt's car was bombed. The following year Judge Doyle was shot, and on his appointment as a judge in January 1984 Carswell QC discovered a bomb strapped to his car.[47]

The Gardiner Committee also evaluated the prison system in Northern Ireland. From 727 inmates at the beginning of 1968, the prison population had nearly quadrupled to 2,848 as of 30 November 1974.[48] The situation was of sufficient concern to spur the Gardiner Committee to write: '[t]he present prison situation in Northern Ireland is so serious that the prison authorities in the remainder of the United Kingdom, despite their own recruitment difficulties, must make even greater efforts to help the Northern Ireland prisons'.[49] As a result of the sudden increase in numbers and the decision, following a hunger strike at Crumlin Road Prison in 1972, to introduce special category status for convicted prisoners, the prison authorities housed seventy-one per cent of the male prisoners in temporary compound prisons, rather than in conventional cellular accommodation. In practice, special category status meant that any convicted prisoner acceptable to a compound leader at the Maze or Magilligan, claiming political motivation and sentenced to more than nine months' imprisonment, was accorded special status. This designation allowed the prisoners to wear their own clothes and removed their work requirement. It accorded them more frequent visits, food parcels and a cash system at the prison canteen. Similar to detainees, the warders segregated special category prisoners according to paramilitary affiliation. As of 30 November 1974, 1,119 out of a total of 1,771 convicted prisoners fell into this category.[50]

The Gardiner Committee found the compounds unsatisfactory, primarily due to the loss of disciplinary control by the prison authorities and a lack of ability to institute rehabilitation programmes. The committee also pointed out that the granting of special status supported the assertion that political motivation separated the acts from ordinary criminal activity, in some sense justifying the crimes committed. Gardiner suggested that its continued operation created expectations of amnesty and was unfair to other non-politically motivated criminals who were subject to prison discipline. SACHR supported the Gardiner Committee's recommendation that the government end special category status at the earliest possible opportunity.

Although Labour had previously stated its intention to phase out special category status, the government claimed in response to Gardiner that such a move would be fruitless in the short term because of the shortage of space and the lack of more appropriate facilities. Rees commented: 'If we abolished special category status tomorrow the effect on the real situation in prison would be minimal. The prisoners would still be in the compounds. I would not announce a procedure which cannot be carried out'.[51] Labour announced that it planned to have 200 individual cells ready by November 1975 and a further 300 by October 1976.[52] Between January 1975 and the time the additional cells were to be completed in November, the number of special category prisoners increased from 1,092 to 1,465.[53] Of the 1,465 prisoners, approximately 900 were republican and around 600 loyalist.[54] Within four months of the debate on the 1975 Emergency Provisions Act, Labour announced that it would finally be ending special category status. The new conditional release scheme would begin on 1 March 1976 and be fully operational by 1 July 1976.[55] The scheme increased remission for sentences of one year or less from one-third to one-half.[56] Within a month, in his first speech as Secretary of State for Northern Ireland,

Mason confirmed that there would be no return to special category status.[57] The accelerated releases, in concert with the new prison building programme, made it possible for the government to end the special status. The prison system accommodated individuals sentenced for offences committed after 1 March 1976 in regular cells.

Following the Gardiner Report, Labour introduced two emergency statutory instruments: on 11 November the government enacted the 1975 Northern Ireland (Emergency Provisions) Regulation, which had the effect of requiring drivers to lock and immobilise unattended vehicles. Failure to do so became a criminal offence under the 1973 EPA and rendered the offender liable to imprisonment for up to six months, a fine of up to £400, or both. The opposition officially welcomed this instrument, although it was recognised in the debates that it would be extremely difficult, if not impossible, to enforce the regulation. The underlying principle justifying these restrictions on private property was not that the owner might endanger his or her property by not locking it, but that by being careless in the care of such property, he or she might endanger a third party. In the first ten months of 1975, 6,674 motor vehicles had been stolen. Of these, 273 were used for terrorist-type crimes.[58] This was an ongoing problem in the province. In 1972, 9,659 cars had been stolen; this decreased to 5,496 in 1973, but subsequently increased to 5,700 in 1974 and to 6,674 in first ten months of 1975.[59] The immediate effect of the statute was a sharp reduction in stolen cars and a drop in police hours required to record and trace such crimes.

The second instrument, the Northern Ireland (Emergency Provisions) Act 1973 (Amendment) Order 1977, provided that the new offences described became scheduled offences. It made provision, however, for the Attorney General to direct that an otherwise scheduled offence not be treated as scheduled with relation to a specific case. The 1977 order also closed a small loophole that had hitherto existed, ensuring that the concealment of a scheduled offence be considered a scheduled offence in and of itself. Not only did the government issue orders under the emergency measures, but it continually refined the ordinary statutes in an effort to counter Northern Irish terrorism. For instance, the Criminal Law (Amendment) (Northern Ireland) Order 1977 created new offences relating to hoax bombing and death threats by telephone. The maximum penalty for the first was five years imprisonment on indictment and for the second ten years. The order also provided for the penalty for the statutory offence of conspiracy to murder to be increased from ten years to life imprisonment and for offences under section 3(1) of the Explosive Substances Act 1883 from twenty years' imprisonment to life.

THE H-BLOCK CAMPAIGN

Significant repercussions accompanied the withdrawal of special category status. Republican prisoners in the Maze Prison swiftly responded by refusing to wear prison-issued clothing. Wrapped only in their bed covers, the initial 'blanket protest' quickly escalated. In the spring of 1978 some three hundred republican prisoners refused to wash, leave their cells or use the toilet facilities. Many prisoners covered the walls with their own excrement and destroyed cell furniture. This protest attracted worldwide publicity. In August 1978 the Catholic Archbishop of Armagh, Dr Tomás (later Cardinal) Ó Fiaich, urged the British government to do something about the 'inhuman conditions' in the prisons. Roy Mason, Secretary of State for Northern Ireland, declared that the government would not change its policy. Concern that the republican campaign was making some impact in the United States, in late 1978 and early 1979, Labour stepped up its publicity drive against the H-Block protesters, allowing journalists into the Maze to report on conditions in the prison, (although they were denied access to those protesting). In 1980 the situation reached a crisis as seven republican prisoners began a hunger strike to demand access to their own clothing, excuse from prison work, freedom of association, extra recreational facilities, more visits and letters, and restoration of remission lost on protest. The new Conservative Party's Secretary of State for Northern Ireland, Humphrey Atkins, insisted that no special category status would be reinstated, but that prison conditions could be addressed on humanitarian grounds. On 18 December 1980 the first strike ended with one prisoner, Sean McKenna, in a severely weakened condition. Discussion on prison reform indicated by Atkins and in clandestine contacts between the republican movement and the British government, however, broke down. On 1 March 1981, five years after the initial phasing out of special category status had begun, Bobby Sands began a second hunger strike. Joined by other prisoners, in the course of the campaign ten republicans died – seven from the Provisional IRA and three from the Irish National Liberation Army. Sands, elected MP for Fermanagh-South Tyrone in the April 1981 by-election, was the first to die. Some 70,000 people attended his funeral, the cortege stretching from Twinbrook, West Belfast, to Milltown Cemetery.

Thatcher remained adamant throughout the strikes that no concessions would be made. On Sands' election to the House of Commons, the Conservative government introduced the 1981 Representation of the People Bill to prevent Sands from taking his seat. In Thatcher's steadfast refusal to grant any political status to those convicted of terrorist offences, she received broad support in Britain. A MORI poll in May 1981 indicated that 92 per cent of English and Welsh voters rejected political status.[60]

The tense atmosphere and high levels of violence accompanying the H-Block campaign prompted the continuation of emergency measures. Fifteen RUC members, eight soldiers and seven UDR members died in bombings and shootings. An additional thirty-four civilians were killed, including seven who died as a result of injuries caused by plastic bullets fired by the police or army. In the Republic some two hundred people suffered injuries during a riot, when Gardaí prevented an H-Block march from passing the British Embassy.

When James Prior became Secretary of State for Northern Ireland in September 1981, his first commitment outside Government Offices was a visit to the Maze. The families of four hunger strikers had already intervened to save the prisoners' lives and the six remaining hunger strikers had been informed that their relatives would also intervene. This factor brought the hunger strikes to an end. Within three days of the last strikers accepting food, Prior announced that all prisoners would be allowed to wear their own clothes and that fifty per cent lost remission would be restored. Although it hinted at improvements in the remaining areas, the Conservative government refused directly to meet the other demands. It was not until 1990 that the government was to announce greater freedom of association for inmates. In the interim, the publicity generated by the H-block Campaign served to jump-start Sinn Féin's entry to the political arena.

The 1978 Northern Ireland (Emergency Provisions) Act

During this tumultuous time Britain retained emergency measures with minimal to no opposition in Parliament. The 1975 EPA remained in place until 1978 when the government passed the 1978 Northern Ireland (Emergency Provisions) Act.[61] This statute consolidated the 1973 EPA, the 1975 EPA and the 1974 Northern Ireland (Young Persons) Act. No inquiry precipitated the creation of the 1978 statute, and the House of Commons' committee and report stages of the Bill and the third reading were conducted without debate. What had been 'exceptional' in 1973 became perceived as 'normal' and less dramatic, and – albeit 'regretably' – 'necessary' in the continued tense climate of Northern Ireland. The 1978 statute included the same procedural arrangements as those required by the previous measures. The 1978 EPA became subject to biannual renewal and sections contained in the legislation could only lapse through order. Renewed at six month intervals, for nine years the 1978 EPA remained unamended.

This is not to say that there was no discussion outside of Parliament as to the effectiveness or appropriateness of the exceptional measures in place: SACHR did annually review the emergency legislation.[62] In its report for 1979 SACHR recommended the elimination of detention and the insertion of a clause specifically prohibiting the use of threats of violence during interrogation.[63] SACHR also suggested that section 2(2), which placed the onus for bail on the defendant rather than the prosecution, should lapse and be granted on the same basis as in non-scheduled offences. SACHR held that the existent provisions breached the principle of innocent until proven guilty. The significant difference between the number of arrests made and charges under sections 11 and 14 increased concern that the statute was being used to gather information and to harass the nationalist community. Nevertheless, SACHR did not have conclusive evidence to demonstrate this. In order to address this issue the Commission suggested that 'reasonable' suspicion be introduced into section 11. The powers had originally been invoked as a preliminary to detention. As detention had ended, the powers had become used as a means to question individuals on general affairs with a view towards re-arrest under section 13 with regard to a particular offence. Since particular offences were rarely mentioned in arrest under section 11, SACHR considered it crucial that the minimum requirement be for the officer to have reasonable grounds for suspecting the individual was involved in terrorist activity. The Commission also advocated that a test of reasonableness be inserted into section 14, concerning arrest by members of the army.

On 17 July 1980 Lord Elton announced that the Conservative government did not propose to renew the powers of internment. Five days later, Humphrey Atkins, who had been appointed Secretary of State for Northern Ireland in May 1979, expanded on this statement in the House of Commons, saying that the reintroduction of detention without trial, at that point, would only exacerbate the situation in Northern Ireland. He did maintain, however, that the government needed to retain the option in the event that the situation in the North changed. Even if the government allowed the powers to lapse, by section 33(3)(c) of the 1978 EPA, the Secretary of State had the authority to bring section 12 back into force for a period not exceeding six months. Although the order would immediately become operative, it would be subject to the affirmative resolution procedure.[64]

While the Conservative government allowed the provision for detention to lapse in 1980, the government refused to adopt the other changes advocated by SACHR. The Executive announced that the provisions for bail were instituted to meet an exceptional situation that still had not altered. Refusing to insert the prohibition on threats of violence as a check against the admissibility of coerced statements, Atkins claimed that the courts were already interpreting section 8(2) of the 1978 EPA in that manner.

During both the July and December 1980 renewal debates, Labour attempted to spur the government to initiate a judicial review of the 1978 EPA, arguing that five years had passed since Gardiner's Review.[65] The government rejected the proposal, stating that it would only create unrealistic expectations among those opposing the legislation.[66] The following year Labour again demanded an inquiry. J.D. Concannon stated: 'The Labour Party's view, as ratified at this year's conference, is that we should have an urgent and independent review of the Northern Ireland (Emergency Provisions) Act 1978 to ensure that the powers that it confers upon the security forces are consistent with the preservation of civil liberties and human rights, balanced by the maintenance of law and order'.[67] Labour simultaneously pursued the institution of a review for the 1976 PTA.[68] Areas that the party advocated be explored included the operation of the Diplock courts, procedures of arrest and interrogation, changes in the admissibility of evidence, the removal from the schedule of certain offences and the onus of proof relating to possession of firearms.

Finally, in June 1982 the Tories announced that an inquiry would be established. The government did not appoint someone to head the review until 1983 though, and it did not present the final report to Parliament until April 1984. The government claimed that the reason for the delay was that it was awaiting the results of the Jellicoe review. John Patten asserted: 'Unfortunately . . . [the EPA review] is closely linked with the review of the Prevention of Terrorism (Temporary Provisions) Act by Lord Jellicoe, which has taken a little longer than we expected. As the two reviews are closely linked, I believe that my Right Hon. Friend the Secretary of State was right to take long and deep soundings to find the right person to conduct the EPA review'.[69] Although the party abstained in the 1982 and 1983 renewal debates, Labour planned to oppose in 1984 the continuation of the 1978 EPA. Labour objected to the limited terms within which the inquiry had been forced to operate as well as the lack of urgency demonstrated by the government in arranging a debate on the resultant Baker Report. Labour also contended that the government had not given due consideration to the inquiry's recommendations, particularly with regard to bail and removal from the schedule.[70]

THE SUPERGRASS SYSTEM

Although not directly codified in emergency legislation, the supergrass system that operated in the early 1980s should be mentioned as a complement to, and as a result of, emergency legislation introduced to counter Northern Irish political violence. As was already discussed, following the end of detention without trial, increased pressure was placed on the security forces to secure convictions. The British government directed alterations in the rules governing the admission of evidence and the elimination of the jury system towards this end. In the aftermath of the Bennett Committee Report, however, the extraction of confessions became more difficult.[71] Roy Mason, Secretary of State for Northern Ireland, had established the three person committee to examine the interrogation procedures used by the RUC and the operation of the complaints procedure in Northern Ireland. His decision to establish the inquiry followed the publication of an official Amnesty International inquiry into seventy-eight complaints of ill-treatment by individuals held at Castlereagh. Lead by Judge Harry Bennett, QC, and English Crown Court Judge, the Committee reported in 1979. It went outside its terms of reference to cite cases where medical evidence had ascertained that individuals had sustained injuries while in police custody. The Labour government accepted two of the main recommendations of the Bennett Committee – the installation of closed-circuit TV in interview rooms and access to a solicitor. Nevertheless, one government minister emphasised in Parliament that only fifteen cases out of approximately 3,000 individuals detained from 1977 to 1978 had reflected the presence of non-self-inflicted injury. Controversy surrounded the report, on the publication of which two doctors involved at the interrogation centres made public their concerns about the ill-treatment of prisoners.

Following the Bennett Report, as Dermot Walsh noted: 'the policy of securing convictions on confession alone consequently lost the viability it once had, a fact which seems to have prompted the security forces to concentrate their efforts on enlisting the services of informers'.[72] The RUC Chief Constable, John Hermon, viewed the use of 'converted terrorists' as an entirely justified way to bring paramilitaries to book. Both the police force and the Conservative government in Britain defended the use of accomplice evidence as well-established in English law. The aim of the introducing informers on a widespread basis and creating the supergrass system was to reduce the level of violence in the province by initiating prosecutions against large numbers of individuals.

Although there had been about four paramilitary supergrasses in the years leading up to 1981,[73] from the arrest of Christopher Black, a slew of similar trials ensued. November 1981 to November 1983 witnessed at least seven loyalist and eighteen republican supergrasses resulting in almost 600 individuals being arrested and charged with terrorist offences in Northern Ireland.[74] A number of those providing 'evidence' retracted their statements before the trials began.[75] The supergrass system garnered minimal support in the nationalist community and came under direct attack by the Irish government and British Labour politicians. It also attracted significant criticism from lawyers in Northern Ireland, particularly when the prosecution resorted to a Bill of Indictment to avoid witnesses having to give evidence at both the preliminary hearings and the actual trials. Those attacking the use of supergrasses accused the RUC of using blackmail and intimidation and offering large sums of money to encourage individuals to speak out in court against 'fellow terrorists'. The RUC granted police protection, immunity from prosecution and the means to start a new life outside of Northern Ireland to a number of those who agreed to testify.

The use of supergrasses swiftly declined as a result of their minimal impact on levels of violence, a more critical stance by the judiciary and recognition that the use of the trials was bringing the law further into disrepute.[76] In 1986 the Court of Appeal reversed the convictions of eighteen individuals jailed on the word of the Provisional IRA supergrass Christopher Black. Peter Archer, Labour front-bench spokesman on Northern Ireland, announced that this decision represented the 'last nail in the coffin' of a discredited system.[77] From the withdrawal of statements by thirteen of the supergrasses in 1983 – with the help of whom some 300 people had been charged – emphasis returned to emergency legislation to counter provincial violence. It is not the intent of this book to delve into these matters in great detail; extensive studies on the operation of the supergrass system have been conducted elsewhere.[78] In the end such trials served as a temporary complement to emergency measures introduced by Westminster to counter Northern Irish political violence.

BAKER

Returning to the review initiated by the government in 1983, the resultant Baker Committee noted that there was something incongruous about an 'emergency' lasting for nearly twenty years. Nevertheless, it concluded that 'any provision of the EPA which may save even one life or bring even one guilty terrorist to conviction and sentence should be retained until the paramilitary forces foreswear terrorism unless there is a powerful convincing reason for repeal or amendment'.[79] Baker viewed the emergency measures as a mechanism by which the individuals and their property could be protected. The aim of the EPA was supported by appeal to this principle. Baker recommended that the Act's title be changed to 'The Protection of the Peoples Act' – because that is 'what it really is'.[80] Although advocating some adjustments, Baker found the vast majority of provisions under the 1978 EPA to be necessary in the fight against terrorism. The comprehensive report examined preliminary trial, procedures for bail, provisions relating to young persons, Diplock courts and their mode of trial, the appeals process, provisions governing accomplices, delays in the trial process, the admission of evidence, detention powers, contributions to and concealment of terrorists, powers of arrest, search and seizure, police complaints procedures, army arrest powers, powers of entry and search, compensation, powers to stop and question, powers of interference with rights of property and highways, proscribed organisations, scheduled offences, public order powers, definitions, the duration of the 1978 EPA and renewal requirements, statistics relating to the operation of the legislation, the current state of the prison system and various sentences imposed as a result of convictions under the Act. While this chapter does not discuss Baker's findings and his reasoning in support of his recommendations in each one of these areas, it highlights some of the more important changes advocated by the committee.[81]

Overall, the suggestions put forth reflected the gradual tightening of emergency measures to try to project a more regular or normal standard of legislation. Throughout this period there were numerous calls in the House of Commons for a tightening of emergency measures. For instance, in June 1978 McNair-Wilson commented:

> I accept that there are special circumstances in Northern Ireland where violence is at a level which can be described only as unreasonably high and where the threat of violence is ever present. Any further erosion of the usual safeguards of the law is fraught with danger. That is the check on any suggestion that I might make that these powers should be amended. At the same time, I believe that we must consider whether there are amendments that could be made which would catch that special category of people who continue to dominate the violence in Northern Ireland.[82]

This reflected the trend, begun by the Diplock Commission, at pursuing convictions through the court system. This tendency had been illustrated by Labour's policy of criminalisation. Roy Mason, Secretary of State for Northern Ireland commented in 1978: 'I am committed to the principle of fair and effective enforcement of the law by bringing terrorists to justice through the courts. This principle has been the firm foundation of our security effort since it was put forward by the Ministerial Committee on Law and Order in Northern Ireland which reported in the middle of 1976'.[83] The British government expected the 'terrorist threat' to continue for some time. The 15 December 1978 Glover Report, conducted by the Director General Ordinance Services at the Army School of Ammunity, analysed future terrorist trends in Northern Ireland. It suggested, 'Only . . . continued direct rule offers any real prospect of political calm and hence waning support for the terrorist during the next five years. Under any other scenario republican fears of a Protestant ascendancy being re-established would enable the Provisional Irish Republican Army to pose as the defenders of the minority interest'.[84] The Glover Report continued: 'there is a strata of intelligent, astute and experienced terrorists who provide the backbone of the organisation'. It concluded:

> Our evidence of the calibre of rank and file terrorists does not support the view that they are merely mindless hooligans drawn from the unemployed and unemployable. PIRA now trains and uses its members with some care. The Active Service Units . . . are for the most part manned by terrorists tempered by up to ten years of operational experience . . . The mature terrorists, including for instance the leading bomb makers, are usually sufficiently cunning to avoid arrest. They are continually learning from mistakes and developing their expertise. We can therefore expect to see increased professionalism and the greater exploitation of modern technology for terrorist purposes.[85]

The British government sought to address this threat by incarcerating paramilitary members. Owing to the increasing 'professionalism' of the paramilitaries, however, the legal rules would have to be somewhat altered. The Conservative Party continued this strategy into the 1980s. As Humphrey Atkins, the Secretary of State for Northern Ireland, commented in 1980: 'The Government's policy for the elimination of terrorism remains the restoration of normal policing throughout Northern Ireland and the arrest, preferring of charges, and conviction, on proven evidence, by the courts of those who commit criminal acts'.[86]

For example, with regard to bail, like the SACHR, the Baker Commission advocated that section 2(2) of the 1978 EPA be amended in order to shift the initial onus for opposing bail to the prosecution. 'It is a fundamental principle of English Law and also a minimum requirement of justice under the European Convention of Human Rights that an accused person is presumed innocent until proven guilty. Accordingly there must be a presumption in favour of bail and in favour of the liberty of the subject. We believe this subsection destroys the presumption of innocence.' The National Council for Civil Liberties presented this argument both to Gardiner and to Baker. Hitherto the responsibility rested on the defence to demonstrate either that there would be no danger posed to the public by granting bail to the defendant, or that to keep the individual in custody would create undue hardship. Simultaneously, also with regard to bail, Baker recommended that the RUC be added to the armed forces with regard to being allowed to be remanded by a resident magistrate on bail into police custody. Gardiner had considered the same recommendation but rejected it on the grounds that the police did not have the resources to arrange for one of their own members to be held in safe custody during remand, thus such a change would result in (the appearance at least of) discriminatory treatment. However, Baker considered that the risk to the police and their families while held on remand at Crumlin Road Prison outweighed the perceived discrimination and supported including the RUC in the exemptive measure. In addition, Baker recommended that the Supreme Court judge or trial judge retain the sole powers to grant bail in scheduled cases, unless the Crown specifically consented to an application to the resident magistrate. The report also suggested that the phrase included as section 2(4) of the 1978 EPA, which provided that 'nothing in this section shall prejudice any right of appeal against the refusal of a judge to grant bail', be dropped from the statute, as no appeal was possible anyway, short of the introduction of further evidence for consideration. Finally, Baker advocated that a further study be instigated to enable courts to remand for twenty-eight to thirty days in the case of scheduled offences, rather than to require an individual to appear before a resident magistrate every seven days, as was required by the 1978 EPA. The re-drafting of section 2(2) was to be completed in accordance with the 1976 Bail Act, by virtue of which the accused was to be granted bail unless the judge was satisfied that the defendant would not meet particular conditions.

Although Baker considered various options for the mode of trial, including a return to jury trial, or a court composed of three judges, two judges, or a judge with assessors or resident magistrates, he concluded that in the light of the continuing threat to jurists and the limited strength of the Northern Ireland Bar the mode of trial be left unchanged. In order to reduce the growing pressure on Diplock courts, however, Baker suggested that all scheduled offences triable summarily or that offences carrying a maximum sentence of imprisonment of five years or less be capable of being certified out. Furthermore, kidnapping, false imprisonment, robbery and aggravated burglary should be capable of being removed from the schedule. The report suggested that the Director of Public Prosecutions in Northern Ireland be granted the authority to certify out any of the above cases. This would have the added advantage of extending jury trial to a greater number of offences and returning the province closer to a situation of normality. The 1978 EPA's requirement that all trials on indictment of a scheduled offence be held only at the Belfast City Commission provided additional stress on the system. Concluding that the court accommodation in Belfast was inadequate for the present needs, Baker suggested that section 6(1) of the Act be amended to arrange for the holding of such proceedings in other venues. Further addressing the significant amount of time elapsing between charge and committal to trial, he suggested that any prisoner held in custody twelve months or longer be granted bail without surety.

On the subject of the admissibility of evidence, Baker recommended that section 8 of the 1978 EPA be amended to disallow statements derived where the 'threat of violence' or the 'threat of intimidation' had been used.[87] The government since 9 February 1975 had issued no detention order. Although the report recognised that the situation in the North could change at any time, it recommended that section 12 be repealed. The Baker Committee suggested that the different powers of arrest in the 1978 EPA and the 1976 Prevention of Terrorism (Temporary Provisions) Act (PTA)[88] be standardised and preferably, incorporated into one act designed to address terrorism. Where the 1978 EPA allowed for an initial period of detention for seventy-two hours, the 1976 PTA permitted only a forty-eight hour period, with the option of extending it up to seven days. Baker opted for a blend of the two, with a forty-eight hour initial period and the option of extension. He suggested that this change either be incorporated into a new EPA or be built into a new act consolidating arrest powers under the 1978 EPA and 1976 PTA. A second inconsistency between the two statutes lay in the latter's use of 'reasonable suspicion' to effect arrest. In order to standardise the two measures, Baker advocated the insertion of 'reasonable suspicion' into sections 11(1) and 13(1) of the 1978 EPA, governing police powers of arrest without warrant and section 14(1) and 14(3)(b), empowering the military to arrest without warrant and enter and search premises in the process of effecting arrest. Baker also suggested that 'reasonably suspected' be substituted for 'suspected' in section 15(2) of the 1978 EPA, authorising any member of HM Forces on duty or any constable authorised by an officer of the RUC to enter any dwelling-house to search for munitions or transmitters. He advocated that the security forces be empowered to detain any or all of the occupants in a premise during the exercise of such searches and suggested that the duration of the search should be limited to four hours or less.

In addition to five of the original six organisations banned under the 1973 EPA, by 1984 the British government had added the Red Hand Commandos, the Ulster Freedom Fighters and the Irish National Liberation Army (INLA) to the list.[89] Margaret Thatcher, the British Prime Minister, banned the INLA on 3 July 1979 in direct response to Airey Neave's murder. Four months earlier the INLA claimed responsibility for a car bomb that killed Neave as he drove out of the House of Commons car park. The mastermind behind Thatcher's bid for Conservative leader and director of her private office from 1975, Neave's death signalled a hardening in Thatcher's policy towards Northern Ireland and the entrenchment of Conservative strategy for nearly a decade. The provisions banning these groups had been used in a number of prosecutions under the 1978 EPA. 1979 witnessed ninety-eight prosecutions under section 21. In 1980 there were 107, in 1981 there were seventy-one, in 1982 there were 137 and in 1983 there were 108.[90] The primary aim of proscription, however, was to express the outrage of the majority of citizens, 'at the barbarous acts of these organisations, and at the revolting glee with which they claim responsibility for the organisation, usually with personal anonymity, together with their public displays in particular areas'.[91] Outlawing such associations was as much of importance in trying to avert public outrage being expressed through public disorder as in symbolically allowing the majority to express moral condemnation of the activities of the organisations. This use of emergency measures as a way to 'send a message' to those using violence continued to characterise Westminster's treatment of Northern Irish violence. Both in the North and in Great Britain, the start of debates on emergency measures often began with a litany of the atrocities that had recently occurred. The legislation, particularly the PTA (to be discussed in the next chapter), bore a representational or moral import, that terrorism was not to be tolerated and that individuals had the right not to be confronted with offensive reminders of the terrorist organisations. Proscription served particularly in this way.

Baker attacked the insertion of 'for political ends' in the definition of terrorism, arguing, quite rightly, that this denied the efforts of the government to present terrorist violence as purely criminal. As a result, the report recommended that more thought be given to standardising a definition for use in both the EPA and the PTA that ignored the motivation of the crime and focused on the means itself. Finally, with regard to the duration of the statute, similar to Jellicoe's recommendations for the Prevention of Terrorism Act, (see discussion, chapter five), Baker suggested that the measure be subject to renewal every twelve months with a maximum duration of five years. In addition, the report advocated that quarterly statistics be published on the operation of the 1978 Act, as were issued at the time for its Prevention of Terrorism counterpart.

Parliament debated the Baker Report on 20 December 1984, simultaneously with consideration of the renewal of the 1978 EPA.[92] The Conservative government received the report in a favourable manner, while remaining sceptical about the need to implement the proposed bail reforms, the exclusion of threats of violence, the rationalisation of police arrest powers and the increased scope for the removal from the schedule of offences. Although Labour abstained the previous year in the 1978 EPA renewal debates, in 1984 the party divided the House over the government's delay in presenting the Baker Report for debate. Peter Archer expressed the Opposition's irritation:

> On 22 July 1982, the then Secretary of State finally responded to [calls for a review of the 1978 EPA] with an announcement that there was to be a review. There was a further nine-month delay before he announced who was to undertake it. Then the general election caused a further delay . . . We tried to exercise patience. We did not expect a debate at once. We hoped that the Government would read the report and consider it carefully, but as month succeeded month we began to wonder whether perhaps the Government were slow readers.[93]

Other Labour MPs expressed dissatisfaction with both the Conservative government's seeming reluctance to initiate a review of the Act as well as more substantive issues, such as the length of remand and declining acquittal rate in Diplock courts. Approximately 90 per cent of those arrested under the EPA between January and October 1980 had been released without charge. Labour MPs expressed concern that this served to alienate the very people whom the government was trying to 'win over'. Concerning the possible 'case hardening' of Diplock judges, MPs noted in the Commons that in 1973 judges acquitted 57 per cent of those involved in contested cases. In 1976 the number decreased to 35 per cent, and by 1981 it had reached 33 per cent.[94] Labour also expressed dissatisfaction at the use of the EPA as a means to gather information. Stuart Bell, Labour spokesman on Northern Ireland from 1984 to 1987, noted: '72 per cent of the Cobden sample of people held under the emergency legislation in 1981 were not questioned about any specific offence. A high percentage were clearly not suspected of involvement in any specific offence, but were detained solely for the purpose of information gathering'.[95] Labour also objected to uncorroborated accomplice evidence being employed in the supergrass trials. Archer stated: 'A further matter in which we have found ourselves unable to share Sir George's conclusions relates to the supergrass trials . . . it has caused great anxiety, and may indeed be the most important single factor in the widespread feeling of frustration and dissatisfaction . . . with the administration of justice in Northern Ireland'.[96] Other parties in the House of Commons shared the Opposition's concerns.[97] Labour threatened to oppose the renewal of the 1978 EPA again, unless the government took the Baker Report into consideration and returned to the House with proposals for new legislation.

The Tory government responded to Labour's concerns by announcing in June 1985 that a new act would be drafted. Prior to the introduction of the new bill in 1987, the government instituted minor changes through the Northern Ireland (Emergency Provisions) Act 1978, (Amendment) Order 1985.[98] This instrument gave the Attorney General greater discretion to certify out particular cases from being considered scheduled offences. The order applied only to blackmail, kidnapping, false imprisonment and offences carrying less than a five year penalty. The government rejected Baker's proposal to certify out robbery or aggravated burglary and determined that as a result of the Attorney General's accountability to the House of Commons, the ability to remove from the schedule certain cases should not be extended to the Director of Public Prosecutions. The government also rejected Baker's suggestion that new measures provide for a jury to be discharged in a case that had been certified out, in the event that the judge believed harassment or intimidation to be at work. This was seen as risking bringing the courts into disrepute.

Anglo-Irish Relations

In the midst of the hunger strikes of the early 1980s, a meeting between the British Prime Minister, Margaret Thatcher, and the Taoiseach of the Irish Republic, Charles Haughey, precipitated a structure for Anglo-Irish consultations. The two leaders commissioned joint studies on citizenship rights, security matters, economic cooperation, possible new institutional structures and measures to encourage mutual understanding.[99] The report issued the following year recommended the possible establishment of four tiers of institutional cooperation: a ministerial, Anglo-Irish

Intergovernmental Council; a parliamentary tier; an advisory committee; and an Anglo-Irish Encounter Organisation. Thatcher and Garrett FitzGerald, Haughey's successor, endorsed the report, and the two governments quickly established the Anglo-Irish Intergovernmental Council. July 1983 witnessed the further establishment of the Encounter Organisation to plan high-level Anglo-Irish conferences.

While Britain was making these efforts to bridge relations with the Republic of Ireland, it simultaneously pursued a devolved assembly in Northern Ireland. In November 1979 Atkins proposed that the four main constitutionalist parties meet to consider ways in which an elected assembly in the province could be granted limited powers.[100] The Democratic Unionist Party, Alliance Party and SDLP agreed to participate in the discussions, in the light of which the government published a White paper in July 1980.[101] No agreement was reached during the discussions. However, in April 1982 the Conservative government published a third White Paper: *Northern Ireland: a framework for devolution*, which proposed a new seventy-eight member assembly elected by single transferable vote.[102] The subsequent 1982 Northern Ireland Act provided for the establishment of a new assembly, as outlined in the White Paper. SDLP members refused to take their seats in the assembly, on the grounds that no Irish dimension had been enshrined in the Act in any concrete way. Sinn Féin also refused to take their seats, and the Ulster Unionists withdrew in November 1983, following a terrorist attack on a church in County Armagh in which three people had been killed. Although the Ulster Unionists returned in May 1984, the boycotts resulted in the assembly being unable to assume the breadth of powers envisaged in the 1982 Act. In order to address the 'Irish dimension' and in response to Sinn Féin's electoral success following the Hunger Strikes, in May 1983 Fianna Fáil, Fine Gael, the Labour party and the SDLP launched the New Ireland Forum. Although participation was open to 'all democratic parties which reject violence and which have members elected or appointed to either House of the Oireachtas or the Northern Ireland Assembly', in practice only nationalist parties participated. Discussion centred on three proposals: joint sovereignty between Britain and the Republic over Northern Ireland, Federation, with subsidiary regional parliaments in Belfast and Dublin, and a unitary State, with a revised and liberalised constitution. Britain vociferously rejected each proposal, with Thatcher's infamous response to each alternative: 'Out . . . out . . . out!'

In some measure a response to the Irish government's open disapproval of Britain's plans for rolling devolution, and following on the New Ireland Forum, the British and Irish governments engaged in extensive confidential negotiations. These meetings resulted in 1985 with the signing of the Anglo-Irish Agreement. By far the most significant development in Anglo-Irish relations since 1920, this Agreement was to spur the peace process and lay the groundwork for the acceleration of talks in the mid to late 1990s. In the Anglo-Irish Agreement the two governments pledged themselves to a closer working relationship with regard to the affairs of Northern Ireland. The two countries lodged the document with the United Nations. The joint communiqué issued following the signing stated as the Anlgo-Irish Agreement's aims: to promote peace and stability in the North, to reconcile the two traditions in Ireland, and to create a new climate of friendship and cooperation in combating terrorism. In the last capacity, the Anglo-Irish Agreement can be seen as a complement to – and a justification of – emergency measures introduced by Westminster. The 1973 EPA had had only limited affect: violence, albeit on a lesser scale than in 1972, still existed in Northern Ireland. The British government initiated the Anlgo-Irish Agreement in the midst of the H-Block campaign, the strikes themselves a potent sign that the republican menace remained unassuaged. By enlisting the help of the Republic Britain formally recognised the limits on its attempt to resolve the conflict alone. An 'international', political process was necessary. In focusing the Anglo-Irish Agreement on combatting terrorism in the North, Britain simultaneously sought to legitimate its own efforts to introduce stringent counter-terrorist measures. The involvement of the Republic would not be to bolster the republican movement in the North, but rather to validate the nationalist tradition while rejecting the use of violence on the part of the paramilitaries. In this way the Anglo-Irish Agreement can be seen as a complement to the extensive web of emergency powers that had been continued by the British government from unionist administration of the North.

The most significant feature of the Anglo-Irish Agreement lay in the creation of a joint ministerial conference of British and Irish Ministers. Backed by a permanent secretariat at Maryfield, close to Stormont, this body was to monitor political, security, legal and other issues of concern to the nationalist minority. Although this body was not formally a joint authority, as it reserved for Britain the final say regarding the affairs of Northern Ireland, it represented a significant change in British attitude. Thatcher's forcible claims in 1982 that her government lay under no obligation to consult the Irish Republic on matters affecting Northern Ireland stood in stark contrast to the establishment of the Inter-governmental Conference and the reservations made in the Anglo-Irish Agreement that the Republic could put forward proposals on behalf of the minority where major legislation or policy was involved (for example, the protection of human rights, the prevention of discrimination in areas such as cultural heritage, electoral arrangements, flags and emblems, the avoidance of social and economic discrimination and a possible bill of rights). In this manner, the Anglo-Irish Agreement actually provided for the Republic to make representations on areas that had been deeply impacted by the operations of emergency legislation during the reign of the Northern Parliament. As was discussed in chapter two, the 1922–43 Special Powers Act had been exercised in a manner that suspended the civil liberties of the minority population. Measures preventing gatherings, assemblies and processions, the publication of nationalist propaganda, the flying of the Tricolour, the wearing of the Easter Lily and the singing of a soldier's song clearly fell within the new remit of the Southern government. Likewise, discrimination in electoral arrangements, introduced as part of the emergency climate of the 1920s could be addressed by the South. Ironically, while the Anglo-Irish Agreement served to validate emergency law in its rejection of terrorism and enlistment of the Republic to defeat political violence in the North, if it hadn't been for the existence of such drastic measures in the past, it is open to question whether either the emergency legislation or the introduction of the Republic in a role of championing the nationalist cause would even be necessary.

Predictably, within Northern Ireland nationalists welcomed the Anglo-Irish Agreement. Equally foreseeable, unionists protested the role given to the Republic in the internal affairs of Northern Ireland. Mass demonstrations, the simultaneous resignation of fifteen Members of Parliament, and subsequent by-elections resulted. In February 1987 unionists presented a 400,000 signature petition to the British government calling for a referendum on the Agreement. The Thatcher government remained steadfast. With a second UWC-style strike failing to get off the ground, the Anglo-Irish Agreement stood. Precedent was set for Irish involvement in the affairs of Northern Ireland. Britain enlisted the help of the Irish government to try to defeat terrorism and end Northern Irish political violence. Together with strict emergency measures, the government hoped to open up a way to discussions that would accommodate both communities in Northern Ireland. In the meantime, security measures could be addressed north and south of the border in the form of counter-terrorist legislation.

THE 1987 NORTHERN IRELAND (EMERGENCY PROVISIONS) ACT

On 16 December 1986 Tom King, Secretary of State for Northern Ireland from 1985 to 1989, presented the Northern Ireland (Emergency

Provisions) Bill to Parliament for its second reading. The new statute implemented a number of Baker's recommendations: Part I set a five year maximum life on the Act, subject to annual renewal. The first deadline was set for 22 March 1988, to coincide with that of the 1984 Prevention of Terrorism (Temporary Provisions) Act. This enabled Parliament 'to consider, at roughly the same time, all the emergency legislation that applies in Northern Ireland and help to consider the Prevention of Terrorism Act in its full United Kingdom context'.[103] As was previously mentioned, SACHR had suggested this alteration. Many of the additional changes introduced by the Conservative's mitigated the more extreme aspects of the 1978 EPA: section 1 shifted the responsibility for bail applications concerning scheduled offences from the defence to the prosecution. The power to certify out particular cases remained in the hands of the Attorney General, however, and applied only to those offences detailed in the 1986 order. The government rejected Baker's suggestion that a right to bail be granted after twelve months' remand, but in an effort to try to speed up the trial process, the government amended section 6 of the 1978 EPA to permit trials of scheduled offences to be held at Crown courts outside Belfast. Likewise, the government altered section 5A to empower the Secretary of State to set limits on the number of days allotted to preliminary proceedings.[104] Section 4 included the threat of violence, as well as violence itself, as a basis for declaring a statement inadmissible. The 1987 EPA also reduced the initial period of detention from seventy-two hours to forty-eight hours and required that subsequent applications for extension of detention detail the reason for the time period, up to five days, requested. The new statute guaranteed right of access to a solicitor within forty-eight hours of arrest, as well as the right of the individual in custody to inform someone of his or her whereabouts.[105] These safeguards went beyond those provided to individuals detained under ordinary law. Section 23 included 'reasonable' suspicion for powers of search and arrest where none previously had been required.[106] The government instituted this last change to enable the UK to meet the requirements laid out by Article 5(1)(c) of the European Convention for Human Rights, which required reasonable suspicion to enact a lawful arrest.[107]

Although these alterations indicated a narrowing of the gap between ordinary law and emergency provisions, the government also introduced some more stringent measures. Section 2 increased the maximum period for the holding of persons remanded into custody before appearing in front of a judge, from seven to twenty-eight days. Section 6 included the search for specialised receivers as sufficient reason for security forces to enter and search dwellings and premises and to stop and search vehicles without a warrant. Sections 7 and 9 extended provisions of the PTA to Northern Ireland relating to proscription that previously only applied to Great Britain. It became an offence to arrange or to assist in arranging a meeting to support a proscribed organisation, or to behave in a public place in a manner indicating support for a proscribed organisation. The statute introduced new certification requirements for security services 'to prevent persons or companies from operating to the benefit of paramilitary organisations under the guise of offering private security guard services'.[108] The government included this clause in the first of many subsequent efforts to address paramilitary protection rackets posing as security firms. The government also extended the category of individuals against whom it was unlawful to collect information, to include present and former elected representatives in Northern Ireland.[109] With only slight alterations, the legislation maintained the ability to close roads and the provisions regarding rights of compensation.[110] The government also maintained various other provisions, such as the police power to enter and search premises to arrest suspected terrorists. King stated that powers of detention would not be relinquished. His rationale reflected the same reasons presented in 1980: should the powers be required, the Secretary of State would be in a position to take immediate action. In its thirteenth annual report SACHR expressed discontent that the government was retaining powers of detention. SACHR also suggested that arrest powers should be limited to reasonable suspicion of involvement in a scheduled offence, that the Attorney General be allowed to certify out any scheduled offence on a case by case basis, and that emergency powers should be consolidated into a single act.[111] In accordance with Baker's recommendations, the government agreed to establish an annual, independent review of the operation of the 1987 EPA, as had been in existence since 1985 for the 1984 PTA.

SUPPLEMENTARY PROVISIONS

Following the enactment of the 1987 EPA, in October 1988 Douglas Hurd, Home Secretary and previously Northern Ireland Secretary of State, issued a broadcast ban on any individual indicating support for Northern Irish paramilitary organisations. The government lifted the ban during the election campaigns and for parliamentary proceedings. Precipitating the introduction of the ban were incidents of violence and IRA publicity. Sir Kenneth Bloomfield served as the head of the Northern

Ireland Civil Service from 1984 to 1991. Immediately following an IRA bombing of his home, Gerry Adams appeared on BBC Radio Ulster's 'Talkback' programme. Hurd sent a notice on the 19th of the month to the BBC and IBA requiring them to abstain from broadcasting any statements made by proscribed organisations, by representatives of Sinn Féin, Republican Sinn Féin, the Ulster Defence Association or by any individual whose statements supported or invited support for these associations. His missive read:

1. In pursuance of section 29(3) of the Broadcasting Act 1981, I hereby require the Independent Broadcasting Authority to refrain from broadcasting any matter which consists of or includes: any words spoken, whether in the course of an interview or discussion or otherwise, by a person who appears or is heard on the programme in which the matter is broadcast where – (a) the person speaking the words represents or purports to represent an organisation specified in paragraph 2 below, or (b) the words support or solicit or invite support for such an organisation, other than any matter specified in paragraph 3 below.

2. The organisations referred to in paragraph 1 above are – (a) any organisation which is for the time being a proscribed organisation for the purposes of the Prevention of Terrorism (Temporary Provisions) Act 1984 or the Northern Ireland (Emergency Provisions) Act 1978; and (b) Sinn Féin, Republican Sinn Féin and the Ulster Defence Association.[112]

The government's logic was similar to that by which it had banned the organisations in the first place – statements made by paramilitaries were offensive to viewers. Perhaps of more serious concern was the government's second worry, that paramilitaries were able to use the media to influence the public and, in particular, to spread fear in the population. Labour opposed the broadcasting ban, asserting that 'causing offence' was not enough to justify its enactment. This clearly contradicted Labour's previous claim in 1974 that proscription was justified on precisely these grounds. Labour rightly suggested in 1988, however, that such a ban would be a tremendous propaganda coup for the paramilitaries. Far from damaging their campaign, it would be seen as an oppressive measure on the part of the State. The prohibition applied to all statements from individuals associated with the named organisation and not only to statements relating to terrorism. The ban came under considerable fire from the media, which, in the event, opted to use a voice-over to convey the sentiments of the individuals on whom the ban had been placed.

Hurd followed this ban with the introduction of new official secrets' legislation aimed at addressing the situation in Northern Ireland. For the first time the government formally acknowledged MI5's role in Northern Ireland. The legislation empowered the Northern Ireland Secretary of State to authorise specific burglaries or bugging by MI5 agents. Placing the security services on a statutory basis for the first time, the legislation also aligned the Secretary of State's powers with those of the Home Secretary. This clearly indicated a growing importance of MI5 in counter-terrorist operations. Although the statute established a special tribunal to deal with complaints about MI5 behaviour, it specifically stated: 'no entry on, or interference with, property shall be unlawful if it is authorised by a warrant issued by the Secretary of State'. The break-ins were to be directed towards securing information 'likely to be of sub-stantial value' in helping MI5 to discharge any of its functions. Critics of the legislation focused on the virtual impossibility of lodging a successful complaint, as it would be an offence under the statute for any MI5 officer or government official to reveal anything about the operation of the organisation.[113]

In the same year that Hurd enacted the media ban and together with formal recognition of the secret services counter-terrorist activities in Northern Ireland and Great Britain, the Conservative government introduced restrictions on the suspect's right to silence. This suggestion had been raised previously by Ian Paisley in the House of Commons: '. . . another step must be taken. Can a person remain silent when it is put to him in a court of law "Are you or are you not a member" of a particular proscribed organisation? If he is not prepared to answer, that should be part of the case against him. My legal friends tell me that that would be a possible way of making such a law effectual'.[114] A narrow manifestation of the common law principle that no individual should be required to incriminate him or herself, the right to silence in criminal proceedings generally referred to the rule that if a person, while being interrogated, omitted to mention a particular fact that might have exculpated them, but subsequently brought this fact up at the trial, the court of jury could not infer that what they said was untrue. Diplock judges therefore had been required to direct themselves not to draw any inference from an accused's silence, even in a situation in which an innocent individual could reasonably be expected to claim his or her innocence. The 1988 Criminal Evidence (Northern Ireland) Order altered this right to silence by allowing the court to draw inferences of guilt from an accused's decision to remain silent. In a written answer on 20 October Tom King, Secretary of State for Northern Ireland, announced that the law on the right to silence in Northern Ireland was to be changed and that a draft Order in Council had already been laid. King highlighted the four circumstances in which a different inference could be drawn:

> First is the 'ambush' where, having remained silent during police questioning, the accused offers an explanation of his conduct for the first time at his trial when he might reasonably have been expected to offer it when being questioned. The second provides that once the prosecution has established that there is a case to answer, the accused should be warned that he will be called to give evidence and that if he should refuse to do so the court may draw such inferences as would appear proper.
>
> The other two situations are covered in provisions which have the same effect as provisions in the Criminal Justice Act enacted by the Irish Parliament in 1984. One allows a court to draw such inferences as would appear proper from an accused's failure or refusal to explain to the police certain specified facts such as substances or marks on his clothing. The other makes similar provision where an accused fails or refused to account to the police for his presence at a particular place.[115]

The following Month the Order was debated in both the House of Commons and the House of Lords.[116] The government asserted that the alteration was justified due to suspects' refusal to answer questions during trials, and that the change had to be examined against the increased protection of suspects generated by the 1987 EPA. From 1987 to 1991 Labour consistently voiced its concerns over the retention of powers of detention, lengthy remands, the Diplock court system and incursions into a suspect's right to silence.[117] However, Parliament annually renewed the statute in the face of Labour opposition, through 1990. During this time, violence in the North remained largely constant. Ninety-three deaths in 1987 were followed by the same number in 1988. The following year the number dropped to sixty-two, but in 1990 it rose again to seventy-six. These numbers were a far cry from the 467 deaths resulting from political violence in 1972.[118] Following the Anglo-Irish Agreement, attempts by King to engage unionists in 'talks about talks' met with little success. On 8 November 1987 an IRA bomb at Enniskillen during a Remembrance Day Service killed eleven and injured sixty-three. The event reignited concern over security in Northern Ireland. Security issues continued to dominate in 1988 with the killing of three IRA members in Gibraltar in March and the murder of three mourners by a loyalist gunman during the subsequent funeral in Milltown Cemetery. Later that month two British army corporals were attacked and killed when their car intercepted the funeral cortege of an IRA member in Andersontown, West Belfast.

It later emerged that in January 1988 John Hume, leader of the nationalist Social Democratic and Labour Party (SDLP), and Gerry Adams, who had succeeded Ruairí Ó Brádaigh as president of Provisional Sinn Féin (PSF), initiated talks at the request of a third party. The discussion soon widened to involve other members of the two parties and the exchange of position papers ensued. The SDLP's aim was to persuade the republican movement that the Anglo-Irish Agreement marked the beginning of British neutrality *vis-à-vis* Northern Ireland, thus rendering violence unnecessary and the development of a more sophisticated strategy paramount. In a March 1988 letter to Gerry Adams Hume suggested that although Britain wanted to withdraw from the North, it could not:

> The objectives of the Provisional Republican Movement are a British withdrawal from Ireland or a declaration of intent to do so within a given period. In our view there is no difference in practice between those objectives because once a declaration of intent is made then the effect is no different from an actual departure. The political vacuum is immediately created and as all experience of such situations show the vacuum will be filled immediately by force as each section of the community moves to secure its position. This route is the route of maximum risk.[119]

A surge in PIRA violence in the summer of 1988 resulted in calls from the Ulster Unionist Party and the Democratic Unionist Party for the introduction of internment against Republicans, and by September 1988 the talks between the SDLP and PSF had broken down. Thatcher's assertion that she would be 'very reluctant' to see its return was undermined by successive Northern Ireland Secretaries of State referring to it as an option. The broadcast ban, official recognition of the role of MI5 in the North, and the restrictions in an individual's right to silence provided interim measures in an attempt to avoid a reintroduction of internment.

THE 1991 NORTHERN IRELAND (EMERGENCY PROVISIONS) ACT

In preparation for the expiry of the 1987 EPA, the government in 1990 commissioned Viscount Colville to examine the operation of the 1978 and 1987 EPAs.[120] Similar to the guidelines assigned to previous reviews, Colville's terms of reference accepted the continuing need for emergency powers. Largely in line with his recommendations, the resultant 1991 Northern Ireland (Emergency Provisions) Act (EPA) more or less reenacted the existing provisions.[121] Three times as long as the original legislation, the statute combined the 1978 EPA and the 1987 EPA, regulations under the 1978 Act, and sections 21–24 of the Prevention of Terrorism (Temporary Provisions) Act. This consolidation clearly indicated the growing standardisation of emergency powers between Great Britain and Northern Ireland. The 1991 EPA also created a number of new offences that Peter Brooke, Secretary of State for Northern Ireland, claimed would help materially to defeat terrorism.[122]

From 1989 Brooke had been working to initiate talks in Northern Ireland. Hampered by the Anglo-Irish Agreement, unionists agreed to enter discussions in return for a decline in the number of intergovernmental meetings. From April 1991 to November 1992 what came to be known as the Brooke-Mayhew talks (Sir Patrick Mayhew replacing Peter Brooke in 1992 as Secretary of State for Northern Ireland) ensued. The Ulster Unionist Party, Democratic Unionist Party, Social Democratic and Labour Party and the Alliance Party participated in these discussions. The three-strand talks were launched on 20 March 1991. (Strand one dealt with the relationship of the communities in Northern Ireland, strand two focused on relationships in the whole of Ireland, and strand three focused on possible inter-governmental arrangements.) Bolstering his position in these talks, Brooke took a strong line in Parliament against paramilitary violence.

As well as the creation of new offences, Part I of the new Act replaced without significant amendment Part I of the 1978 EPA, providing for the continuation of the category of scheduled offences and the Diplock court system. Included in this section were provisions for bail, rules on the admissibility of confessions, reversal of the onus of proof with regard to firearms and explosives offences and the granting of remission for persons convicted of scheduled offences.[123]

Part II of the new Act replaced, with minor amendments, Part II of the 1978 Act. It conferred powers on the security forces to enter and search premises without a warrant to search for munitions, radio transmitters and receivers, and persons unlawfully detained, as well as to arrest terrorists. Powers of arrest and seizure, powers to stop and search, and powers of entry and interference with rights of property and roads were also included in Part II. In accordance with Colville's recommendations, the Conservative government inserted two new measures into this section. First, it became an offence to interfere with or to construct bypasses around closed border crossings.[124] This section resurrected Regulation 9 of the 1922–43 SPAs, which stated: 'If any person without lawful authority, damages or interferes with any barricade or road block or other obstruction, erected . . . on behalf of the civil authority he shall be guilty of an offence'.[125] Section 25(2) of the 1991 EPA similarly stated, 'A person is guilty of an offence if, without lawful authority or reasonable excuse . . . he interferes with . . . works executed in connection with the closure or diversion of any highway specified in an order under this section'. Local residents' attempts to remove barriers and to construct bypasses along the border with the Republic precipitated the reinsertion of these powers into emergency legislation. The new provisions of the 1991 EPA further enabled members of HM Forces to seize for up to four hours any item being used to interfere with road closures. Secondly, the security forces became empowered to examine any documents or recorded data found in the course of a search. If *in situ* examination was not possible, the document could be removed and examined elsewhere for up to ninety-six hours. Although the statute specified that the document could not be reproduced, it did not make it an offence to do so. After vigorous lobbying by Northern Ireland's Law Society and Bar Council, SACHR, and other organisations, the government inserted two safeguards into this section: (a) documents which the security forces had reasonable cause to believe were legally privileged could not be examined, and (b) a written record of all examinations conducted was required.

Part III of the new Act, drawn from Part III of the 1978 EPA, provided for proscription and offences relating to membership of and support for proscribed organisations. It included provisions relating to the unlawful collection of information likely to be of use to terrorists, training in the making or use of firearms or explosives, and the wearing in public places of masks, hoods, or any article intended to conceal identity. The 1987 EPA created the additional offence of directing a terrorist organisation.[126] The government inserted this clause during the final committee stage in the House of Commons. Supposedly an attempt to get at the 'godfathers' of terrorism, it was widely viewed as simply providing a platform from which the government could be seen to be doing something. Brice Dickson, Professor of Law at the University of Ulster, described this clause as 'symbolic law making'.[127] Clive Walker and Kiron Reid concluded in *Criminal Law Review*: 'The government seems to have been more concerned with being seen to respond (. . . to the "godfathers" supposedly directing terrorism) than to pass effective laws'.[128] Kevin McNamara, Labour front-bench spokesman on Northern Ireland, commented for the Opposition: 'Someone felt that the Government had to appear tough – the proposal is nothing but an emotional spasm, and we should get rid of it'.[129] In response to challenges from the Social Democratic and Labour Party and the Ulster Unionist Party, Peter

Brooke was unable to give any convincing examples of situations in which an individual could be prosecuted under the new provision, but not under other sections.[130] In accordance with Colville's recommendation, the government also inserted a new offence of possessing items intended for terrorist activities.[131] Colville had supported shifting the onus of proof to those holding such items to disprove the suspicious circumstances in which they were found. Although Colville had envisaged it applying outside an individual's home,[132] the government imposed no such limitation as, 'the police and armed forces have plenty of evidence of homes being used in Northern Ireland for the construction of improvised explosive devices – mortar bombs and other weapons'.[133]

In contravention of Colville's recommendation, the government retained provisions for detention without trial in Part IV of the 1991 EPA. The argument for doing so rang a familiar note:

> The Government are determined to keep available a comprehensive range of responses to terrorist violence in the Province. Although the precise circumstances in which detention would be reintroduced are not at present identifiable, and while there are no current plans to do so, the Government continue to believe that the outright repeal of the provisions would be mistaken, especially as, should the introduction of internment ever be needed, it may well be needed quickly, which would not be possible without the necessary powers on the statute book.[134]

The maintenance of provisions relating to detention without trial demonstrated the lasting effects of the 1922–43 SPAs. Labour objected to its retention on the grounds that 'an emergency power should not be saved up for a rainy day'.[135] During the report stage of the 1991 Emergency Provisions Bill, McNamara stated: 'The Opposition are convinced that [the inclusion of detention without trial] was a serious mistake which undermines the credibility of efforts to create a normal and democratic society in Northern Ireland. It represents a commitment by the Government to cling to every last ounce of arbitrary executive authority. It is a hangover from the Special Powers Act'.[136]

Providing for the regulation of security guard companies, long seen as a front for paramilitary racketeering, Part V of the new legislation re-enacted, with amendments, Part III of the 1987 EPA. The government designed the alterations to enforce the anti-racketeering provisions inserted in the 1987 EPA. Section 39 of the 1991 EPA further empowered the police to enter the premises of security firms and to require that a full record of all employees be produced. The Tory government also re-enacted word for word Part II of the 1987 EPA, detailing the statutory rights for persons arrested and detained under the terrorism provisions. The government added an additional section, empowering the police to take fingerprints without consent. This brought the law with regard to fingerprinting into line with England and Wales. Article 61 of the Police and Criminal Evidence Order 1989 stated that no person's fingerprints could be taken without the consent of the individual involved. The order only applied to cases specified by the section, exempting its application to persons detained under counter-terrorist legislation. The 1991 EPA altered the law so that Article 61 applied to such arrests. Prints could only be taken without the consent of the individual if a police officer not below the rank of superintendent authorised it and was satisfied that the prints would determine whether the individual was involved in acts of terrorism or was subject to an exclusion order, or if the officer had reasonable grounds for believing that the individual was involved in terrorism and the taking of fingerprints would confirm or disprove this suspicion.

Directly harkening back to the 1922 SPA, the government re-enacted provisions governing the Secretary of State's ability to make regulations for promoting the preservation of the peace and the maintenance of order.[137] In previous EPAs the power only applied to Parts I–IV of the Act. In 1991 Members of Parliament hotly contested the insertion of this section. Although Colville held that the powers should be confined as before, the government maintained its position by claiming that, as there were more provisions in the 1991 statute than in any previous EPA, less scope existed for invoking the power. Dickson later correctly commented in depth about the rather dubious nature of this logic.[138] Also included in Part VI were new grounds on the basis of which the Secretary of State could reject applications for licenses for new explosives factories and magazines.[139] The government took these measures from Part IV of the 1989 PTA.

Part VII included new, extensive powers to confiscate terrorist proceeds, particularly those derived from racketeering operations. Additional measures in Part VII and schedule 4 required Crown courts to make confiscation orders if certain conditions were met. These alterations reflected those included in the Criminal Justice (Confiscation) (Northern Ireland) Order 1990 with regard to drug related offences.[140] This section continued the government's efforts to get at the finances of terrorist organisations. The government once again enacted provisions for compensation, as well as various supplementary provisions. Through sections 61 and 62 the government attempted to alleviate charges that were being levied against the government and the security forces in Northern Ireland that emergency powers were being abused. Section 61(1) required the Secretary of State to make codes of practice regarding detention, treatment, questioning and the identification of individuals detained. It also allowed the Secretary of State to make additional codes for police powers to stop and to question citizens, to arrest individuals, to enter and search premises, to seize property and to close roads. Section 62(1) granted a similar discretion to the Secretary of State to issue codes regarding army powers. 'The distinction between mandatory and discretionary codes results from the government's wish to be seen to be responding to increased concern about police procedures at the terrorist holding centres.'[141]

The government rejected Colville's suggestion that the 1989 PTA and the 1978/1987 EPA be consolidated. Although the government claimed that it would consider Colville's recommendation that terrorist offences be 'certified in', rather than the reverse, it did not accept that the time was appropriate to implement the change. It hesitated similarly about Colville's recommendations that terrorist interviews be videotaped and that an alternative charge to manslaughter be introduced for members of the security forces accused of the use of undue force. The government did agree, however, with Colville's finding that certain powers from the 1978 EPA be allowed to lapse.[142] The powers of security forces to require assemblies of three or more people to disperse, the Secretary of State to close licensed premises and the RUC to impose directions on the conduct of funerals were allowed to expire in the 1991 EPA, with the exception of one portion of the RUC's power that was retained. (The provision that remained was drawn from schedule 3 and empowered the police to require people taking part in funerals to travel by car.) Although Labour opposed the Bill at its second reading, the party abstained on the third reading, which resulted in a divided House of 103 votes to 3.[143]

The 1996 Northern Ireland (Emergency Provisions) Act

Parliament annually renewed the 1991 EPA until the statute's replacement in 1996. Meanwhile the Conservative government continued to support the legislation in the face of Labour opposition. In early 1992 John Major, the British Prime Minister, conducted an extensive review of Northern Ireland and intelligence gathering. This resulted in Kenneth Clarke, the Home Secretary, announcing that the security service, MI5, would henceforward take responsibility for all anti-Provisional IRA intelligence in Great Britain. This entailed a significant reorganisation, as the role had previously been filled by Scotland Yard's Special Branch, since it had begun as the Irish Special Branch to counter Irish-related political violence in Great Britain. MI5 already had responsibility, though, for monitoring loyalist paramilitary activity in Great Britain.

The new organisation did not receive universal welcome. Lord Holme, spokesman for the Liberal Democrats, remained 'dubious' about the change, while Dr Brian Feeney of the SDLP put it more strongly, claiming that the change signified 'a victory for the IRA'.[144] Dublin greeted the alteration with scepticism, amid reports by Fianna Fáil TDs that the former Taoiseach, Charles Haughey, had been targeted by MI5. Although reports of infighting between the different security bodies ensued, it soon emerged that the Conservative government would be maintaining the RUC Special Branch. Britain appointed a second RUC Deputy Chief Constable and acquiesced to the RUC Chief Constable, Sir Hugh Annesley's, suggestion that a new national anti-terrorist unit be established for the United Kingdom. This body would provide a single focus for the RUC, the Garda Síochána, Scotland Yard, MI5 and European and American security forces.

On 20 March 1993 the IRA exploded bombs in Warrington that killed two children and raised significant concern. An enormous IRA bomb the following month at Bishopsgate in the City of London led to the introduction of further security precautions. It also accelerated the Conservative government's plans to 'act as reinsurer of last resort for non-domestic property in mainland Great Britain'. The 1993 Reinsurance (Acts of Terrorism) Act placed the government in this position. In October of the same year an IRA bomb on the Shankill Road killed ten people. In retaliation, loyalists not only killed five Catholics, but on Halloween, the UFF's retaliatory shooting at the Rising Sun in Greysteel killed seven and injured eleven more. In response to these events, which brought to twenty-three the number of people killed in one week, increased calls for peace began to reverberate throughout the province. In November, as authorities seized a shipload of Semtex, detonators and 300 assault rifles from Poland intended for the UVF, the situation in the North appeared increasingly hopeless.

In this context, on 15 December 1993 the British and Irish governments jointly issued the Downing Street Declaration, which, in effect, continued strand two of the 1990 Brooke Initiative. The Downing Street Declaration reaffirmed the commitment of the two governments to the right of self-determination, based on the consent of the majority in both parts of Ireland. It expressed support for the three-stranded basis agreed to in the Brooke initiative as well as the requirement that any participants in the talks process renounce violence:

> The British and Irish governments reiterate that the achievement of peace must involve a permanent end to the use of, or support for,

paramilitary violence. They confirm that, in these circumstances, democratically mandated parties which establish a commitment to exclusively peaceful methods and which have shown that they abide by the democratic process, are free to participate fully in democratic politics and to join in dialogue in due course between the Government and the political parties on the way ahead.[145]

This clear plea for an end to violence was preceded by the Secretary of State, Patrick Mayhew's written guarantee that the British government had no 'selfish strategic or economic interests in Northern Ireland'.[146] This attempt to demonstrate the distance between Britain and the North opened up the possibilities that future negotiations might address.

Following the Declaration, in January 1994 Sinn Féin began to call for clarification on statements contained therein. Seen as a stalling tactic that would only result in any response being subsequently used to justify continued violence, the British government refused to treat the republican request seriously. Loyalists, in turn, greeted the document with some trepidation, suggesting, nevertheless, that it was a work, 'of some ingenuity'. In the light of the widespread favourable reception of the Downing Street Declaration Sinn Féin instituted a series of four public meetings to gauge republican public opinion with regard to the Declaration and the advisability of abandoning the armed struggle in order to pursue constitutionalist politics. Posturing throughout the following months and calls for clarification from both republicans and loyalists resulted in Autumn 1994 with the declaration of cease-fires by the Provisional IRA and the Combined Loyalist Military Command. The paramilitaries called the cease-fires in order to ensure their inclusion in the talks process.

Although bombings ceased, other paramilitary activities continued. During the summer of 1995 seventy-eight attacks were mounted on churches, chapels, Orange Halls and Gaelic Athletic Association property. Throughout the year there were 143 such attacks in total, forty-eight attributed to loyalists and ninety-five to republicans.[147] Punishment beatings, transfers of weapons and collection of paramilitary funding also continued. Sixteen months after the official cease-fire the Provisional IRA suddenly resumed its campaign in Britain with an explosion in the Docklands area of London. This action impacted Parliament's consideration of the 1996 Northern Ireland (Emergency Provisions) Act (EPA).[148] In order to meet the threat of renewed republican hostilities the Conservative government reintroduced some of the provisions initially omitted from the Bill. During his introduction of the 1996 Emergency Provisions Bill, Sir Patrick Mayhew announced that the government had appointed Lord Lloyd of Berwick to lead a review to examine the consolidation of British anti-terrorist legislation. John Rowe had advocated this move in his annual appraisal of the EPAs.[149] Stating that Lord Lloyd's inquiry would be taken into consideration for drafting new legislation, the government limited the 1996 EPA to a two year life-span, subject to annual renewal. As previously, the Act did not allow Parliament to amend the statute in the intervening period. 'As to there being no power to amend the Act annually, for which we are criticised in the amendment, no predecessor statute, I believe, has ever incorporated such a power, and it would not be practicable to introduce one now.'[150] The government included the majority of measures previously incorporated under the 1991 EPA into the new legislation with a few notable changes.

The 1996 EPA introduced measures to provide for the silent video recording of interrogations. This provision had been advocated by Colville in 1990 and by Rowe in 1994 and 1995. Under the advice of the RUC Chief Constable, the government rejected Rowe's recommendation that audio recording be included. The Ministry argued that the insertion of such measures would severely curtail the willingness of suspects to give information to the police. Under the new provision the Secretary of State for Northern Ireland became empowered to issue a code of practice in relation to video recording, although violations of the code by the security forces would not constitute an offence against the Act. The 1996 EPA also departed from the previous statute in its omission of provisions for countering terrorist finances. The government announced that section 57, schedule 5 of the 1991 EPA had been incorporated into article 49 and schedule 2 of the 1995 Proceeds of Crime (Northern Ireland) Order, making its presence in emergency legislation unnecessary.[151] This alteration signalled the further normalisation of emergency measures, as the powers relating to the government control of financial matters became applied to all criminal activity. In accordance with Rowe's recommendation, the 1996 EPA also removed from the list of scheduled offences items which had not been used in conjunction with terrorist cases.[152] The Act increased the number of offences capable of being certified out: offences listed under section 8 and section 10 of the 1969 Theft Act (Northern Ireland)[153] (robbery with violence and aggravated burglary) were included in this section.

Noting that section 8 of the 1991 Act, which allowed the Secretary of State for Northern Ireland to set custody time limits, had still not been implemented, the government announced that the 1996 EPA would not include similar provisions. The measure had first been introduced in the 1987 EPA, at which time the Secretary of State for Northern Ireland had asserted that before the provision would be put into effect, he would have to be assured that it would not result in the release on bail, or the discharge, of any person indicted for serious terrorist crime. Determining that the circumstances in the North made such a position untenable, the government had not enacted the provision. In his review of emergency measures Rowe claimed that the statutory scheme was too rigid for Northern Ireland. In place of the previous measures the government implemented a new section in broader form with less detail, permitting regulations to set the time limits and the circumstances in which they could be extended by the court.

Like its predecessor, Part II of the Bill related to powers of arrest, search and seizure. Departing from the 1991 EPA, it created a new offence of failing to stop and be searched when required to do so by a member of HM Forces. Previously, police officers could stop and search for munitions or transmitters, but anyone failing to do so was not committing an offence under the Act. The Bill repealed some of the powers relating to arrest, entry, search and seizure; however, the Canary Wharf bombing and a second explosion in Aldwych spurred the government to reintroduce provisions it had initially planned to omit. The offence of directing a terrorist organisation was retained in Part III, as were powers of proscription, while provisions relating to proof of possession of information likely to be of use to terrorists were strengthened – evidence of proximity would be treated as proof unless demonstrated otherwise. This alteration reflected the shift in onus of proof as had been previously applied to explosives, firearms and ammunition. Powers of detention under Part IV, and provisions relating to private security services in Part V were also retained, as were the measures in Part VI relating to individuals in custody. Part VII of the 1996 Northern Ireland (Emergency Provisions) Bill removed measures relating to the government's discretionary power to make codes of practice in relation to the police and armed forces' powers of arrest, search and seizure. Mayhew claimed: 'Such codes have not been issued during the lifetime of the current Act; the powers are being used less frequently, particularly the powers of stop, search and seizure, and we have no plans currently to implement those provisions'.[154] Part VIII altered the life-span of the Bill and required annual enactment. In a new move, the legislation provided for the separation of the powers of arrest, search and seizure for the police and army, to allow the army powers to be more easily suspended in the event that affairs in the North became secure.

Labour introduced a motion into the Commons to refuse a second reading of the 1996 Emergency Provisions Bill. The party contended that the government had failed to implement Rowe's recommendations regarding the audio tape recording of interviews. It also objected to the retention of provisions relating to internment, citing recommendations from Gardiner (1975), Baker (1984), Colville (1990), Rowe (1994–5) and SACHR (1980–96) to drop powers of executive detention. The party criticised the government for failing to introduce any mechanisms for amending the legislation at the annual renewal. In addition, the party objected to the government's determination to 'certify out', rather than to 'certify in' scheduled offences, as well as the failure to establish a full-time legal advice unit at holding centres in Northern Ireland. Although Labour opposed the legislation during the second reading and committee stage, it did not divide the House on the third reading, claiming that some sort of counter-terrorist legislation was necessary to protect the life and property of individuals in Northern Ireland.

The principle of *salus populi suprema lex* repeatedly surfaced, throughout the debates on the new bill, both in support of government measures and in reflection of the Opposition's position. Thomas McAvoy asserted: 'I fully support the Labour Front Bench position, which is to support the Government so long as the Government are clearly acting in the interests both of the people of Northern Ireland and of the rest of the United Kingdom'.[155] MPs overtly stated that while negotiations left the constitutional structure of the North open to discussion, the immediate priority for Westminster was the welfare of the people within the United Kingdom. Marjorie Mowlam, the Labour party's front-bench spokesperson on Northern Ireland from 1988 to 1990, stated: 'Constitutional parties on both islands are prepared to work for a negotiated settlement . . . the people of Northern Ireland and Great Britain must be protected; their security is paramount'.[156]

In December 1995 the Conservative government invited Lord Lloyd of Berwick to conduct a review of counter-terrorist legislation in the United Kingdom. His terms of inquiry were:

> To consider the future need for specific counter-terrorism legislation in the United Kingdom if the cessation of terrorism connected with the affairs of Northern Ireland leads to a lasting peace, taking into account the continuing threat from other kinds of terrorism and the United Kingdom's obligations under international law; and to make recommendations.[157]

At the time the government commissioned the inquiry, the cease-fires in Northern Ireland had been in existence for nearly seventeen months, and it looked as though there might be some prospect for peace in the province. On 9 February the situation suddenly changed, with the IRA bombing of Canary Wharf. Nevertheless, the inquiry went ahead, still based on the supposition that lasting peace could be achieved in Northern Ireland. Lloyd therefore focused on the possibility of 'other kinds of terrorism'. His analysis of the legislation in place departed from previous reviews by its reference to both the Prevention of Terrorism Act and the Emergency Provisions Act (although Colville had previously reviewed the operation of each statute separately, they had not been considered together). Lloyd's appointment indicated the narrowing of ground with regard to British and Northern Irish emergency measures. It also signalled the normalisation of extraordinary powers and the possibility of permanent counter-terrorist legislation. As his report deals with both the PTA and the EPA, chapter six looks at his contributions to the evolution of emergency legislation in the United Kingdom in more detail.

Conclusion

The 1973–96 Northern Ireland (Emergency Provisions) Acts maintained many of the provisions introduced and employed by the Unionist government from 1922 to 1972. By the end of 1996 measures relating to detention, restriction and internment, the closing of licensed premises, proscription, the prohibition of meetings and assemblies, powers of entry, search and seizure, the blocking up of roads, the collection of information on security forces, the control of cars and the ability of a government minister to take whatever steps deemed necessary to maintain order and to preserve peace were still on the statute book. The British government added drastic new measures, such as the removal of juries, changes in rules governing admissibility and new measures for young offenders. These were introduced and altered in accordance with government inquiries, international standards, independent reviews and pressures within Parliament. In spite of initial claims by the government that the emergency measures would be temporary, they became ensconced in the Northern Ireland legal system. Chapter seven examines why this occurred. In the interim the attention is focused on additional provisions introduced by Britain to counter Northern Irish political violence. Throughout consideration of the 1973–96 EPAs Westminster also grappled with the introduction and operation of emergency measures in Great Britain. Chapter five focuses on the 1974 Prevention of Terrorism (Temporary Provisions) Act and its various mutations through 1996.

CHAPTER FIVE

Emergency Powers in Great Britain 1939–1996

THE 1973 EPA focused on violence in Northern Ireland. Throughout 1973 and 1974, however, the IRAs bombing campaign in Great Britain steadily gained momentum. In 1973 eighty-six explosions occurred, killing one and injuring more than 380 people. The first ten months of 1974 witnessed another ninety-nine incidents, resulting in seventeen deaths and 145 injuries.[1] The campaign reached a climax on 21 November 1974. Explosions at two pubs in Birmingham left twenty-one people dead and 160 injured. Public revulsion immediately following the incident spurred Westminster to introduce emergency legislation. Four days later the Home Secretary presented a report to the Cabinet outlining measures to be included in a Prevention of Terrorism Bill. The government based the document on draft contingency plans that had been drawn up in 1973 to deal with the transfer of violence to Great Britain. Although the Provisional Irish Republican Army (PIRA) was conducting republican paramilitary operations in Britain, the British government did not distinguish between PIRA and the Official Irish Republican Army. Therefore, the draft included powers to proscribe the Irish Republican Army (IRA), to exclude individuals from Great Britain and the United Kingdom and to restrict movement from Ireland.[2] The Home Office derived the Bill from three sources. Proscription came from the 1922–43 SPAs and, later, the 1973 EPA. Special police powers and exclusion resembled provisions of the 1922–43 SPAs and the 1939 PVA, and controls placed on individuals travelling from Ireland adapted sections of the 1971 Immigration Act.[3] Having examined in detail in chapters one through four the 1922–43 SPAs and 1973 EPA, this chapter first considers the 1939 PVA, which introduced powers later incorporated into the 1974 Prevention of Terrorism (Temporary Provisions) Act (PTA).[4]

THE 1939 PREVENTION OF VIOLENCE (TEMPORARY PROVISIONS) ACT

In 1939 the Chamberlain government responded to the IRA's mainland bombing campaign with the Prevention of Violence (Temporary Provisions) Act (PVA).[5] Republican operations began in January of that year with a letter delivered to the Dominions Office declaring that unless Britain withdrew all troops from Northern Ireland before 16 January, the IRA would retaliate. Explosions on 16 January compelled the Dominions Office to forward the information to Scotland Yard. (The document had not initially been treated as a serious threat.)[6] From January to July some 127 terrorist incidents shook Great Britain. Fifty-seven of these were in London and seventy outside the city.[7] Although the IRA began by targeting property, as the campaign progressed emphasis shifted to incurring casualties. This, combined with the threat of impending war, forced the Conservative government to introduce sweeping emergency powers. 'I have here a photograph of [the IRA's "S" Plan] in my hand, and I shall be perfectly ready to show it to any Right Hon. or Hon. Gentleman who wishes to see it', thundered Sir Samuel Hoare, Secretary of State for the Home Department, at the Second Reading of the Bill. 'It is a very carefully worked out plan, the kind of plan that might be worked out by a General Staff, setting out in detail the way in which an extensive campaign of sabotage could be successfully carried out against this country.' Hoare outlined a plot to destroy areoplane and munitions factories, to damage water supplies, to interfere with the drainage system, and to tamper with the fire brigade, transport systems and essential services. Most significantly, he amplified these claims with veiled references to foreign *agents provocateurs*: 'the campaign is being closely watched and actively stimulated by foreign organisations'. Hoare added: 'I would ask the House not to press me for details. It would not be in the public interest to divulge them but they must accept my assurance that these are not unchecked suspicions founded upon gossip, but definite conclusions reached upon reliable data'. He concluded: 'Can Parliament safely adjourn without strengthening the forces of law and order?'[8]

The 1939 Prevention of Violence Bill swept through both Houses of Parliament in two days. Every Member of Parliament who spoke began their initial statements by deploring the use of violence for political ends. Assertions such as 'Terrorist methods will achieve nothing',[9] and 'terrorism as an instrument is repudiated by every party and by every individual in this House',[10] were added to by claims that the IRA was a fascist organisation: 'For three years Fascism in every country – the IRA are only a form of Fascism – has been fighting against democracy and liberty, and it is quite time that we took powers, the only powers that they will understand, to resist violence'.[11] Conspiracy was everywhere. Speaking for the Opposition, Arthur Greenwood surmised: 'There have been attacks upon trains. There have been mysterious large-scale fires; and naturally, as a politician and therefore having a suspicious mind, I have wondered whether those mysterious fires might have been caused, not by accident, but by design'. He continued: 'The Right Hon. Gentleman talked very guardedly – quite rightly so – of foreign Powers. I do not intend to ask him who provides the money for this campaign. If this be veiled, indirect aggression, then the situation we are facing becomes even more serious'.[12] Just as the Unionist MP, Robert Lynn, claimed during the introduction of the 1922 Special Powers Act, 'We are living not in normal, but in very abnormal times',[13] seventeen years later and in Great Britain Samuel Hoare claimed: 'We are living in altogether abnormal times. The Government are convinced that in the interests of the State the Bill must be passed without delay'.[14] Members from Northern Ireland cited the 1922 Special Powers Act, under which approximately thirty individuals had been interned since the beginning of the year, and encouraged British parliamentarians to adopt more stringent measures. Sir Hugh O'Neill stated: 'Members in this House, probably, do not realise that in Northern Ireland we have been faced with a terrorist campaign of this nature on and off, without much intermission during the whole of the last 20 years . . . In order to meet that situation special legislation had to be introduced'. By O'Neill's own words, the 1922 SPA had not rid the North of the republican campaign, yet he went on to assert his desire that the British emergency measures would have precisely this effect: 'In common with Members in all parts of the House I dislike these special measures which aim at impinging upon the liberty of the subject, but in times of crisis you have to bring in special measures to deal with that crisis and I hope, when the Bill becomes law, it will have the desired effect and that this ill-judged campaign of violence and outrage will be successfully overcome'.[15]

The 1939 Bill targeted Irish immigrants to Great Britain. Its long title read: 'An Act to prevent the commission in Great Britain of further acts of violence designed to influence public opinion or Government policy with respect to Irish affairs; and to confer on the Secretary of State extraordinary powers in that behalf; and for purposes connected with the matters aforesaid'.[16] It obtained three central powers for the Home Secretary to exercise at his discretion: registration, expulsion and prohibition. Similar to restriction orders under Regulations 23A and 23B of the 1922–43 SPAs, the 1939 Act authorised the Home Secretary to order individuals reasonably suspected of complicity to register with and to report regularly to the police.[17] Echoing the Special Powers Regulations, the draft Bill also provided for restrictions on the distance a person could travel from a set place and required that individuals provide personal details to the police. It granted wide powers of discretion to the police and Home Secretary to alter conditions and to impose new ones. The Lord Chancellor, however, insisted that these extended provisions would be considered unduly oppressive, and that the House of Commons would be shocked at the proposal 'to tether a suspect to a particular place without any legal proceedings'.[18] As a result, the Home Affairs Committee deleted the travel restrictions but maintained the requirement for individuals so named by the Home Secretary to register with the police.

For individuals classified as non-residents, or those who had been resident in Great Britain for less than twenty years, the 1939 Bill empowered the Home Secretary to issue expulsion or prohibition orders, excluding them from Great Britain.[19] Before its introduction the draft Bill limited resident requirement for expulsion to less than ten years. However, after having been informed that it would only cover two-thirds of the suspects that had already been targeted for action under the statute, Chamberlain insisted to the Cabinet that the requirement be extended to twenty years. This time frame came under fire in the House of Commons. In his introduction of the Bill, Hoare noted that 'The individuals with whom we shall be dealing will in the main be recent arrivals to these shores'. Arthur Henderson, offering an amendment in committee to change the time of residence to five years, asked the Home Secretary for clarification: 'I should like to ask the Home Secretary why he has fixed on a dividing line of 20 years. There might be cases of one person who had lived in this country for 21 years, and another person who had lived in this country for 19 years'. Hoare admitted: 'The period of 20 years is an arbitrary decision to a great extent', but he went on to note that the list of people already assembled for orders to be made against them included a number of individuals who would not have been affected by a five, ten, or fifteen-year requirement.[20]

The Home Secretary, in consultation with the Northern Ireland government, decided to include powers of expulsion to both Éire and Northern Ireland. Should the Irish government have objected or refused their citizens, new powers, such as internment, would be considered.[21] The Prevention of Violence Bill did not originally include a mechanism to appeal exclusion orders. (It had been dismissed by the Cabinet as either posing an obstacle to the authorities or constituting 'a piece of humbug.')[22] Members of the House mounted a considerable challenge during the second reading and committee stages. Dingle Foot of the Liberal Party pointed out: 'If a man is innocent, what method is open to him under the Bill of establishing his innocence?'[23] The powers afforded to the Home Secretary to exclude a person on the basis of evidence unavailable to the accused and unchecked by the judicial process was seen as a violation of the 'right of an accused person to establish his innocence before an impartial authority'.[24] To do this was to discard protections painstakingly constructed through history. 'Are we then to throw away all those functions and customs that we have set up in order to protect the individual until he has been proved guilty?'[25] Even the 1914–15 Defence of the Realm Acts, the 1922 Special Powers Act and the Republic of Ireland's Offences Against the State Act allowed for mechanisms of appeal. Case after case was cited of, specifically, Irish immigrants, who had been wrongfully accused in the past but had later been exonerated by the judicial system. 'There has never been a Bill before which has abolished trial by jury and destroyed the right of every man to be presumed innocent until he is proved guilty. It seems almost unbelievable that we are passing this Bill today, without a Division, and passing it through all its stages in a couple of days.'[26] Members further objected on the grounds that the Home Secretary would inevitably adopt a cautious approach and expel innocent men, rather than risk further violence in Great Britain. This claim was somewhat backed up by assertions in the House of Commons. For instance, Sir Joseph Nall stated: 'It is much better to deport a dozen innocent persons than to allow one innocent person to be killed'.[27] Moreover, the very introduction of the Bill underscored the probability that the Home Secretary would act in precisely this way. Through its proposals, the government sought to circumvent the judicial process in order to err on the side of caution. The Home Secretary had essentially said: 'I must have this legislation at once, because a war might break out, and in those circumstances I am not going to take any risk'.[28] With the whole point of the proposed legislation to counter the possibility of violence, and with the Home Secretary thus answerable to the House for any violence that might occur in the absence of his exercise of the new powers, it was entirely likely that the Home Secretary would, indeed, send an innocent person away, rather than risk the death or injury of British citizens.

During the committee stage members proposed a number of amendments to try to insert some sort of a judicial review into the process, to include provisions to make the suspect aware of the nature of the charges brought against him or her and to give the individual the chance to respond. In the event, the government rejected any formal role for the judiciary, saying 'This is, and in our view should remain, an executive act'. The whole point of obtaining extraordinary powers was because the ordinary course of law was somehow insufficient to remove suspects from society. However, the government did eventually accept that the individual should have the opportunity to respond. Section 1(6) was inserted during the committee stage in the House of Commons and amended during the Lords' consideration of the statute. The final clause allowed the individual served by either an expulsion or registration order to make representation to the Secretary of State within forty-eight hours, stating any objections to the order. The statute required that at the time of the order being served, the individual be informed of his or her right to make representations and be made aware of the grounds on which the order was being made: '(a) by reason of his being concerned in the preparation or instigation of such acts of violence as aforesaid; or (b) by reason of his knowingly harbouring another person so concerned'.[29] (Any more detailed information provided to the respondent might compromise the source of the information.) On receiving representation the Secretary of State was required, 'unless he consider[ed] the reasons to be frivolous', to refer the matter to an advisor. The advisor, appointed by the Secretary of State, could be neither a police officer nor a member of a government department; however, legal training was not required.[30] As a result of objections raised during the committee stage of the Bill, the Secretary of State was required to report to Parliament every three months the number of expulsion, registration and prohibition orders which he had made, as well as the total number of individuals in respect of whom such powers were made. This provision was inserted to provide a mechanism for Parliament to maintain some degree of scrutiny regarding the Secretary of State's executive powers.

As well as powers of registration, expulsion and prohibition, the 1939 Bill empowered the police to arrest without warrant and detain an individual reasonably suspected of falling under the provisions of the statute for an initial period of forty-eight hours and thereafter, with the authorisation of the Secretary of State, for a period of five more days.[31] The Conservative government introduced this last clause during the report stage. Prior to its inclusion, police powers of detention extended only to forty-eight hours. This was seen to be an insufficient period in which to determine whether charges should be proffered against individuals briefly present in the country. Explosions that occurred concurrent with parliamentary consideration of the Bill prompted the government to introduce extended powers of detention through amendments considered by the House of Lords. Samuel Hoare claimed: 'if we had had these powers two days ago it is very likely that we might have forestalled one or other . . . of those outrages'.[32] These powers, however, failed to stop a subsequent IRA attack in Coventry on 25 August 1939 in which five people were killed. This incident was far more devastating than the violence in evidence prior to the statute's introduction. The additional clause extending detention to seven days was moved and agreed to with minimal debate in the House of Commons.[33] The statute also allowed for powers of search without warrant in cases where a police superintendent, or higher-ranking officer bore reasonable grounds for believing that it was an emergency and in the best interests of the State that the police enter and search premises.[34] Here, many of the concerns raised by Members of Parliament related to the ability of police officers to exercise the powers on British citizens. During the committee stage Leslie also introduced an amendment to require that the police reveal the date and time of such searches and any items removed during the search. 'We all know that the Irish are extremely clannish and that young Irishmen like to lead a communal life. The result is that quite a crowd of them will board together.' He continued: 'Surely it is not too much to expect that when the police ransack the belongings of the individuals in that house, they should give a list stating that they have been there and taken from the house certain articles, so that nobody else would be suspected of doing what the police have done'.[35] The committee rejected the amendment.

The Bill originally included provisions for establishing an elaborate system of port controls, with a visa and passport system. Although the government removed these sections during Cabinet discussions, the Home Office kept them on hand in case they became necessary to secure the passage of the Bill. The Cabinet also considered powers of pro-scription but decided against this power. Hoare provided insight into this decision: 'So far as I know, there is no list of members of the IRA, certainly no circulated list of the members, and I do not believe it would be possible in one case out of a hundred to prove that this or that suspect was a member of the IRA'.[36] In spite of pressure from some Members of Parliament to introduce identity cards for individuals coming from Ireland, the Home Office rejected this power. Hoare asserted:

> In the first place, there is the very large number of men and women constantly passing between Ireland and these shores, [second] the narrowness of the passage between Ireland and Scotland, the ease with which people may pass backward and forward between Southern and Northern Ireland and from Northern Ireland to these shores; and thirdly, the fact that a passport without full knowledge about the

bearer of the passport is of no use at all. The mere fact that a man carries a passport or an identity card is no check unless you have some information about him from the place from which he comes.[37]

The government also eliminated internment from the Bill. Samuel Hoare announced: 'I am opposed to the method of internment. I think it looks, and is, much too like the system of concentration camps . . . One of the difficulties of internment is that to intern a man may be comparatively easy, but it is a much more difficult problem to know when and how to release him'.[38] Nevertheless, as noted above, the Cabinet retained the option of introducing internment in the event that the region to which IRA suspects were deported refused their admission.

Members of Parliament expressed concern that the extensive powers incorporated into the Bill would not be used in the manner in which they were intended:

> We have had experience of the operation of the Official Secrets Act, which was passed into law for one purpose and in the course of time most shamefully used for other purposes. We have had experience of the administration of the famous Defence of the Realm Act, that most unfortunate dame who covered a multitude of innocences which were converted into sins that nobody had ever suspected. It is from the point of view of the possible future use to which this Bill might be put . . . that we have to examine the Bill very carefully.[39]

It was not that ordinary criminal law had been utterly ineffective in the face of the IRA campaign: by Hoare's own admission, sixty-six individuals had been convicted by the ordinary processes of law. In addition, the police had seized 1,500 sticks of gelignite, 1,000 detonators, two tons of potassium chlorate and oxide of iron, seven gallons of sulphuric acid and four cwts. of aluminum powder.[40] Furthermore, the Bill was seen to be 'only tinkering with a very great problem indeed, which will not be dealt with by such provisions'.[41] Another member added: 'My criticism of this Bill is . . . that all your repression and gaoling and deportation will never solve a problem like this. You have to see what causes the problem, and apply your mind to solving the reason'.[42] Members also voiced concern that anti-Irish sentiment in the population would cause false accusations to be made, leading to the deportation of innocent people. 'Under this Bill what will happen is that every man who is Irish and working will be liable to be informed against, not because he had done anything wrong, but because he is thought to have taken the job of somebody else. Who, having represented a Glasgow seat, has not received letters from the unemployed complaining that the Irish are working?'[43]

In spite of these objections, Parliament passed the Bill through all its stages in two days. Having already composed a list of individuals against whom the government wanted to proceed, the Home Secretary immediately exercised his powers. In the first two months Hoare issued 113 expulsion orders, twenty-five registration orders and ten prohibition orders. By the end of May 1940 the government had made a total of 167 orders.[44] Westminster clearly intended for the 1939 Act to operate for a limited time. As Hoare initially noted: 'It is a temporary Measure to meet a passing emergency. We have expressly restricted the duration of the Bill to a period of two years'.[45] Attempts in committee to limit the period of the Bill to one year met with no success, however, with a later amendment permitting a motion to be made in either House for the repeal of the act to be swiftly scotched. Godfrey Nicholson commented on the later amendment: 'I think this is one of the most inhuman proposals one could conceive. There is already plenty of exempted business in this House. One of the curses of Parliamentary life is that one never gets enough sleep, and that there should be more exempted business is a terrible prospect. Seriously, exempted business is one of the banes of Parliamentary life, and I hope the House will reject the proposal'.[46] And so the Bill retained its two year duration. While the IRA's mainland campaign ceased in the same year the statute was enacted, the 1939 Act did not expire until 1953 and was not officially repealed until 1973.[47] In 1951 Geoffrey Bing moved during the Expiring Laws Continuance debates that the 1939 Act be allowed to expire. Unsuccessful, in 1952 he introduced a similar motion. Bing noted: 'A great deal of water has flown under the bridges since [the enactment of this measure.] It is really extraordinary that we should be re-enacting such a Measure, after the experience we have had'. The experience he meant was the Second World War: 'Whatever else might have happened, and whatever else this country might have suffered as a result of violence in respect to Irish affairs, it is only a tittle compared with the violence we suffered at the hands of the Germans'.[48] Bing noted that in his introduction of the Bill for the Conservatives, Samuel Hoare (by 1952 Lord Templewood) asked the House to accept his promise that, 'these powers will not be exercised a day longer than they are actually required'.[49] Assurances from the Home Secretary and from civil servants failed to compensate for the obvious absence of Irish-related terrorism:

> Once that legislation has been imposed each Home Secretary finds it peculiarly convenient, and every civil servant finds it a particularly good example, to define how useful this particular repressive power

has been. But one cannot judge repressive powers on the use which they have been in any particular case. One could devise a whole series of repressive powers applying to motorists which, no doubt, would enable us to decrease the number of road accidents, but to justify them on that ground, without considering the broader grounds of freedom, would be quite alien to the way in which we look at things here.[50]

There had been no terrorist incidents over the past few years that would justify the retention of the powers. The government pointed to just this absence of violence in vindication of the measures. John Hay spoke for the Conservatives: 'Hon. Gentlemen should not overlook that it may well be that the very existence of the Act has had some effect in preventing further outbreaks of violence'.[51] Since the Act had been introduced, expulsion orders had been made against 190 individuals, registration orders against twenty-nine, and prohibition orders against seventy-one. At the time of the debates, some 112 expulsion orders and sixty prohibition orders remained in force.[52] Sir David Maxwell Fyfe, Secretary of State for the Home Department, announced that he would have been prepared to allow the Act to expire at the end of 1952, were it not for the effect that it would have of cancelling the orders currently in operation. A number of prohibition orders had recently been introduced against individuals released from British prisons. Thus, although there had been some overall reduction in the number of prohibition and expulsion orders over the past year, and the elimination of any registration requirements the year before, it was yet necessary to retain the powers for the remaining suspects. It was not until the following year that the government allowed the 1939 Prevention of Violence (Temporary Provisions) Act to expire, and, as previously stated, the government did not repeal the statute until 1973.

THE 1974 PREVENTION OF TERRORISM (TEMPORARY PROVISIONS) ACT

Like the 1939 Act, Parliament directed the 1974 Prevention of Terrorism Bill at countering IRA operations in Great Britain. The Labour government sought to reduce levels of violence by introducing proscription and by limiting the movement of persons into and within the United Kingdom. The Bill outlawed the IRA, provided for extensive border checks with the Republic, extended powers of arrest and detention and introduced exclusion orders. In contrast to the earlier statute, however, and like the 1973 EPA, the 1974 PTA became subject to biannual parliamentary review. In spite of the sweeping powers that it authorised, the legislation passed through Parliament with remarkable speed. The government introduced it on Wednesday, 27 November, and sent it through its second reading and remaining stages between Thursday afternoon and the early hours of Friday morning. The bill went to the Lords on the same day and entered onto the statute book within eight days of the bombing. Some members took exception to the speed with which such measures were being passed: 'The most sensible course for the House to take would be, by whatever procedural means available to it, to put aside this proposed legislation for at least a month and then consider it further. Cooler counsel might then prevail, and reason, which is the proper master for us to serve, might dominate our decisions'.[53] Another member asserted: 'I feel that this legislation has been introduced in a mood of panic. This House ought not to legislate in such a mood, and I regret that we are doing so. If anyone doubts that there is a mood of panic abroad, he has only to listen to the hysterical clamour from the Conservative benches for the return of hanging'.[54] It was noted in the House of Commons that by the second reading, even the Chairman of Ways and Means had been unable to consider all the amendments proffered in the Bill. This was not unlike the passage of the 1939 PVA, also passed in an atmosphere of immediacy, in which the actual text of the Lords' amendments was unavailable to Members of the House of Commons during their consideration of the Lords' amendments.[55] During the 1974 consideration of the Prevention of Terrorism Bill, it was suggested that in the interests of time the government should indicate which amendments would be selected. This would help to shorten Members' speeches in the second reading.[56] Members in the Commons asserted: 'both haste and anger are ill counsellors, especially when one is legislating for the rights of the subject'.[57] Again, this echoed concerns voiced during consideration of the 1939 PVA, such as, 'This is panic legislation . . . when this House is in a hurry and deeply moved, when it is unanimous, this House is nearly always wrong'.[58]

Nevertheless, in the light of the urgency surrounding the Birmingham bombs, from its introduction in 1974 the Prevention of Terrorism Bill captured overwhelming bipartisan support. Representing the Opposition, Edward Heath responded to Roy Jenkins' introduction by stating: 'We strongly support the proposals [the Home Secretary] has put before the House this afternoon and are grateful for his readiness to keep an open mind on the other measures which he has mentioned'.[59] The need to be *seen* as responding to the attacks on 21 November heightened the Members' sense of importunity and, indeed, played a key role throughout the debates:

The British public will not have much confidence in or respect for a House of Commons which is not prepared to grant the authorities powers which . . . they need . . . Nor would the public have much confidence in us if we did not share their outrage at the public glorification of mass murder . . . If we were to stand by and ignore the sense of outrage of many people . . . we would be very much out of tune with the people we represent.[60]

Not only did Members of Parliament feel the need to reflect and address the public outrage at the republican bombings in Great Britain, but the implementation of emergency legislation was viewed by a number of MPs as necessary to prevent reprisals against the Irish population in Great Britain. By being seen to attack the Irish problem head-on, Members claimed that they would diffuse the anti-Irish sentiment steadily growing in Great Britain.[61] At the same time the action had to be seen as equitable: '[My constituents] will . . . expect the action to be fair and to be seen to be fair. I implore the Home Secretary to heed the request made from both sides of the House that the action taken must be seen to be fair'.[62] Two bombings in London during the debates on the Bill further underscored the urgency of the measures proposed. Since 1 January 1974 there had been thirty bombings in Great Britain, with forty deaths and about 396 injured.[63] As with previous measures, the timing of the violence coincided with parliamentary consideration of emergency powers. Discussion in the House of Commons largely followed that of the Cabinet when first considering the measures. While it was recognised by all parties to the discussion that the powers being adopted by the House were harsh, they were time and again declared justified on account of the current situation.[64] During the Cabinet discussion it was recognised that the powers posed were more stringent than any other powers that had been introduced in Britain during peacetime. A number of Cabinet Ministers, such as Harold Wilson and Elwyn Jones, responded by asserting that the country was in a state of war against the IRA. Underlying the sentiment was the understanding that the 'very first function of any government is the maintenance of life and property, and there is real doubt in this country at the moment whether the government have the means to ensure the maintenance of life and property'.[65]

Powers of Proscription

Part I of the resultant 1974 Prevention of Terrorism (Temporary Provisions) Act allowed for the proscription of organisations involved in terrorism connected with Northern Irish affairs.[66] Pressure for the proscription of the IRA in Great Britain had been steadily increasing throughout the year.[67] The government modelled this section on the 1973 EPA, which had been drawn from the 1922–43 SPAs, which in turn, had been taken from the 1920 ROIR and 1914–15 DORAs. Proscription was seen as an effective means to control open membership of the IRA in Northern Ireland.[68] The 1974 Act defined terrorism as, 'the use of violence for political ends [including] any use of violence for the purpose of putting the public in fear'.[69] This wording replicated that of the 1972 Detention of Terrorists Order, introduced under the 1922–43 SPAs. The inclusion of powers of proscription in the 1974 statute departed from the rationale previously employed by Westminster in its consideration of the 1939 PVA. At the introduction of the Prevention of Violence Bill the Home Secretary had stated:

> Why should we not proscribe the IRA as an illegal organisation and make it a criminal offence for anyone to be a member of it? The answer to that question is a simple one. So far as I know, there is no list of members of the IRA, certainly no circulated list of the members, and I do not believe it would be possible in one case out of a hundred to prove that this or that suspect was a member of the IRA. I set aside, therefore, that method for dealing with this emergency.[70]

The inclusion of proscription in the 1974 statute was based on its use in acknowledging the offence caused to individuals in the United Kingdom for being forced to witness public support for the IRA. At its introduction Roy Jenkins asserted: 'I have never claimed, and I do not claim now, that proscription of the IRA will itself reduce terrorist outrages. But the public should no longer have to endure the affront of public demonstrations in support of that body'.[71]

The decision to limit the 1974 statute to organisations associated with Northern Irish political affairs was based on the understanding that, because proscription was such an exceptional measure, its only justification could be found in the existence of a specific, clear and present danger, such as then existed with regard to the province. Although schedule 1 to the 1974 PTA only proscribed the IRA, the Minister of Home Affairs was given the ability to add and subtract additional names. During the debate, concern was voiced that the inclusion of only a republican organisation would enhance the view that the legislation was only being applied to one community.[72] Loyalist organisations also maintained links within Great Britain. But proscription expressed public aversion to acts of terrorism, and it was the Irish Republican Army that had been responsible for incidents of violence in Great Britain. Certainly, the public outrage that followed the Birmingham bombings supported the use of stringent measures against the IRA. How far such sentiments would bolster limiting free association beyond this republican group was less than clear. Labour noted during the debates that the IRA was already illegal both in Northern Ireland and the Republic. The government refused, however, to consider amendments to include the Ulster Freedom Fighters, the Red Hand Commandos and the Ulster Protestant Action Group.[73] The Home Office's objection to expanding the list – indeed, the very presence of disparate emergency powers between Northern Ireland and Great Britain – underlined the distinction drawn between the two regions. The government also refrained from including Sinn Féin, but for different reasons – the organisation claimed to be a political, not a paramilitary, body. The government claimed that in order to encourage political discussion, the group should not be prohibited. Moreover, the British government had only recently lifted the ban on Sinn Féin in Northern Ireland through the 1974 Northern Ireland (Emergency Provisions) Act 1973 Order. It made little sense to ban an association in Great Britain that had only months before been legalised in Northern Ireland.

Like the 1973 EPA, the 1974 PTA prohibited certain forms of dress, claiming them to be indicative of membership of a proscribed organisation. Members voiced concern with regard to what would be considered prima-facie evidence of membership. The Attorney General suggested that the final analysis rested with the courts.[74] Referring to subsection (6), 'The possession . . . shall be evidence . . . of that person belonging to the organisation', the onus of proof shifted to the defendant to prove that he or she was unaware that the objects indicating membership of a proscribed organisation were in his or her possession.[75] The statute also increased the penalties available in the EPA. As was mentioned, not only was proscription seen as an effective way to reduce open membership of organisations, but banning the groups reflected the 'right' not to be offended: 'The open panoply of IRA activities was such an affront to our people that it had to be banned for that purpose'.[76] This line of argument reflected unionist claims during 1922–72. During that time the Northern Executive claimed nationalist and republican meetings, assemblies, newspapers and films, the Tricolour and 'A Soldier's Song' were offensive to the majority population. The difference between Northern Irish and British invocation of the principle lay in why they were considered objectionable. In Northern Ireland the primary reasoning was that republicanism represented an attack on the Constitution of the State. In Britain, the offensiveness revolved almost solely around the destruction wrought to persons and properties within the State itself.

Powers of Exclusion

Based on the precedent set by the 1939 Prevention of Violence (Temporary Provisions) Act, Part II of the Prevention of Terrorism Act gave the Secretary of State the power to make exclusion orders concerning any person resident in Great Britain. The relevant sections reflected Regulation 14E of the 1914–15 Defence of the Realm Acts, which restricted travel between Britain and Ireland for non-British citizens or for British subjects recently returned from abroad. A permit from the Home Secretary was required thereafter for an individual seeking movement from Great Britain to Northern Ireland.[77] For individuals detained in Scotland consent for exclusion orders was required from the Secretary of State for Scotland. In keeping with the 1939 Act, the government made exempt any citizen of the United Kingdom or Colonies resident in Great Britain for twenty or more years.

Also reflecting the previous preparation of the 1974 Prevention of Terrorism Bill, within an hour of the passage of the 1974 Act, the Special Branch produced a list of individuals they wanted to be made subject to exclusion orders.[78] The right to make representations protesting an exclusion order also derived from the 1939 Act although, unlike the previous statute, the grounds on which the order was being made was not provided to the individual being excluded. Within forty-eight hours of being served with notice of exclusion, the individual served had to make written representations to the Secretary of State setting out his or her grounds of objection. The Secretary of State had the authority to decide whether the appeal was strong enough to be referred to one or more persons nominated by himself. Afterwards the Secretary of State was not bound by the opinion of his or her advisors but was required only to reconsider the case in the light of advice so submitted.

As in 1939, the government repeatedly resisted attempts to insert a system of judicial review into the procedure for representations. Jenkins asserted: 'Exclusion orders are concerned with national security rather than with judicial issues and, distasteful though this may be to me and to others – it involves a particular burden upon [the Secretary of State] for the time being – the final decision must . . . rest with the Secretary of State'. He again stated: 'In the last resort, the decision must be mine. They will be advisors and not adjudicators'.[79]

An additional safeguard inserted into Part II of the 1974 PTA and not present in the 1939 Act prevented an individual from being removed to a place to which he or she had no connection. The practical implication of the section was to allow the Home Secretary to exclude from Great Britain not only Irish citizens, but people from Northern Ireland. During a Cabinet meeting following the Birmingham bombings, reservations over the effect of exclusion were raised. Various expressed concern that individuals who returned to the province would immediately be detained under the more stringent requirements of the Emergency Provisions Act. Merlyn Rees stated: 'We've really got to integrate this with the Northern Ireland powers because my authority is quite different. I have the power to intern without trial and you don't in England, and you're just going to send all your IRA people back to Northern Ireland. The thing would be completely unbalanced as between one set of powers and the other'.[80]

In a broad sense, exclusion did serve to differentiate two parts of the UK. Such an isolation of Northern Ireland, in direct response to the fear created by the mainland bombing campaign, played into the hands of the republican paramilitaries who sought to distance the North from Great Britain. This point was not lost on Members of Parliament, who argued for the principle of reciprocity.[81] During the committee stage in the House of Commons an amendment was offered to enshrine this principle.[82] Unionists voiced concern at maintaining the unity of the United Kingdom:

> The United Kingdom for the purposes of these emergency provisions is divided into two parts, Great Britain and Northern Ireland respectively, and those two parts are treated radically differently, in that the exclusion traffic, if I may so describe it, is one-way traffic from Great Britain to Northern Ireland The natural anxiety which representatives of Northern Ireland feel at any marked differentiation of that kind being made between their part of the United Kingdom and the rest was enhanced by words which fell from the Minister of State in winding-up the Second Reading debate when he said in this context that in Northern Ireland there were available powers of detention which might apply to such persons which were not available and are not being provided inside Great Britain.[83]

The amendment sought to ensure that the power of the Home Secretary to compel a citizen of the UK to repair out of Great Britain into Northern Ireland, or, if in Northern Ireland, not to enter Great Britain, was met by a corresponding power to prevent an individual from Great Britain repairing to Northern Ireland or to return him or her to Great Britain if he or she had moved to Northern Ireland.

Jenkins responded to the requested amendment by stating that the 1939 PVA, on which the provision was based, did not include reciprocal powers. The government also claimed that such abilities were unnecessary, as the vast majority of terrorists in Northern Ireland were from the region. In addition, the government suggested that it would be pointless to exclude individuals from an area as large as Great Britain. Roy Jenkins added: 'It would not be possible to amend the Bill at this stage. By that I do not mean at this stage of the night'. (It was 3.45 a.m. Friday when the amendment was under consideration.) He continued: 'The Bill would require considerable restructuring for such an arrangement to be possible ... It would not be practical at this stage to provide reciprocity between the two parts of the United Kingdom'.[84] Gerry Fitt highlighted the irony of unionist insistence on reciprocity:

> For many years Northern Ireland insisted on going its own way. It had a Special Powers Act. It had different electoral rolls. It had a different system of local government. It had a different system of allocating houses. It wanted to have its own little kingdom in Northern Ireland and it did not particularly want reforms. Indeed, it bitterly resisted attempts when they were first made in 1968, 1969 and 1970 by the Labour government to bring about reform in Northern Ireland. Those attempts met with bitter intransigence by the then Government of Northern Ireland. We hear all this talk about them being United Kingdom citizens who accept United Kingdom standards and that there is no difference between Northern Ireland and the rest of the United Kingdom. That is all so much talk. The people who are responsible for it refused in May this year to observe an edict which had the full support of both sides of this House on the bringing into operation of a power-sharing government.[85]

Undeterred, unionists continued to press the issue. In order to meet the concerns that had been raised by unionists and to extend the 1974 PTA to Northern Ireland, on 5 December 1974 Merlyn Rees made two orders under negative procedure. First, the Prevention of Terrorism (Temporary Provisions) (Adaptation) Order 1974 which made numerous textual changes to the PTA to clarify its application in Northern Ireland. Secondly, the Prevention of Terrorism (Supplemental Temporary Provisions) (Northern Ireland) Order 1974, the counterpart to Britain's Supplemental Temporary Provisions Order which the Home Secretary had made a week previously which established control over entry to and departure from Northern Ireland in the same way that the Home Secretary's order established control over entry to and departure from Great Britain. The only real difference between the two orders lay in the former's application to a land boundary as well as sea and air traffic.[86]

Powers of Arrest and Detention

Part III of the 1974 PTA addressed powers of arrest and detention.[87] Duplicating section 4 of the 1939 PVA, the latter statute provided for the police to arrest without warrant and to detain an individual for an initial forty-eight hours and then five more days with the consent of the Secretary of State.[88] The total length of detention was not to exceed seven days. As will be recalled from earlier in this chapter, the five day extension had been added at the last minute during the Lords' consideration of the 1939 Bill and in direct response to an IRA attack levied at the time of the debates. It had been excused on the grounds that the security forces needed more time to question non-British citizens. By 1974 this power had become unexceptional. The government blatantly noted the security forces' intention to use the power to screen individuals suspected of involvement in terrorism in general, not to question them with regard to specific acts that had occurred. As Roy Jenkins asserted during the second reading of the Bill: 'The power of detention is . . . justified by the grave situation which we face. It is wrong in this situation that the police should have grounds for suspecting that a person is involved in terrorist activities but be unable to detain him to check their suspicions because they do not have evidence of a specific offence'.[89] This measure provided for an extensive amount of intelligence gathering, both with respect to incidents that had occurred, as well as concerning general movements and prevailing conditions within communities.

Part III of the 1974 Act went beyond the 1939 PVA, granting the Secretary of State the power to issue orders requiring the examination of persons entering or leaving Great Britain or Northern Ireland. Two regulations under the 1922–43 SPAs bore similar powers. As previously discussed in chapter two, Stormont introduced Regulation 20[90] and Regulation 37[91] during the IRA's 1956–62 campaign. The first measure required that any individual entering Northern Ireland from anywhere outside Britain demonstrate to the police that their purpose in the North would not be detrimental to the maintenance of peace. The second provision stipulated that any individual disembarking at any port in Northern Ireland obtain official permission before doing so. The 1974 statute obliged travellers to produce documents when requested. These provisions ran parallel to those found in the 1971 Immigration Act. Part II, schedule 5 of the 1974 PTA empowered police officers of the rank of superintendent and above to authorise searches under emergency circumstances. This provision duplicated section 4(4) of the 1939 PVA. Unlike the 1939 Act, which initially had a two year life-span, the 1974 PTA was to be renewed every six months through affirmative procedure, as were any orders issued with regard to the proscription of organisations or the duration of the Act itself. All other orders were to be treated by negative procedure.

In sum, the provisions included under the auspices of the 1974 PTA reflected measures previously taken to combat Northern Irish political violence. Drawing as it did on the 1939 PVA, the 1922–43 SPAs, and the 1973 EPA, very little could be considered either new or innovative about the statute. The justification offered by the government in its introduction of the Act revolved around the need to protect – and to be seen as protecting – the life and property of citizens in the UK. For this reason, some aspects of the 1974 PTA, such as proscription, were largely presentational in character: proscription reflected the abhorrence of the population to the use of violence for political ends. This implied that terrorism – and public support for it – was not to be tolerated. As a result, the statute served a dual purpose, both conveying the disgust felt by the electorate at viewing displays of support for republicanism and attempting to prevent the occurrence of such acts, through powers of exclusion, arrest and detention. Although the government intended the statute as a temporary measure, the import attached to its enactment and the continuing crisis in Northern Ireland helped to sustain it long beyond its intended life.

Additional Powers under Deliberation

The 1974 PTA was significant both in what it incorporated and in what was discussed but not included in its auspices. The additional powers under scrutiny drew on previous experience of the use of emergency measures to quell Northern Irish violence and influenced later decisions taken by the British government. Although the introduction of identity cards was carefully considered in Cabinet meetings and discussed in both the House of Commons and the House of Lords, the government decided not to introduce them. Having learned from the difficulties surrounding the implementation of Regulation 1A of the 1922–43 SPAs, the primary argument against their introduction revolved around the high demand that identity cards would place on resources in a manner disproportionate to any results that might be achieved. While such a programme would take a considerable amount of time and effort to implement, it would be easy for terrorist organisations to forge cards and it would be difficult to police. The government suggested that such a system would actually provide a measure of security for those carrying forged documents and stated that it did not want to divert its efforts from what it viewed as more effective means of combatting terrorism.[92] This same decision had been reached in 1939 during consideration of the Prevention of Violence Bill. In lieu of identity cards, the 1974 PTA allowed the Secretary of State to make an order providing for control of travel into and out of Great Britain. Such an order could include the demand to produce some form of identification. In the meantime, the government announced that it would keep the identity card system under review.

As has already been mentioned, the demand for reintroducing capital punishment was high after the Birmingham bombs.[93] A Harris poll conducted at the time determined that about eighty-eight per cent of the public favoured its introduction for terrorist offences,[94] and during the debates approximately 170 Members of Parliament joined a coalition urging the restoration of capital punishment for terrorist acts.[95] Westminster had only recently revoked the death penalty in Great Britain and Northern Ireland. Given the contentiousness of the issue, and the desirability of a speedy passage for the Prevention of Terrorism Bill, the government decided not to include the sentence in the statute. In its stead Members of Parliament suggested that terrorism be considered a treasonable offence, thus warranting capital punishment. Although unused, the death penalty still existed for treason and piracy, as derived from the 1351 Treason Act[96] and the 1837 Piracy Act.[97] Only three people, all during times of war, had been executed in the twentieth century in Great Britain for treason.[98] The 1351 Treason Act provided capital punishment for 'imagining the death of the King,' and for 'slaying a justice of assize'. It was designed to address rival claimants to the throne or situations of war with foreign powers. Section 3 of the 1848 Treason Felony Act later made it a felony 'to levy war against Her Majesty, within any part of the United Kingdom, in order by force or constraint to compel her to change her measures or counsels, or in order to put any force or constraint upon or in order to intimidate or overawe both Houses or either House of Parliament, or to move or stir any foreigner or stranger with force to invade the United Kingdom'.[99] In the absence of a modern principle of treason and unwilling to imply that importance was being attached to terrorist activities by treating them as treasonable,[100] the government resisted efforts to redefine terrorism as acts of treason or treason felony and thus subject to capital punishment. In a separate motion, each House resolved by a majority of 152 votes that 'reintroduction of the death penalty would neither deter terrorists nor increase the safety of the public'.[101] The IRA's campaign in Great Britain abated immediately following the passage of the PTA, but a renewal of bomb attacks in mid 1975 produced an even greater demand for the death penalty.[102] Parliament again refused, but by a smaller majority.[103]

During the House debates on the 1974 PTA the demand for censorship also increased. A week before the Birmingham bombs, Mary

Holland had interviewed IRA leader, Dáithí Ó Conaill, on Thames Television's Weekend World. In the course of the interview Ó Conaill announced that the IRA planned to step up its campaign on the mainland. He stated: 'The British Government and the British people must realise because of the terrors they wage in Ireland they will suffer'. Ó Conaill went on to declare that violence would escalate.[104] Members in the House of Commons and the House of Lords interpreted this as an order from the IRA to Active Service Units on the mainland to commence with the Birmingham bombings.[105] The government observed that there existed no precedent of direct government intervention in the media in Britain. Appeal was made, however, to the Irish Republic's decision to ban material emanating from proscribed organisations. The Ministry of Posts and Telegraphs in the Republic of Ireland had sent a letter to RTE which read: 'I hereby direct you to refrain from broadcasting any matter of the following class: any matter that could be calculated to promote the aims or activities of any organisation which engages in, promotes, encourages or advocates the attaining of any particular objective by violent means'.[106] Nevertheless, the British government repeatedly deflected calls for the implementation of censorship.[107] In the committee stage of the Bill an amendment was proposed to make it an offence to '[arrange] a broadcast, newspaper article or other publicity knowing that the purpose or consequence might reasonably be expected to support, sustain or to further the activities of a proscribed organisation or a person belonging or professing to belong to a proscribed organisation'.[108] Members suggested that it was inconsistent to proscribe organisations and then to allow members to appear in interviews on television.[109] The Opposition threatened to divide the committee over this amendment unless the government gave the strongest assurance that they would ensure that the broadcasting authorities were aware of the sentiments of the House.[110] Both the Home Secretary and the Attorney General provided this assurance. Under the BBC Charter and the 1981 Independent Broadcasting Act, the BBC and the Independent Broadcasting Authority had the responsibility to maintain proper standards and to ensure that nothing included in programmes would be likely to incite to crime, lead to disorder or be offensive to public sentiment.[111] The broadcasting authorities were also required to treat controversial and political matters with due impartiality. This was supported by the 1964 Television Act which required the television authority to ensure 'that nothing is included in the programmes which offends against good taste or decency or is likely to encourage or incite to crime or to lead to disorder or to be offensive to public feeling'.[112] Labour argued that, once the IRA became proscribed, such broadcasts would be regarded as inappropriate. Claiming that the broadcasting authorities would respond to requests from the government to refrain from such airings, Labour threatened that if they resisted the pressure from the government, the executive could issue directives to the broadcasting authorities and in the last resort fire the chairmen and the governors.[113] Although this issue was duly dismissed, its occasional appearance throughout the following decade, accompanied by various programmes and interviews showing republican supporters, guaranteed its revival in the late 1980s.

INTERIM DEVELOPMENTS

Following the enactment of the 1974 PTA republican violence in Great Britain plummeted. As noted in the previous chapter, just before Christmas the Provisional IRA announced a cease-fire. Although the truce broke down on 16 January, it was renewed soon thereafter, and from the end of January until consideration of the renewal order in May there were no further terrorist incidents in Great Britain. It was widely assumed, however, that in the event of a resumption of violence, republican operations on the mainland would continue. Supporting this view was a shooting on 26 February in Hammersmith that led to discoveries of a PIRA bomb factory. On 19 May 1975 Roy Jenkins introduced the Prevention of Terrorism (Temporary Provisions) Act 1974 (Continuance) Order 1975. This statutory instrument extended the 1974 PTA for another six months. Reflecting the decreased urgency owing to the lull in violence, the debating chambers in the House of Commons were far from full: only 171 votes were cast on the 1974 PTA renewal, as opposed to 269 six months previously.[114]

During discussion of the renewal order the government updated the House on actions taken under the 1974 statute. With only one individual convicted under the measures governing the proscription of organisations, ministers reiterated that the purpose of banning associations was to protect individuals from being confronted with offensive displays. Besides, the idea that severe measures would eliminate a backlash against the Irish population in Britain once again surfaced:

> The primary object of [proscription] was to remove what was widely regarded as an affront to the British people, and, against the background of incidents which showed signs of leading to an unjustified but none the less dangerous backlash against the Irish community as a whole, it seemed, and will still seem, to many people intolerable that it

should be lawful to collect money for the IRA and to parade with banners proclaiming support for it.[115]

Members of Parliament noted during the debates in the House of Commons that following the introduction of the 1974 statute a better atmosphere prevailed between the British and Irish living in Great Britain.

With regard to Part II of the 1974 PTA, some fifty-one exclusion orders had been made since its enactment. Forty-four of those had been served on the individuals concerned, thirteen of whom made representations objecting to the order. Members of Parliament raised a number of specific cases during the debates where individuals who had been served exclusion orders had not been informed of their right to make representation.[116] After consultation with his advisors, the Secretary of State subsequently withdrew five of these orders. The Home Secretary appointed Lord Alport and Ronald Waterhouse, QC to serve in the capacity of advisors for the making of exclusion orders. The Home Secretary enforced the remaining thirty-nine exclusion orders, which entailed the removal of twenty-two people to Northern Ireland and seventeen to the Irish Republic.[117] Although Members of Parliament had expressed concern that individuals returned to Northern Ireland would subsequently be interned, none of the twenty-two was imprisoned on arrival in the province. This trend continued.

As of 1 August 1978, 100 persons had been excluded from Great Britain and returned to Northern Ireland. Thirteen of these were detained on their arrival, twelve of whom were released after questioning. Only one person was later charged with offences committed in the North.[118] This might have been due in part to the programme of executive release of detainees, which was being carried out in the North. The government first announced the programme on 9 July 1974. Since that time, the Secretary of State had released seventy-one detainees in Northern Ireland. The commissioners had released another ninety-nine. During the same period, the government had issued about eighty-seven new interim custody orders.[119] Members of Parliament highlighted the contradiction in carrying out the releases while maintaining emergency powers. The central claim for maintaining detention was that the individuals thus imprisoned were a threat to society; however, to then release them suggested that this threat had been exaggerated.[120] Gerry Fitt stated: 'I have been told by the former Secretary of State and the present Secretary of State that they are convinced that many of the people interned in Northern Ireland since the introduction of the Act were guilty of murder . . . of the heinous brutal murder of a colleague of mine . . . since then, these people have appeared before the commission and the commission has released them . . . Who is wrong? Who is right?'[121]

Releases continued throughout the 1975 cease-fire as both a political concession to the republican paramilitaries and the drawing to a close of the controversial system of indefinite detention. Members of Parliament also suggested that the detention of individuals under the 1973 EPA was only valid for individuals suspected of terrorism in Northern Ireland itself; thus, to intern them on arrival would be contrary to the statute. While the overall exemption of excluded individuals from detention orders somewhat alleviated the concern on the part of unionists that the North was being treated differently from the rest of the United Kingdom, the one-way traffic went some way towards giving the impression that Northern Ireland was becoming a dumping ground for suspected terrorists. With regard to the wider powers of arrest, the Home Secretary had not refused any requests from the police, authorising extended detention in ninety-one cases.[122] In relation to the final section of the 1974 PTA, the port authorities had detained 224 people for examination. Thirty-two of these were held for more than forty-eight hours and twelve were subsequently excluded from Great Britain.[123]

In response to back-benchers' criticism that the 1974 PTA had in fact no practical effect and that the lull in violence was due more to a change in PIRA strategy than to British emergency measures, Jenkins announced during the May renewal of the 1974 PTA that unless substantial parts of the Act could be dropped, the government would not seek by order a renewal of the 1974 Act in November 1975. As well as criticism relating to the effectiveness of the statute, there was widespread concern that the 1974 PTA represented a large incursion into civil liberties. The National Council for Civil Liberties issued a report highlighting aspects of the statute and specific case examples where abuses of civil liberties had occurred. This report was repeatedly mentioned during the debates on the extension of the legislation.[124] The Opposition insisted new legislation be prepared that would reflect a more thorough review than that initially given the 1974 PTA, and would open the possibility of amendments which otherwise could not be introduced during renewal of the 1974 Act.

By November 1975, with a renewal of sectarian and intra-factional paramilitary hostilities, the government was not, in fact, of the opinion that any major changes in the 1974 PTA could be made. Towards the end of the month, the second reading of the 1976 Prevention of Terrorism (Temporary Provisions) Bill proceeded in conjunction with a renewal order to maintain the powers until the passage of the new

Act.[125] Points that had been raised previously were once again broached during the House debates: the (questionable) effectiveness of the legislation and the (unquestionable) inroads into civil liberties. Additionally, the significant difference between the number of arrests and the number of charges increased suspicion that the 1974 PTA was being employed to harass left-wing organisations and individuals sympathetic with the republican movement. The security forces were making extensive use of detention powers under both the 1978 EPA and the 1976 PTA to gather intelligence information. Parliamentarians widely recognised the use of the measures for this purpose. For instance: 'What we Conservatives would not support is any modification in the Northern Ireland (Emergency Provisions) Act. In particular, we feel it essential for the security forces to retain the power under this Act to hold suspects for up to three days without preferring charges. This provision, coupled with the powers available under the Prevention of Terrorism (Temporary Provisions) Act, secures a vital period for information to be obtained and put together by those involved in intelligence work'.[126] Of approximately 1,200 people detained under the 1974 PTA through 1975, only twenty-six were subsequently charged with serious offences. Twenty-five more were charged with minor crimes, ranging from intent to defraud the tax inspector to wasting police time.[127]

THE 1976 PREVENTION OF TERRORISM (TEMPORARY PROVISIONS) ACT

With the two year time-span imposed on the operation of the 1974 PTA, in 1976 the government introduced a strikingly comparable Prevention of Terrorism Bill. The Ministry argued that the situation had altered little and that emergency powers were still required. Having introduced the initial Act into an atmosphere of panic, more time was available to Parliament in 1976 to more carefully consider the provisions. The 1976 Prevention of Terrorism (Temporary Provisions) Act (PTA) retained measures providing for the proscription of organisations.[128] The government claimed that clauses 1 and 2 of the 1974 Act had been successful in preventing public displays of support for the IRA. The new statute rearranged the section addressing exclusion orders, with the changes made more of an alteration of form than of substance. The subordinate legislation introduced under the 1974 Act, to provide Northern Ireland with the ability to exclude individuals who were not United Kingdom citizens, became part of the primary legislation. Although Parliament recognised that the insertion of reciprocity was not likely to have any practical effect, it was seen as necessary to support unionist demands that Northern Ireland be treated as an equal within the United Kingdom. Jenkins observed:

> The position as I now see it is that I do not believe that this clause is likely to have any practical effect . . . However, I am quite aware that, should a case arise in which it was right to make such an exclusion order, there could be objections of principle to our not being able to do so. This could arouse a feeling of grievance, lack of equality of treatment or lack of proper respect for the unity of the United Kingdom.[129]

In line with claims made during the debates over the 1939 PVA, the government maintained that exclusion was, and could only be, an executive procedure. 'It would be wrong to attempt to disguise in quasi-judicial dress what is inevitably an executive procedure.'[130] Nevertheless, the first dilution of the provisions relating to exclusion came with the 1976 Act: the time limit for making representations against exclusion orders increased from forty-eight hours to ninety-six hours after notice that the order had been served. Additionally, in the event that the individual had not already been removed from the UK with his or her consent, the right to a meeting with an advisor was made absolute, rather than being dependent on whether the Secretary of State determined the request to be 'frivolous' – language drawn directly from section 1 of the 1939 PVA.

The gradual 'softening' of provisions of the Act marked its progression throughout the subsequent twenty-four years. Such alterations, however, took place within a relatively static structure which had been elicited from previous measures. The government left unchanged both the twenty-year residential exemption and the powers of seven day detention.[131] Clause 10 of the new statute duplicated section 8 of the 1974 PTA, enabling the Secretary of State to make orders providing for the examination of travellers entering or leaving Great Britain or Northern Ireland. Immediately following the enactment of the 1974 PTA, detailed powers regarding traffic at ports had been claimed through the Prevention of Terrorism (Supplemental Temporary Provisions) Order 1974. This reflected provisions of the 1971 Immigration Act. This government re-enacted this order under clause 10 of the 1976 PTA.

Two of the changes in the new statute increased its stringency and reflected the growing normalisation of emergency powers. First of all, the government extended the period of review to once every twelve months, instead of six as previously. Although still a 'temporary measure', this implied greater longevity of its use in Great Britain. The government justified this alteration by claiming that the November 1975 discussion offered Parliament a more detailed examination of the measure than when the statute was rushed through Parliament the previous year. The new statute allowed for sections of the Act to be dropped by amending order. The second significant alteration related to the addition of two new sections designed to clamp down on general support for terrorist activity. Section 10 made it an offence to solicit or invite others to give money or property, knowing or suspecting that it would be used for terrorist means. This section targeted paramilitary front organisations that did not openly support or fund terrorist groups. Section 11 made it an offence to withhold information from the security forces that might be of assistance in preventing terrorist activities or securing the apprehension of individuals engaging in terrorist acts. This measure appears to have been based on section 5 of the 1967 Criminal Law Act (Northern Ireland):

> Where a person has committed an arrestable offence, any other person who, knowing or believing that the offence or some other arrestable offence has been committed, and that he has information which might be of material assistance in securing the prosecution or conviction of an offender for it, accepts or agrees to accept for not disclosing that information any consideration other than the making good of loss or injury caused by the offence, or the making of reasonable compensation for that loss or injury, shall be liable on conviction or indictment to imprisonment for not more than two years.[132]

Although the Opposition technically supported the 1976 Prevention of Terrorism (Temporary Provisions) Bill, a core of Labour backbenchers and Gerry Fitt of the SDLP vociferously asserted that the Bill did not go far enough in protecting civil liberties. The government deliberately excluded any opponents of the 1976 PTA from the committee stage of House deliberations. As well as discontent at the provisions of the statute, members expressed increasing concern that temporary legislation was becoming permanent. A shift similar to that which occurred under the unionist regime in Northern Ireland following the introduction of the 1922 SPA gradually emerged in Westminster: the justification for the continued use of the measure changed from the need for action in the face of immediate, widespread violence to the need for maintaining the measures in order to avert the recurrence of the violence. Instead of the government having to demonstrate the necessity of the emergency measures, those opposing the legislation became required to prove that its withdrawal would have no adverse effect on society. Whitelaw's assertion during the 1976 debates, that the reduction of mainland terrorism since the introduction of the legislation provided sufficient reason for its renewal, echoed Craig's 1928 claims during debates on the extension of the 1922 SPA. Fueling this shift was the increasing emphasis being placed on the criminalisation of terrorist violence: 'Just as there is no military solution to the political problems in Northern Ireland, there is no political solution to the military problem'.[133] Emergency measures became seen as a permanent element of the military or strategic defeat of terrorism. In this respect, to some degree, the British government may have played into republican hands. This point was made in Westminster:

> The passage of the original Act was merely a gesture. We felt that we had to be seen to be doing something, and that was all . . . the Prevention of Terrorism (Temporary Provisions) Act did nothing relevant to what is basically a political problem. It has taken us one more dangerous, but not yet fatal, step down a slope which is very slippery. Having embarked on that path, it is necessary for the State to go on justifying it by saying, 'We did it for a good reason. What is more, we shall strengthen those provisions for the same good reason, and, when the next step fails, we shall strengthen them again.' That is simply following the delusion that, being ever more repressive, we might one day be successful. However, that is to play the Provos' game for them.[134]

Soon after the passage of the 1976 PTA, the government supplemented it with the Prevention of Terrorism (Supplemental Temporary Provisions) Order 1976.[135] Although the Prevention of Terrorism (Supplemental Temporary Provisions) Order 1974 had provided for authorities to require landing and embarkation cards to be produced by all travellers between Great Britain and Ireland, the actual completion of the forms was voluntary. The chief officer of police in the district in which the port was located was empowered to determine whether travellers should be asked to complete the forms. The filling out of the cards was seen as being part of the collection of low-level intelligence. The 1976 Order clarified examination powers at ports and the documentation necessary for travel between Great Britain and Northern Ireland. The statute left discretionary powers up to the port authorities, however, as to whether travellers had to complete landing and embarkation cards. A second order issued on the same day required that any individual traveling between Great Britain and Northern Ireland produce either a valid passport with a photograph or some other document satisfactorily establishing identity or citizenship.[136] In 1977 the Prevention of Terrorism (Supplemental Temporary Provisions) (Amendment) Order provided a standard landing and disembarkation card, overprinted with reference to the Prevention of Terrorism (Temporary Provisions) Act as authority for their issuance. The chief officers of police still made their own decisions as to whether it would be helpful to use the cards or not, depending to a large extent on the scale and flow of passenger traffic. The aim of the order was simply to make it clear, when the cards were used, the authority under which they were employed. The government recognised outright that people could fill in the cards with false information. As a result, corroborative information on identity continued to be required under section 6 of the 1976 PTA.

SHACKLETON

On 27 March 1976 an explosion at the Ideal Home Exhibition in London injured eighty-five people, one of whom subsequently died. This was the latest incident in a series of republican attacks in Great Britain during the early months of 1976. In May of that year republicans forwarded a series of letter bombs to well-known individuals and civil servants in Britain. After this there was a period of calm and no more terrorist incidents took place during 1976. On 29 January 1977, however, approximately fourteen incendiary devices exploded in the Oxford Street area of London. Although no serious casualties resulted, extensive damage to property ensued. Within a week two bombs exploded in Liverpool, leading to the discovery of more explosive materials. These incidents convinced Westminster to extend the 1976 PTA for another year. Nevertheless, the interest that the initial PTA debate had attracted in 1974 had steadily eroded. Opening the debates in 1976 Merlyn Rees stated: 'I must confess that I am tempted to move the motion formally, so that we can all go home, because there does not appear to be anyone present who is interested in the business. I see that one Hon. Member has now entered the Chamber, so I shall have to stay'.[137]

In spite of their rather questionable attendance record at the annual debates, consistent efforts by Labour back-benchers to raise questions about the effectiveness and impact on civil liberties of the 1974 and 1976 PTA aided in establishing a 1978 review of the statute.[138] The Labour government, however, refused to instigate a wide-ranging review of the legislation, as had been conducted by the Gardiner Committee. Instead, Rees established a review led by Lord Shackleton, '[a]ccepting the continuing need for legislation against terrorism, to assess the operation of the Prevention of Terrorism (Temporary Provisions) Acts 1974 and 1976, with particular regard to the effectiveness of this legislation and its effect on the liberties of the subject and to report'.[139] The narrow terms of reference of the inquiry angered those opposing the 1976 PTA, but dissatisfaction caused only a handful of additional votes to be cast against the 1976 PTA renewal in 1978.[140] The government presented the Shackleton Report to Parliament in August 1978.[141] Having been commissioned subsequent to the 1976 Act and first lengthy parliamentary review of the PTA, and bearing such narrow terms of reference, it was unlikely that the Shackleton Report would have much of an impact on the emergency measures. As expected, it did not. For the most part, Shackleton agreed with the measures in place under the 1976 PTA.

The Shackleton Report recommended no alteration with regard to powers of proscription and only minor changes in relation to powers of exclusion and detention. Shackleton reiterated that the primary aim of proscription was to avoid causing offence.[142] Its largely presentational purpose was underscored by only two convictions having been secured under section 1.[143] Although Shackleton did not recommend that any additional groups be proscribed, soon after the release of the Shackleton Report and as a result of Airey Neave's murder, in July 1979 Thatcher outlawed the Irish National Liberation Army (INLA).[144] With regard to exclusion, Shackleton suggested that the government institute a general review of exclusion orders to determine if any of them should be revoked. He also advocated a re-evaluation of whether the State was prepared to give financial assistance to the family and friends of those excluded. Shackleton cited the broad police support for the continuation of exclusion and suggested that the insertion of a judicial process would fail to meet the principled criticisms levied against exclusion. As for the type of evidence on which exclusion orders were made, Shackleton reported:

> The police often find that the person concerned will say nothing at all to them. They realise that there can be several reasons for this and indeed the person concerned is not bound to say anything. But the police cannot rule out the possibility that he has been trained in what might be called 'anti-interrogation' techniques and that this may be an indication of involvement in a terrorist organisation.[145]

This evidence – the silence of the individual questioned – might be teamed with forensic evidence in providing the basis of information on which an exclusion order was made. Shackleton suggested: 'where . . . the police believe that the person concerned has been handling explosives, but they know that the information is not strong enough to serve as evidence on which a prosecution could be based, they may nevertheless think it relevant to the question of exclusion'.[146] He noted that further information which might be taken into account in making an exclusion order included the nature and extent of a person's associations – for instance, whether or not a person was known to 'mix' with people engaged in terrorism. 'Much depends on whether the associations appear to involve contact with dangerous and hardened terrorists. Information in this respect, although not evidence of involvement in terrorism, may, together with other information, strengthen the police in the view that the person concerned would present a danger in Great Britain.'[147]

Although these examples of the type of evidence that were used for exclusion orders were meant to convey the impression that the information was relevant, Shackleton failed in this purpose. Drawing attention to such an amalgamation of evidence as a basis for exclusion merely highlighted the power's discretionary nature. Using one's silence or friends as a basis for removal from one's home provided dubious grounds for 'evidence' of paramilitary membership. Denied the freedom to choose where to live within the UK, individuals thus excluded had no access to the nature of the information assembled against them and no recourse to a judicial process to protest at the making of the order. The impact on family life and job security was undeniable. Further, it made little sense to exclude an individual from Scotland, Wales or England on the grounds that he or she was a terrorist, and then to allow him or her to go free in Northern Ireland. At best this insulted those who lived in Northern Ireland, treating the region as a dumping ground for criminals. At worst this threatened security within the North. Either way, it highlighted a distinction drawn between Northern Ireland and the rest of the United Kingdom, in that what might be acceptable for Northern Ireland (i.e., the free movement of suspected terrorists) would not be tolerated in Great Britain.

Shackleton's endorsement of exclusion reflected the government's 'zero-tolerance' policy towards terrorism in, particularly, Great Britain. The aim was not merely to try to keep terrorist incidents from occurring, but to prevent them altogether. Shackleton suggested that the measures necessary to prevent terrorism may indeed appear to be drastic, but, having regard to their object, such measures could be permitted. He pointed to the exercise of the powers at the highest level and he claimed that the adviser system had not been completely ineffectual. Although the advisor provided no real redress, the Secretary of State had refrained from enforcing orders that the advisor had recommended be revoked. Inconvenience or disruption to individual lives could be excused, as Shackleton concluded: 'welfare considerations cannot override the needs of the security of society as a whole'.[148]

By 1 June 1978, 960 people had been detained in Great Britain under section 12 of the 1976 PTA, 487 people in Northern Ireland under the same section and 2,299 additional people under port powers.[149] These numbers were in addition to the detentions of up to seventy-two hours under the 1978 EPA. (From 29 November 1974 until 1 June 1978, a total of 8,399 people were detained under the 1978 EPA in Northern Ireland.)[150] Extended detention beyond the initial forty-eight hour holding period seems to have been exercised almost solely at the discretion of the police, with no checks instituted by the Home Secretary or the Secretary of State for Northern Ireland. Only once in Northern Ireland and on no occasion in Great Britain had a request for extended detention been denied. Shackleton recommended that these powers be retained and made the norm, with port powers of detention brought into line with section 12. In 1976 the Prevention of Terrorism (Supplementary Temporary Provisions) Order had extended port powers of detention beyond the seven day period. Aside from being an excessive amount of time for which to imprison someone with no formal charge, port authorities had only rarely exercised this option. Responding to complaints lodged by detainees at the miserable conditions in which they were held, Shackleton recommended that the facilities in which detainees were kept be improved. He also strongly suggested that the 'fullest possible' record of interviews be maintained.

Shackleton's most significant recommendation was that measures relating to the withholding of information be allowed to lapse. Section 11 made it an offence for an individual with the knowledge of acts or individuals involved in acts of terrorism not to inform the security forces. This provision resulted from a back-bench amendment to the 1976 Bill, proposed under the assumption that individuals with information on terrorist activity should be placed under the strongest possible obligation to disclose such information to the police. Against this consideration was the view that the measure was a step towards a society where individuals were expected to inform, under fear of prosecution. Section 11 was not consistent with the principle that individuals should not have to incriminate themselves. Members of Parliament also suggested that the distinction between suspicion and sure knowledge could lead to false implications. By 1 June 1978, section 11 had been used in twenty-four cases in Northern Ireland, with six convictions resulting. In one case the charge was withdrawn, leaving seventeen cases still pending.[151] Due to considerations regarding civil rights and the limited use that had been made of this measure, Shackleton recommended that it be allowed to lapse.[152]

Section 10 of the 1976 PTA made it an offence to give or receive money or property in connection with acts of terrorism. By 1 June 1978, some fifteen individuals had been charged in Great Britain under this section, four of whom had been convicted and one acquitted. At the time of the review, the remaining ten cases were still pending.[153] Shackleton suggested that these powers be retained and that the government provide a regular and consistent flow of information, possibly in the form of a quarterly report, in order to evaluate the working of the act and to draw relevant inferences. Finally, he highlighted the argument that at certain times some rights had to be suspended to protect others:

> I conclude by reference to the truism that basic civil liberties include the rights to stay alive and to go about one's business without fear. A society will always seek to defend itself against threats to its security. We must be prepared to forego some of our civil liberties for a time if that is the cost, on the best assessment we can make, of preserving the essentials.[154]

The essentials – the right to life and property – had to be protected. In creating this 'hierarchy' of rights, Shackleton echoed justifications provided in Parliament in relation to the severe inroads into civil liberties that resulted from the PTA. Chapter seven returns to this point.

In March 1979 Parliament debated the Shackleton Report simultaneously with the renewal of the PTA. The government chose to implement Shackleton's recommendation with regard to the review of exclusion orders. In the renewal debates in 1979 the Home Secretary announced a system of review to be instituted three years after the making of the initial order. By the end of 1982, fifty-nine orders had been reviewed or were in the process of being reviewed in Great Britain. This included both individuals approached by the government as well as those wrote in themselves, or had their Member of Parliament or lawyer write in, to request review. Of the fifty-nine, twenty orders were revoked, twenty-eight confirmed, and eleven were still under consideration at the end of 1982.[155] In March 1979 the government also amended section 10(1) in order to limit detention at ports to forty-eight hours, with a five day extension conditional on application to the Home Secretary. Labour also embarked on improvements in the conditions in which detainees were held. In response to Shackleton's suggestion that a more regular statistical summary of the operation of the legislation be implemented, the government instituted a series of quarterly bulletins of statistics published by the Home Office (pertaining to Great Britain) and the Northern Ireland Office (relating to Northern Ireland). Contrary to the recommendation, the government retained section 11, concerning the withholding of information. The government also rejected calls for financial help for families and friends of individuals excluded, on the basis that it would encourage terrorist couriers while being of minimal help in alleviating the hardship on those concerned.

CALLING FOR A REVIEW: THE JELLICOE REPORT

A Labour government with Conservative support passed the 1976 PTA, and as the Tories came to power in 1979 the new government continued to back the measures. MPs and various organisations external to Parliament increasingly raised concern at the inroads into civil liberties posed by the emergency statutes. The government contended, though, that the provisions for renewal provided sufficient parliamentary monitoring of the emergency measures. As the 1980s dawned, however, a growing faction within the Labour Party began to challenge the previous bipartisan approach. In 1981, during the renewal debate on the 1976 PTA, Roy Hattersley, the shadow Home Secretary, tabled a motion that an inquiry into the PTA be established to evaluate the extent of its use and possible amendments which could be made.[156] He called for a review to be conducted under the same terms of reference as the Shackleton Report: 'This evening, the Opposition ask only that [the PTA] should be re-examined, as it was in 1978, when Lord Shackleton was invited by my Right Hon. Friend to look at its provisions and operation'.[157] The Liberal Democrats, the Social Democratic and Labour Party, the Ulster Unionist Party and the Democratic Unionist Party all backed calls for a review. The main purpose for a new inquiry was not to re-evaluate whether emergency legislation should exist, but rather to provide the House with more information, particularly on the subject of the operation of the measures dealing with proscription, exclusion and detention. Labour asserted that it would divide the House if the request for an inquiry were denied. The Home Secretary, William Whitelaw, replied that, with only two and a half years having elapsed since the Shackleton Report, such an inquiry would be of little use. In response to the government's refusal to institute a review, forty-four Members of Parliament voted against renewal of the 1976 PTA – the highest number to oppose the measure since its creation.[158]

The following year, Labour once again demanded a review of the legislation. Of particular concern was the use of emergency powers for interrogation and intelligence gathering operations: powers of arrest under section 11 of the EPA had been applied, on average, 2,000 times per year between 1975 and 1980. Security forces released without charge about three-quarters of all those arrested under section 11. It was widely suspected that section 12(1)(b) of the PTA was being employed in a similar manner, as security forces released without charge approximately fifty-five per cent of individuals arrested under section 12. As one commentator noted: 'The object seemed to be to build up and maintain an intelligence file on the individual and the community in which he or she lived'.[159] Similar charges were levied against the use of army arrest powers under section 14 of the EPA: out of 1,504 arrests between June 1980 and May 1981, the military only passed 418 on to the RUC. The rest were released without charge.[160] The use of interrogation to gain information occurred within a context in which growing emphasis was being placed on the conviction of terrorists. The so-called 'supergrass' system, discussed in chapter four reflected this focus. The decision to rely on informers as a means of identifying operatives and securing convictions against terrorists was most likely related to the perceived difficulty in obtaining confessions as a result of the implementation of the Bennett Committee Report. By 1982 more than twenty potential supergrasses had been recruited. The series of mass trials of those they identified began in 1983.[161]

Altering its position, in 1982 the government agreed to a review of the 1976 PTA. William Whitelaw stated:

> I agree that enough time has now passed since Lord Shackleton finished his work to make a further review worthwhile. We agree that the review ought not to focus on whether or not we need the Act . . . the review will deal with the operation of the Act both in Great Britain and in Northern Ireland. As with the Shackleton inquiry, it will be carried out by one person, taking evidence in private but with a report to be published in full.[162]

The government chose Lord Jellicoe, a former SAS officer and head of the Security Commission, to lead the inquiry. The Tory government presented his findings to Parliament in February 1983.[163] Its directions duplicated those given to Lord Shackleton, with the committee instructed that it 'ought not to focus on whether or not [the UK] need[s] the Act'.[164] The government narrowly defined the terms of reference: 'Accepting the continuing need for legislation against terrorism, to assess the operation of the Prevention of Terrorism (Temporary Provisions) Act 1976, with particular regard to the effectiveness of the legislation and its effect on the liberties of the subject, and to report'.[165] It directed Jellicoe to focus exclusively on the PTA and not other emergency measures. In the opening paragraph Jellicoe agreed with the limits imposed by his terms of reference: '[I]f special legislation effectively reduces terrorism, as I believe it does, it should be continued as long as a substantial terrorist threat remains'.[166] The Provisional IRA's increasing use of the car bomb in the early 1980s and the tumult surrounding the hunger strikes were enough to make numerous Members of Parliament reluctant to diminish in any way the powers contained in the EPA.[167] Jellicoe suggested that such legislation could remain in force only if it met three limiting principles: (a) its aims could not be achieved by the use of the general law, (b) unacceptable inroads into civil liberties would not occur, and (c) effective safeguards would be provided 'to minimise the possibility of abuse'.[168] Not surprisingly, on all three counts Jellicoe found the 1976 PTA sufficient. Although noting that the time afforded the discussion in Parliament for the annual renewal of the 1976 PTA was inadequate for full consideration of the emergency measures, that the Act could not be amended, and that annual renewal had become an anecdotal recitation, Jellicoe advocated that the PTA be renewed annually for a maximum of five years. Any new counter-terrorist legislation would require a new bill. A review of the Act's operation as well as consideration of possible amendments should precede re-enactment of the legislation. Jellicoe also recognised the falsity of the insertion of 'Temporary Provisions' in the title to the Act and suggested that it be dropped.[169]

Lord Jellicoe concluded in his review that 'proscribing an organisation is unlikely to impair substantially its capacity for carrying out terrorist attacks or to deter those most deeply involved in its activities'. Rather, its main advantage was to 'enshrine in legislation public aversion to organisations which use and espouse, violence as a means to a political end'.[170] Under this definition it was questionable whether loyalist organisations would ever be banned, as, owing to the isolation of loyalist violence in relation to Northern Ireland and the Republic, they might not arouse sufficient public offence. Jellicoe suggested that the measure's presentational value had been relatively successful, as there had been few public demonstrations or displays of support staged for either the IRA or the INLA.[171] Nevertheless, the financial aspects linked to proscription had had less of an effect. Jellicoe reported that prosecutions under section 10 in Great Britain had been more frequent and had resulted in a higher proportion of convictions than those under sections directly linked to proscription. In relation to the republican orientation of proscribed organisations, he suggested that new groups only be added to the list in the presence of a clear and demonstrable need. Jellicoe dismissed 'symmetry' – either between Northern Ireland and Great Britain or republican and loyalist paramilitary organisations – as a sufficient reason to add associations. The Jellicoe Report concluded that provisions relating to proscription held some benefit and should be retained.

Jellicoe regarded exclusion orders as the most severe of the Act's powers and an inadequate substitution for criminal prosecution, particularly in the light of the impact of such orders on individuals and their families. However, he concluded that 'the exclusion of some people under these powers has materially contributed to public safety in the United Kingdom and that this could not have been achieved through the normal criminal process'.[172] From 29 November 1974 until 1982, applications for 337 exclusion orders were presented to the Minister of Home Affairs. Of these, the Minister subsequently issued 292 orders.[173] As for the operation of the reciprocal powers, until the end of 1982, the Secretary of State issued twenty-four exclusion orders, seven of which excluded persons from Northern Ireland to Great Britain, and seventeen from the United Kingdom as a whole. Eleven of the twenty-four orders had been made during the tumult surrounding the hunger strikes in 1981.[174] Although the frequency of exclusion orders had declined, Jellicoe recommended that the measure be retained for use in extreme cases, subject to regular reviews and the possibility of abolition.

Jellicoe advocated four main changes to the provisions governing exclusion. First, 'citizens of the United Kingdom and Colonies should not be liable to exclusion from that part of the United Kingdom in which they are settled'. This entailed changing the normal length of residence immunising an individual from exclusion, from twenty years to three years. Second, Jellicoe suggested that the exclusion orders be issued for a fixed, three year period, rather than indefinitely. Renewal should become subject to a new application by the police, with the responsibility placed on the Home Secretary for finding justification for extending detention rather than on the individual to prove that the order should be revoked. Third, Jellicoe advocated that the period in which an individual could make representations protesting the exclusion order should be extended from ninety-six hours to seven days, with the right to a personal interview with the Home Secretary's advisor after exclusion occurred. Information about this right to make representations should be issued to the individual in writing, and the individual should be asked to sign to acknowledge receipt of this information, although no indication would have to be given at this point as to whether he or she intended to make representations. The fourth recommendation was that all applications for the exclusion of citizens of the UK and Colonies 'should include the direct views of the police in both the "excluding" and the "receiving" territory on the merits of exclusion'.[175] In a minor amendment, Jellicoe followed Shackleton in recommending that the phrase 'unless he considers the grounds to be frivolous', still retained from the 1939 PVA, be dropped from section 7(4) of the PTA relating to representations.

More than half of Jellicoe's report focused on police powers under the 1976 PTA. This reflected his efforts to emulate the Police and Criminal

Evidence Bill and to build on the implementation of the Bennett Committee Report, which focused on the RUC's interrogation and complaints procedures. Chapter four discussed this committee in more detail. Jellicoe's attempts to bring emergency powers into line with ordinary legislation reflected the 'normalisation' of emergency law. Although he advocated changes in the more extreme aspects of the statute, Jellicoe nevertheless held that the range of special powers should be maintained. In accordance with the conclusions reached by various previous inquiries, Jellicoe found no conclusive proof that the powers of arrest in the 1976 PTA proved essential in the fight against terrorism. However, it had not been demonstrated that the powers were *not* effective.[176] As a result, on account of the support of the police for continuing the powers of arrest, Jellicoe recommended only minor changes to the existing provisions. Walker criticised this conclusion by citing that Jellicoe's admission, that '[t]here can be no clear proof that the arrest powers . . . are, or are not, an essential weapon', raises doubts as to whether emergency measures met the limiting principles. Most terrorist offences were already arrestable under the 1967 Criminal Law (Northern Ireland) Act.[177]

This echoed the transfer of onus of proof evidenced in both the 1922–43 SPAs and the 1973–96 EPAs. The burden fell on individuals to demonstrate that the power was ineffective or not necessary in order to secure their appeal, rather than on those seeking the powers to demonstrate their effectiveness or clear need. Between 29 November 1974 (when the 1974 Act came into force) and the end of 1982, 5,555 people had been detained in Great Britain. Exclusion orders had been issued against 261, with 394 more charged with criminal offences. This put at only 12 per cent the number of people detained under the Act who subsequently were either excluded or charged. In other words, the security forces released nearly 90 per cent without further action.[178] Although the overall trend in the annual number of individuals detained was declining, and the annual number excluded or charged was increasing, the overall low percentage of convictions arising from the use of these powers did nothing to allay the fears of the opponents of the legislation that they were being used for intelligence gathering and harassment.

Jellicoe suggested that the use of detention for gathering information was legitimate. His report recommended, though, that any period of extension for detention be secured at the time of the extension, along with justification for the period by reference to the results anticipated. The Secretary of State should then grant an extension of detention for the five day period only when satisfied that the full period of time requested would be necessary. The possibility of granting an initial period less than five days and then extending it to a period of up to five days in an additional extension should be maintained. Jellicoe further advocated that the Home Office closely scrutinise extension applications to make sure that they were used only in cases in which they were clearly required. Jellicoe found a higher proportion of extended detentions granted to individuals arrested in Northern Ireland under section 12 of the 1976 PTA than the number of extensions granted in Great Britain. He suggested that the reason for this was that in Northern Ireland, with seventy-two hour detention available under the 1978 EPA, the rationale for employing the 1976 PTA was precisely the fact that the individual could be detained for up to seven days. In Northern Ireland powers of arrest under the 1976 PTA could be used in place of, or in addition to, the 1978 EPA. The advantage of the latter was that it did not require reasonable suspicion. This choice was unavailable in Great Britain.[179]

Perhaps not surprisingly, Jellicoe omitted consideration of the extensive powers of search and left powers of arrest and detention unchanged. He did recommend some minor alterations to improve the situation of those subject to them. As had been recommended previously by the Bennett Committee, Jellicoe advocated that a printed notice of rights be provided to individuals in custody, with access to a solicitor after the first forty-eight hours and every forty-eight hours thereafter guaranteed. After forty-eight hours a uniformed custody officer should remind the individual of the right to a solicitor and enquire whether he or she wished to exercise this right. Jellicoe suggested that the reply be documented and the suspect invited to sign it, with refusal to sign appropriately noted. He advised that there were some instances in which an Assistant Chief Constable might have reasonable grounds for believing that a private interview between the suspect and his or her solicitor might harm evidence or witnesses, lead to the alerting of other terrorist suspects not yet arrested, hinder the recovery of property or prejudice the gathering of intelligence.[180] Under these circumstances, Jellicoe recommended that the Assistant Chief Constable be permitted to exercise the 'uniformed inspector' proviso in which a uniformed inspector not connected with the case be present during the meeting. Jellicoe suggested that financial support for legal advice be provided in cases exceeding forty-eight hours and that the physical premises be improved, creating better accommodation and exercise facilities. He also advised that any person detained at a police station under the 1976 PTA be allowed to consult privately with a solicitor at any time during the detention (excluding the enactment of the 'uniformed inspector' proviso as detailed above) and that the security forces immediately inform a friend or relative of the detainee about the fact and place of his detention 'unless an officer of superintendent rank or above believes on reasonable grounds that such consultation or notification would have one of the four consequences' noted above.[181]

Significantly, Jellicoe recommended that powers of arrest and detention be extended for use in combatting international terrorism. This in part reflected developments in the international community. The timing of the report coincided with the release of the European Commission of Human Rights' decision on the application of *McVeigh, O'Neill and Evans* v. *United Kingdom*.[182] In its findings the Commission widened the discretion of states to take measures deviating from the ordinary process of law enforcement in dealing with terrorist matters without violating the European Convention on Human Rights. Jellicoe's recommendation that terrorist powers be extended to deal with international terrorism reflected the sanction extended by the international community:

> The major trend of terrorism within the United Kingdom is its increasing 'internationalisation'. This has two aspects: the growing international links of those terrorist groups which are associated with Northern Ireland, and the increase in the number of terrorist incidents in Great Britain unconnected with Northern Ireland . . . It does . . . seem strange to me that the Act's powers of arrest and extended detention . . . have not been made available for use against terrorism from other sources.[183]

As a result, Jellicoe advocated that the powers of arrest in section 12(1)(b) 'should be available for use against suspected international terrorists of any group, cause or nationality, but that it should not be so available in respect of domestic terrorism unconnected with Northern Ireland'.[184]

Jellicoe recommended that port powers remain largely as they had been under the 1976 PTA, with however, stricter requirements for the completion of landing and embarkation cards. To establish standard procedures between the different ports, he suggested that training sessions be conducted for inspectors with regard to the questioning of suspected terrorists and that a study be undertaken to determine the number of police personnel, the quality and amount of equipment and the facilities for physical accommodation at airports and sea ports serving destinations within the Common Travel Area. Jellicoe suggested that it be clearly stated or posted that the questioning of travellers was taking place in accordance with the 1976 PTA. It also recommended that immigration officers receive training similar to that of Special Branch port officers regarding the powers enshrined in the 1976 PTA and relating to terrorism concerning Northern Ireland.

THE 1984 PREVENTION OF TERRORISM (TEMPORARY PROVISIONS) ACT

Parliament debated the Jellicoe Report simultaneously with the PTA renewal orders in March 1983.[185] For the first time Labour officially opposed renewal of the Act. The party found that, according to Jellicoe's test under which emergency measures were justified – when their aims could not be achieved by use of the general law, when they made no unacceptable inroads on civil liberties and when effective safeguards were provided to prevent abuse – the 1976 PTA failed. Out of the 5,555 people picked up in Great Britain in 1975 under the 1976 PTA, only twenty-eight had been sentenced to terms of imprisonment greater than one year. Labour recognised that this seriously undermined the confidence of the Irish-Catholic community in Great Britain and its willingness to cooperate.

> The report has failed singularly to satisfy the counter-balancing argument that Lord Jellicoe set up. It fails to show that the Act continues to be effective. It does not show that the Act's aims cannot be obtained under the general law. It shows clearly that the Act makes unacceptable inroads into our civil liberties. It is for that reason, among others, we shall vote against the renewal of the Prevention of Terrorism (Temporary Provisions) Act 1976.[186]

During the debates, the government indicated that it accepted many of Jellicoe's recommendations for immediate implementation. With reference to alterations in powers of arrest and exclusion orders, however, the government withheld comment.

On 24 October the new Prevention of Terrorism Bill received its second reading in the House. The 1984 Act introduced a number of measures to ensure that seven day detention powers would be exercised sparingly. It allowed more than one extension after the first forty-eight hours up to a period of five days in order to encourage the police to apply for shorter periods of detention. The decision to extend detention was to be made only by the Secretary of State and not a junior minister, unless circumstances made it impossible.[187] Under the new act the police became required to submit a follow-up report after extension had been granted.[188]

Labour opposed the statute, arguing that the justification for the measure had changed since it was first instituted in 1974. What had been defended as a temporary response to an emergency situation had become fixed in British legislation. This was partly a result of the government's attempt to normalise what had previously been considered political violence. By claiming the violence to be ordinary criminal activity, the government could not maintain that extraordinary circumstances prevailed. This, in turn, led to a watering-down of emergency measures in order to align special legislation more closely with ordinary law. Under these circumstances the onus shifted from needing to demonstrate the effectiveness of emergency measures to having to show their ineffectiveness to gain their repeal. Reverting back to the initial onus, Labour moved an amendment which stated that the Opposition rejected the Bill as a result of Jellicoe's failure to uncover any clear proof of the effectiveness of the measures. Furthermore, the Opposition held that the emergency provisions actually fostered support for terrorism. Parliament defeated the amendment by 302 votes to 144, but the point stood – Labour refused to fall into step with the government's efforts to extend the PTA.

The House of Commons passed the 1984 Prevention of Terrorism (Temporary Provisions) Act by 291 votes to 46, with the Labour front bench abstaining.[189] Drawing on Jellicoe's recommendations, the new statute introduced three new safeguards in relation to exclusion. First of all, it limited the period of exclusion to three years, after which time the Secretary of State could renew the order. This improved the informal review system established in 1979, by virtue of which exclusion orders were made indefinitely with the option of a subject requesting a review after three years. Not only did the change make an administrative concession a legal right, but it transferred the burden of proof to those wanting the exclusion order to continue. During discussion in the House of Commons the Home Secretary guaranteed that he would not accept the application for additional exclusion orders to be issued as a routine matter: 'If the events during the three years . . . indicate that nothing fresh has occurred . . . if all that is being relied on is material which led to the making of the initial application – I envisage making a fresh exclusion order only in the rarest of circumstances'.[190] Secondly, the government exempted British citizens resident in Great Britain for three or more years prior to consideration of exclusion. Similarly, an individual resident in Northern Ireland for three or more years could not be excluded from the province. This radically altered the twenty year requirement that had been adopted as a legacy of the 1939 PVA. Thirdly, clause 7 established an absolute right of appeal for individuals to meet with an advisor to make representations protesting the issuance of exclusion orders. The government extended the length of time within which such meetings were arranged from ninety-six hours to seven days after the initial order was made. This aimed at encouraging individuals against whom exclusion orders had been made to make representations to the Home Secretary's advisors. In contrast to section 12, exclusion orders could only be made in relation to terrorism connected to Northern Ireland. This included issuing such orders to individuals from the Republic of Ireland. Other cases could be addressed under the 1971 Immigration Act.

Part IV extended powers of arrest to international terrorism but exempted domestic terrorism aside from that related to Northern Ireland. The government offered two justifications for this alteration: (a) the new powers were consistent with the 1978 Suppression of Terrorism Act, and (b) non-Irish terrorism was viewed as a growing threat. With the protection of life and property the first function of the State, the government claimed that the inclusion of international terrorism in the statute's auspices was entirely warranted. Opponents of the section claimed that extraordinary powers were not required: between 1977 and 1986 only a dozen or so non-Irish terrorist murders had occurred.[191] Further, while diplomatic immunity might have hampered investigations in these cases, there was nothing in section 12 of the new Act to overcome this problem. Although not entirely supported by the Tory party, the definition of terrorism continued to include the 'use of violence for political ends'. This seemed to contradict the criminalisation of the violence – an aspect emphasised by the listing of offences in the schedule to the Act not by motivation but by the acts themselves. The government made the 1984 PTA subject to annual renewal, but, in accordance with Jellicoe's recommendation, limited its duration to five years. Although Jellicoe had proposed this limitation to emphasise the temporary nature of the statute, he also had proposed that the actual words 'Temporary Provisions' be dropped from the title. The government retained this phrase in order to diminish fears of the legislation's becoming increasingly long-lived. In response to concern that Parliament was not adequately informed about the ongoing operation of the Act, the government appointed an independent monitor from December 1984 to provide an annual review of the 1984 PTA. The government also announced during the second reading of the Bill that it would be introducing the Police and Criminal Evidence Bill, which would give effect to Jellicoe's recommendation that people held under the PTA be given the same rights as any other detainee. The Bill provided for access to legal advice and for the notification of a relative or friend concerning a detainee's whereabouts. In accordance with Jellicoe the government also asked HM's

Inspectorate of Constabulary to conduct a study of police work at ports. the Home Office distributed circulars to the police to warn them against the exercise of emergency powers for customs or immigration purposes[192] and to recommend that at the beginning of every examination a suspect be handed a notice of his rights.[193] This last action sought to make it clear that an examination had commenced and that the twelve hour detention period had begun. In sum, the 1986 PTA mitigated some of the more objectionable aspects of police powers and exclusion orders. The government accepted fifty-three out of Jellicoe's fifty-nine recommendations. However, the alterations did nothing to change the fundamental nature of the emergency statute.

REVIEW AND DEVELOPMENT

From 1984 to 1988 the annual renewal debates for the 1984 PTA mostly involved a reiteration of established Government and Opposition positions. The Conservatives claimed that the measures were necessary to fight terrorism in Great Britain. Although the provisions represented an incursion into civil liberties, such actions could be justified in order to protect more basic rights, such as the right to life. The government considered its first duty to be the protection of the life and property of British subjects. Although Labour continued to oppose the legislation, it was on the grounds that because of the other civil liberties' issues raised, there was not sufficient violation of primary principles, such as right to life, to warrant the extension of emergency measures. The party contended that in the light of the small percentage of arrests that subsequently led to charges, the statute apparently was being used to gather information and to harass republican sympathisers. This view was not far off the truth. During the 1987 renewal debate the shadow Home Secretary announced that, of those arrested under the 1984 PTA, only 5 per cent were subsequently charged.[194] In 1989 the head of the Metropolitan Police's anti-terrorist squad wrote that the PTA 'permits the detention of suspected terrorists in order to obtain intelligence and/or evidence'.[195] Nevertheless the Northern Ireland Office's *Guide to Emergency Powers* instructed police that it was necessary to caution an individual concerning to their rights 'only when the detainee is suspected of an offence and when questions are put for the purpose of obtaining evidence to be put in court'.[196] Not all individuals detained, though, were held in relation to specific offences that had been committed. Interestingly the use of arrest and interrogation as an intelligence gathering exercise seems to have been upheld by the courts in *ex parte Lynch*.[197] Jackson, however, offers a differing interpretation: '*Lynch* is a decision about the procedure to be followed by arresting officers on arrest and is not a decision on the grounds for the exercise of a power of arrest'.[198] Labour claimed that 'normal' legislation would be sufficient to pursue prosecutions.

As was mentioned earlier, the government agreed during the renewal debates to appoint someone to monitor the operation of the emergency measures on an annual basis. The information provided by the review body was to help facilitate Parliament's yearly consideration of the statute. Cyril Philips conducted the first two reviews.[199] With regard to exclusion, Philips noted that a Secretary of State considered all applications and signed all orders. His second review, submitted in January 1986, reported that the overall number of exclusion orders had decline. As previous inquiries had found, the government had only occasionally invoked the power to exclude from Northern Ireland. The Home Office instituted a review of exclusion orders which revealed that a shift in their use had occurred: 'Whereas the majority of exclusion orders were [in the 1970s] being made against people resident in Great Britain, that number in recent years has declined significantly and the power has been mostly invoked against individuals travelling to Great Britain'.[200] Philips suggested that such orders were becoming less and less important in the fight against terrorism and suggested that the strategy of transferring suspected terrorists within the UK was becoming obsolete. In addition, the introduction of the 1984 Police and Criminal Evidence Act provided the police in England and Wales with significant powers, possibly making the use of exclusion orders unnecessary.[201] For these reasons, Philips recommended that Parliament reconsider the need for sections 4 and 5 of the 1984 PTA, phasing out their use by the secretaries refraining from issuing any new exclusion orders. He suggested that this be done with an eye towards repealing the measure. The government rejected this advice on the grounds that, while the power infringed civil liberties and was in principle objectionable, it did not contravene the European Convention on Human Rights and was necessary to maintain the fight against terrorism.[202]

As with previous reviews, Philips found that applications for extension of detention for less than the maximum of five days were considerably more frequent in Great Britain than in Northern Ireland, where the full detention period was more often requested. Correspondingly, although some applications for extended detention had been rejected in Northern Ireland, none had been refused in Great Britain. Of those arrested and detained in Northern Ireland under section 12 of the 1984 PTA, approximately 24 per cent were then charged with some criminal offence. In Great Britain this number was at 20 per cent, the highest amount recorded since the institution of the measures.[203] In reviewing claims against the use of detention measures under the 1984 PTA, Philips found allegations that the powers were being used as a convenient means of removing political activists from the streets; nevertheless, he was satisfied that the powers were being used in accordance with their aim.

From 1986 to 1994, Viscount Colville conducted the annual 1984 PTA reviews.[204] Representations made to him each year regarding objections to exclusion orders, proscription, and the powers of arrest and detention largely reflected those previously submitted to Philips and repeatedly submitted to the Standing Advisory Commission on Human Rights. As with Philips, Colville's terms of reference 'accept[ed] the continuing need for legislation against terrorism'. In his first report of 5 February 1987, Colville repeated his predecessor's call for an end to exclusion orders. Douglas Hurd's response, however, was similar to that given to Philips: 'Your report acknowledges that [exclusion] is used sparingly . . . The fact that a power is used rarely does not mean it is not necessary. I believe it is right only to employ this power in cases where I am sure that excluding the person will prevent acts of terrorism'.[205] In the Commons debate in 1987 on the renewal of the 1984 PTA, Hurd took it one step further: 'The justification of these powers, as opposed to the ordinary powers of the criminal law, is that they enable the police to prevent horrors before they happen'.[206]

The following year, Colville proposed that exclusion orders be replaced by tighter immigration procedures.[207] The government rejected this suggestion as well as Colville's assertion that the legislation should be made more permanent and that the annual renewal debates should be eliminated.[208] Colville advised, however, that the provisions governing proscription continue to be subject to annual renewal. Colville's 1987 Report examined in detail the 1984 Criminal Justice Act which, in conjunction with other factors, led to the introduction of the 1988 Criminal Evidence (Northern Ireland) Order.[209] This measure allowed adverse inference to be drawn from the silence of the accused.[210] The change derived from the Criminal Law Revision Committee's eleventh report in 1972, which recommended a curtailment regarding the right to silence. The upsurge in terrorist violence in the summer of 1988 precipitated the introduction of the Criminal Evidence (Northern Ireland) Order. The government rushed through Parliament in late October and early November 1988 through Order-in-Council procedure.[211] In his report submitted in 1990, Colville recommended that the provisions relating to internment be dropped altogether. Colville's reviews began to focus increasingly on the use of the 1984 PTA in combating international, in addition to Northern Irish, terrorism.[212] As a result, he placed greater emphasis on port powers and, in particular, on the operation of the 1984 Prevention of Terrorism (Supplemental Temporary Provisions) Order. In his report of 1987 Colville advocated that a new act be drafted to incorporate special powers aimed at combating international terrorism, as the provisions dealing with it from the 1984 PTA proved insufficient for the purpose.[213] Colville also paid greater attention to the operation of ordinary criminal law and, especially, powers of arrest and inter-rogation under the 1984 PACE. Although no charges had been brought under the provisions of the 1984 PTA dealing with proscription, Colville noted in his 1987 report that lifting the ban on the IRA and INLA would be impossible. 'Any such decision by Parliament would be seen as a recognition of something; there would be many views as to that of which it would be a recognition. The most dangerous would be a perception that the leading merchants of Irish terrorism were no longer disap-proved.'[214] He added: 'It may be, too, that there is a deterrent effect which prevents such things as parades and fund-raising. Most of the public would applaud this result'.[215] Although the 1986 Public Order Act might have precluded the necessity for including proscription in the 1984 PTA, Colville suggested that it was 'too late', and, in the event, the provisions governing proscription could not be repealed. Retained, then, for its presentational effect, proscription reflected the public abhorrence and condemnation of proscribed organisations and acted to discourage public displays of support for them.[216] Colville examined proscription in light of the increasing emphasis on international terrorism, but he concluded that proscription would prove too inflexible a weapon to employ in countering international terrorist organisations.

THE 1989 PREVENTION OF TERRORISM (TEMPORARY PROVISIONS) ACT

Colville's report, submitted on 30 January 1989, coincided with Parliament's consideration of the new Prevention of Terrorism (Temporary Provisions) Bill.[217] Much of the statute remained unchanged. Parliament re-enacted with minimal alteration measures relating to proscription, forty-eight hour detention with up to five days' extension granted by the Secretary of State, powers of arrest, controls at the ports and three year exclusion orders. The offence of failing to provide information regarding terrorist activity also remained. The new statute did, however, make changes in five areas. First, although it retained annual renewal, the government removed the Act from its previous five year constraint and gave it an unlimited life-span. Second, the statute reduced remission from a maximum of one-half the sentence to one-third for individuals sentenced for more than five years for a scheduled offence. Individuals released, if convicted of an additional scheduled offence, became required to serve the portion of the previous sentence that had been waived. This alteration sought to increase the deterrent affect of the statute and to bring Northern Irish policy into line with that of Great Britain.[218] Third, the government adopted Colville's recommendation for additional provisions relating to the finances of proscribed organisations. In accordance with the 1987 report, the 1989 Prevention of Terrorism (Temporary Provisions) Act (PTA)[219] granted courts greater powers to examine bank accounts and seize assets, with the onus of proof on the defendant to explain the origin of the monies present. In 1987 Colville recommended that renewed interest be given to legislation enabling bank balances to be frozen and information concerning bank accounts revealed. Unconsciously harking back to Regulation 18C of the 1922–43 SPAs, Colville claimed the 1986 Drug Trafficking Offences Act as the impetus for the idea.[220] These measures were designed to help combat the increasing 'laundering' of paramilitary funding through otherwise 'legitimate' business concerns. Under the 1989 PTA it also became an offence for an individual to handle the finances of a terrorist organisation. However, this measure was not expected to be particularly effective, largely because of the sophisticated nature of paramilitary laundering schemes. Owing to the inclusion of clauses designed to curtail terrorist funding, Labour did not oppose the Bill outright on the second reading, but chose to abstain. The statute eased the prosecution's burden of proof: the individual giving money need only reasonably suspect, instead of intend, the purpose for which the monies were to be used. Fourth, the power to search premises for weapons and equipment was altered. Applicable only in Northern Ireland, section 21 followed a recommendation from Baker's 1984 Review and provided for security forces to restrict individuals in an area in which a search for munitions or transmitters was being conducted. This alteration responded to a decision in *Toner and Oscar* v. *Chief Constable of RUC and MoD* [unreported] in which the judge held that four hours' detention of a family during a search amounted to false imprisonment. Finally, the 1989 PTA also improved the safeguards with regard to fingerprinting. Like its predecessor, the statute permitted any police, prison officer or anyone authorised by the Secretary of State, to take whatever steps reasonably necessary to photograph, measure or otherwise identify the individual in custody. Safeguards in section 61 of PACE became applicable (with some modifications) to the 1989 PTA.[221]

THE 1996 PREVENTION OF TERRORISM (ADDITIONAL POWERS) ACT

Although the 1989 statute enabled Parliament to suspend any of the Act's provisions, subsequent reports submitted by Viscount Colville and (from 1994) J.J. Rowe,[222] did not recommend any significant alterations. From 1990 to 1994 eleven deaths resulted in Great Britain from IRA attacks.[223] The republican and loyalist cease-fires in 1994 once again prompted a detailed examination of emergency powers in Great Britain. In December 1995 the government commissioned Lord Lloyd to conduct an inquiry 'to consider the future need for specific counter-terrorism legislation in the United Kingdom if the cessation of terrorism connected with the affairs of Northern Ireland leads to a lasting peace'.[224] Reflecting the trend towards greater discussion of international terrorism as exemplified in the annual reviews, the inquiry was to take into account the continuing threat from other kinds of terrorism. In addition, because of the various cases that had arisen in the European Court of Human Rights, the inquiry was instructed to consider alterations in the emergency measures in the light of the United Kingdom's obligations under international law.

Soon after the appointment of the Lloyd Commission, the republican cease-fire ended; nevertheless, the inquiry went ahead, with the final report presented to Parliament in October 1996. The report took into consideration both the 1973–96 Northern Ireland (Emergency Provisions) Acts (EPAs)[225] and the 1974–89 PTAs. The government predicated the review on the assumption that Northern Irish political violence would end. The following chapter examines Lord Lloyd's contribution in more detail. The resurgence of hostilities following the Docklands bombing in London in February 1996, together with the severe changes advocated by the inquiry, prompted the Conservative government to shelve the document until after the 1997 General Election. In 1996 Labour altered their position to abstain from voting on the 1989 PTA, rather than to oppose its renewal outright. With the public climate, following the breakdown of the Provisional IRA cease-fire, generally supportive of the introduction of stricter measures, and with Labour's recent decision not to oppose the Act in 1996, the government decided that it would be a propitious time to introduce more extensive powers for the police.

Approximately three weeks after the extension of the 1989 PTA, the government introduced a bill designed to increase police powers. On 1 April the Home Secretary announced to Parliament that the government sought five additional powers. Four of them transferred powers, comparable to those granted to the police in Northern Ireland under the 1996 EPA, to police in Great Britain. These included the ability of police to stop and search pedestrians for terrorist items within a designated area (which had been specified as a search zone for up to twenty-eight days), the power for police to seek a magistrates' warrant to search non-residential premises for material likely to be of use to a terrorist organisation, statutory power for the police to cordon off an area, and the ability of the police to impose temporary parking restrictions in response to a general threat to targets, such as government buildings or royal residences. The fifth power, previously unavailable in either Northern Ireland or Great Britain, enabled the police to search unaccompanied freight at ports. These changes to the Prevention of Terrorism Act demonstrated the further normalisation of emergency powers enshrined in the 1973–96 EPAs. Having been in existence in the province to deal with an exceptional situation, they were being sought under different circumstances for implementation throughout the United Kingdom.

Some similar powers had already seeped their way into ordinary criminal law. From 1992 to 1994 a number of IRA car bombings had prompted the police to set up mobile road checks in metropolitan areas of Great Britain and to construct a perimeter around London. It was unclear at the time whether the powers under the PTA justified the establishment of this 'ring of steel'. The 1994 Criminal Justice and Public Order Act sought to rectify the situation. The statute amended the Prevention of Terrorism Act, enabling police to stop and search vehicles and persons at random to try to prevent instances of Irish and international terrorism. The powers of search introduced by the government in the 1996 Prevention of Terrorism (Additional Powers) Act empowered the police to stop and search pedestrians in any area authorised by a police constable of the ranking of superintendent or above.[226] The Act demanded that such designation be committed to writing 'as soon as possible' and reported to the Secretary of State 'as soon is reasonably practicable'.[227] The measures specifically stated: 'A constable may exercise his powers under this section whether or not he has any grounds for suspecting the presence of articles of [a terrorist-related] kind'.

The 1996 Act also introduced new powers of search for non-residential premises. The legislation empowered a justice of the peace to issue a warrant to search premises if two criteria were met: that he or she held reasonable grounds for believing that material likely to be of value to an investigation could be found on one or more of the premises specified in the application, and that the material did not include items subject to legal privilege, excluded material or special procedure material. Not only could an officer approach a justice of the peace for these powers, but a procurator fiscal could, for the purposes of a terrorist investigation, apply to a sheriff for a warrant.[228]

The new statute empowered the police to impose a cordon 'if it appears to a police officer of at least the rank of superintendent that it is expedient to do so in connection with an investigation into the commission, preparation or instigation of an act of terrorism'.[229] The power to impose a police cordon applied only to acts of terrorism related to Northern Ireland, or any other terrorist act unless 'connected solely with the affairs of the United Kingdom or any part of the United Kingdom other than Northern Ireland'.[230] The initial authorisation of the cordon was not to exceed fourteen days but an officer of the rank of superintendent and above could extend the period up to twenty-eight days. Powers of entry, search and seizure within the cordoned area could be exercised at any time and on multiple occasions, with further power extended to the police to impose parking restrictions and to remove vehicles. The area had to be marked as far as was reasonably practicable.

The legislation also extended further port powers to the authorities to search unaccompanied materials arriving or leaving from Northern Ireland or Great Britain in order to determine whether they were being used in the commission of terrorist acts. The 1974 PTA had introduced the power to examine individuals arriving in or leaving the UK. Authorities exercised the majority of port powers within the Common Travel Area (CTA): Great Britain, Northern Ireland, the Republic of Ireland, the Isle of Man and the Channel Islands. For example, prior to the cease-fires, in 1993 nearly 131 million passengers travelled through British ports. Authorities examined 928 thousand of these people, about 634 thousand of those at CTA ports. The post-cease-fire period did little to change this emphasis. Of 167 million passengers in 1995, 719 thousand were examined, with 444 thousand at CTA ports. Although CTA traffic constituted some sixteen per cent of total passengers travelling through the United Kingdom, the CTA ports witnessed over sixty per cent of all examinations.[231] Section 4(A) of the 1996 Prevention of Terrorism (Additional Powers) Act extended these powers to searching goods originating from the CTA and abroad. The statute empowered the port authority to board any ship or aircraft or enter any vehicle, use reasonable force to carry out his/her functions and retain for up to seven days anything found on the search.

Parliament met the introduction of the 1996 Prevention of Terrorism (Additional Powers) Bill with some resistance, as, typically, the government aimed to push the new statute through all its stages in a matter of two days.[232] However, ultimately, the Opposition supported the Act. The Conservatives invoked a guillotine motion whereby clauses of the statute left undiscussed would automatically pass into law. The rationale offered by the government was that, with the anniversary of the 1916 Easter Uprising drawing near, the other commitments which Members of Parliament had on Holy Thursday and Good Friday, and the 'reasonableness' of the powers requested in the new statute, it was necessary to rush the legislation through Parliament. As no time limit was given on the length of the statute, Parliament would have no opportunity to discuss it in greater length. Significantly, no information had been issued by the Home Office indicating impending difficulties over the holiday period. The first time news of the statute reached the House was in the week in which the Bill was introduced. As a result, a number of members – and the Liberal Democratic party – opposed the rushed measures. Nevertheless, the 1996 Prevention of Terrorism (Additional Powers) Bill passed into law in April 1996.

CONCLUSION

The 1974 Prevent of Terrorism (Temporary Provisions) Act swiftly became subsumed in British legislation. Soon after its enactment the onus shifted from those supporting emergency measures to prove that they were imperative, to individuals seeking to repeal the legislation needing to demonstrate that an emergency no longer existed. Although Westminster instigated various reviews from 1974 to 1996, the basic provisions remained largely unchanged. During the next four years a blending of the EPA and PTA and more detailed consideration of permanent counter-terrorist law emerged. The following chapter considers in more detail the joint evolution of these measures from 1996 to 2000.

CHAPTER SIX

Counter-Terrorist Legislation 1996–2000

LORD LLOYD'S REVIEW differed significantly from previous inquiries into the use of emergency legislation. His terms of reference included all counter-terrorist legislation in the United Kingdom, and not just either the EPA or PTA. He also was the first reviewer to be directed to take into account the United Kingdom's international obligations both to the 1950 European Convention on Human Rights and the 1966 International Covenant on Civil and Political Rights. This reflected a growing concern in Britain about the international attention being drawn to domestic counter-terrorist legislation. In part, this increasing awareness of the international arena stemmed from cases brought against Britain at the European Court in Strasbourg. Although both the European Convention and the International Covenant signified obligations of equal standing, because of the former's right of individual petition, in Lloyd's words: 'The European Convention in particular has impinged on the United Kingdom's counter-terrorist efforts in Northern Ireland'.[1] On several occasions the UK had been taken to court for the operation of its emergency powers.

As was discussed in chapter three, in 1976 the European court determined in *Ireland* v. *UK* that the five techniques employed by Britain in 1971 constituted torture and that other treatment used by the police was inhuman and degrading. In *Brogan and Others* v. *UK*, four people, detained between four and seven days under the PTA on suspicion of involvement in Northern Irish terrorism, submitted complaints to the European Commission on Human Rights that the UK's actions violated the convention.[2] Article 5, paragraph 3 of the convention demanded that anyone arrested 'be brought promptly before a judge or other officer authorised by law to exercise judicial power and . . . be entitled to trial within a reasonable time or to release pending trial'.[3] In November 1988 the European Court ruled that even the shortest period for which one of the four individuals had been held, four days and six hours, violated the convention. Because no provisions existed in the UK through which the government could compensate the individuals, the court found Britain in violation of Article 5, paragraph 5, which stipulated that anyone who had been the victim of arrest or detention should have an enforceable right to compensation. The British government insisted that it needed to retain seven day detention and examined two possible courses of action: either a judicial element could be inserted into the procedure through which the seven day detention was extended, or the UK could derogate under Article 15.[4] In December 1988 Britain announced that it would pursue the second route and a year later it reaffirmed the derogation, stating that it would be maintained as long as deemed necessary.[5] The derogation read:

> There have been in the United Kingdom in recent years campaigns of organised terrorism connected with the affairs of Northern Ireland which have manifested themselves in activities which have included repeated murder, attempted murder, maiming, intimidation and violent civil disturbance and in bombing and fire raising which have resulted in death, injury and widespread destruction of property. As a result, a public emergency within the meaning of Article 15(1) of the Convention exists in the United Kingdom.[6]

Although *Brannigan & McBride* v. *UK* subsequently challenged the validity of this derogation, once again contesting the length of detention, the court found in the UK's favour.[7] According to the preconditions for derogation, that there existed a 'war or other public emergency threatening the life of the nation', that the derogation was 'strictly required by the exigencies of the situation', and that measures were not inconsistent with the State's other international obligations, the court determined that the derogation was valid.[8] Simultaneously, the court noted its concern about the long-term, apparently unexceptional character of the 'emergency' in Northern Ireland. Not only did it appear that the normal course of government could operate, but a formal declaration of emergency was not in place. Although the EPA and the PTA assumed a continuing need for extraordinary powers, only four official states of emergency had been declared in Northern Ireland in the post 1972 period. They were issued under the 1926 Emergency Powers Act (Northern Ireland) and the 1964 Emergency Powers (Amendment) Act (Northern Ireland).[9] Terence O'Neill issued the first state of emergency on 10 February 1972. The British government formally withdrew this decree just over nine months later. However, on the same day, 16 November 1973, the government issued a second declaration. The British government withdrew it the following May. On the same day it was withdrawn a third state of emergency was declared. This time the declaration lasted only four months. Five years went by before the fourth state of emergency was issued and the declaration only lasted for three days. The British government issued it on 11 January and formally withdrew it on 14 January 1979.[10] The European Court's scepticism over the long-term, apparently unexceptional nature of the emergency in the United Kingdom led to increased efforts on the part of Britain to make clear what internal challenges it faced.

Following *Ireland* v. *UK* and *Brogan and Others* v. *UK, Fox, Campbell and Hartley* v. *UK* became the third finding by the European Court of Human Rights that Britain's counter-terrorist legislation violated the European covenant. This case focused on requirements of 'suspicion' versus 'reasonable suspicion' and the use of arrest to gather information.[11] At the time Lloyd began his inquiry the court was further considering *Murray* v. *UK*, with the decision rendered in February 1996.[12] In Northern Ireland, the Codes of Practice made under Section 61 of the EPA empowered the police to waive a detainee's access to a solicitor for the first forty-eight hours of detention. Once having granted access, the police could impose further delays for up to forty-eight hours before allowing additional meetings. The measure prohibited the presence of a solicitor during the police interview. In *Murray* the court found that this denial of access to a solicitor, combined with the trial court's right to draw adverse inferences from silence while being questioned, violated the detainee's right under Article 6 of the European Convention of Human Rights.

In addition to the derogation lodged with the European Court, the United Kingdom also deviated from Article 5 of the International Covenant on Civil and Political Rights. In a letter of 23 December 1988 duplicating virtually word for word the derogation entered in respect of the European Court, Britain noted the terrorist situation in the UK and defended its use of detention. The treatment of detainees also received widespread international attention. In 1991 the UN Committee against Torture examined allegations of ill-treatment of terrorist suspects in police custody. It expressed 'grave concern about the regime governing detention'. Lloyd noted that the UN Human Rights Committee called in 1995 for the UK government to take further steps to permit the early withdrawal of its derogation from Article 4 of the International Covenant on Civil and Political Rights and to 'dismantle the apparatus of laws infringing civil liberties which were designed for periods of emergency'.[13] He concluded that 'The existence of the emergency legislation has, itself, caused some damage to the UK's international reputation in the field of human rights'.[14]

THE LLOYD REVIEW

As a result of such intense scrutiny in the international arena of Britain's domestic legislation, John Major's government instructed Lloyd to take particular notice of the United Kingdom's international obligations, particularly in its consideration of permanent measures, wherein no 'emergency' could be claimed. Lloyd's terms of reference also differed from his predecessors in that the review did not demand an immediate, continuing need for counter-terrorist law. It assumed a cessation of hostilities with regard to Northern Ireland. In doing so, it drew more attention to other types of terrorism existing in the United Kingdom. For example, Lloyd noted that the day following the Birmingham bombing, four men hijacked a British Airways VC-10 en route to Calcutta. The hijackers forced the crew to fly the plane to Tunisia where they demanded that fifteen terrorist prisoners be released. One passenger died before negotiations concluded. Lloyd noted approximately eighty international terrorist incidents that had occurred in the United Kingdom between 1975 and 1995. More than 300 people died in these events and scores more were injured. The vast majority of deaths in these cases occurred with the bombing of Pan Am over Lockerbie, Scotland in 1988. Lloyd cited Scottish nationalist extremist groups who had engineered some forty-seven 'terrorist type attacks' – mainly letter bombs – since the mid 1970s. Welsh nationalist extremist use of arson against unoccupied holiday homes and incendiary devices in packages registered roughly 188 additional incidents since 1975. Lloyd cited another 100 incendiary devices planted by animal rights extremists.

Not only had these events happened in the past, but Lloyd estimated the likelihood of future international terrorist attacks in the United Kingdom as high. Drawing heavily on research conducted by Paul Wilkinson of St Andrews University, Lloyd asserted that the threat from international terrorism would grow in the future. He cited political instability, inter-ethnic conflicts, and state-sponsored terrorism as motivating factors. The advent of chemical and biological weapons and increasingly sophisticated technology presented the possibility of widespread damage. Consequently, '[a]s the "weapon of the weak" terrorism is likely to remain an attractive option to those engaged in regional power struggles, facilitated by the ever-increasing international freedom of movement of people, goods and information. The UK . . . is particularly liable to be caught up in these struggles because of the number of communities of foreign nationals who live, or seek sanctuary, here'.[15] Lloyd cited various sources of international support for the introduction and use of counter-terrorist measures. For instance, the Summit of Peacemakers convened at Sharm El Sheikh in Egypt following four suicide bombings in Israel in early 1996 resulted in the commitment of world leaders:

> To promote coordination of efforts to stop acts of terror on bilateral, regional and international levels; ensuring instigators of such acts are brought to justice; supporting efforts by all parties to prevent their territories from being used for terrorist purposes; and preventing terrorist organisations from engaging in recruitment, supplying arms; or fund-raising.[16]

A P8 Ministerial meeting in Paris on 30 July 1996 similarly focused on terrorism and on taking measures to address the threat. Lloyd surveyed approximately twenty countries and found that eleven of them made specific provision for terrorist crime in their domestic statutes.[17] From these considerations, he concluded that some sort of permanent counter-terrorist legislation was necessary.

Lord Lloyd advocated that counter-terrorist measures be consolidated into a single act, instead of maintaining separate measures for Northern Ireland and Great Britain. He recommended the elimination of the Diplock courts, the ending of internment and the withdrawal of powers of exclusion. His decision to suspend these powers hinged on a lasting peace in Ireland – by far the most cogent terrorist threat faced by the United Kingdom. Since 1969 more than 3,200 people had lost their lives and over 40,000 had been injured as a result of the conflict.[18] Special powers should only be relinquished once this threat had been neutralised. Lloyd recommended a slight change in the definition of terrorism. His suggestion that 'terrorism' be defined as, 'The use of violence for political ends, and includes any use of serious violence for the purpose of putting the public or any section of the public in fear', drew on the current definition under the Prevention of Terrorism Act. He also advocated further definition of 'political ends', 'terrorist act', 'terrorist organisation' and 'terrorist offence'. Lloyd envisaged a new act in which the list of 'terrorist offences' could be set out in a schedule to the Act. For any case to come before a court of law in which a similar offence was alleged, if the prosecution could demonstrate that the necessary terrorist element was present, the offence would be tried under the counter-terrorist statute. The types of offences to be listed included acts of murder, violations of the 1883 Explosives Act, the 1982 Taking of Hostages Act, the 1978 Internationally Protected Persons Act and offences such as hi-jacking under the 1982 Aviation Security Act.[19] Also included would be the offences already in the EPA and PTA, such as directing a terrorist organisation, membership of a terrorist organisation, being concerned in the preparation of an act of terrorism, financial offences under the PTA, travelling equipped for terrorism, collecting information for the use of terrorists and any display of support in public for a proscribed organisation. Up until the inquiry the powers of the EPA and PTA had been used to varying degrees. Schedule 2 of the 1996 EPA detailed the organisations proscribed in the North: the IRA, INLA, UDA, UVF and UFF. The PTA only listed two organisations: the IRA and the INLA. As will be recalled from chapter five, the PTA only applied to organisations connected with the affairs of Northern Ireland. Most significantly, Lloyd advocated a new offence of 'conspiring in the UK to commit a terrorist offence abroad'. This last measure was to be introduced later in the year as a Members' Bill. Unsuccessful, the Labour government later implemented it via the 1998 Criminal Justice (Terrorism and Conspiracy) Act. This legislation is discussed in greater detail later in the chapter.

The 1984 Police and Criminal Evidence Act had obtained extensive powers for the police forces.[20] For Lloyd, these capabilities rendered many of those powers included, particularly in the PTA, irrelevant: 'Since "being concerned in the preparation of an act of terrorism" will itself be a terrorist offence there will be no need for any special power of arrest such as currently exists under [the] PTA', he wrote.[21] Powers of detention for questioning should be slightly longer than those accorded under PACE: from thirty-six hours, a forty-eight hour detention period with an extension for up to a maximum of four days on application, *ex parte*, to the Chief Metropolitan Magistrate in England and Wales, or to the Sheriff Principal for Lothian and the Borders in Scotland. (No such office existed in Northern Ireland, thus rendering a new appointment necessary.) Aside from the period of initial questioning, 'all other procedures, including taping of interviews, fingerprinting, taking of intimate samples, access to legal advice and the right to have someone informed of the person's arrest should be in accordance with PACE and any current code of practice issued under PACE'.[22] Lloyd recommended a drastic reduction in powers of detention at ports, from twenty-four hours to six hours, after which time the passenger either be arrested or released. He further suggested that police powers at ports of entry 'should be subject to a code of practice issued by the Secretary of State, which should, in normal times, reduce random examination to a minimum. In other words the power should normally only be exercised where there is an intelligence lead or in accordance with guidelines'.[23]

With regard to evidence, Lloyd suggested that sections of the 1985 Interception of Communications Act be amended to allow the prosecution to adduce evidence gained by telephone intercepts when relevant. He also advocated extending the power to order forfeiture of property and money to apply to all funds held by the convicted terrorist, unless it could be demonstrated that the articles did not derive from criminal activities of any sort. In order to sanction properties further, five day renewable restraint orders should be exercised by the Crown Court rather than the High Court. Lloyd further recommended that an individual convicted of a terrorist offence be treated differently at sentencing time, with the statute directing that the court take that fact into account when imposing a sentence. Drawing on the Italian government's success with the pentiti trials, Lloyd further stated: 'having regard . . . to the difficulty of obtaining evidence to convict terrorists, there should be a statutory discount of between one-third and two-thirds on what would have been the sentence of the court in every case where an accomplice gives evidence against a fellow terrorist'.[24] In the 1970s the Italian government had made little progress in defeating the Red Brigade. General Dalla Chiesa convinced the authorities in 1980 to introduce the pentiti statutes, allowing considerable reduction in sentences in return for cooperation with the police. 389 pentiti had come forward by 1982, of whom seventy-eight agreed to cooperate. By 1985 the Italian government had imprisoned 1,200 'terrorists'.[25] France, Germany and Spain introduced similar legislation soon thereafter. The Northern Ireland security forces' attempt to introduce similar measures in the province in the early 1980s failed miserably. The notorious supergrass trials (discussed in chapter four) did not make it into Lloyd's report. Instead he focused on foreign experiences with remission of sentences in return for information.

In many ways responding to the European Court of Human Rights' comments on the 'unexceptional' nature of the 'emergency' in the United Kingdom, Lloyd wrote:

> The new legislation should be confined to what is needed in the way of permanent legislation to meet the foreseeable terrorist threat. It should not attempt to cater in advance for emergencies, which may take a form which cannot now be foreseen. A number of additional powers are mentioned in this review which might be needed in the case of an emergency. These ought to be the subject of public discussion in advance of the emergency, but should not be capable of being brought into force otherwise than by way of primary legislation, following a formal declaration of an emergency.[26]

His case for the maintenance of some sort of permanent legislation rested on two assumptions: 'that terrorism presents an exceptionally serious threat to society' and 'that terrorists have proved particularly difficult to catch and convict without special offences and additional police powers'.[27] Terrorism was further distinguishable from 'ordinary' crime in its impact on members of the public, use of lethal force, creation of fear, aim of securing political objectives through methods that undermined democratic structures of government, and use by well-trained individuals backed by sophisticated organisations. Because of the peculiar threat presented to government by terrorism, special powers should be maintained. This conclusion ignored that a great portion of the threat posed was, precisely, the loss of a lifestyle, which emergency measures also destroyed.

The Conservative government presented a lukewarm (at best) response to Lord Lloyd's report. In Parliament Michael Howard, the Home Secretary, stated:

> We accept some of Lord Lloyd's recommendations relating to extra-territorial jurisdiction; as for the generality of his recommendations, which were made on the assumption that there was a lasting peace in Northern Ireland and which indicate the legislative framework that he thinks would be appropriate in those circumstances, we have said that, as that assumption has not yet been fulfilled, we see no need to state our attitude to those recommendations at this stage.

His political dance continued: 'We shall continue to keep [Lord Lloyd's recommendations] under review. If and when . . . the assumption that Lord Lloyd was asked to make comes about, we will consider what decisions to make in the light of the circumstances at the time'.[28] In other words, the resurgence in IRA activity (the absence of which predicated all recommendations in the report), the significant changes advocated by the document, and the coming of a general election, meant that the report would be shelved until a more propitious time.

POLITICAL MANOEUVRES

In the interim, the Northern Ireland talks process stumbled forward. Immediately following the Docklands bombing the British and Irish governments met at 10 Downing Street to condemn the resurgence in paramilitary violence. The Anglo-Irish communiqué issued by the British Prime Minister, John Major, and the Taoiseach, John Bruton, indicated deep regret at the resumption of violence and agreement that the continuation of ministerial talks with Sinn Féin required the restoration of the cease-fire. The governments agreed to conduct 'intensive multilateral consultations' before the all-party negotiations commenced on the 10 June.[29] The communiqué required that all parties participating in the June negotiations 'make clear at the beginning of the discussions their total and absolute commitment to the principles of democracy and non-violence set out in the report of the [Mitchell Commission]. They would also have to address, at that stage, its proposals on decommissioning'.[30] The two governments planned to conduct formal negotiations between the 4 and 13 March in order to reach agreement on proposals for an elective process leading to the all-party negotiations, construct the basis, participation, structure, format and agenda of the negotiations themselves, and determine whether parallel referendums on the peace process should be held in Northern Ireland and the Republic. In his address to the House of Commons following his meeting with Bruton, Major emphasised that any party engaged in violence would be excluded from the negotiations and that the result of the negotiations would be presented in a referendum to the people of Northern Ireland before being presented to Parliament.

In April 1996 the Conservative government introduced the Northern Ireland (Entry to Negotiations, etc.) Bill into Parliament. The legislation established a framework for electoral arrangements for negotiations. On the same day that the Bill was introduced, the government published *Northern Ireland: Ground Rules for Substantive All-Party Negotiations*.[31] In addition to laying out the ground rules for the negotiations (confidentiality, establishment of agenda items, procedures, etc.), this paper emphasised that violence on behalf of negotiation participants would not be tolerated:

> If during the negotiations, any party demonstrably dishonoured its commitment to the principles of democracy and nonviolence set out in the report of the International Body by, for example, resorting to force or threatening the use of force to influence the course or the outcome of the negotiations, or failing to oppose the efforts of others to do so, it would no longer be entitled to participate in the negotiations.[32]

Paragraph 9 of the document directly stated that neither the British nor Irish governments would admit Sinn Féin to the negotiations until the IRA restored its cease-fire of August 1994. In the 30 May elections the political arms of the paramilitary movements gained a number of seats: Sinn Féin captured seventeen, the Progressive Unionist Party (the political arm of the UVF) obtained two, and the Ulster Democratic Party (the political arm of the UDA) gained a further two. Constitutionalist distribution included thirty seats for the Ulster Unionist Party, twenty-four seats for the Democratic Unionist Party, twenty-one seats for the Social

Democratic and Labour Party, seven for Alliance, three for the United Kingdom Unionist Party and two for the Women's Coalition. In the absence of a cease-fire, the governments excluded Sinn Féin from the initial talks.

From June 1996 to March 1997 those party to the negotiations made minimal progress on the issue of decommissioning of weapons by paramilitary organisations, a preliminary issue to negotiations. Meanwhile, Parliament maintained powers in the PTA through the Prevention of Terrorism (Temporary Provisions) Act 1989 (Continuance) Orders. In his annual review of the legislation, John Rowe recommended that the PTA be continued for a further twelve months. Michael Howard, Secretary of State for the Home Department, noted in his introduction of order that although the statute had been intended as a temporary measure, it had to be maintained to meet the threat that continued to be posed by the IRA:

> It is now 23 years since the prevention of terrorism legislation was first enacted. The present Act was passed in 1989 and, like its predecessors, it was intended to be a temporary measure made in response to an exceptional threat. Very regrettably, the threat we face from terrorism remains as great today. Within our midst, a callous, murderous minority remains determined to use violence to achieve its end . . . we must consider the need for its provisions against the background of a continuing campaign by the Provisional IRA in Great Britain, and a return to violence in Northern Ireland. The past 12 months reveal an all too familiar legacy of the destruction of lives, families, homes, livelihoods and communities.[33]

Following the Docklands bombing, further IRA incidents in Great Britain had culminated in the bombing of Manchester city centre. On Saturday, 15 June 1996 more than 200 individuals were injured in a 3,300 lb IRA bomb. In Northern Ireland two car bombs in October 1996 injured a further thirty-eight people inside Thiepval barracks in Lisburn. On 12 February the IRA shot Lance Bombardier Stephen Restorick while checking a car at a vehicle checkpoint in Bessbrook. A growing convergence between British and Irish security policy steadily emerged. Disgust at these acts was expressed on both sides of the Irish sea. Members of Parliament noted that the Taoiseach had vociferously condemned the murder and had indicated that the Irish authorities would do everything within their power to cooperate with the British government to bring an end to terrorism. The IRA's cease-fire of August 1994 was seen as a sham. David Wilshire asserted: 'The original Sinn Féin-IRA so-called cease-fire was not progress and was no reason to abandon the powers in the Act. It was nothing more than a tactical manoeuvre. It was never a real step towards the permanent peace that we need before the recommendations in Lord Lloyd's report can be implemented . . . [The IRA] needed time to regroup and re-equip, to recruit and train again, and to target again'.[34] Michael Howard emphasised that in order for the IRA to join the talks process, 'it must deliver an unequivocal cease-fire, and it must stop its paramilitary activities. It must abandon violence for good'.[35] Even then, counter-terrorist legislation would be maintained for some time. Wilshire stated:

> Three things will have to happen before we no longer need to debate the renewal of the PTA. First, there must be an end to all violence, not just some violence. Last time there was simply a reduction in the number of murders, and torture continued. Reinstating that position will not be sufficient to make the Act unnecessary. Secondly, there must be a verifiable declaration that all violence has ended forever. The weasel words that we heard last time simply will not be enough to make renewing the Act cease to be a fact of life. The third thing that must happen before we can stop having the annual debates is a decommissioning of all arms and explosives. I must make it clear that I direct those remarks not at Sinn Féin-IRA alone; they apply equally to all terrorism. Terrorism is evil and there can be no compromise with it.[36]

Throughout this time, the security forces continued to make use of emergency powers. In 1996 they detained some eighty-four people under the PTA. Of the twenty-three people held beyond the initial forty-eight hour period, the security forces subsequently charged thirteen with terrorist-related offences. In Northern Ireland, the RUC detained 569 people under the Act, holding forty-eight of those beyond the initial forty-eight hours. The police subsequently charged twenty with terrorist-related offences and an additional 135 detainees with other offences. The government defended the non-judicial process through which detention was extended, repeated the all-too-familiar argument that the decision to extend detention beyond the initial forty-eight hours often depended on sensitive information that could not be revealed to a suspect or to his or her legal advisor without compromising the intelligence source. Furthermore:

> Any new procedure that allowed a court to make what amounts to an executive decision on information not presented to the detainee or his legal adviser, and without the giving of reasons or the possibility of an appeal, would represent a radical departure from the principles that govern judicial proceedings in an adversarial system. It would create a real risk of undermining judicial independence, as the judiciary would be perceived as part of the investigation and prosecution process.[37]

The new powers obtained by the 1996 Prevention of Terrorism (Additional Provisions) Act had been used to mask security force information and not necessarily to directly enable the forces to obtain specific materials. Howard commented: 'The police have told me of the use they have made in recent investigations of the power to search, under warrant, non-residential premises without having to specify the one in which they believe the terrorist material for which they are looking may be found'.[38]

The Tories used the occasion of the renewal of the PTA to reprimand Labour for blocking a Private Member's Bill on conspiracy and incitement.[39] In 1997 Nigel Waterson had introduced the Bill to implement Lloyd's suggestion to extend British jurisdiction to acts of conspiracy and incitement relating to offences committed abroad. Backed by the Conservative government, the Bill addressed a wide variety of offences, including those of a sexual nature. The Home Office issued a press release that asserted: 'This measure will be an important tool in the fight against football hooliganism, organised crime and foreign extremists. However, it will not prevent critics of a regime here from criticising the actions of a foreign government. Freedom of speech will be unaffected'.[40] In what was referred to as a 'dual criminality test', the act would have to be an offence under both UK law and the law of the country in which it was either committed or in which it was intended to be committed. Speaking in support of the Bill, Timothy Kirkhope, the Home Office Minister, emphasised that the Bill did not breach the principal of extra-territoriality, as the conspiracy would have to occur within the United Kingdom. Although both the Government and the Opposition formally supported the Bill, concern arose that the statute could lead to the imprisonment of individuals fighting despotic governments overseas. Donald Anderson of the Labour Party inserted into the debate during the Second Reading: 'There are many dictatorships and tyrannical Governments in this world. Are we to say that someone who has fled to this country from that tyranny is stopped thereby from seeking to overthrow by word or action that tyrannical government?'[41] He cited Nelson Mandela and other individuals that had fought injustice in their countries. During the committee stage, Anderson, Sir Ivan Lawrence and Alun Michael, Labour front-bench spokesman, introduced amendments to ensure that prosecution could only be instituted with the consent of the Attorney General. Unsupported by the Conservatives, the members withdrew the amendments. At the third reading Kirkhope suggested that with the authority of the Attorney General, the Director of Public Prosecutions issue instructions that would dictate the level at which all cases under the Bill would be considered. Cases that might give rise to policy concerns, such as those connected with international politics, would be forwarded to the DPP for consultation between he and the Attorney General. During the same discussion George Galloway stated his opposition to the Bill on account of its potential for changing political asylum in the United Kingdom. Forced to a division, less than forty members were present and so the Bill failed to receive a third reading. Two weeks later Galloway invoked a procedural advice that resulted in the Bill's demise. On 28 February he moved that strangers do withdraw. Again, with less than forty members of the Conservatives present, the Bill was stood over. With the general election drawing near, the dissolution of Parliament resulted in the defeat of the Bill.

Aside from discussion of the Waterson Bill, the balance of the 1997 renewal debates degenerated into mud-slinging over past votes on counter-terrorist legislation and Labour's plans for future counter-terrorist law. Jack Straw of Labour pledged to introduce the judicial element into detention procedures. Citing Lord Colville and Lord Lloyd's conclusions that the judicial element should be introduced, Straw's electioneering concluded: 'That will be part of an overall strategy by us to ensure that the judicial system in all parts of the United Kingdom commands the greater confidence of all law-abiding citizens, including those of all communities in the north of Ireland'.[42] Straw reiterated Labour's revilement of exclusion orders, yet he emphasised that the House should 'promptly establish some permanent arrangements that balance the need to deal with terrorism and the need to protect civil liberties'. He finished: 'The House is united in its determination to fight terrorism with every means consistent with a democratic nation founded on the rule of law. The provisions of anti-terrorist legislation are tough and, in many ways, unpalatable, but they are necessary to deter and defeat those who, in Lord Lloyd's words, "seek to wage war on society" and they have our support'.[43]

In his final speech to the House of Commons, Richard Needham, the longest-serving Northern Ireland Minister, again noted the importance of working with the Irish Republic not just to fight terrorism in Northern Ireland, but to introduce social, economic and political initiatives to address the inequalities in the North. He emphasized the importance of the police and the army in becoming involved in these initiatives. 'Tough and difficult decisions will have to be made on both sides of the border in both communities if the present appalling levels of personal violence and intimidation are to be dealt with.' He blamed the IRA for the Troubles in Northern Ireland: 'We are here today because the IRA has us here. The IRA's return to violence is perverse. If the cease-fire proved anything, it proved that, without violence, the economic border disappears . . . when the economic border disappears – there is no police, no Army, no Customs – social integration is bound to follow [and] political change is bound to come'. Needham finished:

> I do not know what that political change will be, because it may take years. When that change comes, it will be built on mutual respect for the differing traditions and cultures of Ireland's communities, both north and south. I know that violence enshrines hatred and division, but it also enshrines the border . . . The IRA is primarily responsible for the violence. It is to blame for the divisions within Northern Ireland and within Ireland. If the IRA really wants to get rid of the border, all it has to do is get rid of violence. Until it does that, it will remain the implacable enemy of all of us who live in the British Isles.[44]

Ken Maginnis, Ulster Unionist MP for Fermanagh-South Tyrone and former B Special and Major in the Ulster Defence Regiment, complained during the debates about the lack of time afforded Members of Parliament for their comments. He argued for the development of a more extensive counter-terrorist strategy, of which the PTA represented one part. 'I do not apologise for the Act; I believe that it must stay, and that it must be strengthened by whichever party comes to power after 1 May.'[45] He also argued for a reintroduction of the broadcast ban. Séamus Mallon, SDLP MP for Newry and Armagh, followed Maginnis' comments with the opposite sentiments. It was precisely because of the emergency legislation and the manner in which the statute was being applied that he had lost his faith in the integrity of the law and the system of justice. He cited the continued detention of Roisín McAliskey, a woman being held in London pending extradition proceedings to Germany. She had been subjected to approximately sixty strip-searches while she was seven months pregnant and on remand. Kevin McNamara added to Mallon's statements: 'Does my Hon. Friend agree that the mental torture that this woman is undergoing in not knowing whether she will be able to have and hold her child after her confinement is a form of torture that only a pregnant woman in prison can suffer?'[46] To this Rupert Allason, MP for Torbay, stated: 'She should have thought of that before she started bombing people'.[47]

Labour and Emergency Law

Two weeks after the House passed the order continuing the 1989 PTA, John Wheeler, the Minister of State for the Northern Ireland Office, dramatically opened the debate on the 1997 draft Northern Ireland

(Emergency and Prevention of Terrorism Provisions) (Continuance) Order. 'Under cover of darkness, the terrorists continued their nightly punishment attacks, and behind the scenes they continued to train, to organise and to plan more evil', he began. Wheeler cited the effectiveness of the EPA in providing the police with the powers necessary to secure weapons. Five significant arms caches had been uncovered in December, nine in January, eight in February and four in the first week of March. Included in these finds were about seventeen mortars and rocket launchers, over 5,000 lbs of explosives, a number of firearms (including several automatic weapons), and nearly 2,500 rounds of ammunition.[48] Wheeler noted the continuing pattern of violence and agreed with Rowe's conclusion in an independent report on the operation of the EPA in 1996, that 'undoubtedly the powers and provisions of the Act are required for another year. There is continuing terrorist activity, and there is a real threat of more of it'. Wheeler also drew attention to Rowe's contention that the provisions of the EPA had been used 'fairly and carefully'. Rowe had neither seen examples of the statute's abuse nor been told of any. This assertion was upheld by the reports of the independent commissioners for the holding centres, Sir Louis Blom-Cooper and Dr Bill Norris, and by the independent assessor of military complaints procedures, David Hewitt. In their reports the assessors urged the extension of the EPA for a further twelve months. Like Michael Howard before him, Wheeler danced around the government's impression of Lloyd's recommendations, with the exception of noting that the government intended, per Lloyd's recommendation, to strengthen existing controls on terrorist finances.

Familiar arguments for altering the system to 'schedule in' terrorist offences arose. Tony Worthington, the parliamentary Under-Secretary of State for Northern Ireland, brought attention to the appendices of Rowe's report. He suggested that between 1990 and 1996 cases had virtually been 'certified in' to the Diplock courts. In 1990 the Attorney General removed 51 per cent of 908 offences from scheduling. In 1996 he removed some 85 per cent of 1,522 offences from the Diplock courts. Not only were cases increasingly scheduled out, but in 1996 of 170 offenders, 128 pleaded guilty. This led Worthington to conclude prematurely that the services of a jury would not have been necessary in those 128 cases. His analysis can be questioned on the grounds that it is unknown whether, in a non-Diplock court situation, the same individuals would have pleaded guilty. Moreover, the number of cases certified out was most definitely affected by the decreased levels of violence in the North with the maintenance of the CLMC cease-fire.

As with every previous debate on emergency legislation, unionist representatives from Northern Ireland expressed heartfelt disgust towards the IRA and recounted the fear in the province towards the IRA. Ian Paisley urged that the powers available to the security forces through the legislation be used with greater rigour than presently. 'Many more soldiers, police officers and civilians will be sacrificed in a war with terrorism that should have been won years ago . . . I urge the Government – whatever Government are in power – to take the next vital step and start enforcing those measures, so that they have a greater effect against the terrorist.' Paisley upbraided leaders who would consider inviting Sinn Féin to the Talks:

> I said to Bill Clinton, 'You would not bring the murderers from Oklahoma to the White House. You would not shake hands with them. You would not say, "Keep your guns." You would not say, "There is a place for you in government."' Says I, 'What do you think of me? You've said you want to know how an Ulsterman ticks. How I tick is the way you would tick. You would kick me out of this room if I suggested such things. Well, I feel like kicking you out of the room when you shake hands with Gerry Adams, his hands stained with the blood of five of my European constituents who lost their lives in the Shankhill road.'[49]

Both he and William Ross of the UUP emphasised the continuing need for emergency measures. Ross thundered: 'The IRA has not gone away. It never went away. It simply threw a fairly thin smokescreen round itself. Some people were foolish enough to believe that, but we on this Bench were never among those who believed what the IRA said'. He continued: 'We have lived among IRA members, we know them and we have had to put up with their horrors, in the present case for nearly 30 years. Some of us in the B Specials, such as myself, in the 1956-61 campaign went out and fought them in the roads, controlled the roads and beat them. I believe that they could be beaten again'.[50] Other members agonised over continuing such extreme measures but concluded that they were necessary: '[The] circumstances [in Northern Ireland] justify powers that in other circumstances would undoubtedly be regarded as draconian. These powers should not be maintained for an instant longer than is necessary. They should be grudgingly tolerated. We in this place, and our successors, should work with all the power available to us to withdraw them at the earliest possible date. They represent a serious incursion into the rights of the citizens of the United Kingdom'. The legislation should continue only as long as the terrorist threat remained: 'Why is it that the powers continue to be justified? That is the position only because it appears that the cancer of terrorism lies still at the heart of life in Northern Ireland. The powers contained in the order will not eliminate that cancer; at the very best they may contain it. Unless and until a political settlement that commands the support of the entire community of Northern Ireland is achieved, we are likely to face the sort of terrorist activity that so affects our judgment of these issues'.[51] The House passed the Order.

Labour won the 1997 General Election with a landslide victory and the new government immediately focused on Northern Ireland. Tony Blair appointed Marjorie Mowlam as Secretary of State for Northern Ireland. On 16 May Blair made a speech offering to arrange government contact with Sinn Féin in advance of a cease-fire, but maintaining that Northern Ireland was to remain part of the United Kingdom.[52] The following month he issued a statement setting out the government's position on decommissioning. Blair announced that substantive talks would begin in September 1997 and conclude in May 1998, with or without Sinn Féin's participation. Together with the Irish government, the British government established an Independent Commission on decommissioning to oversee the reduction of arms. On 19 July the IRA declared a restoration of its cease-fire. Just over a month later Mowlam announced that Sinn Féin could join the talks process, as they had met the requirements of the 1996 Northern Ireland (Entry to Negotiations) Act.[53] By mid-September Sinn Féin had affirmed its commitment to non-violence and the Mitchell principles, and soon thereafter Mowlam announced the beginning of substantive negotiations. Although the UUP, SDLP, Alliance Party, Sinn Féin, UDP, PUP and Women's Coalition were in attendance, the DUP and UKUP refused to attend. They had formally withdrawn from the process in July 1997 over the Drumcree marches.

As the talks got underway, the House of Commons for the first time debated the possible permanent introduction of counter-terrorist legislation. Jack Straw, Home Secretary, introduced the discussion, intended to allow Members of Parliament to comment in advance of the introduction of new legislation. Straw indicated that some of the power currently in place would not be included in any new statute. Exclusion fell into this category. While 248 orders for exclusion operated in 1982, by 1994, just before the first cease-fire, the number had dropped to seventy-four. No orders were made during 1996 or 1997, and by 2 May 1997 exclusion orders had been maintained in only twenty-two cases. During the first six months of the Labour government, Straw renewed orders against only two of the cases and either revoked or allowed to lapse the other ten he was required to consider. He announced: 'I am minded to allow the powers to lapse when the [PTA] comes up for renewal next year. In the light of the recent developments in Northern Ireland, I have come to the conclusion that, at present, the exercise of these powers is no longer expedient to prevent acts of terrorism in relation to each of the 12 outstanding orders. I have therefore today revoked the last 12 orders'.[54] Reflecting the continuing tendency of counter-terrorist law to apply to only one portion of the Northern Ireland population, ten of those twelve remaining orders applied to republicans and only two to loyalists. This was in spite of the fact that loyalist paramilitary violence in Northern Ireland exceeded that of republican militants prior to the August 1994 cease-fires. In 1992 republicans killed thirty-six people and loyalists killed thirty-nine. The following year a further thirty-six people died as a result of republican violence, as opposed to forty-eight deaths resulting from loyalist attacks.[55] Labour proposed that both the PTA and EPA be replaced with permanent counter-terrorist legislation throughout the UK. 'Like Lord Lloyd, the Government envisage that some existing powers will be confirmed and placed on a permanent footing; that some will be strengthened; and that others will substantially be changed. For example, it has long been our view that there should be a judicial element in the extension of detention process.'[56] Furthermore, Straw suggested that the Labour government – with the support of Ronnie Flanagan, the RUC Chief Constable – would seek to suspend powers of internment. Straw announced the government's intent to publish a consultation paper in early 1998, laying out in more detail the government's recommendations. In the interim, he indicated that Labour would seek the extension of the PTA in March 1998 and the re-enactment of the EPA, with amendment.

Having voted against the renewal of the PTA from 1983 to 1995, and abstaining in 1996 and 1997, Labour came under fire from the Opposition. Straw responded that Labour's position had always been that anti-terrorist legislation was needed. For example, in 1994 Tony Blair had stated: 'it is not in dispute, and never has been, that we need anti-terrorist legislation'.[57] However, the type of measure that had been implemented was what lay in dispute. In an interesting twist of justification, the government suggested that a base of sufficiently strong, permanent anti-terrorist legislation was necessary 'to cope with both periods of relative peace in terms of the internal threat and emergencies such as the failure of the cease-fire, and to deal with the continuing international terrorist threat'.[58] So instead of having temporary measures to meet a temporary emergency, it had simply become a good idea to have some sort of counter-terrorist legislation.

The House of Lords held a similar discussion, wherein the possibility of permanent counter-terrorist legislation was generally welcomed.

Concern regarding the past operation of unamendable renewal orders, piecemeal approaches to emergency legislation and the nature of past measures as being instituted in the wake of specific terrorist outrages, underscored the Lords' desire to have the opportunity to debate at some length a permanent counter-terrorist bill. Both Houses were quite eager to proceed with legislation that would be consistent throughout the whole of the United Kingdom, instead of continuing with two statutes that differentiated between Northern Ireland and Great Britain.

THE 1998 NORTHERN IRELAND (EMERGENCY PROVISIONS) ACT

Within weeks of the brief announcement of the possible future introduction of permanent counter-terrorist law, Adam Ingram, the Minister of State for the Northern Ireland Office, opened the second reading of a Northern Ireland (Emergency Provisions) Bill. This Bill aimed 'to ensure that the criminal justice system and the security forces in Northern Ireland continue to have available the measures that they need to counter terrorism; and to protect the rights of individuals directly affected by the operation of the counter-terrorism provisions'.[59] The Bill not only provided for the extension of the 1996 EPA (due to expire in August 1998), but it also introduced additional amendments to the existing provisions.

It was not that violence had totally ceased in Northern Ireland. Although the CLMC cease-fire had held since August 1994 and the IRA had declared a new cease-fire in July 1997, the emergence of Continuity IRA and the Real IRA suggested that paramilitary violence would continue. On 30 October, while Parliament considered the permanent enactment of counter-terrorist legislation, the Continuity IRA left a bomb in a public office in the Department of the Environment in Derry. Only the detonator exploded. Had the Semtex and petrol ignited, extensive damage could have been caused. The organisation planned the attack to undermine the Talks process.

The Northern Ireland (Emergency Provisions) Bill extended the life of the 1996 EPA until August 2000, with the temporary provisions subject to annual renewal. Ingram noted that should a lasting peace be established in the meantime, the Secretary of State could suspend a number of the provisions. The Bill retained the schedule of terrorist offences, the mode of trial for such offences, the Diplock courts, additional powers of arrest, search and seizure for the police and army, specific offences against public security and public order (including offences relating to involvement with proscribed organisations), regulatory provisions for the private security industry in Northern Ireland, the regime for terrorist suspects held under section 14 of the PTA in holding centres, and the appointment of the independent assessor of military complaints procedures.[60] The Bill amended the EPA in three ways: clause 2 amended schedule 1 of the 1996 EPA, increasing the number of offences that the Attorney General could certify out, thus allowing for more cases to be tried by a jury. Clause 3 repealed sections 36 and 3, which provided for the executive detention or internment of terrorist suspects. Clause 5 provided for the audio recording of police interviews with terrorist suspects. The first amendment represented a step on the road to the eventual elimination of the Diplock system. Although Labour claimed to want to replace the Diplock court system with a return to jury trial, it judged that the time was not right for such a change. Pending the appropriate moment, the government sought to reduce the potential number of cases that would be sent to the Diplock courts. Some of the offences listed in the schedule to the EPA automatically went to the Diplock system, regardless of whether they were linked to terrorism. The Bill therefore amended the schedule to add to the number of scheduled offences that could be certified out at the discretion of the Attorney General and thus be subject to jury trial. Making or possessing a petrol bomb, throwing or using a petrol bomb, possessing a firearm with the intent to endanger life, the use or attempted use of firearms and causing explosions became eligible for certifying out. In the government's view, only offences that were PTA or EPA offences would be automatically tried in the Diplock system. All other scheduled offences committed in, for example, a domestic or non-emergency context would be eligible to be certified out for trial by jury. Labour had been advocating for years a certifying in procedure. However, when the opportunity to institute the change came, the party determined that it would be 'too complex and could cause difficulties if the judicial system became involved in judgments about what should be subject to a jury trial'.[61] Séamus Mallon of the SDLP pointed out the incongruity in the argument: 'Does [the minister] accept that at present about 85 per cent of scheduled cases are certified out by the Attorney General's office and that certifying in the other 15 per cent would be less onerous than certifying out 85 per cent?'[62] Ingram responded that 'the problem for the Attorney General's office is not only work load, but the way in which it could be compromised in making judgments about jury trials'.[63] McNamara's pursuit of Mallon's point brought no clearer answer from the government.

On internment the government once again outlined Labour's objections:

The truth is that the powers [of internment] are draconian. [I]nternment did not represent an effective counter-terrorism measure in the past; does not represent one now; and is not likely to do so in the future. The reality is that internment involves a decision by Government to deprive individuals of their liberty without trial and without the normal safeguards that the law provides for the protection of the accused . . . it has never been seen as a means of achieving stability within the community. The Government believe that the effect would be quite the reverse: it would increase community tension; cause serious damage to respect for the rule of law; strengthen the terrorist organisations; create political prisoners; and ultimately prolong the violence.[64]

Labour's decision to remove executive powers of extended detention came under considerable fire from the Tories. Numerous members voiced their concern that when and if the powers were needed the government would not have them available. They appealed to the Republic of Ireland's 1939 and 1940 Offences Against the State Acts, suggesting 'it ill behoves this House to remove internment from the statute book when our friends south of the border are not planning to do the same'. Andrew MacKay, speaking from the Opposition Front Bench, claimed: 'The history of Irish republicanism is littered with historic and bitter divisions. Does the Minister imagine that, in the event of an overall settlement, there will not be people in Northern Ireland . . . who . . . cry betrayal and return to violence?'[65] Ingram reiterated Labour's position: 'Internment creates divisions. It brings friends to the terrorist movement'.[66] McNamara added:

It is a matter of record that the worst disturbances – the killings, the shootings, the explosions – from both sides of the community took place while internment was in force. Only when the present Lord Rees started the process of ending internment in Northern Ireland did the incidents start to decrease. The reason was that internment . . . became a recruiting cry, a rallying cry, for Provisional Sinn Féin. 'Armoured cars and tanks and guns came to take away our sons' was sung in clubs throughout Northern Ireland. The issue united a peaceful community against the Government because no matter how many people from the other side might later have been interned, internment was regarded as patently unfair. The arrest of people in such circumstances was seen as fundamentally unjust.[67]

Unionist Members of Parliament emphasised that the threat from republican terrorism remained. Maginnis noted: 'Gerry Adams stood in front of the city hall in Belfast and said, "The IRA hasn't gone away, you know". In Coalisland, Martin McGuinness said, "We intend to smash

British rule in Northern Ireland". Only last weekend, a leading spokesman for IRA-Sinn Féin addressed a meeting of 150 IRA men in county Armagh. He referred to what would happen if the talks ended and said, "Whenever that does happen then we simply go back to what we know best".[68] Yet, as nationalist politicians from Northern Ireland reminded the House, the use of internment, throughout the history of republican agitation, had been unsuccessful. Séamus Mallon commented: 'Many of us are products of a society or an environment that has experienced internment. Let us not forget that we had internment in the 1920s, 1930s, 1940s, 1950s, 1960s and 1970s; it was not thought up only in the 1970s. Internment failed in each of those decades: it failed to give peace, it failed to solve security problems and above all it failed to have the political effect that it was intended to have'.[69] David Trimble, leader of the Ulster Unionist Party, in an amendment signed by the Opposition front bench, tried to amend the Bill so as to retain powers of internment. Pushed to a vote, the house divided on the amendment with 118 in favour of retaining powers of internment and 223 against.

Acting under the advice of the independent commissioner for the holding centres, Sir Louis Blom-Cooper, and his deputy, Dr Bill Norris, as well as Lord Colville in his previous reviews of emergency legislation, Labour introduced audio recording to document interviews of terrorist suspects in the holding centres. The government sought to provide protection to interviewees and police officers against claims of verbal abuse, intimidation and harassment. 'It will also assist the judicial process by providing the best possible record of interviews conducted, in the event that a criminal case ensues.'[70] The Bill also made a minor amendment to the existing provision on silent video recordings, a power inherited from the Conservatives and not yet implemented in Northern Ireland. The decision to introduce audio recording had been slow to arise because of claims that by creating a record of the interview, a suspect would be less likely to become an informer. With the defence attorneys privy to any audio recordings of the suspect, the implication was that nothing could take place in the interrogation centres that might be of assistance to the police in turning a suspect into an informer.

Although no amendments were tabled in committee, members expressed concern at the procedure followed for consideration of the legislation. The Standing Committee on 25 November addressed the Bill from 4.30 in the afternoon until 5.00 a.m. the following morning. During the report stage in the House of Commons, Trimble introduced an amendment to allow evidence obtained from intercepted telephone communications to be used in the prosecution of terrorist cases. Citing

Lord Lloyd's report, Trimble noted that the United Kingdom was one of the few countries where wire taps were not allowed as evidence in court. Further,

> not allowing intercepted telephone communications to be admitted in evidence is highly illogical, given that other intercepted conversations are admissible. If a bug is placed inside a house and a conversation is tape recorded or transmitted by some wireless device to somewhere else and recorded there, that intercepted conversation is admissible in evidence. People can be wired up with recording devices attached to their body, and the conversations that they have with other people are admissible.[71]

Trimble had raised this suggestion during the government's 30 October announcement that it intended to introduce permanent counter-terrorist legislation into the House. At the time the Home Secretary had replied:

> The Hon. Gentleman asked about Lord Lloyd's proposals in respect of section 9 of the Interception of Communications Act 1985. That is a complicated issue. Lord Lloyd sought to distinguish between interception evidence that arose in respect of a national security investigation – which he said should be adducible in evidence – and other interception evidence, from a customs, police or security service intercept, in respect of the investigation of a serious crime, which he said should not be adducible in court. That is one of the most complex of Lord Lloyd's recommendations. Many take the view that it is very difficult to draw the distinction in practice. There is much to be said on both sides of the argument about whether intercept evidence should be adducible in court.[72]

Objecting to amendments being tabled at such a late stage, Ingram requested that Trimble withdraw the amendment. Trimble also withdrew a second amendment that would have made the audio recordings available only to the judge.

Set against the Northern Ireland political process, the Bill was a 'tactical but regrettable requirement'. Lembit Opik of the Liberal Democrats continued: 'It will not solve the problems of Northern Ireland, but it might provide the space for them to be solved'.[73] This reading ignored the integral role that emergency measures played in the continuation of the conflict. Somehow emergency legislation, its alteration of the judicial system, relaxation of rules of evidence, extensive powers of entry, search, seizure, and arrest, and disparate application to the communities in Northern Ireland could be separated from the Troubles. Political 'advances' were to be made independent of the legislation. The Bill, backed by Labour, the Conservatives and the Liberal Democrats, passed into law. During the debates Worthington announced that silent video recordings had commenced in Castlereagh. The government aimed to bring the silent video recording code of practice into operation in January 1998. On 15 February 1998, in conjunction with an order directing that the code of practice for silent video recording be instituted, Marjorie Mowlam issued the 1996 Northern Ireland (Emergency Provisions) Act (Silent Video Recording of Interviews) Order 1998.[74] Having laid the code of practice before Parliament, the Secretary of State specified in the order that all interviews held by the police of persons detained under section 14(1) of the 1989 Prevention of Terrorism Act after midnight 10 March be subject to silent video recording. Subject to annual renewal, in 1999 Labour once again introduced orders relating to the code of practice and the silent video recording of interviews. The details of both this code of practice and the subsequent audio code of practice, were drawn up in consultation with the RUC.

Following a number of sectarian killings linked to the Ulster Freedom Fighters, (UFF) in January 1998 the Ulster Democratic Party (UDP) left the talks. The Northern Ireland office subsequently met with UDP officials and indicated that 'if over a period of weeks a complete unequivocal and unqualified UFF cease-fire were demonstrated and established . . . the Governments would consider the possibility of the UDP rejoining the negotiations'.[75] Just prior to the UDP rejoining the talks on the 23 February, the British and Irish governments concluded that the IRA's involvement in two recent murders required the suspension of Sinn Féin from the talks. They indicated, however, that Sinn Féin could return to the talks on the 9 March if clear evidence existed that the IRA cease-fire was being 'fully and continuously observed'.[76] In the event, Sinn Féin did not return to the talks until the 23 March, amid much opposition from UUP members calling for Sinn Féin's permanent exclusion following further suspected IRA violence.[77] Immediately prior to the commencement of substantive negotiations, Ronnie Flanagan, the RUC Chief Constable, publicly stated that the IRA had not been involved in the incidents.[78]

The day after the Commons debate on the continuation of the 1989 PTA, the government published the draft decommissioning scheme. Both Houses debated the 1998 Northern Ireland Arms Decommissioning Act 1997 (Amnesty Period) Order within the month.[79] In August 1997 the British and Irish governments had signed the agreement establishing the Independent International Commission on Decommissioning. The following month the governments appointed General John de Chastelain as chair, and Ambassador Donald Johnson and Brigadier Tauno Nieminen as members. By the end of 1997 the Commission issued its recommendations for decommissioning. In consultation with the members of the talks sub-committee on decommissioning, the British and Irish governments brought the proposals forward into draft schemes, enabling voluntary decommissioning. The order introduced into Parliament in March extended the maximum duration of any amnesty period. (The 1997 Act required that any amnesty period end before 27 February 1998.) Any person choosing to hand in arms in accordance with the scheme would be granted amnesty in respect of the offences set out in the schedule of the 1997 Act. Ingram emphasised in the Commons that the non-statutory decommissioning scheme had to retain the power to set the dates, so as to remain flexible in the talks process.

In March 1998 and March 1999 the Labour government continued the 1989 PTA.[80] In both instances and in accordance with Rowe's annual recommendations, the government maintained powers related to proscribed organisations, financial assistance for terrorism, powers of arrest, detention and control of entry, powers related to search and seizure, restricted remission for sentences of scheduled offences and requirements for explosives factories, magazines and stores. Significantly, the government opted to drop exclusion powers. Although the Labour government had not yet introduced their White Paper on proposals for permanent counter-terrorist legislation, the 1998 discussion in Parliament centred on financial measures and communications intercepts that could be built into counter-terrorist law. A lack of violence failed to convince Labour that further counter-terrorist measures should be relaxed. Although punishment beatings and republican and loyalist violence had continued throughout 1997, no incidents of international terrorism were reported within Great Britain. Nevertheless, MPs cited the possibility of their occurrence – and the continued violence related to Northern Ireland – as reason enough to continue the PTA. Tragedy underlined both renewal debates. In 1998 one Catholic and one Protestant, Philip Alan and Damian Treanor, had been murdered by paramilitaries while having a drink together in Poyntzpass, Northern Ireland. The 1999 debates were immediately preceded by the murder of Rosemary Nelson, a republican lawyer. This case is discussed in further detail later. On the same day that the 1998 debates took place, Britain and Ireland held an Anglo-Irish Intergovernmental Conference from which a joint statement was issued inviting the parties in the political process to reach agreement by Easter 1998 to pave the way for referendums in the North and South in May.[81] After further posturing by all parties in the talks, from early April intensive negotiations began. Finally, on the 10 April the parties finally reached the Belfast Agreement.

The Belfast Agreement

A milestone in the history of Anglo-Irish relations, the Belfast Agreement verified that Northern Ireland would remain a part of the United Kingdom for as long as the majority so wished. Having regard to the nationalist tradition, if a majority consented to the establishment of a united Ireland, the British and Irish governments would give effect to that wish. The Belfast Agreement made provision for a Northern Ireland Assembly that would be given responsibility for devolved matters. As with the 1920 Government of Ireland Act, which was to be replaced by new legislation, excepted and reserved matters would remain with the British Parliament. A North-South Ministerial Council would address issues of mutual interest, with accountability to the Assembly and to the Irish Parliament. The Belfast Agreement further established a British-Irish Council and replaced the Anglo-Irish Agreement with a new British-Irish Agreement. This last document addressed constitutional issues, created a British-Irish Intergovernmental Conference, and continued the meetings between the Northern Ireland Secretary of State and the Irish Foreign Minister. The Belfast Agreement also formally closed the Anglo-Irish Secretariat at Maryfield. In direct response to the criticism levied against the British government for its human rights record in Northern Ireland – much of which arose as a result of the emergency measures introduced by the government to address 'political' violence both in the province and in Great Britain – the Belfast Agreement included 'a range of measures to enhance the proper protection of basic human rights including a new independent Human Rights Commission in Northern Ireland to consult and advise on the scope for defining rights supplementary to those in the European Commission of Human Rights which the Government are already in the process of incorporating into our law across the UK'.[82] Significantly, the Belfast Agreement also committed both the British and Irish governments 'to reducing the profile of security measures and emergency legislation as the threat to peace and good order reduces'.[83] Still, however, emergency legislation was seen as somehow outside the purview of the political process, an unfortunate but necessary measure that could be used to address violence when political routes failed. The Belfast Agreement also addressed decommissioning, police reforms and the accelerated release of prisoners.

Within two weeks of the agreement, on 23 April 1998 the British Parliament passed the Northern Ireland Negotiations (Referendum) Order. By the time of the debates, the Ulster Unionist Party Council had approved the agreement by a majority of 72 per cent.[84] The SDLP,

Alliance Party, Northern Ireland Labour Party, Women's Coalition, the Ulster Democratic Party and the Progressive Unionist Party also supported it. The DUP and UKUP remained opposed to the negotiated settlement. On the 18 April Gerry Adams informed Sinn Féin's Ard Fheis that 'when the vote was taken [at the plenary session of the talks] I did not vote and Sinn Féin has yet to make a decision on this document. I had previously made it clear that our negotiating team would report back to the ardchomhairle which would assess the document in the context of our peace strategy and that we would approach this development in a positive manner'.[85] Within two weeks *An Phoblacht* reported:

> The leadership of Oglaigh na hÉireann have considered carefully the Good Friday document. It remains our position that a durable peace settlement demands the end of British rule in Ireland and the exercise of the right of the people of Ireland to national self-determination. Viewed against our republican objective . . . this document clearly falls short of presenting a solid basis for a lasting settlement . . . However, the Good Friday document does mark a significant development . . . Accordingly, we will carefully monitor the situation . . . We are mindful of our responsibilities and of the need for continued vigilance during these challenging times. We are aware, also, of those who will resist any dynamic for change. They need to face up to the reality that peace demands justice, equality and national rights for the people of Ireland. We commend the efforts of Sinn Féin.[86]

At a special conference on 10 May Sinn Féin voted to approve the Belfast Agreement and to allow its delegates to take up their seats in the new Northern Ireland Assembly. The party began to campaign for a 'yes' vote in both referendums. However, a new republican organisation, the 'Real IRA', issued statements on 9 May indicating that a terrorist campaign would continue. Other breakaway paramilitary organisations, the Continuity IRA, the 32 County Sovereignty Committee and the Loyalist Volunteer Force, also remained opposed to the Belfast Agreement.

In the resulting referendum, of the 81.1 per cent of Northern Ireland voters that turned out to participate, 71.12 per cent voted yes to the Belfast Agreement. In the Republic of Ireland, where only 56.3 per cent of the voters went to the polls, 94.39 per cent voted yes.[87] Concerns that the 71 per cent in favour of the agreement in the North were predominantly Catholic were somewhat offset by an RTE Prime Time/Lansdowne exit poll which showed that support for the agreement reached 55 per cent among those who described themselves as unionists and 48 per cent among those who described themselves as either unionist or loyalist. In the subsequent assembly elections the UUP took the most seats with twenty-eight members elected to the new body. The SDLP was close behind with twenty-four. The DUP finished just ahead of Sinn Féin, with twenty seats to Sinn Féin's eighteen. The Alliance Party obtained a further six seats, UK Unionists garnered five, and the Independent Unionists gained three. Both the Progressive Unionists and the Northern Ireland Women's Coalition obtained two seats apiece.[88] Perhaps more surprising than the distribution of seats in the North was the percentage share of first preference votes among the parties. Here the SDLP edged out the UUP with 21.96 per cent of first preference votes to the UUP's 21.26 per cent. Again, the DUP and Sinn Féin ran neck and neck with 18.13 percent going to the DUP and 17.63 per cent transferred to the republican party. The new assembly had until 31 October 1998 to determine the affairs that would be allocated to a north-south body. Mowlam announced that the new assembly would develop the departments and portfolios over the summer, allowing the executive to be appointed soon thereafter, thus permitting the ministers to begin to develop a programme for government and a plan for issues to be included in north-south cooperation. David Trimble soon became the First Minister, with Séamus Mallon of the SDLP as the Deputy First Minister.

THE 1998 CRIMINAL JUSTICE (TERRORISM AND CONSPIRACY) ACT

As the negotiations for the first assembly progressed, on the 15 August 1998 the Real IRA detonated a 300 lb car bomb in Omagh that resulted in twenty-eight deaths and over 200 injuries.[89] A telephone warning at 2.30 p.m. to Ulster Television announced a bomb close to the courthouse in Main Street. The RUC moved people to the other end of town, where the bomb actually exploded. As Blair scathingly acknowledged, the Real IRA's aim in setting the device was to derail the Northern Ireland talks process:

> We have known tragedy in Northern Ireland many times before; but this was an indiscriminate attack on a whole community, bringing nothing but further grief to the long-suffering people of Northern Ireland. It was a deliberate attempt, by a small group of extremists with no moral or political support anywhere, to wreck the Good Friday Agreement and the foundation for a lasting and peaceful Northern Ireland which the agreement offers . . . The aim of those bombers was, as I say, not just to kill innocent people but to strike at the very heart of the peace process.[90]

The most devastating attack in the course of the Troubles, within a fortnight Tony Blair and the Taoiseach, Bertie Ahern, announced that the

British and Irish parliaments would be recalled to introduce more stringent counter-terrorist legislation.[91] In a speech at Omagh on the 25 August, Blair cited the recalling of Parliament as a necessary step, as the only 'legally watertight' way to proceed against the splinter terrorist organisations would be to proceed by way of primary (rather than secondary) legislation. 'There is a clear need, now that it is plain that we are dealing with this small, wholly unsupported, wholly unrepresentative, residual group of extremists, to tighten our law in relation to what is needed to secure a conviction for membership of a proscribed terrorist organisation.' In addition to new measures directed at terrorism connected with the affairs of Northern Ireland, the reconvening of Parliament provided the opportunity 'to put through a further piece of anti-terrorism legislation which has been fully prepared for some time but has not yet been legislated for, in respect of those planning to commit terrorist acts abroad'.[92] The alterations in British law closely mirrored those to be passed in the Republic of Ireland.

The subsequent Criminal Justice (Terrorism and Conspiracy) Bill introduced four essentially new powers into the UK: the opinion of a police officer was to become admissible in court as evidence of membership of particular terrorist organisations; courts would be allowed to draw inference from a suspect's refusal to answer questions during the course of an investigation into membership of a proscribed organisation; on conviction any assets used in the furtherance of a proscribed organisation would be subject to forfeiture; and it would become an offence to conspire in the UK to commit terrorist or other serious offences in a foreign country. Both Blair and Ahern openly acknowledged the new measures as 'Draconian'. Nevertheless, both governments planned to push the measures through their parliaments in a matter of two days. All-party support for the measures was pledged for the Bill in the British House of Commons.

On the 1 September 1998, less than twenty-four hours before the Bill's consideration in the House of Commons, the Labour government made the Bill available to Members of Parliament. In his press release coinciding with the publication of the draft Bill, Jack Straw stated:

> Terrorism is a major threat to our safety and the democratic system we cherish. It is vital we have at our disposal effective and practical measures to counter this threat and bring to justice those who persist in the use of violence. It is also unacceptable for terrorists and other criminals to use the UK as a base for committing offences overseas and this Bill would for the first time give us a wide-ranging power to take action against those who abuse the freedoms we enjoy in the UK.[93]

He added that the Bill did not fulfill the commitment he undertook in October 1997 to consider permanent counter-terrorist legislation for the United Kingdom. The legislation to be enacted on 3 September would again be temporary and subject to annual renewal, pending the introduction of permanent counter-terrorist measures. Mowlam in turn emphasised that the legislation was designed to complement the peace process in Northern Ireland. It was to impact only a particular segment of Northern Irish society:

> Effective anti-terrorist legislation, consistent with the level of threat, is essential to underpin the Good Friday Agreement and to allow peace to flourish in Northern Ireland. The police and the courts must have the power to bring to justice those groups and individuals who show blatant disregard for democracy and peace. We have made it clear that this Bill is specifically aimed at those groups and individuals.

Many of the powers introduced in the 1998 Criminal Justice (Terrorism and Conspiracy) Bill applied to a list of organisations that were to be specified by the Secretary of State. Proscription, as will be recalled from chapters one to five, had a long history in relation to affairs in Ireland, North and South. Most recently, under the 1989 PTA only two organisations, both republican, had been proscribed in the UK – the IRA and the INLA. Under schedule 2 of the 1996 EPA, the British government proscribed twelve organisations. These included the IRA, Cumann na mBan, Fianna na hÉireann, Red Hand Commando, Saor Éire, Ulster Freedom Fighters, Ulster Volunteer Force, INLA, Irish People's Liberation Organisation, Ulster Defence Association, Loyalist Volunteer Force and Continuity Army Council. The 1998 Northern Ireland (Sentences) Act, introduced in the context of the Northern Ireland political process, also drew on the function of outlawed organisations. The Sentences Act permitted the release on licence of certain prisoners serving in Northern Ireland.[94] The statute allowed the Secretary of State to designate as a specified organisation any group believed to be concerned with terrorism connected with the affairs of Northern Ireland, or in promoting or encouraging it, or any organisation that has not established or is not maintaining a complete and unequivocal cease-fire.[95] Section 3(9) added that in designating particular organisations the Secretary of State should take into account whether the group:

(a) is committed to the use now and in the future of only democratic and peaceful means to achieve its objectives;
(b) has ceased to be involved in any acts of violence or of preparation for violence;

(c) is directing or promoting acts of violence by other organisations;
(d) is cooperating fully with any Commission of the kind referred to in section 7 of the Northern Ireland Arms Decommissioning Act 1997 in implementing the Decommissioning section of the agreement reached at multi-party talks on Northern Ireland set out in Command Paper 3883.

On 30 July 1998 Mowlam introduced an order under the Act designating as specified organisations the Continuity Irish Republican Army, the Loyalist Volunteer Force, the Irish National Liberation Army and the 'Real' Irish Republican Army.[96] Mowlam clearly stated that the IRA's absence from the 1998 Order did not influence its status as a proscribed organisation under both the 1989 PTA and the 1996 EPA.

On the same day Mowlam issued the order designating the specified organisations, she appointed the first ten Sentence Review Commissioners. Sir John Blelloch and Brian Currin served as the first joint chairmen of the commission. In order to be eligible for review, prisoners had to apply to the body to obtain declarations that they would be eligible for release. Prisoners released under the Act became subject to conditions, included in which were that they did not support specified organisations and that they did not become concerned in the 'commission, preparation or instigation' of acts of terrorism connected with the affairs of Northern Ireland. If it appeared to the Secretary of State that an individual released on licence under the Act was likely to break or had broken one of the conditions placed on their release, the measure empowered her to suspend the licence. At this point the person could then be detained in pursuance of the sentence, pending consideration of the case by the Sentence Review Commissioners who could then confirm or revoke the licence.[97] By the time Parliament began consideration of the Criminal Justice (Terrorism and Conspiracy) Bill, some four hundred and forty-six prisoners had applied for release under the scheme.[98]

The 1998 Criminal Justice (Terrorism and Conspiracy) Bill specified in its first section that strictures under the Act applied to individuals charged with membership of one of the specified organisations. Inference could be drawn from the silence maintained by an individual so charged. It will be recalled from chapter four that the law regarding the right to silence significantly changed in 1988 with the issuance of the Criminal Evidence (Northern Ireland) Order. This order amended criminal law to allow the courts in Northern Ireland to draw whatever inferences might be proper from the fact that an individual accused of a crime had remained silent. The right to silence also had been amended in Britain through the 1994 Criminal Justice and Public Order Act, which allowed inferences to be drawn from an accused's failure to mention facts when questioned or charged, silence at the trial itself, failure or refusal to account for particular items, substances, or marks found in his or her possession or in any place where he or she was at the time of arrest, or failure or refusal to account for his or her presence at a specific location. The statute required that corroborative evidence be provided, and that 'nothing in these provisions should prejudice the operation of provisions in any other enactments preventing any answer or evidence given by a person in certain specified circumstances from being admitted in evidence against him or some other person in any civil or criminal proceedings'.[99]

In *Murray* v. *UK*, mentioned earlier, the European Court had held that Murray's lack of access to an attorney during the first four days of police detention amounted to a violation of Articles 6.1 and 6.3 (c) of the European Convention. A subsequent vote, however, held fourteen to five that there had been no breach of Articles 6.1 or 6.2 of the Convention arising from the drawing of adverse inferences from the defendants silence. Later in 1996 the European Court held in *Saunders* v. *UK*, that the prosecution's use during Ernest Saunders' trial of statements given under legal compulsion under the 1985 Companies Act infringed Saunders' right not to incriminate himself.[100] The *Times Law Report* of the case noted that '[t]he court stressed that the right not to incriminate oneself, like the right to silence, was a generally recognised international standard which lay at the heart of the notion of a fair procedure under Article 6 of the Convention. The right, which had close links with the presumption of innocence contained in Article 6.2, was primarily concerned with respecting the will of the accused to remain silent'.[101] Legal commentators disagreed over whether the specific provisions of the 1994 Act relating to the right to silence might be found in breach of the European Covenant. The Home Office Research and Statistics Directorate had closely monitored the effects of the 1994 provisions. In February 1998 Alun Michael, the Home Office Minister, reported that there had been a significant reduction in the use of the right to silence during police interviews. The directorate determined that individuals accused of serious offences still exercised their right of silence more frequently than 'other criminals'.

In Britain and Northern Ireland the Bill ensured that an accused person could not be convicted solely on the basis of inference drawn from failure to mention facts. New section 2A(3)(b) of the PTA and new section 30A(3)(b) of the EPA, as specified in clauses 1 and 2 of the 1998 Bill, allowed for the testimony of a police officer of or above the rank of superintendent regarding an accused's membership of a specified organisation to be admissible as evidence in court. Similar to the provisions on the waiving of the right to silence, this testimony alone would not be sufficient to convict a terrorist suspect. However, under the 1998 Act, inference drawn from an accused's silence in conjunction with evidence of membership in a specified organisation as provided by an officer's testimony became sufficient evidence to lead to a committal for trial, to a finding that a person has a case to answer, or to a conviction. Scottish law required that two sources of evidence prove every fact necessary for the Crown to prove its case before a court could convict. Thus, the new section 2A(10) of the PTA provided that in any proceedings in Scotland related to membership of a specified organisation, 'where the court of jury drawn as inference . . . any evidence that he belongs or, as the case may be, belonged to the organisation shall be sufficient evidence of that matter'.

Clause 3 of the new Bill extended powers of arrest and detention for up to seven days to individuals suspected of being involved in specified ways with any of the number of organisations proscribed. The section applied to offences committed before, on, or after the day on which the Act came into force. The fourth clause focused on enabling courts to order the forfeiture of money of property controlled by or in the possession of persons convicted of membership and other offences under section 2 of the PTA or section 30 of the EPA, who, at the time of their offences belong to organisations which are specified organisations. ('For the purposes of this section property includes property wherever situated and whether real or personal, heritable or moveable, a thing in action or other intangible or incorporeal property.')[102] The standard of proof required to determine whether property was controlled by or in the possession of individuals would be the equivalent of that applicable in civil proceedings.

The remaining clauses of the Bill focused on international terrorism and bore no relation to the Northern Irish political situation. As Blair announced in the introduction of the Bill, these clauses had been prepared for some time. In general, the jurisdiction of courts in the United Kingdom is restricted to offences committed within the territory of the United Kingdom, whether by British citizens or individuals from abroad. With but few exceptions, (for example, murder), British courts do not claim jurisdiction over British nationals abroad. In the event that a British national is accused of an offence in another country, the typical course of action is for the individual to be extradited to face proceedings in the other country. In the years leading up to the introduction of the 1998 Bill, there had been increasing calls for the jurisdiction of UK courts to be extended to allow British courts to try individuals from the UK who had committed acts with children abroad that would be regarded as sexual offences under British law. Although deploring such acts, the Conservative government had been reluctant to extend the jurisdictional powers of British courts in this way. The Home Office Minister, David Maclean, said in a Written Answer on 11 February 1994:

> The Government deplore sexual offences against children wherever they occur. Our own law against such abuse is rightly severe. However, our courts' jurisdiction is territorially based rather than nationally based; and we have no plans to extend their jurisdiction over paedophile offences committed by British citizens abroad. We believe that such jurisdiction would be largely unenforceable in practice and that where such offences have been committed abroad it is right for the country concerned to enforce its own law.[103]

An extension of the law on conspiracy and incitement had been proposed in December 1995.[104] John Marshall subsequently introduced a Private Member's Bill, which became the 1996 Sexual Offences (Conspiracy and Incitement) Act. Applying to all parts of the United Kingdom, this act facilitated the prosecution of individuals who sexually exploited children overseas or encouraged others to travel abroad to conduct sexual offences. The Conservative government simultaneously initiated an inter-departmental review to examine the extra-territorial jurisdiction of the courts in the United Kingdom. That the police force in the United Kingdom had no powers of investigation in other countries, and that British courts could not compel foreign witnesses to appear were seen as constituting barriers in extra-territorial jurisdiction. Similarly, if the civil authorities where the offence was alleged to have been committed were unwilling or unable to provide sufficient evidence, British authorities would have difficulty conducting an investigation.[105] Because of the implications for UK courts in terms of procedures and rules of evidence, the report of the inter-departmental review, published on 23 July 1996, suggested that the government refrain from broad implementation of extra-territorial jurisdiction. The Home Office issued a Press Notice on the same day in which six criteria would have to be met for such jurisdiction to be granted: (1) the offence would have to be serious, (2) witnesses would have to be available, (3) international agreement would have to be obtained that the particular conduct was reprehensible and concerted action was necessary, (4) action must be required because of the vulnerability of the victim, (5) the extension would be in the interests of the UK's international reputation and (6) a danger would result if no action were taken to deal with the offence.

Clauses 5–8 of the 1998 Criminal Justice (Terrorism and Conspiracy) Bill harkened back to Waterson's Private Member's Bill. These sections provided UK courts with extra-territorial jurisdiction over acts committed or intended to be committed abroad. All offences, and not just acts related to terrorism, came under the auspices of the Bill. Clause 5 amended the 1977 Criminal Law Act to make it an offence in England or Wales to commit or to conspire to commit an offence abroad. The dual criminality test proposed by Waterson applied. The only real differences between this clause and Waterson's Bill lay in the removal of 'incitement' to commit offences outside the UK (a broader offence than 'conspiracy'), the exemption of individuals working for the British government from being found guilty of any offence under the Act and the requirement that the Attorney General approve all prosecutions under the Act. With regard to the last point, the Bill empowered the Home Secretary to provide by order that the consent of the Attorney General was not necessary in cases of a particular description. Such an order would have to be approved by both Houses through affirmative procedure. Clauses 6 and 7 extended the measures to Northern Ireland and Scotland, amending the 1983 Criminal Attempts and Conspiracy (Northern Ireland) Order and the 1995 Criminal Procedure (Scotland) Act.

During the debates in the House of Commons on the 1998 Criminal Justice (Conspiracy and Terrorism) Bill, the government admitted that the aim of the legislation was to make it easier to obtain convictions for membership of terrorist organisations 'by changing the rules of evidence in a way that is tough but is fully thorough, and fully in line with the rule of law and our commitments under the European Convention'. Blair openly acknowledged that the government was 'taking the opportunity of Parliament's recall to put into law long-held plans to make a criminal offence of conspiracy to commit offences outside the UK'.[106] He unabashedly stated that the government had been waiting for a time when public emotion was running high in order to introduce the powers: 'we have been waiting for the right opportunity . . . [and] I think that, after the events of the past few weeks, that feeling is stronger rather than weaker'.[107] Not only had the Omagh bombings enraged the population, but the recent attacks on the US embassies in Nairobi and Dar es Salam in early August 1998, when nearly 300 people lost their lives, underlined the importance of addressing acts of conspiracy.[108] In his introduction of the Bill Blair concluded: 'There are few more important challenges to democracy, and therefore to this House, than terrorism in all its forms. We must fight it vigorously wherever it appears, while holding fast to our democratic principles and the rule of law'.[109] In this case, the rule of law involved a waiving of the right to silence and the admission of the statement of a police officer as evidence of membership in a proscribed organisation. All Members of Parliament put on the record their disgust at the acts undertaken by the Real IRA, and a number advocated that more extreme powers – such as internment and identity cards – be placed on the books. Members, particularly unionists from Northern Ireland, expressed deep concern at the apparent separation between 'good' and 'bad' terrorist organisations. Robert McCartney, the renegade UK Unionist from North Down, stated: 'There seems to be a distinction between small terrorist groups committing acts of terror with no political support and larger groups of terrorists who may, broadly speaking have such support'. He noted that since the Belfast Agreement had been signed, thirty-seven people had been killed. Both loyalist and republican paramilitaries had been responsible for a further twenty-nine punishment shootings and approximately fifty-seven punishment beatings. He observed: 'We are entering a two-tier system of terrorist opposition and a two-tier system of the administration of justice, and many people would regard that as a grave mistake'.[110]

This two-tier system was justified in the distinction of emergency powers from the political process. William Hague stated on behalf of the Opposition: 'I believe that people expect us to do two things in the wake of Omagh. One is to take what security measures we responsibly can to try to deal with the small remaining groups engaged in terror. The second is to continue with the political process'.[111] The assumed relation between the legislation and the talks process centred on the use of the legislation to, as Blair put it, 'mop up the last recalcitrant and renegade terrorist groups that are prepared to threaten the future of Northern Ireland'.[112] Claims that the 'renegade' terrorist groups had no support in Northern Ireland echoed those of previous generations. Some sixty years previously Wedgwood Benn stood in the same place and announced that the group responsible for the mainland bombing campaign, 'has no support in Ireland. It has no support among the Irish in this country, and Mr DeValera has said quite plainly that he denies utterly the right of this small group of people to speak on the partition issue'.[113] Yet the same small republican organisation thought to be of no consequence became ultimately the parent organisation of some of those groups that Blair sought to 'mop up'. The 1998 Bill withheld protections available to ordinary citizens from those organisations who rejected the talks process and persisted in a violent campaign. Parliamentarians viewed the situation as different from that which prevailed in the early 1970s. Then, too, the IRA was not a strong organisation; however, the emergency measures introduced breathed life into the movement. The Labour government rejected internment in 1998 precisely for this reason. Blair said: 'If we [introduced internment] the danger would be precisely the danger to which we have drawn attention, that there would be set up a series of reactions in other parts of the community that would undermine the very thing that we want to achieve'.[114] And yet, he simultaneously held that because the 'renegade' terrorist groups were so small and had no political base, the exercise of powers in the 1998 Act would *not* generate widespread support. Blair was less than clear as to what made the introduction of the powers included in the 1998 Bill any different than the situation that would result if powers of internment had been reinstated.

For Members of Parliament in 1998, the talks process had changed everything. The new threat was so small, so minimal, it was claimed, that extreme measures against renegade terrorists would bolster and not weaken the political process. Yet, the threat also was significant enough for both the Irish and British governments to introduce Draconian measures. In Northern Ireland minimal protest met the introduction of the more severe measures. The Real IRA, Continuity IRA and Loyalist Volunteer Force had failed to be convinced by other measures. Even Sinn Féin, in a clever strategy, protested only half-heartedly. Significantly, the new measures placed Sinn Féin in a win-win position. The legislation was not directed at them, and if it backfired, they could take advantage of the situation, claiming that they had protested the measure which was another instance of 'British injustice'. This point was lost to Parliament. The introduction of such measures at the inception of a political settlement laid shaky ground on which to build a democratic system.

The introduction of the 1998 Bill also signified a change in the definition of emergency powers. Paddy Ashdown, leader of the Liberal Democrats, unconsciously used language harkening back to the introduction of the 1922 SPA, the 1939 PVA, the 1973 EPA and the 1974 PTA: 'The Government can count on our support, because we believe that these are exceptional times, which require exceptional actions'.[115] He went on to define 'exceptional times' in a manner completely different from how it had previously been regarded:

> First, having maintained the cross-party unity on Northern Ireland matters that has subsisted in the House for 25 years, it would be wrong to allow it to be destroyed by the blood and atrocities of Omagh. The second reason is precisely parallel legislation is now going through the Irish Parliament . . . Finally, the atrocity committed on that terrible day in Omagh was not against the actions of a single

government which one group of people may or may not support, but was designed to undermine and destroy the sovereign will of the Irish people, who, in a referendum, overwhelmingly expressed the desire for peace. We cannot allow that to succeed.[116]

So, what made it different from the earlier 'exceptional times' was that where the Northern Ireland Executive had been faced with a civil war over the border, and where in 1972 violence had erupted in the North, in 1998 the political parties in Britain had established a history of agreeing to emergency measures and so the instigation of an act of violence should not be allowed to interrupt that agreement. Secondly, the Irish Republic simultaneously introduced Draconian measures. Members of Parliament repeatedly cited this fact as justification for the introduction of the extreme measures in Britain. Thirdly, the Real IRA sought to overturn a democratic process of government. Thus, democracy should strike back through the introduction of extraordinary powers. Claims that the measures should be 'focused, targeted, and responsibly done',[117] rang hollow in the legacy of emergency powers in Ireland. Norman Godman inserted into the debate: '[the Prime Minister] must take cognisance of the genuine and utterly legitimate concerns of many people that the implementation of the legislation might harm the civil liberties of decent ordinary citizens. We need sustained, methodical police investigation on both sides of the border to track down these dreadful, evil people. The Government must fulfill their promise of the early creation of a human rights commission for Northern Ireland with strong investigative powers'.[118] Concern existed in Parliament at the way in which the powers would be exercised. A number of MPs noted that the manner in which special powers had been exercised previously had been one of the problems with such legislation. Chris Mullin drew attention to the climate into which such powers would be introduced:

> We have to bear in mind the climate in which the powers will be exercised. Interviews with terrorist suspects are not yet audio recorded, solicitors are routinely excluded from interviews, the courts operate without juries and the judiciary is peculiarly close to the security forces. Moreover, the Police and Criminal Evidence Act 1984, which is designed to safeguard the rights of suspects, does not apply in terrorist cases. It is still possible in Northern Ireland to send someone down for life on the word of a single informer or an unrecorded or uncorroborated statement obtained after hours of relentless interrogation in Castlereagh. That is the background against which the Bill will be implemented. There is a serious possibility that mistakes will be made and that the provisions will be seen by some as an opportunity to settle

> old scores. I would not be surprised to find a few people on the list who were not members of terrorist organisations, but were just being called in for a conversation to remember times past . . .

The manner in which the statute might be used in a court would bring disrepute to the law:

> I do not understand how it will be possible to defend oneself against an allegation. The superintendent will say in court that he is certain that the suspect is a member of a terrorist organisation. He will then be asked the basis of his assertion. He will have to say that unfortunately all his material is covered by public immunity, and then sit down. That will not look very good. A lot of people will be watching. The superintendent may not even know the suspect whom he is fingering. He may be relying on material supplied from south of the border, or on the word of junior officers, who themselves may be relying on the word of a third party whose identity they are not at liberty to disclose. The scope for error or abuse is enormous . . .

Finally, the use of the powers in the Bill might serve to recruit individuals to the movement and to alienate the police even further:

> A lot of doors will be knocked down as a result of the Bill. Most of those at whom it is targeted . . . will not simply sit at home waiting to be lifted; most of them will disappear. A lot of the doors that get knocked down will be the wrong doors. In addition, mistakes will be made. Some of the intelligence will be out of date and there will be cases of mistaken identity. Before we know where we are, we shall be back to alienating a much wider section of the community than those against whom the Bill is targeted. The image of the RUC already leaves a certain amount to be desired. Policing by consent, which we all want, will be more difficult to achieve.[119]

As with previous emergency measures introduced into Westminster, the procedure through which the 1998 Bill was laid before Parliament afforded virtually no time for debate and discussion. Immediately following the motion on the proceedings the second reading of the Bill commenced. Clerks could accept notices of amendments, new clauses and new schedules to be moved in committee at the table before the second reading. Immediately after the second reading the Bill was to be committed to a committee of the whole House, which had three hours to conclude its debate on clauses 1 through 4. The remaining proceedings had to be brought to a conclusion within three more hours (or within a total of six hours after the conclusion of the proceedings on the second reading). After the House of Lords considered the Bill, on the 3

September the House had only one hour to conduct its proceedings on any messages brought forward.

Many MPs objected to the haste with which Parliament was being asked to consider the measure. Richard Shepherd commented:

> This is a land of laws and of due process, and that due process applies to the House of Commons. I am here only because of the liberties secured for me by preceding generations. We are all conscious of that as elected representatives of defined parts of this realm. This is important, therefore, because the process by which we conduct our business is the very process that has secured our liberty . . . In the face of terrorism, we should not abandon the freedom to discuss these matters.[120]

Shepherd pointed out that the Bill had only been made available to the members on the evening previous, and that, owing to the recent general election, it was a new House of Commons. He asked why the House had been so urgently recalled to consider legislation that had been prepared for many months. 'This is no way for the House to conduct its business. The Government are acting manipulatively'.[121] Comments again harkened back to those issued by parliamentarians when previous emergency measures, such as the 1972 Detention of Terrorists Order, or the 1974 Prevention of Terrorism Act, had been rushed through Parliament. Gwyneth Dunwoody stated:

> I have grave reservations about the speed with which this Bill is to be debated . . . I believe that the House of Commons ought to give itself time to think . . . I am aware of the pressure on Members as a result of the horrendous and appalling events, but I hope that we will think seriously that when we rush through legislation and cease to put on the statute book ideas and views that have been properly tested by the time to debate, to examine and, indeed, often to understand what we are doing, we are not fulfilling our proper task. I have very grave reservations about the way in which our proceedings today are being organised.[122]

Ian Paisley commented: 'Why bring us all here and then more or less say, "Snub your nose at the House of Lords for it does not matter what it says anyway"? If we had any respect for the other House we would wait and hear its report and debate it'. He noted that in spite of attempts to get a copy of the Bill, it was not until late the night before that he was able to get a copy. He added, 'Members should bear in mind the fact that the Bill affects all my constituents: it does not affect only people who call themselves the Real IRA. Anybody can be lifted under the terms of the Bill. Therefore I, as a representative of those people have a right to defend their interests, and where should I defend them? I should do so in this House.' Paisley concluded: 'The leader of the Social Democratic and Labour party made a similar point when he said that his party would like more time to consider the Bill. In the circumstances, I should have thought that we should have as much time as possible to consider it, and there are ways in which that could be done'.[123] Tony Benn also voiced his strong objections:

> We say that the Bill attacks civil liberties, but the attack on civil liberties has already begun because Members of Parliament are being denied the time to examine the Bill, to consult their constituents and experts, and to refer to the initial Acts of Parliament that are being amended ... We are being used to rubber-stamp what a Government have decided to do ... Whatever the merits of the Bill ... it is an absolute affront to the House and to those whom we represent to say that we have to pass the motion by 10 pm.[124]

John Hume of the SDLP was sufficiently concerned about the time afforded the debate to announce that for that reason he would be unable to support the Bill. Every MP from Northern Ireland who spoke voiced their strong objections to the time being afforded the discussion. Some MPs lamented that the language used in the Bill was indecipherable. The back benches demonstrated a remarkable cross-party consensus that the Bill was too hasty, 'This is rushed legislation, and I suspect that it will be bad legislation', Andrew Robathan commented.[125] The government countered that much of the Bill had been prepared for some months – and that the time normally afforded debates on emergency measures was even less. The Bill also was credited with providing a way to immediately take action against those responsible for the Omagh bombing. Straw asserted: 'We cannot and must not let such groups succeed'.[126] As Kevin McNamara noted: 'Everyone wants the people who were involved in Omagh to be brought to justice. The Bill will not result in anyone being charged with the terrible offence that took place there. It might bring the perpetrators to prison by virtue of their being members of a particular organisation, but it will not result in anyone being charged with that offence, and I want people to be charged with it and imprisoned'.[127] Perhaps most important was the need to be seen as doing *something* and doing it at the same time as the Irish government did it. David Winnick stated: 'In view of the criticism, which a number of people have made, that the Government are going too far, what would have been the position if, following the terrible tragedy at Omagh, and against the background of what the Irish Government are proposing at this very moment in the Irish Parliament, the British Government had taken no further action against terrorism?'[128] Tony Blair echoed his sentiments: 'People simply would not understand it if the Irish Government were meeting today and the Dáil was meeting in session passing laws that allow them to act against these terrorist groups in the Republic of Ireland, and we were not meeting here to do the same in the United Kingdom's House of Commons'.[129]

A storm of criticism accompanied the government's introduction of the Act. A statement signed by dozens of lawyers in Ireland and a number of attorneys in Great Britain stated: 'Existing emergency legislation and its application has consistently led to violations of human rights and . . . its continued use has contributed greatly to a public lack of confidence in the rule of law'. Chris Mullin introduced the statement into the Commons, noting the lawyers' astonishment at the changes in admissibility of a police officer's statement regarding membership in a specified organisation. Mullin added that in such cases, the corroboration could come from another policeman: 'The one who has to go to court and assert with complete confidence that so and so is a member of a terrorist organisation will be a superintendent. The guy who tells him that during interview in the interrogation centre a chap sat silently or did not respond to questioning is likely to be a constable or even a sergeant. The corroboration will not be very serious if it consists of no more than a superintendent and a sergeant corroborating each other.'[130] Following Parliament's enactment of the measure, the *Economist* wrote: 'It is alarming to hear the leaders of two democracies boasting about how "Draconian" their new security measures are. That adjective is usually a term of abuse, denoting the intolerably harsh and unjust. But Tony Blair and Bertie Ahern, the British and Irish Prime Ministers, seem to think that such laws are now what is needed to bring real peace to Northern Ireland'.[131] The 1998 Criminal Justice (Terrorism and Conspiracy) Act further demonstrated the internationalisation of counter-terrorist law. Clive Soley noted the move towards the globalisation of the issue:

> We are developing a global approach to dealing with terrorism. It is profoundly difficult to get that approach right, because terrorism challenges both democracies and autocracies. The name of the game is to try to find a way of dealing with terrorism that is directed at countries that are capable of change in a democratically legitimate way. A matter that we must consider in the longer term, and one of the things for which I commend the Government, is their signing up to the international criminal court, which probably offers the long-term solution to dealing with terrorism. If we can deal with the problem on an international basis and, in the not-too-distant future, arrive at an

international approach to terrorism . . . we shall have achieved something positive. The danger is that, because we have all been brought up in a world that is polarised and stuck in the past, we are trying to legislate on the basis of those past experiences. The world has changed dramatically and will continue to do so. We should look for an international structure if we are to tackle the problem in the right way in the future.[132]

Just before Christmas the government issued the consultation paper, 'Legislation Against Terrorism', inviting responses by 16 March 1999. In the document the Labour government claimed to have 'come to the conclusion that any new counter-terrorism legislation should be designed to combat serious terrorist violence of all kinds. It proposes therefore that the powers in the new legislation should be capable of being used in relation to any form of serious terrorist violence whether domestic, international or Irish'.[133] As with Lord Lloyd's report, the consultation paper spoke nefariously about possible future threats and the need to not just be vigilant, but to construct a legislative framework to empower the authorities to act swiftly and decisively with regard to counter-terrorist measures. The complete absence of a current threat to Britain failed to dissuade the government that a future possibility might exist wherein a threat could be initiated on British soil. The White Paper cited terrorist attacks on abortion clinics in the United States as an example. It continued: 'Although there have been no comparable attacks in the United Kingdom, the possibility remains that some new group or individual could operate in this way in the future, threatening serious violence to people and property here'.[134] Conor Gearty appropriately commented on this 'final section of determined pessimism in which the whole argument takes on an air of unreality, as though its authorship had been appropriated by the combined talents of Nostradamus and Dr Strangelove'. Gearty noted that if subsequent counter-terrorist legislation took on the form suggested by the consultation paper, 'a whole new category of political activists will be ensnared in the penumbral world of the "terrorist", where the ordinary rule of law does not apply'.[135] The consultation paper suggested that terrorism be redefined as 'the use of serious violence against persons or property, or the threat to use such violence, to intimidate or coerce a government, the public or any section of the public for political, religious or ideological ends'. Further, 'serious violence would need to be defined so that it included serious disruption, for instance resulting from attacks on computer installations or public utilities'.[136] Britain's emergency response to Northern Irish terrorism, drawn largely from the Special Powers Acts, provided a precedent for the permanent introduction of broad-sweeping powers. Hitherto, the measures applying only to Northern Ireland were far wider than those limited to the United Kingdom. Even the 1998 Criminal Justice Act distinguished between the first four clauses, which were applicable only to the North, and the last four clauses, operable throughout the United Kingdom to address international terrorism. The measures that had been introduced in Great Britain, and which had become gradually more acceptable as a response to terrorism *per se*, were now to be enshrined in permanent legislation to meet the possibility of future domestic and international terrorist threat.

Throughout the following year the British government repeatedly moved back the deadline for the devolution of power to the new power-sharing administration. The IRA refused to begin disarming, while unionists refused to allow Sinn Féin entry to the new government before the IRA decommissioned. Bertie Ahern, somewhat surprisingly for his position as a Fianna Fáil TD, showed increased sympathy for Trimble's position on decommissioning. In the midst of efforts to break the deadlock over the decommissioning of weapons, on 15 March 1999 the Red Hand Defenders, a loyalist splinter group bitterly opposed to the Belfast Agreement, set an explosive device that killed the well-known republican lawyer Rosemary Nelson. Fears that a new round of violence would erupt were ignited when two days later Frankie Currie, a loyalist, was shot dead on Belfast's Shankill Road. The incident appeared later to have been the result of an intra-loyalist feud.[137] Nelson, the lawyer for the Garvaghy Road residents' group, had been an outspoken critic of the RUC. In response to Nelson's claims that the RUC had made repeated threats on her life, a United Nations special investigator, Param Cumaraswamy, included Nelson's claims in a report on Pat Finucane, a Belfast lawyer, who had been killed in 1989 and who also was identified with republican clients. On the basis of the report the UN had placed Nelson's name on a list of lawyers around the world whose lives were in danger. Nelson's previous claims added to the pressure for the fundamental reform of the Royal Ulster Constabulary and undermined government efforts to persuade Sinn Féin to decommission its arms. The republican body claimed that their supporters feared that the predominantly Protestant security force was in collusion with loyalist paramilitaries. In response to these fears, Ronnie Flanagan immediately brought in the Chief of Police of Kent to supervise the murder investigation. He also formally requested help from the United States Federal Bureau of Investigation. Republicans and human rights campaigners demanded an independent investigation, arguing that successive investigations by English detectives into the RUC, such as that conducted by John Stalker, had been suppressed. Following this incident, in mid-May 1999 the British and Irish governments issued a dramatic U-turn in policy over decommissioning. After a marathon negotiation session at 10 Downing Street, Tony Blair and Bertie Ahern proposed appointing ministers to the power-sharing executive before any move on weapons. The international decommissioning body headed by John de Chastelain would then liaise with the representatives of paramilitary groups and report back.

A 1998 report on victims of the troubles prepared by Sir Kenneth Bloomfield, the former head of the Northern Ireland Civil Service, led to the establishment of the Commission for the Location of Victims' Remains. Jointly directed by Bloomfield and by the former Tánaiste, John Wilson, the commission provided limited amnesty for individuals involved in the abduction and killing of the victims. In May 1999 the IRA revealed the whereabouts of at least nine past victims.[138] Still, emergency legislation and its inequitable application to the communities in Northern Ireland continued to be of concern. At the 1999 Ard Fheis Gerry Adams cited the annual marches in Drumcree, Nelson's murder, the Robert Hamill case and the release of Lee Clegg as demonstrating 'the corrupt nature of the British judicial system in the North and the unacceptability of the RUC'. He added: 'It is . . . important to point out that there have been no changes to the Emergency legislation. All such laws in place before the signing of the Agreement are still in place. In fact more Draconian laws have been introduced since then in both States on this island'.[139]

During the 1999 PTA renewal debates members recalled that fifty-five deaths over the past year had been caused by terrorist attack. Sir Norman Fowler spoke for the Opposition:

> Even in the event of the agreement succeeding, the terrorist threat is likely to remain at a high level, perhaps for some time . . . the Omagh bombing in 1998 – the single worst atrocity of the past 30 years – was carried out by a republican splinter group; and the murder of Rosemary Nelson is the work of another splinter group. The terrorist threat remains, but it is by no means confined to Northern Ireland: there are other forms of domestic terrorism and the problems of international terrorism . . . Not only has the threat from such groups increased in recent years, but they have access to increasingly sophisticated weapons and methods.[140]

With the same concerns in mind, Jack Straw outlined Labour's future plans:

> As is widely recognised, the time has come to put anti-terrorist legislation on to a permanent footing. We envisage legislation that is flexible enough to be able to respond to the ever-changing nature of

terrorism, that is effective and proportionate to the threat that the UK faces, that protects the rights of individuals and that complies with our international commitments.

He added,

We hope and expect that, by the time new legislation is introduced, the threat from Irish terrorism should have diminished to the point at which no additional special powers are necessary to combat it. If the security situation suggests that some particular measure is needed, it will be included in a temporary additional section of the Act, subject, as the prevention of terrorism Act is at present, to annual independent review and to Parliament's annual approval to its staying in force.

Straw concluded,

Whatever the circumstances in Northern Ireland, we shall ensure that powers necessary to the security forces in Northern Ireland and in the rest of the UK will be on the statute book and will be available.[141]

CONCLUSION

From 1922 to 1972 the Northern Ireland Parliament responded to political violence by the introduction and operation of extensive emergency powers. On the proroguement of Stormont, Britain largely incorporated these powers into the 1973 EPA. From 1939 similar, although in many ways less drastic measures, applied in Great Britain. Repealed in 1973 and re-enacted in 1974, these powers, like the EPA, were directed against Northern Irish violence. For their use of these powers the British government came under a storm of criticism abroad. United Nations reports, cases before the European Court of Human Rights, and attention from non-governmental organisations such as Amnesty International and Human Rights Watch brought attention to British domestic law. Even in the House of Commons members lodged frequent complaints about the manner in which the security forces exercised such measures. Of particular concern was the way in which the powers were being used to 'trawl' for potential terrorists, resulting in the curtailment of the freedom of the population and the construction of an enormous database on the Northern Irish population in the North and Irish subjects in Great Britain.[142] Clearly, the vast majority of the measures had been introduced in a panic mode: the 1922 SPA, 1939 PVA, 1972 Detention of Terrorists Order, 1974 PTA and 1998 Criminal Justice (Terrorism and Conspiracy) Act were all distinguished by being rushed through Parliament at an unbelievable pace. Likewise, the same emotive forces that led to the, arguably, irresponsible swiftness with which such measures were put into place, drove severe and much cited miscarriages of justice. In October 1989 the Director of Public Prosecutions (DPP) freed one woman and three men who had been jailed for life for the Guildford and Woolwich pub bombings engineered in 1979 by the Provisional IRA. The DPP announced at the time that it would be wrong for the Crown 'to seek to sustain' the convictions of Carole Richardson, Paul Hill, Gerard Conlon and Patrick Armstrong on the basis of confessions that they had later retracted.[143] The Irish government, numerous politicians, legal experts, Church advocates and journalists had campaigned on their behalf. Such distinguished people as Lord Scarman, Lord Devlin, Cardinal Basil Hume and the former Northern Ireland Secretary of State, Merlyn Rees, had drawn international attention to the prisoners. The release of the Guildford Four prompted the government to take a more serious look at the case of the Birmingham Six, who were released in 1991. Six men from Northern Ireland had been arrested immediately following the same event that spurred the introduction of the 1974 PTA: the 1974 bombing of two pubs in Birmingham in which twenty-one people died. Theirs became 'the most prolonged and intense campaign in British legal history to demonstrate a miscarriage of justice'.[144] In 1977 two priests, Father Denis Faul of Dungannon and Father Raymond Murray of Armagh, wrote a book, *The Birmingham Framework*, in which they argued the innocence of the six men. Other Catholic clergy publicly supported the campaign, as did numerous Irish government ministers. After seventeen years in prison, two hearings in the Appeal Court and an appeal to the House of Lords, a third Appeal Court determined that fresh evidence cast doubt on the scientific evidence and that some police had, during the trial in 1975, deceived the court. Holding that their convictions were 'no longer safe and satisfactory', the six were released.

Kenneth Baker, Home Secretary, immediately announced a Royal Commission on Criminal Justice to try to address the damage done to the court system. The republican movement received a tremendous boost from the outcome of the Birmingham Six proceedings, and the numerous human rights organisations that had lobbied against the imprisonment of the men were vindicated. Incidents such as these demonstrated the danger of the use of emergency powers; yet not only did Britain retain the provisions, but by the end of the 1990s the government considered making permanent counter-terrorist legislation. This was in spite of the fact that the previous counter-terrorist measures had been justified repeatedly by claims to their temporary nature. The final chapter examines why such temporary measures became gradually entrenched in the United Kingdom from 1922 to 2000.

CHAPTER SEVEN

Temporary Permanence:
Emergency Powers 1922–2000

THROUGHOUT THE twentieth century the United Kingdom maintained extensive emergency powers to address Irish and Northern Irish political violence. In 1922 the Northern Ireland government incorporated the 1914–15 Defence of the Realm Acts and the 1920 Restoration of Order in Ireland Acts into the 1922–43 Special Powers Acts (SPAs). Unionists initially defended the Special Powers Act by claiming its use as a distinctly provisional measure necessary to secure law and order. Section 12 of the statute limited the duration of the legislation to one year, unless otherwise determined by the Northern Parliament. By April 1928, however, in spite of a drastic reduction in violence, the government began calling for the permanent entrenchment of the 1922 SPA and in 1933 the Northern Parliament made the statute indefinite. Direct rule did little to eliminate emergency law: the 1973 Northern Ireland (Emergency Provisions) Act (EPA) simply renamed the vast majority of Special Powers Regulations. Around the time of the statute's introduction, Merlyn Rees, the Northern Ireland Secretary of State, claimed: 'The [1973 EPA] makes emergency provisions and is by its nature temporary, to cover the period of an emergency'.[1] The government limited the legislation to a two year duration, at the close of which Parliament had to vote to extend the powers. In spite of claims that the Act would be temporary, it remained in force for twenty-seven years.

Not only did emergency legislation become a permanent feature of the Northern Ireland legal system, but for fifty-seven years Westminster retained emergency provisions aimed at countering Northern Irish violence in Great Britain. The 1939 Prevention of Violence (Temporary Provisions) Act (PVA) was intended as an interim statute. At its introduction Samuel Hoare, the Home Secretary, stated: 'We have tried to make it clear . . . that the Bill . . . is a temporary measure to meet a passing emergency. We have expressly restricted the duration of the Bill to a period of two years'.[2] Although the IRA's mainland bombing campaign ceased within a year of the statute's introduction, it was not

306

until 1953 that the 1939 Act was allowed to expire, and it was not repealed until 1973. Largely in response to the Birmingham bombings, in 1974 Westminster reintroduced powers contained in the 1939 Act, with the addition of proscription, a provision employed under the 1922–43 SPAs and the 1973 EPA. Again, this legislation was intended to be in place for a limited period. During his introduction of the 1974 Prevention of Terrorism Bill, Roy Jenkins, the Home Secretary, insisted: 'I do not think that anyone would wish these exceptional powers to remain in force a moment longer than is necessary'.[3] Mechanisms were built into the statute to prevent it from remaining on the books simply as a result of inertia: unless specifically continued by Parliament the Act would expire after two years. Nevertheless, the 1974 Prevention of Terrorism (Temporary Provisions) Act (PTA) from belied its title, as not only did it reintroduce measures in place from 1939 to 1973, but it continued in force for more than a quarter of a century after its initial introduction. Jenkins later wrote: 'I think that the Terrorism Act helped to both steady opinion and to provide some additional protection. I do not regret having introduced it. But I would have been horrified to have been told at the time that it would still be law nearly two decades later . . . it should teach one to be careful about justifying something on the ground that it is only for a short time'.[4]

Why is it that emergency law, although repeatedly intended to be temporary in nature, became firmly entrenched in the British Constitution? These wide-sweeping measures alienated a significant portion of the population, exacerbated the conflict, contributed to the suspension of the Northern Ireland Parliament, allowed for significant miscarriages of justice and a weakening of British civil liberties and resulted in drawing international attention to and condemnation of British domestic legislation. Yet, still the powers remain on the books. This chapter examines these questions and proposes that a confluence of factors perpetuated emergency measures in the United Kingdom beyond their intended life. First of all, the nature of emergency legislation – its formal structure, duplication of existing criminal offences, symbolic importance and perceived effectiveness – certainly contributed to the retention of the Special Powers. Secondly, historical considerations played a role in the maintenance of counter-terrorist law. The sheer persistence of the Northern Ireland conflict, reinforced by deep divisions in the province and the sporadic resurgence of paramilitary activity, contributed to the retention of such measures. Britain's previous use of emergency law in Ireland set a precedent for exercising the powers. Facilitating their repeated introduction and use was the perception in Westminster that

Northern Ireland was somehow different from the rest of the United Kingdom, and as a unique place with its own history, counter-terrorist legislation was, although regrettable, somehow acceptable in, particularly, the Northern Ireland context. Finally, although general boundaries were set on the extent to which both the Northern Ireland and British governments could go in introducing extraordinary powers, within these limits there was a fair amount of leeway and, at times, overt support, for the maintenance of emergency law. The boundaries were somewhat wider for the Northern Ireland government than for Westminster. In part this was symptomatic of the underlying justification for the measures: the Northern Executive appealed to reasons of state to justify its use of extraordinary State power. In Britain a Lockean appeal to the right to life and property underlay demands for the retention of emergency powers. A gradual dilution of the more extreme aspects of emergency measures might have occurred, but within certain bounds Westminster maintained a significant degree of latitude. A 'hierarchy of rights' emerged that lent further credence to the maintenance of emergency law. This hierarchy was also supported in the international arena, as was the introduction of some sort of emergency legislation. Thus, although in certain respects Britain was found in violation of the European Convention for the Protection of Human Rights and Fundamental Freedoms, it was not the existence of counter-terrorist law *per se* that was under attack. Even in the cases where the UK violated the Covenant, the State was allowed to derogate in recognition of the terrorist challenge it faced. Tension in the international arena between State sovereignty and self-determination further undermined attempts to develop concrete standards for addressing domestic terrorism. This provided the United Kingdom with flexibility in the introduction and retention of emergency law.

CHARACTERISTICS OF EMERGENCY LEGISLATION

Formal Considerations

One factor that was certainly conducive to the continuation of the emergency measures – even if it did not actively encourage the extension of them – was the formal impeccability of the legislation. Had the provisions represented a significant departure from established, accepted norms, it would have been more likely for pressure to increase on the government to withdraw the statutes. This formal consistency obtained for emergency measures a legitimacy they otherwise might have lacked and bolstered their acceptability as a means to counter Northern Irish violence.

Emergency legislation provided sets of general rules that governed affairs within the States. Far from being decided on an *ad hoc* basis, the legislation both supplied and made provision for the further introduction of legal codes.[5] In the post 1924 period the Northern Ireland government did introduce numerous regulations aimed at preventing particular events from occurring. However, once introduced the statutes remained on the books for possible further application to similar cases. For example, in 1931 the East Tyrone Republican Association attempted to erect a monument in Carrickmore, County Tyrone to commemorate former IRA activists. In order to prevent the construction of the statue, Dawson Bates issued Regulation 8A. Even after the monument had been destroyed, this regulation remained on the books for application to similar events. In order to prevent the republican McKelvey Club from camping near Carnlough in the summer of 1933, the Northern Ireland Attorney General amended Regulation 4. Although the camp was never held and the Northern government never issued the order banning the club from camping in that place, the amended regulation remained on the statute books. In 1954 the Minister of Home Affairs directed that two newspapers, *The United Irishman* and *Resurgent Ulster* be banned. In the absence of any measure specifically authorising such prohibition, the Ministry issued Regulation 8 under the 1922–43 SPAs.[6] Again, this measure became part of the Special Powers Regulations. Such regulations became a standard that the Northern Ireland government later applied to similar cases, and so while such regulations might have been introduced to prevent particular events from occurring, they were not introduced on merely an *ad hoc* basis and they were incorporated into the Special Powers statute.[7]

Both the Northern Ireland and British governments ensured that all emergency measures were clearly promulgated to the affected parties. The Northern Executive regularly published all statutory instruments introduced under the 1922–43 SPAs in the *Belfast Gazette* and the four main northern newspapers. The Minister of Home Affairs also frequently directed that the information be issued to provincial radio stations. In addition, for orders relating to the prohibition of meetings or assemblies in a particular area, the government issued copies of the statutory instruments to the local papers. All regulations made under the legislation had to be laid before both Houses of the Northern Ireland Parliament soon after their creation. The publication of regulations was subject both to section 1(4) of the 1922 SPA and to section 4(1) of the 1925 Rules Publication Act (Northern Ireland).[8] The Northern government also periodically ordered reprints of the 1922–43 SPAs and all regulations issued under the Acts. Similarly, the British government clearly disseminated emergency law. HMSO published the acts, and the *London Gazette* carried notice of any statutory instruments introduced under their auspices.

Britain's efforts to publicise emergency law did fall short of those exerted by the Unionist government. A few explanations are possible: in contrast to the British government, the Northern Executive, particularly after the civil disorder had abated, directed regulations towards preventing particular acts from occurring. For instance, republican assemblies, the circulation of printed material and the construction of monuments involved many people in the province and represented events underway. As the aim of the Unionist government was to prevent the occurrence of the events themselves, it lay in their best interests to ensure that those involved be adequately informed of the law. In order to accomplish this, the government made use of various media and official sources. Adjunctively, by ensuring that the regulations were clearly promulgated, the strength of the Northern government, in contrast to the vacillation seen as characterising previous British rule of Ireland, could be seen more distinctly.

A second explanation revolves around the extremity of the measures themselves. The need for the publication of the laws depends to some extent on the degree to which the requirements of the rules depart from generally agreed perceptions of right and wrong.[9] Certainly the perception within the nationalist and republican communities with regard to the moral acceptance of commemorating nationalist or republican holidays, rallying for a united Ireland, or disseminating literature in accordance with these views, radically differed from the commonly agreed standards within the unionist block. It was not obvious that such events should be banned. In contrast, provisions such as those in the 1973 EPA relating to murder or attempted murder would have fallen more clearly within the understood moral norms of the entire community.

A third explanation relates to the principle of marginal utility, which limited the extent to which the requirement of publicisation could apply. It simply would not make sense to use all the State's resources to try to educate every citizen as to the complete meaning of every statute that could possibly be applied to that individual.[10]

Not only did the UK's size in relation to Northern Ireland here play a role, but the relatively marginal status of legislation concerning Northern Irish affairs in relation to the other daily concerns of individuals in Great Britain was also of relevance. Northern Irish legislation – along with the exercise of British legislation relating to Northern Irish affairs – applied to only a minority of the overall population in the UK.

Further, the relative constancy of the 1973–98 EPAs and 1974–96 PTAs suggests that there was very little new about which the population had to be informed. This contrasts with the more than 100 regulations introduced by the Northern Ireland government, covering powers which ranged from internment to prohibitions on the flying of the Tricolour. These considerations aside, neither government made a secret of the emergency provisions adopted, as the laws were generally available to the population in both Northern Ireland and Great Britain.

Emergency legislation introduced in the Northern Irish context avoided retroactive application. For the most part, emergency law also met requirements of clarity: it maintained accepted norms relating to legislative drafting and language. The one measure which challenged this formal criterion lay in the 1922 SPA's provision for an individual to be found in violation of the statute 'if any person does any act of such a nature as to be calculated to be prejudicial to the preservation of peace or maintenance of order in Northern Ireland'. This wording implied unpredictability and the possibility of inconsistent law. It failed to indicate clearly particular instances in which an individual could be found in violation of the statute. Nevertheless, although in this respect the provision was open to challenge under a principle of fairness, its formal qualities met the other standards. The Unionist government refrained from acting on this provision, preferring instead to issue regulations and to establish precedent through the codification and retention of statutory instruments. As a result, this clause received minimal attention and did not become a target for opponents of the statute. Instead, attention tended to be drawn towards the discretionary power of the Minister of Home Affairs to issue regulations – a power frequently employed during the tenure of the Northern Parliament.

Emergency measures neither contradicted themselves nor placed what could be considered blatantly unreasonable demands on the population. Special powers were employed as a practical means to achieve the aim of the governments – defence of the Northern Irish constitutional structure and protection of citizens and property within the United Kingdom. The specific requirements of the provisions themselves – proscription or otherwise – were not beyond reach. Emergency enactments did not represent a frequent departure from some previous state of affairs. As will be discussed in more detail later, the nineteenth century Coercion Acts, 1914–15 DORA and 1920 ROIA predated the introduction of Northern Irish emergency law. The Northern Ireland government incorporated these statutes into the 1922 SPA and Britain later included many of the same powers in the 1973 EPA. Even the 1974 PTA found precedent in the 1939 PVA, which itself had been on the statute book for thirty-four years. Within the provisions themselves there was also a fairly high degree of constancy: although numerous regulations were introduced under the 1922–43 SPAs, there were very few changes to the statute itself. The additional measures served to clarify the original intent of the government in protecting the constitutional status of the North. From 1972 to 2000, amendments to the 1973 EPA and 1974 PTA largely centred on cosmetic alterations to the existing statutes, leaving the vast majority of provisions included in the 1973 and 1974 Acts still there in 2000. Few new powers were introduced, and even fewer existing powers were relinquished.

As a final formal consideration, discrepancies between the law as written and the law as administered were not apparent. The powers might have been implemented in a way that alienated communities or portions of the population, but the powers exercised by the security forces, the Secretary of State, the courts, and others entrusted with the administration of the legislation reflected the powers enshrined in the statutes themselves. Congruence was maintained between official action and the rules, so although the judicial procedure altered under the measures, procedural due process and rights of appeal were followed in accordance with requirements under the legislation. The ability of official action to relate directly to the declared legal standard was further ensured by the enforceability of the statutes. From 1922 to 1972 the RUC Inspector General repeatedly emphasised that unless the regulations could be administered by the police force, they should not be introduced. This rationale prevented the enactment of provisions relating to renderings of 'A Soldier's Song', wearing of the Easter Lily and the prohibition of various meetings and assemblies. Likewise, from 1972, the vast majority of rules issued by the British government could be put into effect. There was one possible exception to this standard: the 1975 Northern Ireland (Emergency Provisions) Regulation required drivers to lock and immobilise unattended vehicles. Parliament explicitly recognised that the provision would be difficult, if not impossible, to enforce.[11] In Westminster Members of Parliament justified the measure by citing the responsibility borne by drivers to ensure that their vehicles were not employed to the detriment of third parties. While this provision did not hold individuals accountable for conditions beyond their control, it did border on a parliamentary enactment not entirely enforceable. This regulation stood as an anomaly, though, as the civil authorities could implement the vast majority of emergency measures. This contributed to the consistency between statutory form and official action.

In sum, the structure of emergency measures suggests that in fact the 1922–43 SPAs, 1939 PVA, 1973–98 EPAs and 1974–96 PTAs demonstrated a significant degree of formal legitimacy. The extent to which emergency law fully satisfied these principles may have varied slightly; but for the most part the legislation met the standards. In addition to satisfying these criteria, the procedures through which emergency measures were enacted were, for the most part, consistent with the manner in which other statutes passed into law. The powers enshrined in the legislation may have deviated from other standards – this, was precisely one of the distinguishing characteristics by virtue of which they were considered emergency law – however, the statutes were enacted according to proper parliamentary procedure. This formal correctness engendered a reassuring sense of legitimacy, thus contributing to the retention of special powers long beyond their temporary invocation. Had the emergency measures violated these principles, their acceptance within Northern Ireland and Great Britain might have stood in greater question.

Criminal Law and Emergency Measures

A second feature of the emergency legislation introduced in the Northern Irish context, particularly by Westminster post 1972, was that, while some civil rights otherwise protected were violated, many of the acts prohibited by the statutes were already forbidden under criminal law. This reflected the nature of republican strategy: acts were orchestrated to undermine law and order, thus increasing the insecurity of the citizens and moving the State towards ungovernability. As a result, offences already tended to be covered by criminal statutes. What made these undertakings terrorist was the motivation and organisation of entities using them for political or ideological ends. In this respect the government used emergency legislation to reject the use of violence for political means by (a) highlighting the aims of individuals engaging in such behaviour, (b) increasing penalties associated with otherwise ordinary criminal activity, and (c) altering the manner in which the State addressed transgressions of the law. Scheduled offences under the 1973 EPA included violations of common law, such as murder, manslaughter, arson and riot, and infringements of already existent criminal statutes.[12] What caused these acts to be incorporated into emergency legislation was the aim of the government to defeat terrorism (particularly republican), defined in the 1973 EPA as 'the use of violence for political ends [including] any use of violence for the purpose of putting the public or any section of the public in fear'.[13] Under the 1973 EPA, summary conviction or conviction on indictment, while applied to offences in ordinary law, carried tougher penalties than otherwise could be levied. In addition, the pursuit of charges for crimes scheduled under the 1973 EPA was conducted within a specially constructed judicial setting. Not only did Diplock courts adjudicate cases relating to scheduled offences, but under both the 1973 EPA and the 1978 EPA, the government held trials for indictment of a scheduled offence only at the Belfast City Commission or the Belfast Recorder's Court. In accordance with Baker's recommendations, in 1987 the British government amended section 6 of the 1978 EPA to allow scheduled offences to be tried at Crown courts outside of Belfast. From 1973 through 2000, the government altered provisions of the EPAs relating to scheduled offences on only two occasions. The 1985 Northern Ireland (Emergency Provisions) Act 1978 (Amendment) Order granted the Attorney General greater discretion to certify out cases relating to kidnapping, false imprisonment and offences carrying less than a five year penalty. The Conservative government subsequently incorporated this order into the 1987 EPA. (The government rejected Sir George Baker's other proposals to certify out robbery or aggravated burglary, or to extend to the Director of Public Prosecutions the ability to remove from the schedule certain cases.) Although this alteration allowed the Attorney General to certify out specific cases, after the formation of the 1973 EPA, Westminster never actually removed any of the scheduled offences from the statute. The second alteration arrived with the 1998 EPA. Although Labour stopped short of altering the system to 'certifying in', the government extended the possible offences that could be certified out to making or possessing a petrol bomb, throwing or using a petrol bomb, possessing a firearm with the intent to endanger life, the use or attempted use of firearms, and causing explosions. Only offences that represented violations of the PTA or EPA were to be automatically tried in the Diplock system. All other scheduled offences committed in, for example, a domestic or non-emergency context, would be eligible to be certified out for trial by jury.

Not only were offences already cited in other statutes appended to emergency legislation, but some of the measures introduced under the 1922–43 SPAs, 1973–98 EPAs and 1974–96 PTAs gradually influenced ordinary law. For instance, Regulation 4 of the 1922 SPA empowered the Civil Authority to ban meetings, assemblies and processions. At its repeal in 1951, the Northern Ireland government introduced the Public Order Act, which became the primary vehicle through which the Civil Authority prohibited marches and processions.[14] The government used this statute, amended in 1963 and again in 1970, in largely the same way in which it had previously exercised Regulation 4.[15] Regulation 24C of the 1922–43 SPAs prohibited the display of the Tricolour. Responding to widespread support from the unionist population, in 1954 the government incorporated the measure into the Flags and Emblems (Display) Act (Northern Ireland).[16] As the Republic of Ireland had been recognised in the interim, the new statute did not follow Regulation 24C in banning the Tricolour outright. Instead, it forbade interference with the flying of the Union Jack and empowered the security forces to ban any flags or emblems likely to lead to a breach of the peace. More recently the Criminal Evidence (Northern Ireland) Order 1988 limited an individual's right to silence.[17] 'The Order was prompted primarily by the need to encourage those who were suspected of terrorist activity to answer questions when there was not enough evidence to convict them',[18] and it reflected the widespread belief among the security forces that maintaining silence was evidence of training in 'anti-interrogation techniques'.[19] The British government aimed the provision at individuals suspected of involvement in terrorist activity or paramilitary financial affairs;[20] but, because the Conservative government enacted it by means of the Order in Council procedure, the measure applied to all criminal suspects in Northern Ireland. The impact of emergency measures can also be seen in the powers incorporated into the 1984 Police and Criminal Evidence Act. Reflecting steps taken by Westminster to counter republican violence in Great Britain, '[t]he widely increased police powers within the Police and Criminal Evidence Bill suggest that the emergency nature of the [PTA] will to an even greater extent be subsumed within everyday police practice'. A gradual blurring of the line occurred between emergency law and regular statutes. The 1994 Criminal Justice and Public Order Act amended the PTA. This statute extended to Britain the offence of possessing any article in circumstances giving rise to reasonable suspicion that it was to be used in the commission of Irish or international terrorism. The burden of proof shifted to the defence to demonstrate, on the civil balance of probabilities, that the item was not intended to be used for terrorist purposes. By far the most cogent example would be the 1998 Criminal Justice (Terrorism and Conspiracy) Act, which codified in a non-temporary statute even more extensive powers than had existed under the emergency legislation. The waiving of the right to silence, the admission of police testimony as evidence, and extended powers of forfeiture all went beyond what previously had been in place. Yet such powers were not emergency powers; they were part of a criminal statute. From trying to deny the extreme nature of the powers assumed by the government, by 1998 Blair boasted that the new statute was 'Draconian'.

As a result, 'what was abnormal in 1982 becomes normal in 1983; likewise emergency measures become standard and unexceptional'.[21] The norms shifted so as to incorporate what had up to now been emergency measures into ordinary law.

In brief, the gradual impact of emergency measures on ordinary legislation was accentuated by the incorporation of already existing statutes into emergency measures. Because many of the crimes cited in the 1973 and subsequent EPAs were a permanent feature of ordinary criminal legislation, their inclusion did not represent a significant point of departure. What was unusual about their appearance was the focus of the measures on the political intent behind the actions themselves, the alteration in penalties associated with engaging in such activities with terrorist intent, and the court system through which cases relating to breaches of the measures were conducted.[22] These elements recognised the unique nature of the challenge being mounted against the State and indicated rejection of the use of violence for political ends, thus lending emergency law an import that served to entrench the measures beyond their intended life.

Import of Emergency Legislation

As republican violence reached the mainland both in the late 1930s and again in the early 1970s, broad support grew within Great Britain for the introduction of more stringent measures. Terrorism was seen as an attack on democracy and democratic institutions. Tony Blair summed up sentiments repeatedly voiced in Parliament: 'There are few more important challenges to democracy, and therefore to this House, than terrorism in all its forms. We must fight it vigorously wherever it appears, while holding fast to our democratic principles and the rule of law'.[23] In addition to any practical inroads that the Special Powers provided, terrorist legislation also symbolised the rejection of non-democratic methods of achieving political objectives. Violence would not be tolerated. This was true throughout Britain's twentieth century consideration of counter-terrorist law. In 1939 Arthur Greenwood stated: 'I should like to express my view emphatically, and irrespective of the political motives behind the IRA campaign, that terrorist methods will achieve nothing. I do not believe that in these days the people of this country, having witnessed the use of terrorism abroad, will ever have solutions of political problems forced upon them against their will'.[24] The role of counter-terrorist law as a statement in and of itself influenced the willingness with which parliamentarians passed such measures. In urging

fellow members to pass the 1974 Prevention of Terrorism Bill Lord
Hailsham stated: 'Apart from [the Bill's] practical value . . . its moral
impact is hardly less important and would, I fear, be considerably
blunted if we did not accede to the Government's request to enable the
Bill to receive the Royal Assent so as to place it on the Statute Book
tomorrow . . . I would suggest to pass it without amendment'. He later
added: 'If one yields to terrorism of this kind other terrorists in Britain
will draw the obvious moral that the gun and the bomb pay off because
the British do not have the courage to resist them'.[25] Members of both
Houses of Parliament repeatedly emphasised that counter – terrorist law
demonstrated not just the government, but society's rejection of the use
of violence for political ends. Because of this, any repeal or repudiation
of the measures enacted assumed new import. In the absence of a
cessation of terrorist activity, repeal might have indicated a level of
acceptance either of some degree of violence or of terrorism as a means
to a political goal. Furthermore, no real indication was given in any of
the statutes as to what circumstances would have to change, or to what
extent, in order to justify their repeal. This made it less than clear as to
when the legislation could be rescinded without altering the initial
connotation entailed in its enactment. The Birmingham bombings
provided the main impetus behind the enactment of the 1974 PTA.[26] The
need to be *seen* to be responding to this event – and indeed, to the slew
of terrorist incidents in Britain immediately preceding Birmingham – was
as important as the specific aspects of the statute itself. The government's
first duty was to protect the life and property of its citizens; it had to be
seen as acting in accordance with this aim. Proscription under the
1974–96 PTAs served in this capacity.

The main purpose underlying the introduction of proscription in
Great Britain was to reduce the affront caused to the public by seeing
overt support for republican organisations.[27] The Jellicoe Report
emphasised this point, noting that proscription bore both a practical and
presentational value: 'At the least practical level it enshrines in legislation
public aversion to organisations which use, and espouse, violence as a
means to a political end'.[28] If the government prohibited public displays
in support of proscribed organisations, public outrage and disorder
might likewise be avoided. Lord Shackleton juxtaposed considerations
of civil liberties with the moral disapprobation assigned to republican
paramilitary activity. While freedoms should not be lightly infringed, the
great offence caused by seeing support for the IRA outweighed other
considerations. Reviews of the 1973–98 EPAs expressed similar
sentiments. For example, Baker wrote in 1984: 'Proscription is an

expression of the outrage of the ordinary citizen, who comprises the overwhelming majority, at the barbarous acts of these organisations, and at the revolting glee with which they claim responsibility for the organisation, usually with personal anonymity, together with their public displays in particular areas'.[29] From 1974 to 1996 only ten charges were brought under the provisions of the 1974–96 PTAs governing proscription. This contrasted sharply with the number of similar charges brought in Northern Ireland under the 1973–96 EPAs.[30] The variance can be further understood in the context of the aim of the Northern Ireland government. As will be discussed shortly, from 1922 to 1972 any expression of republicanism represented an attack on the constitutional position of the North. In defence a significant number of charges were brought for violations of the provisions related to proscription. In Britain, by contrast, it was used sparingly, serving instead as an indicator of public outrage and relatedly, a possible preventer of civil disorder stemming from the outrage. It was not until the introduction of the 1998 Criminal Justice (Terrorism and Conspiracy) Act that the government began to focus more directly on 'specified' (a sort of ultra-proscribed) organisations. The content of this statute, the list of proscribed entities, became a mechanism for 'mopping up' recalcitrant paramilitaries that refused to enter the negotiations. Introduced in the wake of the Omagh bombing, the inflammatory language employed by parliamentarians again highlighted the fact that the use of specified organisations – and the relaxation of rules of evidence and property rights for those suspected of membership in such groups – was a statement of the appalling nature of terrorist violence. However, this legislation went beyond a merely presentational benefit, by actually waiving the rights of individuals suspected of membership. It was not simply an offence in and of itself to belong to one of these organisations. The statute reflected a status of suspect to whom a second tier of justice applied. Because of the implicit moral aversion demonstrated towards terrorism by the introduction of such measures, once in place they became difficult to rescind. Although Colville noted the limited use made of the measure within the bounds of the legal system, he recoiled from recommending its repeal. He was afraid that it would be perceived as 'a recognition . . . that the leading merchants of Irish terrorism were no longer disapproved'.[31]

Britain's failure to include loyalist paramilitaries in PTA provisions relating to proscription further emphasised that the primary function of the provision was to express public outrage and, adjunctively, to avoid civil disorder. Numerous cases of loyalist paramilitary activity occurred in Britain from 1972 to 2000. *Hamilton* v. *HM Advocate* addressed

Ulster Defence Association (UDA) activities in Dumfries, Scotland. In *Sayers* v. *HM Advocate* the Crown prosecuted members of the Ulster Volunteer Force (UVF) in Glasgow. The collection of gun-running funds for the UVF was subsequently dealt with through *Walker, Edgar and Others* v. *HM Advocate*, with further UDA activity in Scotland arising under *HM Advocate* v. *Copeland, Robertson and Others*, *Forbes* v. *HM Advocate* and *Reid* v. *HM Advocate*.[32] These cases challenged Shackleton's insistence that, 'the Protestant extremist groups are not engaged in violence against the community in Great Britain and . . . their activities are not in any way comparable to those of the IRA'.[33] Walker notes the dubious basis of this reasoning and concludes that, 'The true basis for proscription under Part I is the prevention of public offence and disorder. Thus, it is not the paramilitary activity in Britain *simpliciter* which justifies listing but the degree of resultant public outrage. In fact, loyalist criminality in Britain has not provoked public condemnation to the same degree as republican misdeeds'.[34]

The inability to revoke emergency measures once enacted was tied directly to the moral import assumed in their enactment. Withdrawing it would have been akin to surrendering to terrorism: 'I welcome the legislation because it is a signal to the men of violence that the Government will not weaken in their fight'.[35] From 'emergency provisions' the statutes became 'anti-terrorist legislation'.[36] This verbiage demonstrated a rejection of terrorism, which became inextricably linked to the renewal of emergency measures. In the annual debates on the PTA, the Opposition went out of its way to indicate that by opposing the legislation, it was by no means going soft on terrorism. Roy Hattersley stated: 'I hope that our debate today will be conducted on the understanding that, whatever our disagreements, we all occupy . . . common ground. Certainly I do not propose . . . to accuse the Home Secretary of being negligent in the cause of civil liberties, and I suspect that neither he nor his Minister will want to accuse us of being irresponsible in the face of terrorism'.[37] Similarly, calling for an inquiry into the operation of the emergency measures risked being seen as retiring from the fight. In suggesting that the government institute a review of the emergency measures, the Opposition stated:

> My Right Hon. and Hon. Friends supported the motion calling for an inquiry, but there should be no misunderstanding about our reasons. We do not believe that there should be any lowering of our guards against terrorist activity and the continuing threat of it. Our vote did not signify any complacency or moral weakness, faced as we are by deadly, clandestine groups in our midst.[38]

In 1996 Labour decided not to oppose the renewal of the Prevention of Terrorism Act. The party announced during the House of Commons' consideration of the 1996 EPA that, primarily due to the retention of provisions relating to internment, it would be opposing the Bill on the second reading but would not divide the House on the third reading. Some sort of emergency legislation was necessary. Barry Porter of the Conservatives immediately seized on the implication of this position: 'I do not believe that many people in Northern Ireland, certainly in terrorist organisations, will read the details of the Opposition's reasoned amendment . . . the headline will be, "Labour Party votes against anti-terrorist legislation"'.[39] Nick Hawkins put the point in an even more partisan fashion: 'Unless and until [the Labour Party] support the Government on every piece of anti-terrorist legislation, the voters of Britain will never take seriously any of the weasel words of Labour spokesmen from the leader downwards on the strength of the Labour Party's policy on crime. If the Opposition will not support us on measures against terrorism, they cannot be taken seriously'.[40]

With the import carried by the enactment of emergency measures, their repeal might have been interpreted as meaning either that rejection of paramilitary violence had altered, or that the threat was no longer relevant. From 1973 to 2000, however, there were no sustained breaks in paramilitary activity in either Northern Ireland or Great Britain. Even after the 1994 cease-fires, punishment beatings, movements of arms and racketeering continued, suggesting that paramilitary activity was not so much ended as funneled into other channels. Either violence still existed within society, in which case the moral import of the enactment of emergency measures proved a stumbling block to removing them, or a cessation in violence had occurred. In the latter case the onus was on those opposing emergency legislation to demonstrate that the threat no longer remained. This transferred the burden of responsibility from those seeking to extend anti-terrorist law to those seeking to repeal it. This transition guaranteed the survival of emergency measures beyond their temporary intent. The situation was reinforced by the fact that the British government made the repeal of the Prevention of Terrorism Act ultimately dependent on a solution to the Northern Irish political situation: 'Until it is resolved and until there is an end to the threat, we must be able to look for the protection that the [PTA] provides'.[41] MPs repeatedly cited this as a reason for voting for the renewal of emergency legislation. For instance, during consideration of the 1996 EPA, David Wilshire stated: 'I [support the Bill] for one clear and simple reason – the conditions that originally made the emergency powers necessary have still not gone away . . . in Northern Ireland, there is still no universal renouncement of violence for political ends'.[42] The cease-fires from 1994 to 1996 and in the post 1997 period did not diminish this threat: 'The PTA will remain necessary even if the temporary cease-fire is reinstated'.[43] Another MP, A.J. Beith, added: 'Even if the cease-fire were continuing, we would have to keep in place some emergency measures for quite some time'.[44] Members of Parliament from Northern Ireland repeatedly supported the use of extraordinary powers. Trimble stated: 'It is important that we do not lose the protection that the Prevention of Terrorism Act and the Northern Ireland (Emergency Provisions) Act provide with regard to terrorist acts. It is not wise to leave the United Kingdom without some permanent protection'.[45] Why? Because, 'There is always a need to be cautious when dealing with terrorism . . . it is, to a great extent, unpredictable. There is always a danger of resurgence'.[46] As long as this threat remained, '[i]t would be criminally irresponsible to foreswear [*sic*] the use of the power of internment'.[47] At worst, repeal of such measures might be seen as an invitation to the paramilitaries to step up their campaign.[48] Not only did these dangers exist, but no politician would want to be seen as responsible for violence should it occur after the legislation had been repealed.

The extension of the 1984 Prevention of Terrorism Act to international terrorism made the statute's repeal even more remote. Between 1984 and 1996 more than 21 per cent of those detained under either the 1984 or the 1989 PTA and subsequently charged with an offence were involved in international terrorism. In 1995 the number rose to 50 per cent. In Parliament this led one MP to comment that it was vital for Britain to 'continue to have on the statute book legislation which will enable a democratic society to respond to the ever-present threat of international terrorism, regardless of the situation in Northern Ireland'.[49] During his introduction in the renewal debates in 1996, Michael Howard, the Home Secretary, agreed that 'there is always likely to be terrorism of an international kind . . . the manifestations of it are increasing; and . . . the need for the [PTA] in order to counter them therefore remains'.[50] To base the withdrawal of a temporary statute on the cessation of international terrorism undermined the Act's claim to transient status and placed repeal even further beyond reach. The 1998 Criminal Justice (Terrorism and Conspiracy) Act further codified the use of emergency legislation to counter international terrorism. The first four clauses of the act were meant to address an emergency in Northern Ireland; the second four clauses had nothing to do with the North and applied, instead, to international terrorist acts. Together they became a statement of Britain's rejection of the use of violence for political ends wherever such acts might occur. Thus, as long as violence continued, either in relation to Northern Ireland or with regard to international disputes, the use of emergency legislation as a condemnation of terrorist techniques added to the propensity of such legislation to remain in force.

Impact on Violence

Not only did emergency legislation carry with it a moral import, but the perceived effectiveness of the measures also lent itself to encouraging the continued use of the legislation. Declining levels of violence followed the introduction of the 1922 SPA, 1939 PVA, 1973 EPA and 1974 PTA. A high of eighty murders and fifty-eight attempted murders in April 1922 plummeted to one murder and eleven attempted murders by September of that year. These numbers continued to fall throughout the balance of 1922 and into 1923.[51] Within a year of the introduction of the 1939 PVA the IRA's campaign had come to a close. Similarly, immediately following the introduction of the 1973 EPA, the number of deaths and injuries in Northern Ireland decreased. From a total of 467 deaths in 1972, the number dropped to 250 in 1973, and 216 in 1974. Injuries correspondingly decreased from 4,876 in 1972 to 2,651 in 1973 and 2,398 in 1974.[52] Following the devastating attacks in Birmingham in which twenty-one people lost their lives, over the next five years, there were only twelve total fatalities in all of Great Britain that resulted from republican violence.[53] There is the question as to what degree special powers were responsible for these decreases. The increased effectiveness of the security forces, improved intelligence, growing rejection by the communities in Northern Ireland of the use of violence for political ends, the 1974 IRA cease-fire, the drying up of IRA funding from the United States, greater selectivity of terrorists in choosing targets, greater cross-border cooperation with the Republic, internal dynamics within the republican movement and increased media attention may all have played significant roles in helping to reduce the violence. However, statistics available on the operation of, particularly, the 1973 EPA and 1974 PTA suggest that wide use was made of provisions relating to the collection of information during the first few years of the statutes' operation. Under the 1973 EPA 4,141 people were arrested in 1975, 8,321 in 1976 and 5,878 in 1977.[54] *Pari passu*, the armed forced detained 1,067 people in 1975 under the 1974 PTA, 1,066 in 1976 and 853 in 1977.[55] This brought to well over 21,000 the number of people held for questioning over the three year period under powers provided by emergency legislation. From its introduction in 1974 until its renewal in 1996, some 27,000 people were arrested under the PTA alone. Although fewer than 15 per cent were subsequently charged with a crime,[56] the information gathered from such techniques most likely had a significant impact on levels of violence in both Northern Ireland and Great Britain. Certainly under the 1922–43 SPAs, which were considerably more far-reaching than their post 1972 counterparts, Northern Ireland suffered significantly less in terms of statistical eruptions of violence. Northern Ireland MPs highlighted this fact in Westminster. For example, Paisley commented: 'I am trying to suggest that for 50 years there was comparative peace in Northern Ireland. I am stating as a fact that there were fewer people killed in the past 50 years than there have been in the past three years, even in the past year, or perhaps even in the past five months'.[57] In Stormont the effectiveness of the 1922–43 SPAs actually became the basis for the shift in the justification of the measures: they came to be defended as a means of maintaining the status quo rather than as a means of establishing law and order. This same alteration marked British defence of emergency measures: their efficaciousness became a reason for their retention. The security forces tended to support the extension of such measures as part of their arsenal in the fight against terrorism. Once the powers had been gained, those wielding them were unwilling to see them diminished. This was picked up in Parliament during the 1981 renewal of the PTA: 'It is my impression that once a government have these powers in their control they are very reluctant to give them up'.[58] As time passed and security forces became more familiar with the operation of the statute significant alterations might further be seen as inconvenient.

In summary, a number of aspects of emergency legislation itself likely contributed to the longevity of measures with regard to Northern Ireland. First, emergency legislation was formally consistent with other types of legislation. Second, many of the offences introduced under the statutes were already in place under ordinary law. Third, in the light of the moral disgust articulated through the enactment of emergency laws, it became politically undesirable (particularly against a background of continuing violence) to repeal them. Whenever a lull in violence occurred, opponents of the legislation had to prove that a threat no longer existed. As I shall discuss in a moment, both the nature of the Northern Irish situation and the complexion of terrorism made it difficult to demonstrate the absence of a threat. Finally, the perceived effectiveness of the legislation lent itself to justification for the entrenchment of emergency measures in the Northern Irish and British Constitutions.

HISTORICAL CONSIDERATIONS

Internal Divisions and the Physical Force Tradition

The political situation into which the Northern government and Westminster introduced emergency powers was of utmost importance in the retention of the legislation. The sheer complexity and depth of the conflict ensured that any attempt to address the political situation would be fraught with difficulty, thus lending an apparent permanence to the mere existence of the conflict itself. To some extent, emergency law can be seen to mirror the permanence of this division. From the inception of the Northern Ireland State, politics in the North had been built around deep ethnic divisions and divergent political aspirations. This situation continued throughout the life of the Northern Parliament. Housing distribution, employment patterns, education, inter-personal relationships and social activities all cut along ethnic lines.[59] Divergent constitutional aspirations further underlay the Catholic-Protestant divide. The two communities drew on historical events to interpret the social and political structure: the twelfth century Norman invasions, sixteenth century surrender and Regrant Treaties and Nine Years' War, and seventeenth and eighteenth century plantations and penal laws provided grounds for the republican struggle. The sixteenth century risings by the Irish Catholics, 1689 Siege of Derry, 1690 Battle of the Boyne and agrarian risings throughout the eighteenth century provided the basis for loyalist claims. Repeated reference to past events served to justify not just the republican view of the British government as an outside force, but physical force organisations as a 'legitimate' means to rid the country of British presence. From Theobold Wolfe Tone and the 1791 Society of United Irishmen to the Young Ireland movement, Fenian Brotherhood, Irish Republican Brotherhood and the Defenders, republican violence was directed against the State and its institutions. In turn, the counter-revolutionary tradition sought to uphold the authority of the State. The Planters' home guards in the 1780s, the Rifle clubs, and Young Ulster at the end of the nineteenth century professed devotion to the British Crown. These physical force organisations both emphasised and further entrenched divisions between the communities. By the time of partition and throughout Unionist government of the North, two very different histories had been constructed, which further reinforced divisions within the province.

The entrenched ideologies of the two dominant ethnic groups, and in particular the two extremes, lent its own dynamic to the maintenance of emergency law from 1922 to 1972. Because the central issue at stake rested on the constitutional status of the North, minority aspirations threatened the foundation of the State. Any attempt on the part of nationalists or republicans to gain power or to garner support for a united Ireland was perceived as an attack on the Northern Irish Constitution. As defenders of the State unionists immediately exercised their authority to secure the Northern government: emergency legislation was hailed as critical in order to gain control of the North. To have lost control, particularly at the time of partition, would have meant not just civil disorder, but a change in the structure of government. Because of the political aspirations of both nationalism and republicanism, the threat to the constitutional position of the North remained long after the violence had subsided. With the physical force tradition bearing a protracted history in Irish affairs, the possibility of its return, certainly openly advocated by republicanism, and the occasional, actual revival of violent attacks, was enough to remind unionists of the threat in their midst, emergency measures had to be maintained.

Developments in the South heightened unionists' anxiety: just over the border a distinctively Irish, Catholic State was being formed. As will be recalled from chapter one, in the 1932 Free State General Election, Eamonn deValera and Fianna Fáil gained control of the Southern Parliament. Having vigorously opposed the 1921 Treaty, deValera lifted the ban on the IRA, released all IRA prisoners, demanded that Britain return monies paid for Land Annuities, abolished the oath of allegiance from the Dáil and dropped the Union Jack as the Irish flag. DeValera encouraged northern nationalists to boycott Stormont and he continually raised the issue of partition with the British government. The changes in the South emphasised the lack of acceptance of the Treaty and with it, the border, as well as the Irish and Catholic nature of the State. Fianna Fáil eliminated the right of appeal from Irish courts to a judicial committee of the Privy Council in London, ended British citizenship for Irish citizens and instituted a number of laws that reflected the teachings of the Catholic Church. The number of Protestants in the South plummetted. In 1940 veiled offers of British support for Irish unity in exchange for Éire's entry into the Second World War further angered and alarmed northern politicians. The Northern Executive steadily maintained and expanded its emergency powers.[60]

Following the Second World War the Northern government did withdraw some of the Special Powers Regulations. Nevertheless, the Act itself remained in force, and within a few years the government swiftly re-enacted the provisions that had been repealed. One explanation for the slight relaxation in emergency law lay in the impact of politics during the war. Having demonstrated loyalty in contrast to the South's neutrality, northern unionists could look upon their continued links with Britain with increased confidence. Churchill, an implacable Orange supporter, led Westminster in passing the 1949 Ireland Act, which confirmed Northern Ireland's position within the United Kingdom as long as such links were backed by a majority in the Northern Parliament. Unionists firmly controlled both the provincial Parliament and the local governmental structures, and so the threat of nationalists gaining control of these institutions was as remote as ever. Together with the lack of an immediate threat from the IRA and the relative calm that existed in Northern Ireland, unionists slightly relaxed the emergency provisions. The dawn of the IRA's 1956 campaign, however, resulted in the swift re-enactment of emergency measures.

As Britain assumed direct rule, the conflicting aims of the communities in Northern Ireland continued to influence the existence of emergency law. Just as a threat had existed during the operation of the Northern Parliament, violent opposition faced Britain. While Westminster did not share unionists' immediacy in terms of the impact on the survival of the British (versus Northern Irish) State, Britain too became caught in the deep provincial divisions. The long history of republicanism and loyalism and their surrounding ideologies made it difficult for Westminster to address the situation by means of ordinary legislation. Successive British governments thought that the 'terrorist threat' could somehow be contained, with those advocating violence separated from the, particularly republican, community. The Diplock courts, the withdrawal of special category status, the advent of supergrass trials and the media ban were all attempts to remove suspected terrorists from communities which were steeped in a history of conflict. But the fact remained that these were communities that had formed from and that identified with a long history of conflict. To a great extent, the sheer persistence of the conflict and the deep nature of the divisions in the North, ensured that there was a situation which had to be addressed. In the light of the complexity and the depth of the grievances involved, emergency legislation was one – albeit imperfect – way in which the State could address at least the violent manifestation of divergent aspirations. It was a stop-gap measure until, at the best of times, political 'progress' could be made. In the absence of any aspiration for political progress, at the worst of times it simply became an end in and of itself.

Prior Emergency Measures

Not only was there a history of division and a physical force tradition, but there was a long history of Britain enacting emergency measures in Ireland. This precedent played a role in influencing, on the State side at least, the acceptability of utilising emergency legislation to address Northern Irish affairs. Between 1800 and 1921 more than 100 Coercion Acts were employed in Ireland.[61] The government designed these statutes to minimise violence and to establish law and order. 'An Act for the Suppression of the Rebellion which still unhappily exists within this Kingdom, and for the Protection of the Persons and Properties of His Majesty's faithful subjects within the same',[62] preceded 'An Act for the Suppression of Rebellion in Ireland, and for the Protection of the Persons and Property of His Majesty's Faithful Subjects there'. These were succeeded by statutes such as, 'An Act for the More Effectual Suppression of Local Disturbances and Dangerous Associations in Ireland',[63] and 'The Protection of Life and Property in Certain Parts of Ireland Act'.[64] In response to the land war agitation of the late nineteenth century, in 1881 the British government enacted the Protection of Person and Property (Ireland) Act[65] and the following year the Prevention of Crime (Ireland) Act.[66] The preamble of the latter statute highlighted the purpose of emergency measures in the Irish context: 'Whereas by reason of the action of secret societies and combinations for illegal purposes in Ireland the operation of the ordinary law has become insufficient for the repression and prevention of crime, and it is expedient to make further provision for that purpose, [this statute is now] enacted'. Like the 1973 EPA, this legislation allowed for the suspension of trial by jury in cases of treason, murder, attempted murder, manslaughter, aggravated crimes of violence against the person, arson and attacks against the dwelling-home. The statute was the first to make an offence of intimidation. Like the 1922–43 SPAs, it included powers against rioting, unlawful associations, curfew, freedom of movement, and newspapers advocating offences against the Act and it empowered security forces to search for illegal documents and arms. It withdrew privilege against self-incrimination, with magistrates enabled to summon witnesses and compel them to answer questions under oath. The 1887 Criminal Law and Procedure (Ireland) Act,[67] which drew on previous coercion measures, allowed magistrates to engage in inquisition proceedings and empowered the Attorney General to conduct interrogation in private: 'Whereas it is expedient to amend the law relating to the place of trial of offences committed in Ireland, for securing more fair and impartial trials, and for relieving jurors from danger to their lives or property, and business', trials could be transferred to different counties where a 'more fair and impartial trial' could be held with or without a special jury. The same concerns addressed by Lord Diplock in 1972 were at issue in the nineteenth century. The 1887 Act also allowed the Lord Lieutenant and Privy Council to proscribe organisations. The government passed various Peace Preservation (Ireland) Acts throughout the nineteenth century. Other statutes adjusted the judicial procedure and tightened explosives and firearms measures.[68] The 1914–15 Defence of the Realm Acts (DORAs) and the 1920 Restoration of Order in Ireland Act (ROIA), as highlighted in chapter one, provided further precedent for the Northern Ireland government's adoption of emergency law. Not only did these statutes support the introduction of some sort of emergency statute, but the specific provisions introduced under the DORAs and ROIA became incorporated into Northern Irish and British law. In short, Britain historically addressed the unrest by punctuating the rule of Ireland through the introduction of special powers. This created an internal legitimacy in the continued use of similar measures immediately following partition and through direct rule. Britain's application of similar measures from 1972 to 2000 was further helped along by the perception in Westminster of Northern Ireland as a place apart.

Perceptions from Westminster

In Westminster the view that Northern Ireland bore a unique history within which special powers were acceptable or even necessary played a key role in annual consideration of emergency legislation. Members of Parliament frequently cited this history as justification for maintaining extraordinary powers. For example, responding to Labour's withdrawal of the powers of internment from the EPA, Andrew MacKay asserted:

> The history of Irish republicanism is littered with historic and bitter divisions. Does the Minister imagine that, in the event of an overall settlement, there will not be people in Northern Ireland, on both sides, who, following many precedents, cry betrayal and return to violence? Recent days have shown the potential for that to happen if a comprehensive settlement falls short of what is expected by some in the republican movement. Does he not believe that, in such a scenario, the power to intern may prove necessary?[69]

In 1972 one Member of Parliament commented: 'I have great sympathy with those who have protested in this debate that the order provides for internment in another and more sophisticated form. But internment has been one of the facts of Irish history and one of the means for securing the State in Ireland, north or south'.[70] Another MP asserted: 'We have never been able to maintain a Northern Ireland State, since its very inception, without some kind of repressive law'.[71] Northern Ireland was different from the rest of the UK; it was a place apart. In 1979 Humphrey Atkins, the Secretary of State for Northern Ireland, stated: 'Northern Ireland, for reasons that cannot be undone, is not like any other part of the United Kingdom. New structures of government must be based on recognition of that fact'.[72] Atkins later added: 'I hope that it will be clear to the House that the Government are, and will continue to be, sensitive to the special problems of Northern Ireland'.[73] In response to pro-testations in 1978 that the powers in the 1975 EPA would not accepted in England, J.D. Concannon, the Minister of State for Northern Ireland, replied: 'Of course, but the same situation does not apply in England'.[74] Discussing the elimination of juries in the 1973 EPA, during the committee stage of the Bill, A.W. Stallard asserted: 'the . . . impression I got . . . was that . . . this step would never be taken here but that it was good enough for Northern Ireland'.[75] More than two decades later similar sentiments were still being voiced. In 1996 Kevin McNamara pointed out: 'no one in Britain will undergo the [EPA] procedures that apply in Northern Ireland'.[76] Some comments bordered on blatant racism with regard to the view of the Irish and Ireland. During the introduction of the 1939 Prevention of Violence Bill, Colonel Wedgwood commented: 'There is no chance of appeasing [Irish] terrorism. All parties in the House are agreed that we shall never consent to putting the Protestants of Ulster under the domination of the Catholics of Southern Ireland'.[77] There might be hope for the future – Clive Soley commented in 1997: 'Is [the Hon. Member] so pessimistic and full of doom and gloom that he must assume that Northern Ireland will never be a normal society again? . . . It is a small but important step to say to the people of Northern Ireland, unionist and republican, that they are not killing each other as they used to so let us keep moving in that direction to make it a normal society once more'.[78] But in the interim special considerations had to apply. Commenting about the government's decision to introduce the Prevention of Terrorism (Temporary Provisions) Bill, Roy Jenkins wrote:

> I always believed in keeping as much as possible of the contagion of Northern Irish terrorism out of Great Britain. I thought we had responsibilities in Northern Ireland, both to uphold security and to assuage the conflict, but I did not think they extended to absorbing any more than we had to of the results of many generations of mutual intolerance.[79]

Tom Litterick commented: 'I view with trepidation the prospect of discussing the internal affairs of a foreign country. Ulster is a foreign country. I have been there and it is, in every sense, unmistakably a foreign country'.[80] Northern Ireland was alien territory with its own ingrained history. Litterick added: 'We should remember that we cannot allow ourselves to be swayed too much by our sometimes frantic considerations of present events because, as the House should know, present events are very similar in Ireland to what has gone on before. There is nothing exceptional about them'.[81]

Reflecting the perception of emergency legislation as somehow acceptable in the Northern Irish context were the brevity and perfunctoriness of the renewal procedure. In the House of Commons debates tended to be held late at night, rarely lasting more than ninety minutes. In the Lords they were even shorter and less detailed.[82] Not only was the time allocated to the consideration of emergency legislation limited, but, after the introduction of the 1973 EPA, Parliament appended the renewal of other statutes to the debates surrounding emergency measures. Within a few years the renewal of the 1974 Northern Ireland (Young Persons) Act[83] and the 1974 Northern Ireland Act, were being considered concurrent with the retention of the 1973–5 EPAs.[84] This allowed for even less direct discussion of the emergency measures at hand. In addition, attendance at the annual renewals steadily eroded in the years following the introduction of emergency law. Despite the minimal time and attention afforded the discussion of emergency legislation in Northern Ireland, the powers incorporated into the EPA were significantly more far-reaching than those of the PTA. Extensive powers of stop and search, the waiving of the right to silence, extended detention, the establishment of Diplock courts, denial of access to a solicitor and broad-sweeping powers of entry, search and seizure applied only to Northern Ireland. It was not until the mid 90s that some of these powers began to appear, in muted form, in legislation applying to Great Britain. Even the 1998 Criminal Justice (Terrorism and Conspiracy) Act limited its first four clauses to apply the encroachment of judicial standards only to Northern Ireland. Clauses allowing the testimony of a police officer to be admitted as evidence, extending powers of detention and internment, empowering the government to exercise greater leverage in forfeiture of property and impacting a suspect's right to silence all applied only to Northern Irish organisations specified by the Secretary of State for Northern Ireland. Along with the procedures followed with respect to both the EPA and PTA, this further reflected the general view in Westminster of the acceptability of applying emergency law to the North.

SETTING OF BOUNDARIES

Reason of state versus Salus Populi Suprema Lex

As well as the characteristics of emergency legislation itself and the historical considerations that played a role in the enactment and continuation of counter-terrorist law, both Northern Ireland and Westminster operated within certain boundaries that were defined by the justification used to defend the use of extraordinary State power. In 1922 in Northern Ireland, the justification took the form of reason of state, which created a fairly wide area within which the government could manoeuvre. On the assumption of direct rule, Westminster adopted many of the Special Powers Regulations; however, there was a difference in justification and consequently, the particular provisions were retained. Westminster primarily appealed to the principle of *salus populi suprema lex*[85] to support its use of the measures. Drawing on a Lockean concept of rights and the duty of the State to protect life and property, the government's objective varied from that pursued by the unionist regime. Rather than to retain at all costs the constitutional structure of Northern Ireland, Britain sought to ensure the welfare of the people within the United Kingdom. The scale of the danger posed to Britain differed from that confronting the Northern government, and certainly Westminster did not view the constitutional structure of Northern Ireland as written in stone. The underlying justifications offered for the introduction and retention of these measures go some way towards explaining not just how the measures evolved within certain boundaries, but how emergency statutes became embedded in both Northern Ireland and Great Britain.

Following partition, the survival of Northern Ireland depended on entrenching the border with the South. The overriding issue was whether the Northern Province, distinguished by the 1920 Government of Ireland Act and subsequent Anglo-Irish Treaty, would survive. Unionists claimed that 'exceptional times, requiring exceptional measures' existed. Robert Lynn exclaimed: 'We are living not in normal, but in very abnormal times . . . Is civilisation going to be allowed to exist, or is there going to be anarchy?'[86] Hugh Smith Morrison, Unionist MP for Queen's University added: 'I say, we cannot help ourselves. We are up against a wall, and we must make a fight for our lives'.[87] Reason of state adopted the character of national necessity. It was not merely *acceptable* that the Northern Parliament act decisively; the majority viewed it as the government's *responsibility* to take such steps as were required to secure the constitutional structure of the North. The measures immediately implemented addressed the civil disorder surrounding partition. Levels of violence in the North dropped. However, the threat to the constitutional structure remained. Nationalism and republicanism sought to secure a united Ireland, a goal that undermined Northern Ireland's position within the United Kingdom. As chapter two demonstrated, the Special Powers Regulations adopted from 1922 to 1972 continued to be aimed at protecting the body politic, but the immediate justification for the measures shifted. From being hailed as necessary to establish law and order, the Special Powers became considered critical to maintaining peace, and the types of provisions employed altered. In spite of this shift, the government's main defence stood unchanged. Reason of state continued to provide the underlying justification for the use of emergency law. Aspirations to a united Ireland challenged the existence of the body politic, but the exact manner in which the government responded to this challenge varied. One of the defining characteristics of reason of state is the variable character it assumes in its invocation by different political entities. As Meinecke wrote: 'The State is . . . an individual structure with its own characteristic way of life; and the laws general to the species are modified by a particular structural pattern and a particular environment'.[88] Distinct constitutional orders contribute to the principles that orient subsequent behaviour. Such principles may alter with changes in circumstances, but they nevertheless, find cohesion with the basic aim of the body politic. 'For each State at each particular moment there exists one ideal course of action.'[89] As the circumstances in Northern Ireland, Great Britain, and the Irish Free State changed, the course chosen by the Northern government in the name of necessity also altered. The actions taken by the Northern Executive bore both this individual character as well as a general quality: they were a product of the moment, adapted to the needs of the State. In this capacity they infringed liberal-democratic considerations of rights and liberties. At the same time they were general, in that they arose from an impulse common to all bodies politic.

One of the dangers inherent in invoking reason of state is that the very means employed to preserve the political community destroys relationships within its bounds. In Northern Ireland, where emergency measures were adopted from the beginning of the provincial government, this was the case. Although James Craig asserted in 1921 that 'the rights of the minority must be sacred to the majority', and that 'broad views, tolerant ideas, and a real desire for liberty of conscience' would guide the Northern government,[90] in response to internal and external developments and reflecting the character of the emergency measures employed, he asserted in 1932: 'Ours is a Protestant government and I am an

Orangeman'.[91] By the outbreak of the civil rights marches in the late 1960s, the 1922–43 SPAs had become one of the central grievances of the minority community. Morality and law had to be taken into account, for the 'well-being of the State is secured not solely through power, but also through ethics and justice; and in the last resort the disruption of these can endanger the maintenance of power itself'.[92] Certain rules and standards had to be followed in order for Northern Ireland to preserve itself and to grow. Here reason of state provided a fulcrum for the balance of conflicting impulses; for while justice might have been suspended, it was one of the very elements on which the government depended for its perpetuity. A careful balance had to be struck between the two extremes. Thus, while the government was willing to take steps perceived as necessary to secure its existence, it stopped short of acting in such a manner as to antagonise its loyal followers. The doctrine of reason of state replaced fidelity to the Crown as the impetus for action; loyalty itself was conditional on the protection of the Northern Ireland Constitution.

In the discussion surrounding reason of state, one historical assumption has been that a difference, or even a discontinuity exists between the normal state of affairs and extraordinary circumstances, which preclude viewing the exception as a foundation of normality. In the case of Northern Ireland, however, the permanence of emergency law suggests that far from being an exception, it became the norm. The doctrine, as a response to the constitutional challenge being mounted by republicanism, became embedded in the foundation of the government. For Westminster too, emergency law became a permanent feature of its legislation with regard to Northern Ireland, but a different rationale underlay the retention of extraordinary powers. In contrast to the Unionist government's outlook, Britain's response to Northern Irish political violence, particularly in the post 1972 period, was rooted primarily in the principle of *salus populi suprema lex*. The border was a negotiable issue. Violence within the State was not.

This appeal differed from that made to justify emergency measures during the two World Wars. At the beginning of the First World War, the British Executive issued a proclamation which asserted the Crown's, 'undoubted prerogative and the duty of all . . . loyal subjects . . . in times of imminent national danger to take all such measures as may be necessary for securing the public safety and the defence of [the] Realm'. In this instance, similar to the situation in which the Northern Ireland government had previously found itself, necessity authorised the State to take whatever steps were deemed essential to protect its existence.

Although parliamentary influence over the administration of defence regulations gradually increased, the rationale underlying both prerogative and parliamentary action revolved around reason of state. *Raison d'état* likewise formed the basis of Westminster's adoption of the 1939 Emergency Powers (Defence) Act.[93] This statute granted the government the ability by order in council to 'make such Regulations . . . as appear to [it] to be necessary or expedient for securing the public safety, the defence of the realm, the maintenance of public order and the efficient prosecution of any war in which His Majesty may be engaged, and for maintaining supplies and services essential to the life of the community'.[94] The scope of this language differed substantially from that adopted in emergency legislation enacted by Britain in relation to Northern Ireland. With some 16,000 statutory instruments introduced under the 1939 Act, its import was more widespread than the impact of emergency statutes designed to counter the challenge being mounted by Northern Irish political violence.[95]

Following the establishment of the North, Britain largely distanced itself from Northern Irish affairs. Westminster allowed emergency statutes enacted throughout the United Kingdom during the course of the war to lapse. In their place Britain drafted the 1920 Emergency Powers Act, which enabled the government to address industrial agitation.[96] This statute significantly differed from emergency powers adopted by Britain during both the First and Second World Wars, at which times the government invoked reason of state as the primary justification for defence statutes. In contrast, the 1920 Act reflected more accurately the basic principle employed in Britain's later attempts to address Northern Irish political violence. The 1920 Emergency Powers Act empowered the government to make regulations by order in council and to confer whatever powers were considered 'necessary for the preservation of the peace, for securing and regulating the supply of food, water, fuel, light and other necessities, for maintaining the means of transit and locomotion, and for any other purposes essential to the public safety and the life of the community'.[97] It was not until 1964 that the statute was extended to Northern Ireland by means of the Emergency Powers (Amendment) Act (Northern Ireland).[98] Until that time, similar measures were provided in the North by Regulation 13A of the 1922–43 SPAs. The 1920 statute was worded broadly so as to give the government the ability to respond to emergencies resulting from a variety of causes, such as natural disasters or attacks on essential supplies or services. Thus, while it was designed to preserve the life of the community as a whole, a second, clear aim was the protection of life and property *within* the community. The Act provided that: 'His Majesty may by proclamation declare that a state of emergency exists if at any time it appears to him that any action has been taken or is immediately threatened by any persons or body of persons of such a nature and on so extensive a scale as to be calculated, by interfering with the supply and distribution of food, water, fuel or light, or with the means of locomotion, to deprive the community, or any substantial portion of the community, of the essentials of life'.[99] In the event of an assault on the material well-being of the population, the government was empowered to take steps for the good of the people.[100]

In 1939 Sir Donald Somervell, the Attorney General, asserted: '[The 1939 Prevention of Violence] Bill takes away in certain circumstances the ordinary safeguards of liberty, but the safety, not only of property but of lives, is threatened by a conspiracy'. He continued: 'We have had six months . . . to deal with that conspiracy by the normal methods of the criminal law . . . [but] normal methods are unable to deal with this attack on life and property'.[101] The Opposition echoed these sentiments. Arthur Greenwood announced: 'it is essential that the State should take all the measures necessary for the protection of life and property'.[102] In 1974 parliamentarians supported this attitude and the duty of government to act in accordance with *salus populi*: 'The justification [for the 1974 PTA] is overwhelming . . . the very first function of any government is the maintenance of life and property'.[103] The House of Lords repeated this view, claiming that the aim of the PTA was 'the protection of life' within the United Kingdom.[104] Emphasising the priority accorded Great Britain, both the 1939 PVA and the 1974 PTA allowed for the exclusion of individuals not just from the United Kingdom, but from Great Britain to Northern Ireland. Although Britain later inserted reciprocal powers into the 1974 PTA to empower the State to exclude individuals from Northern Ireland to Great Britain, the initial actions taken by the government, and certainly, the vast majority of subsequent exclusion orders served, reflected the primacy of the protection of life, and particularly life in Great Britain, as the fundamental aim of the State. Northern Ireland was, somehow, 'a place apart', and far from a foregone conclusion, the border was a negotiable issue. The veiled offers of British support for Irish unity in 1940 lurked behind the 1949 Ireland Act, which hinged union with Great Britain on the consent of a majority in the Northern Parliament. At the outbreak of the Troubles in the late 1960s the British government reiterated this position.[105] The 1985 Anglo-Irish Agreement altered the requirements for constitutional change, placing the onus on a majority of the population in Northern

Ireland. This was again stated in the 1993 Downing Street Declaration and later the 1995 Framework Document. The possibility for changes in the constitutional structure of the North became increasingly evident:

> Both governments recognise that Northern Ireland's current constitutional status reflects and relies upon the present wish of a majority of its people. They also acknowledge that at present a substantial minority of its people wish for a united Ireland. Reaffirming the commitment to encourage, facilitate and enable the achievement of agreement over a period among all the people who inhabit the island, they acknowledge that the option of a sovereign united Ireland does not command the consent of the unionist tradition, nor does the existing status of Northern Ireland command the consent of the nationalist tradition. Against this background, they acknowledge the need for new arrangements and structures . . . to foster the process of developing agreement and consensus between all the people of Ireland.[106]

While the constitutional structure was open to discussion, what was not negotiable was the right of the state to take such actions as were deemed necessary to protect the entitlements of individuals within its auspices. It was this which provided the *fil conducteur* of Westminster's policies.

Similar to debates on the 1939 PVA and the 1974 PTA, discussion in Westminster revolving around the 1973 Northern Ireland (Emergency Provisions) Act recognised that republicans directed violence against a political goal: 'We are debating tonight how a democratic society can legitimately respond to the use of indiscriminate and brutal violence for political ends'.[107] However, the underlying rationale for Parliament's enactment of the legislation was the same as when the IRA mounted its 1939 campaign – the property and life of the citizens existed as the first priority of the government. 'The British Government in this democracy will not be shifted from their chosen and democratic course by bombs or by the threat of bombs, or by any variety of violence. *We shall ensure that all practical measures within the law are taken to protect life and property from evil.* That means that all practical measures have to be available, which is what [the EPA] is all about.'[108] The types of measures used to accomplish this end, such as detention, special courts, increased penalties and extensive powers of arrest, entry, search and seizure, focused on preventing destruction. Missing from the measures were those assumed by the Unionist government that aimed at precluding the public deliberation of support for an all-Ireland State. The closest the British government came to such measures lay in the proscription of organisations and the government's decision in the mid-1980s to enforce a media ban on representatives of proscribed groups. Much of the rationale for these measures lay in the moral statement embedded in such provisions and in the appeal to the right of the citizens not to be offended, and not in the immediate necessity of preventing the overthrow of the Northern State. The constitutional structure of Northern Ireland might have been under attack, but Britain itself was not; rather, its authority in the province was being challenged. This differed significantly from the approach previously taken by the Northern Ireland government, which had claimed to be fighting for its very existence.[109]

While *salus populi* was the dominant theme, it was not exclusive. Unionists in Westminster also frequently stressed that the aim of republicanism was the overthrow of the State:

> A government's first duty is to protect the State and its citizens from attack, whether that attack is mounted from within or from without . . . the Government say that democratic Governments have a grave dilemma. I cannot see that dilemma. *There cannot be any dilemma in the objective of government, which is to protect the citizens and their property and the territory of the State from those who would seek to overthrow that State.* If a Government find themselves in a dilemma, surely the way to resolve that dilemma is to consider what their primary duty is.[110]

For the most part, though, such language was singular to representatives from Northern Ireland. Members of Parliament from Great Britain relied instead almost exclusively on an appeal to the government's duty to protect the life and property of the citizens as justification for emergency legislation. This defence wove its way through both parliamentary debates on the 1973–98 EPAs as well as official reviews commissioned by the government to report on the operation of the legislation.[111] Society's right to defend itself meant, precisely, a right to protect the well-being of citizens. This entailed enacting emergency law: 'Society has a right . . . to protect innocent citizens and to give to the police and the Executive carefully defined exceptional powers, subject to the regular approval of Parliament'.[112] This justification arose from an essentially Lockean concept of the function of the State: political power was to be employed for the good of the citizens and the preservation of their property.[113] While these ideas also underlay Unionist government of the North, it was not the first aim of the State; more critical was the survival of the body politic itself. The initial regulations employed by the Northern government were designed to establish civil order. This adjunctively protected the property of the citizens, and it is largely these measures which Britain adopted post 1972. The Northern State, however, had also implemented provisions that denied a platform to the expression of nationalist or republican ideals. Owing to the disparate aims of the British government, Westminster did not include these later provisions in the 1973 Northern Ireland (Emergency Provisions) Act. While there was overlap in the type of measures adopted by Northern Ireland and later Westminster, different rationales drove the States. Nevertheless, because provisions aimed at establishing civil order met the criteria of both governments, similar emergency powers operated from the inception of the Northern Irish State through the assumption of direct rule.

Likewise, one of the characteristics of reason of state applied to the principle to which Westminster appealed. Aimed at justifying a particular mode of action, *salus populi* was legitimated by its invocation in the name of the public good. Because of the difficulties of determining how the public good was to be defined, its use was open to question. Exactly what constituted the good of the people could be claimed equally by opposing factions. For instance, the civil libertarians' assertions swiftly became overshadowed by the government's demand for urgency. The State's insistence was backed by appeal to information unavailable to the public, and so in order to maintain its legitimacy, the government had to publicly consider constitutional issues. Members of Parliament and government ministers repeatedly weighed the suspension of civil liberties against the exigencies of the situation in question. For instance, Roy Jenkins claimed: 'I have carefully considered the need for this legislation and I am convinced of its necessity. It is right that the balance between civil rights and the need for the protection of our citizens should be weighed up and discussed'.[114] As will be discussed shortly, a priority in liberties became established according to which emergency measures were justified:

> Basic civil liberties include the rights to stay alive and to go about one's business without fear. A society will always seek to defend itself against threats to its security. We must be prepared to forego some of our civil liberties for a time if that is the cost, on the best assessment we can make, of preserving the essentials.[115]

Civil libertarian concerns had to be addressed in order to acknowledge their place in preserving the health of the nation. They acted as a limiting factor on those applying *salus populi* and, to a lesser extent, to those invoking reason of state. Although the Northern Ireland government and Westminster both violated civil liberties, there was a limit to which certain powers could be assumed by the State. Because of the more narrow justification of special powers in Britain, there were more limits on the types of measures that Westminster could introduce. It was recognised in Parliament that the Northern Ireland conflict was 'an extremely difficult war for a democracy such as [Britain] to fight'.[116] Not only did the justification of the measures taken, modified by the liberal, democratic values of society, play a role in limiting the extent to which the government could go, but the apparent boundaries placed on the governments were to some extent symptomatic of the situation itself. In Northern Ireland and Great Britain there was no *need* for the government to take more drastic steps. Within the North the 1922–43 SPAs appeared adequate for the government's aim. In the event that such measures proved wanting, the statute provided for the instantaneous further erection of statutory instruments and in lieu of the introduction of additional measures, empowered the Minister of Home Affairs to deem any action illegal. Broad movement within the legal framework served as a legitimate response to the challenge posed by dissident views. In the early 1970s violence once again erupted and then plummeted in conjunction with Britain's introduction of additional emergency measures. The Ministry claimed that violence would again erupt should emergency legislation be repealed, and so, in spite of the continuation of some level of violence, the measures were seen as effective in their application.

Bound, then, to operate within a generally agreed strata, British politicians felt morally justified in departing from the standards, for in doing so they believed they were acting in accordance with the 'good of the people'. Moreover, as was highlighted in chapters four and five, they ardently wanted to be *seen* to be acting in this manner. All conduct prompted by both reason of state and *salus populi* fluctuates between the two sides: moral and legal considerations inherent in the body politic versus the principle invoked. This middle ground is a difficult one to tread. As Meinecke suggested, the statesman 'should . . . seek, quite coolly and rationally, to ascertain the practical interests of the State and to separate these from any emotional overtones – for hatred and revenge . . . are bad counsellors in politics'.[117] This is more easily said than done, though, as it was emotion that drove the introduction of the 1939 PVA 1974 PTA and 1998 Criminal Justice (Terrorism and conspiracy) Act. During the second reading of the 1939 Prevention of Violence Bill one MP observed: 'This is panic legislation, and I say this, which I think will be confirmed by all Members who have had a long experience of this House, that when this House is in a hurry and deeply moved, when it is unanimous, this House is nearly always wrong'.[118] In 1974 the explosions in Birmingham topped a series of republican operations in Great Britain that had left numerous people dead and many more wounded. Parliament overtly recognised that 'both haste and anger are ill counsellors, especially when one is legislating for the rights of the subject'.[119] Members asserted: 'The most sensible course for the House to take would be, by whatever procedural means available to it, to put aside this proposed legislation for at least a month and then consider it further. Cooler counsel might then prevail, and reason, which is the proper master for us to serve, might dominate our decisions',[120] and, 'I feel that this legislation has been introduced in a mood of panic. This House ought not to legislate in such a mood, and I regret that we are doing so'.[121] Nevertheless, the House did legislate in such a mood. Again in 1998 following the Omagh bombing, the Labour government took the 'opportunity' to rush through Parliament extensive powers. Richard Shepherd protested at both the speed and the emotive nature of the Bill's introduction: 'This is no way for the House to conduct its business. The Government are acting manipulatively. The House does not countenance terrorism, but we have been knee-jerked here. There is much talk about considered, rational legislation, but all too little ability for the House to consider it reasonably'.[122] Gwyneth Dunwoody added:

> I have grave reservations about the speed with which this Bill is to be debated . . . I believe that the House of Commons ought to give itself time to think. In a long career in this House, I have realised that, brilliant though we may be, we are not the repository of all wisdom and that occasionally there are those outside in the United Kingdom who can give us advice and help and point out that what we believe to be targeted and precise may in legislative terms be imprecise, vague and, in the final analysis, not worthy of a democratic assembly. I hope that we will think. I am aware of the pressure on Members as a result of the horrendous and appalling events, but I hope that we will think seriously that when we rush through legislation and cease to put on the statute book ideas and views that have been properly tested by the time to debate, to examine and, indeed, often to understand what we are doing, we are not fulfilling our proper task.[123]

In each situation, however, the emotional response to the immediate event, and the need of the government to act to protect the life and property of those in the United Kingdom, overrode all other concerns and helped to secure extraordinary State power.

Mitigating Measures

While Britain sought to demonstrate that the government would not tolerate terrorist acts, it walked a fine line between allowing what it saw as too much leeway for subversive organisations and violating rights otherwise protected in a liberal, democratic State. A lack of clarity existed as to exactly where the boundary between acceptable measures and unacceptable provisions should be drawn. As a result, Britain's use of emergency law after 1972 underwent some alteration. Although the basic measures remained the same, the specific provisions metamorphosed in response to internal demands, internal reviews and international attention. For instance, the security forces drew the interrogation techniques introduced in the early 1970s directly from British operations in Palestine, Malaya, Kenya, Cyprus and elsewhere. It was not until they were employed in the Northern Irish context, however, within the United Kingdom, that they received widespread attention and condemnation and were subsequently dropped. Because of the State structure, such techniques were unacceptable. By contrast, seven day detention and its disparate application to the minority community in the North continued well into the next decade. Both of these aspects of interrogation were challenged. Nevertheless, partially reflecting the mitigated measures in place, a borderline acceptability was maintained.

Exclusion also underwent dilution – and eventually suspension – during the tenure of direct rule. In response to unionist agitation, Britain included the principle of reciprocity through the 1974 Prevention of Terrorism (Supplemental Temporary Provisions) (Northern Ireland) Order. The British government later incorporated a revised version of this instrument into the 1976 PTA. The time limit for making representations against an exclusion order after being served with notice increased from forty-eight hours to ninety-six hours. In the event that the individual had not already been removed from the UK with his or her consent, the right to a meeting with an advisor was made absolute, rather than being dependent on whether the Secretary of State determined the request to be 'frivolous'. Two years later, in response to Lord Shackleton's recommendation that a survey of exclusion orders be conducted in order to determine if any of them should be revoked, Westminster announced that it would implement a standard review of exclusion orders to be instituted three years after the making of the initial order. In 1982 Lord Jellicoe proposed that the government modify and retain provisions related to exclusion orders.[124] The Conservatives accepted his findings and altered the appropriate provisions in the 1984 Prevention of Terrorism (Temporary Provisions) Act. The statute limited exclusion to a period of three years, after which time the Secretary of State could renew the order. The Act exempted any British citizen resident in Great Britain three or more years prior to consideration of exclusion. Similarly, an individual resident in Northern Ireland for three or more years could not be excluded from the province. Clause 7 made an absolute right of appeal for individuals to meet with an advisor to make representations protesting the issuance of exclusion orders. The statute extended the length of time within which such meetings would be arranged from ninety-six hours to seven days after the initial making of the order. Westminster's later introduction of the 1996 Draft Prevention of Terrorism (Temporary Provisions) Regulations further modified the provisions in accordance with the European Covenant on Human Rights. These changes gradually reduced the more severe effects of exclusion, making the presence of the measure, while still exceptional, more palatable than previously. As Labour gained power in the 1997 elections, exclusion underwent its final demise: the 1998 Prevention of Terrorism (Temporary Provisions) Act 1989 Partial Continuance Order omitted exclusion from its bounds.

Other alterations, such as the extension of the requirement of reasonable suspicion for the exercise of various powers, and the extension to detainees of certain rights they otherwise would hold under PACE, demonstrated the 'normalisation' of emergency law. The mitigation of emergency measures contributed to the entrenchment of the legislation. While many of the measures were diluted, more 'acceptable' powers, such as those relating to the financial support of proscribed organisations, grew more strict. This normalisation, and the growing acceptance of emergency legislation throughout the 1980s and into the 1990s are clear in parliamentary scrutiny of the measures. From the 1976 general review of the PTA until Lord Lloyd's review – which focused on the permanent entrenchment of counter-terrorist law – the terms of reference for independent reports consistently accepted 'the continuing need for legislation against terrorism'.[125] Analysis was based on the operation of the statute, and not on whether the legislation was necessary or appropriate. From the early 1970s the framework was established within which minor adjustments could be made.

Emergence of a 'Hierarchy of Rights'

Emergency legislation introduced in the Northern Irish context led to a clash between liberal principles: put rather simplistically, in the government's efforts to protect certain entitlements – arguably all the entitlements available in a liberal, democratic State – some of these entitlements ended up being violated. In Northern Ireland unionists sidestepped this seeming contradiction. Part of the justification for the

1922–43 SPAs rested on the claim that for those who did not challenge the State, such measures in no way infringed their freedom: 'One great feature about this Act which we now propose to continue is that while it places great powers in the hands of the government in regard to dealing with disorder and the disorderly elements in our midst, it does not tend in any way to infringe on the liberty of any law-abiding subject'.[126] This assertion not only reflected the security which unionists felt that the measure would not be applied to those individuals supporting the constitutional position of the Northern State, but it also ignored the impact of legislation that violated, in any measure, the rights of any citizens in the State. There was no clash between the suspension of entitlements and the right of the citizen to exercise his or her right to such entitlements, because those for whom the rights were suspended were those who had voluntarily given up such entitlements by embarking on a violent campaign against the State and the Constitution of Northern Ireland.

In contrast to assertions in the Northern Parliament, politicians in Westminster openly acknowledged that the 1973–98 EPAs and the 1974–96 PTAs violated the rights of the citizens. Parliament mitigated the impact of conflicting rights by establishing a hierarchy wherein 'lesser' entitlements could be suspended to protect the most important rights – particularly, the right to life and property. MPs justified the establishment of this hierarchy in terms of the duty that the government bore to protect its citizens. As John McQuade asserted: 'If the Government are not to forfeit their right to be called a Government, if the rule of law is to be anything other than a hollow mockery, if the Government are to be entitled to the regard and obedience of their citizens, it is their solemn duty to [respond to the terrorist challenge]'.[127] The citizens bore a right to be protected by the government, a right that in turn placed a correlative duty on the government to create and enforce measures protecting the citizens. This right clearly derived from the most basic one of all, the right to life, which imposed a duty on citizens to abstain from causing death. Britain's obligation to enforce that duty corresponded to a separate entitlement of the citizens to protection from the government, creating a duty for officials to pursue and effectuate individuals' rights. The concurrence of these two rights was a matter of practicality and not logic – one did not necessarily entail the other. The right of the British subject to be protected against other subjects could simply be a nominal right. However, as in any operative legal system, the government officials were under a moral duty and perhaps also a legal duty to take all reasonable steps to avert and rectify violations of basic rights. Not only were the right to life and the duty of others to abstain from taking that life recognised in the international covenants to which the United Kingdom was a signatory, but, as will be discussed, the entitlement of the citizens to expect protection from the government was implicit in the articles delineating derogations. Further, the primacy of the right to life as the most fundamental right within a State, along with the ability of the State to suspend other rights in order to protect that entitlement, was widely recognised as well. A hierarchy of rights emerged in Westminster in which the government was called on to protect the most basic of individual entitlements. Those rights of lesser importance had to be sacrificed in order to protect the more basic rights of the citizenry:

> Where there is a terrorist situation in any country, the rights of the individual in the community have to be surrendered to a degree in order that his real rights may be defended and eventually maintained. We must keep that principle before us. We have to surrender certain rights in Northern Ireland for the greater welfare of the whole community, so that the rights of the individual may be defended.[128]

William Whitelaw, the Secretary of State for Northern Ireland, emphasised in Parliament: '[The PTA] infringe[s] our shared concept of civil liberties. But that is the price which the House has always accepted must be paid for protecting the most fundamental liberty of all – the liberty not to be killed or maimed when going about one's lawful business'.[129] The basic right to life and protection from physical harm was placed even above the right to self-determination: 'More important to most people than the right of self-determination is the right to stay alive – which is why we must accept the necessity, however regretfully, of these emergency powers'.[130]

In its protection of the most basic right – that of the right to life – the British government violated what it considered to be the lesser rights or freedoms of the citizens. To act in this manner, however, was to risk further alienating the population. In the case of Northern Ireland, where the aim of republican paramilitarism was to draw an ever sharper distinction between the State and the citizens, this was a route of maximum possible risk. It was recognised in Westminster that the more egregious violations of civil liberties had done more harm than good. Merlyn Rees stated: 'I feel that the key is internment. Whoever one talks to in the minority group in Ulster, one can be in no doubt that since internment the political situation has changed radically. Internment has hardened attitudes'.[131] Not only was this a risky approach for Westminster to adopt, but Parliament did not seek only to protect the right to life and property. Equally important in the introduction of the statutes was the underlying claim, the right of the citizens *not to be afraid*. Fear clearly drove the introduction of particularly the 1939 PTA and 1974 PVA. It was an emotive response to the threat of violence, and the fundamental human desire to be free of that fear, that lent urgency to the assumption of extraordinary State power. The actual impact that terrorism had on life and property in the United Kingdom was much less than other acts. For example, in each year of the Troubles more people were killed in driving accidents in Northern Ireland than were killed by terrorist violence in the entire thirty years of the Troubles, and the impact of terrorist violence in sheer numbers in Great Britain fell dramatically short of the figures for accident related deaths on mainland Britain. Yet the government did not suspended all civil rights with counter-accident legislation in order to protect the life and property of citizens. Terrorism distinguished itself from these other circumstances in part by the fear associated with the unpredictability, the devastating impact, the political aim and the helplessness associated with terrorist violence. Secondly, it attempted to control the risk associated with the loss of property and life. Terrorism, by its very nature, however, is not a controllable event. By introducing emergency law, the British government sought to gain some sense of control over the situation. In fact, some control was achieved: among other powers, the legislation enabled the security forces to collect information, imprison suspected terrorists and confiscate property that might be used in the commission of terrorist offences. The right not to be afraid played a central role in the adoption and maintenance of emergency legislation. An emotive response to tragic incidents, coupled with the fear associated with indiscriminate and widespread violence, provided further justification for Westminster's introduction – and retention – of emergency law.

The International Arena

Reason of state and *salus populi* provided justification for the general placement of an outer boundary within which the Northern Irish and British States could act. Appeal to liberal principles contributed to the clarification of what was acceptable and what was not acceptable, with the inevitable clash of rights either dismissed (as in Northern Ireland) or rationalised through the establishment of a hierarchy of rights (as in Britain). From 1922 to 1972, as a result of Northern Ireland's structural subservience to Westminster, measures enacted by the Unionist government were largely considered an internal UK matter. As highlighted in chapter one, minimal attention was drawn to the operation of the 1922–43 SPAs either internationally or within Britain itself. This undoubtedly contributed to the retention of emergency law. With the advent of the civil rights marches in the 1960s, however, and the sudden international attention focused on civil rights issues, the Northern Irish situation suddenly stood out. The prominence of the region was aided by the rapidly expanding media industry and highlighted by Westminster's assumption of direct rule. Increasing international attention focused on Northern Ireland and, consequently, Britain's response to events related to provincial affairs. The Republic of Ireland's successful bid to the European court in *Ireland* v. *UK* dramatically demonstrated that Britain could not treat the Northern Ireland conflict as a purely internal matter. As discussed in chapter three, the European court determined that the five techniques employed in the early 1970s to interrogate prisoners violated the European Covenant. Britain subsequently abandoned the five techniques and altered its interrogation procedures. Following vast international coverage of the Hunger Strikes, the Republic of Ireland became increasingly involved through the Anglo-Irish intergovernmental talks. Irish America took its own steps to thrust the Northern Irish conflict into the spotlight. These changes brought into sharp relief international agreements into which the United Kingdom had entered that related to issues arising under the introduction and operation of emergency measures. These agreements, and the international community at large, both reinforced the introduction of emergency measures and played a minor mitigating role with regard to the more extreme aspects of counter-terrorist legislation.

Various treaties to which the UK was a signatory protected the ability of contracted States to introduce emergency measures in times of need. For instance, Article 4 of the International Covenant on Civil and Political Rights allowed for derogation from obligations under the treaty in times of public emergency.[132] Although the Covenant exempted some articles from derogations, such as those relating to the right to life, the right not to be subjected to torture or to cruel, inhuman or degrading treatment or punishment, and the right not to be enslaved or held in servitude, it allowed for a general derogation to be established. On ratification of the Covenant in 1976, the British government entered a derogation in respect to Northern Ireland. Britain withdrew the derogation in 1984 only to reinstate it in 1988.[133] Similar to Article 4 of the International Covenant, Article 15 of the European Convention on Human Rights and Fundamental Freedoms allowed that 'In time of war or other public emergency threatening the life of the nation any High

Contracting Party may take measures derogating from its obligations under this Convention to the extent strictly required by the exigencies of the situation, provided that such measures are not inconsistent with its other obligations under international law'.[134]

During the introduction of emergency measures, Members of Parliament appealed to the derogations provided by these agreements: 'We know that every human rights convention admits of some circumstances in which ordinary principles may be set aside'.[135] And again, 'the principle [of derogation from the normally accepted principles of the judicial process] is well recognised in the European Convention of Human Rights'.[136] In its exercise of emergency powers after 1972, the United Kingdom government chose to avail itself of the right to derogate from the standards when it was brought before the European Court for violations of the Covenant. *Brogan and Others* v. *UK*, discussed in chapter six, focused on powers of detention under the PTA. The court determined that the length of time four men had been detained, between four and seven days, violated Article 5, paragraph 3 of the Convention. Furthermore, as the UK did not make provision for compensation for the extended detention, the court also determined that the United Kingdom was in violation of paragraph 5 of the same article, which required that anyone who had been the victim of arrest or detention should have an enforceable right to compensation. In December 1988 Britain lodged a derogation under Article 15 of the Convention, citing the attack on life and property within the United Kingdom as justification for the derogation. In spite of the recognition of the long-term, apparently unexceptional nature of the 'emergency' in Northern Ireland, *Brannigan & McBride* v. *UK* subsequently upheld the validity of the derogation, supporting the United Kingdom's use of extraordinary powers. Prior to *Brogan and Others* v. *UK*, *Ireland* v. *UK* stunned the United Kingdom into recognition that their domestic counter-terrorist law would be subject to international censure. *Fox, Campbell and Hartley* became the third finding by the European Court of Human Rights that determined that Britain's counter-terrorist legislation violated the Covenant. This case focused on requirements of 'suspicion' versus 'reasonable suspicion' and the use of arrest to gather information.

These cases, and the international agreements under which they were conducted, became a yardstick by which Britain could measure its incursions into civil rights. Annual reviews directly cited Britain's responsibilities – and allowances afforded the country – by way of its international treaties. In 1972 Lord Diplock sought to adjust existing criminal procedures in a manner consistent with Article 6 of the

European Convention. In his 1975 review of the 1973 EPA Lord Gardiner wrote: 'The British Government has acted legitimately, and consistently with the terms of the European Convention for the Protection of Human Rights and Fundamental Freedoms, in restricting certain fundamental liberties in Northern Ireland'.[137] These findings followed on concerns voiced in the House of Commons that emergency measures introduced by Westminster, and particularly with respect to the Diplock Court system, would lower the UK's standing in the international arena: 'When we sit in and observe trials in [other] countries, our position and the respect in which British law is held in those countries will be severely diminished and hampered'.[138] Parliamentarians and individuals conducting reviews of the counter-terrorist statutes repeatedly inspected the powers under the 1973–98 EPAs and 1974–96 PTAs against recent findings by the European court.[139] Also important was the perception of Britain in the international arena. MPs repeatedly cited the need to maintain Britain's international reputation. In consideration of counter-terrorist statutes laid before Parliament, attention was drawn as to how the international community would perceive the powers. For example, concerning the passage of the 1939 Prevention of Violence Bill, one MP stated: 'I do not think the reputation of our country in the world will be improved by the passage of this Bill. Our ambition is that the name of our country should shine in the world. The reputation of Great Britain is based upon what Great Britain stands for. It is not based only upon the Army, the Navy, and the Air Force. It is based on the belief of people that we stand for liberty'.[140] Annual reviews in the post *Ireland* v. *UK* period repeatedly cited international opinion as an indicator of the acceptability of the assumption of certain powers. For instance, Colville's 1987 review cited the damaging effects of exclusion on the British government's civil rights reputation in the eyes of the international community. This provision's presence prevented the UK from ratifying Protocol 4 of the European Convention on Human Rights, which declared the right to move freely and to choose where to live within one's own country.

While such cases provided a measure for the degree to which certain powers could be assumed, the derogations offered by European treaties inherently supported the introduction of some sort of counter-terrorist measure. The European Convention for the Suppression of Terrorism consigned terrorism and upheld the right of States to take measures to protect themselves against terrorist attack. In May 1973 the Consultative Assembly of the Council of Europe adopted Recommendation 703, which condemned international terrorist attacks. It invited governments of member States 'to establish a common definition for the notion of "political offence" in order to be able to refute any "political" justification whenever an act of terrorism endanger[ed] the life of innocent persons'.[141] The basic rationale was that some crimes were so odious in terms of the methods adopted to obtain certain results, that they should no longer be classified as political offences for which extradition was not possible.[142] The European Convention on Extradition stated that extradition should not be granted in respect of a political offence. The ministers of justice of the member States recommended further action, which resulted in the European Convention on the Suppression of Terrorism. The document removed certain offences from consideration as political offences: any offences under the 1972 Convention for the Suppression of Unlawful Seizure of Aircraft or the 1974 Convention for the Suppression of Unlawful Acts against the Safety of Civil Aviation, any serious offence against internationally protected persons, kidnapping, the taking of hostages or unlawful detention, an offence involving the use of a bomb, grenade, rocket, automatic firearm, letter or parcel bomb if individuals are so endangered, or acting as an accomplice in any of the above offences.[143] Others, listed in Article 2, could be removed from classification as a political offence, notwithstanding their political content or motivation. These offences included acts of violence not covered by Article 1, acts against property, offences creating a collective danger to persons, or accomplices in the aforementioned acts. In expediting extradition, member States relied on the operation of mechanisms that already had been established. This overtly supported member States' measures, placing faith in the mechanisms of the European Commission on Human Rights and Fundamental Freedoms to address any deviation. In the interim, politically motivated terrorism could be made subject to ordinary rules governing extradition.

In 1978 the United Kingdom ratified the European Convention on the Suppression of Terrorism and instilled it as domestic law.[144] Although the first article of the convention technically eliminated the possibility for a requested State to invoke the political nature of an offence in order to oppose an extradition request, Article 13 allowed contracting States to make exceptions with regard to the application of Article 1. 'Any state may, at the time of signature or when depositing its instrument or ratification . . . declare that it reserves the right to refuse extradition in respect of any offence mentioned in Article 1 which it considers to be a political offence, an offence connected with a political offence or an offence inspired by political motives.'[145] Seven of the eighteen initial signatories, including Denmark, France, Germany, Italy, Norway,

Portugal and Sweden, chose to avail of this option. In its derogation, though, France asserted the need to tighten legislation to combat terrorism. The French government's decision to sign the European convention represented: '[T]he logical consequence of the action we have been taking for several years and which has caused us on several occasions to strengthen our internal legislation'.[146] At the time the statement was made, Britain was implementing its policy of Ulsterisation and criminalisation. The international support for the criminalisation of terrorist acts, such as that signified by the European Convention on the Suppression of Terrorism, and the concurrent tightening of counter-terrorist measures within other member States created a context within which the adoption of emergency law reflected an accepted, international norm. The European community openly allowed derogations and introduced conventions to facilitate the transfer of suspected terrorists. As the more extreme aspects of British domestic counter-terrorist measures, such as the torture techniques, extended detention, exclusionary powers and requirements for 'suspicion', fell under the scrutiny of the European Court, a watering-down of emergency measures occurred. Within the boundaries set by the underlying justification for the existence of the statutes, Britain gradually arrived at what was determined to be an 'acceptable level' of the suspension of rights. This circumstance certainly allowed emergency measures to continue well beyond their intended duration.

Aside from the acknowledgment of the right of the States to derogate from their responsibilities in times of 'great need', the judicial curtailment of some of the worst human rights' abuses and general support for the introduction of some sort of domestic counter-terrorist legislation, the international arena has said very little about the issue of, specifically, counter-terrorist law. This fact alone has provided Northern Ireland and Great Britain with a fair amount of leeway within which to legislate, and in the absence of demands for the suspension of emergency legislation, has also served to perpetuate counter-terrorist law. In part, the failure of the international community to act decisively as one voice stems from the inability of State actors to agree to a common definition of 'terrorism'.[147] The aims, structures, targets, strategies and tactics of terrorist organisations vary widely. Cultural and historical considerations may provide a certain amount of concurrence within a particular region, such as Western Europe, as to what constitutes a terrorist act; however, cultural, ethnic, or religious connections between neighbouring States and sub-State movements may blur the distinction between 'terrorism' and 'liberation'. The very characterisation of terrorist acts as 'grave breaches' or war crimes assumes that acts of terrorism during liberation struggle can be distinguished from individual acts of international terrorism; yet the success in making such a distinction is less than clear. The lack of clarity in determining what constitutes a terrorist act reflects the jurisprudential dispute over whether terrorism constitutes its own formal branch of international law, or whether it is simply a manifestation of acts conducted within the auspices of other areas, such as the Law of the Seas or Air and Space Law. Although it is not the intent of this book to delve into the factors influencing international treatment of terrorism and counter-terrorist domestic and international law, some aspects of the principles that form the basis of the structure of the United Nations and the international community do bear mention.[148] Their impact on the international community's lack of guidance on domestic counter-terrorist law has to some extent served to perpetuate emergency measures in the United Kingdom.

The principle of equal rights and the self-determination of a people lay at the heart of the United Nations' Charter. This document also pre-supposed a vision of State sovereignty, territorial integrity and political independence. As the scope of self-determination expanded – particularly in the post 1945 period – these principles came into frequent conflict. While ethnic groups straddle geo-political boundaries, traditional State mechanisms seek to govern the general context of ethnic nationalism. The exercise of the right to self-determination takes place within the geo-political limits.[149] Yet the majority/minority mechanisms present in many of these States often preclude the possibility of minority self-deter-mination. It has never been made clear in the international arena exactly what rights are involved in self-determination. How can international law determine which ethnic groups can exercise this entitlement? How can self-determination be achieved? What constitutes an ethnic group and what should occur if claims of competing peoples come into conflict?

In addition to the vagueness and contradiction inherent in the right to self-determination, the application of the principle of self-determination, if backed at an international level, contradicts the principles of State sovereignty and the territorial integrity of the existing State. The principle of non-intervention encourages States to handle domestic disputes inde-pendent of any international customary law. Yet self-determination suggests that nationalist movements are themselves legitimate actors in the international arena and thus subject to protection under international norms. The 1977 Protocol to the Geneva Conventions of August 1949 addresses the Protection of Victims of International Armed Conflicts, and the International Humanitarian Law of Armed Conflict extends to self-determination. The crucial difference in the 1977 extension of international humanitarian law is that the actions of the States in particular when dealing with domestic armed conflicts is no longer beyond the scope of international inquiry. Furthermore, acts of terrorism perpetuated by or on behalf of people struggling for their right to self-determination constitute a separable and different phenomenon that could be prosecuted under international humanitarian law. However, the UN only regulates States in their use of force. International humanitarian law generally applies between States party to the same treaties or other parties which accept the same treaties. For example, it is applicable to domestic liberation conflicts through States' acceptance of the 1949 Geneva Conventions. Reflective of the aim of States to deny the challenge to State political legitimacy posed by nationalist terrorist movements, ruling governments have stopped short of advocating the application of international humanitarian law to sub, anti-State terrorist organisations. Governments prefer to deal with terrorism as a criminal activity and to prosecute it within a sovereign, domestic framework of penal law.

Certainly, in the case of the United Kingdom, the government made every effort to address the violence through domestic statutes. During unionist control of the North both the Northern Ireland and British governments repeatedly denied the Republic or the international arena any role in what it claimed were the internal workings of the State. It was not until direct rule, *Ireland* v. *UK*, and the international attention suddenly drawn to the Northern Ireland conflict that Britain acknowledged any role that a State external to the UK might have *vis-à-vis* Northern Ireland. By handling the violence as an internal UK matter, the State sought to deny legitimacy to the terrorist organisations. This refusal of States to elevate terrorist organisations to equal status in the international arena prevents international humanitarian norms relating to conduct in war from being applied to the measures adopted by either the terrorist organisations or by the States themselves. If the States were to involve international humanitarian law in wars of self-determination, it might imply that the manner in which the State ensures its own survival no longer lies within domestic jurisdiction. This, of course, violates the principle of State sovereignty. So while most States are prepared to cautiously allow that the right to self-determination is a principle of the UN system and of international customary law, they are not prepared to accept the practical impact of such a concession: the legitimisation of anti-State terrorist organisations, the possible fragmentation of State territory, constitutional alteration, the application of international humanitarian law, the erosion of State sovereignty and limitations on the State's right to self-defence.

CONCLUDING REMARKS

There is very little either new or temporary about emergency measures enacted to combat Northern Irish violence. As the preceding chapters demonstrate, the Northern Ireland government and the British government addressed the conflict through the assumption and exercise of extra-ordinary powers. The justification offered for the introduction and use of such measures, however, failed to provide a sufficient limitation on the extent of the provisions and the way in which such measures would be exercised. Emergency law itself became an intricate part of the political problem. The Northern Ireland government's appeal to reason of state could be defended on grounds of political and moral responsibility, as the legitimate exercise of power in the name of the common good. But this doctrine lay open to abuse. Reason of state degenerated into a technique of domination and became a device to consolidate power – not to defend the body politic against clear attack. It was difficult to gauge at what point necessity ended. In turn, the presence of such measures became interpreted according to a domination doctrine, thus ensuring that the special powers became entangled in the political grievances in the North.

Even after the suspension of Stormont, the British government sought to eradicate terrorism completely. As Tom King expressed: 'If it is our dearest wish that this is the last such outrage that ever occurs in Northern Ireland or in the island of Ireland, and as, if terrorism is to be eradicated, it will be necessary for co-operation of the closest kind between the Irish and British Governments and people to continue, will the Prime Minister accept my support for the fact that Parliament meets today?'[150] It would have been political suicide to suggest that this was not a reasonable goal. But it is one of the unfortunate characteristics of terrorism that a government cannot ensure its eradication if it wants to maintain some modicum of freedom. The British government did attempt to pursue other routes to try to address the (distinctly) political conflict. Tony Blair stated: 'There are few more important challenges to democracy, and therefore to this House, than terrorism in all its forms. We must fight it vigorously wherever it appears, while holding fast to our democratic principles and the rule of law. We must also redouble our efforts to carry through the political settlement in Northern Ireland, which alone can bring lasting peace. That is the approach that I commend to the House'.[151] Somehow violence could be separated from the conflict, and so the government removed emergency legislation from the political discourse. As early as 1939 MPs recommended dealing with terrorism as crime: 'The way that I would suggest is that which should be used in handling the whole problem of crime: to try to remove the causes of crime, and, having done that, to try to create a machine that will be able to take efficient action against people who can be proved guilty of crime'.[152] This separation failed to recognise that the interim statutes imposed 'in the meantime' or 'until such a time as the conflict could be brought to a close' were part of the very grievances that perpetuated the conflict.

Only sporadic recognition was granted to the role of the Special Powers in exacerbating tension in Northern Ireland. In 1939 Benn, reflecting back on his stint as Home Secretary, asserted: 'We have faced that situation of terrorism many times, and we should have learned something about it. Excessive severity, the appearance of injustice, only increases the terrorism . . . the Government must appear to the world to be administering perfect justice'.[153] But exercising indefinite detention, denying access to a solicitor, waiving the right to silence, relaxing the rules of evidence and suspending the right to trial by jury are not ways to be seen as 'administering perfect justice'. The hasty enactment of measures and the disproportionate levying of the powers on the minority population in Northern Ireland ensured that the legislation would become part of the problem. In the annex to Lord Lloyd's report on counter-terrorist legislation, Paul Wilkinson observed:

> The long history of British coercion and repression in Ireland is undoubtedly a significant contributory cause of the recurrent periods of violence and conflict. The often brutal suppression of Irish rights and the discrimination and prejudice suffered by Irish Catholics in almost every sphere of life right down to modern times, undoubtedly helped to fuel support for a succession of bitterly anti-British Irish Republican movements, from Wolfe Tone's United Irishmen . . . to today's Provisional IRA.[154]

As long as policies that provoke claims of injustice continue, attempts to separate emergency powers from the politics of the region will be ineffectual. The long history of emergency law in Northern Ireland and Great Britain reinforces the assumption that it is only through the exercise of such powers that the State can be secured. Yet, part of the reason for the instability and conflict revolved around the very measures implemented to secure the State. This cycle must be broken, as although in the short term such policies may well impact the immediate level of violence, in the long term they do unimaginable damage to the social and political dynamics of the conflict.

APPENDIX A

Murders and Attempted Murders in Northern Ireland November 1921–May 1923

Date	Murders	Attempted Murders
November 1921	17	4
December 1921	19	6
January 1922	13	17
February 1922	37	41
March 1922	67	31
April 1922	35	23
May 1922	80	58
June 1922	45	33
July 1922	7	15
August 1922	3	9
September 1922	7	19
October 1922	1	11
November 1922	1	4
December 1922	1	3
January 1923	–	1
February 1923	1	1
March 1923	1	–
April 1923	–	–
May 1923	–	–

Source: Ministry of Home Affairs, 1923

APPENDIX B

Principal Regulations under the 1922 Civil Authorities (Special Powers) Act (Northern Ireland)

Regulation	Description
1.	Curfew
2.	Government authority to close licensed premises
3.	Prohibition of public meetings, wearing uniforms, carrying weapons, motor cars
4.	Prohibition of meetings, processions and assemblies
5.	Prohibition of military drilling
6.	Security force access to land and property
7.	Security force closure of close roads, lanes, passageways, ferries
8.	Security force possession of land and property, including gas and water resources
9.	Prohibition of possession of petrol
10.	Prohibition of gathering information on the security forces
11.	Prohibition of interference with telegraphic communication
12.	Prohibition of possession of codes or ciphers
13.	Prohibition of injury to railways
13A.	Responsibility to uphold contracts to supply gas, water, other municipal supplies
14.	Construction of perimeters by security forces
15.	Endangering safety of security forces
16.	Prohibition of any act to cause mutiny or disaffection among police
17.	Prohibition of withholding of information and impeding investigations
18.	Security force powers of entry

⟶

Regulation	Description
(cont.)	
19.	Security force powers of entry to prohibit meetings
20.	Government authority to close premises
21.	Security force powers to stop, search, seize vehicles
22.	Furnish Civil Authority with information specified in order
23.	Powers of detention and internment
24.	Proscription of associations
25.	Prohibition of printed material designed or likely to cause disaffection
26.	Prohibition of newspaper circulation
27.	Prohibition on publishing confidential documents
28.	[Administrative re: Orders]
29.	Powers in addition to other powers
30.	Latitude in publishing Orders
31.	[Administrative re: producing permit to show powers under Orders]
32.	Ability to exclude public from court proceedings
33.	Suspension of legal services during state of disorder
34.	Provision for court of summary jurisdiction for offences under Act
35.	Exemption of security forces from application of regulations in exercise of duties

Statutory Rules and Orders Introduced under the 1922–1943 Civil Authorities (Special Powers) Acts (Northern Ireland)

1922 Peace Preservation [Civil Authorities (Special Powers) Act (NI), 1922]

No. 31.   Curfew [Reg. 19]
" 32.   Stopping up of Roads [Reg. 7A]
" 33.   Use of Premises for Discharge of Firearms, etc. [Reg. 18A]
" 34.   Arrest and Detention of Suspected Persons [Reg. 23]
" 35.   Unlawful Associations: Irish Republican Brotherhood, Irish Republican Army, Irish Volunteers, Cumann na mBan, Fianna na hÉireann [Reg. 24A]
" 36.   Amending the Regulations for Peace and Order in Northern Ireland [Regs. 7A, 22A, 23A, 23B]
" 37.   Unauthorised Use of Uniform [Reg. 10A]
" 39.   Photographs and Finger Prints of Arrested Persons [Reg. 23]
" 41.   Detention of Suspected Persons and Removal of Prisoners [Reg. 23, 23B, 23C, 23D]
" 56.   Registration of Lodgers [Reg. 18B]
" 73.   Compensation Rules [Section 11(2)]
" 85.   Persons Detained in any of HM's Prisons by Order of the Civil Authority [Reg. 23]
" 86.   Persons Detained elsewhere than in one of HM's Prisons by Order of the Civil Authority [Reg. 23]
" 87.   Persons Interned [Reg. 23B, 23C]

1923 Civil Authorities (Special Powers) Act (NI), 1922

No. 14.   Access to Bank Records and Authority to Retain Funds [Reg. 18C]
" 48.   Control over Removal and Placement of Internee [Reg. 23B, 23D]
" 58.   Advisory Committee to Minister of Home Affairs for Detention [Reg. 23B]

1930 Civil Authorities (Special Powers) Act (NI), 1922

No. 58.   Cinematograph Film and Gramophone Records [Reg. 26A]

1931 Civil Authorities (Special Powers) Act (NI), 1922

No. 85.   Unlawful Associations [Erection of Monuments or Memorials] [Reg. 8A]
" 119.   Unlawful Associations: Saor Éire [Reg. 24A]
" 120.   Military Exercises and Drill [Reg. 5 (3)]

1933 Civil Authorities (Special Powers) Acts (NI), 1922 and 1933

No. 11.   Membership of Unlawful Associations and Refusal to Recognise Court [Reg. 24B]
" 80.   Prohibition of Assemblies [Reg. 4]
" 88.   Unlawful Associations: The National Guard [Reg. 24A]
" 110.   Examination of Witnesses by Magistrates [Reg. 22B]
" 127.   Display of Republican Flag [Reg. 24C]

1934 Civil Authorities (Special Powers) Acts (NI), 1922 and 1933

No. 5.   Explosive Substances [Reg. 3A]

1936 Civil Authorities (Special Powers) Acts (NI), 1922 and 1933

No. 47.   Unlawful Associations: Cumann Poblachta na hÉireann [Reg. 24A]

1937 Civil Authorities (Special Powers) Acts (NI), 1922 and 1933

No. 156.   Refusal to Recognise Courts [Reg. 22B]

1939 Civil Authorities (Special Powers) Acts (NI), 1922 and 1933

No. 88.   Explosive Ingredients: Potassium Chlorate and Aluminum Powder [Reg. 3B]

1940 Civil Authorities (Special Powers) Acts (NI), 1922 and 1933

No. 51.   Documents of Identity [Reg. 1A(1)]
" 54.   Persons Entering NI [must prove legitimate business] [Reg. 1A(2)]
" 61.   Persons Entering NI [must prove that purpose not detrimental to preservation of peace/maintenance of order in NI. Revoked Order 54 within a week of its enactment] [Reg. 1A(2)]
" 92.   Interned Persons [specifies Inspector General or Deputy Inspector General] [Reg. 23B]

Ministries Act (NI), 1940 – Public Security

No. 69.   Prohibition of Processions [Order prohibiting all public processions other than funerals]
" 155.   Prohibition of Processions (Amendment) [Article 4 of Principal Order]

1942 Ministries Act (NI), 1940 – Public Security

No.   Prohibition of Processions

1943 Civil Authorities (Special Powers) Acts (NI), 1922 to 1943

No. 37.   Restriction of Documents [publishing, printing, distributing, possessing]
" 61.   Increase Terms of Imprisonment and Fines for Violations of Regulations [Regs. 1, 1A, 1B, 2, 9]
" 137.   Circulation of Printed Materials [Regs. 26(1), 26(2)]

Ministries Act (NI), 1940 – Public Security

No.   Prohibition of Processions
" 93.   Prohibition of Processions (Revocation)

1946 Civil Authorities (Special Powers) Acts (NI), 1922 to 1943

No. 193.   Revoking Identity Documents [revoking Order No. 51 1940] [Reg. 1A(1)]

1949 Civil Authorities (Special Powers) Acts (NI), 1922 to 1943

No. 149.   Revoking Regulations [Regs. 1, 1B, 2, 3, 3B, 5, 6, 7, 7A, 8, 9, 10A, 11, 12, 13, 13A, 14, 15, 16,17, 18, 18A, 18B, 19, 20, 21, 22, 22A, 22B, 23, 23A, 23B, 23C, 24, 25, 26, 26A, 27, 31, 32, 34]

1950 Civil Authorities (Special Powers) Acts (NI), 1922 to 1943

No. 48.   Powers to Enter, Search and Seize; Stop Vehicles and Persons and Obtain Response, Arrest without Warrant, Seven Days' Detention, Disposal of Materials Seized Left to Discretion of Civil Authority [Regs. 11, 12, 13, 14, 15, 36]
" 187.   Revoking Regulation 8A(b) [Reg. 8A]

1951 Civil Authorities (Special Powers) Acts (NI), 1922 to 1943

No. 187.   Revoking Regulations [Regs. 4(a), 8A(b), 10, 11(c), 12(c), 13(c), 14(c), 15(c), 24B(d), 24C(e), 29, 33, 36(c)]

1954 Civil Authorities (Special Powers) Acts (NI), 1922 to 1943

No. 90.   [Similar to Order No. 48 1950] [Insertion into Principal Regulations New Regs. 4, 5, 6, 7, 36]

" 179.   Restriction of Documents (publishing, printing, distributing, possessing) [Reg. 8]

1955 Civil Authorities (Special Powers) Acts (NI), 1922 to 1943

No. 176.   Regulation of Roads and Vehicles, Powers of Arrest without Warrant and Twenty-four Hour Detention, Unlawful Associations: Saor Uladh [Regs. 9(1), 10, 24A]
Cited as: CA (SP) Acts (Amending) Regulations (NI) 1955

1956 Civil Authorities (Special Powers) Acts (NI), 1922 to 1943

No. 191.   Powers of Seizure, Arrest and Detention
Cited as: CA (AP) Acts (Amending) Regulations (NI) 1956

" 199.   Curfew, Presence in NI, Information to and on Police, Unlawful Associations: Sinn Féin, Fianna Uladh, Interference in Communications and Railways, Discharge of Firearms, Powers over Road Vehicles [Regs. 19, 20, 21, 22, 24A, 25, 26, 29, 31, 32]
Cited as: CA (SP) Acts (Amending) (No. 2) Regulations (NI) 1956

" 204.   Holding of Explosives in Stores between Sunrise and Sunset [Reg. 3B]

1957 Civil Authorities (Special Powers) Acts (NI), 1922 to 1943

No. 3.   Possession of Land and Buildings [33, 34, 34A]
" 16.   Control of Ships and Passengers [Reg. 37]
" 23.   Explosive Substances [Reg. 3B]
" 45.   Transport of Explosive Substances [Reg. 3C]
" 71.   Extension of Regulations to Armed Forces [Regs. 4, 5, 5A, 6, 7, 20]
" 132.   Forty-eight Hour Detention [Reg. 10]
" 167.   Terms of Imprisonment and Fines for Violations of Regulations [Reg. 3A(a), 3B(b), 3C(c), 5A(d), 19(e), 20(e), 32(a), 33(b), 37(c)]

1966 Civil Authorities (Special Powers) Acts (NI), 1922 to 1943

No. 82.   Limit Railway Traffic [Reg. 5B]
Cited as: CA (SP) Acts (Amending) Regulations (NI) 1966

" 146.   Unlawful Associations: Ulster Volunteer Force [Reg. 24A]
Cited as: CA (SP) Acts (Amending) (No. 2) Regulations (NI) 1966

" 173.   Assembly of Three or More People [Reg. 38]
Cited as: CA (SP) Acts (Amending) (No. 3) Regulations (NI) 1966

Emergency Powers Acts (NI), 1926 and 1964

" 106.   Proclamation of Emergency
" 158.   Revoking Proclamation of Emergency [Revokes 1966, No. 106]
           Cited as: Emergency (Revocation) Regulations (NI) 1966

**1967 Civil Authorities (Special Powers) Acts (Northern Ireland), 1922 to
1943**

No. 42.   Unlawful Associations: Republican Clubs [Reg. 24A]
           Cited as: CA (SP) Acts (Amending) (No. 1) Regulations (NI)
           1967

1969 Civil Authorities (Special Powers) Act (NI), 1922

No. 268.   Fireworks [Reg. 3D]
           Cited as: CA (SP) Acts (Amending) Regulations (NI) 1969

Civil Authorities (Special Powers) Acts (NI), 1922 to 1943

No. 281.   Closing Hour of Premises [Reg. 39]
           Cited as: CA (SP) Acts (Amending) (No. 2) Regulations (NI)
           1969
" 312.   Restriction of Use of Premises [Reg. 38A]
           Cited as: CA (SP) Acts (Amend) (No. 3) Regulations (NI) 1969

1970 Civil Authorities (Special Powers) Acts (NI), 1922 to 1943

No. 198.   Public Processions and Meetings [Reg. 40]
           Cited as: CA (SP) Acts Regulations (NI) 1970
" 214.   Assembly of Three or More Persons [Reg. 38]
           Cited as: CA (SP) Acts (Amending) (No. 2) Regulations (NI) 1970

Emergency Powers Acts (NI), 1926 and 1964

No. 317.   Sabotage, Trespassing/loitering, Arrest without Warrant
           Cited as: Emergency Regulations (NI) 1970

1971 Civil Authorities (Special Powers) Acts (NI), 1922 to 1943

No. 40.   Restriction of Documents [publishing, printing, distributing,
           possessing] [Reg. 8]
           Cited as: CA (SP) Acts (Amending) Regulations (NI) 1971
" 48.   Necessity of Reporting Use of Offensive Weapon [Regs. 23 E, 24]
           Cited as: CA (SP) Acts (No. 2) Regulations (NI) 1971
" 309.   Control over Persons Detained or Interned; Funeral Regulations
           [Regs. 13, 23D, 40]
           Cited as: CA (SP) Act (No. 3) Regulations (NI) 1971

1972 Civil Authorities (Special Powers) Acts (Northern Ireland), 1922 to 1943

No. 18.   Powers of Inspectors of Explosives to Enter, Stop and Search
[Reg. 3]
Cited as: CA (SP) Acts (Amending) Regulations (NI) 1972

Emergency Powers Acts (NI), 1926 and 1964

No. 26.   Various Orders to Address State of Emergency Proclaimed

Northern Ireland (Temporary Provisions) Act, 1972

No. 1632   (N.I. 15) Detention of Terrorists (NI) Order 1972

1973 Civil Authorities (Special Powers) Acts (Northern Ireland), 1922 to 1943

No. 113.   Removal of Republican Clubs from List of Proscribed
Organisations [Reg. 24A]
Cited as: CA (SP) Regulations (Northern Ireland) 1973

Endnotes

PREFACE

1 A.T.Q. Stewart, quoted in Townshend 1983, p. 342, fn. 2.
2 NCCL 1936, Campbell 1994.
3 See for example Buckland 1981, Townshend 1983, Lyons 1985, Follis 1995, Farrell 1976, Bew, Gibbon and Patterson, 1995, Wichert 1991.
4 Lyons 1985, p. 699.
5 Lyons 1985, p. 773.

CHAPTER ONE

1 Memo to Belfast Ulster Volunteer Force from Lt.-Col. W. Spender, 29 October 1920 (PRONI D/1700/5/16).
2 For comprehensive accounts of events precipitating the three Home Rule Bills in Westminster and the establishment of the border 1920–1, see Beckett 1981, pp. 376–461; Foster 1989, pp. 399–535; Lyons 1985, pp. 315–468; Ranelagh 1995, pp. 129–209; and Lee 1989, pp. 1–55. The immediate subsequent history draws from the work of these authors.
3 Buckland 1981, p. 19. Quoting Buckland, 1973, 114.
4 Buckland 1981, p. 20. Quoting Buckland, 1973, 116–117.
5 Government of Ireland Act, 1920, 10 & 11 Geo. V, c. 67. [Hereafter 1920 Government of Ireland Act].
6 Statements of Griffith and Collins, February 1922, State Paper Office, Dublin, S1801/A.
7 *Irish News*, 30 December 1921, 9.
8 Coogan 1987.
9 See for example Buckland 1981, Campbell 1994, Foster 1989 Lee 1989, and Townshend 1983.
10 Minute Sheet Ministry of Home Affairs, Ref. S/266, 1922, PRONI HA/32/1/206.
11 *Ibid.*
12 *RIC Reports*, 10–17 July 1921, PRONI, FIN 18/1/107.
13 Bew et al. 1995. p. 26.
14 *Irish News*, 27 May 1936.
15 *Ibid.*, 31 January 1922.
16 Blythe Papers P24/554, quoted in Darby et al. 1990, p. 34.
17 Kennedy 1988, p. 48.
18 Townshend 1983, p. 343.
19 Gilbert 1975, p. 689.
20 1920 Government of Ireland Act, section 4.
21 *Ibid.*, section 4, paras. 1–14. Recognition of limitations on Stormont's power as provided by the 1920 Government of Ireland Act, as amended, occurred in *McEldowney* v. *Forde*, [1971] A.C. 632, p. 658 (with dissenting opinion by Lord Diplock). The appellant, though, was not contending in this particular case that the challenged regulation exceeded power of Northern Ireland Parliament; rather, such a view was stated as an *obiter dictum* by the court.
22 *Ibid.*, section 6, paras. 1, 2.
23 *Ibid.*, section 5, para. 1.
24 *Ibid.*, sections 40, 41, 47, 48, 49.

25 Samuel Hoare, *HC Debs*, 24 July 1939, Vol. 350, col. 1064.
26 Dennis Herbert, *HC Debs*, 24 July 1939, Vol. 350, col. 1064.
27 Cunningham 1991, p. 3.
28 1920 Government of Ireland Act, section 14, para. 3. The 1918 Representation of the People Act defined the single transferable vote. (Representation of the People Act, 1918, 7 & 8 Geo. 5, c. 64.)
29 *Ibid.*, section 14, para. 5.
30 *Ibid.*, sections 61, 62.
31 Purdie 1990, p. 113.
32 Diary of Sir Henry Wilson, in Gilbert 1977, p. 1774.
33 Bew et al. 1995, pp. 29–33.
34 *HC Debs*, 27 May 1936, Vol. 312, col. 2019.
35 Circular sent out from the divisional commissioner's office of the RIC in Belfast to the district inspectors, PRONI HA/32/1/55.
36 Local Government (Emergency Powers) Act (Northern Ireland), 1921, 12 Geo. V, c. 5.
37 Farrell 1980, p. 83.
38 Local Government Act (Northern Ireland), 1922, 12 & 13 Geo. V, c. 16. [Hereafter 1922 Local Government Act]. Note that this statute consolidated the Local Government (Ireland) Acts 1898 to 1919, in many cases returning procedure to the pre 1919 standard.
39 1922 Local Government Act, Schedule, part III.
40 *Ibid.*, section 7.
41 Farrell 1980, p. 84. Further evidence of gerrymandering in Omagh in 1934 is given in the *Irish News*, 26 May 1936.
42 *Senate Debs NI*, 23 March 1943, Vol. XXVI, col. 65.
43 Arthur and Jeffery 1989, p. 5.
44 Farrell 1980, p. 85.
45 Gallagher 1957, pp. 251–3. Other instances of unionist majorities in local council elections in areas dominated by Catholics are also cited in *Disturbances in Northern Ireland: Report of the Commission appointed by the Governor of Northern Ireland. September 1969, Session 1969/70 Cmd. 532*, para. 229. (Hereafter Cameron Report), and Boyle et al. 1975, pp. 7, 10.
46 Cameron Report, paras. 10, 13. For a discussion of the impact of these measures see Dunn 1995, Donnan and McFarlane 1986, pp. 110–35, Cormack and Osborne 1983, Rose 1971, Kelley and McAllister 1969, pp. 171–90, Gallagher 1957, Farrell 1980, pp. 87–92, Aunger 1975, pp. 1–18, and Whyte 1991, pp. 52–66.
47 Cabinet Conclusions, 31 July 1922, App. C. PRO CAB 43/2, quoted in Townshend 1983, p. 384.
48 *Northern Whig*, 11 January 1946.
49 Farrell 1980, pp. 85–6.
50 Special Constables (Ireland) Act, 1832, 2 & 3 Will. IV, c. 108.
51 Paddy Hillyard, 'Law and Order', in Darby 1986, p. 33.
52 Flackes et al. 1994, p. 437; Farrell 1980, p. 95.
53 *Irish News* 11 February 1922, *Irish Independent* 17 February 1922.
54 Secret Report of Barrington Ward, Cab. 24/138 CP 4193, referenced in Bew et al. 1995, p. 52.
55 Buckland 1981, p. 41.
56 Criminal Procedure Act (Northern Ireland), 1922, 12 & 13 Geo. V, c. 6. [Hereafter 1922 Criminal Procedure Act].
57 1922 Criminal Procedure Act, section 1(3).
58 Protection of Person and Property Act, 1881, 44 & 45 Vict. c. 4
59 Lloyd 1892, p. 229.
60 Prevention of Crime (Ireland) Act, 1882, 45 & 46 Vict. c. 25.
61 PRO CAB/24/109.
62 Campbell 1995. fn 97, pp. 26–7.
63 See for instance Mr McGuffin, *HC Debs NI*, 6 April 1922, Vol. II, col. 398.

64 Townshend 1983, pp. 60, 172.
65 Civil Authorities (Special Powers) Act (Northern Ireland), 1922, 12 & 13 Geo. V, c. 5. [Hereafter 1922 SPA].
66 Buckland 1981, p. 46.
67 For discussion of whether the SPA was *ultra vires* of the 1920 Government of Ireland Act see Palley 1972. pp. 401–4.
68 Expiring Laws Continuance Act (Northern Ireland), 1923, 13 & 14 Geo. V, c. 25; Expiring Laws Continuance Act (Northern Ireland), 1924, 14 & 15 Geo. V, c. 28; Expiring Laws Continuance Act (Northern Ireland), 1925, 15 & 16 Geo. V, c. 19; Expiring Laws Continuance Act (Northern Ireland), 1926, 16 & 17 Geo. V, c. 20; and Expiring Laws Continuance Act (Northern Ireland), 1927, 17 & 18 Geo. V, c. 14.
69 Civil Authorities (Special Powers) Act (Northern Ireland), 1928, 18 & 19 Geo. V, c. 15.
70 Civil Authorities (Special Powers) Act (Northern Ireland), 1933, 23 & 24 Geo. V, c. 12.
71 Civil Authorities (Special Powers) Act (Northern Ireland), 1943, 7 & 8 Geo. VI, c. 2.
72 National Council for Civil Liberties 1936.
73 Contrast *HC Debs NI*, 21 March 1922, Vol. II, col. 95 with *Senate Debs NI*, 22 March 1933, Vol. XV, cols. 128–9.
74 Restoration of Order in Ireland Act, 1920, 10 & 11 Geo. V, c. 31. [Hereafter ROIA].
75 Defence of the Realm Act, 1914, 4 & 5 Geo. V, c. 29; Defence of the Realm (No. 2) Act, 1914, 4 & 5 Geo. V, c. 8; Defence of the Realm Consolidation Act, 1914, 4 & 5 Geo. V, c. 8; Defence of the Realm (Amendment) Act, 1915, 5 & 6 Geo. V, c. 34; Defence of the Realm (Amendment) (No. 2) Act, 1915, 5 & 6 Geo. V, c. 37; and Defence of the Realm (Amendment) (No. 3) Act, 1915, 5 & 6 Geo. V, c. 42. [Hereafter DORA].
76 DORA, section 1.
77 Hadden et al 1990, p. 14. For a comprehensive examination of the operation of both the 1920 Restoration of Order in Ireland Act and the 1914–15 Defence of the Realm Acts, see Campbell 1995 and Cotter 1953.
78 Ref. to Defence of the Realm Consolidation Act, 1914, 5 & 6 Geo. V, c. 8; quoted section taken from 1920 ROIA, section 1.
79 Letter to W.F. Coates from the Minister of Home Affairs, 22 March 1922, PRONI HA/32/1/29.
80 Note on Civil Authorities Act, 1922, PRONI HA/32/1/447.
81 Minute Sheet Ministry of Home Affairs, 23 July 1926, PRONI HA/32/1/447.
82 Minutes from a deputation regarding the retention of Restoration of Order in Ireland Regulations (ROIR) to the Minister of Home Affairs, PRONI HA/32/1/447.
83 Statute Law Revision Act, 1953, 1 & 2 Eliz. II, c. 1.
84 Hugh Smith Morrison, *HC Debs NI*, 21 March 1922, Vol. II, col. 89.
85 Robert Megaw, *HC Debs NI*, 21 March 1922, Vol. II, col. 87.
86 Dehra Chichester, *HC Debs NI*, 28 March 1922, Vol. II, col. 270.
87 Report marked 'secret' at the Ministry of Home Affairs, 29 November 1921, Ref. 2/10, PRONI HA/32/1/29.
88 Robert Megaw, *HC Debs NI*, 21 March 1922, Vol. II, col. 87.
89 Mr Coote, *HC Debs NI*, 28 March 1922, Vol. II, col. 267.
90 Robert Megaw, *HC Debs NI*, 21 March 1922, Vol. II, col. 89.
91 Robert Lynn, *HC Debs NI*, 21 March 1922, Vol. II, col. 91.
92 Mr McGuffin, *HC Debs NI*, 21 March 1922, Vol. II, col. 94.
93 *Senate Debs NI*, 23 March 1943, Vol. XXVI, col. 72. See also the *Belfast Newsletter*, 18 June 1936; the *Belfast Newsletter*, 26 June 1936; and the *Northern Whig*, 3 July 1936.
94 Robert Lynn, *HC Debs NI*, 21 March 1922, Vol. II, col. 91.
95 1922 SPA, para. 1.
96 1920 ROIA, section 1.
97 Richard Best, *HC Debs NI*, 23 March 1922, Vol. II, col. 152.
98 S.R.O. 73/1922, 7.12.22.
99 Notes re section 11 of the Special Powers Act, PRONI HA/32/1/47. For a copy of the Rules see Northern Ireland Statutory Rules and Orders 1922, No. 73; printed in the *Belfast Gazette* 22 December 1922.

100 The publication of Regulations was subject both to section 1(4) of the 1922 SPA and to section 4(1) of the Rules Publication Act (Northern Ireland), 1925, 15 & 16 Geo. V. c. 6.

101 See, for example, comments by Mr Nixon in the Northern Ireland House of Commons during the Committee Stage of the 1943 Special Powers Bill, *HC Debs NI*, 18 March 1943, Vol. XXVI, cols. 352–3.

102 1922 SPA, section 2, para. 2.

103 *Ibid.*, section 2, para. 3.

104 *Ibid.*, section 2, para. 4.

105 Regulation 23 governed powers of detention, while Regulation 4 addressed the prohibition of meetings, assemblies and processions. The following chapter details the operation of these regulations in more detail.

106 S.R.O. 92/1940, 7.8.40.

107 Letter from Ewing Gilfillan, Deputy Inspector General, to J.B. O'Neil, Ministry of Home Affairs, 14 July 1940, PRONI HA/32/1/684.

108 1922 SPA, Regulation 4.

109 Letter from H.C. Montgomery, Secretary to the Ministry of Home Affairs, to Captain Richard Pike Pim, RUC Inspector General, 31 August 1945, PRONI HA/32/1/38.

110 Minute Sheet Ministry of Home Affairs, Ref. S.747, 3 August 1945, PRONI HA/32/1/38.

111 'Detention orders for the signature of the Inspector General or the Deputy Inspector General will be issued from this Ministry to your office as hitherto.' (Correspondence between Ministry of Home Affairs and Charles Wickham, RUC Inspector General, 13 November 1922, PRONI HA/32/1/38).

112 Minute Sheet Ministry of Home Affairs, 8 August 1922, PRONI HA/32/1/38. Note that there were sixty officers at the time.

113 Circular marked 'secret' from the Divisional Commissioner's office, RIC, Belfast to the Commissioner, all County Inspectors and all County Commandants, 1 May 1922, Ref. S/206, PRONI HA/21/1/796.

114 Circular to the RUC detailing the evidence necessary to prosecute cases under the Special Powers Act, Ref. S. 153/11, 30 May 1922, PRONI HA/32/1/37.

115 Letter sent to Charles Wickham, RUC Inspector General, from Major E. W. Shewell in response to a telephone inquiry as to whether police officers were still authorised to prosecute cases under the Special Powers Act, February 1926, PRONI HA/32/1/30.

116 Letter from Charles Wickham, RUC Inspector General, to the Ministry of Home Affairs, 13 December 1941, PRONI HA/32/1/796. Chapter two introduces a more detailed analysis of Regulation 1A.

117 Letter from H.C. Montgomery to Ewing Gilfillan, Ref. S.1094, PRONI HA/32/1/796.

118 Memo at the Ministry of Home Affairs from John MacDermott, Attorney General, 17 February 1942, PRONI HA/32/1/796.

119 Letter marked 'secret' from the Assistant Secretary, Ministry of Home Affairs to Charles Wickham, RUC Inspector General, Ref. S. 1094, 20 February 1942, PRONI HA/32/1/796.

120 For a general discussion of this case see the *Belfast Newsletter*, 16 July 1942, the *Northern Whig*, 9 June 1942, and the *Belfast Telegraph*, 8 June 1942.

121 For further discussion of this provision see *HC Debs NI*, 28 March 1922, Vol. II, cols. 248–9.

122 Robert Megaw, in point of clarification as to operation of legislation, *HC Debs NI*, 21 March 1922, Vol. II, col. 98.

123 Larceny Act, 1916, 6 & 7 Geo. V, c. 50; Explosive Substances Act, 1883, 40 & 47 Vict. c. 3; Firearms Act, 1920, 10 & 11 Geo. V, c. 43; Malicious Damage Act, 1861, 24 & 25 Vict., c. 97; regulations relating thereto listed under Civil Authorities (Special Powers) Act (Northern Ireland), 1922, c. 5, sections 4 and 5.

124 See for example *Irish Independent,* 10 August 1922 and Farrell 1980, pp. 155–6.

125 Buckland 1977, pp. 206–210 and Campbell 1995, pp. 312–13.

126 Buckland 1981, p. 47.

127 *HC Debs*, 14 May 1973, col. 1028.
128 Letter from Samuel Watt, Permanent Secretary Northern Ireland Ministry of Home Affairs to Richard Best, Northern Ireland Attorney General, 20 March 1922, PRONI HA/32/1/29.
129 Hugh Smith Morrison, *HC Debs NI*, 21 March 1922, Vol. II, col. 104.
130 *Ibid.*, 23 March 1922, Vol. II, col. 159.
131 Richard Best, *HC Debs NI*, 23 March 1922, Vol. II, col. 159.
132 *Ibid.*, col. 160. See also Regulation 16 of S.R.O. 1530/1920, 13.8.20.
133 Letter marked, 'confidential' from the Divisional Commissioner's office, RIC Belfast, Ref. S/153/2, 1 May 1922, PRONI HA/32/1/30.
134 Civil Authorities (Special Powers) Northern Ireland Act, 1922, instructions for guidance of police, 14 April 1922, PRONI HA/32/1/30.
135 As prescribed by section 4(1) of the Rules Publication Act (Northern Ireland), 1925, 15 & 16 Geo. V, c. 6.
136 Criminal Evidence Act (Northern Ireland), 1923, 13 & 14 Geo. V, c. 9.
137 Memo from Sir Richard Dawson Bates, Minister of Home Affairs, 1928.
138 Letter from Charles Wickham, RUC Inspector General, to the Ministry of Home Affairs, 20 January 1933, PRONI HA/32/1/617.
139 Memo to the Parliamentary Secretary and the Minister of Home Affairs, 7 February 1928, Ref. S. 153/26.
140 Memo from the Law Department to the Ministry of Home Affairs, 18 January 1928.
141 For the decision to make the 1922 Act permanent see Cabinet meeting minutes, 27 September 1927, PRONI HA/32/1/29, and Cabinet meeting minutes, 19 April 1928, PRONI HA/32/1/47.
142 Kennedy 1988, p. 161.
143 Buckland 1981, p. 85.
144 Kennedy 1988, p. 161.
145 *Ibid.*, pp. 151–2.
146 *Senate Debs NI*, 25 April 1933, Vol. XV, cols. 161–70.
147 Second reading in the Senate, 1928, PRONI HA/32/1/619.
148 Correspondence between Harris, Ministry of Home Affairs and Arthur Queckett, Minister of Finance, 23 and 24 February 1933, PRONI HA/32/1/619.
149 Memo at the Ministry of Home Affairs, Ref. S.747, 12 October 1937, PRONI HA/32/1/38.
150 See Coogan 1987, pp. 164–308, Farrell 1980, pp. 152–3, and discussion, chapter five.
151 S.R.O. 13/1922, 22.5.1922, B.G. 26.5.1922. Unlawful organisations extended to include Cumann Poblachta na hÉireann by S.R.O. 47/1936.
152 Letter from John MacDermott, Attorney General, to Sir Richard Dawson Bates 12 November 1942, PRONI HA/32/1/855.
153 Civil Authorities (Special Powers) Act (Northern Ireland), 1943, 7 & 8 Geo. VI, c. 2.
154 Precedent existed for the provision of different punishments for the same offence, according to whether or not the case was dealt with summarily or on indictment. See, for instance, Defence (General) Regulation 92.
155 Letter from Charles Wickham, RUC Inspector General, to the Ministry of Home Affairs, 13 December 1941, PRONI HA/32/1/796.
156 S.R.O. 61/1943, 27.5.43.
157 The statutory instrument adjusted Regulations 1, 1A, 1B, 2 and 9.
158 Memorandum for the Cabinet submitted by the Minister of Home Affairs regard to the trial of members of the Irish Republican Army, November 1942, PRONI HA/32/1/855.
159 *Ibid.*
160 Minute Sheet Ministry of Home Affairs, 17 February 1943, PRONI HA/32/1/855, and Memo from John MacDermott, Attorney General, 19 February 1942, PRONI HA/32/1/855.
161 Civil Authorities (Emergency Powers) Acts, 22 June 1936, PRONI HA/32/1/619.
162 Statement from the Ministry of Home Affairs regarding the Civil Authorities (Special Powers) Acts (Northern Ireland), *c.*1938, PRONI HA/32/1/619.

CHAPTER TWO

1 The 1922–43 Civil Authorities (Special Powers) Acts [Hereafter 1922–43 SPAs] included the Civil Authorities (Special Powers) Act (Northern Ireland), 1922, 12 & 13 Geo. V, c. 5, [Hereafter 1922 SPA], the Civil Authorities (Special Powers) Act (Northern Ireland), 1933, 23 & 24 Geo. V, c. 12, and the Civil Authorities (Special Powers) Act (Northern Ireland), 7 & 8 Geo. VI, c. 2.
2 Letter from the Imperial Secretary to the Under Secretary of State, Home Affairs, 21 June 1923, PRO HO 267/362.
3 *Senate Debs NI*, 25 April 1933, Vol. XV, col. 166.
4 S.R.O. 1949, No. 147, 1950, No. 187 and 1951, No. 187.
5 Northern Ireland (Emergency Provisions) Act, 1973, Eliz. II, c. 53.
6 Second reading in the Senate, 1928, PRONI HA/32/1/619.
7 Statement from the Ministry of Home Affairs regarding the Civil Authorities (Special Powers) Acts (Northern Ireland), *c.*1938, PRONI HA/32/1/619.
8 Civil Authorities (Emergency Powers) Acts, 22 June 1936, PRONI HA/32/1/619.
9 Weekly reports from Charles Wickham, RUC Inspector General, to the Ministry of Home Affairs 24 July 1923–24 December 1923, PRONI HA/32/1/41.
10 See Appendix B for a list of the principal regulations under the 1922 Civil Authorities (Special Powers) Act (Northern Ireland).
11 Restoration of Order in Ireland Act, 1920, 10 & 11 Geo. V, c. 31 [Hereafter 1920 ROIA].
12 1922 SPA, section 25.
13 Richard Best, *HC Debs NI*, 23 March 1922, Vol. II, col. 184.
14 1922 SPA, para. 1.
15 S.R.O. 34/1922, 20.5.22.
16 S.R.O. 41/1922, 6.7.1922, B.G. 7.7.1922.
17 National Council for Civil Liberties 1936.
18 *Location and conditions* S.R.O. 34/1922, 20.5.1922, B.G. 26.5.1922; *change of location* S.R.O. 41/1922, 6.7.1922, B.G. 7.7.1922.
19 Instructions regarding Form 38A were contained in a letter from H. Toppin, Ministry of Home Affairs, to Charles Wickham, RUC Inspector General, Ref. S.153/2, 10 July 1923, PRONI HA/32/1/30.
20 S.R.O. 34/1922, 20.5.1922, B.G. 26.5.1922.
21 S.R.O. 41/1922, 6.7.1922, B.G. 7.7.1922.
22 S.R.O. 39/1922, 23.6.1922, B.G. 30.6.1922.
23 S.R.O. 36/1922, 1.6.1922, Supplement to B.G. 2.6.1922.
24 Temporary circular marked 'Secret' and ordered to be destroyed on the 1 March 1938, dated 28 January 1938, Ref. 24/8960.38, PRONI HA/32/1/621.
25 Letter from Charles Wickham, RUC Inspector General, Ref. S.B. 24/5943, 22 March 1923, PRONI HA/32/1/307.
26 'Or an advisory committee' added by S.R.O. 58/1923, 17.11.1923, B.G. 7.12.1923; otherwise governed by S.R.O. 36/1922, 1.6.1922, B.G. 2.6.1922. [Emphasis added].
27 Report on internments in Northern Ireland 1922–4, 6, PRONI HA/32/1/46.
28 Minute Sheet Ministry of Home Affairs entitled, 'Return of Internees', 11 January 1923, PRONI HA/32/1/39.
29 S.R.O. 48/1923, 30.10.1923, B.G. 2.11.1923.
30 S.R.O. 41/1922, 6.7.1922, B.G. 7.7.1922.
31 *Idem.*
32 *Idem*
33 S.R.O. 85/1922, 24.6.1922.
34 S.R.O. 86/1922, 27.9.1922. The term 'prisoner' maintained the same meaning as assigned in Section eleven of 1898 Prison Act. (S.R.O. 48/1923, 30.10.1923, B.G. 2.11.1923).
35 See, for instance, National Council for Civil Liberties 1936, and *Disturbances in Northern Ireland: Report of the Commission appointed by the Governor of Northern Ireland*, September 1969. Session 1969/70 Cmd. 532. [Hereafter Cameron Report].
36 Order for internment, 28 June 1922, PRONI HA/32/1/155.

37 Letter marked 'secret' and sent by divisional commissioner's office, Ref. S.B. 24/5788, 30 May 1922, PRONI HA/32/1/148.
38 Report on internments in Northern Ireland 1922–4, p. 1, PRONI HA/32/1/46.
39 Minute Sheet Ministry of Home Affairs entitled, 'Return of Internees', 11 January 1923, PRONI HA/32/1/39.
40 Farrell 1980, p. 64, Minute Sheet Ministry of Home Affairs, 11 January 1923, PRONI HA/32/1/39, and Report on internments in Northern Ireland 1922–4, p. 5 PRONI HA/32/1/46.
41 Farrell 1980, pp. 62, 58.
42 Report from Charles Wickham, RUC Inspector General, Ref. S.208.4, 21 October 1922, PRONI HA/32/1/81.
43 Records relating to Daniel Dempsey, a clerk in the General Post Office, PRONI HA/32/1/155.
44 Records relating to Edward Kelly, a Spirit Grocer, PRONI HA/32/1/155.
45 Certificate advocating internment, PRONI HA/32/1/155.
46 Report on Internments in Northern Ireland 1922–4, p. 4, PRONI HA/32/1/46.
47 Ibid., p. 5.
48 Extracts of letters censored from Larne internment camp and S.S. *Argenta* for period 29 January to 4 February 1923, PRONI HA/32/1/92.
49 Letter from H. Toppin, Ministry of Home Affairs, to Charles Wickham, RUC Inspector General, Ref. S.208/25, 16 July 1923, PRONI HA/32/1/92.
50 Letter from the RUC Deputy Inspector to the Ministry of Home Affairs, Ref. 24/7268a, 8 August 1923, PRONI HA/32/1/92.
51 Extracts of letters censored from Larne internment camp and S.S. *Argenta* for period 3 June 3 to 1 September 1923, PRONI HA/32/1/92.
52 Letter from the Ministry of Home Affairs to Charles Wickham, RUC Inspector General, 3 May 1923, PRONI HA/32/1/39.
53 Letter marked 'secret and confidential' from Charles Wickham, RUC Inspector General, to the Ministry of Home Affairs, 24 November 1924, PRONI HA/32/1/39.
54 Minute Sheet Ministry of Home Affairs, Ref. S153/13A, 5 May 1924, PRONI HA/32/1/39.
55 Letter from Charles Wickham, RUC Inspector General, to the Secretary, Ministry of Home Affairs, 18 July 1924, PRONI HA/32/1/39.
56 Minutes from a conference at the Ministry of Home Affairs, 20 June 1924, PRONI HA/32/1/39.
57 Minute Sheet Ministry of Home Affairs, 19 July 1924, PRONI HA/32/1/39.
58 Letter from the Ministry of Home Affairs to Charles Wickham, RUC Inspector General, 22 November 1922, PRONI HA/32/1/306.
59 Memo at the Ministry of Home Affairs, PRONI HA/32/1/308.
60 Memo on exclusion orders, PRONI HA/32/1/308. Note that a number of individuals excluded from all the border counties had given an undertaking to remain outside Northern Ireland for two years.
61 Minute Sheet Ministry of Home Affairs, 21 December 1922, PRONI HA/32/1/307.
62 Minute Sheet Ministry of Home Affairs, Ref. S.364, December 1922, PRONI HA/32/1/307.
63 Letter to District Inspector's office, 18 January 1923, PRONI HA/32/1/307.
64 Report on Internments in Northern Ireland 1922–4, Appendix, PRONI HA/32/1/46.
65 Farrell 1980, p. 200.
66 Boyle et al. 1975, p. 56.
67 *HC Debs NI*, 16th March 1939, Vol. XXII.
68 *Sunday Express*, 22 August 1940.
69 *Belfast Newsletter*, 3 October 1942.
70 This compared with 477 internees in the South. (Farrell 1980, p. 167)
71 S.R.O. 147/1949, 20.8.49.
72 S.R.O. 176/1955, 30.11.55.
73 S.R.O. 132/1957, 10.7.1957.
74 S.R.O. 191/1956, 15.12.1956.
75 By 1958 187 men were interned in the South as well. (Farrell 1980, pp. 216–18)
76 S.R.O. 16/1957, 28.1.1957.

77 Purdie 1990, p. 150.
78 Coogan 1987, pp. 424–5.
79 Bishop and Mallie 1987, p. 72.
80 *Violence and Civil Disturbances in Northern Ireland in 1969: Report of the Tribunal of Inquiry.* Volumes 1 and 2, Session 1972/73 Cmd. 566. [Hereafter Scarman Tribunal].
81 Scarman Tribunal, chapter 3.8.
82 See for instance Arthur 1974, Coogan 1995, Darby 1986, Purdie 1990, *Sunday Times* Insight Team 1972, Townshend 1983 and Wichert 1991.
83 Statement made on the 10 September 1970, reprinted in *Fortnight*, 25 September 1970, 16–17.
84 *Fortnight*, 18 December 1970.
85 *Fortnight*, 16 April 1971, 14.
86 Minutes from a meeting between conservative and unionist MPs at Westminster 28 July 1971, printed in *Fortnight*, 6–31 August 1971, 20.
87 *Fortnight*, 9 July 1971, 18.
88 *Report of the Inquiry into Allegations Against the Security Forces of Physical Brutality in Northern Ireland Arising Out of Events on the 9 August, 1971.* Cmnd. 4823 (Sir Edward Compton, Chairman 1971); *Report of the Committee of Privy Counsellors Appointed to Consider Authorised Procedures for the Interrogation of Persons Suspected of Terrorism.* Cmnd. 4901 (Lord Parker of Waddington, Chairman 1972).
89 Bishop and Mallie 1987, p. 186.
90 *Idem.*
91 *Fortnight*, 1 October 1971.
92 *Fortnight*, 18 December 1970. The nature and extent of internment and the treatment of detainees in August 1971, however, shifted the Republic's stance.
93 *Fortnight*, 3 September 1971, 13.
94 Payment for Debt (Emergency Provisions) Act (Northern Ireland), 1971, Eliz. II, c. 30.
95 *Fortnight*, 1 October 1971.
96 Statistics relating to detention and internment released by the Ministry of Home Affairs, 2 November 1971, *Fortnight*, 12 November 1971, 14.
97 *Fortnight*, 12 November 1971, 14.
98 Spjut 1986, p. 712.
99 Ibid., p. 735.
100 Spjut 1986, p. 738.
101 Detention of Terrorists (Northern Ireland) Order 1922, No. 1632 (N.I. 15).
102 Northern Ireland (Emergency Provisions) Act, 1973, 21 & 22 Eliz. II, c. 53. [Hereafter 1973 EPA]
103 S.R.O. 31/1922, 27.4.22.
104 Revocation S.R.O. 147/1949, 20.8.49, reinstatement S.R.O. 199/1956, 21.12.56.
105 *HC Debs NI*, 23 March 1922, Vol. II, col. 173.
106 S.R.O. 147/1949, 20.8.49.
107 S.R.O. 281/1969, 16.10.69.
108 Firearms Act, 1920, 10 & 11 Geo. V, c. 43.
109 S.R.O. 1530/1920.
110 S.R.O. 5/1934, 11.1.1934, B.G. 12.1.1934.
111 Letter from E.W. Scales, Ministry of Home Affairs, to the Parliamentary Secretary and the Minister of Home Affairs, 3 June 1939, PRONI HA/32/1/684.
112 S.R.O. 88/1939, 16.6.39.
113 S.R.O. 5/1934, 11.1.1934, B.G. 12.1.1934, and S.R.O. 88/1939, 16.6.1939.
114 Letter marked 'confidential' from the Divisional Commissioner's Office, RIC Belfast, to the Secretary, Ministry of Home Affairs, Ref. S/153/2, 1 May 1922, PRONI HA/32/1/30.
115 S.R.O. 32/1922, 18.5.1922, B.G. 26.5.1922.
116 S.R.O. 33/1922, 18.5.22.
117 S.R.O. 36/1922, 1.6.1922, Supplement to B.G. 2.6.1922.
118 Revocation S.R.O. 147/1949, 20.8.49, reinstatement S.R.O. 176/1955, 30.11.1955.

119 B.G. 31.3.1972.
120 S.R.O. 33/1922, 18.5.22, B.G. 26.5.1922.
121 S.R.O. 36/1922, 1.6.1922, Supplement to B.G. 2.6.1922, and S.R.O. 56/1922, 20.9.1922, B.G. 29.9.1922.
122 S.R.O. 14/1923, 13.3.1923, B.G. 16.3.1923.
123 Letter to the District Inspector of the RIC in Newry, 26 May 1922, PRONI HA/32/1/134.
124 Report from Pim to C.G. Markbreiter, Home Office in London, 20 July 1939.
125 Report from Pim to C.G. Markbreiter, Home Office in London, 20 July 1939.
126 Revoked S.R.O. 147/1949, 20.8.49, reintroduced S.R.O. 90/1954, 16.6.54, B.G. 18.6.1954.
127 See discussion, chapter three.
128 Memo at the Ministry of Home Affairs, PRONI HA/32/1/465.
129 The government also occasionally posted notices and sent out broadcasts through the BBC to promulgate clearly the orders banning meetings, assemblies and processions.
130 S.R.O. 80/1933, 30.6.33.
131 Letter from Charles Wickham, RUC Inspector General, to the Ministry of Home Affairs, 23 July 1933, PRONI HA/32/1/596.
132 Revocation 187/1951, 12.10.1951, new governing statute Public Order Act (Northern Ireland), 1951, 14 & 15 Geo. VI, c. 19. See for instance orders issued 13 November 1968, B.G. 15.11.1968 and 11 July 1970, B.G. 17.7.1970.
133 S.R.O. 198/1970, 23.7.1970.
134 S.R.O. 173/1966, 26.7.1966. Regulation 38 was later amended to prevent conflict with section 20(1) of the Interpretation Act (Northern Ireland), 1954, 2 & 3 Eliz. II, c. 33 via S.R.O. 214/1970, 7.8.1970.
135 S.R.O. 312/1969, B.G. 28.11.1969.
136 *HC Debs NI*, 16 March 1948, PRONI HA/32/1/467.
137 Statement prepared for the Northern Ireland Parliament but not used, PRONI HA/32/1/467.
138 For commentary on the 'communist threat' posed by these meetings see the *Northern Whig*, 11 October 1933.
139 Memo from E.W. Shewell at the Ministry of Home Affairs, 16 April 1930, PRONI HA/32/1/465.
140 See, for example, 'A Necessary Precaution', in the *Northern Whig*, 29 March 1932.
141 Minute Sheet S.558, 31 March 1938, PRONI HA/32/1/466. See also memo from the Ministry of Home Affairs, S. 558, 11 March 1948 PRONI HA/32/1/467.
142 See for instance Report of the RUC Inspector General, 27 March 1928, PRONI HA/32/1/465, and *HC Debs NI*, 22 March 1932, Vol. XIV, cols. 537–546.
143 Memo marked 'secret' from the Assistant Secretary, Ministry of Home Affairs to Charles Wickham, RUC Inspector General, Ref. S.558, 31 March 1928, PRONI HA/32/1/465 and Report of the RUC County Inspector, Ref. 26/593, 10 April 1930, PRONI HA/32/1/465.
144 Minute Sheet Ministry of Home Affairs, 30 March 1928, PRONI HA/32/1/465.
145 See for instance Reports from the RUC Inspector General's office to the Secretary, Ministry of Home Affairs, Ref. 26/593, 9 April 1934, 27 April 1934, 2 May 1935, 23 April 1936, 9 April 1937, 2 May 1938, 20 April 1939, 6 May 1939, 8 April 1940, 6 May 1941, 20 April 1942, 5 May 1943, 18 April 1944, 3 May 1946, 14 April 1947 and 4 May 1949, PRONI HA/32/1/467.
146 See, for instance, the *Northern Whig*, 18 January 1935, *Belfast News Letter*, 13 April 1937, The *Northern Whig*, 29 March 1937, the *Irish News*, 12 February 1940, the *Belfast Newsletter* 12 February 1940, Report from the RUC Inspector General's office to the Secretary, Ministry of Home Affairs, Ref. 26/593, 5 May 1943, PRONI HA/32/1/467 and Report from the RUC Inspector General's office to the Secretary, Ministry of Home Affairs, Ref. 26/593, 14 April 1947, PRONI HA/32/1/467.
147 During World War Two the Public Security Order, S.R.O. 69/1940, issued under the Ministries Act (Northern Ireland), banned all processions in Northern Ireland. The 1922–33 Special Powers Acts, however, continued to be used for meetings which did not fall under the order's guidelines. Under pressure from the RUC and immediately prior to this order a number of Orange Lodges suspended marches. The County Grand

Orange Lodges of Belfast, Tyrone, Armagh, and Antrim agreed to smaller demonstrations and church services wherever possible. See the *Belfast Newsletter*, 31 May 1940, the Irish News, 28 May 1940, and the *Northern Whig*, 24 May 1940.

148 Report from the RUC Inspector General's office to the Secretary, Ministry of Home Affairs, Ref. 26/593, 4 May 1949, PRONI HA/32/1/467.

149 Various letters, PRONI HA/32/1/471 and Various letters, HA/32/1/475.

150 Letter from District Master to Minister of Home Affairs, 6 March 1950, PRONI HA/32/1/480.

151 *Londonderry Sentinel*, 10 December 1938, 7.

152 Minute Sheet Ministry of Home Affairs, PRONI HA/32/1/473.

153 Letter from one of the meeting participants to R. Gransden, Stormont Castle, 2 December 1938, PRONI HA/32/1/473. [Emphasis added].

154 Report from Charles Wickham, RUC Inspector General, to the Ministry of Home Affairs, Ref. 24/7508/5, 13 March 1939, PRONI HA/32/1/476.

155 Extract from a speech made by Sir Richard Dawson Bates, Minister of Home Affairs, to the Victoria Unionist Association, 14 December 1938 and quoted in the *Irish News*, 15 December 1938.

156 Memo by Edmond Warnock marked 'confidential', PRONI HA/32/1/465.

157 Notation on back of letter to District Inspector in Armagh from the County Inspector of the RUC, PRONI HA/32/1/468.

158 Report from Charles Wickham, RUC Inspector General, to the Ministry of Home Affairs, Ref. 26/1021/7, 2 October 1934, PRONI HA/32/1/469.

159 Internal memo from the Ministry of Home Affairs, Ref. S. 558, 4 October 1934, PRONI HA/32/1/469.

160 Report marked 'secret' and 'crime special' from Ewing Gilfillan, for Charles Wickham, the RUC Inspector General, to the Minister of Home Affairs, 27 February 1928, PRONI HA/32/1/295.

161 Report from Ewing Gilfillan to the Ministry of Home Affairs, 6 March 1926, PRONI HA/32/1/295.

162 Notes on nationalist and other Members of Parliament, PRONI HA/32/1/465.

163 Letter from RBP 286 to Minister of Home Affairs, 8 March 1948, PRONI HA/32/1/475.

164 Letter from Brown's Dental Depot to Minister of Home Affairs, 9 March 1948, PRONI HA/32/1/475.

165 Letter from the Mitchelburne Club Apprentice Boys of Derry to the Minister of Home Affairs, 13 March 1948, PRONI HA/32/1/475.

166 Letter from D.G. Evans to the Minister of Home Affairs, 4 March 1948, PRONI HA/32/1/475.

167 Questions in the NI House of Commons, Thursday, 8 December 1938.

168 This statute replaced the Public Meeting Act, 1908, 8 Edw. VII, c. 66.

169 Public Order (Amendment) Act (Northern Ireland), 1970, Eliz. II, c. 4.

170 Statement issued on the 23 January 1972 and quoted in *Fortnight*, 9 February 1972, 14.

171 Regulation 26(1) and 26(2), S.R.O. 137/1943, 13.12.43.

172 S.R.O. 147/1949, 20.8.49.

173 S.R.O. 179/1954, 21.12.54.

174 S.R.O. 40/1971, 29.1.71.

175 *Northern Whig*, 17 April 1933.

176 Memo from Attorney General, Ref. S.1223, 9 November 1943, PRONI HA/32/1/874.

177 S.R.O. 137/1943, 13.12.43.

178 S.R.O. 147/1949, 20.8.49.

179 S.R.O. 179/1954, 21.12.54.

180 *Fortnight*, 19 February 1971.

181 S.R.O. 58/1930, 2.5.30.

182 Memo at the Ministry of Home Affairs, 27 May 1930, PRONI HA/32/1/627.

183 Memo from E.W. Shewell at the Ministry of Home Affairs, 27 May 1930, PRONI HA/32/1/569.

184 Oral answer from George Hanna, Parliamentary Secretary, *HC Debs NI*, 29 May 1930, Vol. XII, col. 1630.

185 *Northern Whig*, 24 May 1930.
186 Films banned by the Home Office, PRONI HA/32/1/569.
187 Letter from the Ministry of Home Affairs to Charles Wickham, RUC Inspector General, 13 June 1930, PRONI HA/32/1/640.
188 *Belfast Newsletter*, 28 November 1936 and *Irish News*, 30 November 1936.
189 S.R.O. 85/1931, 25.7.1931, Supplement to B.G. 27.7.1931.
190 Letter from Samuel J. Baird, Secretary of the Newry Unionist Association to James Brown, MP, Warrenpoint, 11 October 1938, PRONI HA/32/1/69.
191 S.R.O. 127/1933, 14.12.1933, B.G. 15.12.1933.
192 Circular Ref. 26/1480, 12 February 1934, PRONI HA/32/1/603.
193 Circular Ref. 26/1480, 2 March 1948, PRONI HA/32/1/603.
194 Letter from the RUC to the Ministry of Home Affairs, Ref. CS.26/1480/16(A), PRONI HA/32/1/603.
195 *HC Debs NI*, 4 December 1934, Vol. XVII.
196 The RUC Inspector General instructed police to comply with this request. (Circular Ref. 24/8960, 5 March 1934, PRONI HA/32/1/621 responding to Circular Ref. 26/1480, 12 February 1934, PRONI HA/32/1/621).
197 *HC Debs NI*, March 1948, Vol. XXXII, col. 488.
198 Letter from Thomas Nelson to William Brian Maginess, Minister of Home Affairs, 4 September 1951, PRONI HA/32/1/603.
199 Letter from the City of Londonderry and Foyle Unionist Association to William Brian Maginess, Minister of Home Affairs, 6 April 1951, PRONI HA/32/1/603. See also Resolution passed by the Strabane District Loyal Orange Lodge, No. 14, 10 September 1954, PRONI HA/32/1/603, and Farrell 1980, pp. 199–200.
200 Letter from William Brian Maginess, Minister of Home Affairs, to 'Brother Burdge' of the Grand Orange Lodge of Ireland, 9 December 1949, PRONI HA/32/1/603.
201 Letter from William Brian Maginess, Minister of Home Affairs, to the City of Londonderry and Foyle Unionist Association, 13 April 1951, PRONI HA/32/1/603.
202 See, for instance, *Belfast Telegraph*, 7 January 1947, *Belfast Newsletter*, 20 November 1946, *Belfast Newsletter*, 14 August 1946, *Irish News*, 31 October 1938, *Belfast Newsletter*, 13 July 1938, *Belfast Newsletter*, 9 March 1938, *Irish News*, 4 June 1937, *Belfast Newsletter*, 29 November 1935, *Belfast Newsletter*, 16 July 1935, *Belfast Newsletter*, 8 May 1935, *Northern Whig*, 26 April 1935, *Belfast Newsletter*, 23 November 1933, *Northern Whig*, 14 September 1934, *Belfast Newsletter*, 21 September 1934, *Belfast Newsletter*, 27 June 1934, and *Belfast Newsletter*, 26 June 1934.
203 Letter from George Hanna, Ministry of Home Affairs to James Gregg, 6 September 1954, PRONI HA/32/1/603.
204 Flags and Emblems (Display) Act (Northern Ireland) 1954, 2 & 3 Eliz. II, c. 10.
205 *First Report of the Standing Advisory Commission on Human Rights. Annual Report for 1974–75*. HC 632, 1975/76, paras. 26–28.
206 Circular issued by Captain Richard Pike Pim, RUC Inspector General, 19 May 1954, PRONI HA/32/1/603.
207 Letter from Charles Wickham, RUC Inspector General, to the Ministry of Home Affairs, 9 November 1935, PRONI HA/32/1/621.
208 Letter from the Parliamentary Secretary to the Prime Minister, 27 November 1935, PRONI HA/32/1/621.
209 See Draft documents, PRONI HA/32/1/603.
210 Letter marked 'secret' from Charles Wickham, RUC Inspector General, to the Ministry of Home Affairs, 19 May 1938, PRONI HA/32/1/603. He echoed these sentiments in a later missive. (Letter from Charles Wickham, RUC Inspector General, to the Ministry of Home Affairs, 3 December 1938, PRONI HA/32/1/621).
211 Letter marked 'secret' from the Ministry of Home Affairs to Charles Wickham, RUC Inspector General, Ref. S.721, 22 January 1938, PRONI HA/32/1/621.
212 See for example the *Irish News*, 15 November 1935, the *Belfast Newsletter*, 1 November 1935, the *Belfast Newsletter*, 29 November 1935, and the *Irish News*, 9 May 1938.
213 *Dublin Gazette*, 3.7.18, 1123.
214 S.R.O. 1530/1920, 13.8.20.

215 S.R.O. 33/1922, 18.5.1922, B.G. 26.5.1922.
216 'Unlawful associations' were defined by section 7 of the Criminal Law and
     Procedure (Ireland) Act, 1887, 50 & 51 Vict., c. 62 and addressed by S.R.O.
     35/1922, 22.5.1922.
217 S.R.O. 11/1933, 14.1.1933, B.G. 20.1.1933.
218 S.R.O. 147/1949, 20.8.49 and S.R.O. 187/1951, 12.10.51.
219 Minute Sheet Ministry of Home Affairs, Ref. S.200, 20 May 1922, PRONI
     HA/32/1/54.
220 S.R.O. 35/1922, 22.5.1922, B.G. 26.5.1922.
221 S.R.O. 47/1936, 8.4.36.
222 S.R.O. 119/1931, 26.10.31; S.R.O. 88/1933, 22.7.33.
223 Organisations banned in the Irish Free State, 21 October 1931, PRONI HA/32/1/586.
224 S.R.O. 176/1955, 30.11.55; S.R.O. 199/1956, 21.12.56.
225 Quoted in Bishop and Mallie 1987, p. 62.
226 S.R.O. 146/1966, 28.6.66.
227 *HC Debs NI*, 28 June 1966; reprinted in Bruce 1992. p. 14.
228 S.R.O. 42/1967, 7.3.67.
229 Boyle et al. 1975, p. 11.
230 S.R.O. 11/1933, 14.1.33.
231 Circular issued by the Attorney General to the RUC, 18 February 1933, PRONI
     HA/32/1/594.
232 Circular issued by Charles Wickham, RUC Inspector General, 13 April 1938,
     PRONI HA/32/1/594.
233 Circular issued by Charles Wickham, RUC Inspector General, 17 November 1937,
     PRONI HA/32/1/594.
234 Circular issued by Charles Wickham, RUC Inspector General, 6 December 1943,
     PRONI HA/32/1/594.
235 S.R.O. 36/1922, 1.6.22, Supplement to B.G. 2.6.22.
236 'The Attorney General considered such a regulation now desirable and suggest it
     should be sent to him through the CCS for his consideration.' (Memo from H.
     Toppin, Ministry of Home Affairs Minute Sheet Ref. 5/153/7, 22 May 1922,
     PRONI HA/32/1/34).
237 Circular issued by Charles Wickham, RUC Inspector General, 19 July 1922, PRONI
     HA/32/1/148.
238 S.R.O. 110/1933, 25.10.33, B.G. 27.10.33.
239 *Report of the Committee Appointed to Review the Provisions of the Restoration of
     Order in Ireland Act, 1920, and of the Regulations Made Under that Act, 1924,*
     Cmd. 2278, p. 7.
240 Emphasis added.
241 1922–43 SPAs, Regulation 22B, section 6.
242 Farrell 1980, pp. 94, 142–3.
243 Report from Pim, Ministry of Home Affairs, to C.G. Markbreiter, Home Office, 20
     July 1939.
244 National Council for Civil Liberties 1936, p. 11.
245 S.R.O. 51/1940, 15.6.40.
246 Extract from draft conclusions of a cabinet meeting held on Saturday, 15 June,
     1940, PRONI HA/32/1/746.
247 Notes on ROIR provisions, PRONI HA/32/1/408. For a discussion on the use of
     identity cards in the second instance, under Regulation 23B, see discussion,
     'Detention, restriction and internment', above.
248 Order issued 19.6.40.
249 Order issued 10.2.43 ref. to S.R.O. 2681/1942, 28.12.42 of the Emergency Powers
     (Defence) Merchant Shipping Regulations.
250 Order issued 15.10.43 ref. to S.R.O. 2561/1942, 16.12.42 of the Emergency Powers
     (Defence) General Regulations.
251 S.R.O. 54/1940, 22.6.40. Similar to Regulation 1A(1), which governed identity
     documents, Regulation 1A(2) was introduced subsequent to increased pressure in
     the Northern Irish House of Commons requesting increased safeguards on travel to
     and from Éire.

252 S.R.O. 61/1940, 29.6.40.
253 Letter from Captain Richard Pike Pim, RUC Inspector General, to the Ministry of Home Affairs, 17 May 1946, PRONI HA/32/1/746 and Letter from Captain Richard Pike Pim, RUC Inspector General, to the Ministry of Home Affairs, 17 June 1946, PRONI HA/32/1/746.
254 S.R.O. 193/1946, 8.11.46.
255 S.R.O. 120/1931, 28.10.1931, B.G. 30.10.1931.
256 S.R.O. 37/1922, 25.5.22
257 Revoked by S.R.O. 187.1951, 12.10.51, reinstated by S.R.O. 199/1956, 21.12.1956.
258 *Irish News*, 1 February 1957.
259 See discussion, chapter three.
260 Firearms Act (Northern Ireland), 1969, 17 & 18 Eliz. II, c. 12.
261 Firearms (Amendment) Act (Northern Ireland), 1971, 19 & 20 Eliz. II, c. 25.
262 Protection of the Person and Property Act (Northern Ireland), 1969, 17 & 18 Eliz. II, c. 29.
263 Explosives Act (Northern Ireland), 1970, 18 & 19 Eliz. II, c. 10.
264 Criminal Justice (Temporary Provisions) Act (Northern Ireland), 1970, 18 & 19 Eliz. II, c. 22.
265 Prevention of Incitement to Hatred Act (Northern Ireland), 1970, 18 & 19 Eliz. II, c. 24.
266 See also *Irish News*, 13 July 1935; *Irish News*, 8 April 1938; and *Irish News*, 29 October 1938.
267 Report from Charles Wickham, RUC Inspector General, to the Ministry of Home Affairs, 30 June 1936, PRONI HA/32/1/619.
268 See, for example, Report from the RUC marked 'secret' and submitted to the Ministry of Home Affairs detailing the movements and meetings of Ronald Kidd, PRONI HA/32/1/619.
269 *Northern Whig*, 17 August 1936.
270 *Sydney Morning Herald*, 8 June 1936, and The *Star* (in Johannesburg), 25 June 1936.
271 *Belfast Newsletter*, 11 June 1936.
272 See, for instance, *Belfast Newsletter*, 10 June 1936, and almost daily articles in the *Northern Whig* and *Belfast Newsletter* May–July 1936.
273 Report from the Ministry of Home Affairs, *c.*1938, PRONI HA/32/1/619.
274 *Belfast Newsletter*, 26 June 1936.
275 *Irish News*, 28 November 1938.
276 *Fortnight*, 25 September 1970, 16.
277 Gerry Fitt, *HC Debs*, 5 July 1973, Vol. 859, col. 835.

CHAPTER THREE

1 For discussion of British involvement in provincial affairs 1969 to 1972 see Palley 1972, pp. 411–45.
2 *Report of the Advisory Committee on Police in Northern Ireland.* October 1969, Cmd. 535. Belfast: HMSO. [Hunt Committee Report].
3 Ulster Defence Regiment Act, 1969, 17 & 18 Eliz. II, c. 65.
4 Firearms Act (Northern Ireland), 1969, 17 & 18 Eliz. II, c. 12; Protection of the Person and Property Act (Northern Ireland), 1969, 17 & 18 Eliz. II, c. 29; Public Order Act (Northern Ireland), 1970, 18 & 19 Eliz. II, c. 4; Explosives Act (Northern Ireland), 1970, 18 & 19 Eliz. II, c. 10; Prevention of Incitement to Hatred Act (Northern Ireland), 1970, 18 & 19 Eliz. II, c. 24.
5 Mr Balniel, Minister of State for Defence, *HC Debs*, 23 September 1971, Vol. 823, col. 212.
6 For discussion of internment and its role in British policy *vis-à-vis* Northern Ireland, see Spjut 1986.
7 McKeown 1989.
8 *Report of the Commission to consider legal procedures to deal with terrorist activities in Northern Ireland.* December 1972, Cmnd. 5185, para. 32. [Hereafter Diplock Report].

 9 See Cunningham 1991, pp. 58–60.
10 Boyle et al. 1975, p. 49.
11 *Fortnight*, 3 September 1971.
12 *Report of the inquiry into allegations against the security forces of physical brutality in Northern Ireland arising out of events on the 9 August 1971.* Session 1971/72 Cmnd. 4823, para. 23.
13 See Brownlie 1972, pp. 501–2 and the Report of Amnesty International, 13 March 1972.
14 Bishop 1978, pp. 160–2. For further discussion on the effectiveness of these methods in countering terrorism, see Parker Majority Report, paras. 18–26, and Gardiner Minority Report, paras. 12–16. [Citation below].
15 Gardiner Minority Report, para. 6.
16 *Report of the Committee of Privy Counsellors Appointed to Consider Authorised Procedures for the Interrogation of Persons Suspected of Terrorism.* Chairman: Lord Parker of Waddington. March 1972. Session 1971/72 Vol. xviii Cmnd. 4901. [Hereafter Parker Majority Report and Gardiner Minority Report].
17 *HC Debs*, 2 March 1972, Vol. 832, col. 743.
18 *Ireland v. United Kingdom of Great Britain and Northern Ireland* (Application No. 5310/71) (1976).
19 Cunningham 1991, p. 63, O'Boyle 1977b, p. 674, and Boyle 1982, pp. 166–9.
20 See *HC Debs*, 30 June 1978, Vol. 952, cols. 1725–1836.
21 1972 N. Ir. 91.
22 *HC Debs*, 23 February 1972, Vol. 821, cols. 1368–1499.
23 Northern Ireland Act, 1972, Eliz. II, c. 10.
24 *HC Debs*, 24 March 1972, Vol. 883, cols. 1839–63.
25 Northern Ireland (Temporary Provisions) Act, 1972, Eliz. II, c. 22.
26 Cunningham 1991, p. 67.
27 This alteration related also to the manner in which security forces employed the powers they were granted under emergency legislation. Dermot Walsh suggests that the changes gave rise to an increase in hostility, alienation and violence. (Walsh 1990, p. 31).
28 See Diplock Report, ch. 4, para. 17, and *HC Debs*, 17 April 1973, Vol. 855, cols. 309–10.
29 European Convention for the Protection of Human Rights and Fundamental Freedoms, 1950. (Hereafter European Convention).
30 Diplock Report, ch. 4, para. 27.
31 The 1972 Detention of Terrorists (Northern Ireland) Order is discussed below.
32 Firearms Act (Northern Ireland), 1969, 17 & 18 Eliz. II, c. 12, and Explosives Act (Northern Ireland), 1970, 18 & 19 Eliz. II, c. 10.
33 See *Reg. v. Flynn and Leonard* (Belfast City Commission 24 May 1972), and *The Queen v. Gargan* (Belfast City Commission, 10 May 1972), digested at 23 *Northern Ireland Legal Quarterly* 343 (1972) and quoted in Bishop 1978, p. 172.
34 *People v. Coffey*, 39 LRANS, 704, 706 (1911), cited in Greer et al. 1990, fn. 18, p. 51.
35 See also Diplock Report, paras. 86, 88.
36 Children and Young Persons Act (Northern Ireland), 1968, Eliz. II, c. 34.
37 *HC Debs*, 17 April 1973, Vol. 855, cols. 380–6.
38 *HC Debs*, 16 November 1972, Vol. 846, cols. 188–9.
39 *HC Debs*, 11 December 1972, Vol. 848, cols. 96–7 highlights attacks on magistrates.
40 *HC Debs*, 25 November 1974, Vol. 882, col. 30.
41 Greer et al. 1990, p. 59, quoting *HC Debs*, 17 April 1983, Vol. 855, cols. 281–2.
42 Greer et. al, 1990, 59, quoting *HC Debs*, 17 April 1983, Vol. 855, col. 282.
43 *HC Debs*, 17 April 1983, Vol. 855, col. 305.
44 See for example *HC Debs*, Standing Committee B, 1972–73, Vol. 2, cols. 29–97.
45 See Boyle et al. 1973, Boyle et al. 1975, and Law Officers' Department 1974.
46 For further discussion of the Diplock Report and later Diplock courts see Boyle et al. 1973, Boyle et al. 1975, Boyle et al. 1980, Greer 1986, Twining 1973, pp. 406–17, Walsh 1983, Korff 1984, Jackson and Doran 1993, pp. 503–20, and Jackson and Doran 1995.

47 Gerry Fitt, *HC Debs*, 6 December 1978, Vol. 959, col. 1563.
48 Cunningham 1991, p. 71.
49 Northern Ireland (Emergency Provisions) Act, 1973, Eliz. II, c. 53. [Hereafter 1973 EPA].
50 Appeal became governed by the Criminal Appeal (Northern Ireland) Act, 1968, 16 & 17 Eliz. II, c. 21, section 8.
51 *HC Debs*, 5 July 1973, Vol. 859, cols. 777–98.
52 *Ibid.*, cols. 735–60.
53 *Ibid.*
54 *Ibid.*, cols. 761–76.
55 1973 EPA, Part 1, section 3.
56 *HC Debs*, 17 April 1973, Vol. 855, col. 283.
57 1973 EPA, Part I, sections 5 and 6.
58 *HC Debs*, 16 April 1973, Vol. 855, cols. 33–4. For discussion of the admissibility of confessions under the EPAs see Greer 1973, pp. 199–210, and Greer 1980, pp. 205–38.
59 1973 EPA, Part I, section 6(2). This last change was made in committee and passed during report stage. (*HC Debs*, 5 July 1973, Vol. 859, cols. 813–15).
60 1973 EPA, Part I, section 7(1).
61 Explosive Substances Act, 1883, 46 & 47 Vict., c. 3, Firearms Act (Northern Ireland), 1969, 17 & 18 Eliz. II, c. 12, and Protection of the Person and Property Act (Northern Ireland), 1969, 17 & 18 Eliz. II, c. 29.
62 *HC Debs*, 17 April 1973, Vol. 855, col. 284.
63 1973 EPA, Part I, section 9.
64 S.R.O. 36/1922, 1.6.1922, Supplement to B.G. 2.6.1922.
65 S.R.O. 147/1949, 20.8.49. Regulations 11 and 12 introduced by S.R.O. 191/1956, 15.12.1956.
66 S.R.O. 132/1957, 10.7.57.
67 See Mr Justice McGonigal in re *McElduff* (1972) N.I. 1, cited in Walsh 1990, p. 29.
68 See for instance Walsh 1990, pp. 27–46.
69 Northern Ireland (Temporary Provisions) Act, 1972, Eliz. II, c. 22.
70 S.I. 1265/1972, 1.11.1972 (N.I. 15).
71 Diplock Report, para. 28.
72 *HL Debs*, 7 December 1972, Vol. 337, col. 445.
73 Part III, section 15 of the schedule to the 1972 Detention of Terrorists Order.
74 Lord Diplock, *HL Debs*, 7 December 1972, Vol. 337, col. 442.
75 *HC Debs*, 11 December 1972; Vol. 848, col. 51.
76 *Ibid.*, col. 102.
77 *Fortnight*, Thursday, 16 November 1972, 19.
78 *HC Debs*, 11 December 1972, Vol. 848, cols. 53–72.
79 *Ibid.*, cols. 101–4.
80 Regulation 23, 1922 SPA.
81 Walsh 1990, p. 32. Section 13 of the EPA provided a special power of arrest for the purpose of bringing suspected terrorists before the courts.
82 1973 EPA, Part II, section 12.
83 Criminal Law (Northern Ireland) Act, 1967, Eliz. II, c. 18.
84 For discussion of the exercise of army powers under the 1973–87 EPAs and 1984 PTA see Walker 1989. pp. 1–33.
85 *HC Debs*, 11 December 1972, Vol. 848, col. 81.
86 *HC Debs*, 5 July 1973, Vol. 859, cols. 736–40.
87 Licensing Act (Northern Ireland), 1971, Eliz. II, c. 3; Registration of Clubs Act (Northern Ireland), 1967, 15 & 16 Eliz. II, c. 27.
88 S.R.O. 32/1922, 18.5.1922, B.G. 26.5.1922.
89 S.R.O. 176/1955, 30.11.1955.
90 Regulation 7A introduced by S.R.O. 36/1922, 1.6.1922, Supplement to B.G. 2.6.1922 and principle Regulation 8.
91 S.R.O. 176/1955, 30.11.1955.
92 S.R.O. 3/1957, 11.1.57.
93 1973 EPA, Part II, sections 10, 11, 12.

94   *Ibid.*, Part II, sections 13, 14.
95   *Ibid.*, Part II, section 15.
96   *Ibid.*, Part II, sections 13(1) and 14(1).
97   *Ibid.*, Part II, sections 13(3), 14(2) and 16(1).
98   *Ibid.*, Part II, section 15.
99   Regulation 18 revoked by S.R.O. 147/1949, 20.8.49; Regulation 4 introduced by
     S.R.O. 90/1954, 16.6.54.
100 1973 EPA, Part IV, section 25.
101 Criminal Justice (Miscellaneous Provisions) Act (Northern Ireland), 1968, 16 & 17
     Eliz. II, c. 28.
102 Regulation 24A enacted by S.R.O. 35/1922, 22.5.1922, B.G. 26.5.1922.
103 Regulation 24 revoked by S.R.O. 147/1949, 20.8.49.
104 *HC Debs*, 17 April 1973, Vol. 855, cols. 365, 382.
105 S.R.O. 113/1973, 11.4.1973. See discussion, chapter three.
106 Public Order Act, 1936, Edw. I, c. 8 & Geo. VI, c. 6, amended by the Public Order
     Act, 1963, 11 & 12 Eliz. II, c. 52.
107 Metropolitan Police Act, 1839, 2 & 3 Vict. c. 47.
108 *Thomas* v. *Sawkins*, (1935) 2 K.B. 249.
109 Emergency Powers (Defence) Act, 1939, 2 & 3 Geo. VI, c. 62.
110 *The Times* (London), No. 21, 1974, 3.
111 Repealed by S.R.O. 187/1951, 12.10.51, re-enacted by S.R.O. 199/1956,
     21.12.1956.
112 1973 EPA, Part IV (1).
113 Prosecution of Offences (Northern Ireland) Order, 1972, S.I. No. 538 (N.I. 1).
114 See *Report of the Working Party on Public Prosecutions*. Cmd. 554 HMSO (Belfast)
     1971.
115 1973 EPA, Part IV, section 29(4).
116 The 1973 EPA replaced both the 1922–43 SPAs as well as the Criminal Justice
     (Temporary Provisions) Act (Northern Ireland), 1970, 18 & 19 Eliz. II, c. 33.
117 S.I. No. 2213. See *HC Debs*, 11 December 1975, Vol. 902, col. 743, and *HC Debs*,
     1 July 1976, Vol. 914, col. 271.
118 In addition to debates on instituting the death penalty during consideration of the
     1974 Prevention of Terrorism (Temporary Provisions) Act, see also *HC Debs*, 6
     December 1978, Vol. 959, col. 1516, *HC Debs*, 2 July 1979, Vol. 969, cols. 949–50,
     HC Debs, 10 December 1980, Vol. 995, cols. 1934–5, and *HC Debs*, 9 December
     1982, Vol. 33, cols. 1058–9.
119 *HC Debs*, 14 May 1973, Vol. 856, cols. 1025–1146.
120 *HC Debs*, 14 May 1973, col. 1028. Capital punishment had been provided for
     previously through the Criminal Justice Act (Northern Ireland), 1966, 14 &15 Eliz.
     II, c. 20.
121 *HC Debs*, 14 May 1973, Vol. 856, col. 1142.
122 *Northern Ireland Annual Abstract of Statistics*, 1972, 1973, 1974.
123 For Commons' consideration of the policy of Ulsterisation see *HC Debs*, 17
     December 1976, Vol. 922, cols. 1933–2048, *HC Debs*, 8 December 1977, Vol. 940,
     cols. 1678–1764 and *HC Debs*, 30 June 1978, Vol. 952, cols. 1727–35 and
     1807–14.

CHAPTER FOUR

1   *HC Debs*, 9 July 1974, Vol. 876, cols. 283–316. See also *HC Debs*, 9 July 1974,
    Vol. 876, col. 1282.
2   Gardiner Report, Introduction.
3   *HC Debs*, 27 June 1975, Vol. 894, cols. 964–6.
4   See for instance The *Irish Times*, 27 May 1975, quoted in *HC Debs*, 13 May 1975,
    Vol. 892, col. 261, *The Times* (London), 20 June 1975, *The Times* (London), 21 June
    1975, *The Times*, (London), 23 June 1975, *The Guardian*, 14 July 1975 and *HC
    Debs*, 26 June 1975, Vol. 894, cols. 826–30.
5   *HC Debs*, 4 November 1975, Vol. 899, col. 234.

6   *HC Debs*, 27 June 1975, Vol. 894, col. 906.
7   Northern Ireland (Young Persons) Act, 1974, Eliz. II, c. 33.
8   *HC Debs*, 26 June 1975, Vol. 894, col. 820.
9   *Report of a Committee to Consider, in the Context of Civil Liberties and Human Rights, Measures to Deal with Terrorism in Northern Ireland.* Chairman: Lord Gardiner. January 1975. Session 1974/75 Cmnd. 5847. [Hereafter Gardiner Report].
10 Gardiner Report, para. 6.
11 'Some of those who have given evidence to us have argued that such features of the present emergency provisions as the use of the Army in aid of the civil power, detention without trial, arrest on suspicion and trial without jury are so inherently objectionable that they must be abolished on the grounds that they constitute a basic violation of human rights.' (Gardiner Report, para. 15).
12 Gardiner Report, para. 15.
13 European Convention, Articles 5 and 17.
14 *Report of the inquiry into allegations against the security forces of physical brutality in Northern Ireland arising out of events on the 9 August 1971.* Session 1971/72 Cmnd. 4823 [Compton Report]; and *Report of the Committee of Privy Counsellors Appointed to Consider Authorised Procedures for the Interrogation of Persons Suspected of Terrorism.* March 1972, Session 1971/72 Vol. xviii, Cmnd. 4901 [Parker Report]. Last citation Gardiner Report, para. 20.
15 Northern Ireland (Emergency Provisions) Act 1973 (Amendment) Order 1974.
16 Northern Ireland (Emergency Provisions) Act 1973 (Amendment) Order 1975 (S.I. 1975, No. 1609). See *HC Debs*, 4 November 1975, Vol. 899, cols. 233–94.
17 *First Report of the Standing Advisory Commission on Human Rights.* Annual Report for 1974–75. HC 632, 1975/76.
18 Prevention of Incitement to Hatred Act, 1970, 18 & 19 Eliz. II, c. 24, and Flags and Emblems (Display) Act (Northern Ireland), 1954, 2 & 3 Eliz. II, c. 10.
19 See, for instance, A.J. Beith, *HC Debs*, 26 June 1975, Vol. 894, col. 838.
20 Criminal Injuries to Persons (Compensation) Act (Northern Ireland), 1968, 16 & 17 Eliz. II, c. 9, and Criminal Injuries to Property (Compensation) Act (Northern Ireland), 1971, Eliz. II, c. 38. Gardiner Report, para. 66.
21 Northern Ireland (Emergency Provisions) (Amendment) Act 1975, Eliz. II, c. 62. [Hereafter 1975 EPA].
22 Gardiner Report, para. 27.
23 Explosive Substances Act, 1883, 46 & 47 Vict., c. 3.
24 Similar concern continued to be raised in the House of Commons. See for example *HC Debs*, 6th December 1978, Vol. 959, cols. 1529 and 1546.
25 Gardiner Report, para. 28.
26 Preliminary hearings were provided for by the Criminal Procedure (Committal for Trial) Act (Northern Ireland), 1968, 16 & 17 Eliz. II, c. 32.
27 Prison Act (Northern Ireland), 1953, 2 Eliz. II, c. 18.
28 Gardiner Report, para. 70. The idea of introducing an offence of terrorism repeatedly arose in the House of Commons. See, for instance, speech by Airey Neave, *HC Debs*, 17 December 1976, Vol. 922, cols. 1943–50.
29 Merlyn Rees, *HC Debs*, 27 June 1975, Vol. 894, col. 891.
30 Gardiner Report, para. 119. [Emphasis added].
31 Gardiner Report, Appendix F and para. 119.
32 Ian Paisley, *HC Debs*, 9 July 1974, Vol. 876, col. 1290. See also *HC Debs*, 9 July 1974, Vol. 876, col. 1288.
33 Gardiner Report, paras. 173–4.
34 Gardiner Report, para. 173. (Emphasis added).
35 Kevin Mcnamara, *HC Debs*, 9 July 1974, Vol. 876, col. 1298.
36 Gardiner Report, para. 176.
37 Gerry Fitt, *HC Debs*, 27 June 1975, Vol. 894, col. 931.
38 Merlyn Rees, *HC Debs*, 27 June 1975, Vol. 894, col. 900.
39 Three extensions of one week each were allowed on top of the seven week total period.
40 Merlyn Rees, *HC Debs*, 27 June 1975, Vol. 894, cols. 894–8.
41 Prevention of Terrorism (Temporary Provisions) Act, 1974, Eliz. II, c. 56.

42   Gardiner Report, para. 72.
43   *Ibid.*, para. 74.
44   *Ibid.*, para. 83.
45   Boyle et al., 1980.
46   *First Report of the Standing Advisory Commission on Human Rights. Annual Report for 1974–75.* HC 632, 1975/76, para. 34.
47   Baker Report, para. 40.
48   Gardiner Report, para. 101.
49   *Ibid.*, para. 114.
50   *Ibid.*, Appendix E.
51   Merlyn Rees, *HC Debs*, 27 June 1975, Vol. 894, cols. 902–3.
52   *HC Debs*, 27 June 1975, Vol. 894, col. 898. The government was awaiting the results of a public inquiry with regard to building a new prison at Maghaberry. In the interim, work was proceeding at the Maze with the construction of new cell block accommodation. Gardiner urged that the 1976 date for completion of the new prison units be moved forward. The committee also found the practice of housing young prisoners in the Maze and Magilligan, in order to conduct jobs around the prisons from which detainees and political prisoners were exempt, to be unsatisfactory. Some eighty-six young prisoners between the age of seventeen and twenty-one were in this category at the time. (Gardiner Report, para. 111).
53   *HC Debs*, 4 November 1975, Vol. 899, col. 235.
54   *HC Debs*, 4 November 1975, Vol. 899, col. 242.
55   *HC Debs*, 4 November 1975, Vol. 899, cols. 239–40.
56   Fourteen per cent of the total convicted prisoners were in this category.
57   *HC Debs*, 17 December 1976, Vol. 922, col. 1938.
58   *HC Debs*, 11 December 1975, Vol. 902, cols. 742–3.
59   *HC Debs*, 11 December 1975, Vol. 902, col. 759.
60   Flackes and Elliott 1994, p. 179.
61   Northern Ireland (Emergency Provisions) (Amendment) Act, 1978, Eliz. II, c. 5. In the interim the Northern Ireland (Various Emergency Provisions) (Continuance) (No. 2) Order 1975 renewed the 1973 EPA, 1975 EPA and the 1974 Northern Ireland (Young Persons) Act. In 1976 these statutes were renewed by the Northern Ireland (Various Emergency Provisions) (Continuance) Order 1976 and the Northern Ireland (Various Emergency Provisions) (Continuance) (No. 2) Order 1976. The following year the Northern Ireland (Various Emergency Provisions) (Continuance) Order 1977 and the Northern Ireland (Various Emergency Provisions) (Continuance) (No. 2) Order 1977, No. 1249, SI 1977 continued the statutes.
62   See footnote, *supra*.
63   *Fifth Report of the Standing Advisory Commission on Human Rights. Annual Report for 1978–79.* HC 433, 1979/80.
64   *HC Debs*, 22 July 1980, Vol. 989, cols. 429–61.
65   See *HC Debs*, 22 July 1980, Vol. 989, col. 440 and *HC Debs*, 10 December 1980, Vol. 995, cols. 1033–4.
66   Cunningham 1991. p. 155.
67   See *HC Debs*, 15 December 1981, Vol. 15, cols. 261–4.
68   See discussion, chapter five.
69   John Patten, *HC Debs*, 9 December 1982, Vol. 33, cols. 1081–3.
70   Cunningham 1991. p. 182. For renewal debates in the interim (before the Baker Report), see *HC Debs*, 12 May 1983, Vol. 42, cols. 975–93 and *HC Debs*, 8 December 1983, Vol. 50, cols. 517–72.
71   Report of the Committee of Inquiry into Police Interrogation Procedures in Northern Ireland by H.G. Bennett. Session 1978/79 Cmnd. 7497.
72   Walsh 1983, p. 63 and Greer 1990, p. 85.
73   Workers' Research Unit, *Belfast Bulletin No. 11* – 'Supergrasses', 1984.
74   Greer 1990, p. 73.
75   Flackes and Elliott 1994, p. 318.
76   Cunningham 1991, p. 158.
77   Flackes and Elliott 1994, p. 318.
78   See particularly Greer 1980, 1986, 1990, 1995.

79 *Review of the Northern Ireland (Emergency Provisions) Act 1978*. By the Rt. Hon. Sir George Baker OBE. April 1984. Session 1983/84 Cmnd. 9222 [Hereafter Baker Report], para. 18.

80 Baker Report, 7–8.

81 For detailed analysis of the Baker Report see Bonner 1984.

82 Mr McNair-Wilson, *HC Debs*, 30 June 1978, Vol. 952, col. 1736. See also *HC Debs*, 6 December 1978, Vol. 959, col. 1559.

83 Roy Mason, Secretary of State for Northern Ireland, *HC Debs*, 6 December 1978, Vol. 959, cols. 1501–2.

84 Glover Report. MOD Forms 102 S25/1182, p. 2.

85 Ibid., p.4.

86 Humphrey Atkins, Secretary of State for Northern Ireland, *HC Debs*, 22 July 1980, Vol. 989, cols. 429–30.

87 Baker's discussion of the admissibility of confessions and his conclusions were heavily drawn from Greer, 1980, which had been submitted to the Baker Committee during its deliberations.

88 Prevention of Terrorism (Temporary Provisions) Act, 1976, Eliz. II, c. 8.

89 Northern Ireland (Emergency Provisions) Act 1978 (Amendment) Order 1979 (S.I. 1979, No. 746). For discussion of the orders proscribing the INLA see *HC Debs*, 2 July 1979, Vol. 969, cols. 925–1070 and *HC Debs*, 25 July 1979, Vol. 971, cols. 741–70.

90 Baker Report, para. 412.

91 *Ibid.*, para. 414.

92 See *HC Debs*, 20 December 1984, Vol. 70, cols. 579–672.

93 Peter Archer, *HC Debs*, 20 December 1984, Vol. 70, col. 585.

94 *HC Debs*, 8 December 1983, Vol. 50, cols. 527–8.

95 Stuart Bell, *HC Debs*, 20 December 1984, Vol. 70, col. 638.

96 Peter Archer, *HC Debs*, 20 December 1984, Vol. 70, col. 593. For a detailed discussion of Labour's concerns, see also Cunningham 1991, pp. 156–84.

97 See for instance John Hume, *HC Debs*, 20 December 1984, Vol. 70, cols. 620–3.

98 The instrument was approved with Labour's support on the 16 January 1986.

99 *Anglo-Irish Joint Studies – Joint Report and Studies*, 1981, Cmd. 8414. HMSO.

100 *The Government of Northern Ireland: A Working Paper for a Conference.* November 1979, Cmd. 7763. HMSO.

101 *The Government of Northern Ireland: Proposals for Future Discussion.* 2 July 1980, Cmd. 7950. HMSO.

102 *Northern Ireland: A Framework for Devolution.* April 1982. Cmd. 8541. HMSO.

103 Tom King, *HC Debs*, 16 December 1986, Vol. 107, col. 1084.

104 Northern Ireland (Emergency Provisions) Act, 1987, Eliz. II, c. 30. [Hereafter 1987 EPA].

105 1987 EPA, sections 15 and 14.

106 1987 EPA, section 6 (amending 1978 EPA, section 11) and 1987 EPA schedule 1 (amending 1978 EPA sections 13, 14, 15).

107 For shortfalls in meeting the European Convention requirements see Jackson 1988, pp. 241–5.

108 Tom King, *HC Debs*, 16 December 1986, Vol. 107, col. 1085. Clause relating to security firms: 1987 EPA, Part III and 1987 EPA, section 10.

109 1978 EPA, section 22 and 1987 EPA, section 10.

110 1987 EPA, section 8 and 1987 EPA, section 12. With regard to roads, for the most part, the changes revolved around a clarification of the legal basis for closures already in force. See *HC Debs*, 8 April 1987, Vol. 114, cols. 310–400. For discussion of the sections on road closure and compensation see Jackson 1988, pp. 238–41.

111 *Thirteenth Report of the Standing Advisory Commission on Human Rights. Annual Report for 1986–87.*

112 Letter from Douglas Hurd to the Independent Broadcasting Authority, 19 October 1988.

113 For discussion of MI5 and MI6 involvement in Northern Ireland and the Republic of Ireland, see Flackes and Elliott 1994, pp. 461–6.

114 *HC Debs*, 25 July 1979, Vol. 971, col. 761.

115 Tom King, *HC Debs*, 20 October 1988, Vol. 138, col. 996; Criminal Evidence (Northern Ireland) Order 1988, S.I. 1987/1988, N.I. 20.

116 *HC Debs*, 8 November 1988, Vol. 140, cols. 182–224, *HL Debs*, 10 November 1988, Vol. 501, cols. 774–803.
117 See for instance *HC Debs,* 1 March 1988, Vol. 128, cols. 883–919.
118 *Northern Ireland Annual Abstract of Statistics*, 1972, 1986–90.
119 Letter from John Hume, Social Democratic and Labour Party, to Gerry Adams, Sinn Féin, 17 March 1988.
120 *Review of the Northern Ireland (Emergency Provisions) Acts 1978 and 1987* by the Viscount Colville of Culross QC. July 1990. Session 1989/90 Cm. 1115. [Hereafter Colville Report, 1989/90].
121 Northern Ireland (Emergency Provisions) Act, 1991, Eliz. II, c. 22. (Hereafter 1991 EPA).
122 *HC Debs*, 20 June 1991, Vol. 193, col. 514.
123 This last provision was drawn from Part VI of the 1989 PTA (see discussion, next chapter).
124 1991 EPA, section 25.
125 S.R.O. 176/1955, 30.11.55.
126 1991 EPA, section 27.
127 Dickson 1992b, p. 617.
128 Walker and Reid 1993, p. 670.
129 McNamara, *HC Debs*, 7 March 1991, Vol. 187, col. 407.
130 Dickson 1992b, p. 617.
131 1991 EPA, section 30.
132 Colville Report, 1989/90, para. 2.7.3.
133 Lord Belstead, *HL Debs*, 19 June 1991, Vol. 527, col. 1693.
134 Peter Brooke, *HC Debs*, 19 November 1990, Vol. 181, col. 30.
135 Colville Report, 1989/90, para. 11.7.
136 *HC Debs*, 7 March 1991, Vol. 187, col. 426.
137 1991 EPA, section 58.
138 Dickson 1992b, p. 622.
139 1991 EPA, section 37(1).
140 For further discussion see Dickson 1992b, pp. 620–1.
141 Dickson 1992b, p. 622; see also *HC Debs*, 20 June 1991, Vol. 193, col. 508.
142 *HC Debs*, 8 March 1989, Vol. 148, cols. 907–9.
143 *Ibid.*, 6 March 1991, Vol. 187, col. 429.
144 Flackes and Elliott 1994, p. 461.
145 *Downing Street Declaration.* 15 December 1993. Cmd. 2442. HMSO, article 10.
146 Ibid., Introductory message.
147 Sir John Wheeler, *HC Debs*, 9 January 1996, Vol. 269, col. 107.
148 Northern Ireland (Emergency Provisions) Act, 1996, Eliz. II, c. 22. [Hereafter 1996 EPA].
149 *Report on the operation in 1993 of the Prevention of Terrorism (Temporary Provisions) Act 1989*. By J. J. Rowe. Session 1993/94 and *Report on the operation in 1995 of the Prevention of Terrorism (Temporary Provisions) Act 1989*. By J.J. Rowe. Session 1995/96.
150 Sir Patrick Mayhew, *HC Debs*, 9 January 1996, Vol. 269, col. 33.
151 For discussion of the degree to which these provisions were consistent see *HC Debs*, 19 February 1996, Vol. 272, cols. 94–5.
152 Sir Patrick Mayhew, *HC Debs*, 9 January 1996, Vol. 269, col. 35.
153 Theft Act (Northern Ireland), 1969, 17 & 18 Eliz. II, c. 16.
154 *HC Debs*, 9 January 1996, Vol. 269, col. 38.
155 Thomas McAvoy, *HC Debs*, 9 January 1996, Vol. 269, col. 86.
156 Marjorie Mowlam, *HC Debs*, 19 February 1996, Vol. 272, col. 89.
157 *Report of the Inquiry into Legislation Against Terrorism.* 4 September 1996, Cm. 3420, p. v.

CHAPTER FIVE

1 Walker 1992, p. 32.
2 Mr Lyons, *HC Debs*, 18 March 1981, Vol. 1, col. 360 and Lord Harris, *HL Debs*, 13 February 1989, Vol. 504, col. 22.

3 Immigration Act, 1971, Eliz. II, c. 77.
4 Adaptations of the 1971 Immigration Act will be addressed in the text explicating the 1974 PTA.
5 Prevention of Violence (Temporary Provisions) Act, 1939, 2 & 3 Geo. VI, c. 50. [Hereafter 1939 PVA].
6 Cabinet meeting notes, PRO Ref. CAB 23.97 1(39), 43–4. See also Lomas 1980, pp. 18–19.
7 *HC Debs*, 24 July 1939, col. 1049.
8 Samuel Hoare, *HC Debs*, 24 July 1939, Vol. 350, cols. 1047–52.
9 Arthur Greenwood, *HC Debs*, 24 July 1939, Vol. 350, col. 1057.
10 Donald Somervell, Attorney General, *HC Debs*, 24 July 1939, Vol. 350, col. 1113.
11 Colonel Wedgwood, *HC Debs*, 24 July 1939, Vol. 350, col. 1080.
12 Arthur Greenwood, *HC Debs*, 24 July 1939, Vol. 350, col. 1058.
13 Robert Lynn, *HC Debs NI*, 21 March 1922, Vol. II, col. 91.
14 Samuel Hoare, *HC Debs*, 24 July 1939, Vol. 350, col. 1057.
15 Hugh O'Neill, *HC Debs*, 24 July 1939, Vol. 350, col. 1063.
16 1939 PVA, section 1(1).
17 *Ibid.*, section 1(3).
18 Lomas 1980, p. 25.
19 1939 PVA, sections 1(2) and 1(4).
20 Samuel Hoare, *HC Debs*, 26 July 1939, Vol. 350, col. 1553.
21 Lomas 1980, p. 24.
22 *Ibid.*, p. 27.
23 Dingle Foot, *HC Debs*, 24 July 1939, Vol. 350, col. 1067.
24 Edmund Harvey, *HC Debs*, 24 July 1939, Vol. 350, col. 1086.
25 F. J. Bellenger, *HC Debs*, 24 July 1939, Vol. 350, col. 1092.
26 Richard Acland, *HC Debs*, 24 July 1939, Vol. 350, col. 1103.
27 Joseph Nall, HC Debs, 24 July 1939, Vol. 350, col. 1577.
28 Paraphrased by D.N. Pritt, *HC Debs*, 24 July 1939, Vol. 350, col. 1078.
29 1939 PVA, section 1(6).
30 *Ibid.*, section 2(1).
31 *Ibid.*, section 4(1).
32 Gearty 1999. p. 23.
33 *HC Debs*, 28 July 1939, Vol. 350, cols. 1864–8.
34 1939 PVA, section 4(4).
35 J.R. Leslie, *HC Debs*, 24 July 1939, Vol. 350, col. 1596.
36 Samuel Hoare, *HC Debs*, 24 July 1939, Vol. 350, col. 1053.
37 Samuel Hoare, *HC Debs*, 24 July 1939, Vol. 350, col. 1053.
38 Samuel Hoare, *Ibid.*, col. 1054.
39 Arthur Greenwood, *HC Debs*, 24 July 1939, Vol. 350, col. 1059.
40 Samuel Hoare, *HC Debs*, 24 July 1939, Vol. 350, col. 1051.
41 Godfrey Nicholson, *HC Debs*, 24 July 1939, Vol. 350, col. 1090.
42 G. Buchanan, *HC Debs*, 24 July 1939, Vol. 350, col. 1097.
43 *Ibid.*, col. 1098.
44 Gearty 1999, p. 23.
45 Samuel Hoare, *HC Debs*, 24 July 1939, Vol. 350, col. 1054.
46 Godfrey Nicholson, *HC Debs*, 24 July 1939, Vol. 350, col. 1600.
47 The 1939 statute was finally allowed to expire by the Expiring Laws Continuance Act, 1953, 2 & 3 Eliz. II, c. 9. The 1939 Act was not repealed, however, until the Statute Law Repeals Act, 1973, 21 & 22 Eliz. II, c. 39.
48 Geoffrey Bing, *HC Debs*, 2 December 1952, col. 1400.
49 Samuel Hoare, *HC Debs*, 26 July 1939, Vol. 350, col. 1598.
50 Geoffrey Bing, *HC Debs*, 2 December 1952, col. 1407.
51 John Hay, *HC Debs*, 2 December 1952, col. 1415.
52 David Maxwell Fyfe, *HC Debs*, 2 December 1952, col. 1419.
53 *HC Debs*, 28 November 1974, Vol. 882, col. 674.
54 *HC Debs*, 29 November 1974, Vol. 882, col. 736.
55 *HC Debs*, 28 July 1939, Vol. 350, cols. 1853–70.
56 *HC Debs*, 28 November 1974, Vol. 882, col. 647.

57 *Ibid.*, 28 November 1974, Vol. 882, col. 667.
58 Mr Benn, *HC Debs*, 24 July 1939, Vol. 350, col. 1104.
59 *HC Debs*, 25 November 1974, Vol. 882, col. 42.
60 *HC Debs*, 28 November 1974, Vol. 882, col. 675.
61 See for instance *HC Debs*, 28 November 1974, Vol. 882, cols. 706, 729–30.
62 *Ibid.*, 28 November 1974, Vol. 882, col. 718. This statement is taken from J.W. Rooker of Birmingham, Perry Bar.
63 *Ibid.*, 28 November 1974, Vol. 882, col. 653.
64 Benn, 1990, 273. For similar sentiments voiced by MPs, see *HC Debs*, 25 November 1974, Vol. 882, col. 35, *HC Debs*, 28 November 1974, Vol. 882, cols. 634, 705.
65 *Ibid.*, col. 648.
66 Prevention of Terrorism (Temporary Provisions) Act, 1974, Eliz. II, c. 56.
67 See, for instance, *HC Debs*, 11 September 1973.
68 *HC Debs*, 28 November 1974, Vol. 882, col. 783.
69 *Ibid.*, col. 365.
70 Samuel Hoare, *HC Debs*, 24 July 1939, Vol. 350, col. 1053.
71 *HC Debs*, 28 November 1974, Vol. 882, col. 636.
72 *HC Debs*, 28 November 1974, Vol. 882, col. 943.
73 *Ibid.*, col. 942.
74 *Ibid.*, col. 806.
75 *Ibid.*, col. 810.
76 *Ibid.*, col. 746.
77 See *HC Debs*, 14 October 1941, Vol. 374, col. 1249 for discussion of criteria for issuance of permits. See also S.R.O. 54/1940 and S.R.O. 61/1940.
78 Workers' Research Unit, 'Rough Justice: the Law in Northern Ireland', *The Belfast Bulletin*, no. 10, (1982), 17, reprinted in Hall 1990 p. 183.
79 *HC Debs*, 28 November 1974, Vol 882, cols. 637 and 639.
80 Benn 1990 p. 273.
81 *HC Debs*, 28 November 1974, Vol. 882, cols. 670, 747–50.
82 *Ibid.*, cols. 848–66.
83 *Ibid.*, col. 849.
84 *Ibid.*, cols. 856–7.
85 *Ibid.*, cols. 859–60.
86 For discussion of the insertion of reciprocity see *HC Debs*, 28 November 1974, Vol. 882, cols. 748–50.
87 For extensive commentary on this section of the 1974 PTA see Street 1975.
88 This section suspended the following provisions: section 38 of the Magistrates' Courts Act 1952, section 29 of the Children and Young Persons Act 1969, sections 10(1) and 20(3) of the Summary Jurisdiction (Scotland) Act 1954, section 132 of the Magistrates' Courts Act (Northern Ireland) 1964, and section 50(30) of the Children and Young Persons Act (Northern Ireland), 1968, 16 & 17 Eliz. II, c. 34.
89 *HC Debs*, 28 November 1974, Vol. 882, col. 641.
90 S.R.O. 199/1956, 21.12.56.
91 S.R.O. 16/1957, 28.1.57. See also Regulation 1B of the 1922–43 SPAs (S.R.O. 61/1940, 29.6.40, Defence of the Realm Regulation 14E (S.R.O. 561/1916), and Defence (General) Regulation 18 (S.R.O. 927/1939).
92 See for example *HC Debs*, 25 November 1974, Vol. 882, col. 34, and *HL Debs*, 28 November 1974, Vol. 882, col. 1513.
93 See for example *HC Debs*, 25 November 1974, Vol. 882, cols. 39, 41, and *HC Debs*, 28 November 1974, Vol. 882, cols. 644, 726, 729, 735.
94 *The Economist*, 6 December 1975, 9.
95 *The Times* (London), 28 November 1974, 1.
96 Treason Act, 1351, 25 Edw. III, c. 2.
97 Piracy Act, 1837, 7 Will. IV & 1 Vict., c. 88.
98 *HL Debs*, 28 November 1974, Vol. 882, col. 1564.
99 Treason Felony Act, 1848, 11 & 12 Vict., c. 12.
100 Law commission Working Paper No. 72, *Treason, Sedition and Allied Offences*, 1977, para. 58.

101 *HC Debs*, 11 December 1974, Vol. 883, col. 518.
102 *New York Times*, 11 December 1975, 15.
103 *The Economist*, 13 December 1975, 21.
104 *HL Debs*, 28 November 1974, cols. 1543–4.
105 See for example *HC Debs*, 25 November 1974, Vol. 882, col. 45; and *HC Debs*, 28 November 1974, Vol. 882, cols. 756–8.
106 *HL Debs*, 28 November 1974, Vol. 882, col. 1544.
107 See for example the Opposition's response to the second reading of the Bill, *HC Debs*, 28 November 1974, Vol. 882, col. 646 and the counter–response in col. 650.
108 *HC Debs*, 28 November 1974, Vol. 882, col. 756.
109 *Ibid.*, cols. 762, 769.
110 *Ibid.*, col. 759.
111 Independent Broadcasting Act, 1981, Eliz. II, c. 68. The 1981 Broadcasting Act consolidated the Independent Broadcasting Authority Act, 1973, Eliz. II, c. 19, the Independent Broadcasting Act, 1974, Eliz. II, c. 16, the Independent Broadcasting Authority (No. 2) Act, 1974, Eliz. II, c. 42, the Independent Broadcasting Authority Act, 1978, Eliz. II, c. 43, and the Broadcasting Act, 1980, Eliz. II, c. 64.
112 Television Act, 1964, 12 & 13 Eliz. II, c. 21.
113 *HC Debs*, 28 November 1974, Vol. 882, col. 780.
114 The 1974 PTA was extended 161 votes to 10.
115 *HC Debs*, 19 May 1975, Vol. 892, col. 1084.
116 *Ibid.*, cols. 1111, 1116–17.
117 *Ibid.*, col. 1085.
118 *Written Answers*, 3 August 1978, Vol. 955, col. 506.
119 *HC Debs*, 5 December 1974, Vol. 882, col. 2075.
120 *Ibid.*, col. 2085.
121 *Ibid.*, col. 2096.
122 *HC Debs*, 19 May 1975, Vol. 892, col. 1088.
123 *Ibid.*, col. 1089.
124 *HC Debs*, 19 May 1975, Vol. 892, cols. 1082–1160.
125 Prevention of Terrorism (Temporary Provisions) Act 1974 (Continuance) (No. 2) Order 1975.
126 Airey Neave, *HC Debs*, 30 June 1978, Vol. 952, cols. 1218–1719.
127 *HC Debs*, 26 November 1975, Vol. 901, col. 912.
128 Prevention of Terrorism (Temporary Provisions) Act, 1976, Eliz. II, c. 8. [Hereafter 1976 PTA].
129 Roy Jenkins, *HC Debs*, 28 January 1976, Vol. 904, col. 443.
130 Roy Jenkins, *HC Debs*, 26 November 1975, Vol. 901, col. 886.
131 1976 PTA, clause 9.
132 Criminal Law Act (Northern Ireland), 1967, 15 & 16 Eliz. II, c. 15.
133 *HC Debs*, 26 November 1975, Vol. 901, col. 927.
134 Tom Litterick, *HC Debs*, 26 November 1975, Vol. 901, col. 968.
135 Prevention of Terrorism (Supplemental Temporary Provisions) Order 1976, S.I., 1976, No. 465, 25 March 1976.
136 Prevention of Terrorism (Supplemental Temporary Provisions) (Northern Ireland) Order 1976, S.I. 1976, No. 466, 25 March 1976.
137 *HC Debs*, 9 March 1977, Vol. 927, col. 1472.
138 For pressures placed on the government to conduct a review see for instance, *HC Debs*, 9 March 1977, Vol. 927, cols. 1491–2.
139 *HC Debs*, 15 March 1978, Vol. 946, col. 550.
140 Prevention of Terrorism (Temporary Provisions) Act 1976 (Continuance) Order 1978.
141 *Review of the Operation of the Prevention of Terrorism (Temporary Provisions) Acts 1974 and 1976*. By the Rt. Hon. Lord Shackleton, KG, OBE. August 1978. Session 1977/78. Vol. xxiii, Cmnd. 7324. [Hereafter Shackleton Report].
142 Shackleton Report, paras. 27–32.
143 Ibid., Appendix E, Table 4.
144 Prevention of Terrorism (Temporary Provisions) Act 1976 (Amendment) Order 1979.

145 Shackleton Report, para. 41.
146 *Ibid.*, para. 42.
147 *Ibid.*, para. 44.
148 *Ibid.*, para. 61.
149 *Ibid.*, paras. 76, 77, and 98.
150 *Ibid.*, fn. 1, p. 23.
151 *Ibid.*, para. 68.
152 For more detailed discussion of considerations involved in the clauses governing the withholding of information including changes in the right to silence, see Walker 1992, pp. 132–44.
153 Shackleton Report, para. 64.
154 *Ibid.*, para. 160.
155 Jellicoe Report, para. 174.
156 *HC Debs*, 18 March 1981, Vol. 1, cols. 336–41.
157 Roy Hattersley, *HC Debs*, 18 March 1981, Vol. 1, col. 336.
158 Cunningham 1991, p. 151.
159 Walsh 1990, p. 35.
160 *Ibid.*, pp. 35–7. See also Hall 1990, pp. 170–81.
161 For detailed accounts of the supergrass system see Greer 1980, Greer 1986, Greer 1987, Greer 1995 and Hadden et al. 1987.
162 William Whitelaw, *HC Debs*, 15 March 1982, Vol. 20, col. 152.
163 *Review of the Operation of the Prevention of Terrorism (Temporary Provisions) Act 1976.* By the Rt. Hon. Earl Jellicoe, DSO, MC. February 1983. Session 1982/83 Cmnd. 8803. [Hereafter Jellicoe Report].
164 William Whitelaw, *HC Debs*, 16 March 1982, Vol. 20, col. 1052.
165 Jellicoe Report, iv.
166 *Ibid.*, para. 1.
167 See, for instance, *HC Debs*, 30 June 1982, Vol. 21, cols. 941–99.
168 Jellicoe Report, para. 9.
169 For commentary on Jellicoe's recommendations see Walker 1983, 485–486 and Bonner 1983.
170 Jellicoe Report, para. 207.
171 Walker argues that proscription violates the 'limiting principles' set out by Jellicoe as, if the provision's object is to reduce public disorder, then republican rallies likely to raise such sentiments could be banned by sections 3 and 5 of the 1936 Public Order Act. (Walker 1983, p. 491)
172 Jellicoe Report, para. 176.
173 *Ibid.*, para. 163, Table 1.
174 *Ibid.*, para. 167. For an account of the hunger strikes see Beresford 1987.
175 *Ibid.*, para. 188.
176 *Ibid.*, para. 55.
177 Criminal Law (Northern Ireland) Act, 1967, 15 & 16 Eliz. II, c. 18. Walker 1983, pp. 486–7.
178 Jellicoe Report, para. 45.
179 See Jellicoe Report, paras. 45–52.
180 Jellicoe Report, para. 110.
181 Jellicoe Report, para. 112.
182 No. 8022/77, 8025/77 and 8027/77. For further discussion of the *McVeigh* case see Warbrick 1983, pp. 757–66.
183 Jellicoe Report, para. 13.
184 *Ibid.*, para. 77.
185 *HC Debs*, 7 March 1983, Vol. 38, cols. 564–642.
186 Mr Marshall, *HC Debs*, 7 March 1983, Vol. 38, cols. 632–3.
187 William Whitelaw, *HC Debs*, 7 March 1983, Vol. 38, cols. 568–9 and Mr Brittan, *HC Debs*, 24 October 1983, Vol. 47, col. 59.
188 This provision had been recommended in the Jellicoe Report, para. 72.
189 Prevention of Terrorism (Temporary Provisions) Act, 1974, Eliz. II, c. 56. [Hereafter 1974 PTA].

190 Mr Brittan, *HC Debs*, Standing Committee D, 15 November 1983, col. 144, quoted in Walker 1984, p. 709.
191 Walker 1984 p. 705. Contrast this with discussion, *HC Debs*, 7 March 1983, Vol. 38, cols. 612–13.
192 Home Office Circular 26/1984, para. 100.
193 Walker 1984, p. 708.
194 Cunningham 1991, p. 202.
195 S. Crawshaw, 'Combating Terrorism', in R.H. Ward and H.E. Smith (eds.), *International Terrorism*. Chicago: O.I. C. J., 1987, 20, quoted in Walker 1992, p. 162.
196 *Guide to Emergency Powers*, 1990, Part IV, para. 49, cited in Walker 1992, p. 162.
197 *Ex parte Lynch* [1980] N.I. 126. See Dickson 1992b, p. 611.
198 Jackson 1988, fn. 36.
199 *Review of the operation in 1984 of the Prevention of Terrorism (Temporary Provisions) Act 1984* by Sir Cyril Philips and Review of the operation in 1985 of the Prevention of Terrorism (Temporary Provisions) Act 1984 by Sir Cyril Philips. [Hereafter Philips 1985].
200 Philips 1985, para. 16. This shift had also been noted by Jellicoe.
201 Police and Criminal Evidence Act, 1984, Eliz. II, c. 60.
202 *HC Debs*, 19 February 1986, Vol. 92, cols. 415–37.
203 Philips 1985, para. 35.
204 *Review of the operation in 1986 of the Prevention of Terrorism (Temporary Provisions) Act 1984*. By the Viscount Colville of Culross QC. Session 1986/87, [Hereafter Colville Report, 1987]; *Report on the operation in 1987 of the Prevention of Terrorism (Temporary Provisions) Act 1984*. By the Viscount Colville of Culross QC. Session 1987/88 Cm. 264, [Hereafter Colville Report, 1988]; *Report on the operation in 1988 of the Prevention of Terrorism (Temporary Provisions) Act 1984*. By the Viscount Colville of Culross QC. Session 1988/89, [Hereafter Colville Report, 1989]; *Report on the operation in 1989 of the Prevention of Terrorism (Temporary Provisions) Acts 1984 and 1989*. By the Viscount Colville of Culross QC. Session 1989/90; *Review of the Northern Ireland (Emergency Provisions) Acts 1978 and 1987*. By the Viscount Colville of Culross QC. July 1990. Session 1989/90 Cm. 1115, [Hereafter Colville Report, 1990]; *Report on the operation in 1990 of the Prevention of Terrorism (Temporary Provisions) Act 1989*. By the Viscount Colville of Culross QC. Session 1990/91; *Report on the operation in 1991 of the Prevention of Terrorism (Temporary Provisions) Act 1989*. By the Viscount Colville of Culross QC. Session 1991/92; *Report on the operation in 1992 of the Prevention of Terrorism (Temporary Provisions) Act 1989*. By the Viscount Colville of Culross QC. Session 1992/93; and *Report on the operation in 1992 of the Northern Ireland (Emergency Provisions) Act 1991*. By the Viscount Colville of Culross QC. Session 1992/93.
205 Letter from Douglas Hurd to Viscount Colville, 5 February 1987.
206 Douglas Hurd, *HC Debs*, 10 February 1987, Vol. 110, col. 264.
207 Colville Report, 1990.
208 Colville Report, 1989.
209 S.I. No. 1987. For detailed consideration of this statutory instrument see Jackson 1989, pp. 105–30, Ashworth and Creighton 1990, and Jackson 1993, pp. 103–12.
210 For more detailed discussion of the relationship of this order to section 18 of the PTA see Walker 1992, pp. 137–8.
211 For concerns voiced regarding the procedure followed see *HC Debs*, 8 November 1988, Vol. 140, cols. 182–221 and Note by the Standing Advisory Commission on Human Rights on the Government's Recent Announcements Affecting Northern Ireland Dealing with Terrorism and Terrorist-Related Activities, 1989, 3–5. The government responded that since it applied to all criminals in Northern Ireland, it was perfectly legitimate to conduct it in such a manner. See Jackson 1989, pp. 107–8.
212 See for instance Colville Report, 1987, paras. 1.4, 2.1, and 2.4.6.
213 Colville Report, 1987, paras. 7.1–7.3.
214 *Ibid.*, 1987, para. 13.1.6.
215 *Ibid.*, 1987, para. 13.1.6.

216 Colville Report, 1989, para. 13.1.6. See also Bonner, 1982. p. 441.
217 As a result of the timing of the document, it was limited mostly to a statistical summary of the operation of the 1984 PTA during 1988.
218 Some discrepancies still existed. See Dickson 1989, pp. 265–6.
219 Prevention of Terrorism (Temporary Provisions) Act, 1989, Eliz. II, c. 4. [Hereafter 1989 PTA].
220 Regulation 18C of the 1922–43 SPAs (S.R.O. 14/1923, 13.3.1923, B.G. 16.3.1923).
221 Bonner 1992, p. 452.
222 *Report on the operation in 1993 of the Prevention of Terrorism (Temporary Provisions) Act 1989.* By J.J. Rowe. Session 1993/94; and *Report on the operation in 1995 of the Prevention of Terrorism (Temporary Provisions) Act 1989.* By J.J. Rowe. Session 1995/96.
223 Poole 1997, p. 162.
224 *Inquiry into Legislation Against Terrorism.* By the Rt. Hon. Lord Lloyd of Berwick. October 1996 Cm. 3420.
225 1973 EPA, Northern Ireland (Emergency provisions) (Amendment) Act, 1975 Eliz. II, c. 62, Northern Ireland (Emergency Provisions) Act, 1978, Eliz. II, c. 5, Northern Ireland (Emergency Provisions) Act, 1987, Eliz. II, c. 30, Northern Ireland (Emergency Provisions) Act, 1991, Eliz. II, c. 24 and Northern Ireland (Emergency Provisions) Act, 1996, Eliz. II, c. 22.
226 Prevention of Terrorism (Additional Powers) Act, 1996, Eliz. II, c. 7.
227 *Ibid.*, Section 1.
228 *Ibid.*, Section 2.
229 Prevention of Terrorism (Additional Powers) Act, Section 4.
230 *Ibid.*
231 Lloyd Report, p. 61.
232 *HC Debs*, 1 April 1996, Vol. 275, cols. 35–45 and *HC Debs*, 2 April 1996, Vol. 275, cols. 156–299.

CHAPTER SIX

1 *Report of the Inquiry into Legislation Against Terrorism*, 4 September 1996, Cm. 3420.
2 Publ Eur Ct. HR, Ser A, No 145–B.
3 *European Convention on Human Rights and Its Five Protocols*, in Brownlie, *supra*, p. 329.
4 Douglas Hurd, *HC Debs*, 6 December 1988, Vol. 143, cols. 210–11. The derogation was an option in *Brogan and Others* v. *UK;* it had not been possible in the first case to come before the court: *Ireland* v. *UK* (1978) 2 E.H.R.R. 25, since the breach established in that case was non-derogable under Article 3.
5 Written Answer by Mr Waddington, *HC Debs*, 14 November 1989, Vol. 160, cols. 209–10, reprinted in S. Marks, 'Civil Liberties at the Margin: the UK Derogation and the European Court of Human Rights', (1995) 15 O.J.L.S., 71.
6 *Derogation from the European Court of Human Rights;* UK Permanent Representative to the Council of Europe Strasbourg, 23 December 1988.
7 Publ Eur Ct. HR, Ser A, No 258-B. For other applications challenging the validity of the derogation, see Application Nos 14672/89, 14705/89, 14780/89, 14880/89, 18317–320/91, 18414/91, 18627–628/91, 19431/92, 19504/92, and 20440/92. Reprinted in Marks, *supra*, fn. 18, p. 71.
8 'The Jurisprudence of the Commission and Court of Human Rights has established the following characteristics of an emergency where Article 15 of the Convention is invoked: (i) the emergency must be actual or imminent, (ii) its effects must involve the whole nation; (iii) the continuance of the organised life of the community must be threatened; and (iv) the crisis or danger must be exceptional in that the normal measures or restrictions, permitted by the convention for the maintenance of public safety, health, and order, are plainly inadequate.' (K. Boyle, 'Human Rights and Political Resolution in Northern Ireland', (1982) 9 Yale Journal of World Public Order, 159). For further discussion of the margin of appreciation granted in

emergency circumstances see C. Feingold, 'The Doctrine of Margin of Appreciation and the European Convention on Human Rights', (1977) 53 *Notre Dame Lawyer*, 90–106 and the European Court. of Human Rights' decision in *Lawless* v. *Ireland* (1961) 1 E.H.R.R. 15. For analysis of *Lawless* see A. Robertson, *Human Rights in Europe* (1st ed., 1977), pp. 51–3, 111–14, 212–21.

9 Emergency Powers Act (Northern Ireland),1926, 16 & 17 Geo. V, c. 5, Emergency Powers (Amendment) Act (Northern Ireland), 1964, 12 & 13 Eliz. II, c. 34.
10 http:\\www.law.qub.ac.uk.
11 For analysis of this case see Finnie 1991, pp. 288–93.
12 *Murray* v. *UK*, Case No 41/1994/488/570, 8 February 1996.
13 Lloyd Report, p. 10.
14 *Idem.*
15 Lloyd Report, p. 5.
16 *Ibid.*, p. 3.
17 The countries surveyed included Argentina, Australia, Austria, Belgium, Brazil, Denmark, Finland, Greece, India, Ireland, Italy, Japan, Netherlands, Norway, Pakistan, Portugal, Russia, Spain, Sweden and Turkey.
18 *Northern Ireland Annual Abstract of Statistics; RUC Chief Constable's Report 1969–1996; Irish Information Partnership.*
19 Explosive Substances Act, 1883, 46 & 47 Vict., c. 3.
20 Police and Criminal Evidence Act, 1984, Eliz. II, c. 60.
21 Lloyd Report, p. xiv.
22 *Ibid.*, p. xiv.
23 *Ibid.*, p. xv.
24 *Ibid.*, p. xvi.
25 *Ibid.*, p. 19.
26 *Ibid.*, p. xvi.
27 *Ibid.*, p. 23.
28 Michael Howard, *HC Debs*, 5 March 1997, col. 922.
29 *HC Debs*, 28th February 1996, cols. 900–2. See also Oonagh Gay and Bryn Morgan, *Northern Ireland: political developments since 1972*. HC Research Paper 98/57, 11 May 1998.
30 *Anglo-Irish Communiqué*, 28 February 1996, para. 12.
31 *Northern Ireland: Ground Rules for Substantive All-Party Negotiations*, HMSO Cmd. 3232.
32 *Ibid.*, para. 17.
33 Michael Howard, *HC Debs*, 5 March 1997, col. 917.
34 David Wilshire, *HC Debs*, 5 March 1997, col. 945.
35 Michael Howard, *HC Debs*, 5 March 1997, col. 919.
36 David Wilshire, *HC Debs*, 5 March 1997, col. 945.
37 Michael Howard, *HC Debs*, 5 March 1997, col. 921.
38 *Ibid.*, col. 922.
39 Northern Ireland (Emergency and Prevention of Terrorism Provisions) (Continuance) Order 1997, S.I. 1114/1997.
40 'Government Backs Plans for Extra Powers for Courts,' Home Office Press Release, 032/97, cited in HC Research Paper 98/87.
41 Donald Anderson, *HC Debs*, 31 January 1997, Vol. 289, col. 585.
42 Jack Straw, *HC Debs*, 5 March 1997, col. 930.
43 Jack Straw, *HC Debs*, 5 March 1997, col. 936.
44 Richard Needham, *HC Debs*, 5 March 1997, cols. 940–1.
45 Ken Maginnis, *HC Debs*, 5 March 1997, col. 950.
46 Kevin McNamara, *HC Debs*, 5 March 1997, col. 952.
47 Rupert Allason, *HC Debs*, 5 March 1997, col. 952.
48 John Wheeler, *HC Debs*, 19 March 1997, col. 1012.
49 Ian Paisley, *HC Debs*, 19 March 1997, col. 1020.
50 William Ross, *HC Debs*, 19 March 1997, col. 1023.
51 Menzies Campbell, *HC Debs*, 19 March 1997, cols. 1024–5.
52 See the *Guardian*, 17 May 1997, 'Peace in their time?', the *Scotsman,* 17 May 1997, 'A Last Chance for Sinn Féin?', and HC Research Paper 98/57, 11 May 1998.

53   Northern Ireland (Entry to Negotiations, etc.) Act, 1996, Eliz. II, c. 11. Statement
     issued as a Northern Ireland Office Press Notice, 29 August 1997, 'Statement by the
     Secretary of State'.
54   Jack Straw, *HC Debs*, 30 October 1997, Vol. 299, cols. 1028–9.
55   Flackes and Elliott 1994, p. 469.
56   Jack Straw, *HC Debs*, 30 October 1997, Vol. 299, col. 1029.
57   Tony Blair, *HC Debs*, 9 March 1994, Vol. 239, c. 300.
58   Jack Straw, *HC Debs*, 30 October 1997, Vol. 299, col. 1031.
59   Adam Ingram, *HC Debs*, 18 November 1997, col. 168.
60   *Ibid.*, col. 172.
61   *Ibid.*, col. 174.
62   Seamus Mallon, *HC Debs*, 18 November 1997, col. 174.
63   Adam Ingram, *HC Debs*, 18 November 1997, col. 174.
64   *Ibid.*, col. 175.
65   Andrew MacKay, *HC Debs*, 18 November 1997, col. 182.
66   Adam Ingram, *HC Debs*, 18 November 1997, col. 182.
67   Kevin McNamara, *HC Debs*, 18 November 1997, col. 184.
68   Ken Maginnis, *HC Debs*, 18 November 1997, col. 189.
69   Seamus Mallon, *HC Debs*, 18 November 1997, col. 193.
70   Adam Ingram, *HC Debs*, 18 November 1997, col. 176.
71   David Trimble, *HC Debs*, 11 December 1997, col. 1216.
72   Jack Straw, *HC Debs*, 30 October 1997, Vol. 299, cols. 1032–3.
73   Lembit Opik, *HC Debs*, 18 November 1997, col. 200.
74   Norern Ireland (Emergency Provisions) Act 1996 (Code of Practice) Order 1998, S.I.
     312/1988 and Norern Ireland (Emergency Provisions) Act (Silent Video Recording
     of Interviews) Order 1998, S.I. 313/1998.
75   Norern Ireland Information Service, 30 January 1998, Meeting wi UDP.
76   Norern Ireland Office, 20 February 1998, Joint Press Statement by theBritish and
     Irish Governments.
77   The *Guardian*, 24 March 1998, 'Sinn Féin returns to talks turmoil', cited in HC
     Research Paper, 98/57 11 May 1998.
78   The *Guardian*, 26 March 1998, 'Find Ulster peace by April 9, parties told', cited in
     HC Research Paper, 98/57 11 May 1998.
79   Norern Ireland Arms Decommissioning Act, 1997, Eliz. II, c. 7.
80   Prevention of Terrorism (Temporary Provisions) Act 1989 (Partial Continuance)
     Order 1998, S.I. 768/1998 and Prevention of Terrorism (Temporary Provisions) Act
     1989 (Continuance) Order 1999, S.I. 906/1999.
81   Norern Ireland Office Press Notice, 5 March 1998.
82   Marjorie Mowlam, *HC Debs*, 20 April 1998, col. 480.
83   *Ibid.*, col. 481.
84   http://www.uup.org. See also HC Research Paper, 98/57 11 May 1998.
85   http://sinnfein.ie/ardfheis/98ardfheis.gerry.html Presidential Address.
86   *An Phoblacht* cited in HC Research Paper, 98/57 11 May 1998.
87   Statistics provided by *Irish Times* at http://www.ireland.com/scripts/special/peace/
     counts/results.cfm.
88   http://www.isreland.com/special/peace/assembly/road/ahead5.htm.
89   Tony Blair, *HC Debs*, 2 September 1998, col. 693.
90   *Ibid.*, col. 694.
91   For Ahern's announcement of the1998 Offences Against the State (Amendment) Bill
     see 'Government Statement on Response to the Omagh Atrocity', *Department of the
     Taoiseach PN*, 19 August 1998. Text of statement also available in Appendix to HC
     Research Paper 98/87.
92   Speech of the Prime Minister in Omagh, 25 August 1998, reprinted in HC Research
     Paper 98/87.
93   Home Office Press Release, 'Draft Criminal Justice (Terrorism and Conspiracy) Bill
     Published', 346/98, 1 August 1998.
94   Norern Ireland (Sentences) Act, 1998, Eliz. II, c. 35.
95   *Ibid.*, section 3(8).

96 Norern Ireland (Sentences) Act 1998 (Specified Organisations) Order 1998, S.I. 1882/1998.
97 Mary Baber and Edward Wood, HC Research Paper 98/87, 2 September 1998. See also HC Research Paper 98/65.
98 Norern Ireland Office News Release, 27 August 1998.
99 HC Research Paper 98/87.
100 Publ Eur Ct. HR, Case 43/1994/490/572.
101 'Right not to incriminate oneself infringed', *Times Law Report*, 18 December 1996.
102 Criminal Justice (Terrorism and Conspiracy) Act, 1998, section 4(6).
103 David Maclean, *HC Debs*, 11 February 1994, Vol. 237, col. 532, cited in HC Research Paper 98/87.
104 See *HC Debs*, 8 December 1995, Vol. 268, cols. 451–2 and *HC Debs*, 2 February 1996, Vol. 270, cols. 1225–1267.
105 See also *HC Debs*, 2 February 1996, Vol. 270, cols. 1249–1254, cited in HC Research Paper 98/87.
106 Tony Blair, *HC Debs*, 2 September 1998, col. 695.
107 *Ibid.*, col. 699.
108 See for instance, Jack Straw, *HC Debs*, 2 September 1998, col. 739.
109 Tony Blair, *HC Debs*, 2 September 1998, col. 695.
110 Robert McCartney, *HC Debs*, 2 September 1998, cols. 710–11.
111 William Hague, *HC Debs*, 2 September 1998, col. 698.
112 Tony Blair, *HC Debs*, 2 September 1998, col. 705.
113 Wedgwood Benn, *HC Debs*, 24 July 1939, Vol. 350, col. 1105.
114 Tony Blair, *HC Debs*, 2 September 1998, col. 712.
115 Paddy Ashdown, *HC Debs*, 2 September 1998, col. 698.
116 *Ibid.*, col. 699.
117 Tony Blair, *HC Debs*, 2 September 1998, col. 700.
118 Norman A. Godman, *HC Debs*, 2 September 1998, col. 710.
119 Chris Mullin, *HC Debs*, 2 September 1998, col. 768.
120 Richard Shepherd, *HC Debs*, 2 September 1998, col. 714.
121 *Ibid.*, col. 715.
122 Gwyne Dunwoody, *HC Debs*, 2 September 1998, col. 716.
123 Ian Paisley, *HC Debs*, 2 September 1998, cols. 716–17.
124 Tony Benn, *HC Debs*, 2 September 1998, col. 717.
125 Andrew Robaan, *HC Debs*, 2 September 1998, col. 721.
126 Jack Straw, *HC Debs*, 2 September 1998, col. 735.
127 Kevin McNamara, *HC Debs*, 2 September 1998, col. 786.
128 David Winnick, *HC Debs*, 2 September 1998, col. 702.
129 Tony Blair, *HC Debs*, 2 September 1998, col. 706.
130 Chris Mullin, *HC Debs*, 2 September 1998, col. 768.
131 *Economist*, 29 August 1998, 'Overreact in haste, repent at leisure.'
132 Clive Soley, *HC Debs*, 2 September 1998, cols. 799–800.
133 *Legislation Against Terrorism: a Consultation Paper*, London, HMSO, Cm. 4178.
134 Ibid.
135 Gearty 1999, p. 26.
136 Legislation Against Terrorism: A Consultation Paper, quoted in Gearty 1999, p. 26.
137 *Economist*, 20 March 1999, 'Why Rosemary Nelson's dea spells trouble for Ulster's police: tragedy of a dea foretold.'
138 *Irish Times*, 29 May 1999, 'Gardaí to start digging for bodies of IRA victims.'
139 http://www.sinnfein/ardfheis/99ardfheis.
140 Norman Fowler, *HC Debs*, 16 March 1999, col. 1006.
141 Jack Straw, *HC Debs*, 16 March 1999, col. 1004.
142 See for instance, *HC Debs*, 18 November 1997, cols. 192 and 199 and *HC Debs*, 11 December 1997, col. 1227.
143 Flackes and Elliott 1993, p. 171.
144 *Ibid.*, p. 97.

CHAPTER SEVEN

1   Merlyn Rees, *HC Debs*, 9 July 1974, Vol. 876, col. 1273.
2   Sir Samuel Hoare, *HC Debs*, 24 July 1939, Vol. 350, col. 1054.
3   Roy Jenkins, *HC Debs*, 28 November 1974, Vol. 882, col. 642.
4   Jenkins 1991, p. 397.
5   The discussion of the formal impeccability of emergency legislation in Northern Ireland and Great Britain claims from Lon Fuller's jurisprudential claims in *The Morality of Law* (Fuller, 1964).
6   S.R.O. 179/1954, 21.12.54.
7   These met what Fuller termed the 'requirement of generality': rules existed. See Fuller 1964.
8   Rules Publication Act (Northern Ireland), 1925, 15 & 16 Geo. V, c. 6.
9   Fuller 1964, p. 92.
10 Fuller 1964, p. 49.
11 *HC Debs*, 11 December 1975, Vol. 902, cols. 742–90.
12 This included statutes such as the Malicious Damage Act, 1861, 24 & 25 Vict., c. 97, Prison Act (Northern Ireland), 1953, 2 Eliz. II, c. 18, Firearms Act (Northern Ireland), 1969, Eliz. II, c. 12, Theft Act (Northern Ireland), 1969, Eliz. II, c. 16, and Protection of the Person and Property Act (Northern Ireland), 1969, Eliz. II, c. 29.
13 1973 EPA, Part IV, section 28.
14 Public Order Act (Northern Ireland), 1951, 14 & 15 Geo. VI, c. 19.
15 Public Order Act (Northern Ireland), 1963, Eliz. II, c. 52 and Public Order Act (Northern Ireland), 1970, Eliz. II, c. 4.
16 Flags and Emblems (Display) Act (Northern Ireland), 1953, 2 & 3 Eliz. II, c. 10.
17 For background on the introduction of the order see Jackson 1989 and 1990. For criticism of the statutory instrument see SACHR, *Fourteenth Report of the Standing Advisory Commission on Human Rights*, HC 394 (988/89) and Ashworth and Creighton 1990.
18 Jackson 1991, p. 413.
19 Home Office Circular, para. 41, cited in Walker 1992, p. 74.
20 Tom King, *HC Debs*, 8 November 1988, Vol. 140, cols. 183–7.
21 Sim and Thomas 1983, p. 75. See also O'Boyle 1977, pp. 160–87.
22 For further discussion of the assimilation of emergency legislation into normal law, see Hillyard 1981, p. 88, Walsh 1982, pp. 53–7, and Bonner 1992, p.473–4.
23 Tony Blair, *HC Debs*, 2 September 1998, col. 696.
24 Arthur Greenwood, *HC Debs*, 24 July 1939, Vol. 350, col. 1057.
25 Lord Hailsham, *HL Debs*, 28 November 1974, Vol. 354, cols. 1509 and 1517.
26 See also *HC Debs*, 28 November 1974, Vol. 882, cols. 634–944 and *HC Debs*, 25 November 1974, Vol. 882, cols. 29–45.
27 Roy Jenkins, *HC Debs*, 28 November 1974, Vol. 882, col. 636.
28 *Review of the Operation of the Prevention of Terrorism (Temporary Provisions) Act 1976*. By the Rt. Hon. Earl Jellicoe, DSO, MC. February 1983. Session 1982/83 Cmnd 8803, para. 207.
29 *Review of the Northern Ireland (Emergency Provisions) Act 1978*. By the Rt. Hon. Sir George Baker OBE. April 1984. Session 1983/84 Cmnd. 9222, para 414. [Hereafter Baker Report].
30 Between June 1978 and the end of 1983, some 537 charges were brought under section 21 of the 1978 EPA. (Baker Report, para. 412).
31 *Review of the Operation in 1986 of the Prevention of Terrorism (Temporary Provisions) Act 1984*. By the Viscount Colville of Culross QC. Session 1986/87, para. 13.1.6.
32 *Hamilton v. HM Advocate* [(1980) S.C. 66]; *Sayers v. HM Advocate* (1982) J.C. 17]; *Walker, Edgar and Others* v. *HM Advocate* [*Times*, 14 March 1986, 2]; *HM Advocate* v. *Copeland, Robertson and Others* [(1987) S.C.C.R. 232]; *Forbes* v. *HM Advocate* [(1990) S.C.C.R. 69]; and *Reid* v. *HM Advocate* [(1990) S.C.C.R. 83]. Cited in Walker, *supra*, p. 57.
33 *Review of the Operation of the Prevention of Terrorism (Temporary Provisions) Acts 1974 and 1976*. By the Rt. Hon. Lord Shackleton, KG, OBE. August 1978. Session

1977/78 Vol. xxiii Cmnd. 7324, para. 110.

34   Walker, *supra*, pp. 57–8.
35   Ian Paisley, *HC Debs*, 19 February 1996, Vol. 272, col. 104.
36   Compare *HC Debs*, 17 April 1973, Vol. 855, cols. 275–392 and *HC Debs*, 18 April 1973, Vol. 855, cols. 627–28 to *HC Debs*, 9 January 1996, Vol. 269, cols. 31–115 and *HC Debs*, 19 February 1996, Vol. 272, cols. 41–108.
37   Roy Hattersley, *HC Debs*, 7 March 1983, Vol. 38, col. 569. See also *HC Debs*, 9 January 1996, Vol. 269, col. 94.
38   Neville Sandelson, *HC Debs*, 18 March 1981, Vol. 1, col. 379.
39   *HC Debs*, 9 January 1996, Vol. 269, col. 43.
40   *Ibid.*, col. 75.
41   Mr Gardner, *HC Debs*, 18 March 1981, Vol. 1, col. 351.
42   David Wilshire, *HC Debs*, 9 January 1996, Vol. 269, col. 54.
43   David Wilshire, *HC Debs*, 14 March 1996, Vol. 273, col. 1147.
44   A.J. Beith, *HC Debs*, 14 March 1996, Vol. 273, col. 1149.
45   David Trimble, *HC Debs*, 8 March 1995, Vol. 256, cols. 379–380.
46   Piers Merchant, *HC Debs*, 9 January 1996, Vol. 269, col. 90.
47   David Trimble, *HC Debs*, 19 February 1996, Vol. 272, col. 96.
48   Brice Dickson makes this last point in Dickson 1992, p. 597.
49   Andrew Hunter, *HC Debs*, 14 March 1996, Vol. 273, col. 1143.
50   Michael Howard, *HC Debs*, 14 March 1996, Vol. 273, col. 1129.
51   Letter from the Imperial Secretary to the Under Secretary of State, Home Affairs, 21 June 1923, PRO HA 267/362.
52   *Northern Ireland Annual Abstract of Statistics and Irish Information Partnership.*
53   Poole 1997, p. 162.
54   *Statistics on the Operation of the Northern Ireland (Emergency Provisions) Act 1991 for 1993.* Northern Ireland Office Statistics and Research Bulletin 1/94. Table 7a, 9.
55   *Statistics on the Prevention of Terrorism (Temporary Provisions) Acts 1974 and 1976 – First Quarter 1980.* Home Office Statistical Bulletin. 29 April 1980. Issue 7/80. Table 1, 5.
56   Mr Canavan, *HC Debs*, 14 March 1996, Vol. 273, col. 1162.
57   See Ian Paisley, *HC Debs*, 8 December 1977, Vol. 940, col. 1736. For an examination of the 1922–43 SPAs as breeding subsequent violence, see Gerry Fitt, *HC Debs*, 18 March 1981, Vol. 1, col. 382 and *Disturbances in Northern Ireland: Report of the Commission Appointed by the Governor of Northern Ireland.* September 1969. Session 1969/70 Cmd. 532, para 229(a).
58   Gerry Fitt, *HC Debs*, 18 March 1981, Vol. 1, col. 382.
59   For more detailed discussion of the entrenched divisions in Northern Ireland see Boulton 1973, Boal and Douglas 1982, Boal and Robinson 1972, Burton 1978 and Darby 1986.
60   Kennedy 1988, pp. 151–2.
61   M. Farrell 1986, p. 1. For other accounts of emergency legislation in Ireland and Great Britain prior to 1921 see Campbell 1994, Osborough 1972, pp. 48–82, and Mulloy 1986.
62   'An Act for the Suppression of the Rebellion which still unhappily exists within this Kingdom, and for the Protection of the Persons and Properties of His Majesty's faithful subjects within the same', 1799, 39 Geo. III, c. 11.
63   'An Act for the more effectual Suppression of Local Disturbances and Dangerous Associations in Ireland', 1833, 3 Will. IV, c. 4.
64   'The Protection of Life and Property in Certain Parts of Ireland Act', 1871, 34 & 35 Vict., c. 25.
65   Protection of Person and Property Act, 1881, 44 & 45 Vict., c. 4.
66   Prevention of Crime (Ireland) Act, 1882, 45 & 46 Vict., c. 25.
67   Criminal Law and Procedure (Ireland) Act, 1887, 50 & 51 Vict., c. 25. This statute was not repealed until the 1973 Northern Ireland (Emergency Provisions) Act.
68   See for example the Peace Preservation (Ireland) Act, 1870, 33 & 34 Vict., c. 9; the Peace Preservation (Ireland) Acts Continuance Act, 1873, 36 & 37 Vict., c. 24; the Peace Preservation (Ireland) Act, 1875, 38 & 39 Vict., c. 14; the Peace Preservation (Ireland) Act, 1881, 44 & 45 Vict., c. 5; and the Peace Preservation (Ireland)

Continuance Act, 1886, 49 & 50 Vict., c. 24.
69 Andrew MacKay, *HC Debs*, 18 November 1997, col. 182.
70 *HC Debs*, 11 December 1972, Vol. 848, col. 80.
71 J. Maynard, *HC Debs*, 2 July 1979, Vol. 969, col. 987.
72 Humphrey Atkins, *HC Debs*, 2 July 1979, Vol. 969, col. 928.
73 *HC Debs*, 2 July 1979, Vol. 969, col. 930.
74 J.D. Concannon, *HC Debs*, 6 December 1978, Vol. 959, col. 1580.
75 A.W. Stallard, *HC Debs*, Standing Committee B, 1972–73, Vol. 2, col. 52.
76 Kevin McNamara, *HC Debs*, 19 February 1996, Vol. 272, col. 61.
77 Colonel Wedgwood, *HC Debs*, 24 July 1939, Vol. 350, col. 1082.
78 Mr Soley, *HC Debs*, 18 November 1997, col. 183.
79 Jenkins, *supra*, p. 377.
80 Tom Litterick, *HC Debs*, 8 December 1977, Vol. 940, col. 1710.
81 Tom Litterick, *HC Debs*, 30 June 1978, Vol. 952, col. 1784.
82 In support of this point see Jellicoe Report, para. 14.
83 Northern Ireland (Young Persons) Act, 1974, Eliz. II, c. 33.
84 See for instance *HC Debs*, 26 June 1975, Vol. 894, col. 814, *HC Debs*, 30 June 1977, Vol. 934, col. 633, and *HC Debs*, 8 December 1977, Vol. 940, col. 1678.
85 'The welfare of the people is the supreme law', Cicero, *De Legibus*, Book III.
86 Robert Lynn, *HC Debs NI*, 21 March 1922, Vol. II, col. 91.
87 Hugh Smith Morrison, *HC Debs NI*, 21 March 1922, Vol. II, col. 89.
88 Meinecke 1957, p. 1.
89 Ibid.
90 *Belfast Newsletter*, 8 February 1921.
91 *Belfast Newsletter*, 13 July 1932.
92 Meinecke 1957, p. 3.
93 Emergency Powers (Defence) Act, 1939, 2 & 3 Geo. VI, c. 62.
94 1939 Emergency Powers (Defence) Act, section 1(1).
95 For discussion of the 1939 Act and the Emergency Powers (Defence) (No 2) Act, 1940, 3 & 4 Geo. VI, c. 20, see Carr 1940, pp. 1309–25, Cotter 1953, fn. 127, p. 403, and Rava 1941, pp. 403–51. For invocation of the doctrine of *salus populi* during the Second World War see *Liversidge* v. *Anderson* [1942] A.C. 206; Heuston 1970, pp. 33–68, Heuston 1972, pp. 161–6, and Lowry 1977, pp. 56–9.
96 Emergency Powers Act, 1920, 10 & 11 Geo. V, c. 55.
97 Section 2(1).
98 Emergency Powers (Amendment) Act (Northern Ireland), 1964, 12 & 13 Eliz. II, c. 34.
99 Section 1(1).
100 For further discussion of the operation of the 1920 Emergency Powers Act, see de Smith 1973, pp. 520–2, J. Bishop 1978, pp. 142–5, Carr 1940, pp. 1309–25, Cotter 1952/53, pp. 382–417, Jeffery et al. 1983, and Morris 1979, pp. 317–52.
101 Donald Somervell, *HC Debs*, 24 July 1939, Vol. 350, col. 1113.
102 Arthur Greenwood, *HC Debs*, 24 July 1939, Vol. 350, col. 1058.
103 Mr Walden, *HC Debs*, 28 November 1974, Vol. 882, col. 648.
104 Baroness Fisher, *HL Debs*, 28 November 1974, Vol. 354, col. 1533.
105 *Joint Declaration* 1969, Article 1.
106 *Frameworks for the Future* 1995, p. 17.
107 Douglas Hurd, *HC Debs*, 19 February 1986, Vol. 92, col. 415.
108 Sir Patrick Mayhew, Secretary of State for Northern Ireland, *HC Debs*, 19 February 1996, Vol. 272, col. 85. [Emphasis added].
109 For application of the doctrine of *salus populi* to detention in Northern Ireland post 1972 see Lowry 1976, p. 261 and O'Boyle 1977, pp. 160–87.
110 William Ross, *HC Debs*, 30 June 1978, Vol. 952, col. 1753. [Emphasis added].
111 See for instance the terms of reference and discussion on the role of emergency measures in the *Review of the Operation of the Prevention of Terrorism (Temporary Provisions) Acts 1974 and 1976*. By the Rt. Hon. Lord Shackleton, KG, OBE. August 1978. Session 1977/78, Vol. xxiii Cmnd. 7324; Jellicoe Report, and Baker Report.
112 Douglas Hurd, *HC Debs*, 19 February 1986, Vol. 92, col. 415.
113 Locke, *Second Treatise*, 1993, para. 171.

114 Roy Jenkins, quoted in Shackleton Report, 3.
115 Shackleton Report, 49.
116 W. Benyon, *HC Debs*, 2 July 1979, Vol. 969, col. 1005.
117 Meinecke 1957. p. 6.
118 Mr Benn, *HC Debs*, 24 July 1939, Vol. 350, col. 1104.
119 *HC Debs*, 28 November 1974, Vol. 882, col. 667.
120 *Ibid.*, col. 674.
121 *Ibid.*, 29 November 1974, Vol. 882, col. 736.
122 Richard Shepherd, *HC Debs*, 2 September 1998, col. 715.
123 Gwyneth Dunwoody, *HC Debs*, 2 September 1998, col. 716.
124 See Jellicoe Report, para. 188.
125 See for instance Shackleton Report.
126 Second reading in the Senate, 1928, PRONI HA/32/1/619.
127 John McQuade, *HC Debs*, 2 July 1979, Vol. 969, col. 948.
128 Ian Paisley, *HC Debs*, 8 December 1977, Vol. 940, col. 1737.
129 William Whitelaw, *HC Debs*, 18 March 1981, Vol. 1, col. 341.
130 John Biggs-Davison, *HC Debs*, 8 December 1977, Vol. 940, col. 1748.
131 Merlyn Rees, *HC Debs*, 25 November 1971, Vol. 826, col. 1661, quoted in *HC Debs*, 11 December 1975, Vol. 902, col. 762. See also *HC Debs*, 17 April 1973, Vol. 855, col. 354.
132 See *International Covenant on Civil and Political Rights 1966*, in Brownlie 1994, p. 127.
133 For the text of this subsequent derogation see http:\\www.law.qub.ac.uk.
134 *European Convention on Human Rights and its Five Protocols*, in Brownlie, *supra*, p. 331. Britain withdrew its derogation under Article 15 in 1984 as part of its criminalisation of terrorist violence. See Jackson, *supra*, p. 235.
135 *HC Debs*, 5 July 1973, Vol. 859, col. 812. See also EPA debates, *HC Debs*, 17 April 1973, Vol. 855, col. 298.
136 *HC Debs*, 5 July 1973, Vol. 859, col. 843.
137 *Report of a Committee to Consider, in the Context of Civil Liberties and Human Rights, Measures to Deal with Terrorism in Northern Ireland*. Chairman: Lord Gardiner. January 1975. Session 1974/75 Cmnd. 5847, chapter 7, no. 4.
138 *HC Debs*, 17 April 1973, Vol. 855, col. 315.
139 See for example *HC Debs*, 19 February 1996, Vol. 272, cols. 42–4, 81–4, 89–90 and *HC Debs*, 14 March 1996, Vol. 273, col. 1160.
140 Mr Benn, *HC Debs*, 24 July 1939, col. 1111.
141 *Explanatory Report*, European Convention on the Suppression of Terrorism, Strasbourg, 27 January 1977, 1977/78 Cmnd. 7031, vol. xiii, 11.
142 For discussion of extradition concerns between the United Kingdom and the Republic of Ireland see M. McGrath 1993, pp. 292–314.
143 Convention for the Suppression of Unlawful Seizure of Aircraft [Treaty Series No 39 (1972), Cmnd. 4956], Convention for the Suppression of Unlawful Acts against the Safety of Civil Aviation [Treaty Series No 10 (1974), Cmnd 5524], and European Convention, Article 1.
144 Suppression of Terrorism Act, 1978, Eliz. II, c. 26.
145 Explanatory Report, para. 31, quote from Article 13.
146 European Convention on the Suppression of Terrorism, 8.
147 In 1937 the world community agreed in principle as to what constitutes international terrorism. Since then, however, States have failed to accept a common definition. For further discussion of this point see for example, Alexander 1976.
148 For further discussion of these matters see Sunga 1997 and Higgins and Flory 1997.
149 Chadwick 1996, p. 3.
150 Tom King, *HC Debs*, 2 September 1998, cols. 702–3.
151 Tony Blair, *HC Debs*, 2 September 1998, col. 696.
152 *HC Debs*, 24 July 1939, Vol. 350, col. 1089.
153 Mr Benn, *HC Debs*, 26 July 1939, Vol. 350, col. 1533.
154 Lloyd Report, Annex.

Bibliography

Addo, Michael K., 'The role of English courts in the determination of the place of the European Convention on Human Rights in English law', *Northern Ireland Legal Quarterly*, 46 (1995), 1–17.

Alexander, Yonah, ed. *International Terrorism: National, Regional, and Global Perspectives*. Praeger Publishers: New York, 1976.

Allan, T.R.S. *Law, Liberty and Justice: the Legal Foundations of British Constitutionalism*. Oxford, 1993.

Anderson, Don. *14 May Days: the Inside Story of the Loyalist Strike of 1974*. Dublin, 1994.

Anderson, Paul and Platt, Steve. 'Whatever happened to civil liberties?', *New Statesman and Society*, 3 November 1995, 14–16.

Apter, David, ed. *The Legitimization of Violence*, New York, 1997.

Arthur, Paul. 'The Brooke Initiative', *Irish Political Studies* (1992), 111–115.

————. 'Three years of the Anglo-Irish Agreement', *Irish Political Studies*, 4 (1989), 105–9.

————. *The Anglo-Irish Agreement: Conflict Resolution or Conflict Regulation?* Jordanstown, 1986.

————. *The People's Democracy, 1968–1973*. Belfast, 1974.

Arthur, Paul and Jeffery, Keith. *Northern Ireland Since 1968*. London, 1989.

Ashworth, A. and Creighton, P. 'The right of silence in Northern Ireland', in J. Hayes and P. O'Higgins, *Lessons From Northern Ireland*, 1990.

Aunger, Edmund. 'Religion and occupational class in Northern Ireland', *Economic and Social Review*, 7 (1975), 1–18.

Barker, Rodney. *Political Legitimacy and the State*. Oxford, 1990.

Bates, T. St. J.N. 'The Shackleton Report on terrorism: some Scottish aspects', *Scots Law Times*, 27 July 1979, 205–8.

Beckett, J.C. *The Making of Modern Ireland 1603–1923*. London, 1981.

Beetham, David. *The Legitimation of Power*. Basingstoke, 1991.

Bell, J. Bowyer. *The Secret Army: the IRA 1916–1979*. Dublin, 1989.

Benn, Tony. *Against the Tide*. London, 1990.

Beresford, David. *Ten Men Dead*. London, 1987.

Bew, P. and Gillespie, G. *Northern Ireland: a Chronology of the Troubles 1968–1993*. Dublin, 1993.

Bew, Paul, Gibbon, Peter and Patterson, Henry. *Northern Ireland 1921–1994: Political Forces and Social Classes*. London, 1995.

Birch, D.J. 'The evidence provisions', *Northern Ireland Legal Quarterly*, 40 (1989), 411–40.

Bishop, Joseph W. Jr. 'Law in the Control of Terrorism and Insurrection: the British Laboratory Experience', *Law and Contemporary Problems*, 42 (1978), 140–201.

———. *Justice Under Fire*. New York, 1974.

Bishop, Patrick and Mallie, Eamonn. *The Provisional IRA*. London, 1987.

Boal, Fred and Douglas, J. Neville, eds. *Integration and Division: Geographical Perspectives on the Northern Ireland Problem*, London, 1982.

Boal, Fred and Robinson, Alan. 'Close together and far apart: religious and class divisions in Northern Ireland', *Community Forum*, No. 3, 1972.

Bonner, David. 'The United Kingdom response to terrorism', *Western Responses to Terrorism*, ed. by Alex P. Schmid and Ronald D. Crelinsten. London, 1993, 171–205.

———, 'Combating terrorism in the 1990s: the role of the Prevention of Terrorism (Temporary Provisions) Act 1989', *Public Law* (1992), 440–76.

———. 'Combating terrorism: supergrass trials in Northern Ireland', *Modern Law Review* 51 (1988), 23–53.

———. *Emergency Powers in Peacetime*. London, 1985.

———. 'The Baker review of the Northern Ireland (Emergency Provisions) Act 1978', *Public Law* (1984), 348–65.

———. 'Combating terrorism: the Jellicoe approach', *Public Law* (1983), 224–34.

———. 'Combating terrorism in Great Britain: the role of exclusion orders', *Public Law* (1982), 262–81.

Boulton, David. *The UVF 1966–1973: an Anatomy of Loyalist Rebellion*. Dublin, 1973.

Boyle, Kevin. 'Human rights and political resolution in Northern Ireland', *Yale Journal of World Public Order* 9 (1982), 156–77.

Boyle, Kevin and Hadden, Tom. *The Anglo-Irish Agreement: Commentary, Text and Official Review*. London, 1989.

———. 'Northern Ireland: conflict and conflict resolution', *Ethnic Conflict and Human Rights, ed. by Kumar Rupesinghe*. Oslo, 1988.

———. *Ireland: A Positive Proposal*. Middlesex, 1985.

Boyle, Kevin, Hadden, Tom and Hillyard, Paddy. *Ten Years on in Northern Ireland: the Legal Control of Political Violence*. Nottingham, 1980.

———. *Law and State: the Case of Northern Ireland*. London, 1975.

———. *Justice in Northern Ireland: A Study in Social Confidence*. London, 1973.

Boyle, Louis. 'The Ulster Workers' Council strike, May 1974', in Darby et al., 1978.

Brewer, John D. *Inside the RUC*. Oxford, 1991.

Brooke, Peter. *Ulster Presbyterianism: the Historical Perspective 1610–1970*. Belfast, 1994.

Brownlie, Ian, ed. *Basic Documents on Human Rights*. 3rd edn. Oxford, 1994.

————. 'Interrogation in depth: the Compton and Parker reports', *Modern Law Review*, 35 (1972), 501–2.

Bruce, Steve. *The Edge of the Union: the Ulster Loyalist Political Vision*. Oxford, 1994.

————. 'Loyalists in Northern Ireland: further thoughts on "pro-state terror"', *Terrorism and Political Violence*, 5 (1993), 252–65.

————. *The Red Hand: Protestant Paramilitaries in Northern Ireland*. Oxford, 1992.

Buckland, Patrick. *A History of Northern Ireland*. Dublin, 1981.

————. *The Factory of Grievances: Devolved Government in Northern Ireland*. Dublin, 1977.

————. Irish Unionism 1885–1923. A Documentary History, Belfast 1973.

Burton, Frank. 'Republicanism: the IRA and the community', *The Politics of Legitimacy: Struggles in a Belfast Community*. London, 1978, 68–128.

Butterworth's Emergency Legislation Service. London, 1939–51.

Campbell, Colm. *Emergency Law in Ireland 1918–1925*. Oxford, 1994.

Canning, P. *British Policy Towards Ireland 1921–1941*. Oxford, 1985.

Carr, Cecil T. 'Crisis legislation in Britain', *Columbia Law Review*, 40 (1940), 1309–25.

Chadwick, E. *Self-Determination, Terrorism and the International Humanitarian Law of Armed Conflict*. Martinus Nijhoff Publishers: The Netherlands, 1996.

Cicero. *On Duties*. Ed. by M.T. Griffin and E.M. Atkins. Cambridge, 1991.

Clark, Gorden L. and Dear, Michael. 'Democracy and the crisis of legitimacy', *State Apparatus: Structures and Language of Legitimacy*. Boston, 1984, 153–74.

Committee on the Administration of Justice. *No Emergency, No Emergency Law: Emergency Legislation Related to Northern Ireland the Case for Repeal*. Belfast, 1995.

————. *A Bill of Rights for Northern Ireland*. Belfast, 1993.

————. *Making Rights Count: discussion, analysis and documentation of international charters of rights and their application to Northern Ireland*. Belfast, 1990.

Clarke, L. *Broadening the Battlefield: the H-Blocks and the Rise of Sinn Fein*. Dublin, 1987.

Coogan, Tim Pat. *The Troubles: Ireland's Ordeal 1966–1995 and the Search for Peace*. London, 1995.

————. The IRA. London, 1987.

Cook, Chris and Stevenson, John. *The Longman Companion to Britain Since 1945*. London, 1996.

Cormack, R.J. and Osborne, R.D. Religion, *Education and Employment: aspects of equal opportunity in Northern Ireland*. Belfast, 1983.

Cotter, Cornelius P. 'Constitutionalizing emergency powers: the British experience', *Stanford Law Review*, 5 (1952/53), 382–417.

Cunningham, M.J. *British Government Policy in Northern Ireland 1969–89: its nature and execution*. Manchester, 1991.

Curtis, L. Ireland: the Propaganda War, the British Media and the 'Battle for Hearts and Minds'. London, 1984.

Daniels, Norman, ed. *Reading Rawls: Critical Studies of A Theory of Justice*. New York, 1980.

Darby, John, ed. *Northern Ireland: Background to the Conflict*. Belfast, 1986.

————. 'Internment without trial, August 1971', in Darby et al., 1978.

Darby, John, Dodge, Nicholas and Hepburn, A.C. eds. *Political Violence: Ireland in a Comparative Perspective*. Belfast, 1990.

Darby, John and Williamson, Arthur, eds. *Violence and the Social Services in Northern Ireland*. London, 1978.

Dearlove, John and Saunders, Peter. *Introduction to British Politics*. London, 1992.

de Smith, Stanley and Brazier, Rodney. *Constitutional and Administrative Law*. London, 1971, 1973 and 1990.

Dewar, Michael. *The British Army in Northern Ireland: 1941–1985*. London, 1985.

Dickson, Brice. 'Criminal justice and emergency laws', *Facets of the Conflict in Northern Ireland, ed. by Seamus Dunn*. London, 1995.

————. ed. *Civil Liberties in Northern Ireland: the C.A.J. Handbook*. 2nd edn. Belfast, 1993.

————. 'Northern Ireland's legal system – an evaluation', *Northern Ireland Legal Quarterly*, 43 (1992), 315–29.

————. 'Northern Ireland's emergency legislation – the wrong medicine?', *Public Law* (1992b), 592–624.

————. 'The Prevention of Terrorism (Temporary Provisions) Act 1989', *Northern Ireland Legal Quarterly*, 40 (1989), 250–67.

————. *The Legal System of Northern Ireland*. Belfast, 1984.

Dillon, Martin. *The Enemy Within: the IRA's war against the British*. London, 1994.

————. *The Dirty War*. London, 1990.

Dixon, Paul. '"A house divided cannot stand": Britain, bipartisanship and Northern Ireland', *Contemporary Record*, 9 (1995), 147–87.

Donnan and McFarlane. 'Informal social organization', *Northern Ireland: the Background to the Conflict, ed. by Darby*, 1986, 110–35.

Doran, Sean. 'The doctrine of excessive force: developments past, present and potential', *Northern Ireland Legal Quarterly*, 36 (1995), 314–41.

Duncanson, Ian. 'Moral outrage and technical questions: civil liberties, law and politics', *Northern Ireland Legal Quarterly*, 35 (1984), 153–79.

Dunn, John. 'The creation of the legitimate polity', *The Political Thought of John Locke: an Historical Account of the "Two Treatises of Government"*. Cambridge, 1969.

Dunn, Seamus. *Facets of the Conflict in Northern Ireland*. London, 1995.

Dunstan, Simon. *The British Army in Northern Ireland*. London, 1984.

Evelegh, R. *Peace-Keeping in a Democratic Society: the Lessons of Northern Ireland*. London, 1978.

Farley, Lawrence T. 'The crisis of illegitimate sovereignty', *Plebiscites and Sovereignty: the Crisis of Political Illegitimacy*. Boulder, 1986, 1–23.

Farrell, M. 'The apparatus of repression', *Field Day Pamphlet*, 11 (1986).

———. *Northern Ireland: the Orange State*. London, 1980.

Feingold, Cora S. 'The doctrine of margin of appreciation and the European Convention on Human Rights', *Notre Dame Lawyer*, 53 (1977), 90–106.

Feldman, David. *Civil Liberties and Human Rights in England and Wales*. Oxford, 1993.

Finn, John E. 'Public support for emergency (anti-terrorist) legislation in Northern Ireland: a preliminary analysis' *Terrorism*, 10 (1987), 113–24.

Finnie, Wilson. 'Anti-terrorist legislation and the European Convention on Human Rights', *Modern Law Review* 54 (1991), 288–93.

Finnis, John. *Natural Law and Natural Rights*. Oxford, 1992.

———. 'Some Professional Fallacies About Rights', *Adelaide Law Review*, 4 (1972), 377–88.

Flackes, W.D. and Elliott, Sydney. *Northern Ireland: a Political Directory 1968–1993*. Belfast, 1994.

Follis, Bryan. *A State Under Siege: The Establishment of Northern Ireland 1920–1925*. Oxford, 1995.

Foster, Roy F. *Modern Ireland 1600–1972*. London, 1989.

Fuller, Lon. *The Morality of Law*. New Haven, 1964.

Gaffikin, F. and Morrissey, M. *Northern Ireland, The Thatcher Years*. London, 1990.

Gallagher, Frank. *The Indivisible Island*. London, 1957.

Galston, William A. *Justice and the Human Good*. Chicago, 1980.

Gearty, Conor, 'Finding an Enemy', *London Review of Books*, 15 April 1999, 23–36.

———. 'The cost of human rights: English judges and the Northern Irish troubles', *Current Legal Problems*, 47 (1994), 19–40.

Gearty, Conor and Kimbell, J.A. *Terrorism and the Rule of Law*. London, 1995.

———. *Terror*. London, 1991.

Gibbons, Thomas. 'Questioning and treatment of persons by the police', *Northern Ireland Legal Quarterly*, 40 (1989), 386–410.

Gilbert, Martin. *Winston S. Churchill*, Companion Vol. IV, Part 3, London, 1977.

Greer, D. Steven. *Supergrasses: a study in anti-terrorist law enforcement in Northern Ireland*. Oxford, 1995.

————. 'The supergrass system,' in Jennings 1990, 73–103.

————. 'Supergrasses and the legal system in Britain and Northern Ireland', *Law Quarterly Review*, 102 (1986), 198–249.

————. 'The admissibility of confessions under the Northern Ireland (Emergency Provisions) Act', *Northern Ireland Legal Quarterly*, 31 (1980), 205–10.

————. 'Admissibility of confessions and the common law in times of emergency', *Northern Ireland Legal Quarterly*, 199 (1973).

Greer, S.C. and White, A. 'A Return to Trial by Jury', in Jennings 1990, 47–72.

————. *Abolishing the Diplock Courts*. London, 1986.

Hadden, Tom, Boyle, Kevin and Campbell, Colm. 'Emergency law in Northern Ireland: the context', in Jennings 1990, 1–26.

Hadfield, Brigid. *Northern Ireland: Politics and the Constitution*. Buckingham, 1993.

————. 'The Anglo-Irish Agreement 1985 – blue print or green print?', *Northern Ireland Legal Quarterly*, 37 (1986), 1–28.

————. 'The Northern Ireland Act 1982: do-it-yourself devolution', *Northern Ireland Legal Quarterly*, 22 (1982), 301–25.

————. 'Committees of the House of Commons and Northern Ireland affairs', *Northern Ireland Legal Quarterly*, 32 (1981), 199–235.

Hall, Peter. 'The Prevention of Terrorism Act', in Jennings 1990, 144–90.

Hamill, D. *Pig in the Middle: The Army in Northern Ireland 1969–1985*. London, 1986.

Harkness, David. *Northern Ireland Since 1920*. Dublin, 1983.

Healey, Denis. *The Time of my Life*. London, 1990.

Heuston, R.F.V. '*Liversidge* v. *Anderson: Two Footnotes*', *Law Quarterly Review*, 87 (1972), 161–6.

————. '*Liversidge* v. *Anderson* in retrospect', *Law Quarterly Review*, 86 (1970), 33–68.

Higgins, Rosalyn and Flory, Maurice, eds. *Terrorism and International Law*. (Routledge: London), 1997.

Hillyard, Paddy. *Suspect Community: People's Experience of the Prevention of Terrorism Acts in Britain*. London: Pluto Press, 1993.

————. 'Political and social dimensions of emergency law in Northern Ireland', in Jennings 1990, 191–212.

————. 'Law and order', in Darby, 1986, 32–60.

————. 'From Belfast to Britain: some critical comments on the royal commission on criminal procedure', *Power and Politics*. London, 1981.

————. 'Police and the penal services', in Darby et al., 1978.

Hofnung, Menachem. 'States of emergency and ethnic conflict in liberal democracies: Great Britain and Israel', *Terrorism and Political Violence*, 6 (1994), 340–65.

Hogan, G. and Walker, C. *Political Violence and the Law in Ireland.* Manchester, 1989.

Hohfeld, W. 'Some fundamental legal concepts as applied in judicial reasoning', *Yale Law Journal,* 23 (1913), 16. [Reprinted in W. Hohfeld, *Fundamental Legal Conceptions as Applied in Judicial Reasoning.* Ed. by W. Cook, 1923, 23–64].

————. 'Fundamental legal conceptions as applied in judicial reasoning', *Yale Law Journal,* 26 (1917), 710. [Reprinted in W. Hohfeld, *Fundamental Legal Conceptions as Applied in Judicial Reasoning.* Ed. by W. Cook, 1923, 65–114].

Holland, Jack and McDonald, Henry. *INLA: Deadly Divisions.* Dublin, 1994.

Houston, Alan Craig. 'Republicanism and reason of state: from royal prerogative to rule of law', presented at workshop on *The Politics of Necessity and Language of Reason of State,* King's College, University of Cambridge, 14–16 April 1993. (Unpublished)

Hume, John. *A New Ireland: Politics, Peace, and Reconciliation.* Boulder, 1996.

International Lawyers' Inquiry into Lethal Use of Firearms by the Security Forces in Northern Ireland. *Shoot to Kill?* Cork, 1985.

Jackman, Robert W. 'Legitimacy and political capacity', in *Power without Force: the Political Capacity of Nation-States.* Ann Arbor, 1993, 95–121.

Jackson, Donald, 'Prevention of Terrorism: the United Kingdom confronts the European Convention on Human Rights', *Terrorism and Political Violence,* 6 (1994), 507–35.

Jackson, John D. 'Inferences from silence: from common law to common sense', 44 *Northern Ireland Legal Quarterly,* 103–12.

————. 'Curtailing the right of silence: lessons from Northern Ireland', *Criminal Law Review* (1991), 404–15.

————. 'Developments in Northern Ireland', *The Right of Silence Debate,* ed. by S. Greer and R. Morgan, Bristol, 1990.

————. 'Recent Developments in Criminal Evidence', *Northern Ireland Legal Quarterly,* 40 (1989), 105–30.

————. 'The Northern Ireland (Emergency Provisions) Act 1987', *Northern Ireland Legal Quarterly,* 39 (1988), 235–57.

Jackson, John D. and Doran, Sean. *Judge without Jury: Diplock Trials and the Adversary System.* Oxford, 1995.

————. 'Conventional trials in unconventional times: the Diplock court experience', *Criminal Law Forum,* 4 (1993), 503–20.

Jamieson, Alison. 'Collaboration: new legal and judicial procedures for countering terrorism', *Conflict Studies,* 257, January 1993.

Jeffery, Keith and Hennessey, Peter. *States of Emergency: British Governments and Strikebreaking Since 1919.* London, 1983

Jenkins, Roy. *A Life at the Centre.* London, 1991.

Jennings, A. ed., *Justice Under Fire: the Abuse of Civil Liberties in Northern Ireland.* London, 1990.

——. 'Shoot to kill: the final courts of justice', in Jennings 1990, 104–30.

——. 'Bullets above the law', in Jennings 1990, 131–43.

Kelley, Jonathan and McAllister, Ian. 'The genesis of conflict: religion and status attainment in Ulster, 1969', *Sociology*, 18 (2), 171–90.

Kennedy, Denis. *The Widening Gulf: Northern Attitudes to the Independent Irish State 1919–49*. Belfast, 1988.

Kenny, John. 'The advantages of a written constitution incorporating a bill of rights', *Northern Ireland Legal Quarterly*, 30 (1979), 189–206.

Keogh, Dermot. *20th Century Ireland: Nation and State*. New York, 1994.

Keogh, Dermot. and Haltzel, Michael H. eds. *Northern Ireland and the Politics of Reconciliation*. Cambridge, 1993.

Klayman, B. M., 'The definition of torture in international law', *Temple Law Quarterly*, 51 (1978), 449–515.

Korff, Douwe. 'The Diplock Courts in Northern Ireland: a Fair Trial?' *Netherlands Institute of Human Rights*, Special No. 3 (1984).

Lee, J.J. *Ireland 1912–1985: Politics and Society*. Cambridge, 1989.

Leigh, L.H. 'Powers of arrest and detention', *Northern Ireland Legal Quarterly*, 40 (1989), 363–85.

Lidstone, K.W. 'The Police and Criminal Evidence (Northern Ireland) Order 1989: powers of entry, search and seizure', *Northern Ireland Legal Quarterly*, 40 (1989), 333–62.

Locke, John. *Two Treatises of Government*. Ed. by Mark Goldie. London, 1993.

——. 'Essays on the law of nature'. Ed. by W. von Leyden. Oxford, 1954.

Lomas, Owen G. 'The Executive and the anti-terrorist legislation of 1939', *Public Law* (1980), 16–33.

Lowry, David R. 'Terrorism and human rights: counter-insurgency and necessity at common law', *Notre Dame Lawyer*, 53 (1977), 49–89.

——, 'Internment: detention without trial in Northern Ireland', *Human Rights*, 5 (1976), 261.

Lyons, F.S.L. *Ireland Since the Famine*. London, 1985.

Maguire, Paul R. 'The Standing Advisory Commission on Human Rights 1973–1980', *Northern Ireland Legal Quarterly*, 32 (1981), 31–61.

Mancias, Peter T. 'The legitimate state', *The Death of the State*. New York, 1974, 38–90.

Maran, R. 'Against torture', *Human Rights Review*, 85 (1979).

Marks, Susan. 'Civil liberties at the margin: the UK derogation and the European Court of Human Rights', *Oxford Journal of Legal Studies*, 15 (1995), 69–95.

McCrudden, J.C. 'Judicial discretion and civil liberties', *Northern Ireland Legal Quarterly*, 25 (1974), 119–46.

McGrath, Margaret. 'Extradition: another Irish problem', *Northern Ireland Legal Quarterly*, 34 (1993), 292–314.

McKeown, Michael. *Two seven six three: an analysis of fatalities attributable to civil disturbances in Northern Ireland in the twenty years between July 13, 1969 and July 12, 1989.* Belfast, 1990.

Meinecke, Friedrich. *Machiavellism: the doctrine of raison d'état and its place in modern history.* Trans. by Douglas Scott. London, 1957.

Miller, Arthur S. 'Reason of state and the emergent constitution of control', *Minnesota Law Review* 64 (1980), 585–633.

Miller, D.W. *Queen's Rebels: Ulster loyalism in historical perspective.* Dublin, 1978.

Morgan, Kenneth O. *The People's Peace.* Oxford, 1992.

Morris, G.S. 'The Emergency Powers Act 1920', *Public Law*, 317 (1979), 317–52.

Mulloy, Eanna. 'Emergency legislation: dynasties of coercion', *Field Day Pamphlet*, 11 (1986).

Murray, R. *The SAS in Ireland.* Belfast, 1990.

National Council for Civil Liberties. *The Special Powers Act of Northern Ireland: report of a commission of enquiry appointed to examine the purpose and effect of the Civil Authorities (Special Powers) Acts (Northern Ireland) 1922 and 1933.* London, 1936.

Nelson, Sarah. *Ulster's Uncertain Defenders: Loyalists and the Northern Ireland Conflict.* Belfast, 1984.

Nelson, William R. 'Terrorist challenge to the rule of law: the British experience', *Terrorism*, 13 (1990), 227–36.

Neumann, Franz L. 'The concept of political freedom,' *Columbia Law Review*, 53 (1953), 901–35.

O'Boyle, Michael P. 'Emergency situations and the protection of human rights: a model derogation provision for a Northern Ireland bill of rights', *Northern Ireland Legal Quarterly*, 28, (1977), 160–87.

———. 'Torture and emergency powers under the European Convention on Human Rights: *Ireland* v. *UK*', *American Journal of International Law*, 71 (1977b), 674.

O'Brien, Brendan. *The Long War: the IRA and Sinn Féin 1985 to Today.* Dublin, 1993.

O'Callaghan, Margaret. *British High Politics and a Nationalist Ireland: criminality, land and the law under Forster and Balfour.* New York, 1994.

O'Day, Alan, ed. *Political Violence in Northern Ireland: Conflict and Conflict Resolution.* London, 1997.

O'Dowd, Liam, Rolston, Bill and Tomlinson, Mike. *Northern Ireland: between civil rights and civil war.* London, 1980.

O'Leary, Brendan. *The Northern Ireland Assembly 1982–1986: a constitutional experiment.* London, 1989.

O'Leary, Brendan and McGary, John. *The Politics of Antagonism.* Athlone, 1994.

———. eds., *The Future of Northern Ireland.* Oxford, 1990.

O'Neill, Terence. *Ulster at the Cross-Roads*. London, 1969.

Osborough. 'Law in Ireland 1916–26', *Northern Ireland Legal Quarterly*, 23 (1), 1972, 48–82.

Owen, Arwel Ellis. *The Anglo-Irish Agreement: the first three years*. Cardiff, 1994.

Palley. 'The evolution, disintegration and possible reconstruction of the Northern Ireland constitution', *Anglo-American Law Review*, 1 (1972), 368–478.

Poole, Michael. 'The Demography of Violence', in Darby, 1986, 151–180.

Provisional IRA. *Freedom Struggle*. [Publisher unknown].

Purdie, Bob. *Politics in the Streets: the origins of the civil rights movement in Northern Ireland*. Belfast, 1990.

Ranelagh, John O'Beirne. *A Short History of Ireland*. Cambridge, 1995.

Rava, Paul B. 'Emergency powers in Great Britain', *Boston University Law Review*, 21 (1941), 403–51.

Robertson, A. *Human Rights in Europe*, 3rd edn. Manchester, 1993.

Rolston, Bill. 'Reformism and sectarianism: the state of the union after civil rights', in Darby, 1986, 197–224.

Rose, Richard. *Governing without Consensus: An Irish Perspective*. London, 1971.

Rosenbaum, A. ed., 'The editor's perspectives on the philosophy of human rights', *The Philosophy of Human Rights: International Perspectives*, 1980.

Rubin, Alfred P. 'Current legal approaches to international terrorism', *Terrorism: an International Journal*, 7 (1984), 147–61.

Ryder, Chris. *The Ulster Defence Regiment: an instrument of peace?* London, 1992.

———. *The RUC: a force under fire*. London, 1989.

Samuels, Alec. 'The legal response to terrorism: the Prevention of Terrorism (Temporary Provisions) Act 1984', *Public Law* (1984), 365–70.

Schiff, D.N. 'The Shackleton review of the operation of the Prevention of Terrorism (Temporary Provisions) Acts 1974 and 1976', *Public Law* (1978), 352–9.

Scorer, C. Spencer, S. and Hewitt, P. *The New Prevention of Terrorism Act: the case for repeal*. London, 1985.

Sieghart, Paul. *The International Law of Human Rights*. Oxford, 1995.

Silkin, Samuel. 'The rights of man and the rule of law', *Northern Ireland Legal Quarterly*, 28 (1977), 3–20.

Sim, Joe and Thomas, Philip A. 'The Prevention of Terrorism Act: normalising the politics of repression', *Journal of Law and Society* 10 (1983), 71–84.

Simmonds, Nigel. 'The analytical foundations of justice', *Cambridge Law Journal*, 54 (1995), 306–41.

———. *Central Issues in Jurisprudence: Justice, Law and Rights*. London, 1986.

Simmons, A. John. *On the Edge of Anarchy: Locke, Consent, and the limits of society*. Princeton, 1993.

————. *The Lockean Theory of Rights*. Princeton, 1992.

————. *Moral Principles and Political Obligations*. Princeton, 1981.

Smith, M.L.R. *Fighting for Ireland? The military strategy of the Irish Republican movement*. London, 1995.

'Special powers extraordinary: the court of appeal in *Forde v. McEldowney*', *Northern Ireland Legal Quarterly*, 20 (1969), 1–18. [Editorial].

Spjut, R. J. 'Internment and detention without trial in Northern Ireland 1971–1975: ministerial policy and practice', *Modern Law Review* (1986), 712–39.

Steinberg, Jules. *Locke, Rousseau, and the Idea of Consent: an inquiry into the liberal-democratic theory of political obligation*. Contributions in Political Science, No. 6. Westport, 1978.

Street, Harry. 'The Prevention of Terrorism (Temporary Provisions) Act 1974', *Criminal Law Review*, (1975), 192–9.

Sunday Times Insight Team. *Ulster*. Middlesex, 1972.

Sunga, Lyal S. *The Emerging System of International Criminal Law: Developments in Codification and Implementation*. Kluwer Law International: The Hague, 1997.

Taylor, Maxwell and Quayle, Ethel. *Terrorist Lives*. New York, 1994.

Taylor, P. *Beating the Terrorists: Interrogation at Omagh, Gough and Castlereagh*. London, 1980.

Thatcher, Margaret. *The Downing Street Years 1979–1990*. New York, 1993.

Townshend, Charles. 'The supreme law: public safety and state security in Northern Ireland', *Northern Ireland and the Politics of Reconciliation*, ed. by Dermot Keogh and Michael H. Haltzel. Cambridge, 1993.

————. *Political Violence in Ireland*. Oxford, 1983.

Tuck, Richard. 'Machiavelli and reason of state,' presented at workshop on *The Politics of Necessity and the Language of Reason of State*, King's College, University of Cambridge, 14–16 April 1993. Unpublished.

————. *Philosophy and Government 1572–1651*. Cambridge, 1993.

Twining, W.L. 'Emergency powers and criminal process: the Diplock report', *Criminal Law Review* (1973), 406–17.

Vecher, A. *Terrorism in Europe: an international comparative legal analysis*. Oxford, 1992.

Viroli, Maurizio. *From Politics to Reason of State*. Cambridge, 1992.

Walker, Clive. 'The governance of special powers: a case-study of exclusion and the treatment of individual rights under the Prevention of Terrorism Act', *University of Leeds' Review*, 38 (1995–6), 115–48.

————. *The Prevention of Terrorism in British Law*. 2nd edn. Manchester: Manchester University Press, 1992.

————. 'Army special powers on parade', *Northern Ireland Legal Quarterly*, 40 (1989), 1–33.

————. 'Political violence and democracy in Northern Ireland', *Modern Law Review* 51 (1988) 605–22.

————. 'The offence of directing terrorist organisations', *Criminal Law Review*, (1993), 669–77.

————. 'Emergency arrest powers', *Northern Ireland Legal Quarterly*, 36 (1985), 145–55.

————. 'Prevention of Terrorism (Temporary Provisions) Act 1984', *Modern Law Review* 47 (1984), 704–13.

————. 'The Jellicoe Report on the Prevention of Terrorism (Temporary Provisions) Act 1976', *Modern Law Review* 46 (1983), 484–92.

Walker, Clive and Reid, Kiron. 'The offence of directing terrorist organisations,' *Criminal Law Review* (1993), 669–77.

Walsh, Dermot P.J. 'Arrest and interrogation,' in Jennings 1990, 27–46.

————. *The Use and Abuse of Emergency Legislation*. London, 1983.

————. 'Arrest and interrogation: Northern Ireland 1981', *B.J.L.S.*, 9 (1982), 53–7.

Warbrick, Colin. 'The Prevention of Terrorism (Temporary Provisions) Act 1976 and the European Convention on Human Rights: the *McVeigh* Case', *International Comparative Law Quarterly* 32 (1983), 757–66.

White, Barry. 'From conflict to violence: the re-emergence of the IRA and the loyalist response', in Darby 1986, 181–96.

Whyte, John. *Interpreting Northern Ireland*. Oxford, 1991.

Wichert, Sabine. *Northern Ireland Since 1945*. Essex, 1991.

Wilkinson, Paul. *Terrorism and the Liberal State*. London, 1986.

Williams, Glanville. 'The interpretation of statutory powers of arrest without warrant', *Criminal Law Review*, 543 (1958), 73–84.

Wilson, Harold. *Final Term: The Labour Government 1974–1976*. London, 1979.

Wolfe, Alan. 'The predicament of liberal democracy', and 'The legitimacy crisis of the state', *The Limits of Legitimacy: Political Contradictions of Contemporary Capitalism*. New York, 1977, 1–10, 322–92.

Zagari, M.P.M. 'Combating terrorism: report to the committee of legal affairs and citizens' rights of the European Parliament', *Western Responses to Terrorism*, ed. by Alex P. Schmid and Ronald D. Crelinsten. London, 1993, 288–300.

Zander, Michael. 'PACE four years on: an overview', *Northern Ireland Legal Quarterly*, 40 (1989), 319–32.

Index